D1460065

THE NEW
PROTECTIONIST THREAT
TO WORLD WELFARE

THE NEW
Protectionist
Threat
TO WORLD WELFARE

EDITED BY

DOMINICK SALVATORE

Fordham University, New York, New York

NORTH-HOLLAND
New York • Amsterdam • London

Elsevier Science Publishing Co., Inc.
52 Vanderbilt Avenue, New York, NY 10017

Distributors outside the United States and Canada:
Elsevier Science Publishers B.V.
P.O. Box 211, 1000 AE Amsterdam, The Netherlands

Library of Congress Cataloging in Publication Data

Salvatore, Dominick.
    The new protectionist threat to world welfare.

    Includes index.
    1. Free trade and protection—Protection. 2. International economic relations.
    I. title.
HF1713.S27 1986   382.7   86–16794
ISBN 0–444–01084–X

Manufactured in the United States of America

TO MADELEINE

CONTENTS

PREFACE

This volume comes at a very crucial time in international economic relations. Never before in the postwar period has the world been closer to an all-out trade war reminiscent of the 1930s, with its devastating effect on world welfare. In this volume, many of the most distinguished economists from all over the world address the issue of the recent deterioration in international economic relations as to causes, effects, and possible solutions. Protectionism is not a short-term and passing issue, but it is likely to remain an important world economic problem for the foreseeable future, no matter how successful the leading nations are in containing its most dangerous and immediate expressions. Indeed, the threat of protectionism is always present and arises from the ever-changing relative international competitiveness of nations.

This volume is an updated and much enlarged version, both in scope and content, of the special issue of the *Journal of Policy Modeling* which I edited on the same topic in the spring of 1985. Since then, there have been significant new developments in this field and, unfortunately, the dismal prediction made in the special issue that international economic relations would worsen has been borne out. Spurred by a trade deficit which may exceed $150 billion in 1986, some three hundred bills have been introduced in Congress calling for protection for the battered American industry against imports of almost every kind and directed at many nations, particularly Japan. Very little has also been accomplished in the United States to reduce the huge budget deficit, which is to a large extent responsible for the dollar overvaluation and the almost irresistible call for protectionism.

Recently, there have been some hopeful signs, however, that could go a long way toward resolving the current impasse. Hoping to avert a possible trade war stemming from mounting protectionist measures at home, the Reagan administration summoned the finance ministers and central bankers of Japan, Germany, France, and England to New York in September 1985 and announced a coordinated effort to intervene in foreign-exchange markets in order to lower the international value of the dollar and to strive to achieve greater international coordination in macroeconomic policies, including faster growth in the major U.S. trade partners. The dollar, which had already declined in value by some 15 percent from the peak achieved at the end of February 1985, mostly under the pressure of market forces, declined another 12 percent by March 1986. Whether the dollar will continue to depreciate gradually by another 20 to 25 percent (as generally desired) remains to be seen. But even if it does, it usually takes many months before it would lead to a significant improvement in the U.S. trade balance.

A second hopeful sign is that a new round of trade negotiations has been approved by the GATT nations and is scheduled to begin in the fall of 1986. The talks will deal especially with nontariff barriers and trade in services. As is well known, it is much easier to resist protectionist measures when trade negotiations are taking place or are scheduled to begin to deal with some of the problems that spur protectionism than in the absence of any such trade negotiations or expectation. Finally, under U.S. leadership, a somewhat new approach to solving the developing nations' debt problem, which stresses growth over austerity and is based on an enlarged flow of resources to developing nations, was presented at the 40th annual meeting of the International Monetary Fund and World Bank in Seoul in October 1985. By stimulating growth and trade, this would also reduce protectionist sentiments.

Whether and to what extent these measures will be successful remains to be seen. However, the expectation of future improvement in the U.S. trade balance may no longer be sufficient to overcome the overwhelming protectionist mood now in Congress. There are also those who feel that the proposed measures address the symptoms rather than the underlying causes of the problem and, without a significant reduction in the U.S. budget deficit, at best, these measures can be partially successful only in the short run. In any event, time seems to be running out in trying to resolve the pressing trade issues that face the world community today within an open trading system under GATT arrangements. This year and the next promise to be full of opportunities and dangers for international economic relations.

This volume would not have been possible without the help

and cooperation of a large number of people. I gratefully acknowledge assistance from: J. Aschheim (George Washington University), M. J. Bailey (University of Maryland and U.S. Department of State), B. Balassa (Johns Hopkins University and World Bank), R. E. Baldwin (University of Wisconsin), J. N. Bhagwati (Columbia University), J. F. O. Bilson (University of Chicago), W. H. Branson (Princeton University), R. N. Cooper (Harvard University), W. M. Corden (Australian National University), A. M. Costa (O.E.C.D.), A. V. Deardorff (University of Michigan), C. F. Diaz-Alejandro (Columbia University), O. Emminger (former President of the Deutsche Bundesbank), G. Feder (World Bank), R. C. Feenstra (Columbia University), G. K. Helleiner (University of Toronto), L. Jones (Federal Reserve Bank of Kansas), L. R. Klein (University of Pennsylvania), M. E. Kreinin (Michigan State University), P. R. Krugman (M.I.T.), L. O. Laney (Federal Reserve Bank of Dallas), R. I. McKinnon (Stanford University), M. Michaely (Hebrew University and World Bank), C. Michalopoulos (World Bank), M. E. Morkre (International Trade Commission), M. Mussa (University of Chicago and Council of Economic Advisers), P. H. Pauly (University of Pennsylvania), C. E. Petersen (University of Pennsylvania), F. Spinelli (Catholic University of Milan), R. W. Staiger (Stanford University), R. M. Stern (University of Michigan), T. Tange (Kanto Gakuin University, Japan), D. G. Tarr (Federal Trade Commission and the World Bank), G. S. Tavlas (I.M.F.), L. V. Uy (World Bank), and my colleagues at Fordham University: Edward T. Dowling, W. T. Hogan, D. McLeod, J. Piderit, and E. Sheehey; and from the United Nations, S. U. Yolah (the Undersecretary General), G. Ohlin (Assistant Undersecretary General), F. Campano, M. D'Angelo, D. Choi, V. K. Sastry, K. P. Sauvant, D. Walker, and C. Wang. C. Cacdac and A. Longobardi provided valuable research assistance. Finally, I would like to express my sincere gratitude to Alan Corneretto, David Dionne, and especially to Christine Hastings of Elsevier Science Publishing Company for their very skillful assistance in the publication of this volume.

Dominick Salvatore
New York, July 1936
Fordham University

CONTRIBUTORS

Joseph Aschheim
George Washington University, Washington, D.C.

Martin J. Bailey
University of Maryland, College Park, Maryland, and U.S. Department of State, Washington, D.C.

Bela Balassa
Johns Hopkins University, Baltimore, Maryland, and World Bank, Washington, D.C.

Robert E. Baldwin
University of Madison–Wisconsin, Madison, Wisconsin

Jagdish N. Bhagwati
Columbia University, New York, New York

John F. O. Bilson
University of Chicago, Chicago, Illinois

William H. Branson
Princeton University, Princeton, New Jersey

Richard N. Cooper
Harvard University, Cambridge, Massachusetts

W. Max Corden
Australian National University, Canberra, Australia

Antonio Maria Costa
Organization for Economic Cooperation and Development, Paris, France

Alan V. Deardorff
University of Michigan, Ann Arbor, Michigan

Carlos F. Diaz-Alejandro*
Columbia University, New York, New York

Otmar Emminger
Former President of the Deutsche Bundesbank, Frankfurt am Main, West Germany

* Deceased in July 1985. G. K. Helleiner completed their joint paper.

Gershon Feder
World Bank, Washington, D.C.

Robert C. Feenstra
Columbia University, New York, New York

Gerald K. Helleiner
University of Toronto, Toronto, Canada

William T. Hogan
Industrial Research Institute, Fordham University, New York, New York

Lawrence R. Klein
University of Pennsylvania, Philadelphia, Pennsylvania

Mordechai E. Kreinin
Michigan State University, East Lansing, Michigan

Paul R. Krugman
Massachusetts Institute of Technology, Cambridge, Massachusetts

Ronald I. McKinnon
Stanford University, Stanford, California

Darryl L. McLeod
Fordham University, New York, New York

Michael Michaely
Hebrew University of Jerusalem, Jerusalem, Israel, and World Bank, Washington, D.C.

Constantine Michalopoulos
World Bank, Washington, D.C.

Morris E. Morkre
International Trade Commission, Washington, D.C.

Michael Mussa
University of Chicago, Chicago, Illinois, and the Council of Economic Advisors, Washington, D.C.

Peter H. Pauly
University of Pennsylvania, Philadelphia, Pennsylvania

Christian E. Petersen
University of Pennsylvania, Philadelphia, Pennsylvania

Dominick Salvatore
Fordham University, New York, New York

Franco Spinelli
Catholic University, Milan, Italy

Robert W. Staiger
Stanford University, Stanford, California

Robert M. Stern
University of Michigan, Ann Arbor, Michigan

Toshiko Tange
Kanto Gakuin University, Yokohama, Japan

David G. Tarr
Federal Trade Commission and World Bank, Washington, D.C.

George S. Tavlas
International Monetary Fund, Washington, D.C.

Lily V. Uy
World Bank, Washington, D.C.

1

The New Protectionist Threat to World Welfare: Introduction

DOMINICK SALVATORE

Introduction

Trade relations among the world's major industrial nations have taken a turn for the worse during the past decade and are now threatened by new and more dangerous forms of trade restrictions, collectively known as the "new protectionism." This phrase, coined in the mid-1970s, refers to a revival of "mercantilism" whereby nations, particularly the industrial nations, attempt to solve or alleviate their problems of unemployment, lagging growth, and declining industries by imposing restrictions on imports and by subsidizing exports. The instruments by which imports are restricted are also somewhat different from and less transparent than traditional import tariffs, and are called nontariff barriers (NTBs). These refer to "voluntary" export restraints, orderly marketing arrangements, antidumping measures, countervailing duties, safeguard codes, and so on. Thus, at the same time that tariffs were and are being reduced as part of the Tokyo Round of trade negotiations and are presently very low on most industrial goods, the number and importance of NTBs have grown rapidly since the mid-1970s and have now become more important than tariffs as obstructions to international trade. It has been estimated (OECD, 1985) that the number of NTBs has quadrupled between 1968 and 1983 and that a typical international transaction now requires 35 copies and 360 documents, largely because of trade restrictions.

From Fordham University, New York, New York.

This new protectionism now represents the greatest threat to the fairly liberal world trading system that was so painstakingly put together over the past four decades and which so well served the world since the end of World War II. That is, the sharp tariff reductions on industrial goods over the past four decades that resulted from successive rounds of multilateral trade negotiations made possible a very rapid expansion of international trade that significantly contributed to the growth of the world economy. Since the mid-1970s, however, the continued reduction of tariffs was more than offset by the rise of NTBs, as industrial nations sought to protect industry after industry from the adjustments required by international trade, in a climate of slow domestic growth and rising unemployment. While not exactly "beggar-thy-neighbor" policies, the rise in NTBs leads to a shrinkage in the volume of trade and to a reduction in the static and dynamic gains from trade that threatens the well-being of the entire world economy.

The new protectionism or neomercantilism is certainly an important recent development in international economic relations, and it is likely to remain so for many years to come. The topic is also closely related to other crucial policy controversies that the United States and other countries are now facing and are likely to continue to face in the foreseeable future. These include proposals for a domestic industrial policy; the calls for correction of the overvaluation of the U.S. dollar; the need to deal with the threat to the mature industrial countries, particularly the United States, emanating from the so-called newly industrializing countries; disagreements on how to solve the world debt problem; and the calls for reform of the international economic system. These are the specific topics around which this volume is organized.

In selecting the topics to be included I sought a balance between theoretical considerations and empirical results, between the real sector and the monetary sector, and between the general and the specific. The list of contributors reads like Who's Who in international economics, and the authors are affiliated with universities and institutions that are at the forefront of research on the topic of this volume (although they write as individuals rather than as spokesmen for the institutions with which they are associated).

In the remainder of this introduction, I will first examine briefly some of the most important examples of the new protectionism and NTBs imposed by the leading industrial nations, especially the United States, and then deal with the relationship between the new protectionism and (1) the need for an industrial policy in the United States, (2) the problems created by the dollar overvaluation and the steps taken to correct it, (3) the challenge to industrial countries (and especially to the United States) arising from the newly industrializing countries, (4) the world debt problem and the plan to defuse it, and (5) the future of the international monetary and trading system—noting in each case the contribution to the specific topic made by the papers included in the volume.

Postwar Trade Liberalization and the New Protectionism

The 1950s and the 1960s saw unprecedented growth in the volume of international trade and in the economies of most countries of the world, particularly the industrial countries. The merchandise trade of industrial countries grew at an average rate of about 8 percent per year, which fueled a growth in real gross domestic product of over 4 percent per year. This period can truly be regarded as a golden age of growth and stability.

The growth of international trade was made possible by successive rounds of trade liberalization achieved under the Dillon Round (1960–1961), the Kennedy Round (1964–1967), and by the Tokyo Round (1974–1977). Tariffs were cut until today they are less than 5 percent on most industrial products. Effective tariffs (that is, tariffs on value added) are somewhat higher than nominal tariffs but are still very low both in absolute terms and by historical standards. Generally resisting the trend toward trade liberalization was trade in agricultural commodities. As is well known, most nations have very elaborate domestic agricultural-support programs and jealously shield their agriculture from outside competition by a powerful array of subsidies, tariffs, quotas, health regulations, and so on.

During the 1970s, the international monetary system suffered a series of shocks, the effects of which are still being felt. The decade began with the collapse of the Bretton Woods system in 1971 because of lack of an adequate adjustment mechanism and an overvalued dollar. This led the United States to impose temporary trade restrictions that were removed when the dollar was allowed to depreciate, as fixed exchange rates were replaced by a flexible exchange-rate system of a sort. Then came the oil shock in the fall of 1973 and 1974, which resulted both in serious balance-of-payments difficulties for most oil-importing countries and in a world inflationary spiral. This led most industrial nations to relax trade restrictions temporarily to ease domestic inflationary pressures.

The general trend toward trade liberalization was soon reversed, however, starting in 1975, when the world faced the deepest worldwide recession since the Great Depression of the 1930s. This gave rise to what has come to be known as the new protectionism, characterized by the imposition of many new nontariff barriers. This fact did not go unnoticed during the Tokyo Round of trade negotiations (1973–1979), and indeed codes were negotiated to restrict and regulate the use of NTBs. These codes, however, were unsuccessful in stemming the tide of new NTBs, to the point where today these represent the most serious threat to the postwar trading system and world welfare.[1]

From 1975 to 1979, world trade grew at about 5 percent per year (as opposed to an average of 8 percent over the previous two and a half decades) and fell to a yearly average growth of about 3 percent from 1980 to 1985. Until now, the slowing of the great trade engine of growth can be attributed mostly to the reduced growth of the world economy rather than to the rise in protectionism (though causality generally runs both ways). The great danger, however, is that the continued proliferation of NTBs will lead to sharp retaliation and result in an actual decline in world trade, as nations revert more and more to bilateral trade deals. This will result in a misallocation of resources internationally, a slowdown in structural adjustments in mature economies and in growth in developing economies, and in an increase in the specter of a trade war in which all nations stand to lose. One study estimated that postretaliation optimal tariffs would be 50 percent or higher, or of the same order of magnitude prevailing in the mid-1930s, following the Great Depression.[2]

NTBs have been applied by industrial nations in a number of mature industries such as the automobile industry, the steel industry, and the textile and other industries that are facing sharp declines in employment, especially in a period (such as the present) of sluggish economic growth all over the world. Trade theory, however, clearly dictates that in cases such as these where divergencies between private and social costs and benefits are domestic, taxation and subsidization at the point of divergence rather than trade intervention is the first-best policy.[3] Yet many people in most nations believe that foreigners are trading unfairly and have gained unjust

---

[1] See, for example, Salvatore (1987c, 1984b). While reliable estimates as to the ad valorem equivalents of the voluntary restraints and for other NTBs are generally lacking, they seem to be substantial. Of course, the greater danger is that they will remain a permanent feature of the international trading system and that they will proliferate, resulting in most trade being managed.

[2] See Hamilton and Whalley (1983).

[3] See Bhagwati (1971). Not everyone subscribes to this, however. The Cambridge Economic Policy Group (CEPG), in particular, believes that in cases of real-wage rigidity, protection represents the only effective way for an industrial nation such as the United Kingdom to escape balance-of-payments and domestic unemployment problems. In the paper included in this volume, however, Spinelli points to some serious weaknesses in the CEPG's analysis and shows that real wages do not appear to be rigid and unresponsive to changes in labor-market conditions, even in the United Kingdom.

trade advantages through all sorts of import restriction and export subsidies. As pointed out by Bhagwati in the next paper in this volume, these days talk is often heard of the need for "fair" rather than "free" trade. Of course, the fact that small and well-organized groups in a nation stand to benefit greatly by protectionist measures at the expense of the mass of "silent" consumers is an important determinant of increased protection.

There is also a danger that trade restrictions inappropriately applied to protect domestic employment during recessionary periods will not be eliminated once the recession ends. There will then be a recession–protection ratchet effect: a recession leads to protection but the end of the recession will not lead to the removal of the protection. Until now, demands for protection have often been successfully resisted by governments with the well-known arguments of the benefits of free trade and for fear of foreign retaliation. The exception is in several mature industrial sectors. The danger is that the list may greatly expand in the future. Even the Reagan administration, in spite of its alleged adherence to the free market and thus to free trade, has imposed significant new trade restrictions in the form of NTBs. The most glaring examples of the new protectionism have been in the automobile industry, the steel industry, and the textile and apparel industries and have been directed primarily at Japan and newly industrializing countries. This experience is briefly reviewed next.

THE AUTOMOBILE INDUSTRY

In April 1981, "voluntary export restraints" (VER) imposed by the United States limited Japanese automobile exports into the United States to 1.68 million cars per year for three years. In April 1984 the restraint was renewed for another year; under it 1.85 million cars were allowed in. Though these restraints were called voluntary, they were essentially quotas by any other name. Japan "agreed" out of fear of still more stringent trade restrictions on its automobile exports to the United States. These restraints were deemed essential at a time when the domestic automobile industry was incurring huge losses and almost one-quarter million of its workers were idled by Japanese imports. U.S. automakers generally used the time wisely to lower break-even points and improve quality, but the cost improvements were not passed on to the consumers, and Detroit reaped profits of almost $6 billion in 1983, $10 billion in 1984, and $8 billion in 1985. Even Japan gained by exporting higher-priced autos and earning higher profits. The big loser, of course, was the American public, which had to pay substantially higher prices for automobiles.[4] In addition, the United States all but abandoned the small-car market. In 1985, the United States decided not to press Japan to continue its quota on auto exports to the United States. Japan, however, in an effort to ease trade frictions with the United States, decided to limit its automobile exports to the United States to 2.3 million units per year, or 24 percent of the U.S. market. At this point, Detroit's strategy is to import a large number of small automobiles from Japan to sell in the United States under American labels while competing in the $10,000-plus-priced automobiles and seeking to thwart the Japanese push to move "up the market." Japanese automobile exports have been even more severely restricted by Italy, France, England, and Germany. Today, practically the entire international trade in automobiles (which is about 8 percent of total trade in manufactures) is managed. An in-depth analysis of Japanese automobile trade with the United States is presented in the paper by Feenstra in this volume.

THE STEEL INDUSTRY

The United States imposed "voluntary" quotas on steel imports from all the leading foreign steel suppliers from 1969 to 1974, orderly marketing agreements (OMA) that reduced imports of specialty steel from 1976 to 1980, and a trigger price mechanism (TPM) from 1978 to speed up and facilitate investigations of dumping—the exporting of steel at prices below domestic prices or below average production costs. In late 1982 the United States negotiated a new voluntary restraint limiting the European Community's steel exports to about 6 percent of the U.S. market. Japan also unilaterally kept its steel exports from exceeding 5 percent of the American market. In spite of these restrictions, steel imports into the United States swelled from 16 percent of the domestic market in 1980 to over 26 percent in 1984. Most of this increase came from newly industrializing countries such as Brazil, Korea, and Spain. Acting on a complaint from domestic steel producers charging foreign steel producers of dumping, the International Trade Commission ruled in June 1984 that the American industry was seriously injured by imports and that trade barriers be raised against steel imports. In the fall of 1984 President Reagan, utilizing the so-called escape clause of the Trade Act of 1974, limited for five years imports of finished steel to 18.5 percent of the domestic market (20.5 percent if semifinished steel is included).[5] Most of the

---

[4] Tarr and Morkre, in their paper included in this volume, estimated that it cost about $240,000 to save each auto worker's job by trade protection.

[5] Nevertheless, steel imports exceeded 26 percent of the U.S. market in 1985, prompting an investigation.

negotiated reduction in steel imports into the United States comes at the expense of newly industrializing countries. The restriction is expected to save 35,000 to 40,000 jobs in the U.S. steel industry.[6] The European Community also has imposed bilateral import quotas on steel since 1972, so that today most trade in steel and iron (which accounts for about 4 percent in total trade in manufactures) is managed. A historical review of protectionism in the steel industry in the major industrial nations is presented in the paper by Hogan in this volume.

TEXTILE AND APPAREL

Trade restrictions in textile and apparel, which account for about 5 percent of world trade in manufactures, have been imposed since the early 1960s by the United States and other industrial nations (for the most part on the exports of developing countries) and, over time, they have become more and more complex and comprehensive. In 1962, the Long-Term Arrangement (LTA) on cotton and textiles, negotiated under the leadership of the United States, restricted imports of cotton textiles from Japan and from developing countries. This was succeeded in 1974 by the Multifiber Arrangement (MFA), which limited the growth of all textile and clothing imports into the United States to 6 percent per year. The renewal of the MFA in 1977 and then again in 1981 reduced the growth of textile and clothing import quotas into the United States and into the European Economic Community (EEC) in general, and reduced imports from "dominant" suppliers even more. As a result, textile and apparel imports into the United States are lower today than in 1971. In 1986, the textile industry was getting a higher degree of protection than any other major U.S. industry, with tariffs averaging over 22 percent, compared with less than 5 percent for all other industries. Nevertheless, employment in the industry declined by over 200,000 since 1980 under the pressure of imports and automation. Prompted by rising imports and a sharp decline in employment, Congress approved legislation in November 1985 that would have placed stringent quotas on textile imports into the United States. The bill, however, was vetoed by President Reagan.

OTHER TRADE RESTRICTIONS

Since the mid-1970s, import restrictions in the form of voluntary or orderly marketing arrangements have been negotiated also on footwear, color television sets, motorcycles, and shipbuilding by the

---

[6] It has been estimated that workers dismissed from the U.S. steel industry suffer, on the average, a loss equal to about 10–15 percent of their lifetime earnings.

United States, Canada, France, the United Kingdom, Italy, and Germany against the exports of Japan, Korea, and Taiwan, among others.[7] It has been estimated that in the early 1980s over half of world trade was subject to some form of NTBs.[8] New trade legislation passed by Congress in the fall of 1984 also gave the government new authority to impose additional restrictions on the exports of nations, such as Japan, that would not lower barriers to American companies selling services such as insurance and technology. By the fall of 1985, some 300 bills had been introduced in Congress calling for protection against imports of almost every kind, from telecommunications to forest products, and directed at many nations, particularly Japan. LINK estimates of the effect that these trade restrictions would have on the U.S. economy and on the rest of the world are presented by Klein, Pauly, and Petersen in their paper included in this volume. These trade restrictions were all aimed at protecting domestic employment against cheaper imports, in the general context of lagging economic growth. This problem is even more serious in Europe than in the United States (see Costa's paper). But, as pointed out in Corden's paper, trade restrictions prevent the needed structural changes required for long-term increases in productivity and growth in both industrial and developing countries. In addition, the rise in protectionist measures could lead to a full-scale trade war that would result in serious welfare losses for all nations. However, as Baldwin points out in his paper, even if the spread of protectionism is checked, it seems inevitable that the world trading system of the future will be characterized by more bilateral deals, with openness in some industries and protection in others.

The New Protectionism and Industrial Policy

The new protectionism is closely related to the controversy over the need for an industrial policy, particularly in the United States. Both stem from lagging economic growth and the substantial loss of jobs in such mature industrial sectors as automobiles, steel, and textiles. The new protectionism also results from the desire on the part of many industrial nations to stimulate the development and growth of high-technology industries, and especially of a national information industry. The latter includes semiconductors, computers, office equipment, telecommunications, programming, and so on. While the United States, as the world leader in the information industry,

---

[7] In the fall of 1985, however, President Reagan rejected the government's International Trade Commission recommendation to grant the battered American shoe industry five years of protection from imports and vetoed an import bill that would have seriously cut back shoe imports into the United States.

[8] See Anjaria et al. (1982).

does not (and need not) protect this industry from foreign competition, most other nations, including Japan, do provide many benefits in the form of trade protection and subsidies to encourage its growth. To counteract this, there is a call for an overall industrial policy in the United States that would also include high-technology industries in order to facilitate their further development and to retain market leadership.

Those in favor of an industrial policy argue that it is essential, among other things, to manage the contraction of older industries along more rational lines. They believe that Japan has been much more successful than the United States in doing so. They fear that without a U.S. industrial policy we may witness the large-scale demise of some older and very large industries, such as steel. Supporters of an industrial policy in the United States point out that employment in U.S. manufacturing has declined by over 10 percent in the past five years and that this is evidence that a process of deindustrialization is taking place in the United States. The steel industry alone has lost nearly 250,000 jobs or almost half its labor force between 1979 and 1985, and it might have collapsed entirely without the "voluntary" import quotas imposed at the end of 1984 that limited for five years steel imports to 18.5 percent of the American market. In short, those in favor of an industrial policy for the United States are convinced that such a policy is needed to rationalize the decline of older industries, to protect them against unfair trade practices (such as dumping and hidden subsidies provided) by other nations, to stimulate the growth of high-technology industries, and to make sure that other nations do not impose unfair restrictions against American high-technology exports in an effort to encourage the development of their own high-technology industries.

Opponents of an industrial policy for the United States believe that such a policy would only delay required structural adjustments and reduce the overall growth of the nation over time. They point out that older industries are facing difficulties and are shrinking not only in the United States but in most other industrial nations. In fact, the economic performance of the United States since 1973 (as measured by the growth of manufacturing production and the growth in productivity, employment, and investments in manufacturing) has been better than that of Germany, France, the United Kingdom and only slightly inferior to that of Japan.[9] It is thus Europe, and not the United States, that is deindustrializing. The relatively better performance of the United States vis-à-vis Europe can be attributed to the greater flexibility, the greater mobility of labor, and more adaptable

---

[9] See Lawrence (1984).

real wages in the United States than in Europe. The problems faced by mature industries in the United States are common to those faced by these same industries in other nations and are due primarily to sluggish domestic growth rather than to imports. It is true that U.S. imports are encouraged and exports are discouraged by the overvaluation of the dollar, but then the solution (as examined in the next section) is to correct the dollar overvaluation rather than restrict imports and argue for an industrial policy. In fact, in his paper Cooper convincingly argues that increased protection and more explicit industrial policies for particular industries will harm other industries and the entire nation in the long run, and it would not succeed in reducing the huge U.S. trade deficit.

Over the long run, the United States and other industrial nations have been losing their comparative advantage (especially to newly industrializing countries) in labor- and capital-intensive products utilizing standardized technologies, but this has been balanced by the growth of high-technology and natural-resource industries in which the United States has a strong comparative advantage.[10] Whatever unfair trade practices are used by other nations should be corrected through trade-liberalizing negotiations and not through import restrictions, which only invite retaliation. The only function for trade restrictions would be to make structural adjustments less disruptive and smoother. But then trade restrictions would have to be temporary and should not be used to prevent adjustment. Yet, even here, trade theory tells us that this is better accomplished by subsidies (which are more efficient and transparent) than by trade restrictions (which are less efficient, run the greater risk of becoming more or less permanent, and lead to retaliation).

Objections to an industrial policy for the United States run not only in terms of the above arguments (that it is not needed and that it would do more harm than good by retarding the needed structural adjustments) but also from a more operational point of view. Specifically, it is argued that it is difficult, if not impossible, to determine precisely what has to be targeted and to evaluate the effect of an industrial policy, once adopted. Krugman, in the paper included in this volume, points out that the usual popular criteria for an industrial policy (to target industries with high value-added per worker or with strong linkages to the rest of the economy, industries which are likely to be internationally competitive in the future, and to balance targeting by foreign nations) are likely to reduce rather than increase growth in the long run by retarding structural adjustments. Further-

---

[10] As pointed out by Kreinin, however, the technological lead of the United States vis-à-vis Japan and Europe is diminishing.

more, countertargeting to combat foreign targeting is detrimental because, in economics, two wrongs simply do not make a right. More sophisticated criteria for targeting are advanced by some economists. One of these is to overcome imperfect markets resulting from economies of scale and externalities. However, market imperfections can be overcome with taxes and subsidies to the particular industries facing economies of scale and externalities, and without the need for an overall national industrial policy. It is argued that much can be done to stimulate growth simply by tax simplification, regulatory relief, lower deficit financing (which crowds out private investments and raises interest rates), and so on.[11]

Krugman also points out that one of the allegedly most successful cases of industrial targeting by Japan, the steel industry, is no success at all. The reason is that the Japanese steel industry has had consistently lower rates of return on investment than the national average and, if anything, the targeting of the steel industry from the 1950s to the early 1970s has reduced Japanese national growth. Schultz (1983) holds similar views.[12] There are, then, many examples of clear targeting failures, such as Synfuel in the United States and the Concorde in the United Kingdom and France. To this, supporters of an industrial policy in the United States reply that comparative advantage can be created by targeting, as has occurred, for example, in the case of synthetic rubber, jetliners, and lunar landers and in the new advanced technology that sprung from them. They also point out that Lockheed, Chrysler, and Continental Illinois were saved by large government loans.

Support for an industrial policy in the early 1980s came from a remarkably broad spectrum of the American public, with the conspicuous absence of most professional economists. What was proposed was the establishment of a development bank to provide subsidized loans to targeted industries. These were to be the older and mature industries, such as steel, and new high-technology industries, such as the information industry. The actual choice of targeted firms, however, would certainly have involved political considerations and most economists feared that such a policy would have slowed national growth by retarding needed structural adjustments. Rapid domestic growth in the United States during 1983 and 1984 reduced considerably demands for a national industrial policy and

---

[11] Heavy industry, however, is deeply troubled by President Reagan's 1985 tax proposal which would abolish the investment tax credit and cut back on accelerated depreciation for new plant and equipment.

[12] In the paper included in this volume, Tange presents evidence indicating that the gain in trade competitiveness of Japan over the United States is due primarily to larger productivity gains in Japan rather than to industrial policy.

the 1984 presidential campaign all but killed the idea, at least temporarily.[13] Adjustment problems have certainly been painful and real in the past, and continued structural adjustments will certainly be required in the future, but most economists reject the conclusion that this necessitates a national industrial policy and believe that such a policy would do more harm than good.[14]

The New Protectionism and Fluctuating Exchange Rates

The new protectionism is also closely related to excessive fluctuations in exchange rates in general and to the large overvaluation of the dollar (until 1985) in particular. Exchange rate volatility, or frequent and large fluctuations of exchange rates about equilibrium levels, by increasing uncertainty in international trade and payments, can lead to demands for protectionist measures.[15] Even more important in giving rise to protectionist pressures are exchange rates that remain overvalued or undervalued for relatively long periods of time. The overvaluation of a nation's currency is equivalent to an import subsidy and an export tax by the nation. Many goods and services that would normally be exported with equilibrium exchange rates would be imported with an overvalued currency. Thus, potential exporters join import-competing producers in demanding protection. These demands are greatly strengthened by displaced workers and their labor unions and are difficult to resist, especially in periods of large unemployment and sluggish growth.

---

[13] Perhaps the idea of an industrial policy is not dead but has simply been overshadowed recently by the widespread call for protectionism. Indeed, there are some who believe that the United States has had in fact an *implicit* industrial policy all along, one that forced a large reallocation of labor from "sunset" heavy industries to more technologically advanced "sunrise" industries, such as the information and the telecommunication industries. This was to be reinforced by the Reagan tax reform plan, which would greatly discourage investments in heavy industries. In the meantime, high-tech industries were to be (and to some extent are being) greatly stimulated by the large defense spending. However, as pointed out by Branson in the paper included in this volume, despite the creation of more jobs in "sunrise" industries than jobs lost in "sunset" ones, the heavy concentration in the loss of jobs in some industries such as steel and textiles and in some regions of the nation has led recently to something amounting to a popular rebellion against imports, as reflected by the flood of bills that have been introduced in Congress to restrict all sorts of imports.

[14] Private industry itself is addressing the problem of structural change. For example, recent contracts between the U.S. automobile manufacturers and the UAW include explicit provisions for laying off workers displaced by new technology and some steel mills are successfully reorganizing under chapter 11 of the federal bankruptcy laws by extracting large wage concessions from labor unions and relinquishing responsibility for pension plans.

[15] See IMF (1984a).

Ironically, protectionist demands arise even in nations with undervalued currencies. An undervalued currency has an effect similar to an import tax, or tariff, and to an export subsidy. Thus persistent currency undervaluation leads to excessive expansion in the domestic production of import-competing and export industries. A subsequent realignment of exchange rates toward equilibrium levels and elimination of the currency undervaluation then lead to increased competition and loss of production and jobs in import-competing as well as in export industries. Having become more or less entrenched during the period of currency undervaluation, these industries and their workers are likely to demand and frequently succeed in receiving protection when the currency appreciates toward the equilibrium level. Thus extended periods of both currency overvaluation and undervaluation are likely to give rise to increased protection against foreign competition.

Bergsten and Cline[16] pointed out that the three periods of greatest protectionist pressures in the United States since the late 1960s coincided with periods of large dollar overvaluations. These were: (1) The period from the late 1960s to 1971, when a dollar overvaluation of about 20 percent (corrected when the Bretton Woods system collapsed and was replaced by flexible exchange rates) led to increased trade restrictions on imports of textiles and steel, and to widespread support for strongly protectionist measures such as the Mills Bill in 1971 and the Burke–Hartke proposal in 1971–1972. (2) The period from 1975–1976, when a dollar overvaluation of about 15 percent (corrected during 1977–1978) coincided with the adoption of the trigger price mechanism (TPM) for steel and other protectionist measures. (3) The dollar overvaluation from 1981 to 1985, which led to new trade protection for automobiles, textiles, and steel. Conversely, periods of near exchange-rate equilibrium in the United States have led to trade liberalizations, such as the passage of the Trade Act of 1974 and the Trade Act of 1979. There is, however, the danger of a ratchet effect, whereby trade restrictions imposed during periods of exchange rate over or undervaluations are not removed when exchange rates return to near equilibrium levels. For example, the extension of trade restrictions to synthetic fibers in the early 1970s (at a time when the United States had a trade deficit in that account) were not removed afterward when the United States achieved a trade surplus in synthetic fibers.

By September 1985 the United States faced a dollar overvaluation of between 35 and 40 percent, was running a trade gap esti-

---

[16] See Cline (1983, chap. 3).

mated at $150 billion for 1985 (the highest in U.S. history), and was facing the strongest protectionist pressures and increase in actual protection since the early 1970s.[17] It has been estimated that the U.S. trade balance declines by about $2.8 billion for every percentage point by which the dollar is overvalued.[18] According to this, the overvaluation of the dollar contributed about $100 billion, or two-thirds of the huge U.S. trade gap in 1985. It has also been estimated that the dollar overvaluation was responsible for more than 3 million jobs lost in import-competing and export industries in the United States, but for an inflation rate that was 3 to 4 percentage points *lower*. Thus, correction of the dollar overvaluation would greatly reduce the demand for trade protection and, at the same time, also reduce the call for an industrial policy (which, as pointed out earlier, has recently been overshadowed by demands for protectionism).[19] At the same time, it is widely believed that the elimination of the overvaluation of the dollar will not lead to a rekindling of inflation in the United States in view of the present decline in petroleum prices and slack in the American economy, and, more importantly, because foreign exporters, having increased their share of the American market in recent years, are not likely to want to relinquish it but will instead accept lower prices and shave profit margins (which, in many cases, have been substantial).

The major contributing factor to the large overvaluation of the dollar during the 1981–1985 period was the huge federal budget deficit of the United States. This kept real (i.e., inflation-adjusted) interest rates higher in the United States than in most other industrial nations and led to large capital inflows into the United States that, in turn, raised the international value of the dollar. To be sure, there were other forces at work (besides higher real rates of interest) that contributed to capital inflows into the United States and to a very strong dollar. These were the greater flexibility of the U.S. economy in relation to the economy of most other industrial nations, the lower rate of inflation, and the higher profitability of investments in the United States than elsewhere.

---

[17] The International Trade Commission, the government agency dealing with trade complaints, had the busiest years ever, with more than 200 cases filed in 1984 and 1985.

[18] See Stern (1983).

[19] The overvaluation of the dollar also seems to have created a two-tier economy in the United States, with strong growth in services (which are less exposed to international trade and in which the United States has a stronger comparative advantage) and slow growth or recession in most other industries exposed to international competition. More generally, the dollar overvaluation has resulted in a significant erosion of business support for a liberal trade policy.

As Emminger points out in his article, international financial flows into the United States have recently grown so much faster than trade flows that, today, movements in exchange rates reflect much more the former than the latter. In the process, the traditional capital-exporting role of the United States, appropriate for its status as a rich developed country, has been entirely reversed and in 1985 the United States returned to the ranks of debtor nations for the first time since 1914. The United States is now financing, directly or indirectly, nearly half of its huge budget deficits with capital inflows. A more in-depth analysis of the relationship between exchange rates, budget deficits, and the new protectionism is presented by Aschheim, Bailey, and Tavlas in their paper in this volume.

Until mid-1985, the Reagan administration kept a hands-off attitude with regard to the dollar exchange rate and was unable or unwilling to do much about the huge budget deficit. By that time, however, it had succumbed to demands for higher protection against foreign competition in textiles (by the extension of the Multifiber Arrangement until 1986), in automobiles (by extending until April 1985 the "voluntary" restriction on Japanese automobile exports), and in steel (by restricting imports until 1989 to 18.5 percent of the American market). Starting in mid-1985 (and after nearly five years of watching the dollar soar in value from the sideline), the Reagan administration began to be very concerned about the serious damage that the high value of the dollar was inflicting on American industry. A growing number of administration officials became convinced that it was next to impossible for American firms to increase productivity sufficiently to overcome the high value of the dollar and that some major steps were urgently required to resist the widespread calls for protectionism.

Finally, in September 1985, the Reagan administration convened in New York the finance ministers and central bankers of Japan, Germany, France, and England and announced a coordinated effort to intervene in foreign exchange markets in order to lower the international value of the dollar and to strive to achieve greater international coordination of macroeconomic policies, including faster growth in the U.S. major trade partners. The dollar, which had already declined in value some 15 percent from the peak reached toward the end of February 1985 (mostly under the pressure of market forces), declined by another 12 percent by March 1986. At this point, the administration in Washington would prefer a further 10 to 15 percent depreciation of the dollar, while most U.S. trade partners are against it for fear of losing too much of their U.S. export market.

A structured program of intervention designed to ensure greater stability of exchange rates and interest rates is presented by Bilson in the paper included in this volume. On the other hand,

McKinnon believes that grossly out-of-line and excessive fluctuations in exchange rates can be avoided only by close monetary coordination among the world's major central banks. As Mussa points out, any other policy that induces trade surpluses or deficits can provide only temporary positive or negative protection to the tradable-goods sector of the economy.

Despite the fact that a great deal of the large dollar overvaluation had been corrected by early 1986, the United States faced another record deficit in 1986. As is well known, it usually takes from 12 to 18 months for a currency depreciation to lead to a substantial improvement in a nation's trade balance.[20] In the meantime, demands for protectionism have not subsided in the United States, even from long-term defenders of free trade. Whether the expectation of future improvement in the U.S. trade balance is sufficient to slow protectionist pressures in Congress remains to be seen. The Reagan administration, for its part, initiated several unfair trade cases against Japan and other trading partners in an effort to derail protectionist legislation in Congress.

The New Protectionism and Newly Industrializing Countries

A great deal of the new protectionism has been directed by the developed countries against the manufactured exports of the newly industrializing developing countries (NICs). These nations (Brazil, Hong Kong, Korea, Mexico, Singapore, and Taiwan)[21] are characterized by rapid growth in gross domestic product (GDP), in industrial production, and in manufactured exports. Over the past twenty years the ratio of the industrial exports of the NICs to the total imports of the developed countries rose from about 1 percent to 4 percent. However, as pointed out by Michaely in the paper included in this volume, it has been the timing and the type of products exported by the NICs that have led to increased trade restrictions by the developed countries (DCs).[22]

The NICs have had, and are gaining, a comparative advantage vis-à-vis developed nations (including Japan) in textiles, shoes, television sets, consumer electronic products, steel, and shipbuilding.

---

[20] In fact, the initial effect will be higher-priced imports and lower-priced exports and would temporarily widen the U.S. trade deficit (the so-called J-curve effect).

[21] Some authors and organizations, such as OECD (1979), include among the NICs other nations such as Argentina, Greece, Portugal, Spain, and Yugoslavia.

[22] The growth of the exports of other non-oil-exporting developing countries and the contribution that these exports have made to the growth and development of these other nations has been much less than for NICs. See Salvatore (1983).

These are the very industries in which sharp cuts in employment have occurred, and are now taking place, in developed countries. This, combined with the fact that these newly industrializing countries have little political power and are not in a position to threaten effective retaliation, has led developed countries to raise many new forms of protection against the manufactured exports of these newcomers. This has occurred in spite of the Generalized System of Preferences (GSP), negotiated by Western European countries and Japan in 1971–1972 and by the United States in 1976, which grants preferential access for the exports of developing countries into developed countries' markets. Exception after exception to the GSP has been "voluntarily" negotiated by the United States and other developed countries in many products, such as textiles, which are of great importance to developing countries. By 1982, the United States had negotiated such bilateral agreements with twenty-nine developing countries, and the European Economic Community with twenty-one. In addition, in the trade legislation passed by Congress in October 1984 (which renewed the GSP trade privileges to developing countries), the President was given authority to deny GSP privileges to the NICs that did not curb their own unfair trade practices and restricted U.S. exports. This condition was included in the face of the increase in the NICs' trade surplus with the United States from just over $2 billion in 1981 to over $20 billion in 1985. However, as Balassa and Michalopoulos point out in their paper in this volume, trade protection by developed and developing countries alike imposes a heavy burden on both.

The NICs have simply been unlucky to be rapidly growing and to have increased their manufactured exports to developed countries at a time when the latter were and are facing large unemployment and slow growth. Had developed countries and international trade been growing in the second half of the 1970s and in the early 1980s as rapidly as they did in the 1950s and 1960s, the growth in the manufactured exports of the NICs to developed countries would probably have been absorbed much more smoothly and without as much of a rise in protectionism on the part of the developed countries. Having emerged in the wake of Japan's great industrial and export success, NICs have also inevitably been drawn into the trade disputes between other developed countries and Japan and have been, to some extent, victimized by the ire of the former nations against the latter. It must be pointed out, however, that while NICs have been, and are still, bitterly complaining against the new protectionism directed against their manufactured exports by developed countries, they are themselves heavily protecting their market against manufactured exports from both developed and other developing countries.

Yet, the anxiety sometimes expressed by developed countries of possibly having continuously to face more developing countries joining the ranks of NICs does not seem warranted. Rapid industrial growth depends on the simultaneous existence of a number of propitious internal factors such as a high rate of savings, availability of skilled labor, political stability, and a flexible economic system (as well as unrestricted access to foreign markets) that are not likely to be easily satisfied by more than a handful of additional countries (if any) over the balance of the decade. Indeed, even some of the current NICs seem to be falling under the weight of political uncertainty (Hong Kong), foreign debt (Brazil), the difficulty in adopting new technologies (Singapore), as well as from reduced access to developed-country markets.[23]

As pointed out by Diaz-Alejandro and Helleiner in the paper included in this volume, it is essential to reassert and enforce the GATT principle of nondiscrimination in trade matters and allow developing countries to increase their exports to developed countries, thereby helping to solve the former's foreign-debt problem and stimulate their development. If this does not happen very soon, we may witness a revival (and justification) of export pessimism and a return to inward-looking policies in developing countries. At present, nearly a third of developing countries' exports to industrial countries are restricted by quotas and other NTBs. The opening more widely of developed countries' markets to developing countries exports depends, however, on solving or dealing with the sectoral unemployment problems in developed countries. In the paper concluding this volume, McLeod and Salvatore examine theoretically the conditions and the degree under which the North loses employment by reducing protection on the South's exports and the impact of indexing the South's debt-service payments to its export revenues.

The New Protectionism and the World Debt

The new protectionism also has important implications for the ability of developing nations to repay or even service their foreign debt. The huge foreign debt of some developing nations, including some NICs such as Brazil, arose as they borrowed heavily from private banks in developed nations to finance their growing capital needs and to pay for sharply higher oil bills since the fall of 1973—all this in the face of slowly expanding exports to developed countries (as the latter entered a period of slow growth). By heavily borrowing abroad, developing countries continued to grow at a relatively rapid pace even during the second half of the 1970s. However, in the early

---

[23] See Turner and McMullen (1982).

1980s their huge and rapidly growing foreign debts caught up with them and large-scale defaults were avoided only by repeated large-scale official intervention by the IMF.[24]

Even Mexico rapidly accumulated a huge short-term foreign debt with foreign banks as it overborrowed against its newfound riches from petroleum. When the price of petroleum started to decline in 1982, Mexico was unable to service its foreign debt (August 1982) and the world was plunged into the so-called debt crisis. At the end of 1985 Mexico had a foreign debt of about $96 billion (more than half of it short-term) and faced an annual interest payment on the debt of $13 billion against a positive trade balance of $8 billion. Comparable figures (in billions) were $104, $12, and $11 for Brazil; $50, $4, and $3 for Argentina; and $37, $2, and $0.7 for Venezuela. These are the most heavily indebted developing countries.[25] By the middle of 1985, Mexico and Venezuela had renegotiated and Brazil and Argentina were in the process of renegotiating their debt repayment schedules and interest payments with their creditor banks in the developed countries, with the help of the IMF and under its general direction. As part of the deal, these nations were required to adopt austerity measures to reduce imports still further and to cut inflation, wage increases, and domestic programs, so as to put domestic growth on a more sustainable basis.

Renegotiation of the foreign debt by the heavily indebted nations, however, only avoided defaults on foreign loans and did not provide a long-term solution to the debt crisis. A long-run solution would necessarily involve increased access for the exports of developing countries to developed-country markets. The strength of the dollar since the early 1980s certainly stimulated the exports of these (and other) nations to the United States. But, as pointed out above, this was neutralized, or more than neutralized, by rising protectionism in the United States and in other developed nations, and high interest rates in the United States made the interest charges on LDCs' foreign debt very onerous. The strong dollar also raised developing countries' costs for petroleum and other imported items priced in dollars. Thus, we see the close links between the new protectionism and the call for an industrial policy in the United States, the huge budget deficit and the high interest rates in the United States, the strong dollar, the U.S. trade deficit, and the world debt problem.

Toward the end of summer 1985, the heavily indebted countries of Latin America began to reject the austerity plans advocated by the IMF as a condition for additional loans and to demand a

---

[24] See Salvatore (1984a, 1987c).

[25] Other heavily indebted nations include Chile, India, Indonesia, Korea, Nigeria, Spain, the Philippines, and Yugoslavia.

renegotiation of existing loans under the threat of default. It was under such circumstances that the United States advanced a new plan to deal with the worsening debt problem at the annual meetings of the International Monetary Fund and World Bank held in Seoul in October 1985. Known as the Baker Plan (for the U.S. secretary of the treasury who introduced it), the plan stressed growth over austerity in developing countries, based on a much increased flow of capital from developed nations and international institutions (primarily the World Bank). Specifically, the plan called for additional loans of $20 billion from commercial banks in developed nations and an additional $9 billion from the World Bank to fifteen heavily indebted developing countries (of which ten are in Latin America) over the next three years. The United States also pressured other developed countries to reduce protectionist measures and to take a larger share of developing countries' exports.[26] Developing countries welcome the plan and the general direction of the new U.S. thinking on the debt problem but feel that it does not go far enough. Specifically, they advocate a reduction in the huge outflow of debt interest payments (which for Latin American countries amounted to $32 billion in 1985).[27] While major American commercial banks (which have the largest concentration of Third World loans at risk) strongly supported the plan from the beginning, European and small American commercial banks seemed reluctant to pour fresh loans on top of troublesome ones.

In the final analysis, the continued and increased capital flows from developed to developing countries that are necessary for growth to resume in the latter countries require improvement in the creditworthiness of developing countries and a major shift in the *composition* of the capital flows.[28] Whereas in the early 1970s developing countries were receiving about one dollar of equity (direct investments) for every dollar of debt, in the early 1980s they were receiving less than 20 cents of equity for every dollar of external debt. It is this excess leverage that led to the debt crisis in the early 1980s. Thus, for the debt problem to be overcome and for sustained growth to resume in developing countries, an increase in the flow of equity capital in the form of direct investments and less reliance on short-term borrowing is required. Stripped of all its rhetoric, the

---

[26] By 1985, the United States was absorbing nearly 60 percent of LDCs' exports, up from 40 percent in 1980.

[27] The depreciation of the dollar since early 1985 brought some relief to debtor nations from their onerous debt-service charges. But it also lowered the value of developing countries' commodity exports, since most commodities are also priced in dollars.

[28] This topic is examined in detail in the paper by Gershon and Uy in this volume and by McDonald (1982).

Baker plan advanced in Seoul seems primarily aimed at avoiding large-scale default on past commercial loans (which at the end of 1985 exceeded $600 billion)[29] and does not seem as radical a departure from the past as it was made to sound to be. Bluntly, the new loans, even if they come in the amounts advocated, will only allow debtor nations to pay service charges on their past debts and avoid widespread default, without leaving much for new development projects. The sharp decline in petroleum prices during the latter part of 1985 and early 1986 will benefit nonpetroleum-exporting nations by reducing their oil bills and inflation, and by stimulating their exports as the growth of industrial countries is stimulated, but it plunged Mexico and other petroleum-exporting countries into an even-greater debt crisis and seems also to have sidetracked the Baker plan.

The New Protectionism and the Future of the International Economic System

The drift toward the new protectionism over the past ten years represents a serious threat to world welfare. Protectionism, in general, and the new protectionism, in particular, is contagious. For example, within months of the negotiated agreement that "voluntarily" restricted Japanese automobile exports to the United States in April 1981, Canada, West Germany, Belgium, the Netherlands, and Luxembourg all extracted similar "voluntary" agreements from Japan.

Reversing the present drift toward protectionism will not be easy. The best antiprotectionist measure is the resumption of rapid expansion by the world economy. A resumption of rapid growth not only will slow the decline of mature industries (such as textiles and steel) in developed nations but also will lead to the creation of many additional job opportunities in the rest of the economy to absorb new entrants into the labor force and to provide employment opportunities for displaced workers from declining industries. This, together with increased assistance (in the form of financial assistance, job retraining, and relocation allowances to displaced workers), would greatly reduce demands for trade protection and arrest or reverse the movement toward protectionism.[30]

---

[29] Of this about two-thirds was short- or medium-term (as opposed to long-term) and owed to commercial banks in developed countries. See World Bank (1985) and United Nations (1985).

[30] To be noted, however, is the fact that the limited adjustment assistance program set up in the early 1960s to aid American workers displaced by imports to retrain for other jobs (which union leaders branded "burial insurance") has practically been allowed to expire by the Reagan administration.

Another important step in avoiding a further drift toward protectionism is for the United States to reduce its huge budget deficit. This would lead to lower interest rates, a further depreciation of the dollar, and reduction in the record U.S. trade deficits, which is a very important cause of the new protectionism in the United States. Future gross currency misalignments and resulting protectionist pressures can be avoided only by effective international monetary cooperation among the leading countries. In the past, however, these nations have simply been unwilling to give up the large degree of autonomy that is required for effective international monetary cooperation.[31] While it is, of course, impossible to predict how the international monetary system might be changed in the future, support is increasing in international monetary circles for the establishment of currency target zones of perhaps plus or minus 10 percent with soft or adjustable margins.

Perhaps more promising as a way to reverse the trend toward greater protectionism is the agreement to begin a new round of multilateral trade negotiations in 1986. As pointed out by Bergsten and Cline,[32] governments find it somewhat easier to resist demands for new trade restrictions when they are engaged in trade-liberalizing negotiations. The crucial problem to be addressed in these new trade negotiations is the current drift toward bilateralism and discriminatory practices in international trade. There is today a serious need for the world to return to GATT's most-favored-nation principle. That is, to the principle that trade restrictions should not discriminate among sources of supply. Trade disputes should be resolved through GATT, not bilaterally. In particular, "voluntary" export restraints, which are bilateral and discriminatory, should be discontinued and replaced whenever possible by more open and transparent devices such as tariffs. As it is, managed trade greatly reduces the volume and the benefits of trade and generally leads to still more trade restrictions.

The new round of trade negotiations is also scheduled to address the question as to how far it is legitimate for nations to promote their high-technology industries by restricting market access, by subsidies to exports and to research and development, and by government procurement provisions favoring domestic suppliers. It seems that most industrial and some developing nations (such as Brazil) are claiming a greater share of high-tech industries than is consistent with world growth of these industries. This not only leads to current trade problems but also sows the seeds for even greater trade prob-

---

[31] See IMF (1984b).

[32] See Cline (1983, chap. 22).

lems in the future. Japan is a case in point. Having targeted the information industry for growth, Japan provides all sorts of trade protection and subsidies to the industry. It has been pointed out that

> leading-edge technology licences coming from Japan are under strict surveillance by the Japanese government. The Japanese provide less access to research results than any other non-communist country, placing government and private laboratories entirely off limits to American executives. At the same time, companies in Japan obtain licences for advanced technology developed in America, often at fire-place prices, frequently from smaller companies and universities, which do not reflect the costs and risks involved in development. [Norris, 1984]

It is now clear that without some international agreement on the development, expansion, protection, and trade in high-technology products by leading nations, the world will see increasing trade tensions in the future.

One of the major aims of U.S. trade policy today is to include trade in services (banking, insurance, telecommunications, data processing, high technology, and so on) in trade negotiations and to force Japan and other nations to open more widely their markets to American exports. As pointed out by Sauvant (1986), liberalizing international trade in services is strongly opposed by some developing nations, under the leadership of Brazil and India, as undermining their own development plans in this crucial field. Negotiations in this area are likely to prove long and difficult, and their success is by no means assured.

Conclusion

Trade policy in the United States over the past thirty years has been marked by continuous tensions. While the United States has generally adhered to the principle of free trade, it has made an increasing number of compromises to protect textiles, automobiles, steel, and other industries in exchange for political support for the general principle of free trade. However, in the process, the United States and the world have slipped more and more toward bilateralism and managed trade. Unless arrested, this process can undermine the entire world trading system and have very serious consequences for world welfare.

As we enter 1986, the greatest danger remains that of a trade war between the United States and Japan. In April 1985, the U.S. House of Representatives overwhelmingly voted to urge President Reagan to block Japanese imports unless Tokyo took prompt and effective action to open its market wider to American exports. A week earlier the Senate had passed a similar measure unanimously. In January 1986, the International Trade Commission ruled unanimously that Japan has dumped or sold computer chips in the United States at below Japanese production costs, and so the administration's "strike force" was set up in September 1985 to expose and fight trade restrictions against American exports by other nations. Under the pressure of imports from Japan and sluggish domestic demand, employment in the semiconductor industry declined by over 50,000 in the United States during 1985. American trade frustrations with Japan today can best be exemplified by the telecommunication industry in which the United States is acknowledged as the world leader—and in which it, nevertheless, had a deficit of about $2.5 billion with Japan in 1985. Although Japanese tariffs are low, Japanese regulatory, testing, product certification, and other barriers effectively restrict American exports of telecommunications, electronics, wood products, and medical and pharmaceutical products. In the fall of 1985 Japan responded with the most ambitious trade-liberalizing program to date, one that still fell far short of American demands.

It must be recognized, however, that under the best of circumstances, opening wider Japan's markets to American products may reduce the U.S. trade deficit by only $10 billion. This is less than 7 percent of the overall U.S. trade deficit in 1985 and 20 percent of its bilateral deficit with Japan.[33] However, unless American frustration with Japanese trade practices is quickly resolved, the danger of trade war remains real. As part of the new trade policy unveiled in September 1985 to improve the U.S. trade balance and derail the protectionist movement in Congress, the Reagan administration set up a $300-million "war chest" to help American exporters compete against the subsidized exports of other nations (particularly those of Japan and France) and to prosecute unfair trade practices by foreign nations in general. In November 1985, Congress approved legislation that would have placed stringent quotas on textile and shoe imports into the United States (President Reagan vetoed it).

There is today a great need for the United States to take the lead in checking the further spread of trade restrictions worldwide. The United States can do so by stimulating its growth, by reducing its budget deficits, and by pushing vigorously for reforms of the present international monetary and trading systems. Japan and Germany can also be of great help by stimulating their economies more and by

---

[33] In the paper included in this volume, Staiger, Deardorff, and Stern estimate with their Michigan Model of production and trade that the elimination of all Japanese tariff and nontariff trade barriers would lead to a significant net increase in employment only in American agriculture.

Japan responding more substantially to American demands for opening wider its economy to imports. Absolutely essential, however, is a strong leadership role by the United States. Without it, the world is likely to slip more and more into protectionism and managed trade, to the detriment of all. Time is clearly running out.

This is an updated, revised, and expanded version of a paper presented at the annual meetings, American Economic Association, Dallas, December 1984, and published in the special issue of the *Journal of Policy Modeling* (Spring 1985), on the same topic, which I edited.

References

Aho, M. C., and Aroson, J. D. (1985) *Trade Talks*. New York: Council of Foreign Relations.

Anjaria, S. J., Iqbal, Z., Kirmani, N., and Perez, L. L. (1982) *Developments in International Trade Policy*. Washington, D.C.: International Monetary Fund.

Balassa, B. (1978) The New Protectionism and the International Economy, *Journal of World Trade Law* 12: 409–436.

Baldwin, R. E. and Krueger, A. O. (eds.) (1984) *The Structure and Evolution of Recent U.S. Trade Policy*. Chicago: University of Chicago Press.

Bhagwati, J. N. (1971) The Generalized Theory of Distortions and Welfare. In *International Trade: Selected Readings* (J. N. Bhagwati et al., eds.). Amsterdam: North-Holland.

———— (1982) *Import Competition and Response*. Chicago: University of Chicago Press.

Bilson, J. F., and Marston, R. C. (1984) *Exchange Rate Theory and Practice*. Chicago: University of Chicago Press.

Branson, W. H. (1980) Trends in United States International Trade and Investment. In *The American Economy in Transition* (M. Feldstein, ed.). Chicago: University of Chicago Press.

Cline, W. R. (ed.) (1983) *Trade Policies in the 1980s*. Washington, D.C.: Institute for International Economics.

Cooper, R. N. (1984) A Monetary System for the Future, *Foreign Affairs* 63: 166–184.

Evans, P. (1985) Do Large Deficits Produce High Interest Rates?, *American Economic Review* 75: 68–87.

Federal Reserve Bank of Kansas City (1986) *The U.S. Dollar—Recent Developments, Outlook, and Policy Options*. Kansas City: Federal Reserve Bank of Kansas City.

Hamilton, B., and Whalley, J. (1983) Optimal Tariff Calculations in Alternative Trade Models and Some Possible Implications for Current World Trading Arrangements, *Journal of International Economics* 15: 323–348.

Hogan, W. T. (1984) *Steel in the United States: Restructuring to Compete.* Lexington, Mass.: Lexington Books.

IMF (1984a) Exchange Rate Volatility and World Trade. Occasional Paper 28. Washington, D.C.: International Monetary Fund.

—— (1984b) The Exchange Rate System: Lessons of the Past and Options for the Future. Occasional Paper 30. Washington, D.C.: International Monetary Fund.

Jones, R. W. and Kenen, P. B. (eds.) (1984, 1985) *Handbook of International Economics,* vols. i, ii. New York: North-Holland.

Krauss, M. B. (1978) *The New Protectionism: The Welfare State and International Trade.* New York: New York University Press.

Krugman, P. R. (1983) Targeted Industrial Policies: Theory and Evidence. In *Industrial Change and Public Policy.* Kansas City: Federal Reserve of Kansas City.

Laney, L. O. (1984) The Strong Dollar, the Current Account, and Federal Deficits: Causes and Effects, *Federal Reserve Bank of Dallas Economic Review* January: 1–14.

Lawrence, R. Z. (1984) *Can America Compete?.* Washington, D.C.: Brookings Institution.

McDonald, D. C. (1982) Debt Capacity and Developing Country Borrowing: A Survey of the Literature, *International Monetary Fund Staff Papers* 29: 603–646.

McKinnon, R. I. (1984) *An International Standard for Monetary Stabilization.* Washington, D.C.: Institute for International Economics.

Michaely, M. (1984) *Trade, Income Levels, and Dependence.* New York: North-Holland.

Norris, W. C. (1984) Halting the Flow of High-Tech Bargains, *The New York Times,* February 26: D3.

OECD (1979) *The Impact of Newly Industrializing Countries on Production and Trade in Manufactures.* Paris: Organization for Economic Co-operation and Development.

—— (1984) *Costs and Benefits of Protection.* Paris: Organization for Economic Co-operation and Development.

Ray, E. J., and Marvel, H. P. (1984) The Pattern of Protection in the Industrialized Countries, *Review of Economics and Statistics* 66: 452–458.

Salvatore, D. (1983) A Simultaneous Equations Model of Trade and Development with Dynamic Policy Simulations, *Kyklos* 36: 66–90.

—— (1984a) Petroleum Prices, Exchange Rates, and Domestic Inflation in Developing Nations, *Weltwirtschaftliches Archiv* 119: 580–589.

—— (1984b) *Theory and Problems of International Economics*. New York: McGraw-Hill.

—— (1985) The New Protectionism and the Threat to World Welfare, *Journal of Policy Modeling* 7: 1–22.

—— (1986) Oil Import Costs and Domestic Inflation in Industrial Countries, *Weltwirtschaftliches Archiv* 121: March.

—— (ed.) (1987a) *African Development Prospects: A Policy Modeling Approach*. New York: Elsevier.

—— (1987b) Import Penetration, Exchange Rates and Protectionism in the United States, *Journal of Policy Modeling* 9.

—— (ed.) (1987c) *International Economics*, 2nd ed. New York: Macmillan.

—— (1987d) The Emergence of New Protectionism with Nontariff Instruments, *Vienna Institute of Comparative Economic Studies—Working Paper Series*, Spring.

—— (1987e) *World Population Trends and Their Impact on Economic Development*. Westport, Conn.: Greenwood Press.

Sauvant, K. P. (1986) *International Transactions in Services: The Politics of Transborder Data Flows*. Boulder, Col.: Westview Press.

Schultz, C. L. (1983) Industrial Policy: A Dissent, *The Brookings Review* 2: 3–12.

Scott, B. R., and Lodge, G. C. (1986) *U.S. Competitiveness in the World Economy*. Boston: Harvard Business School Press.

Stern, R. M. (1983) The Appreciation of the U.S. Dollar and Its Implications for Industrial Policy. Mimeographed. Ann Arbor: University of Michigan.

Turner, L., and McMullen, N. (1982) *The Newly Industrializing Countries: Trade and Adjustment*. London: George Allen & Unwin.

United Nations (1985) *World Economic Survey*. New York: United Nations.

World Bank (1985) *World Bank Development Report*. Washington, D.C.: World Bank.

PART ONE

THE NEW PROTECTIONISM:
AN OVERVIEW

2

Protectionism:
Old Wine in New Bottles

JAGDISH BHAGWATI

Protectionism has always reared its familiar head when unemployment has risen and competition has gotten tough. Both these reasons have certainly contributed to the recent resurgence of the threat to the postwar environment of freer trade that generated rapid growth in both trade and incomes for nearly three decades. The major recession in the first Reagan term and the continuing high levels of unemployment in European countries despite the revival of the U.S. economy are the source of the macroeconomic threat. Moreover, the vast debt carried by Latin America fuels its need for more exports and adds to the difficulties of specific industries in the mature economies that must adjust to the relatively more rapid growth of outward-oriented economies of the Far East. Indeed, the growth of Japan "squeezes" the industries at the upper end of the technological spectrum whereas the growth of the Gang of Four (Taiwan, South Korea, Hong Kong, and Singapore) has been pressuring the industries at the lower end of that scale, resulting in a pincer movement that has fed the demands for protection from these industries.

This paper, however, does not address the specifics of the current protectionist situation as they reflect these economic phenomena. Instead, I choose to discuss here certain new types of arguments in defense of protection that have recently arisen. I divide these arguments into two classes: the ones that have arisen in the developing countries and those that have surfaced in the developed coun-

From Columbia University, New York, New York.

tries.[1] Finally I will examine some of the considerations that must be kept in mind in opening up trade in services.

Arguments in the Developing Countries[2]

The arguments in favor of protection in the developing countries arise essentially in the form of a resurrection of the assertion that the import-substituting (IS) strategy is preferable to the export-promoting (EP) strategy. Raised at the outset of the postwar period, and indeed forming the basic core of the debate over the ideal developmental strategy for the developing countries, this issue was settled in favor of the EP strategy by the remarkable success of the countries (in the Far East) that followed its precepts. Numerous studies, organized by several distinguished economists, led therefore to the demise of the notion that the IS strategy was the appropriate one, among the principal such studies being that done at the World Bank by Bela Balassa (1982); that done at the OECD by Ian Little, Tibor Scitovsky, and Maurice Scott (1970); and those done at the NBER by Bhagwati (1978) and Krueger (1978).

Recently, however, questions have been raised, with influential impact in some developing countries, concerning the advisability of the EP strategy, thus implying the desirability of an inward-looking, protectionist policy stance by the developing countries. As argued below, these are in my view legitimate, though somewhat misplaced, doubts. Their currency, however, is partly due to the "nationalistic" reaction that intellectuals in some of these countries have to the fact that the EP strategy has been turned into an important component of conditionality at the World Bank at a time when many countries are seeking help from the international institutions.

The new sources of protectionist sentiments are basically four-fold.

RECESSION-CUM-DEBT-CRISIS COSTS

During the postrecession years of the late 1970s and early 1980s, it is asserted that the EP countries must have suffered a greater adverse impact than the IS countries in view of their exposure to the external

---

[1] There are also a few *theoretical* arguments that have been advanced in the literature, based essentially on the introduction of market structures such as oligopoly and imperfect competition. In my judgment, their empirical relevance is not great, and several key results supportive of protection are critically dependent on absence of free entry into the market studied. A proper examination of these arguments, however, would take me far beyond the scope that I have defined for the present paper.

[2] The structure of the argument advanced in this section closely follows a recent discussion of the subject in my contribution to the *Festschrift* for Saburo Okita: see Bhagwati (1985).

environment. Insofar as the EP countries were also on a debt-led growth path, the debt crisis and the adjustments imposed by the collapse of the world credit markets would have forced yet greater costs on these countries. IS proponents would therefore feel vindicated.

However, the fact remains that the Far Eastern economies that were into EP strategy in the most pronounced fashion remained the best growth performers even as they slowed down with the rest of the world. In fact, Bela Balassa's (1982) cross-sectional analysis of comparative performance of the EP and IS countries during this lean period suggests little to confirm the suggestion that outward orientation has made countries fare worse. Moreover, the EP countries grew so much better during the many years preceding this lean period that any proper cost–benefit calculus would have to take into account earlier successes and set them off against the later losses (if there were any).

PROTECTION IN THE WORLD ECONOMY

If the world-trade environment is being overwhelmed by protection, would that not be a ground for retreating into the IS strategy? There are really several levels at which this argument can be addressed. First, adjusting for the income effects of the last recession, it is not clear that the *actual* protectionist effect on trade has been sufficiently severe to make us fear that the world trade order has begun to collapse. There are good reasons to infer rather that world trade has shown remarkable resilience in the face of these fears and threats, that the bark has been more evident than the bite, and that the revival of export pessimism may be premature.[3] Second, even if the world markets do not expand rapidly, this does not mean that developing countries will necessarily face, for *individual* decision making, a less than perfectly elastic offer curve: the offer curve may be fully elastic at any point of time while shifting steadily over time toward the developing country's offer curve. In that event, the case for an IS strategy does not legitimately derive from the traditional optimal-tariff-for-a-large-country argument. Third, I should like to emphasize that I do not find persuasive the frequent contention that the Far Eastern economies' EP model cannot be exported because if every developing country exports like them, the world cannot possibly absorb the resulting exports. This argument is often buttressed by raising all developing countries' exports to the same share of GNP as

---

[3] On this point, see the interesting paper of Bela and Carol Balassa (1984) in *The World Economy* which takes, consistently also with work by Anne Krueger and Helen Hughes at the World Bank, an optimistic view of world trade trends in the teeth of protectionist voices and actions.

in the Far Eastern economies. But the EP strategy simply implies eliminating the bias against exports. There is *no reason* to conclude that this would yield, for every country, the same share of trade to GNP as for the small group of current EP countries. Moreover, such extrapolations ignore the fact that trade can occur in all kinds of differentiated products and in unpredictable ways. Export pessimism in the 1950s was in no small part a result of the inability of planners in developing countries to think up, in their armchairs, the possible sources and composition of trade expansion. For example, before the trade in similar products seized our empirical and theoretical attention, who could have not thought that "similar economies" would have less, rather than more, trade with one another? Again, devaluations are often successful in promoting exports of "miscellaneous" items that no bureaucrat or economist can predict but which the opportunity for gainful trade seems often to galvanize. Finally, the fact that rapid trade expansion, if many more countries chose the EP strategy, could put pressure on specific sectors in specific countries cannot be denied. But interestingly, the reaction need not be simply protectionist but may also be to pressure one's rivals into freer trade as, in fact, is happening in the case of Japan at the insistence of Europe and the United States. Expanding trade needs may therefore ensure that the Western leadership may redouble its efforts to keep doors open *and* to open other people's doors.

WAGES AND LABOR MARKETS

A recent argument against the adoption of the EP strategy has been advanced by Gary Fields (1984). Contrasting the Far Eastern economies principally with the countries of the Caribbean, Jamaica included, he has argued in effect that these countries have suffered from excessively high wages that make protection desirable and that their reliance on the EP strategy has therefore been harmful rather than helpful.

   However, Fields does not establish, I am afraid, the basic contention that these countries have an EP strategy in the first place. As has been explained systematically in the Bhagwati (1978) and Krueger (1978) synthesis volumes from the NBER project, the EP strategy simply consists in eliminating the *bias against exports* implied by the (overvalued exchange rates, protection, etc. resulting in the) IS strategy. As far as one can tell, Fields has not produced the evidence on the relative effective exchange rates on exports (EER_x) and on imports (EER_m) that would support his contention that these are EP countries—i.e., that they are characterized by $EER_x \approx EER_m$ rather than by $EER_m > EER_x$ as with the IS countries. In fact, for Jamaica at least, I am assured that my presumption that it is really a classic case of an *IS strategy* is corroborated by such evidence. Fields, like many other commentators who are unfamiliar with the careful and analytical concepts in the literature, seems to have confused the island nature and smallness (with associated high ratios of trade to GNP)[4] of these countries with the altogether different concept of what is an EP strategy.[5]

Besides, note that the theoretical contention that labor market imperfections *may* require a departure from the EP strategy is well known from the work of trade theorists, including Richard Brecher, V. K. Ramaswami, T. N. Srinivasan, Harry Johnson, myself, and others during the 1960s. Their demonstration that the optimal policy intervention in these cases is to intervene in the factor markets directly—see my synthesis (1971) in the Kindleberger *Festschrift*—may of course not be feasible where political or institutional factors inhibit the implementation of such policies. If this case is persuasively established, then a protectionist departure from the EP strategy may well make sense. But I see no such case plausibly established for Fields' Caribbean countries either.

Fields' reliance rather on the argument that wages are kept under control in the Gang of Four countries seems to me to point to a very different general-equilibrium-theoretic argument of microeconomics. The Gang of Four countries appear to have used authoritarian methods to keep trade unions under control and to build on this a successful macro policy of low inflation. The good microeconomics of EP strategy has then been built on the necessary macro foundations without which one would likely lapse into repeated overvaluations, occasional exchange controls, and the attendant inefficiencies of implied import substitution. I have already hinted at this explanation in my NBER synthesis volume (1978), but it is a thesis that requires intensive empirical analysis for validation.

POLITICAL REQUIREMENTS?

Many critics of EP strategy have been worried about the association of this strategy with the authoritarian regimes of the Far Eastern countries. Does this not imply that the iron fist is essential for the adoption and successful implementation of this strategy?

Of course, since many developing countries are unfortunately authoritarian, this would not constitute a barrier to the adoption of the EP strategy. Less cynically, however, the argument simply ig-

---

[4] On four alternative ways of defining these ratios, and their conceptual underpinnings, see the important recent paper by Padma Desai (1984).

[5] Thus an EP strategy is wholly consistent with a "low" ratio of trade to GNP, however defined.

nores the fact that many totalitarian countries (e.g., the USSR) have been on the IS strategy, whereas within the Far Eastern economies the degree of authoritarianism varies, and not necessarily monotonically with respect to their economic performance. It is possibly safe to say that there are no necessary or sufficient conditions to be found here.

I would venture, however, to suggest the modest hypothesis that it has been hard for democratic countries such as India to transit from their early IS strategy, and easy for the less democratic and more authoritarian countries of the Far East to embrace the EP strategy after a brief IS phase, simply because pluralistic democracies may find it much harder to dismantle the controls, protection, etc. that inevitably accompany the IS strategy—because, in turn, these policy instruments carry patronage and confer on the politicians the power to collect funds for their reelection, so that the economic regime under the IS strategy tends to become a critical source of political power. By contrast, in authoritarian regimes, the political power is seized directly, freeing the rulers to shift to the EP strategy with its diminished patronage potential.[6]

A "satisficing" political theory has recently been advanced by John Ruggie (1983) and his associates, all distinguished political scientists, suggesting that the advantages of an EP strategy cannot be exploited by political regimes that cannot successfully address the distributional conflicts and tensions that would follow from this strategy. Fundamentally, this appears to me to be a persuasive argument as far as the acceptance or political feasibility of any developmental strategy is concerned. Where I part company from Ruggie and his associates is in the implied contention that the EP strategy leads to *more* such demands on the political system. An IS strategy, while relatively insulating the system from external disturbances, may create yet more tensions if the resulting loss of income expansion accentuates the zero-sum nature of the other policy options in the system. Therefore, I would rather convert the Ruggie thesis from its current version into the necessary and valid caveat that, in pursuing *any* developmental strategy, one must consider its compatibility with the political structure and resilience of the country. And this particular caveat is, I would stress, not one that I would address only to EP-strategy proponents.

The caveat does imply, in my view, that those who seek to include the EP strategy as a necessary ingredient of conditionality imposed by the World Bank or the IMF, as is, for example, the case with many Structural Adjustment Loans from the Bank, should be

---

[6] I have advanced this hypothesis in Bhagwati (1978), drawing on elements of the argument in Bhagwati and Krueger (1973).

urged to exercise some caution lest their prescriptions be counter-productive because of ignored political prerequisites. The unduly harsh witticism aimed at the distinguished Nicholas Kaldor, that political upheavals follow his advisory missions, is an excellent corrective to those who fail to place their economic prescriptions in their political context.

Arguments in the Developed Countries

Let us turn now to the arguments for protection that have arisen in the developed countries.

SHIFT TO THE SERVICE ECONOMY

Interestingly, the rise of modern service industries, reflecting the rapid growth of the information technologies, has led to two protectionist arguments, each in fact diametrically opposed to the other in its intellectual foundations.

On the one hand, we have the demand, especially from Nicholas Kaldor and his associates in Cambridge, for "reindustrialization," a sentiment supported in the United States by the sociologist Amitai Etzioni. The main contention of Kaldor seems to be that there are externalities associated with industrialization that would be lost otherwise. In particular, Kaldor's (1966, 1975) views seem to rest on the so-called Verdoorn (1949) finding that growth of productivity is higher in the manufacturing sector, a finding that also led him to recommend the Selective Employment Tax to Chancellor of the Exchequer Mr. Callahan to shift employment into manufactures. I am afraid, however, that this argument erroneously identifies low productivity with services as against manufactures, reflecting the identification by British economists of services with inefficient retailing and other traditionally low-productivity sectors in their economy. The argument is totally misleading when it comes to modern, highly progressive service sectors.[7]

On the other hand, many intellectuals and policymakers in the developed countries have begun identifying high-tech and information industries-cum-services as the cutting edge of the modern age, and this has led to the demand that, no matter what the market dictates, governments should assure that their nations get these activities established domestically through implicit or explicit protection. This is reminiscent of the demand for protection of manufac-

---

[7] I have discussed this issue, and the possible reasons underlying the prevalence of these views in Britain, in an article in *The World Economy* (Bhagwati 1984). I might warn the reader that there is also a macrotheoretic rationale advanced in Cambridge, England, for protection.

tures in the developing countries in the postwar years: few developing countries would have been willing to let the market (that is, comparative advantage) assign them to a purely primary-product specialization. For this reason I find this to be a potentially difficult area for GATT to monitor effectively. Politicians will simply be obdurate, I am afraid, in the face of advice from economists on this question.

DEFENSE

Surprisingly, the traditional argument for protection in order to promote defense industries has recently been revived by Paul Seabury (1983), a distinguished political scientist, in the context of the basic or smokestack industries and therefore in favor of "reindustrialization," for the United States. It is best to let him talk:

> Indeed, in light of the deteriorating state of its basic industries, the United States has a clear need for a coherent industrial policy, but for reasons wholly unrelated to those usually offered. The necessity for a U.S. industrial policy arises not from domestic economic considerations—however large these may currently loom—but rather from strategic–military concerns. As the only genuine guarantor of security for both itself and the Free World as a whole, the United States simply cannot afford to allow its industrial base to wither away. . . . The American industrial base constitutes the strategic core of Free World defenses. Those who, whether in the interests of free trade or a "high tech" boom, are content to remain untroubled by the demise of the U.S. basic industry would do well to remember Solon's stern warning to Croesus: Sir, if any man hath better iron than you, he will be master of all this gold. (1983, pp. 5–6)

This argument sounds wholly implausible to me, even though Seabury examines in detail the ways in which lack of domestic capacities in the basic industries might impact on conflagrations between the superpowers. He really would have to discount the possibility of drawing on supplies from the U.S. allies during such episodes. He would also have to ignore the possible policy option of storing supplies that may not be so accessible: nuts and bolts, not just tanks and oil, are capable of being stored. And if the shift to high-tech and modern services is indeed advantageous, I doubt immensely that the storage costs of "sensitive" basic-industry items would outweigh the costs of forgoing such a shift of specialization in response to shifting comparative advantage. Besides, there is also the "systemic" point that the United States cannot invoke this argument for protecting its basic industries without having serious impact on the "rule of law," as embodied in GATT. Can anyone seriously believe that the other GATT members would accept such an argument by the United States without cynicism? GATT is under enough pressure as it is without the United States, a principal actor on the scene, resorting to protection on such an implausible argument.[8]

THREAT OF PROTECTION TO INDUCE FOREIGN INVESTMENT: QUID PRO QUO DFI

A rather remarkable development in the developed countries in recent years has been the use of the *threat* of protection to induce foreign competitors in specific industries to invest in one's own country. This is reminiscent of the developing countries, especially those following the IS strategy, using *actual* protection to induce such investment inflows into specific sectors.

This type of direct foreign investment (DFI) is evident from the GM–Toyota deal in the United States, apparently prompted by the threat of domestic-content protection—which was very real prior to the imposition of VERs (voluntary export restrictions) on exports of autos by Japan to the United States. The quid pro quo for Toyota in this deal, which benefits General Motors and creates jobs for the United Auto Workers (UAW) union, is evidently the conversion of General Motors to a free-trader stance in local U.S. politics: this is manifest from the fact that GM alone among the U.S. automakers has been arguing against the extension of the auto VERs. Therefore I like to call this type of investment quid pro quo DFI.[9]

This model has its attractions and, I am afraid, will draw in more imitators as unions try to protect their specific jobs by threaten-

---

[8] Since Seabury does not really go into the question of alternative ways in which such protection may be provided, I should remind the reader that the theory of noneconomic objectives recommends that defense industries be protected not by tariffs but by domestic production subsidies.

[9] It may be of interest to the readers to note that this quid pro quo deal, which promotes joint investments and hence is a specific DFI "type," may be contrasted with another DFI type I developed in Bhagwati (1972) in a review of Vernon's work and have later elaborated in Bhagwati (1982). This type of DFI, which I christened the MPI (Mutual Penetration of Investment), involves mutual investment by GM in Toyota to produce the small cars the Japanese are better at, and by Toyota in GM to produce the large cars the Americans are better at, for reasons of historical specialization. This idea was suggested to me by the Dunlop–Pirelli DFI deals, where each bought into the other's specialization. I was contrasting the MPI model with Vernon's celebrated "product-cycle" model and predicting that the MPI model would be the wave of the future, just like *trade* in "similar products." For the time being, however, it seems to be partly displaced from the center stage by the model type that I am discussing in the text, where the foreign competitors' quid pro quo comes not from their investing in your specialized knowhow, but rather simply from getting you on their side in an otherwise-difficult-to-avoid threat of protectionist actions.

ing protection as an inducement to the foreign producers to manufacture here rather than there.

OPENING UP TRADE IN SERVICES[10]

The GATT has provided the liberal trading order, facilitating the
phenomenal postwar growth of world commerce. But it oversees
only trade in goods.

Services, now estimated at up to a quarter of world trade, have
no corresponding compact that defines the rules and procedures to
govern their trade. For half a decade now, the United States has led
efforts to fill this vacuum. But, at the November 1982 GATT inter-
ministerial meetings and in early October 1985 in Geneva, important
developing countries led by Brazil and India adamantly opposed
these initiatives.

This confrontation is unfortunate. It sours relations between
the developing countries and the United States just as the former
have changed from impassioned rhetoric to pragmatism and the latter, as in Mr. Baker's policy moves at Seoul, has turned from ideolog-
ically inspired rigor mortis to necessary intervention. It also threatens to push the United States, through ire and impatience, into
opting yet again for bilateral and regional moves, reinforcing the
fragmentation of the world trading system away from multilateralism.

Developing countries must therefore be brought on board in the
negotiations on international transactions in services. How can this
be done?

The key lies in recognizing that, despite the occasional rhetoric
on behalf of world efficiency from having a service trade compact,
U.S. negotiators have unwittingly tended to press U.S. advantages in
services instead of seeking mutuality of interests within the broad
service sector itself. This has much to do with the factors that have
propelled the United States into its catalytic role on service trade.

Certainly the force of the economic philosophy of free trade,
and the obvious logic that it should apply to service transactions as
well, has been important. However, the principal thrust has come
from lobbying by particular service sectors. In particular, successful
political pressure has resulted from the global outreach desired principally by multinational banks and by corporations in the new "telematics" sector, and later by companies providing insurance, accounting, and other business services.

---

[10] This section is based on my article in *New York Times*, "U.S. Should Heed
Third World Demands," November 10, 1985, p. F3.

In turn, arguments of national interest have served to buttress the efforts of these special-interest lobbies. U.S. export advantage is increasingly seen as having shifted to service transactions. It is therefore considered unfair to have U.S. markets open to goods while foreign markets are closed to U.S. services. This is simply another instance of the increased demands for "aggressive reciprocity" and "level playing fields." Also, the insistence on opening foreign markets to service sectors is part of the "grand alternative" to a protectionist response to the American trade-deficit problem.

But the immediate consequences of these origins of American interest in service trade negotiations have been untoward. In particular, the United States has focused energies mainly on those sectors in which Americans happen to have the exporting edge. This has therefore encouraged the notion that service trade is for U.S. export benefit, goods trade for that of the developing countries. Accordingly, the U.S. negotiators have tended to argue that the mutuality of interests in trade negotiations must come from developed-country gains on trade in services and developing-country benefits from trade in goods. Goods-trade concessions to developing countries have been seen as the quid pro quo for their service trade concessions to the United States.

But the more articulate developing countries find these aspects of the U.S. position unfair and hence unacceptable. If service negotiations are going to reflect the export interest of the developing countries, what do *they* get? The United States has suggested offering "rollbacks" of VERs, "standstill" on new protection on goods of interest to the developing countries. But the developing countries see all recent and threatened trade barriers on goods as de facto violations of GATT obligations anyway. Protectionist rollbacks and standstills on goods trade are seen, therefore, not as concessions but as acceptance of existing GATT obligations. In short, since services are a *new* area not contemplated as subject to the original GATT protocol, they think they are being offered a raw bargain: an unrequited concession on services masquerading as a quid pro quo agreement.

We must recognize the legitimacy of this view. We should therefore look for service sectors where the developing countries have the export edge. The quid pro quo must be sought within the service sector itself. Among the most obvious services where many developing countries have recently developed such trading advantage is in the construction sector.

South Korea, India, the Philippines, Egypt, Pakistan, and a growing number of developing countries are already waiting to redo in the developed countries what they have been doing in the Middle

East: building highways, hospitals, schools and playgrounds, using skilled and unskilled labor from home. Indeed, South Korea has formally applied to the European Economic Community (EEC) to enable its firms to enter the community in this fashion.

Conceptually these are indeed services, and international transactions in them cannot legitimately be excluded from a services compact. Willingness to include them and related transactions in the negotiations we seek would help convince the developing countries that the emerging discussion of the rules designed for service transactions will be even-handed.

There is also an added advantage in enlarging the scope of service trade negotiations in this way to accommodate services where the developing countries have the export advantage. It would alert us instantly to the obvious difficulties we must face in moving toward a free market in such services as construction. In so doing, it would equally bring home to the United States that the developing countries too have serious difficulties with opening their markets fast and fully to services in which we have the export advantage instead.

Thus banking raises issues of fiduciary and monetary control, whereas telematics is generally regarded—not just by India and Brazil but also by France and Japan—as a field that simply cannot be left to the marketplace.

In short, we cannot realistically expect that such service sectors can be brought altogether under a GATT-type "rule of law" trade regime. "Who gets what," not just "what rules do we play by," becomes a critical question. Quantity outcomes become relevant. The analogy has to be partly with armaments negotiations: we would not expect nation-states to leave the location of defense production to be determined by market forces.

It is therefore evident how we should proceed. The scope of the negotiations must be augmented to include service transactions such as construction where the developing countries enjoy export advantage. Generous quantity-outcome safeguards should be permitted in sensitive sectors such as banking, telematics, and construction. Developing countries would then recognize true mutuality of advantage and fairness, rather than the current force majeure, in the service trade compact the United States seeks. This could indeed bring them on board.[11]

---

[11] The issues considered above have been analyzed in greater depth in my Tenth Annual Lecture of the Geneva Association, delivered at the London School of Economics on November 28, 1985, and to be published, along with discussants' comments, by the Association Internationale pour l'Etude de l'Economie de l'Assurance.

quick

References

Balassa, Bela (1982) *Development Strategies in Semi-Industrial Economies.* Baltimore: Johns Hopkins University Press.

—— (1983) External Shocks and Adjustment Policies in 12 Less Developed Countries: 1974–76 and 1979–81. Paper presented to the Annual Meeting of the American Economic Association, San Francisco, December.

—— and Balassa, Carol (1984) Industrial Protection in the Developed Countries, *The World Economy* (7)2: 179–196.

Bhagwati, Jagdish N. (1971) The Generalized Theory of Distortions and Welfare. In *Trade, Balance of Payments and Growth: Essays in Honour of Kindleberger* (J. Bhagwati et al., eds.). Amsterdam: North-Holland.

—— (1972) Review of *Sovereignty at Bay* by Raymond Vernon, *Journal of International Economics* 2: 455–459.

—— (1978) *The Anatomy and Consequences of Exchange Control Regimes.* Cambridge, Mass.: Ballinger & Co.

—— (1982) Shifting Comparative Advantage, Protectionist Demands, and Policy Response. In *Import Competition and Response* (J. Bhagwati, ed.). Chicago: Chicago University Press.

—— (1984) Splintering and Disembodiment of Services and Developing Nations, *The World Economy* 7(2): 133–144.

—— (1985) Export Promotion as a Development Strategy. In *Essays in Honor of Saburo Okita* (T. Shishido and R. Sato, eds.). Boston: Auburn House.

—— and Krueger, Anne O. (1973) Exchange Controls, Liberalization and Economic Development, *American Economic Review* (May) 419–427.

Desai, Padma (1984) How Should the Role of Foreign Trade in the Soviet Economy be Measured? Working Paper No. 42. New York: International Economics Research Center, Columbia University.

Fields, Gary (1984) Employment, Income Distribution and Economic Growth in Seven Small Open Economies, *Economic Journal* 994: 74–83.

Kaldor, Nicholas (1966) *Causes of the Slow Economic Growth of the United Kingdom.* Cambridge, Eng.: Cambridge University Press.

—— (1975) Economic Growth and the Verdoorn Law: A Comment on Mr. Rowthorn's Article, *Economic Journal* 85: 891–896.

Krueger, Anne Osborne (1978) *Liberalization Attempts and Consequences.* Cambridge, Mass.: Ballinger & Co.

—— (1982) *Trade and Employment in Developing Countries: Synthesis and Conclusions.* Chicago: University of Chicago Press.

Little, Ian, Scitovsky, Tibor, and Scott, Maurice (1970) *Industry and Trade in Some Developing Countries.* London: Oxford University Press.

Ruggie, John Gerard (ed.) (1983) *The Antinomies of Interdependence: National Welfare and the International Division of Labor.* New York: Columbia University Press.

Seabury, Paul (1983) Industrial Policy and National Defense. *Journal of Contemporary Studies* 2: 5–15.

Verdoorn, P. J. (1949) Fattori che regolano lo sviluppo della produttivita del lavoro, *L'Industria* 1: 3–11.

3

The Revival of Protectionism in Developed Countries

W. MAX CORDEN

There is evidence of the revival of protectionist attitudes in developed countries, notably the United States and Western Europe. This essay reviews some aspects of this protectionist renaissance, focusing particularly on the relationship between protection and macroeconomic events and policies.

Protection and Macroeconomic Policies

RECESSIONS BRING PROTECTION

From 1980 to 1982 the developed world passed through a major recession created essentially by tight monetary policies designed to squeeze inflation out of the system. During this period protectionist pressures increased, and there were also some increases in actual protection. This experience raises the important issue of the connection between two sets of government policies—protection policies and macroeconomic policies. One has to consider the case where the latter may have induced a recession or may have failed to prevent a recession caused by other factors and where the recession in turn has induced pressures to increase protection.

Policies of monetary tightness squeeze profitability and reduce employment, one aim—perhaps the primary one—being to moderate wage increases. If the moderation in wages anticipated the mone-

From the Australian National University, Canberra, Australia.

tary squeeze, or at least followed it very closely, then profitability and employment would not need to fall, and the desired decline in the rate of inflation could be brought about without cost. But we know that profits do get squeezed and employment does fall. The declines in the rates of inflation in the United States, Japan, Germany, and Britain were brought about at considerable cost, especially in Britain. Additionally, if a country's monetary contraction is significantly greater than that of other countries (so that its real interest rate rises relatively), its real exchange rate is likely to appreciate and the decline in profitability and employment will be greater, the adverse effects being focused on the export and import-competing sectors of the economy. This was the experience both in the United States and in Britain.

Pressures for protection, direct and indirect, are then inevitable. The protection may take the form not of tariffs, quotas, or voluntary export restraints (VERs), but of subsidization of private industries or the covering of losses of publicly owned industries, as in the case of British Steel. Recessions, whether policy-induced or not, always give rise to increased pressures for protection.

This experience suggests that contradictions in government policy can arise here. The central bank and ministry of finance bring about a profitability squeeze which the ministry of industry—pushing for protection—seeks vainly to reverse. If the latter were successful one would have to ask whether the original macroeconomic policy was justified: the profitability squeeze was meant to moderate wage increases, and these will not be moderated if the squeeze is avoided by protection. But in fact, in an overall sense protection cannot undo what macroeconomic policy has created. It can only reshuffle the consequences. For example, with given fiscal and monetary policies, subsidies to particular industries must be balanced by fewer funds elsewhere. If taxes are raised, this may lead to increased wage demands, again offsetting the initial effects. Furthermore, protection to help some import-competing industries which have suffered from appreciation will lead to greater appreciation than otherwise, and so increase the adverse effects on other import-competing as well as export industries.

These considerations do not rule out a role for microeconomic policy, including specific subsidies or even tariffs, but they do raise a question about protectionist policies designed to negate or soften the effects of macroeconomic policies.

A recession—whether policy-induced or otherwise—may lead to increases in protection in spite of the implicit contradiction just discussed. The danger is then that protection will not be reduced once the economy recovers, since reducing protection may require a much more prolonged period of prosperity. Long-term costs are then imposed in the form of adverse effects on resource allocation and on the degree of competition. If protectionist pressures at a time of recession cannot be resisted, such adverse long-term effects must be taken into account when framing short-term macroeconomic policies. A temporary recession has then adverse long-term effects not only through the fall in investment that it brings about and through the loss of work experience of the temporarily unemployed but also through the recession-protection ratchet effect: a recession increases protection, but the following boom does not lower it to the same extent.

The association of increased protection with recessions or depression has also led some people to believe that protection can actually cause recessions. The association of the two in the 1930s helps to explain the free-trade movement in developed countries in the 1950s and 1960s. Others again think that protection can moderate a recession because of the favorable effects on employment in particular industries. In fact, it is not obvious that protection can either contribute to or moderate a recession. It can, of course, raise the inducement to invest in particular industries, but one must balance against this the indirect opposite effects in other industries.

PROTECTION AND GROWTH

While the relationship between protection and recession goes only one way—recessions tending to increase protection but protection not necessarily moderating or intensifying recessions—the relationship between low long-term growth and protection is clearly two-way. Widespread protection is likely to lower the long-term growth rate, especially if it is designed to protect losers from change rather than just consisting of a system of fixed tariffs or subsidies. It reduces the flexibility of the economy, and hence the productivity of capital and labor. At the same time, low growth—and especially a shift of gear to a lower growth rate—means that adjustment between industries is difficult since *relative* losers may also have to be *absolute* losers, since fewer alternative job opportunities become available and since fewer resources are available to compensate losers. People become more security-minded, protection being part of an implicit "industry insurance system." Hence it has been much easier to reduce protection at times of high growth.

Looking ahead, it seems likely that the ending of the recession will somewhat reduce protectionist pressures. It will certainly provide an opportunity for policymakers who appreciate the virtues of freer trade but find it difficult to resist political pressures. An interesting question is whether capacity utilization in the world steel industry will improve, so allowing a reduction of protection in one of the most sensitive areas in the United States and the European Community. There is little reason to expect a complete restoration of employment levels in the U.S. and European steel and automobile industries owing to various long-term factors, so some pressures for protection of these two major industries are likely to continue. Furthermore, the underlying OECD growth rate is likely to stay low so that it would be optimistic to expect a dramatic change in attitudes.

PROTECTION AND THE EXCHANGE RATE

In the days of fixed exchange rates it was often said that a move to floating rates would obviate the need for tariffs and quotas to deal with balance-of-payments deficits. In the immediate aftermath of the first oil shock it was usual to congratulate OECD countries for having avoided a revival of protectionism, the credit being given (at least to some extent) to exchange-rate flexibility.

   If one thinks of devaluation as a policy instrument that switches demand from foreign to home goods and, within the latter, from tradeables to nontradeables, and switches output from supplying the domestic market to exports, then tariffs, tighter import quotas, export subsidies, and so on are substitutes for devaluation. The standard argument is that they are inferior substitutes because they create distortions *within* the tradeable goods (import-competing plus exporting) sector. Tariffs and quotas favor only import substitution relative to nontradeables, while devaluation or depreciation makes both import substitution and exporting more profitable relative to nontradeables, so that they are not antitrade-biased. Furthermore, devaluation (or depreciation in a floating rate regime) has a uniform effect on the import side—being like a uniform ad valorem tariff—and so avoids the distortions between different import-substituting activities which result from differential tariffs or from any system of import quotas.

   It is thus an important argument in favor of exchange-rate flexibility that it is likely to reduce or eliminate the need to use tariffs, quotas, and similar devices for balance-of-payments reasons. Comparing two ways of improving the balance of payments (while simultaneously maintaining the level of demand for domestically produced goods and services in total)—the way of devaluation and the way of tariffs or quotas—the former has a more favorable resource allocation effect.

   It must be stressed that, for a given level of utilization of domestic labor and capacity, any improvement in the current account of the balance of payments requires a fall in aggregate expenditure, since the initial excess of expenditure over output has to be reduced if the current account is to improve. It is widely understood that this is so in the case of devaluation, but it is also true if tariffs or import quotas were, instead, to be used. Thus trade restrictions are not painless ways of improving the balance of payments.

We have considered here the case where a country has to improve its competitiveness because the balance of payments needs to improve. The argument also applies to the case where a change in the balance of payments is not needed but where a country is losing competitiveness owing to its inflation rate exceeding that of its trading partners. Exchange-rate depreciation can then restore competitiveness. If such exchange-rate adjustment were not possible the resultant losses in profitability and employment in the export and import-competing industries would inevitably generate protectionist pressures.

ADVERSE EFFECTS
OF EXCHANGE-RATE FLUCTUATIONS

This standard approach views the exchange rate as a policy instrument. It implies that the exchange rate is neither fixed nor freely floating, but rather is managed so as to attain desired competitiveness or balance-of-payments outcomes. The rate could be pegged in the short run, with occasional or frequent policy decisions that alter the peg. A system of managed floating, with frequent interventions in the foreign exchange market by central banks, could also have the same result. But we must now consider a somewhat different situation, one where the exchange rate floats—possibly with some "leaning against the wind" intervention—and fluctuates over the medium term because of varying pressures originating in the capital market. There will then be changes, possibly very large ones, in competitiveness. This might be called the U.S. problem—on which a number of economists, notably Bergsten and Williamson (1983), have focused recently.

Whenever the United States loses competitiveness, pressures for U.S. protectionism intensify. The yen–dollar rate is particularly important in this respect. There have been three periods when the dollar appears to have been overvalued relative to the yen in terms of purchasing power parity (meaning some average longer-term real exchange rate). The overvaluation in the late 1960s and early 1970s gave rise to the Mills and Burke–Hartke bills, import controls on steel, and finally, in 1971, the import surcharge. The Burke–Hartke bill, if enacted, would have imposed strict quantitative limits on the levels and rates of growth of all imports into the United States. The overvaluation of the 1976–1977 period led to major trade conflict between the United States and Japan. Finally, the most recent overvaluation has led to voluntary export restraints on Japanese cars and numerous protectionist proposals in Congress.

It is implied in this view that fluctuations in exchange rates originating in the capital market, especially in the yen–dollar rate, always generate pressures for increased protection in the United States when the dollar is in its real appreciation phase—when U.S. competitiveness has declined—but that this is not offset by reductions in protection when the dollar is in its real depreciation phase. Thus an asymmetry or ratchet effect is implied. When times are bad for U.S. import-competing industries they succeed in getting more protection, but when times become good this protection is not dismantled. There is possibly some tendency toward such a ratchet effect, though it has to be borne in mind that "protectionist pressures" do not always lead to actual increases in protection. Furthermore, one must also look at the Japanese side of the coin. There have in the last few years been some modest reductions of protection in Japan (how much being hard to assess) and it seems very plausible that this has been caused not only by political pressure from the United States but also by the improved competitiveness of Japanese industries owing to yen depreciation.

Medium-term fluctuations in exchange rates in response to forces originating in the capital market are not necessarily inappropriate. A country's exchange rate may appreciate because there is a transfer of long-term capital into the country based on correct expectations of favorable investment opportunities relative to other countries. Thus the United States has lately been seen by investors as a "safe haven." The exchange rate may also appreciate because of short-term capital inflows (or incipient inflows) that reflect particular expectations of prospective monetary and fiscal policies, expectations that may be perfectly rational given available information.

If the resultant loss in competitiveness leads to protectionist pressures the question arises to what extent the exchange rate itself should be altered through exchange market intervention—which may be difficult, in any case, if market expectations are very firm—and to what extent effort should be put, rather, into resisting the protectionist pressures, while allowing the exchange rate to fluctuate. If the market expectations turn out to be justified, some reallocation of resources induced by the exchange-rate signals will also be justified. But this does not rule out an argument in favor of the monetary authorities forming a medium-term view about an exchange rate and, if this view differs from the market, sometimes cautiously acting on it.

THE U.S. BUDGET DEFICIT AND THE DECLINE
IN U.S. COMPETITIVENESS

The immediate question for the United States is whether the real appreciation of the dollar relative to the yen and to various European currencies, notably the DM, is here to stay for some time or is likely to be reversed in due course.

The upturn in the U.S. economy will raise private U.S. savings. While it might also be expected to raise U.S. private investment, on balance there might be some increase (in real terms) in the net financial surplus of the U.S. private sector. The upturn should also in due course eliminate the cyclical part of the U.S. fiscal deficit. On the other hand, the structural budget deficit will increase because of tax cuts and higher defense spending. On balance it seems highly unlikely that the private sector net financial surplus will be sufficient to finance the large budget deficit. Of course, if there were no international capital mobility and exchange rates were freely floating, the private surplus would have to finance the public deficit. This would be brought about by real interest rates rising until sufficient private investment were crowded out for the private surplus to reach the level of the budget deficit. Furthermore, if the deficit were financed with monetary expansion, inflation might raise savings and also reduce the budget deficit.

In any case, with an open capital market it is inevitable—and desirable from the U.S. point of view—that the higher interest rates will draw in capital from abroad. Inevitably the United States will have to finance some of its budget deficit from foreign savings. If it did not do so and the structural budget deficit attained the sorts of levels being currently expected there would have to be a significant decline in private investment relative to its normal recovery level in the United States. The United States must thus run a current account deficit, this being the way in which foreign savings become absorbed into the United States.

One wishes that this simple connection between U.S. fiscal policy and the external balance were more widely understood in the United States.[1]

Real appreciation is part of the mechanism by which a current-account deficit is brought about. The United States has to lose competitiveness if it is to generate the current-account deficit which is the counterpart of the capital inflow. There has to be some shift of resources, at least at the margin, away from export and import-com-

---

[1] An excellent exposition of these issues, making many of the key points stressed in the present paper, appeared in Council of Economic Advisers (1983), chap. 3.

peting industries toward nontradeables. Clearly there will be gainers in the United States—above all the industries stimulated by the extra defense spending and those benefiting from the extra consumer spending resulting from the tax cuts—but there will be losers, namely employees and the owners of capital in the tradeable goods industries, especially the more marginal ones. In addition, of course, there are gainers and losers from higher interest rates. Inevitably losers seek protection, irrespective of gainers elsewhere.

If this is a correct assessment, there are three implications:

1. We face the prospect of continued or even increased protectionist pressures in the United States.
2. It needs to be widely understood that the decline in U.S. competitiveness is a by-product of expansionary fiscal policy—an inevitable one—and does not reflect any particular inadequacies of U.S. industries. Such inadequacies may well exist although they need not lead to a general loss of competitiveness, but only to a loss of competitiveness on the part of particular industries, offset—through the mechanism of exchange-rate adjustment—by a gain in competitiveness of other industries. It would seem appropriate that those whose taxation and spending policies have generated the deficit go to some trouble to explain that an overall loss of U.S. competitiveness is necessary. In doing so they may be able to moderate some of the protectionist pressures.
3. If some increase in protection is a predictable by-product of real appreciation, while real appreciation in turn is a by-product of an increased fiscal deficit, then there is a reason to reduce the fiscal deficit additional to the usual reasons. It is usually argued that a large deficit would tend to crowd out private investment, might lead to the incurring of undue interest commitments eventually payable by the U.S. taxpayer, and would have adverse effects on developing-country debtors and new borrowers. To this is now added the resource misallocation cost resulting from extra protection.

If the increase in U.S. protection turned out to be significant, it could not alter the *average* effect on U.S. import-competing and export industries of the fiscal deficit. It could only shelter particular industries or sectors at the expense of others. If an increase in particular imports is prevented by protection, other imports will have to increase even more, and so other import-competing industries will be even more adversely affected and the decline in exports will have to be greater. The key point is that the higher the level of protection for particular sectors the greater the real appreciation of the dollar will have to be to yield the required current-account deficit. The cost of protection to the United States results from the distortions set up within the U.S. tradeables sector and in distorting relative tradeables prices facing U.S. purchasers. Foreign suppliers of protected products will certainly lose, but foreign suppliers of other products will actually gain, benefiting from an even higher real appreciation.

OECD Protection and the Developing Countries

PROTECTION AND THE DEBT PROBLEM

The effects of OECD protection on the developing countries are crucial. To start with, the relationship between OECD protection and the developing countries' debt will be discussed. It seems obvious that if the indebted developing countries are to meet their interest obligations and eventually to repay at least some of their debt they must be allowed to increase their exports. It also seems obvious that it is in the interests of the developed countries, and especially their financial system, that the debt issue be resolved without open or implicit default.

It might be argued that improvements in a current account can be brought about as much by reductions in imports as in increases in exports. Clearly the indebted developing countries may need to operate on both fronts. But if OECD countries were unwilling to accept substantial extra imports of manufactures from developing countries, then the latter would be forced to bring about the necessary balance-of-payments improvements mainly by reducing their own imports from OECD countries. This would mean that the necessary improvements would be brought about at greater cost to the developing countries. They would be deprived of the potential benefits of further exploiting their comparative advantage in labor-intensive products.

More specifically, there tends to be some minimum requirement of imported components and raw materials for domestic manufacturing production (at least in the short run), so cutting imports beyond a point is likely to lead to increased unemployment. Furthermore, reduced imports would raise the cost of living, so tend to raise nominal wages to compensate, and hence lead to reduced employment in the manufacturing industry owing to higher wage costs. It follows that the indebted countries will have to increase their exports—and to be allowed to do so by OECD countries—if they are to bring about the necessary balance-of-payments improvements at tolerable cost.

How important is this issue for the principal debtors? In the case of a number of products exported by them OECD protection must have reduced their income substantially. The Community's Common Agricultural Policy has had an adverse effect on Argentinian agricultural exports. Some of the debtor countries are substantial exporters of textiles and clothing. The Republic of Korea is a debtor country and obstacles have been placed by the United States on its exports of textiles, clothing, and color television sets. In addition to these products, Community countries have restricted imports from Korea of steel products and (in the case of France at least) many other goods. Its footwear exports generally meet trade obstacles in the Community on a whole range of primary product exports. Japan has quotas on footwear imports. These are just examples.

Perhaps more important in the case of several of the countries are the actual and expected obstacles against products which would form the basis of a feasible export expansion program. The potential for expanding exports of labor-intensive goods of various kinds would seem to be very large. I shall return to this point below.

THE EFFECTS OF OECD PROTECTION
ON THE DEVELOPING COUNTRIES

Until a few years ago one could say clearly that OECD protection in the manufacturing sector grossly discriminated against developing countries, especially the more successful exporters among them. This is in spite of the Generalised System of Preferences, which has had a modest effect compared with the various and complex restrictions imposed under the umbrella of the Multi-Fibre Arrangement (MFA).

It really seems outrageous that over a long period of time severe limits have been placed on imports of textiles and clothing from developing countries. It appears that these restrictions, if anything, have been strengthened since the renewal of the MFA in 1981. This arrangement provides a framework for bilateral agreements (utterly contrary to the most-favored-nation GATT principle) and is the basis for numerous VERs. At the end of 1982 the United States had bilateral agreements with twenty-two developing countries, mostly embracing all textiles and textile products (clothing), and the Community with twenty-nine. The full implications of the 1981 MFA renewal are unclear (since much will depend on actual bilateral agreements reached under its umbrella) but it endorses continued quantitative restrictions arranged bilaterally, especially against the most successful suppliers. Furthermore, the complexities of the arrangements are likely to inhibit exporters, especially the less experienced ones.

Textiles and clothing are by no means the only products from developing countries that have suffered from restrictions, but it is here that the comparative advantage of developing countries seems particularly strong. The Common Agricultural Policy also has an adverse effect on many developing countries which are exporters of wheat, beef, rice, and sugar. It is worth noting that some developing countries which are importers of products the Europeans export at heavily subsidized prices are gainers. This would include particularly major grain importers. It cannot be said that the Common Agricultural Policy clearly discriminates against developing countries since it has a significant adverse effect on temperate-zone exporters such as Australia, Canada, and New Zealand (though Argentina is also in that group). In addition, because of restrictions imposed primarily on Japanese exports in recent years, one cannot say for sure that overall protection by the United States and the Community discriminates against developing countries. But it does discriminate against particular labor-intensive products, and, in any case, in some fields at least, it puts a severe limit on export expansion by developing countries.

The importance of these protectionist policies directed against exports from developing countries can perhaps be overstated.[2] After all, manufactured exports from developing countries to OECD countries have continued to increase and rose steadily, even relative to world trade, over the whole postwar period. It is worth noting that in 1970 the share of developing-country imports in the total (apparent) consumption of manufactured goods in industrial countries was 1.7 percent and by 1980 it had risen to 3.4 percent. In the United States it rose from 1.3 percent to 2.9 percent. So protection may have slowed the growth of exports somewhat but did not halt it. Even exports of textiles and clothing have steadily increased.

Taking a broad view, the severest restrictions have clearly been applied in the field of clothing and textiles. Even here some suppliers have managed to cope with the restrictions by upgrading their products: when restrictions are on a quantitative basis it pays to export higher-value products. This, of course, is not necessarily an economically sound adjustment for a country that may have a comparative advantage in low-value, low-quality products. In addition many developing countries have widely diversified their exports, moving into areas where there have been rather fewer or looser restrictions: machinery and nonmetallic mineral products (including china and glassware), and miscellaneous goods such as sports equipment, toys, and musical instruments. Furthermore, extensive import

---

[2] The following discussion draws on Hughes and Waelbroek (1981) and Hughes and Krueger (1983).

controls have been imposed on products from the Far Eastern exporters and nevertheless they have increased their shares of the OECD market. Restrictions on footwear imports into most OECD countries have not been as tight as for clothing and textiles, although Japan has strict quotas, the Community has negotiated VERs with Korea and Taiwan, and tariffs are still moderately high (averaging 13 percent in the major developed countries).

On the other hand, the possibilities of export expansion are very great. There are widespread restrictions on imports of consumer electronics from developing countries, notably Korea, and yet these must be regarded as having a major potential for growth. Developing countries clearly have a comparative advantage in textiles, clothing, and footwear and yet still have only a small part of the market of OECD countries. (In 1976 the developing countries had about 2 percent of the total U.S. market for textiles and 10 percent of the market for clothing, though, of course, they had a much larger share of imports. In 1980 the share in the market of a group of eleven industrial countries as a whole—including the main ones—was 5.4 percent for textiles and just over 16 percent both for clothing and for footwear.) Not only are there possibilities of further expansion from the major existing exporters but there are also many potential exporters around the world who could, after an initial infant-industry period, become suppliers of such goods to the industrial countries without subsidization. But they are likely to be discouraged by the prospects of restrictions as soon as they manage to break into a market.

PROTECTION BY DEVELOPING COUNTRIES

Perhaps the worst aspect of the continuance of such protection and the revival of protectionist sentiments in the developed countries is that it may lead to a revival of export pessimism in developing countries, leading again to inward-looking policies.

In the 1950s export pessimism was fashionable, especially in India and Latin America, and, arguably, led to severely growth-inhibiting import-substitution policies. For a long time it was widely believed that there was little hope of breaking into the markets for manufactured goods of the developed countries so that, if developing countries were to build up their manufacturing industries, they would have to do so by replacing imports. On the basis of such beliefs some highly uneconomic industries were built up in many countries, for example India and Brazil. Partly as a result of the successes of the new industrial countries, as well as of academic and World Bank research and writing, there has been a gradual shift of opinion, leading to some modest tendencies to liberalization in many developing countries and a realization of the disadvantages of import-substitution policies. The experiences of Korea and Taiwan seemed to justify export optimism. In fact, in major countries the shift of policies has not been so great. But the danger is that this tendency will now be reversed.

There are really two separate issues here. One is whether protection in developed countries justifies protection by developing countries. It might be noted here that most developing countries have much more all-embracing systems of protection—and, on the average, at much higher rates—than OECD countries have. If the OECD rates of protection were *given*, there would be no case for developing countries keeping their protection just because of OECD protection. This is a well-known proposition of trade theory: one country's protection does not justify another's. Protection by a trading partner lowers the real income both of the partner and at home, and protection at home would add to the income loss both at home and in the partner country.

The matter would be different if OECD protection consisted of fixing the quantity of (rather than rates of protection on) imports from developing countries. It would then pay the latter to restrict their exports so as to obtain the highest possible prices, given the fixed quantity they can export. An indirect form of export restriction is through quotas and tariffs on imports (with the exchange rate then adjusting to bring exports down to the reduced level of imports). But, of course, such an extreme situation does not really exist. Thus there is still a case for these countries in general reducing their trade restrictions.

The second issue is crucial. In practice, it has been difficult to persuade policymakers and the general public in developing countries to liberalize their trading arrangements. The protectionist arguments used have been prevalent in developed countries as well, and are very similar. They are the types of arguments that have been analyzed by economists for over two hundred years and generally have been found wanting. If there is a revival of protectionist attitudes in developed countries, if it *seems* that OECD protection has greatly increased (though it may not actually have done so) and if it is possible to obtain ready-made arguments from intellectuals and policymakers in developed countries in favor of protection, then it is quite likely that the liberalization trend in the developing world would be reversed. This would reinforce a tendency to such reversal in countries facing severe debt problems. Increased protection by developing countries themselves—or even a failure to continue liberalization trends—may do them more harm than have the possibly modest increases in protection in Europe and the United States, but the latter may encourage the former.

Some Arguments for Protection

It is worth looking briefly at some arguments for protection currently popular in the United States and Europe.[3] The main argument from the point of view of politicians is presumably that protection may raise the incomes of particular groups in their countries or—more important—may avoid falls in incomes that might otherwise take place, and that these groups have political influence. But a variety of arguments is used to show that either fairness or the national interest justifies such protection. With regard to the national interest, the implication is that there is some *national* gain—either that there will be no significant losers from protection but only gainers or that over time losers could be compensated and a net gain would remain.

In fact, no new arguments for protection have been developed in recent years. Indeed, some of the currently popular arguments were advanced in the nineteenth century in the United States, notably the "pauper labor" argument. One of the more acceptable arguments in current conditions is for the imposition of temporary restrictions to modify a sudden import surge that might impose serious and unexpected injury on some domestic industry. This will be referred to later in connection with a possible safeguard code and GATT Article XIX. Here let us look briefly at the employment argument, the pauper labor argument, the fairness argument, and the dumping argument. Subsequently I shall consider the supposed "problem" of Japan.

THE EMPLOYMENT ARGUMENT

Protection of an industry may contribute to preserving employment in that industry. At the same time there is evidence that the actual declines in employment in particular industries (such as textiles, clothing, automobiles, and steel) that have taken place in the United States and Western Europe have not been primarily caused by increases in import shares. In the United States in particular, declines in rates of change in overall demand for various industries' products as well as labor productivity growth have been quantitatively much larger in their impact on employment (as shown in Krueger, 1980). Nevertheless, if import competition is significant and the volume of

---

[3] One argument not discussed here is the infant-industry argument. This is used currently by advocates of protection for high-technology or "sunrise" industries. This argument has slightly more to be said for it than some of the other arguments discussed here but is not as widely applicable as often believed. It is analyzed in Corden (1974), chapter 9.

imports is large, common sense suggests sufficient protection could offset the adverse employment effects of these other factors.

The weakness of the employment argument is that it is narrowly partial equilibrium, focusing only on particular industries. One should note the adverse effects, for example, of protection of steel on steel-using industries. Higher steel costs reduce effective protection (protection related to value added) for the automobile industry and will tend to reduce employment there, and this could more than offset the gains in employment in the steel industry. More important are the general equilibrium effects operating through effects on wage levels and the exchange rate. Here let us note the oft-neglected exchange-rate aspect.

If protection of some industries is increased and yet the balance of payments is not to change, then—given the average level of nominal wages as well as foreign costs—the exchange rate has to appreciate. And this will have an adverse effect on employment in those tradeable-goods industries where protection has not increased. To consider the case where the general level of protection for import-competing industries is reduced, such reduction would have to be associated with depreciation of the exchange rate and thus would have beneficial effects on employment in export industries. This is not to deny the possibility of transitional unemployment effects: the demand for labor in one set of industries may fall while that in others increases, but labor may not readily move, and in the short run the former industries may shed labor before the latter absorb extra labor. But such a problem suggests simply the need for temporary measures to foster adjustment, not protection designed to prevent change.

In addition there may be some general real wage rigidity. If initially there is unemployment because real wages are too high, then, if protected industries are labor-intensive relative to nonprotected industries, an increase in protection would raise overall employment. The gain in employment in the protected industries would more than offset the losses in the nonprotected industries. But here it must be noted that United States exports, not import-competing industries, tend to be relatively labor-intensive (though there are measurement problems which require this to be stated with caution) so that, given the real-wage rigidity assumption, a general rise in tariffs or imposition of quotas, as proposed for example in the famous Burke–Hartke bill, would actually lower U.S. employment overall. In any case, the real-wage rigidity model is too simple. If the nation as a whole gains from a particular measure (that is, nonlabor and labor incomes combined rise), there is scope through the tax system for maintaining after-tax real wages while lowering pretax real wages to the levels required for full employment.

THE PAUPER LABOR ARGUMENT

The pauper labor argument is that protection should be imposed on goods originating from countries where wages are low. In fact, in many developing countries labor costs per unit of output are not relatively low, since the benefits of low wage costs are offset by low labor productivity. But let us suppose that labor costs per unit are low for particular products, presumably labor-intensive ones. This simply means that these countries have a comparative advantage in such products. There must be other products where costs are relatively high, for otherwise they would be only exporting, not importing. If they were only exporting, then presumably they would need to alter their exchange rates unless they were primarily interested in importing bonds—that is, lending money—rather than importing goods and services.

Another version of this argument is that it is "immoral" to buy goods produced by cheap or "sweated" labor. On the basis of such an argument some labor unions have advocated restricting imports from Hong Kong, for example. Yet if the demand by the United States for Hong Kong products fell, Hong Kong producers would either have to lower their prices—and hence in due course the wages they paid—in order to unload more exports on other markets or unemployment in Hong Kong would increase.

FAIRNESS ARGUMENT

To industrialists faced with competition from imports produced in more favorable conditions than at home, such competition seems "unfair." Thus one gets the view that conditions—wages and other factors affecting the cost of labor—should be equalized around the world. In the extreme this could be interpreted to mean that protection should offset all comparative advantage differences, so that all trade would cease. More plausibly it may be meant that the flow of trade should depend purely on differences in managerial efficiency and entrepreneurial skill, all other factors being offset by protection. In any case, the appropriate analysis is the same as in the case of the pauper labor argument.

But there is one complication. Suppose foreign governments subsidize certain industries or the exports of certain products. They may provide indirect assistance, as Britain does when it meets the losses of publicly owned industries, or the United States does through its defense spending or its space program. One country may pump funds into research and development, another into its educational system, a third into its agricultural sector, and a fourth into reviving its steel industry. Does this mean that it is in other countries' interests to engage in countervailing protection?

If a country is concerned only with maximizing its national income and neither with sectional interest nor with fairness, then such protection is *not* to its advantage. The various interventions by country A should be taken as given by country B when the latter formulates its optimal policy, at least unless it can induce country A to change its policies in more favorable directions. But some intervention policies by country A may actually be favorable for A's trading partners, for example, policies that lower the prices of A's exports relative to its imports. In the case of unfavorable policies, such as tariffs that restrict the flow of trade, if B responds by imposing tariffs of its own, this increases the cost of protection. All this must be qualified for the case where the foreign interventions are expected to be temporary, in which case they can either be ignored or some temporary offsetting measure might be applied to avoid short-term dislocations.

DUMPING

Dumping generally means that a country exports its products at prices lower than it sells them at home. Naturally the competing industries abroad will seek to get the country to raise its export prices or will try to persuade their own governments to impose countervailing duties. Yet there is no logical argument for such reactions. It should not really be of interest to either the import-competing producers of a country or its purchasers of imports at what prices these goods are sold to purchasers in the foreign country. In general a nation benefits when its imports become cheaper relative to its exports, even though import-competing producers may lose. If there is a sudden fall in the price or a surge of imports there may be some argument for temporary protection, but this has little or nothing to do with whether the price charged to consumers in the supplying country is above or below the import price.

The "Japan Problem"

There is great concern in Europe and the United States about the growth of Japanese exports and, even more, there is fear—even paranoia—about their prospective growth. A good deal of the revival of protectionism has been directed against Japan, notably in the case of motorcars, steel, and consumer electronics.

Partly this appears to be connected with trade and current-account balances. Japan has a large and recently growing trade surplus with the United States. This is reduced but not eliminated when services are allowed for; that is, when the focus is on the current rather than the trade account. But world trade is not meant to be balanced bilaterally, so clearly one must at the minimum look at Japan's overall current account.

In the twelve years from 1970 to 1981 Japan ran current-account deficits in four years, balance in one, and surpluses in the other seven. The two big surplus periods were 1971–1972 and 1977–1978. There was a modest surplus in 1982. But the surpluses were low as proportions of Japanese GNP—the maximum was 2.5 percent in 1971, and in 1977 and 1978 they were only 1.6 percent and 1.7 percent. In general, changes in the Japanese overall current account have been closely correlated with bilateral current-account movements with the United States, and the explanations can be largely found in the relationships between Japanese and the U.S. macroeconomic policies. Essentially there have been two explanations: divergences in overall macroeconomic demand levels or pressures (in 1977–1978, the United States followed expansionary and Japan relatively contractionary policies) and divergences in the monetary-fiscal policy mix, as recently.

Apart from these cyclical movements there does appear to be some general tendency for the Japanese current account to be in surplus, a surplus substantially larger than required to maintain constant the real value of Japan's foreign financial assets.

These current-account surpluses are not necessarily matters for concern. The Japanese household sector has a very large savings ratio by world standards, and even though most of these savings are absorbed by Japanese private investment and by the big Japanese budget deficits, there is on average still something left over for the rest of the world, so that Japan as a nation tends to be a net buyer of financial assets in exchange for goods. This is not necessarily a bad thing. It tends to lower world interest rates. It is the obverse of the situation of most developing countries and of the prospective United States situation. In fact, if the United States is to become a large net borrower on the world capital market as the result of her budget deficit there will have to be net lenders—countries that run current-account surpluses—and Japan must be the premier candidate for this role, a role in which it is practiced and which, for some time, its cautious citizens saving massively for their old age are eager to fulfill. There are surely gains from international trade in financial assets against goods, as there are in goods-goods trade. There are, furthermore, plenty of similar examples from the history of countries that ran surpluses over long periods, notably Britain in the nineteenth century.

There seem to be two problems connected with Japan's impact on the world.

The first is that a large, high-growth, high-productivity country, by the very fact of its importance and of the changes it generates in the rest of the world, provokes fears. These fears were provoked by the United States in the 1950s. For those who do not understand the law of comparative advantage there is the fear that this country is getting better at everything—and presumably will end up only exporting and not importing. There is also the feeling that, just because the country happens to have the world's highest productivity growth rate now, this must go on forever—even though Japan's growth rate has actually slackened dramatically since 1974.

The second problem is the true problem. There are losers as well as gainers both from longer-term Japanese economic expansion (with a given current-account balance) and from periods (like 1971–1972, 1977–1978, and 1981–1984) when there is a substantial Japanese current-account surplus. In the former long-term-growth case, the gainers are the consumers of Japan's export products and the suppliers of food and raw materials; while in the latter episodes the gainers include those consumers as well as borrowers who can draw indirectly on Japanese savings. But the focus, inevitably, is on the losers. They are the competitors with Japanese exports, above all. The problem is particularly acute when these exports expand suddenly.

In Japan, unlike other countries, a deflation of domestic demand leads very quickly to a significant increase in exports, so that variations in Japanese domestic macroeconomic policy manifest themselves in variations in exports. From 1975 to 1981 the volume of Japanese exports increased 71.5 percent while import volume rose only 21.4 percent. Just to show how quickly exports can change, in 1976 export volume was 43 percent above 1973. It is no wonder that competitors in other countries were unhappy.

But it is not difficult to explain these developments. Japan suffered a sharp deterioration in its terms of trade owing to the two oil price shocks and compensated by pushing exports. A big current-account deficit in the first half of 1974 had by the second half of 1974 been turned into a surplus. Taking the whole period from 1975 to 1981, when export volume increased 71.5 percent and import volume rose only 21.4 percent, the country's terms of trade deteriorated 52 percent.

The reaction to these developments has been increased protectionism outside Japan. In particular, the two oil shocks have created major adjustment problems, some of which have manifested themselves indirectly through increased competition from Japan in certain products, as Japan has sought to avoid large current-account deficits.

It has to be accepted that rapid expansion of Japanese export volume—however justified by the rise in its import prices—inevitably generates protectionist pressures in other countries. So it may be advisable in such situations for Japan to moderate rapid export expansion and accept temporarily larger current-account deficits even though such restraint is in the interests neither of consumers in other countries nor of borrowers.

Finally, one might look rather carefully at the full implications of proposals that Japan open its own markets further to imports from the United States and Europe. First it must be stressed that this would have an adverse effect on third countries, such as Australia and many developing countries, if it led to discrimination in favor of the United States (and there are some signs that this is happening). Apart from that, reductions in Japanese protection would have favorable efficiency effects on the standard grounds that more of the benefits of comparative advantage differences would be reaped. But the source of current complaints has been the surge in Japanese exports. If Japan accelerated its growth rate or opened up its markets more, its imports would increase, which would inevitably lead to more exports. There is no reason why the current account would disappear or even turn into a deficit, since this depends on the aggregate savings–investment balance, which is only very indirectly affected by changes in Japanese protection levels, if at all. The tendency would be for the yen to depreciate in real terms even more, thus improving Japanese competitiveness and, no doubt, generating increased pressures from U.S. and European industries for protection. It is doubtful that these pressures would be moderated by the knowledge that the Japanese have reduced their own protection. The industries in the United States that benefit from the extra sales to Japan need not be the same ones that would lose from a new Japanese export expansion.

Changes in Rules and Changes in Attitudes

Much of the current policy discussion on international trade issues is concerned with institutions and rules. Among the developed countries the postwar movement toward the freeing of trade was built around GATT, and GATT itself was built around the most-favored-nation principle—the principle that tariffs and quantitative import restrictions should not discriminate among sources of supply. Only agriculture and textiles were left out of this process. It seems that GATT is being bypassed more and more, and a feature of the "new protectionism" is that it is discriminatory, leading to bilateral arrangements, and that it involves devices that are not subject to GATT rules and procedures.

Various proposals for changes have been made. In general Americans tend to favor extending and tightening rules, ensuring that "codes" are obeyed, and so on, while the Europeans are inclined toward more pragmatism, which at the moment means letting every country be as protectionist as it wants, subject only to some limitations that can be rather easily bypassed. The GATT ministerial meeting of November 1982 came up against this conflict and no progress was made, whether to slow up the existing movement toward more protectionism, to tidy it up and make it more transparent (the latter needed especially with regard to VERs), to enforce and extend the new subsidies code agreed upon at the Tokyo Round, or to extend regulations to include trade in services (as the United States wished).

The most urgent need seems to be to bring the various nontariff restrictions that now exist—the VERs, the quotas, and especially the bilateral arrangements under the auspices of the MFA—within the ambit of GATT rules. Some allowance must be made for the desire of countries to impose at least temporary restrictions on particular imports when there is a sudden inflow likely to impose substantial damage on particular domestic industries (even though such an import surge would benefit consumers or industries that use these imports as inputs).

Article XIX of GATT is a famous article that provides for quotas on these grounds but sets certain conditions. Restrictions must be nondiscriminatory, must be temporary, and must be justified to GATT. Countries imposing restrictions under that article must notify the affected parties in advance and must consult with them, are expected to compensate countries against which affected action is taken, and could be subject to retaliatory action in the form of the withdrawal of equivalent concessions by adversely affected exporters. Countries have bypassed Article XIX by inducing suppliers to accept VERs or what are called "orderly marketing arrangements," of which the MFA is the main case. Suppliers have agreed reluctantly because the alternatives would probably not be Article XIX restrictions but unilaterally imposed import quotas which would be even less satisfactory from the exporters' point of view.

Attempts at the Tokyo Round negotiations or later to negotiate a new "safeguards code," involving a revision of Article XIX to make it more acceptable and to bring much of the new protectionism within its ambit, have failed. The main obstacle was the determination of the European Community to preserve the principle of selectivity—discrimination among countries—something that is not acceptable to most developing countries and probably also not to the United States. It is well known that the United States was the original protagonist of the principle of nondiscrimination, having viewed the British preferential system of the prewar years with great disfavor. But perhaps there is a deeper reason why no agreement has been reached to bring the various existing unilateral or bilateral safeguard arrangements within GATT rules. The major nations simply see no reason to subject their policies to international scrutiny.

Two additional difficulties in getting an improvement in the situation in the near future can be expected. First, the recovery from the recession is likely to be modest with much overall unemployment remaining, especially in Europe. In particular, the automobile and steel industries are unlikely to be able to restore earlier profitability and employment levels owing to earlier excess investments, undue high real-wage levels, and various structural factors. Second, it will be difficult to work out "bargaining down" arrangements (new versions of the earlier tariff reduction negotiations) in the case of nontariff barriers, notably VERs, essentially because of their nontransparency and the measurement problems they present.

In spite of the difficulties, it could be argued that the central problem is one of attitudes. If attitudes became less protectionist, agreements would be readily reached and it would be found easy to strengthen GATT. If they harden—if protection becomes the new conventional wisdom—then surely in time the attitudes will be reflected not just in a maintenance of the new protectionism but in increased actual protection and thus in a substantial movement away from the open trading system. The greatest concern must be about protection that is designed to prevent adjustment in OECD countries to export expansion by developing countries.

Essentially, protection as currently practiced in developed countries involves protecting one sector of an economy at the expense of others, with the nation as a whole losing, at least in the long term. The gains from protection are usually very visible, perhaps concentrated on one industry, while the losses are more indirect and thinly spread. The understandable argument for protection is that it helps a particular sector, this being a sufficient argument for the relevant lobby. But, as noted above, it is often argued incorrectly and yet persuasively that there are *national* gains—in particular that, in the absence of protection, employment lost at one end of the economy as a result of an inflow of imports will not be compensated by employment gains elsewhere. As a result, it is usually thought by noneconomists that protection yields national gains at the expense of foreign suppliers, thus providing the basis for trade negotiations. The central message that economists regularly preach, but fail to convey, is that protection is likely to inflict a loss on the protecting nation itself. Yet it is a message that—if understood—should carry a lot of weight.

The question thus arises why attitudes have become more protectionist and how a shift in attitudes back to a belief in the gains from trade can be fostered. While this issue seems to arise particularly in the European Community, none of the developed countries seem immune from the revival of protectionist sentiment. It is certainly not difficult to find protectionists in the United States Congress or in the U.S. labor movement. If a shift back to a belief in the advantages of relatively free trade does not occur it is at least possible that the fairly open world trading system in manufactures that we had until the early 1970s will be gradually eroded with long-term adverse effects for the world economy, and especially for the growth of many developing countries.

This is a revised version of W. M. Corden, *The Revival of Protectionism*, Occasional Paper No. 14, The Group of Thirty, New York, 1984.

References

Anjaria, S. J. et al. (1982) *Developments in International Trade Policy*. Occasional Paper No. 16. Washington, D.C.: International Monetary Fund.

Bergsten, C. F. and Cline, W. R. (eds.) (1983) *Trade Policy in the 1980s*. Washington, D.C.: Institute for International Economics.

———— and Williamson, J. (1983) Exchange Rates and Trade Policy. In *Trade Policy in the 1980s* (C. F. Bergsten and W. R. Cline, eds.). Washington, D.C.: Institute for International Economics.

Corden, W. M. (1974) *Trade Policy and Economic Welfare*. Oxford: Clarendon Press.

———— (1980) Relationships Between Macroeconomic and Industrial Policies. *The World Economy* 3: 167–184.

Council of Economic Advisers (1983) *Annual Report*. Washington, D.C.: U.S. Government Printing Office. Chap. 3.

Frank, I. (1981) *Trade Policy Issues of Interest to the Third World*. Thames Essays No. 29. London: Trade Policy Research Centre.

Hindley, B. and Nicolaides, E. (1980) *Taking the New Protectionism Seriously*. Thames Essays No. 28. London: Trade Policy Research Centre.

Hughes, H. and Waelbroek, J. (1981) Can Developing Country Exports Keep Growing in the 1980s? *The World Economy* 4: 127–148.

Hughes, H. and Krueger, A. O. (1983) Effects of Protection in Developed Countries on Developing Countries' Exports of Manufactures. In *The Structure and Evolution of Recent U.S. Trade Policies* (R. Baldwin, ed.). Chicago: University of Chicago Press.

Keesing, D. B. and Wolf, M. (1980) *Textile Quotas Against Developing Countries.* Thames Essays No. 23. London: Trade Policy Research Centre.

Krueger, A. O. (1980) Protectionist Pressures, Imports, and Employment in the United States. Working Paper No. 461. Cambridge, Mass.: National Bureau of Economic Research.

Lal, D. (1981) *Resurrection of the Pauper-Labour Argument.* Thames Essays No. 28. London: Trade Policy Research Centre.

4

Empirical Aspects of Protectionism: Results From Project LINK

LAWRENCE R. KLEIN, PETER H. PAULY,
AND CHRISTIAN E. PETERSEN

Introduction

For more than five years, Project LINK researchers have been looking into the worldwide effects of protectionism.[1] This research was done as a forewarning of things to come. The world is now confronted with increasing manifestations of protectionism, both actual and potential. It is the purpose of the present paper to reexamine the issues involved and to try to estimate new quantitative effects in the light of the present state of the world economy, a state in which Japanese and German surpluses have reappeared on an enlarged scale, in which the bilateral balance between Japan and the United States or between Japan and the Common Market have grown to bothersome dimensions. These new developments have generated some protectionist movements or have made the threat of protectionism even more serious.

Protectionism has become a worldwide problem. The effects on developing countries, although currently less publicized, are equally worrisome. Since protectionism generally hurts imports in total, and therefore restrains world trade, it hurts exports by developing countries, for they depend on capturing their share of world trade in order to generate export earnings. These earnings, in turn, are crucial at the present time. They are the mainstay of debt servicing. We are in the curious position of telling the developing countries that they are

---

From the University of Pennsylvania, Philadelphia.

[1] See, for example, Klein and Su (1979), Bollino, Pauly, and Petersen (1983), and Klein, Pauly, and Petersen (1985).

exporting too successfully to us (OECD countries) and of restricting this flow through protectionism. At the same time we want developing countries to continue to service their debts at a time when LDC debt has destabilized the world financial system. This, in a macro sense, is contradictory.

The main concern of this chapter will be to show that restrictions of international trade will generate worldwide losses in activity and to obtain quantitative estimates of the extent of these losses. Trade restrictions (and liberation) can take many forms. It can involve bilateral or regionally restricted trade. These measures are used to deal with very specific problems such as the Japanese current surplus with the United States. Changes in the tariff rate are easy to understand and easy to implement, from a statistical point of view, but nontariff barriers are growing in importance and, in a sense, currently represent the most serious impediment to trade performance. To put such barriers into models it becomes necessary to quantify them. A straightforward way to do that is to find an equivalent tariff rate that would restrict entry of goods, in the first instance, by the same amount as the restraint of the nontariff barrier. Our calculations with the LINK system using tariff instruments are, therefore, only indicative. We use this instrument mainly because of its ease of statistical manipulation and note that real progress will have to be made through the calculation of equivalent tariff reductions, corresponding to nontariff barriers.

While the first LINK results on protectionism dealt with *tariff increases*, subsequent investigations were concerned with opposite effects, namely *trade liberalization*. For the most part, analyses of this kind are symmetric; our subsequent analysis therefore examines cases of both tariff reductions and increases with the understanding that the corresponding opposite effects would be roughly symmetric.

In this chapter, we examine three broad classes of trade policies through tariffs:

1. unilateral protection through import surcharges imposed by a single country vis-à-vis the rest of the world;
2. multilateral trade restrictions resulting from a joint tariff imposed by one group of countries on another;
3. worldwide trade liberalization represented as a joint reduction of tariff rates by all trading partners.

Prior to these empirical results, in the next two sections, we summarize the theoretical background of the tariff debate and the relevant structure of the LINK system. Finally, we evaluate our empirical findings; nine appendixes contain detailed tables for the nine scenarios presented in the text.

The Theoretical Background

The theory-of-international-trade message is clear and persistent. More than two hundred years ago, Adam Smith concluded that free trade should be the guiding principle, and David Ricardo, in the early nineteenth century, elaborated the theory of comparative advantage. According to Smith, there should be an international division of labor, and goods/services should move between nation pairs unfettered by barriers to trade. This was a distinct shift from mercantilist philosophy that emphasized the desirability of nations achieving a favorable balance—that is, an export surplus which is impossible for all to accomplish simultaneously. Adam Smith noted well-recognized exceptions for infant industries, national defense, and other exigencies.

Correspondingly, in the more recent theoretical literature, tariffs are generally viewed as instruments capable of altering resource allocation, even though direct interventions on a national level, such as direct subsidies, are clearly the more preferable means to achieve such goals. Only occasionally[2] have tariffs been advocated for purposes of managing aggregate demand and supply, such as the use of import restrictions to reduce unemployment.

Following Mundell (1961), the international literature has advanced further arguments for the claim that, under flexible exchange rates, a tariff is contractionary. While initially this was assumed to be due to the existence of a Laursen-Metzler effect, other transmission channels have subsequently been found possible as well. More recent studies[3] have gone beyond the static framework of traditional international trade theory. While the long-run contractionary effects are quite robust, there appears to be an intertemporal trade-off in that in the short run gains in output and employment are possible.

For any reasonable empirical analysis of protectionist measures it is imperative that the direct and indirect, real and monetary effects are properly represented. The LINK system is driven by imports. The way to change world activity in trade, production, and employment is to change imports. Since protectionist measures generally restrict imports, except in the case of some export subsidies, they result in the loss of trade, production, and jobs. Consequently, in an overall sense, the LINK simulations show that protectionism is unfavorable for a healthy world economy. It reduces growth in world trade, pro-

---

[2] Most prominently has this been advocated by the Cambridge Economic Policy Group, see Cripps and Godley (1978).

[3] See Eichengreen (1981). A good survey can also be found in Corden (1971) or Baldwin (1984).

duction, and employment. In a sense, we offer a macroeconomic supplement to the theoretical analysis of Smith and Ricardo.[4]

Just as important as the real channels are the monetary effects of a tariff, particularly the effects on exchange rates. There has been a substantial debate about the likely response of currency rates to a tariff. The primary change in relative prices should cause an appreciation of the currency for the tariff-imposing country; the improvement in the trade balance should only accentuate that effect. Secondary effects such as an endogenous policy response of monetary authorities or a fundamental change in market expectations can, however, change the direction of the effect dramatically.

Exchange-rate models have, over the past few years, not proven to be accurate in the short run. Their critical role in assessing the effects of various protectionist measures makes it, however, necessary that the *long-run* response of the system reflects changes in fundamentals in accord with economic theory.

Tariffs in the LINK System

The LINK system brings together major macroeconometric models for seventy-nine countries or regions of the world in a consistent world model for studying global economic problems. The system includes a broad range of different models with widely diverse characteristics. The technical linkage, however, imposes a certain homogeneity across the models. The most important mechanism linking different economies is the international flow of merchandise exports and imports. The centerpiece of linkage, and the technique by which consistency of merchandise trade flows is maintained, is the world trade matrix, an accounting design that lays out the intercountry and interregional trade flows on a bilateral basis. Lack of bilateral data makes it impossible to provide that same mechanism for services as well as capital flows. Monetary linkages in the system therefore assume the form of direct linkages via exchange rates and interest rates, while service linkages are still to be implemented.

In an interrelated world, exports of the *i*th country are linked to partner countries' imports, and import prices of any country are linked to partner countries' export prices. The guiding principle of the structure of the LINK system regarding merchandise trade is that two world identities should hold, simultaneously.

---

[4] For a similar conclusion, see the general equilibrium studies such as Brown and Whalley (1980) or Whalley (1985).

$$\sum_{i=1}^{n} (PX)_i * X_i = \sum_{i=1}^{n} (PM)_i * M_i \tag{1}$$

$$\sum_{i=1}^{n} X_i = \sum_{i=1}^{n} M_i \tag{2}$$

with

PX_i = export price of country i
X_i = export volume of country i
PM_i = import price of country i
M_i = import volume of country i

In Eq. (1) we impose the condition that the current value of world exports equal the current value of world imports, and in Eq. (2) we impose the condition that the volume of world exports equal the volume of world imports. Both equations are expressed in a common denominator. In practice this denominator is usually U.S. dollars, but it could be gold, SDRs, ECUs, or any other international unit. Essentially, what the procedure amounts to for an individual country in the system is that the national model is required to generate import volumes and export prices, while the linkage procedure provides a consistent set of export volumes and import prices to be passed back into the model. These transformations are performed for four subgroups of commodities: SITC01 (food, beverages, and tobacco), SITC24 (basic materials), SITC3 (mineral fuels), and SITC59 (manufactures and miscellaneous).

The vector of import prices in domestic currency (by commodity group) in Eq. (1) above can be expressed in the following way, with appropriate allowance for tariff rates,

$$PM_j^k = (1 + t_j^k) \sum_{i=1}^{n} a_{ij}^k PX_i^k * S_j \tag{3}$$

PM_j^k = import price of country j, for commodity k, in domestic currency
t_j^k = LINK estimate of average tariff rate for k in j
a_{ij}^k = country i's share of j's imports (element of trade share matrix)
PX_i^k = export price of country i for commodity k, in common denominator currency
S_j = exchange rate, local per common denominator currency

A tariff simulation involves an appropriate change in t_j^k, taking account of the change in tax collections that is induced by the duty change. The simulation (scenario) with the change in tariff rate is then compared with the baseline simulation, in which rates are kept at their prevailing (expected) values.

Unilateral Protection: U.S. Import Surcharges

At the present time, especially in the United States and also in Western Europe, we are experiencing a drift towards protectionism because many older, well-established industries are fading in overall importance or in competitiveness with newly developing areas of the world. Primary examples are textiles, apparel, television, shoes, steel, and automobiles. Producers and trade unionists engaged in these lines of activity ask for protection, either through direct exclusion, quotas, tariffs, subsidies, or a variety of nontariff barriers. The argument is usually that protection for one single sector is small in the total economy and contributes little to price indexes or GNP values. There is also an appeal, in most cases, to save domestic jobs. Finally, there is frequently an argument that only temporary relief is wanted because the affected sector simply needs time and resources to modernize and become an effective international competitor again.

BROAD-BASED SURCHARGES

The most widely discussed protectionist proposal in the United States calls for the imposition of a three-year sliding import surcharge with rates of 20 percent, 15 percent, and 7 percent, respectively. The surcharge, by assumption, will be imposed on all goods from all countries without exception. There appears to be some discussion to limit the measure to dutiable goods only, which would exclude about 30 percent of all imports; this is, however, not part of the present study.

It turns out that the effects of such a policy are, to a large extent, determined by domestic and foreign policy responses, by expectations of exporters and importers as well as by foreign exchange traders around the world. In this context, several crucial issues will be examined.

1. The effects of a surcharge will depend on whether or not there will be retaliation of some kind from trading partners. Opponents of a surcharge argue that such a course of events will be more than likely, citing recent remarks particularly from Common Market representatives. They also warn that such retaliation could lead to a severe disruption of world trade, and subsequently a world depression, just as retaliation against the

Smoot-Hawley tariffs in the 1930s may have contributed to the worsening of the subsequent depression. On the contrary, proponents argue that the desire to retain U.S. markets—and the temporary nature of the proposed U.S. measure—would lead foreign countries to prefer not to retaliate. One of the scenarios presented below will thus examine the effects of a foreign retaliation *in kind.*

2. Any tariff will most likely be accompanied by adjustments in policy instruments both domestically and abroad. In particular, the effectiveness of such a tariff will depend critically upon the Federal Reserve response and monetary policies abroad. The central issue is whether the FED can be expected to accommodate the domestic price increase or to maintain a fixed supply of unborrowed reserves. In the latter case, the interest-rate response to a surcharge will be ambiguous, since the reduction in transactions demand for money and the reduction in federal borrowing requirements may well be compensated by the effects of inflationary expectations. The general result, however, is for an interest-rate decline because of the implied decline in velocity.

3. Market participants on goods, money, and international foreign exchange markets are highly responsive to any U.S. policy measure. Given the volatility of present financial markets, any major policy shift cannot but have significant impacts on these markets. In particular, market reactions will differ depending on whether or not such a policy will be perceived to be a promising attempt to tackle the fundamental disequilibria. While there is some indication that a surcharge will contribute to a deficit reduction both in the trade balance and the federal budget, such a measure may, on the other hand, also be interpreted as an attempt to avoid the necessary domestic adjustment by taxing foreigners. Under such circumstances the net effect on market confidence may well be negative.

In addition to these aspects, which will be analyzed in this study, there is some debate about the extent to which the surcharge will be passed through to consumers in terms of higher prices for imported goods. Proponents of the surcharge proposal argue that the percentage pass-through can be expected to be close to zero, based on the assumption that a *preannounced temporary* surcharge will induce foreign exporters to absorb the losses (or reductions in profit margins) in order to maintain market shares. Econometrically, it turns out to be rather difficult to obtain such a response in a given model. While there are endogenous reactions of export prices in affected countries, the zero pass-through assumption would imply a change in behavior and would have to be imposed exogenously. In addition to this technical aspect, it remains questionable whether foreigners would be prepared to be taxed by U.S. authorities for a period of a few years to finance the federal deficits without some form of price adjustment.

The previous two issues lead directly to the final and most important aspect of these scenarios: the exchange-rate response to a temporary surcharge. There has been a substantial debate about the likely response of currency rates to a tariff. In the absence of any definite policy reaction—and disregarding market sentiments—the changes in fundamentals should unambiguously cause an appreciation of the dollar. The major factor underlying this movement would be the trade balance improvement. One of our scenarios will be based on this assumption.

A contrasting view can, however, quite easily be established. A depreciation caused by either a precipitous capital outflow or an easing of monetary policy is quite possible. Some economists think that the effect of a surcharge on the dollar's exchange value would be to trigger a capital flight causing the dollar to fall and interest rates to rise—via "crowding out"—together with restrictive central bank monetary policy in the face of higher domestic prices.

A preferred scenario, however, is that the deficit reduction that would follow the collection of the surcharge by the Treasury would pave the way for easier monetary policy (in compensation for the deficit reduction), lower interest rates, and a depreciating dollar. Such a scenario broadly corresponds to a "soft-landing" view of the impact of a surcharge while the former would mimic a "crash-landing" case. Both variants, while assuming that these effects dominate the improvement in the trade balance, are associated with quite different interest-rate movements and, consequently, rather contrasting assessments of the effectiveness of a surcharge.

Exchange-rate models have, over the past few years, not proven to be accurate in the short run. The forecast record reflects the inability to trace back the present strength of the dollar to market fundamentals. Rather than relying on a model of endogenous exchange-rate response, we have *imposed* alternative reactions in our various scenarios.

To assess the impact of a unilateral surcharge under various alternative assumptions, we therefore examined the following scenarios:

Scenario 1. Sliding surcharge (20 percent, 15 percent, 7 percent)
Scenario 2. Sliding surcharge with foreign retaliation
Scenario 3. Sliding surcharge, 10 percent dollar appreciation

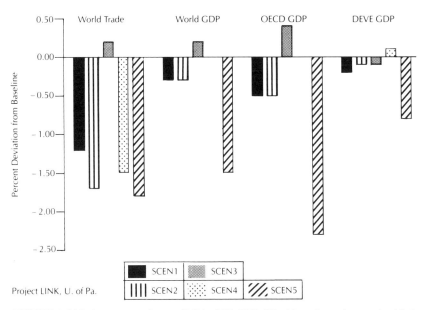

FIGURE 1. U.S. import surcharge (20%, 15%, 7%): World trade and growth, third-year effects.

Scenario 4. Sliding surcharge, 10 percent dollar depreciation, interest-rate decline (180 basis points)

Scenario 5. Sliding surcharge, 10 percent dollar depreciation, interest-rate increase (200 basis points)

The results are summarized in Appendixes 1–5 and Figures 1 and 2.

Standard economic theory suggests that a country that levies a tariff potentially suffers from two types of cost. A production cost results from the fact that domestic and foreign firms allocate their resources in response to distorted prices for their goods, rather than to the true international market prices. A consumption cost occurs since consumers will end up purchasing fewer goods—without benefit of import substitution—than they would have preferred to purchase if they had been free to buy at the international market price. Evaluating such hypotheses, however, requires an explicit welfare analysis, while in this study we shall concentrate on standard macroeconomic aggregates. The analysis in terms of trade balance and price effects, impacts on real activity, and the federal deficit, while not completely capturing the spirit of traditional welfare concepts, is much more in line with the current political debate.

The most important conclusion to be drawn from the basic surcharge scenario without retaliation (no exchange rate and policy reaction) is that, while an immediate reduction of the federal deficit

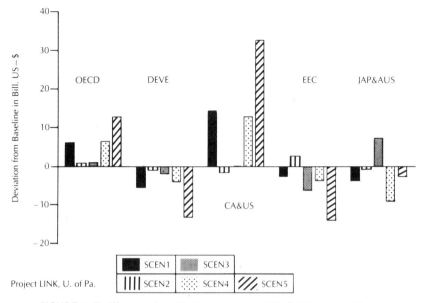

FIGURE 2. Tariff scenarios: Trade balance in U.S.-$, third-year effects.

and a significant trade balance improvement can indeed be expected, it will lead to a loss of real activity to the extent that domestic production and existing stocks cannot fully compensate for the loss of imported goods at favorable prices. Assuming a full pass-through, consumer prices will rise by about 0.6 of one percent. If both Canada and the LDCs were exempt from the surcharge, the effects on the federal deficit and the trade balance would be substantially reduced, in effect by more than half. In that case, our results indicate that there would be even a slight increase in GNP, caused by the redirection of trade to Canada, which indirectly benefits U.S. exports. Finally, a surcharge against Japan alone would generate only a minor trade balance shift, with slight improvements in the federal deficit; the *real* effects of such a policy are hardly discernible. It is noteworthy that in the long run, in all cases, a slight reduction in consumer prices can be expected. While a surcharge will be inflationary in the short- and medium-term, the recessionary effects on wage and price increases potentially more than compensate the initial inflationary effect.

A closer look at the final three scenario results reveals the crucial importance of the exchange-rate response to a surcharge. Compared with the base case, the additional exchange-rate reaction can induce a wide range of variation. Should the surcharge be accompanied by an appreciation of the effective dollar rate, short- and medium-term effects on trade balance and government budget, as well as effects on real activity, would be only slightly altered; the inflationary effect could be expected to be less pronounced in the short run and even more favorable in the long run due to lower import price increases. For both cases involving an exchange-rate depreciation caused by either a loss in confidence in the U.S. economy or an interest-rate–induced-capital outflow, the differences are even more striking. In the soft-landing scenario, the negative impact on activity of a surcharge would be more than compensated for by the stimulating effects of easier monetary policy and the resulting depreciation. Higher economic activity would improve the federal budget even further, while the trade-balance effect would be smaller, caused by induced imports. Contrary to that, in the hard-landing scenario, the interest-rate increase, caused by a shortage of funds following a capital outflow, will—both in the short- and medium-term—slow down economic activity. In addition, it will be inflationary. The loss in real activity will ultimately lead to a further deterioration of the federal budget situation.

The imposition of a surcharge, under any policy and/or exchange-rate response, reduces world trade. The reduction is most pronounced when there is full retaliation, or when the secondary effects of an induced recession in the United States generate a further decline in trade activities. The effects on GNP growth in the OECD area range from 0.1 to 0.7 of one percent in the first year. Compared with a baseline forecast of about 3-percent growth in 1986, the worst case represents a substantial reduction in economic activity. While a multilateral tariff is clearly inflationary, this effect would be greatly reduced in the case of a dollar depreciation, due to lower import prices in the majority of OECD countries.

The primary and secondary effects of a U.S. surcharge will tend to reduce LDC growth slightly. The reduction is, however, relatively small and a major effect on the debt status of certain countries can only be expected in the case of scenario 5, where the U.S. interest-rate increase is expected to be reflected fully in LIBOR.

Over the five-year horizon of our simulations, the effects are, on average, much less pronounced. As is the case for the United States, the initial recessionary effect of a surcharge tends to improve growth rates in the medium-term. An inventory cycle, combined with adjustments in domestic spending, ultimately reverses the initial GNP losses. Average growth rates over the simulation period are affected only marginally; similarly, reduced inflation in the medium term compensates for initial tariff-related price increases.

On an aggregate level, long-run effects on world activity, trade, and inflation do basically occur only in the hard-landing scenario. In that case, the interest-rate increase is responsible for a persistent reduction in activity.

In all these simulations, a surcharge turns out to reduce the trade deficit and generate federal revenues, as expected. The initial effects on domestic activity, world trade, and world GNP are also unambiguously negative. In the medium-term, the effects are, however, rather diverse, depending upon the adjustment of other policy variables, market expectations, and exchange rates. In the long run, with favorable exchange-rate adjustments, a surcharge may improve GNP in the United States while reducing the federal deficit substantially. The hard-landing scenario, on the other hand, portrays a surcharge as generating significant GNP losses combined with a deterioration of the federal budget situation. Also, retaliatory actions from trading partners would, in all scenarios, reduce the effectiveness of a surcharge appreciably. In that case, the revenue effect would be reduced to almost half of its original size, while the trade balance effect would even be reversed; GNP losses would end up being substantially higher without the benefit of more than just a marginal reduction in the inflationary effect.

Macroeffects are examined in this analysis. Individual sectors or industries may gain at the expense of others. At the world level, some countries may gain at the expense of others, but the United States does not appear to be a gainer.

SELECTIVE SURCHARGES

In the context of the surcharge discussion, the question has come up as to whether there is a need to exempt certain countries from a surcharge, based on good trade relations and/or other economic and political criteria. For example, it is often argued that the indiscriminant imposition of a surcharge against *all* trading partners may place a particular burden on debt-ridden developing countries. Following that view, there is a nonnegligible possibility that the imposition of trade barriers vis-à-vis certain countries may trigger an avalanche of defaults with unpredictable repercussions on the United States. Also, it is argued that—under any circumstances—Canada must be exempted.

Based on these arguments, and since much of the debate is centered around the bilateral trade relationships between the United States and Japan, much of the debate has recently focused on selective surcharges. The proposal being examined here deals with a temporary surcharge along the lines of the previous proposal, but limited to Japan, Korea, Taiwan, and Brazil, on the grounds that these countries stand out with respect to their bilateral trade surpluses with the United States.

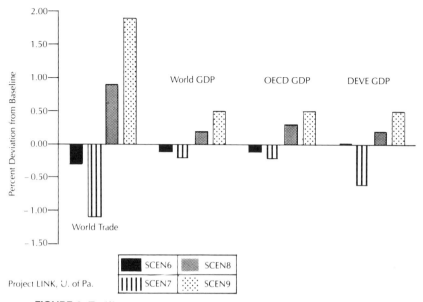

FIGURE 3. Tariff scenarios: World trade and growth, third-year effects.

The results of this scenario are summarized in Appendix 6 and Figures 3 and 4. It turns out that the effects on real world activity are almost negligible. Import substitution away from goods originating in the Pacific Basin area leads to a moderate improvement of growth prospects in the EEC area and in other OECD countries. The initial gain for the United States is eventually wiped out, mostly as a result of higher prices in response to the surcharge. World trade is reduced by up to 0.3 of one percent annually. Clearly, such a measure contributes to an improvement of the U.S. trade balance (by between $7 billion and $10 billion annually). It also reduces the federal deficit by about $15 billion annually. While such a policy may seem to offer a relatively painless way of generating additional federal revenues and at the same time improving the trade balance without appreciable effects on world activity, this evaluation ignores the potential political implications of selective surcharges.

Multilateral Regional Tariffs

Frequently the policy discussion with regard to international trade focuses on regional balances rather than bilateral relationships. One such example is the North–South perspective: how would broad-based tariffs imposed by the OECD area affect the developing countries, or, alternatively, would a tariff reduction on the part of OECD

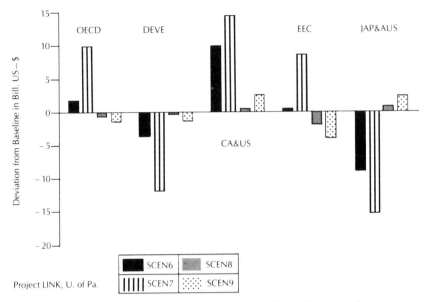

FIGURE 4. Tariff scenarios: Trade balance in U.S.-$, third-year effects.

vis-à-vis the Third World be an effective means of development policy?

To address these issues, the LINK system was used to simulate the effects of a temporary 20-percent surcharge on OECD imports of manufactured goods from Asia and Latin America. For the purposes of this scenario Japan was excluded from OECD and, as part of Asia, treated as an affected country. The results are summarized in Appendix 7 and Figures 3 and 4.

While, not surprisingly, the effects on real world activity are relatively moderate, the implied redistribution of activities is quite substantial. Japan loses more than 1 percent of real GNP annually. The effects on the rest of Asia and on Latin America are in the range of about 0.5 to 0.8 percent of GNP, reflecting the lower share of manufactured goods in exports from these regions. The EEC area benefits from import substitution, leading to a GNP increase of about one-third of one percent. The implied trade balance improvement for the OECD as a whole (excluding Japan) amounts to about $20–25 billion annually.

The more interesting interpretation, of course, is related to a corresponding reduction in trade barriers in the OECD area for developing countries' exports. According to our calculations such a tariff reduction could improve the trade balances in affected exporting areas by about $10 billion annually; the beneficial effect would clearly be substantially larger if Japan were exempted from this policy. Such a tariff reduction would indeed contribute substantially to an improvement of foreign-exchange earnings of developing countries. Such an effect would be most desirable for the major debtors in Asia and Latin America.

Worldwide Trade Liberalization

Against the background of protectionist scenarios presented in the preceding sections, we now examine the potential effects of global tariff reductions. Specifically, we evaluate the effects of 5-percent reductions of tariff rates for SITC categories 01 and 24, and for SITC categories 5–9. This is, of course, a purely arbitrary expository value. We could have 10-percent reductions, or even larger. But at those rates, the volume of production would not be strikingly larger, or not large enough to have much impact on the world economy. The scenario values may be as much as a full percentage point higher, and this represents the most significant policy input. The results are summarized in Appendixes 8 and 9 and Figures 3 and 4.

On a global scale, the results are unambiguous. Tariff reduction leads to an improvement in total world production and trade. Tariff increases would lead to corresponding reductions in production and trade. The results however are uneven. Some individual countries gain or lose.

The developing countries fare relatively better when tariffs are lowered than do either OECD or socialist countries. But the average gains are expected to be quite modest. For manufacturing duty changes, OECD production (GDP) responds by about one-half of a percentage point. The lowering of trade balances for OECD and non-OPEC developing countries occurs because they both have high marginal propensities to import. As liberalization leads to increased trade volume and increased GDP (in both regions) these two groupings of countries respond by importing much more than before. They are expected to import so much that their trade balances move in a negative direction.

Protectionism, as implemented in scenarios of the LINK system, generally lowers world GDP and trade, but these are aggregative findings, and some countries benefit at the expense of others. It is often the protecting country that makes explicit gains, but these are overbalanced by losses somewhere else. The same thing is true within a country; some people gain, while others lose.

Losers may be identified as those who are displaced or, in many cases, the public at large who have to pay a higher price for domestic goods. Price measures are most meaningful for OECD countries. Prices are rigidly controlled in most of the socialist countries and are poorly estimated, if at all, on a regular basis, in the developing countries. We, therefore, pay most attention to OECD pricing.

For two years running, the simulation shows a fall in the inflation rate, and then the estimates change course. Instead of declines in the inflation rate after two years, there is a reversal. It should be emphasized that the only statistically significant results are those for the first two years under the influence of trade liberalization. After two years, the changes are negligible. To hold down a comprehensive price measure for two years by about 20–30 basis points is worth looking at, but the remaining years of the scenario have inflation rates that are hardly changed. The difference from the baseline fluctuates by only 0.02 to 0.05 percentage points—or only two to five basis points, and the estimation accuracy would not be strong enough to distinguish these values from zero.

Tariff reduction, or more generally, trade liberalization, is apparently one of the more powerful instruments for enhancing trade volume. It is the kind of policy that will be needed in order to do much for developing-country export earnings—earnings that are used for capital imports.

Summary

It has been the purpose of our calculations to evaluate the importance of tariff-related barriers to international trade for world trade, real activity, trade balances and prices, as well as for the economic welfare of individual countries. The results by and large confirm elementary economic theory: the imposition of tariffs reduces world trade and real activity, increases prices worldwide, and consequently generates welfare losses for all participants. Correspondingly, reductions in the level of tariffs can be expected to generate benefits worldwide, even though the gains are not distributed evenly; accommodating policies are therefore desirable. With regard to unilateral protectionism along the lines of the currently debated import surcharges the results are equally unambiguous: while such a tariff may generate short-run gains for the protecting country, the medium-term effects via domestic inflation and reductions in world trade more than wipe out the initial benefit. While these conclusions are to some extent conditional on other policy responses, the general direction of effects appears to be robust across a large number of alternative scenarios.

References

Baldwin, R. E. (1984) Trade Policies in Developed Countries. In *Handbook of International Economics*, vol. I (R. W. Jones and P. B. Kenen, eds.). Amsterdam: North-Holland, pp. 571–619.

Bollino, C. A., Pauly, P., and Petersen, C. E. (1983) Tariffs and Global Development: Further Results From Project LINK, paper presented at LINK Fall Meeting, University of Tsukuba, September 1983.

Brown, F., and Whalley, J. (1980) General Equilibrium Evaluations of Tariff-Cutting Proposals in the Tokyo Round and Comparisons with More Extensive Liberalization of World Trade, *Economic Journal* 90: 838–866.

Corden, W. M. (1971) *The Theory of Protection.* Oxford: Clarendon Press.

Cripps, F., and Godley, W. (1978) Control of Imports as a Means to Full Employment and the Expansion of World Trade: The U.K. Case, *Cambridge Journal of Economics* 2: 327–334.

Eichengreen, B. J. (1981) A Dynamic Model of Tariffs, Output, and Employment Under Flexible Exchange Rates, *Journal of International Economics* 11: 341–359.

Klein, L. R., Pauly, P., and Petersen, C. E. (1985) Import Surcharges, U.S. Deficits, and the World Economy. Project LINK, University of Pennsylvania, April, 1985.

Klein, L. R., and Su, V. (1979) Protectionism: An Econometric Analysis from Project LINK, *Journal of Policy Modeling* 1: 5–35.

Mundell, R. (1961) Flexible Exchange Rates and Employment Policy, *Canadian Journal of Economics* 27: 509–517.

Whalley, J. (1985) *Trade Liberalization Among World Trading Areas.* Cambridge, Mass.: MIT Press.

APPENDIX 1
SUMMARY OF WORLD ECONOMIC ACTIVITY— PROJECT LINK

```
Temporary Surcharge (20 , 15 , 7 %)
       - No Retaliation -

GDP pct. deviations: (scenario - baseline) / baseline
Priv. Cons. Defl.  : differences in growth rates from baseline
Trade Balance      : abs. differences from baseline in bill. US $
Unemployment       : rate deviation from baseline
```

Variable		1st Year	2nd Year	3rd Year	4th Year	5th Year
			----------- OECD -------------			
GDP	pct. dev.	-0.2	-0.4	-0.5	-0.2	0
PCDEFL.	abs. diff.	0.3	0.1	-0.2	-0.3	-0.3
TBAL.	abs. diff.	6.78	8.12	5.91	1.39	-1.04
UNEMPL.	rate diff.	0.1	0.1	0.1	0.1	0.1
			--------- CANADA + USA --------			
GDP	pct. dev.	-0.2	-0.5	-0.6	-0.3	0.1
PCDEFL.	abs. diff.	0.6	0.2	-0.4	-0.5	-0.4
TBAL.	abs. diff.	13.78	17.59	13.86	5.20	0.44
UNEMPL.	rate diff.	0.2	0.4	0.4	0.3	0
			-- JAPAN + AUSTRALIA + N.ZEA. ---			
GDP	pct. dev.	-0.2	-0.4	-0.4	-0.2	-0.1
PCDEFL.	abs. diff.	0	0	-0.2	-0.1	-0.1
TBAL.	abs. diff.	-3.34	-4.70	-3.98	-1.86	-0.65
UNEMPL.	rate diff.	0	0.1	0	0	0
			------------ EEC ------------			
GDP	pct. dev.	-0.2	-0.3	-0.2	-0.1	-0.1
PCDEFL.	abs. diff.	0.1	0	-0.1	-0.1	-0.1
TBAL.	abs. diff.	-2.73	-3.46	-2.84	-1.42	-0.67
UNEMPL.	rate diff.	0	0.1	0	0	0
			-------- EUROPE non-EEC --------			
GDP	pct. dev.	-0.1	-0.3	-0.3	-0.2	-0.1
PCDEFL.	abs. diff.	0	0	-0.1	-0.2	-0.1
TBAL.	abs. diff.	-0.93	-1.32	-1.16	-0.58	-0.21
UNEMPL.	rate diff.	0.1	0	0.1	0	0
			---- DEVELOPING COUNTRIES -----			
GDP	pct. dev.	-0.1	-0.2	-0.2	-0.1	-0.1
TBAL.	abs. diff.	-6.49	-7.67	-5.51	-1.11	1.19
			--------- OPEC --------			
GDP	pct. dev.	-0.1	-0.1	-0.2	-0.2	-0.2
TBAL.	abs. diff.	-1.93	-2.43	-2.03	-0.76	0.20
			--------- AFRICA --------			
GDP	pct. dev.	-0.2	-0.3	-0.4	-0.3	-0.3
TBAL.	abs. diff.	-0.20	-0.13	0.02	0.17	0.20
			-------- ASIA -------			
GDP	pct. dev.	-0.1	-0.2	-0.2	-0.1	-0.1
TBAL.	abs. diff.	-1.93	-2.53	-1.56	0.14	1.07
			--------- LATIN AMERICA ------			
GDP	pct. dev.	-0.2	-0.2	-0.2	-0.1	0
TBAL.	abs. diff.	-2.30	-2.39	-1.77	-0.55	-0.17
			----------- CMEA ------------			
GDP	pct. dev.	0	0	0	0	0
TBAL.	abs. diff.	-0.22	-0.38	-0.39	-0.23	-0.08
			----------- WORLD ----------			
GDP	pct. dev.	-0.1	-0.3	-0.3	-0.2	0

APPENDIX 2
SUMMARY OF WORLD ECONOMIC ACTIVITY—
PROJECT LINK

```
Temporary Surcharge (20 , 15 , 7 %)
        - Full Retaliation -
```

GDP pct. deviations: (scenario - baseline) / baseline
Priv. Cons. Defl. : differences in growth rates from baseline
Trade Balance   : abs. differences from baseline in bill. US $
Unemployment   : rate deviation from baseline

Variable		1st Year	2nd Year	3rd Year	4th Year	5th Year
			OECD			
GDP	pct. dev.	-0.3	-0.5	-0.5	-0.2	0.1
PCDEFL.	abs. diff.	0.7	0.1	-0.4	-0.5	-0.3
TBAL.	abs. diff.	-7.80	-2.83	0.73	3.09	0.67
UNEMPL.	rate diff.	0.2	0.3	0.2	0.1	0
			CANADA + USA			
GDP	pct. dev.	-0.8	-0.8	-0.7	-0.1	0.2
PCDEFL.	abs. diff.	0.8	-0.1	-0.6	-0.7	-0.4
TBAL.	abs. diff.	-15.37	-7.51	-1.64	3.12	-0.96
UNEMPL.	rate diff.	0.5	0.9	0.8	0.3	-0.2
			JAPAN + AUSTRALIA + N.ZEA.			
GDP	pct. dev.	0.2	-0.1	-0.3	-0.2	0
PCDEFL.	abs. diff.	0.4	0.1	-0.2	-0.3	-0.2
TBAL.	abs. diff.	1.10	-0.15	-0.40	-0.17	0.67
UNEMPL.	rate diff.	0	0	0	0	0
			EEC			
GDP	pct. dev.	0.2	0	-0.3	-0.3	-0.1
PCDEFL.	abs. diff.	0.3	0.3	0	-0.2	-0.3
TBAL.	abs. diff.	4.64	4.03	2.51	0.08	0.13
UNEMPL.	rate diff.	0	0	0	0.	0
			EUROPE non-EEC			
GDP	pct. dev.	0	-0.1	-0.3	-0.3	-0.2
PCDEFL.	abs. diff.	0.8	0.2	-0.2	-0.5	-0.2
TBAL.	abs. diff.	1.74	0.78	0.27	0.05	0.78
UNEMPL.	rate diff.	0	0	0.1	0.1	0
			DEVELOPING COUNTRIES			
GDP	pct. dev.	0	-0.1	-0.1	0	0
TBAL.	abs. diff.	6.38	1.90	-1.04	-2.88	-0.77
			OPEC			
GDP	pct. dev.	1.1	1.2	0.8	0.2	0
TBAL.	abs. diff.	4.64	2.17	-0.76	-3.40	-3.43
			AFRICA			
GDP	pct. dev.	-0.2	-0.6	-0.9	-0.9	-0.8
TBAL.	abs. diff.	0.26	0.33	0.51	0.64	0.77
			ASIA			
GDP	pct. dev.	0	-0.1	-0.1	0.1	0
TBAL.	abs. diff.	1.40	0.15	0.27	0.77	2.03
			LATIN AMERICA			
GDP	pct. dev.	-0.5	-0.4	-0.2	0	0
TBAL.	abs. diff.	0.03	-0.71	-0.96	-0.79	-0.11
			CMEA			
GDP	pct. dev.	0	0	0	0	0
TBAL.	abs. diff.	1.22	0.70	0.13	-0.23	0.14
			WORLD			
GDP	pct. dev.	-0.2	-0.3	-0.3	-0.1	0.1

L. R. Klein, P. H. Pauly, and C. E. Petersen

APPENDIX 3
SUMMARY OF WORLD ECONOMIC ACTIVITY— PROJECT LINK

```
                   Temporary Surcharge (20 , 15 , 7 %)
          - 10 % Dollar Depreciation , U.S. Interest Rates down 2 % -

GDP pct. deviations: (scenario - baseline) / baseline
Priv. Cons. Defl.  : differences in growth rates from baseline
Trade Balance      : abs. differences from baseline in bill. US $
Unemployment       : rate deviation from baseline
```

Variable		1st Year	2nd Year	3rd Year	4th Year	5th Year
			---------- OECD ----------			
GDP	pct. dev.	-0.2	0.1	0.4	0.8	1.0
PCDEFL.	abs. diff.	-0.2	-0.4	-0.7	-0.5	-0.3
TBAL.	abs. diff.	7.51	6.31	0.81	-6.49	-10.01
UNEMPL.	rate diff.	0.1	-0.1	-0.3	-0.4	-0.5
			-------- CANADA + USA --------			
GDP	pct. dev.	0.3	0.8	1.3	1.9	2.2
PCDEFL.	abs. diff.	0.3	0	-0.7	-0.5	-0.1
TBAL.	abs. diff.	7.82	9.43	0.15	-15.16	-24.40
UNEMPL.	rate diff.	0	-0.3	-0.8	-1.3	-1.6
			-- JAPAN + AUSTRALIA + N.ZEA. ---			
GDP	pct. dev.	-1.0	-1.1	-1.0	-0.7	-0.6
PCDEFL.	abs. diff.	-0.6	-0.4	-0.5	-0.3	-0.1
TBAL.	abs. diff.	4.09	4.75	7.05	10.64	13.27
UNEMPL.	rate diff.	0.1	0.1	0.1	0	0
			----------- EEC -----------			
GDP	pct. dev.	-0.7	-0.5	-0.4	-0.3	-0.2
PCDEFL.	abs. diff.	-0.6	-1.0	-0.8	-0.5	-0.4
TBAL.	abs. diff.	-3.45	-7.85	-6.43	-2.88	-0.35
UNEMPL.	rate diff.	0.1	0.1	0	0	0
			-------- EUROPE non-EEC -------			
GDP	pct. dev.	-0.9	-1.2	-1.0	-1.0	-1.0
PCDEFL.	abs. diff.	-1.5	-0.9	-0.8	-0.9	-0.7
TBAL.	abs. diff.	-0.68	0.15	0.20	1.01	1.51
UNEMPL.	rate diff.	0.1	0.2	0.3	0.4	0.4
			---- DEVELOPING COUNTRIES ----			
GDP	pct. dev.	-0.1	-0.1	-0.1	-0.1	-0.1
TBAL.	abs. diff.	-8.40	-7.24	-2.06	4.92	8.18
			-------- OPEC -------			
GDP	pct. dev.	-0.8	-0.6	-0.5	-0.4	-0.3
TBAL.	abs. diff.	-0.31	0.15	2.51	5.35	7.38
			-------- AFRICA --------			
GDP	pct. dev.	-0.2	-0.6	-0.9	-1.1	-1.3
TBAL.	abs. diff.	-0.39	0.35	0.98	1.57	2.04
			-------- ASIA -------			
GDP	pct. dev.	0	0	0.1	0.1	0.3
TBAL.	abs. diff.	-5.22	-5.84	-4.75	-3.07	-3.15
			-------- LATIN AMERICA ------			
GDP	pct. dev.	-0.2	-0.3	-0.4	-0.5	-0.6
TBAL.	abs. diff.	-1.66	-1.05	0.14	2.02	2.91
			-------- CMEA ----------			
GDP	pct. dev.	0	0	0	0	0
TBAL.	abs. diff.	0.86	0.92	1.15	1.35	1.39
			---------- WORLD ----------			
GDP	pct. dev.	-0.2	0	0.2	0.4	0.6

APPENDIX 4
SUMMARY OF WORLD ECONOMIC ACTIVITY—
PROJECT LINK

Temporary Surcharge (20 , 15 , 7 %)
 - 10 % Dollar Appreciation -

GDP pct. deviations: (scenario - baseline) / baseline
Priv. Cons. Defl.   : differences in growth rates from baseline
Trade Balance   : abs. differences from baseline in bill. US $
Unemployment   : rate deviation from baseline

Variable		1st Year	2nd Year	3rd Year	4th Year	5th Year
				OECD		
GDP	pct. dev.	0.7	0.3	0	-0.1	-0.1
PCDEFL.	abs. diff.	0.7	0.1	-0.4	-0.5	-0.3
TBAL.	abs. diff.	6.56	8.12	6.24	1.71	-1.32
UNEMPL.	rate diff.	0.1	0.1	0.1	0	-0.1
				CANADA + USA		
GDP	pct. dev.	0.6	0	-0.4	-0.6	-0.4
PCDEFL.	abs. diff.	0.8	-0.1	-0.6	-0.7	-0.4
TBAL.	abs. diff.	17.19	17.91	12.59	4.58	0.16
UNEMPL.	rate diff.	0.3	0.4	0.5	0.3	0
				JAPAN + AUSTRALIA + N.ZEA.		
GDP	pct. dev.	0.4	0.4	0.4	0.7	0.9
PCDEFL.	abs. diff.	0.6	0.4	0.3	0.2	0.1
TBAL.	abs. diff.	-8.76	-10.45	-9.25	-6.94	-5.97
UNEMPL.	rate diff.	-0.1	0	-0.1	-0.1	0
				EEC		
GDP	pct. dev.	0.4	0	0.1	0.3	0.4
PCDEFL.	abs. diff.	0.7	1.0	0.6	0.4	0.3
TBAL.	abs. diff.	-1.09	2.48	3.89	4.09	3.92
UNEMPL.	rate diff.	0	0	0	0.	-0.1
				EUROPE non-EEC		
GDP	pct. dev.	0.6	0.7	0.6	0.9	1.2
PCDEFL.	abs. diff.	1.5	0.9	0.6	0.6	0.7
TBAL.	abs. diff.	-1.01	-2.02	-1.21	-0.22	0.46
UNEMPL.	rate diff.	0	-0.2	-0.2	-0.3	-0.4
				DEVELOPING COUNTRIES		
GDP	pct. dev.	0	0	0.1	0.3	0.4
TBAL.	abs. diff.	-4.75	-6.12	-4.17	0.14	2.99
				OPEC		
GDP	pct. dev.	0.6	0.5	0.5	0.6	0.7
TBAL.	abs. diff.	-2.86	-3.02	-2.76	-1.28	-0.37
				AFRICA		
GDP	pct. dev.	-0.1	0.1	0.4	0.8	1.2
TBAL.	abs. diff.	-0.02	-0.46	-0.68	-0.86	-1.26
				ASIA		
GDP	pct. dev.	-0.2	-0.2	-0.1	0.1	0
TBAL.	abs. diff.	0.65	0.33	1.62	3.44	5.60
				LATIN AMERICA		
GDP	pct. dev.	-0.1	0.1	0.3	0.7	1.0
TBAL.	abs. diff.	-2.78	-3.01	-2.35	-1.21	-1.05
				CMEA		
GDP	pct. dev.	0	0	0	0	0
TBAL.	abs. diff.	-0.82	-1.02	-1.05	-0.69	-0.26
				WORLD		
GDP	pct. dev.	0	-0.1	0	0.2	0.4

L. R. Klein, P. H. Pauly, and C. E. Petersen

APPENDIX 5
SUMMARY OF WORLD ECONOMIC ACTIVITY—
PROJECT LINK

```
               Temporary Surcharge (20 , 15 , 7 %)
        - 10 % Dollar Depreciation , U.S. Interest Rates up 2 % -

GDP pct. deviations: (scenario - baseline) / baseline
Priv. Cons. Defl. : differences in growth rates from baseline
Trade Balance     : abs. differences from baseline in bill. US $
Unemployment      : rate deviation from baseline
```

Variable		1st Year	2nd Year	3rd Year	4th Year	5th Year
			---------- OECD ----------			
GDP	pct. dev.	-0.7	-1.7	-2.3	-2.3	-2.0
PCDEFL.	abs. diff.	0	0.1	-0.3	-0.5	-0.7
TBAL.	abs. diff.	7.86	11.84	12.64	10.42	10.02
UNEMPL.	rate diff.	0.2	0.4	0.6	0.8	0.8
			------- CANADA + USA -------			
GDP	pct. dev.	-0.6	-2.3	-3.2	-3.2	-2.8
PCDEFL.	abs. diff.	0.8	1.1	0.1	-0.2	-0.7
TBAL.	abs. diff.	12.24	26.54	32.41	29.06	27.52
UNEMPL.	rate diff.	0.3	0.9	1.6	1.8	1.6
			-- JAPAN + AUSTRALIA + N.ZEA. ---			
GDP	pct. dev.	-1.1	-1.5	-1.7	-1.7	-1.6
PCDEFL.	abs. diff.	-0.6	-0.5	-0.7	-0.6	-0.4
TBAL.	abs. diff.	2.25	-0.79	-2.73	-2.22	-1.40
UNEMPL.	rate diff.	0.1	0.2	0.1	0.1	0.1
			---------- EEC ----------			
GDP	pct. dev.	-0.8	-0.7	-0.8	-0.8	-0.8
PCDEFL.	abs. diff.	-0.6	-1.0	-0.8	-0.6	-0.6
TBAL.	abs. diff.	-5.16	-12.30	-14.21	-13.31	-12.61
UNEMPL.	rate diff.	0.1	0.1	0.1	0.2	0.2
			------- EUROPE non-EEC -------			
GDP	pct. dev.	-0.9	-1.5	-1.4	-1.6	-1.7
PCDEFL.	abs. diff.	-1.5	-1.0	-0.9	-1.0	-0.9
TBAL.	abs. diff.	-1.18	-1.41	-2.65	-3.01	-3.47
UNEMPL.	rate diff.	0.2	0.2	0.4	0.4	0.5
			---- DEVELOPING COUNTRIES ----			
GDP	pct. dev.	-0.3	-0.6	-0.8	-1.0	-0.9
TBAL.	abs. diff.	-9.00	-12.67	-13.26	-10.86	-10.34
			-------- OPEC --------			
GDP	pct. dev.	-0.9	-1.0	-1.3	-1.7	-1.9
TBAL.	abs. diff.	-1.22	-3.93	-5.34	-5.84	-5.64
			-------- AFRICA --------			
GDP	pct. dev.	-0.2	-0.7	-1.2	-1.6	-1.8
TBAL.	abs. diff.	-0.49	0.07	0.50	0.92	1.29
			-------- ASIA --------			
GDP	pct. dev.	-0.1	-0.3	-0.5	-0.6	-0.4
TBAL.	abs. diff.	-5.12	-6.50	-6.10	-4.40	-4.86
			------- LATIN AMERICA -------			
GDP	pct. dev.	-0.3	-0.7	-1.0	-1.2	-1.2
TBAL.	abs. diff.	-1.80	-2.28	-2.50	-1.86	-1.54
			---------- CMEA ----------			
GDP	pct. dev.	0	0	0	0	0
TBAL.	abs. diff.	0.56	0.23	-0.02	-0.22	-0.44
			---------- WORLD ----------			
GDP	pct. dev.	-0.5	-1.1	-1.5	-1.6	-1.4

APPENDIX 6
SUMMARY OF WORLD ECONOMIC ACTIVITY—
PROJECT LINK

Temporary Surcharge (20 %) on US Imports
from Japan, Korea, Taiwan, and Brazil

GDP pct. deviations: (scenario - baseline) / baseline
Priv. Cons. Defl. : differences in growth rates from baseline
Trade Balance : abs. differences from baseline in bill. US $
Unemployment : rate deviation from baseline

Variable		1st Year	2nd Year	3rd Year	4th Year	5th Year
				OECD		
GDP	pct. dev.	0	-0.1	-0.1	-0.1	0
PCDEFL.	abs. diff.	0.1	0.1	0.1	0	-0.1
TBAL.	abs. diff.	-1.10	0.30	1.66	0.19	-0.94
UNEMPL.	rate diff.	0	0	0	0.1	0
				CANADA + USA		
GDP	pct. dev.	0.1	0	-0.2	-0.3	-0.1
PCDEFL.	abs. diff.	0.2	0.2	0.1	-0.2	-0.4
TBAL.	abs. diff.	6.15	8.03	9.78	3.17	1.08
UNEMPL.	rate diff.	0	0	0	0.1	0.2
				JAPAN + AUSTRALIA + N.ZEA.		
GDP	pct. dev.	-0.6	-0.6	-0.4	0.4	0.6
PCDEFL.	abs. diff.	-0.2	0	0.2	0.2	0.4
TBAL.	abs. diff.	-8.34	-8.31	-8.88	-0.04	0.02
UNEMPL.	rate diff.	0.1	0	0	-0.1	-0.1
				EEC		
GDP	pct. dev.	0.2	0.2	0.2	0	0
PCDEFL.	abs. diff.	0	0	0.2	0.2	0.3
TBAL.	abs. diff.	0.31	0.02	0.30	-2.19	-1.10
UNEMPL.	rate diff.	0	0	0	0.1	0
				EUROPE non-EEC		
GDP	pct. dev.	0.1	0.1	0	-0.2	-0.3
PCDEFL.	abs. diff.	0	0	0	-0.1	-0.1
TBAL.	abs. diff.	0.75	0.64	0.44	-0.76	-1.00
UNEMPL.	rate diff.	0	0	-0.1	0	0
				DEVELOPING COUNTRIES		
GDP	pct. dev.	0	0	0	0	0.2
TBAL.	abs. diff.	-1.36	-2.50	-3.64	-1.71	-0.94
				OPEC		
GDP	pct. dev.	0	0	-0.1	-0.2	-0.3
TBAL.	abs. diff.	-0.10	-0.08	0.03	0.31	0.79
				AFRICA		
GDP	pct. dev.	0.1	0	0	-0.1	-0.2
TBAL.	abs. diff.	0.11	0.09	0.04	-0.14	-0.16
				ASIA		
GDP	pct. dev.	0	0	0.1	0.2	0.3
TBAL.	abs. diff.	-1.41	-2.16	-2.98	-0.78	-0.68
				LATIN AMERICA		
GDP	pct. dev.	-0.2	-0.2	-0.3	-0.2	-0.1
TBAL.	abs. diff.	-0.01	-0.20	-0.41	-0.58	-0.42
				CMEA		
GDP	pct. dev.	0	0	0	0	0
TBAL.	abs. diff.	0.34	0.28	0.07	-0.60	-0.68
				WORLD		
GDP	pct. dev.	0	0	-0.1	-0.1	0

L. R. Klein, P. H. Pauly, and C. E. Petersen

APPENDIX 7
SUMMARY OF WORLD ECONOMIC ACTIVITY—
PROJECT LINK

```
                   Temporary Surcharge (20 %) for SITC59
                 OECD (excl. Japan) vs. Asia and Latin America
GDP pct. deviations: (scenario - baseline) / baseline
Priv. Cons. Defl.  : differences in growth rates from baseline
Trade Balance      : abs. differences from baseline in bill. US $
Unemployment       : rate deviation from baseline
```

Variable		1st Year	2nd Year	3rd Year	4th Year	5th Year
			----------- OECD -----------			
GDP	pct. dev.	0.1	-0.1	-0.2	-0.3	0
PCDEFL.	abs. diff.	0.2	0.2	0.2	0	-0.1
TBAL.	abs. diff.	5.61	7.06	9.89	0.16	-2.34
UNEMPL.	rate diff.	0	0	0	0.1	0.1
			-------- CANADA + USA --------			
GDP	pct. dev.	0.2	0	-.3	-0.5	-0.2
PCDEFL.	abs. diff.	0.3	0.3	0.1	-0.3	-0.5
TBAL.	abs. diff.	10.60	12.40	14.38	2.60	0.03
UNEMPL.	rate diff.	0	0	0	0.1	0.3
			-- JAPAN + AUSTRALIA + N.ZEA. ---			
GDP	pct. dev.	-1.1	-1.2	-0.9	0.6	1.0
PCDEFL.	abs. diff.	-0.2	-0.1	0	0.3	0.7
TBAL.	abs. diff.	-13.97	-14.86	-15.30	-0.05	-0.29
UNEMPL.	rate diff.	0.1	0.1	0.1	-0.1	-0.1
			----------- EEC -----------			
GDP	pct. dev.	0.4	0.3	0.3	-0.1	0
PCDEFL.	abs. diff.	0.1	0.2	0.3	0.2	0.3
TBAL.	abs. diff.	6.33	7.29	8.46	-1.34	-1.59
UNEMPL.	rate diff.	0	-0.1	-0.1	0.1	0
			-------- EUROPE non-EEC --------			
GDP	pct. dev.	0.3	0.3	0.1	-0.4	-0.5
PCDEFL.	abs. diff.	0.3	0.1	0	-0.5	-0.2
TBAL.	abs. diff.	2.56	2.21	2.32	-1.00	-0.60
UNEMPL.	rate diff.	0	0	-0.1	0	0
			---- DEVELOPING COUNTRIES -----			
GDP	pct. dev.	-0.4	-0.6	-0.6	-0.2	-0.2
TBAL.	abs. diff.	-8.58	-9.55	-11.79	-0.48	1.52
			-------- OPEC --------			
GDP	pct. dev.	0	-0.1	-0.3	-0.5	-0.5
TBAL.	abs. diff.	-0.66	-1.01	-0.94	-0.07	0.96
			--------- AFRICA ---------			
GDP	pct. dev.	0.1	0.1	0	-0.3	-0.3
TBAL.	abs. diff.	0.15	0.07	-0.01	-0.28	-0.23
			-------- ASIA --------			
GDP	pct. dev.	-0.6	-0.8	-0.7	-0.1	0
TBAL.	abs. diff.	-6.07	-5.90	-7.49	1.28	1.73
			-------- LATIN AMERICA ------			
GDP	pct. dev.	-0.4	-0.6	-0.8	-0.5	-0.5
TBAL.	abs. diff.	-2.09	-2.48	-2.89	-0.62	-0.28
			--------- CMEA ----------			
GDP	pct. dev.	0	0	0	0	0
TBAL.	abs. diff.	0.78	0.41	0.04	-1.44	-1.13
			----------- WORLD ----------			
GDP	pct. dev.	0	-0.2	-0.2	-0.2	0

APPENDIX 8
SUMMARY OF WORLD ECONOMIC ACTIVITY—
PROJECT LINK

Worldwide Tariff Reduction of 5 % for SITC 01 and 24

```
GDP pct. deviations: (scenario - baseline) / baseline
Priv. Cons. Defl.  : differences in growth rates from baseline
Trade Balance      : abs. differences from baseline in bill. US $
Unemployment       : rate deviation from baseline
```

Variable		1st Year	2nd Year	3rd Year	4th Year	5th Year
			----------- OECD ------------			
GDP	pct dev.	0.2	0.2	0.3	0.3	0.3
PCDEFL.	abs. diff.	-0.3	-0.1	0	0	0
TBAL.	abs. diff.	-0.22	-0.55	-0.63	-0.57	-0.15
UNEMPL.	rate diff.	-0.1	-0.1	-0.2	-0.2	-0.2
			-------- CANADA + USA --------			
GDP	pct. dev.	0.2	0.1	0.2	0.2	0.2
PCDEFL.	abs. diff.	-0.1	0	0	0	0
TBAL.	abs. diff.	0.28	0.20	0.42	0.48	0.62
UNEMPL.	rate diff.	0	-0.1	-0.1	-0.1	-0.1
			-- JAPAN + AUSTRALIA + N.ZEA. ---			
GDP	pct. dev.	0.1	0.2	0.2	0.2	0.3
PCDEFL.	abs. diff.	-0.2	-0.1	0	0	0
TBAL.	abs. diff.	0.47	0.57	0.67	0.74	0.82
UNEMPL.	rate diff.	-0.1	-0.2	-0.3	-0.4	-0.4
			----------- EEC ------------			
GDP	pct. dev.	0.2	0.4	0.6	0.6	0.6
PCDEFL.	abs. diff.	-0.6	-0.3	-0.2	-0.1	-0.1
TBAL.	abs. diff.	-0.44	-1.39	-1.88	-1.93	-1.73
UNEMPL.	rate diff.	0	-0.1	-0.1	-0.2	-0.2
			-------- EUROPE non-EEC --------			
GDP	pct. dev.	0.2	0.3	0.3	0.3	0.3
PCDEFL.	abs. diff.	-0.2	0	0	0	0
TBAL.	abs. diff.	0.04	0.19	0.15	0.14	0.15
UNEMPL.	rate diff.	0	0	-0.1	-0.2	-0.4
			---- DEVELOPING COUNTRIES -----			
GDP	pct. dev.	0.1	0.1	0.2	0.2	0.3
TBAL.	abs. diff.	-0.26	-0.29	-0.27	-0.34	-0.62
			-------- DEVEL. non-OIL --------			
GDP	pct. dev.	0.1	0.1	0.2	0.2	0.3
TBAL.	abs. diff.	-0.24	-0.41	-0.55	-0.62	-0.68
			-------- DEVEL. OIL ----------			
GDP	pct. dev.	0	0.1	0.1	0.2	0.3
TBAL.	abs. diff.	-0.02	0.11	0.28	-0.27	0.05
			----------- CMEA ------------			
GDP	pct. dev.	0	0	0	0	0.1
TBAL.	abs. diff.	0.35	0.70	0.81	0.76	0.72
			----------- WORLD ------------			
GDP	pct. dev.	0.1	0.2	0.2	0.2	0.2

L. R. Klein, P. H. Pauly, and C. E. Petersen

APPENDIX 9
SUMMARY OF WORLD ECONOMIC ACTIVITY—
PROJECT LINK

Worldwide Tariff Reduction of 5 % for SITC 5-9

```
GDP pct. deviations: (scenario - baseline) / baseline
Priv. Cons. Defl. : differences in growth rates from baseline
Trade Balance     : abs. differences from baseline in bill. US $
Unemployment      : rate deviation from baseline
```

Variable		1st Year	2nd Year	3rd Year	4th Year	5th Year
				OECD		
GDP	pct. dev.	0.2	0.5	0.5	0.5	0.5
PCDEFL.	abs. diff.	-0.3	-0.2	0	0.1	0.1
TBAL.	abs. diff.	-0.54	-1.53	-1.40	-0.40	0.98
UNEMPL.	rate diff.	-0.1	-0.2	-0.3	-0.4	-0.4
				CANADA + USA		
GDP	pct. dev.	0.1	0.1	0.1	0	-0.1
PCDEFL.	abs. diff.	0	-0.1	0	0.1	0.1
TBAL.	abs. diff.	1.93	2.23	2.48	3.45	5.14
UNEMPL.	rate diff.	0	-0.1	-0.2	-0.1	-0.1
				JAPAN + AUSTRALIA + N.ZEA.		
GDP	pct. dev.	0.1	0.2	0.3	0.3	0.4
PCDEFL.	abs. diff.	0	0	0.1	0.1	0.1
TBAL.	abs. diff.	0.29	1.54	2.33	3.04	3.88
UNEMPL.	rate diff.	-0.1	-0.2	-0.3	-0.4	-0.4
				EEC		
GDP	pct. dev.	0.6	1.2	1.4	1.5	1.7
PCDEFL.	abs. diff.	-0.6	-0.6	-0.2	-0.1	-0.1
TBAL.	abs. diff.	-1.65	-3.89	-3.97	-3.96	-5.04
UNEMPL.	rate diff.	-0.1	-0.2	-0.3	-0.3	-0.3
				EUROPE non-EEC		
GDP	pct. dev.	0.2	0.3	0.4	0.6	0.8
PCDEFL.	abs. diff.	-0.1	-0.1	0	0.1	0.3
TBAL.	abs. diff.	-0.55	-1.12	-1.35	-1.56	-1.42
UNEMPL.	rate diff.	0	-0.2	-0.4	-0.5	-0.7
				DEVELOPING COUNTRIES		
GDP	pct. dev.	0.2	0.4	0.5	0.7	0.8
TBAL.	abs. diff.	-0.27	-0.65	-1.26	-2.29	-3.89
				DEVEL. non-OIL		
GDP	pct. dev.	0.1	0.3	0.5	0.6	0.7
TBAL.	abs. diff.	-0.41	-0.98	-1.35	-1.62	-1.90
				DEVEL. OIL		
GDP	pct. dev.	0.2	0.5	0.8	1.3	1.7
TBAL.	abs. diff.	0.14	0.33	0.09	-0.67	-1.99
				CMEA		
GDP	pct. dev.	0	0.1	0.1	0.1	0.2
TBAL.	abs. diff.	1.02	1.99	2.41	2.66	2.84
				WORLD		
GDP	pct. dev.	0.2	0.3	0.4	0.4	0.5

5

The New Protectionism: A Response to Shifts in National Economic Power

ROBERT E. BALDWIN

Introduction

The international trading economy is in the anomalous condition of diminishing tariff protection but increasing the use of nontariff trade-distorting measures. The former trend is the result of the staged tariff cuts agreed on in the GATT-sponsored Tokyo Round of multilateral negotiations concluded in 1979. The latter trend, however, is taking place largely outside the framework of GATT and threatens to undermine the liberal international trading regime established after World War II.

This paper relates the new nontariff protectionism to significant structural changes in world industrial production that have brought about a decline in the dominant economic position of the United States, a concomitant rise to international economic prominence of the European Economic Community and Japan, and the emergence of a group of newly industrializing developing countries (NICs). The first two sections describe the rise of the United States to a dominant position in international economic affairs in the immediate postwar period and indicate the types of "hegemonic" actions taken by this country. "Shifts in International Economic Power" explains how changes in trade, finance, and energy have led to modifications in national trade policy behavior, particularly on the part of the United States. We then speculate about the nature of the international regime that is evolving under the present pattern of economic power among nations. The paper's final section is a summary and conclusion.

From the University of Wisconsin–Madison, Madison, Wisconsin.

The Rise in U.S. Hegemony

The role of the United States in the evolution of the modern trading system has been central. Although this country became an important trader on the world scene after World War I, it gave little indication at the time of a willingness to assume a major international leadership role. The American share of the exports of the industrial countries rose from 22.1 percent in 1913 to 27.8 percent by 1928 (Baldwin, 1958), but during this period the United States chose political and economic isolation by rejecting membership in the League of Nations and by erecting in 1930 the highest set of tariff barriers in its peacetime history. The failure of the London Economic Conference of 1933 due to the inward-looking economic position of the United States marks the low point of U.S. internationalism in the interwar period.

A major policy reorientation toward participation in international affairs began to occur in the United States during the late 1930s and especially in World War II. More and more political leaders and the electorate generally began to accept the view of key policy officials in the Roosevelt administration that continued international isolationism would bring not only renewed economic stagnation and unemployment to the American economy but also the likely prospect of disastrous new worldwide military conflicts. Consequently, active participation in the United Nations was accepted by the American public, as were the proposals to establish international economic agencies to provide for an orderly balance-of-payments adjustment mechanism for individual nations and to promote reconstruction and development. International trade had long been a much more politicized subject, however, and all that was salvaged (and then only by executive action) from the proposal for a comprehensive international trade organization was the General Agreement on Tariffs and Trade (GATT).

The economic proposals initiated by the United States were not, it should be emphasized, aimed at giving this country a hegemonic role. They, instead, envisioned the United States as one of a small group of nations which would cooperate to provide the leadership necessary to avoid the disastrous nationalistic policies of the 1930s. The envisioned leadership group included the United Kingdom, France, China, and it was hoped, the Soviet Union.

Hegemony was thrust upon the United States by a set of unexpected circumstances. First, the failure of the United Kingdom to return to anything like its prewar position as a world economic power was unforeseen. U.S. officials thought, for example, that the U.S. loan of $3.75 billion to the United Kingdom in 1946 would enable that country to restore sterling convertibility and to return to its earlier prominent international role. But the funds were quickly exhausted and it was necessary to restore exchange control. The 1949 devaluation of the pound was equally disappointing in its failure to revitalize the country. Economic reconstruction in Europe also proved much more costly than envisioned. The resources of the International Bank for Reconstruction and Development proved much too small to handle this task and massive foreign aid by the United States became necessary. The U.S. economy also grew vigorously after the war rather than, as many expected, returning to stagnant conditions.

The failure of either China or the USSR to participate in the market-oriented international economy placed an added leadership burden on the United States. But perhaps the most important factor leading to U.S. hegemony was the effort by the Soviet Union to expand its political influence into Western Europe and elsewhere. American officials believed they had little choice from a national viewpoint but to assume an active political, economic, and military leadership role to counter this expansionist policy, an action that most noncommunist countries welcomed.

Hegemonic Behavior

The significant expansion of productive facilities in the United States during the war coupled with the widespread destruction of industrial capacity in Germany and Japan gave American producers an enormous advantage in meeting the worldwide pent-up demands of the 1940s and 1950s. The U.S. share of industrial country exports rose from 25.6 percent in 1938 to 35.2 percent in 1952 (Baldwin, 1958). (The combined share of Germany and Japan fell from 24.0 percent to 11.4 percent between these years.) Even in a traditional net import category like textiles, the United States maintained a net export position until 1958.

Static trade theory suggests that a hegemonic power will take advantage of its monopolistic position by imposing trade restrictions to raise domestic welfare through an improvement in its terms of trade. However, like the United Kingdom when it was a hegemonic nation in the nineteenth century, the United States reacted by promoting trade liberalization rather than trade restrictionism. A restrictionist reaction might have been possible for a highly controlled, planned economy that could redistribute income fairly readily and did not need to rely on the trade sector as a major source of employment generation or growth, but the growth goals of free-market firms together with the nature of the political decision-making process rule out such a response in modern industrial democracies.

Industrial organization theory emphasizes that firms in oligopolistically organized industries take a long-run view of profitability and strive to increase their market share. By doing so, they try both to prevent new competitors from entering the market and possibly causing losses to existing firms and old competitors from increasing their shares to the point where others might suffer progressive and irreversible market losses. U.S. firms organized in this manner seized the postwar competitive opportunities associated with American dominance to expand overseas market shares both through increased exports and direct foreign investment. The desire of U.S. political leaders to strengthen noncommunist nations by opening up American markets and providing foreign aid complemented these goals of U.S. business, and business leaders actively supported the government's foreign policy aims. Even most producers in more competitively organized and less high-technology sectors such as agriculture, textiles, and miscellaneous manufactures favored an outward-oriented hegemonic policy at this time, since they too were able to export abroad and were not faced with any significant import competition.

The United States behaved in a hegemonic manner on many occasions in the 1950s and early 1960s. As Keohane (1984, chapter 8) emphasizes, in doing so, it did not coerce other states into accepting policies of little benefit to them. Instead, the United States usually proposed joint policy efforts in areas of mutual economic interest and provided strong incentives for hegemonic cooperation. In the trade field, for example, U.S. officials regularly pressed for trade-liberalizing multilateral negotiations and six such negotiations were initiated between 1947 and 1962. But the United States traded short-term concessions for possible long-run gains, since the concessions by most other countries were not very meaningful in trade terms due to the exchange controls they maintained until the late 1950s. The U.S. goal was to penetrate successfully the markets of Europe and Japan as their controls were eased and finally eliminated.

One instance where the United States did put considerable pressure on its trading partners to accept the American viewpoint was in the Kennedy Round of multilateral trade negotiations. At the initial ministerial meeting in 1963, U.S. trade officials—with President Kennedy's approval—threatened to call off the negotiations unless the European Community accepted the American proposal for a substantial, across-the-board tariff-cutting rule. Members of the Community had regained much of their economic vitality and the United States wanted economic payment for its earlier nonreciprocated concessions and its willingness to support a customs-union arrangement that discriminated against the United States.

In the financial area the $3.75 billion loan to the United Kingdom in 1946, the large grants of foreign aid after 1948 under the

Marshall Plan, and the provision of funds to help establish the European Payments Union in 1948 are examples of hegemonic leadership by the United States. American leaders envisioned the postwar international monetary regime to be one with fixed and convertible exchange rates in which orderly adjustments of balance-of-payments problems would take place. When the International Monetary Fund (IMF) proved inadequate to cope with the magnitude of postwar payments problems, the United States provided financial aid until the affected countries were strong enough economically for the IMF to assume its intended role. A U.S. hegemonic role was also exercised in the energy field, as American companies, with the assistance of the U.S. government, gained control over Arab oil during the 1940s and 1950s.

Shifts in International Economic Power

TRADE COMPETITIVENESS

The hegemonic actions of the United States, aimed at maintaining the liberal international economic framework established largely through its efforts and at turning back the expansion of the Soviet Union, succeeded very well. By 1960 the export market shares of France, Germany, Italy, and Japan had either exceeded or come close to their prewar levels. Among the industrial countries only the United Kingdom failed to regain its prewar position by this time. The restoration of peacetime productive capabilities in these countries meant that the exceptionally high market shares of the United States in the early postwar years declined correspondingly. The 35.2 percent U.S. export share of 1952 had dropped to 29.9 percent by 1960, a figure that was, however, still higher than its 1938 share of 25.6 percent (Baldwin, 1962).

For manufactured products alone, the picture is much the same. The U.S. world export share decreased from 29.4 percent in 1953 to 18.7 percent in 1959, while the shares of Western Europe and Japan rose from 49.0 percent to 53.7 percent and from 2.8 percent to 4.2 percent, respectively (Branson, 1980). The export market share of Western Europe remained unchanged in the 1960s, but the Japanese share continued to rise and reached 10.0 percent in 1971. At the same time the U.S. share of world exports of manufactures fell to 13.4 percent by 1971.

While aid from the U.S. government played an important part in restoring the trade competitiveness of the European countries and Japan, the governments of these nations themselves were the prime driving force for revitalization. The French government, for example, formulated an industrial modernization plan after the war and two-thirds of all new investment between 1947 and 1950 was financed from public funds. Similarly, the British government under the Labour Party created an Economic Planning Board and exercised close control over the direction of postwar investment, while even the relatively free-market-oriented German government channeled capital into key industries in the 1950s. Government investment aid to the steel, shipbuilding, and aircraft industries and the use of preferential government policies to promote the computer sector are other examples of the use of trade-oriented industrial policies in Europe during this period.

Japan is perhaps the best-known example of the use of government policies to improve international competitiveness. During the 1950s and 1960s the Japanese government guided the country's industrial expansion by providing tax incentives and investment funds to favored industries. Funding for research and development in high-technology areas also became an important part of the government's trade policy in the 1970s. Governments of newly industrializing developing countries use industry-specific investment and production subsidies to an even greater extent than any of the developed nations in their import-substitution and export-promotion activities.

Not only had the prewar export position of the United States been restored by the late 1960s, but the period of an absence of significant import pressures in major industries with political clout had also come to an end. Stiff competition from the Japanese in the cotton textiles industry was evident by the late 1950s, and the United States initiated the formation of a trade-restricting international cotton textile agreement in 1962. A broad group of other industries also began to face significant import competition in the late 1960s. The products affected included footwear, radios and television sets, motor vehicles and trucks, tires and inner tubes, semiconductors, hand tools, earthenware table and kitchen articles, jewelry, and some steel items.

Trade-pattern changes in the 1970s and early 1980s were dominated by the price-increasing actions of the Organization of Petroleum Exporting Countries (OPEC). This group's share of world exports rose from 18.2 percent in 1970 to 27.3 percent in 1980 (Economic Report of the President, 1985). By 1984 OPEC's share, however, had fallen to 23.5 percent as the power of the cartel declined. During this period the U.S. export share fell from 13.7 percent to 10.9 percent, while that of the European Community dropped from 36.1 percent to 30.7 percent. Japan, however, managed to increase its share from 6.1 percent to 8.4 percent. The latter figures reflect Japan's continued strong performance in manufacturing. That country's share of industrial countries' manufacturing exports rose from 9.9 percent in 1971 to 15.3 percent in early 1984 (U.S. Department of Commerce, 1985).

The 1970s and early 1980s were a time of relative stability in the U.S. manufacturing export share, with this figure rising slightly—from 19.6 percent in 1971 to 20.1 percent in 1984. In contrast, the European Community's manufacturing export share declined from 59.9 percent in 1971 to 54.6 percent in 1984. Another major development of this period was the increase in the manufacturing export share of the developing countries from 7.1 percent in 1971 to 11.0 percent in 1980.

An important feature of the shifts in trading patterns of industrial countries in the 1970s and 1980s has been that not only have labor-intensive sectors like textiles, apparel, and footwear continued to face severe import competition but that large-scale oligopolistically organized industries such as steel, automobiles, and shipbuilding have had to contend with such competition. Machine tools and consumer electronic goods have also come under increasing import pressure.

The decline in the dominance of the United States in trade policy matters became apparent in the Tokyo Round of multilateral trade negotiations as well as when the United States proposed a new negotiating round in 1982. As it had in the Kennedy Round, the United States proposed an across-the-board linear tariff-cutting rule at the outset of the Tokyo Round, whereas the European Community again proposed a formula that cut high tariff rates by a greater percentage than low duties. This time the United States did not prevail. The other industrial nations treated both the United States and the Community as major trading blocs whose negotiating objectives must be satisfied. The result was a compromise duty-cutting rule that met the U.S. desire for a deep average cut and at the same time produced the significant degree of tariff harmonization sought by the European Community. At the 1982 GATT ministerial meeting the United States again called for a new multilateral exercise that included as major agenda items negotiations aimed at reducing export subsidies in agriculture and barriers to trade in services. The Community and the developing countries both rejected the U.S. proposals, and it has become clear that the United States can no longer determine the pace at which such negotiations will be held.

INTERNATIONAL FINANCIAL
AND OTHER ECONOMIC CHANGES

As a decline in the dominant trade-competitiveness position of the United States became increasingly evident in the 1960s, both the United States and many other countries became dissatisfied with the

U.S. role in international monetary affairs. Since the supply of gold in the world increases only slowly, the demand for additional international liquidity that accompanied the rapid growth in world trade had to be met by greater holdings of dollars, the other official form of international reserves. However, as these holdings grew, a number of countries became concerned about the freedom from monetary and fiscal discipline that such an arrangement gave the United States and they resented the seigniorage privileges it granted. The United States also became increasingly dissatisfied with its inability to change the exchange rate of the dollar as a balance-of-payments adjustment means. Another indication of the decline in U.S. hegemony was the creation in 1969 of a new form of international liquidity in the International Monetary Fund (IMF): Special Drawing Rights (SDRs), designed to reduce the dependence of the international economy on the dollar.

The shift to a flexible exchange-rate system in 1971, however, was the clearest manifestation of the decline in U.S. dominance in the monetary field. Although the results of this action have not given countries the expected degree of freedom from U.S. financial influence, the role of the dollar as a reserve and vehicle currency has declined. Another institutional change directed at reducing the monetary influence of the United States was the formation of the European Monetary System in 1979.

The difficulties faced by the industrial nations in the energy field as a consequence of the success of OPEC have already been mentioned, but the importance of this shift in economic power is hard to exaggerate. This development was an especially devastating blow to the international economic prestige of the United States.

Trade Policy Responses to the Redistribution of National Economic Power

The nonhegemonic members of the international trading regime (i.e., countries other than the United States) responded to the inevitable industry disruption caused by the shifts in comparative cost patterns in a manner consistent with their earlier reconstruction and development policies. With the greater postwar emphasis on the role of the state in maintaining full employment and providing basic social welfare needs, these governments intervened to prevent increased imports and export market losses from causing what they considered to be undue injury to domestic industries. Assistance to industries such as steel and shipbuilding injured by foreign competition in third markets took the form of subsidies. These included loans at below-market rates, accelerated depreciation allowances and other special tax benefits, purchases of equity capital, wage subsidies, and the payment of worker social benefits. Not only had such activities been an integral part of the reconstruction and development efforts of the 1940s and 1950s, but the provisions of the GATT dealing with subsidies other than direct export subsidies also did not rule out such measures.

Because of the difficulties of modifying the tariff-reducing commitments made in the various earlier multilateral trade negotiations, import-protecting measures generally did not take the form of higher tariffs. By requiring compensating duty cuts in other products or the acceptance of retaliatory increases in foreign tariffs, increases in tariffs could have led to bitter disputes and the unraveling of the results of the previous negotiations. Therefore, to avoid such a possibility, governments negotiated discriminatory quantitative agreements outside of the GATT framework with suppliers who were the main source of the market disruption. For example, quantitative import restrictions were introduced by France, Italy, the United Kingdom, and West Germany on Japanese automobiles as well as on radios, television sets, and communications equipment from Japan, South Korea, and Taiwan (Balassa and Balassa, 1984). Flatware, motorcycles, and videotape recorders from Japan and the NICs of Asia were also covered by such import restrictions of various European countries. In the agricultural area, which had been excluded from most of the rules of the GATT, governments did not hesitate to tighten quantitative import restrictions (or restrictions like those under the European Community's Common Agricultural Policy that have the same effect) or provide export subsidies to handle surpluses produced by high domestic price-support programs.

In the United States the disrupting effects of the postwar industry shifts in competitiveness throughout the world produced basic policy disputes that continue today. Except for the politically powerful oil and textile industries, up until the latter part of the 1960s import-injured industries were forced to follow the administrative track provided for import relief under the escape-clause provision of the GATT. Moreover, many of the industry determinations by the International Trade Commission were rejected at the presidential level on foreign policy grounds—namely, the need for the hegemonic power to maintain an open trade policy. Industry subsidies provided by foreign governments, though subject to U.S. countervailing duty laws, were also largely ignored by the executive branch for the same reason.

The official position of the United States began to change under the strong import pressures of the late 1960s. As their constituents described the competitive problems they were facing, fewer members of Congress accepted the standard argument that a liberal U.S. trade policy was essential to strengthen the free world against com-

munism. The intensity of congressional views on trade issues is
indicated by the rejection by that body of President Lyndon Johnson's 1968 request for new trade authority and by the near-approval
in 1970 of protectionist legislation. The growing unwillingness of
U.S. allies to accept the unquestioned leadership of the United
States in international political, military, and economic affairs also
caused officials in the executive branch to question the traditional
American position on trade policies.

The view that gradually gained the support of the major public
and private interests concerned with trade matters was that much of
the increased competitive pressure on the United States was due to
unfair foreign policies such as government subsidization, dumping
by private and public firms, preferential government purchasing procedures, and discriminatory foreign administrative rules and practices relating to importation. This argument had appeal for several
reasons. No new legislation was required to provide import relief; a
stricter enforcement of long-existing domestic legislation seemed to
be all that was necessary. After a material injury clause was introduced into the U.S. countervailing duty law in 1979, these laws also
were consistent with the provisions of the GATT dealing with unfair
trade practices. Consequently, a stricter enforcement of U.S. unfair
trade laws was unlikely to lead to bitter trade disputes with other
countries. By placing the blame for their decline in competitiveness
on unfair foreign actions, U.S. managers and workers could avoid
the implication that this decline might be due to a lack of efficiency
on their part. Finally, government officials could maintain that the
United States was still supporting the rules of the liberal international regime that the country had done so much to fashion.

The emphasis on the greater need for fair trade is evident in the
1974 legislation authorizing U.S. participation in the Tokyo Round
of multilateral negotiations. In reshaping the proposal of the president, the Congress stressed that the president should seek "to harmonize, reduce, or eliminate" nontariff trade barriers and tighten
GATT rules with respect to fair trading practices. Officials in the
executive branch supported these directives not only on their merits
but because they deflected attention from more patently protectionist policies as well.

The new codes that were approved in the Tokyo Round by no
means fully satisfied those who stressed the need for fairer trade, but
their provisions and the attention that the subject received established the framework for many U.S. trade policy actions that have
followed the conclusion of these negotiations. There has been a
marked increase recently in the number of antidumping and countervailing duty cases, determinations in such cases rising between
1981 and 1983 from 21 to 50 in the United States and from 31 to 58

in the European Community (Moore, 1985). Another indication of the greater use of these statutes to gain import protection is the increased number of ITC injury findings in antidumping cases, from 8 in the 1961–1964 period to 32 between 1980 and 1983. The most important protectionist action taken by the United States since the late 1960s—the gradual tightening of controls over steel imports—has also been justified mainly on the grounds of unfair trade practices by foreign producers. For example, the trigger price mechanism (TPM) introduced by President Carter in 1978 that in effect established minimum import prices for steel was designed to offset foreign dumping. When a series of voluntary export-restraint agreements with leading steel-exporting nations was concluded in late 1984, a spokesperson for the U.S. Trade Representative stated: "We are responding to unfair trade in the U.S.; defending yourself against unfair trade is not, in our opinion, protectionism" (*New York Times*, December 19, 1984).

The unfair trade argument has been used in support of most other trade-restricting or trade-promoting actions taken by the United States in recent years. The textile and apparel sectors have been described by government officials as "beleaguered" by disruptive import surges, thus justifying more restrictive import controls. Similarly, when temporary orderly marketing agreements (OMAs) were negotiated in the 1970s with selected East and Southeast Asian countries, the implication conveyed was that these were responses to unfair export activities of these nations. Even the Japanese voluntary export restraints on automobiles were sometimes justified by American industry and government officials on the grounds that industry's competitive problem was in part due to the unfair targeting practices of the Japanese government. On the export-promoting side, it is routinely claimed that subsidized export credits through the Export-Import Bank and special tax privileges to exporters establishing Foreign Sales Corporations are necessary to counter unfair foreign practices in these areas. In short, fair trade arguments using such phrases as the need for "a level playing field" or "to make foreign markets as open as U.S. markets" have become the basic justification for the greater use of trade-distorting measures by the United States.

The Future of the International Trading Regime

The United States fared well economically in its hegemonic role: American exporters and investors established substantial foreign market positions from which they are still benefiting greatly. The open trade policy that U.S. officials were able to maintain for so long also promoted growth and resource-use efficiency and thus extended the period of U.S. economic dominance. But the postwar recovery of Europe and Japan and the emergence of the NICs brought an inevitable relative decline in U.S. economic and political power. The comparative economic position of Western Europe also receded from its postwar recovery level as Japan and the NICs grew more rapidly. The outcome has been an increase in industrial-country protection that takes the form of nontariff trade-distorting measures.

No country or country group is likely to assume a dominant role in the world economy during the rest of the century. Japan seems to be the most likely candidate for this leadership role with its highly competitive industrial sector, but it appears to be too small economically to be a hegemonic power. Moreover, like the United States in the 1920s, Japan is still quite isolationist. Government officials and businesspeople are conditioned by the disastrous outcome of the country's expansionist efforts in the 1930s and 1940s and by its past history of inwardness. Furthermore, when a potential hegemonic nation first demonstrates its competitive strengths over a wide range of products, certain traditional sectors (such as agriculture) that are faced with difficult adjustment problems tend to be able to prevent the national commitment to trade openness required by a dominant economic power. This occurred in the early stages of both the British and the American rise to economic dominance and is now keeping Japan from making a commitment to openness commensurate with its competitive abilities. In addition, Japanese consumers have not yet developed the taste for product variety needed to make Japan an important market for foreign manufactured goods. The European Community possesses the size and resources to be the dominant economic power, but the very diverse economic nature of its members and the severe structural adjustment problems faced by almost all of them preclude a hegemonic role for this economic bloc.

The United States remains the country most able to identify its trading interests with the collective interests of all. However, a number of the industries that were the most competitive internationally during the rise of U.S. hegemony have become victims of their success. The relatively high profits these oligopolistically organized industries were able to maintain provided the investment funds needed to take advantage of the expanding market opportunities at home and abroad. But their economic structures were also favorable to the development of powerful labor unions that wished to share these profits through higher wages. The outcome was wage increases in these industries that far exceeded wage increases in manufacturing in general. Consequently, as other countries developed their productive capabilities, these American industries found themselves penalized by above-average labor costs and an institutional framework that made it very difficult to adjust to the new realities of international competition. Management in some of these industries also failed to keep up with the most advanced practices. Another very important feature of these industries is their ability to obtain protection by exerting political pressure at the congressional and presidential levels, if they fail to gain it through administrative routes involving the import-injury, antidumping, and countervailing duty laws.

As a consequence of these developments, protectionism has gradually spread in the United States as such industries as steel and automobiles have come under severe international competitive pressures. European governments are faced with even stronger protectionist pressures for similar reasons and have also moved toward more restrictive import policies. As Mancur Olson (1983) has argued, organized common interest groups such as these industries tend to delay innovations and the reallocation of resources needed for rapid growth.

There seems to be no reason why the recent trend in nontariff protectionism at the industry-specific level will not continue in the United States and Europe and become more important in Japan. But one should not conclude from this that the present international trading regime will turn into one where protectionism is rampant. There are—and will continue to be—dynamic, export-oriented industries in the older industrial countries that will seek access to foreign markets and see the relation between this goal and open markets in their own country. Moreover, such industries will have considerable political influence, as U.S. high-technology and export-oriented service industries have demonstrated. These sectors will continue to provide the United States, Western Europe, and Japan with the economic power that makes international openness a desirable trade policy objective. Consequently, none of these trading blocs is likely to adopt a policy of general protection.

But will not creeping protection at the industry level eventually bring a de facto state of general protection? This is, of course, a real possibility. However, this conclusion need not follow because protection usually does not stop the decrease in employment in declining industries. Even politically powerful industries usually have only enough political clout to slow down the absolute fall in employment. Furthermore, while employment tends to increase due to the fall in imports from the countries against which the controls are directed, offsetting forces are also set in motion. These include a decrease in expenditures on the product as its domestic price tends to rise; a shift in expenditures to noncontrolled varieties of the product, to either less or more processed forms of the good, and to substitute products; a redirection of exports by foreign suppliers to more expensive forms of the item; and, if the import controls are country-specific, an increase in exports by noncontrolled suppliers. The larger industry profits associated with the increased protection are also likely to be used to introduce labor-saving equipment at a more rapid pace than previously.

The continued decline in employment after increased protection is well-documented from histories of protection in particular industries (e.g., United States International Trade Commission, 1982). In the European Community and the United States even such politically powerful industries as textiles and apparel and steel have been unable to prevent employment from falling despite increased import protection.

There are many factors that determine an industry's effectiveness in protection-seeking. Its size in employment terms is one important factor. With declining employment an industry is likely to face diminution of its political power because of a fall in its voting strength and an attendant decrease in its ability to raise funds for lobbying purposes. The decline in the political power of the U.S. agricultural sector as the farm population has declined is an example that supports this hypothesis. It seems likely, therefore, that highly protected industries such as textiles and apparel will gradually lose their ability to maintain a high degree of import protection. Consequently, in older industrial nations the spread of protection to sectors in which newly industrializing countries gradually acquire international competitiveness may be offset by a decrease in protection in currently protected sectors. Counterprotectionist pressures also build up as industry-specific protection spreads. The stagnating effect of this policy becomes more obvious, as do the budgetary and economic efficiency costs. A state of affairs may thus be reached in which protectionism will not increase on balance in the current group of industrial countries or only at a very slow rate. Meanwhile, export-oriented high technology and service sectors will encourage continued international cooperation to maintain an open trading regime.

Even if this sanguine scenario takes place, the international trading regime is likely to operate quite differently than it did in the years of U.S. dominance. Industrial countries will seek short-run economic reciprocity in their dealings with each other. In particular, the United States will no longer be willing to trade access to the American market for acquiescence to U.S. international political goals and the prospect of long-term penetration of foreign economic markets. The developing countries and nations with special political relationships with particular major trading powers will probably continue to be waived from the full-reciprocity requirement but their trade benefits from this waiver will be closely controlled. Greater emphasis will be placed on bilateral negotiations in reducing nontariff trade distortions, though these negotiations may still take place at general meetings of GATT members. The articles and codes of the GATT will provide the broad framework for such negotiations, but the variety and discriminatory nature of nontariff measures make true multilateral negotiations too cumbersome. Bilateral negotiations will also be used to a greater extent in handling trade disputes. The GATT dispute-resolution mechanism will be utilized by smaller countries in their dealings with the larger trading nations and by the larger nations to call attention to actions by one of their members that are outside of generally accepted standards of good behavior. These means of settling disputes do not differ essentially from the practices followed throughout the history of the GATT.

Greater discrimination in the application of trade restrictions and in the granting of trade benefits is another feature of the emerging international trading regime. The safeguard provisions of the GATT, for example, will probably be modified to permit the selective imposition of quantitative import controls on a temporary basis. It will be justified, at least implicitly, on the grounds that injury-causing import surges from particular suppliers represent a form of unfair competition and thus can be countered with discriminatory restrictions under GATT rules. Greater state assistance for the development and maintenance of high technology and basic industries will be another characteristic of the international trading order likely to evolve during the rest of the century. The governments of industrial countries as well as developing nations will continue to insist on the use of subsidies to develop a certain minimum set of high-technology industries and to maintain a number of basic industries domestically on the grounds that these are needed for a country to become or remain a significant economic power.

The international trading regime described above is not one to gain favor with economists. It will not yield the degree of static economic efficiency or economic growth that economists believe is achievable in an open, nondiscriminatory trading order. But this is an essay on the most likely nature of the future international trading order and not on the regime economists would most like to see evolve. Free trade is not a politically stable policy in an economic world of continuing significant structural shifts involving severe adjustment problems for some politically important sectors and the demands of infant industries for special treatment. But neither is general import protection a politically stable state of affairs in modern industrial democracies with dynamic export sectors. Politically stable conditions in this type of world economy involve openness in some industries and protection in others with the set of industries in each category changing over time. The particular mix of openness and import protection can vary significantly, depending on such factors as the country distribution of national economic power and the pace of structural change. The present situation in which there are three major industrial trading powers plus a rapid rate of new technology development and international transfer of old technology suggests that the currently evolving trading regime will be characterized by a greater degree of government control and private cartelization than has existed throughout most of the postwar period.

Summary and Conclusion

The new protectionism threatening the international trading regime is related to significant structural changes in world production that have brought about a decline in the dominant economic position of the United States, a concomitant rise of the European Community and Japan to international economic prominence, and the emergence of a highly competitive group of newly industrializing countries.

The trading regime expected to develop after World War II involved a shared responsibility on the part of the major economic powers for maintaining open and stable trading conditions. However, the unexpected magnitude of the immediate postwar economic and political problems thrust the United States into a hegemonic role. U.S. economic dominance manifested itself in the trade, finance, and energy fields and enabled American producers to establish strong export and investment positions abroad. Yet, by facilitating the reconstruction and development of Western Europe and Japan as well as the industrialization of certain developing countries, U.S. hegemonic activities led eventually to a marked decline in the American share of world exports and a significant rise of import competition in both labor-intensive sectors and certain oligopolistically organized industries. These developments also significantly diminished the leadership authority of the United States.

Most industrial countries responded to the inevitable market disruptions associated with these shifts in comparative advantage by providing extensive government assistance to injured industries in the form of subsidies and higher import barriers. Such behavior was consistent with the extensive role the governments of these countries played in promoting reconstruction and development. For the hegemonic power, the United States, the policy adjustment has been more difficult. However, government and business leaders have gradually adopted the view that unfair foreign trading practices are the main cause of the country's competitive problems. By focusing on more vigorous enforcement of U.S. statutes and GATT rules on fair trade they are able to press for import protection and still maintain their support for the type of open trading regime the United States did so much to establish after World War II. Attention has also been diverted from the role that high labor costs and inefficient managerial practices in certain industries play in explaining these problems.

No other trading bloc seems able or prepared to become a hegemonic power. However, free trade is not a politically stable policy in a dynamic economic world in the absence of such leadership. Without the foreign policy concerns of the dominant power, domestic sectors injured by import competition and the loss of export markets are able to secure protection or other forms of government assistance through the political processes of industrial democracies. Nevertheless, these industries are unlikely to be able to prevent market forces from halting the decline in employment in the industries and thus an erosion of their political influence. General protectionism is also not a politically stable policy in a rapidly changing economic environment. Politically important export industries that are able to compete successfully abroad will press for the opening of foreign markets and realize the need to open domestic markets to achieve this result.

While it is possible that particular protectionism will continue to spread and bring about an essentially closed international trading order, a more sanguine outcome, involving the support of the three major trading powers (the United States, the European Community, and Japan) seems possible. This is the emergence of a regime characterized by more trade-distorting government interventions than at the height of American hegemonic influence and by the existence of a significant group of government-assisted industries. However, while new industries will be added to this group, assistance will be withdrawn from others as they lose political influence so that, on balance, the list does not increase over time or does so only very slowly. Such a regime will not yield the growth and efficiency benefits of an open trading system, but at least it will not lead to the disastrous economic and political consequences brought about by the type of trading order prevailing in the 1930s.

References

Baldwin, R. E. (1958) The Commodity Composition of Trade: Selected Industrial Countries, 1900–1954, *The Review of Economics and Statistics* 40: 50–68.

Balassa, B. and Balassa, C. (1984) Industrial Protection in the Developed Countries, *The World Economy* 7: 179–196.

———— (1962) Implications of Structural Changes in Commodity Trade. In *Factors Affecting the United States Balance of Payments*, Part 1. Washington, D.C.: Joint Economic Committee, 87th Congress, 2nd Session.

Branson, W. (1980) Trends in U.S. International Trade and Investment Since World War II. In *The American Economy in Transition* (M. Feldstein, ed.). Chicago: University of Chicago Press.

Economic Report of the President (1985) Washington, D.C.: U.S. Government Printing Office.

Keohane, R. O. (1984) *After Hegemony: Cooperation and Discord in the World Political Economy*. Princeton, N.J.: Princeton University Press.

Moore, M. (1985) Import Relief from Fair and Unfair Trade in the United States and the European Community. Madison, Wis.: Department of Economics, University of Wisconsin.

Olson, M. (1983) The Political Economy of Comparative Growth Rates. In *The Political Economy of Comparative Growth Rates* (D. C. Mueller, ed.). New Haven: Yale University Press.

United States Department of Commerce (1985) *United States Trade: Performance in 1984 and Outlook*. Washington, D.C.: U.S. Department of Commerce, International Trade Administration.

United States International Trade Commission (1982) *The Effectiveness of Escape Clause Relief in Promoting Adjustment to Import Competition*, USITC Publication 1229. Washington, D.C.: United States International Trade Commission.

6

The Need for New Multilateral Trade Negotiations: Why Is It Urgent to Complete the GATT Round Successfully?

ANTONIO MARIA COSTA

Introduction

Trade policies unite and divide nations no less than foreign policy. In the first half of the 1980s trade policies have swung mostly in the direction of either growing government intervention or growing threat of such intervention; as a consequence, commercial issues have been increasingly contentious on international agendas. In order to defuse the situation our countries need to complete successfully and urgently the new GATT Round of Multilateral Tariff Negotiations (MTNs) launched in 1986. The alternative to an improved trade environment could be a trade war among the world's major trading areas. The erosion of the trade system—which the new round will hopefully halt—has many causes and no country is innocent. The recession, certain policies to sustain the recovery, the heavy indebtedness of major countries, and structural deficiencies in the working of many of our economies have all translated into growing threats to the open multilateral trade regime which our countries established in the postwar period.

The new GATT Round is needed on at least two accounts. First, it is needed to reverse the prevailing mood favoring protectionism. Unless the liberalization process among our countries proceeds further, the system is bound to backslide into some form of mercantilism. Second, the round is required because liberalization and multi-

Special Counselor in Economics to the Secretary General (OECD), Paris.

TABLE 1.
Implied Elasticity of Trade with Respect to Income, 1960–1985
(average values for the 24 OECD countries)

	1960–1968	1969–1973	1974–1979	1980–1981	1983	1985
Growth of						
Real Income	5.1	4.8	2.7	0.9	2.6	2.7
Real Export	8.1	10.0	5.1	1.6	2.4	4.3
Implied Elasticity	1.6	2.1	1.9	1.8	0.9	1.6

lateralization of trade flows will once again contribute to economic growth, as has happened since World War II. Indeed, for the OECD region the three decades since the 1950s have been characterized by a high (implicit) elasticity of trade with respect to income. Only during the recession years that followed the two oil shocks and in the 1982–1983 biennium did elasticity fall to unity or below. Otherwise, it generally hovered at around twice that level, as shown in Table 1.

Several forces have fostered the liberalization process since the end of World War II. In Europe, the formation of free trade areas (EFTA and especially the EEC) created trade among member countries. Both areas also diverted some trade from the outside, still with an overall likely net positive effect (Balassa, 1973). At the same time, successive rounds of trade negotiations (first held at Annecy, France; at Torquay, England; and in Geneva, Switzerland) brought about further trade liberalization and multilateralization through the wider applications of the most-favored-nation (MFN) clause. Both the Dillon (1960–1961) and the Kennedy (1964–1967) Rounds cut tariffs on manufactured goods by approximately one quarter. The Tokyo round (1973–1979) cut tariffs on the average by another 25 to 30 percent. It also established important new codes for the regulation and/or elimination of nontariff barriers. Hundreds of additional bilateral agreements have also been put into operation on the occasion of these rounds, and outside them, leading to the situation of the early 1980s when world trade, especially for manufactured goods, encountered fewer obstacles than at any time in the past. According to GATT (1984) and OECD (1985d) sources, today the average MFN tariffs on industrial imports for the two dozen major industrial countries is about 5 percent. Whalley (1982), Stern and Deardorff (1981), Krueger (1978), Cline et al. (1978), and Balassa and Kreinin (1967) among others have attempted to quantify the impact of the postwar trade liberalization process.

Suddenly, after the turn of the 1980s, the chemistry of the situation seems to have changed. What has happened since then explains why we need the sixth GATT Round launched in 1986. The forces now at play to increase the pressure toward government intervention in trade include both *macroeconomic* issues and *structural* issues concerning the working of our economic systems. This, of course, leaves aside the fact that the current mood favoring protectionism and trade interventionism is something more than a symptom of, and a partial response to, structural deficiencies and cyclical economic imbalances.

To an extent the new roots of protectionism can be found in an ill-defined realm where psychological, social, economic, political and even strategic considerations coexist in loose partnership. These include widespread concerns, especially in Europe, about high unemployment and poor economic prospects; an often-unacknowledged desire to shield established socioeconomic patterns, jobs, and life-styles; the fear of losing, once and forever, activities and skills that took generations and resources to build; generic definitions of national security, especially in the food- and defense-related areas; xenophobic response to uncontrollable events taking place abroad; and, in the ultimate instance, a reaction to broadly perceived changing balances of power worldwide.

Metaeconomic arguments aside, the present wave of measures to interfere with trade flows reflects more tangible goals. For example, some OECD economies are at present hard-pressed to buy time during the process of transition to higher industrial competitiveness (Abernathy, 1983; Stirling and Tochelson, 1985). In this perspective, the requirement, strongly felt by politicians, to minimize social costs and political tensions during periods of structural adjustment acquires significance. The borderline between more- or less-objectionable protection is often quite fuzzy. Yet we all are aware that there is a clear vicious circle: protectionism paralyzes structural adjustment and weakens competitiveness, becoming once again a source of protectionism (OECD, 1985d). In most cases, whether a given trade measure is indeed the least-cost means to foster and assist the restructuring of production, or whether it is a form of accommodation of the forces least interested in—and agreeable to—such transformation, is a difficult question. It largely depends on specific circumstances. Certainly there is ample evidence that the protectionism we know of late—especially the type implemented by means of illiberal, non-tariff measures such as quantitative import restrictions (QIRs), voluntary export restraints (VERs), and orderly marketing agreements (OMAs)—is often the result of pressure by narrowly focused but highly effective interest groups. From their vantage point, the microeconomic benefits stemming from shielded market positions (where economic rent is high) outweigh the long-term, economywide cost from poor resource allocation. In protected economies, as we all know, costs are widely shared but benefits are not.

In this paper I shall not address any of the issues just mentioned. I shall follow a more general approach, seeking to identify unresolved structural problems, inadequate economic policy stances, and poor economic conditions that in my view are responsible for the current mood favoring trade management and intervention—and that will make the new GATT Round all the more necessary.

The bulk of the study concerns the two dozen member countries of the Organisation for Economic Co-operation and Development (OECD). Together these countries account at present for about four-fifths of world trade. Their trade regimes, economic policies, and industrial structures are sufficiently similar to justify an overall approach to the subject. Also, while these countries have created the most liberal trade area in the entire world (or perhaps because of that), the recent deterioration in trade attitudes has mostly been on their part. For reasons related to well-known differences in the nature and strength of the recovery and in the economic structures, the pressure for trade intervention in the United States differs significantly from that in Europe: the roots of protectionism are simply quite different on the two sides of the Atlantic. The case of Japan is relevant for the interrelation between Japan's growing international competitiveness and its macroeconomic policies. Matters of more direct concern to the LDCs deal with the ongoing adjustment process in their economies as a consequence of and response to the debt problem. I shall concentrate on four major policy issues that make the current GATT negotiations quite crucial.

The urgent preoccupation in the United States for a new round is studied in the next section. Here the emphasis is on the exchange rate of the U.S. dollar; on the uneven economic recovery in the early 1980s (weak in 1983, very strong in 1984, followed again by a weak 1985); the blend of policy instruments used to promote it; the unwinding of macroeconomic imbalances in the domestic and external accounts; the resulting movement of capital resources; and its implications for world trade.

The case of Europe is then addressed. After two decades of growth without inflation (the 1950s and the 1960s) and a decade of stagnation with inflation (the 1970s), in the first years of the 1980s Europe's economy entered a period of noninflationary stagnation. Prospects have much improved since. Europe needs the new GATT Round to consolidate this improvement. In this discussion, emphasis is placed on the dilemmas arising from the trade requirements of some of the world's most open economies, especially those in the EEC, as well as on the constraints posed by high unemployment, slowly improving economic growth, and on the ongoing process of industrial adjustment.

Japan is dealt with in "Japan's International Competitiveness: Virtue or Vice?" This paper considers critically the reasons given by the rest of the world to justify efforts to curb Japan's ability to compete on markets for manufactures. The emphasis is on trade, exchange rate, and macroeconomic conditions, including the commercial policies of partner countries, affecting Japan's degree of comparative advantage and ability to gain world market shares consistent with this advantage. The real question is rather simple: Is the high degree of Japan's competitiveness the result of effective industrial and macroeconomic policies, facilitated by a consensus-oriented society? Or is it the artificial consequence of a mixture of discrimination against imports and careful handling of economic aggregates to manipulate the yen exchange rate and, therefore, of discrimination in favor of exports? Paraphrasing Salieri's opening statement in *Amadeus*: Is Japan doing what the rest of the world suspects?

The final focus is on the developing countries in terms of external debt and adjustment. Here the urgency of a successful new GATT Round is justified on the basis of the disquieting situation of some of the most heavily indebted LDCs, which are progressing in major adjustment programs during a period of poor trade trends (low external demand and deteriorating terms of exchange of primary commodities), adverse monetary conditions (high interest rates and low creditworthiness), and until recently uneven growth performance in the industrial world.

The conclusions submit the view that the successful conclusion of the new GATT negotiations is needed by the entire world, to bring forward greater multilateralism and nondiscrimination and to improve the general rules of behavior providing for stability, transparency, and predictability to the benefit of the entire world. It is therefore the responsibility of all countries to work individually and jointly to make sure that the new GATT Round will proceed fast and effectively.

Trade Implications of Macroeconomic Imbalances in the U.S. Recovery

Two policy situations in the United States have been linked, in one way or another, to trade intervention and protectionism: (1) the macroeconomic policies pursued in the recovery and (2) the external and internal financial imbalances which have accompanied these policies.

THE U.S. POLICY MIX (AND POLICY AIM) IN THE
ECONOMIC RECOVERY

Historically there is little proof that governments (and people) have learned a great deal from each other or, for that matter, from their own experience. Yet, before us is at least one solid piece of evidence that history has taught OECD countries something: in a sensible application of what they learned in 1973–1974 after OPEC-I, OECD governments responded to OPEC-II with generally nonaccommodating monetary policies. Aware of the lasting damage that was being inflicted on their economies by high rates of price increases, and concerned about the further inflationary consequences of higher energy costs, the principal focus for most OECD countries was the goal of restraining inflationary pressures (OECD, 1984; EEC, 1984).

Results were much as governments intended and those their economies badly needed: the price pressure was reversed. Policy also ushered in a period of high nominal interest rates; in turn, the decline of inflation increased real rates (see Figures 1 and 2). However, because of a certain degree of monetary accommodation on the part of the U.S. Federal Reserve beginning in late 1982 (when the seriousness of the LDC debt was first manifested and the recession was at its trough), U.S. interest rates fell by several percentage points in the first half of 1983. In the meantime, inflation continued to decline and output growth resumed. From summer 1983 to the beginning of 1984 interest rates remained stable, although in real terms at levels quite high by postwar standards. In mid-1984 interest rates in the United States increased again but eased somewhat in the second half of the year and in the first half of 1985. Since then, they have declined again, especially so in early 1986. What is behind the current prolonged turbulence in financial markets and what are the implications for the recovery of the OECD economy, for world trade and the LDCs' debt?

The strong reflationary effect of the U.S. budget deficit in the first half of the 1980s undoubtedly played a significant role in promoting the U.S. recovery, already under way for a number of other reasons: the monetary move just mentioned; the wealth effect induced by the rapid decline of inflation; the cyclical reduction of the saving propensity during the downturn; the productivity gains brought about by labor shedding; and the cooperation of labor unions in keeping real-wage costs stable or even lowering them. Since early 1986 the reflationary effect of U.S. fiscal policy has been reversed by Congressional legislators concerned with budget balancing (the Gramm-Rudman-Hollings fiscal stabilization act of 1985) (see Figure 2).

Historically, the swings of the saving ratio (to GNP) in the

United States as much as in other industrial countries have been particularly significant in their dimension as well as their countercyclical impact. Responding to the contraction of real wealth due to higher inflation and increased uncertainty, the composite savings ratio of OECD countries showed a rising trend from the late 1960s to the mid-1970s. This was followed thereafter by a decline and an upward movement again in 1980–1981 (see Table 2). Since 1982 the savings rate has again tended to decline, with several forces at play. In the United States in particular, the more stable and predictable economic environment has reinforced favorable expectations and business confidence. The recovery of output (see Figure 3) and the improved employment outlook induced households to increase their consumption in anticipation of even higher income streams (IMF, 1985).

THE U.S. EXTERNAL AND INTERNAL FINANCIAL IMBALANCES

The prolonged large fiscal deficits in the United States carry both domestic and international implications. Because of financing requirements of the private sector, especially during this period of recovery and reabsorption of idle capacity, internal and external imbalances are likely to remain significant. Thus real interest rates may continue to remain high, relative to the growth rate of the economy. The high cost of capital would also seriously undermine the efforts of heavily indebted LDCs to service their debt.

Moreover, the United States would require a continuous, even growing, flow of capital from abroad. This would continue to have an impact on availability and cost of capital resources abroad, where investment is needed to support economic activity. It is actually due to major inflows of foreign capital that the United States so far has been able to avoid the vicious circle into which many European economies were drawn during the period of growing government expenditure and fiscal imbalances. In order to finance the deficits, European countries were forced to cut productive investment while restricting the expansion of monetary aggregates to restrain inflation. Employment fell, and so did income and tax revenues; thus the deficits increased, setting into motion a perverse train of events. On the other hand, financial adjustment was delayed (in Italy, France, and in most southern European countries) wherever the inflation differential remained stubbornly high. Now all this is being undone as more and more countries in Europe are progressing toward fiscal austerity and the containment of government dissaving (see below).

During the entire first half of the 1980s, the prolonged and sustained flow of capital resources to the United States has spurred trade interventions to the extent that the resulting high U.S. dollar

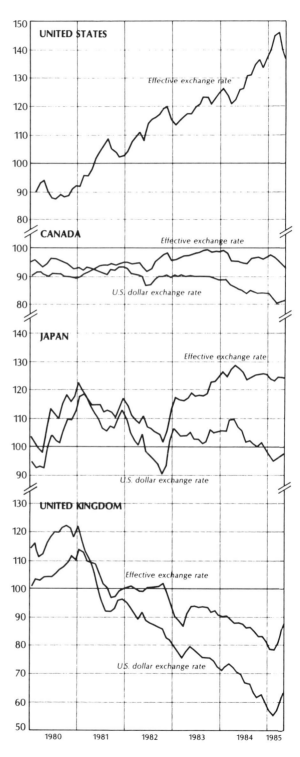

FIGURE 1. Indices of monthly average U.S. dollar and effective exchange rates. (*Source: I.M.F. World Economic Outlook, September 1985.*)

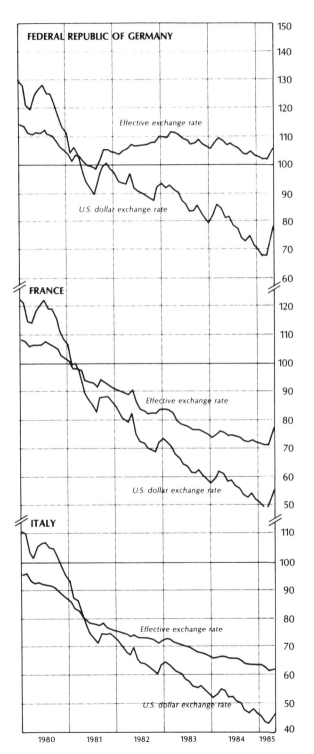

FIGURE 1. Continued.

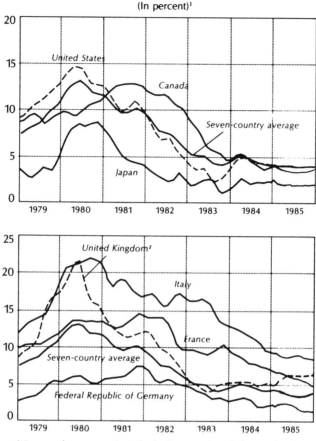

(In percent)[1]

[1] Average of consumer price index for three months ended in month indicated over corresponding three months a year earlier.
[2] The figures for the second half of 1979 and the first half of 1980 were affected by the approximately 3¼ percent increase in value-added tax rates, with effect from June 18, 1979.

FIGURE 2. Major industrial countries: Consumer price inflation, 1979–March 1985. (*Source: I.M.F.*)

rate has continued to erode the competitiveness of the U.S. economy. Higher interest rates have hurt business prospects at home via the cost of capital, and on foreign markets via the exchange rate. As a consequence, it is no surprise that the high U.S. dollar rates have been accompanied in the United States by strong pressure in favor of protectionism. In particular, we have witnessed a growing shift from a regime of *fixed* protection through tariffs and duties to a flexible form of *containment* protection implemented by means of administrative procedures. In this regard, one senses a sharp contrast between a nonaccommodating monetary policy intended to restrain inflation and income growth and a certain benign neglect of protec-

TABLE 2.
General Government Indebtedness and Public Sector Claims
on Private Savings

	Gross Debt Outstanding (as percentage of nominal GDP)			Debt Interest Payments		
	1970	1980	1986*	1970	1980	1986*
United States	46.2	40.1	50.4	1.2	1.3	3.4
Japan	12.0	52.9	68.6	0.6	3.2	3.1
Germany	18.4	32.5	41.1	1.0	1.9	2.4
France	29.4	29.1	38.7	1.1	1.6	3.1
United Kingdom	86.2	55.5	55.3	3.9	5.6	4.6
Italy	44.4	65.3	109.4	1.7	6.2	10.9
Canada	53.7	45.9	73.0	3.8	5.6	7.3
Average (OECD Seven)	39.6	42.9	56.0	1.4	2.5	3.7

	Budget Deficit (as percentage of net private savings)		
	1975	1980	1986*
United States	62.4	22.0	74.9
Japan	17.1	28.2	5.4
Germany	55.9	35.4	10.6
France	20.2	− 2.6	46.3
United Kingdom	76.1	42.8	28.8
Italy	69.4	47.5	97.1
Canada	24.1	20.8	41.4
Average (OECD Seven)	45.6	25.2	40.2

* Estimate.

tionism, which keeps import prices and the price of import-competing industries high and indirectly stimulates wage demand.

The successful completion of the new GATT Round is needed by the United States on several accounts. The drain of saving from the world pool to finance public-consumption expenditure in the United States; the growth of claims on future generations caused by rising U.S. domestic indebtedness; and the flow of capital from the rest of the world toward a U.S. economy already relatively better endowed with it—these three major tendencies which have been manifested in the U.S. recovery between 1981 and early 1985 have implied a pattern of resource allocation over time and space and among users that could not—and should not—be sustained for long. Already in the second half of 1985, under the impulse of an international agreement struck in New York among the five major OECD countries (part of the G5 group), normal equilibrating mechanisms were set in motion. Active intervention on foreign-exchange markets by the central banks of the G5 have brought about a substantial

(Percentage changes)[1]

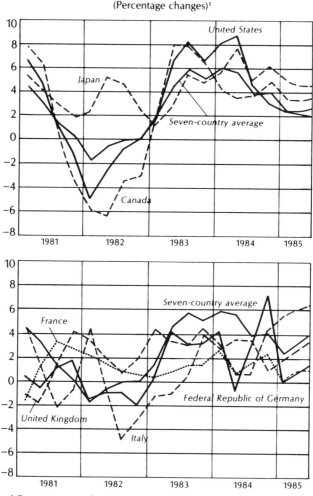

[1] Current quarter relative to two quarters previously; seasonally adjusted annual rates.

FIGURE 3. Major industrial countries: Real GNP, 1981–1985. (*Source: I.M.F.*)

depreciation of the U.S. dollar with respect to the Japanese yen and, to a lesser extent, the ECU's currencies. But before the correction of the dollar value will be felt on trade and economic activity, a lot of additional harm will be done to export-competing industries in the United States.

The flow of capital to the United States to the extent we have known in the past few years, with its extraordinary impact on the dollar exchange rate, has not occurred because the United States *alone* pursued policies conducive to such a flow. The U.S. dollar appreciation between 1980 and 1985 was due to causes far more far-reaching than simply interest-rate differentials. Foreigners should recognize that the U.S. recovery in both 1983 and 1984, through income impulses and strong demand in world markets, has played a major role in the restoration of growth conditions within the OECD area and elsewhere. It has also inspired confidence among investors at home and abroad. Foreigners should also acknowledge that capital tends to flow naturally and in large volume where equity and financial returns are highest and where economic performance is superior—at least as long as it remains so. The rest of the world has a long way to go to catch up in this regard, if it intends to keep its own savings at home.

The resolution of the United States federal debt problem—intrinsically a domestic U.S. problem with a major impact, of course, on the U.S. economy itself—will have to be dealt not only with resolve but also with gradualism. It has to be staged so that any deflationary impact on the U.S. economy (and that of the rest of the world) will be compensated by improved growth conditions elsewhere, most notably in Europe, where the recovery is younger and weaker. It will also have to be accompanied by a process of *reliberalization of trade*—thanks to the new GATT impulse—so that sectors which sought, and were granted, shelter during this period of high dollar rates will continue the process of adjustment.

Can a New GATT Round Pull Europe Out of Noninflationary Stagnation?

The most frequently heard term about economic prospects in the Old World is *Europessimism*. In my view, Europe's economic outlook—though not without cause for concern especially with respect to the high level of unemployment—seems to warrant a more appropriate code word: *Eurorealism*. In fact, the continuing slack and occasional crises in some traditional manufacturing activities coexists in Europe with regained strength in many other productive sectors. Furthermore, it is not accurate to portray the situation in the smokestack activities of European countries exclusively in negative terms. In the course of the past few years there have been examples of constructive attitudes developing between the social partners throughout the Continent. There is also growing evidence of new industrial programs and of major efforts, some sponsored by the European Community, for rationalization and restructuring of capacity (in steel, for example). But there is something even more significant than that: the European economy is showing a healthy turnaround in a number of structural areas.

EUROPE'S RECOVERY IS SLOW
BUT RESTS ON SOLID FOUNDATIONS

In the first place, the rate of *inflation* has declined substantially almost everywhere. In some countries (Germany, the Netherlands, Denmark, and Switzerland, for example) the decline has been so marked as to have generated *price stability* for the time being. In other countries previously known for structural inflation in the two-digit range (the United Kingdom, Italy, and France), the decline in the rate of price rises has been remarkable, without any sign that at present this accomplishment is under threat. For example, in 1986 the *private consumption deflation* for the major four European economies may be about one fourth the average of the decade that followed OPEC-I:

	1972–1982	1984	1986
Germany	5.2	2.4	0.0
France	10.6	7.4	2.0
United Kingdom	13.7	5.0	4.5
Italy	17.1	10.8	5.0
Major 4 European countries	9.9	6.6	2.25

In the second place, *fiscal deficits* are progressively under control in a number of countries of middle and northern Europe, although not so in some Mediterranean ones. Non-Europeans should recognize this. In a period of high and growing unemployment it has been socially quite costly to contract government dissaving. Yet, the current general orientation of our societies toward greater market liberalization; reduced role of the public sector in economic activity; and awareness of the constraint that large public debts pose to the effectiveness of macroeconomic policy were all translated by European governments into a drive for lower budget deficits. For example, by 1986, the *general government financial imbalances*, though still negative, will look much better in several major and minor European countries than they did at the turn of the 1980s. *Fiscal deficits* (as a percentage of GDP) during the recession and in the early phase of the recovery have been as follows:

	1982	1984	1986
Germany	3.3	1.9	0.7
United Kingdom	2.3	3.8	3.4
France	2.6	2.5	3.0
Italy	12.7	13.4	13.1
Smaller European countries	5.0	4.5	4.0

The recovery generally increases government revenues, while the lower burden of built-in stabilizers reduces government expenditure. In fact, according to OECD secretariat estimates (OECD, 1986a), structural budget deficits in some major European countries have already been in surplus for quite some time. Elsewhere in Europe they are moving toward restraints.

Finally, in Europe during the past few years there has been a pause in the long-term trend toward greater labor share in value-added. It is too early to judge whether the trend has actually reversed. Yet, under the impact of lower employment, higher productivity, and relatively moderate wage demand, both profitability rates and *business return* have increased. It is hard to say whether higher profit margins will trigger and generalize the recovery of capital formation: a phenomenon noticeable already in countries like Germany and the United Kingdom. But it will certainly help. Among the various determinants of investment trends—sales expectations in domestic markets, export prospects, user cost of capital, and rate of return on assets—the latter is perhaps a more significant indicator of the *timing* of the cyclical variation of investment. Although the current reversal of the trend in relative factor prices in Europe may not be a good predictor of the overall level of investment, it has historical significance. There are also those who see in this an overall indication that the foundations of the current recovery in economic activity are solid and possibly noninflationary. For example, in 1985 the growth of *hourly earnings in manufacturing* for the major four European countries was, depending on the situation, half or less the rate of increase experienced in the preceding ten years:

	1973–1983	1984	1985
Germany	6.3	2.4	4.0
France	14.4	8.1	6.2
United Kingdom	15.1	8.8	9.1
Italy	21.1	9.6	8.0
OECD Europe	13.0	7.2	6.6

All this has significant consequences for the new GATT Round, since in no other region of the world do trade and macroeconomic conditions interact as forcefully as in Europe, especially the European Community. During the past twenty years, export and import volumes have grown at about 6.5–7 percent on average, almost twice as much as real domestic product. At present, however, European countries individually, and also some jointly in the context of the EC, face difficult challenges in three interrelated areas: slow economic growth and poor employment prospects, structural adaptation in traditional manufacturing, and evolution of production toward high-technology areas.

EUROPE'S POOR EMPLOYMENT PROSPECTS

The growth rate of real GNP in Europe in the 1985–1986 biennium is likely to be about 3 percent or, on average, more than three times higher than in the previous biennium (which was itself about twice as high as was experienced in the 1981–1982 biennium). Notwithstanding, in 1984 real income grew in Europe at about one-third the rate of growth in the United States. In 1985 Japan's growth of income outperformed Europe's by 2 to 1. In 1986, given the fact that the rate of increase in productivity is not likely to be much lower than the growth rate of real income—mostly, as we shall see, on account of large-scale labor shedding—labor demand in Europe is likely to increase, but only marginally. However, because large, though declining, cohorts will keep reaching working age and inflate the labor supply, employment prospects will deteriorate. According to OECD secretariat estimates, there are almost 20 million people out of work in Europe (OECD, 1985).

Some economists believe that the major European obstacle to greater trade liberalization (and to the GATT Round) is Europe's unemployment problem. Because of this, it is useful to look at Europe's unemployment more closely. In the first place, present macroeconomic policies and cyclical conditions are not conducive to greater labor demand. In order to bring structural fiscal deficits under control, government expenditure is being checked almost everywhere, a subject already dealt with above. Business fixed capital formation, which as usual declined during the recession, is at present recovering. However, adverse business prospects in many traditional sectors, unit labor costs in manufacturing much higher than in the United States or Japan, high interest rates, and the claim of resources by government dissaving (in Italy and other Mediterranean countries especially) are all direct or indirect constraints to labor demand (see Figure 4).

Second, current European unemployment is caused by the accelerated introduction of new capital-intensive technologies. It is hard to judge whether the rate of introduction of capital-deepening processes is today faster than relative-factor price movements would justify. Certainly, the trend toward growing substitution of labor by means of fixed assets has not slowed down in the face of large excess of labor and considerable wage moderation. This is perhaps the response of the business sector to a number of structural problems besieging labor markets: poor labor cost responsiveness to business prospects, scarce flexibility of manpower management in relation to

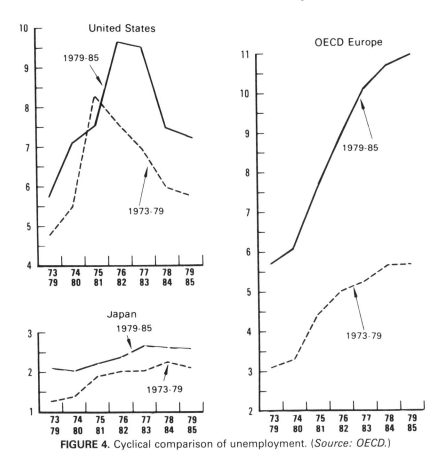

FIGURE 4. Cyclical comparison of unemployment. (*Source: OECD.*)

the economic cycle, inadequate geographical and skill mobility, and an insufficient incentive system based on pay differentials. Furthermore, profit-sharing, workers' equity participation, part-time employment, and other measures useful to promote job motion through adaptability, while preserving social consensus, have so far found limited application in Europe.

Third, there is ample evidence available of the continuing trend toward factor substitution in Europe. To relate this phenomenon to factor price trends is naturally more difficult. Figure 5 shows the number of people employed and the capital stock utilized per unit of output in the industrial sector of four major European countries (Todd, 1984). In the figure, movement toward the origin of the interpolated lines would indicate a gain in resource efficiency through lower use of both factors of production. Movement toward either axis would indicate a bias in factor usage in *favor* of that factor and *against* the other. In all four countries the tendency toward

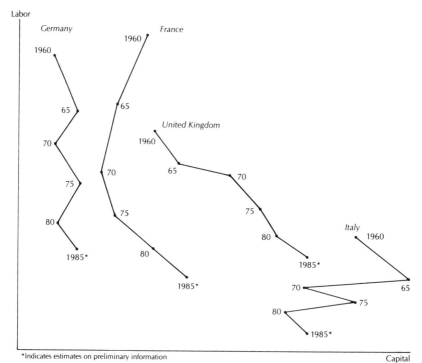

*Indicates estimates on preliminary information   Capital

FIGURE 5. Labor and capital requirements per unit of output for four European countries (1960–1985). (*Source: Todd (1984) updated.*)

substitution of labor by capital is well pronounced. What is perhaps most remarkable is that the updating of this figure to cover the recent past does not show that the generalized trend toward higher capital/labor ratios slowed under the impact of growing excess labor supply (see Table 3).

TABLE 3.
Employment, Unemployment, and Productivity in Major OECD Countries in 1985

	GNP Growth	Employment Growth	Productivity Growth	Unemployment Rate
Germany	2.5	0.5	1.7	8.25
France	1.4	−0.3	1.3	10.50
Italy	2.3	0.5	2.0	10.50
United Kingdom	3.7	1.2	2.5	11.50
OECD Europe	2.4	0.3	2.0	11.00
United States	2.3	2.0	0.5	7.00
Japan	5.0	1.0	4.0	2.50
OECD Total	2.7	1.0	1.7	8.50

Annual percentage variations in volume terms, when applicable.

EUROPE'S DRIVE FOR STRUCTURAL ADAPTATION

Perhaps the explanation of all this is to be found in the adjustment process taking place in a number of major manufacturing sectors. The origins of the process are remote, and I am obliged to make a short historical digression. We all know that Europe's economy, especially its labor markets, failed to adjust to OPEC-I. To a large extent, overlooking intercountry differences, governments pursued policies in the second half of the 1970s that insulated incomes and purchasing power from worsening terms of trade and wealth losses. The burden of adjustment was transferred from the real sector to the fiscal sector through a battery of subsidies and demand support policies. The rate of unemployment was artificially maintained in the 4.2–5.5 percent range between 1975 and 1980, on average a good third less than in the United States (where the range was 5.7–8.3 percent during the same period). OPEC-II made this type of policy unsustainable. Product markets responded quite elastically to low demand conditions: since 1982 the *price* adjustment in the economy at large has been quite strong, giving rise to a period of accelerated contraction of inflation. In labor markets the high degree of wage rigidity in the phase of cyclical downturn produced a situation where *quantity* (namely employment) had to adjust. The watershed was reached in winter 1983, when massive labor shedding took place and employment started to fall even more rapidly than output. During the past triennium European unemployment has increased over a percentage point (for an average of 2 million jobs) a year. The resulting productivity gains have contributed to the decline of inflation and the recovery of business margins. At the end of 1985 unemployment was still at about 11 percent in Europe, approximately 40 percent more than in the United States and more than four times more than in Japan. No surprise, then, to find that unemployment problems are a priority on policy agendas.

EUROPE'S QUEST FOR A TECHNOLOGY POLICY

The question of European technology also carries implications for trade. A number of sources have documented that Europe is lagging behind major partner countries in the development of new technologies. The matter is serious since ground lost in the product markets of the future, those that represent a source of growth, will eventually worsen the future competitive position of Europe, reducing the scope of growth even more. Statistics on the world-market share in trade of high-technology products provide some useful indication of the changing comparative advantage in this area (see Figure 6). According to EC sources (Albert and Ball, 1984), the European share two decades ago was in line with the OECD average; at present it is

15 percent below. On the other hand Japan, which at that time was 30 percent below the OECD average, is at present 40 percent above and is clearly the pacesetter. Little wonder that after the oil shock and the employment shock it was said that Europe was suffering from a veritable technology shock. In Table 4 the evolution of comparative advantage in high-technology trade for the period 1963–1984 is reported, with a clear indication of the growing gap between the European Community, the United States, and Japan.

The rigidity of the European production system and labor markets and the low competitiveness of European industry have been important causes—structural in nature—of a growing feeling in favor of protection. This is perhaps a new application of protectionism, which under fixed exchange rates was used mostly for balance of payments purposes and in conditions of underdevelopment was used mostly to shelter new industries. This new application could be called defensive to the extent that it is mostly intended to accommodate a multiplicity of well-established interests threatened by foreign competition. But the question of industrial restructuring is no less important, nor the social strain associated with it less heavy, especially in those societies slower to accommodate change. To a significant extent, the traditional *infant*-industry argument for protection has been expanded to accommodate an *aging*-industry argument for protection in the OECD economy.

It is my claim that current efforts toward industrial restructuring and rationalization of capacities—including the labor force—are examples of a positive response to evolving international conditions. Policies to reduce inflation are equally important. They need to continue with determination and to be supported by the new trade negotiations within GATT. As long as the process goes on unemployment will be high. But unless the process, at home and abroad, goes on with unmitigated determination, unemployment will never decline.

Japan's International Competitiveness: Virtue or Vice?

To the average Western traveler the Orient is a place of mystery and dreams. To the average Western producer the Orient is a place of tough and real competition. Indeed, in Europe and the United States there seems to be an uneasy feeling of worried admiration toward Japan and a few highly successful NICs of the Far East. Their growth in real income and export has been characteristically faster than anywhere else in the world.

As a matter of economic welfare (leaving ethics aside), foreigners should all welcome the economic success of the Pacific. It

TABLE 4.
Evolution of Comparative Advantage in High-Technology Trade 1963–1984

	1963	1970	1978	1984
France	0.93	1.00	0.96	0.88
Germany	1.20	1.06	0.99	1.00
Italy	0.83	0.87	0.65	0.60
United Kingdom	1.02	0.94	0.92	1.00
European Community (average)	1.01	0.94	0.88	0.87
United States	1.27	1.18	1.27	1.19
Japan	0.72	1.07	1.27	1.37

Source: Cardiff (1984), EEC (1984).
(OECD average = 100)

improves the overall terms of trade in Europe and the United States; it enriches the basket of goods available on world markets; it stimulates competitiveness and better quality; it reduces the real cost of all tradeable goods and, in general, inflation. Admittedly, in the short term it does have negative consequences on certain sectors. These sectors, however, are undergoing the adjustment process for the reasons indicated above, not because of Japan and its neighboring NICs.

I will address three broad points: whether Japan's trade level and pattern reflect the country's postulated comparative advantage; whether its exchange-rate policies are designed so as to influence current-account balances; and whether the first two points could be construed as evidence of indirectly managed trade.

JAPAN'S COMPARATIVE ADVANTAGE: NO FOUL PLAY

The pattern of Japan's external trade can be easily explained (Cline, 1983). No doubt, Japan's agricultural sector is highly protected—as is that of the United States and, even more, that of the European Community. Similarly, the specialization in production of goods intensive in primary commodities should be excluded, given Japan's poor natural-resource endowment and distance from supply centers. On the other hand, given the highly skilled labor force, the social consensus prevailing in its cohesive society, and its geographic distance from major trading partners, it is only good economics to conclude that the country's comparative advantage has to be in medium- and high-technology manufactures (Corden, 1983). (Refer to Figure 6 for a firsthand impression of Japan's growing specialization and Europe's despecialization.) The real question, therefore, is not whether, in a totally free trade environment, Japan's trade basket would be different from the one we presently know. The question is whether

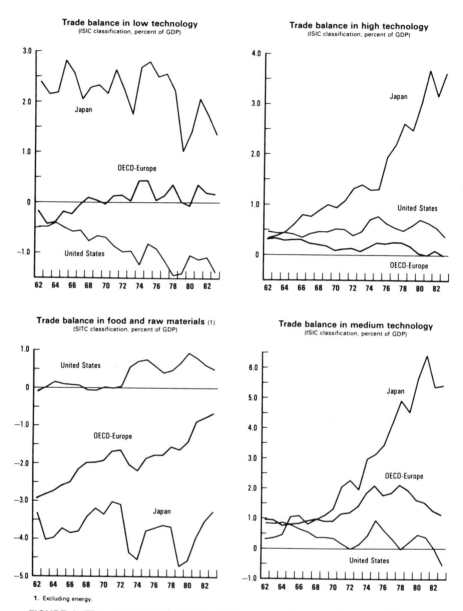

FIGURE 6. The response of trading patterns to technological change. (*Source: O.E.C.D.* Economic Outlook *n.37 [June 1985].*)

its import volume would be greater. The answer is obviously affirmative—but so would be its export volume.

The reason is simple. During the past ten years Japanese households have had a propensity to save which was almost double that in Europe (with Italy a significant exception) and triple that of the

TABLE 5.
Sectoral Financial Balances as Percentage of GDP in 1986
(estimates)

	United States	Japan	Germany	France	United Kingdom	Italy
Public Sector	−3.4	−2.2	−1.3	−3.4	−2.7	−12.8
Foreign Sector	2.3	−2.6	−1.0	1.4	−0.5	0.7
Household Sector	2.4	11.1	6.3	4.5	2.4	13.2
Corporate Sector	−1.3	−6.4	−4.0	−2.6	0.9	−1.1

United States. In 1985, for example, the savings ratios (to GDP) in major OECD countries were:

Japan	17.6
United States	4.9
Germany	11.9
France	13.0
United Kingdom	11.6
Italy	24.2
Canada	13.6

At present, the government's relatively large dissaving claims a relatively small percentage of Japan's exceptionally high saving. The business sector—with a gross operating surplus in manufacturing that is about 50 percent of value added (twice as much as the U.S., one and a half times that of the EC)—manages to absorb another part. The rest joins the pool of world saving, taking along a handsome merchandise-account surplus (see Table 5). It also contributes to lower world interest rates. Therefore even full trade liberalization is not likely to change Japan's current-account configuration to any significant extent. It might nevertheless bring about a higher level of both imports and exports, improving the terms of trade of Europe and the United States. Broadly, this is what happened after OPEC-I. Therefore, the reciprocity argument frequently raised by the United States and the EC vis-à-vis Japan, and the restrictions imposed unilaterally on exports from Japan, can be added to the roster of the systemic causes of neomercantilism.

THE RELATIONSHIP BETWEEN THE YEN EXCHANGE RATE AND JAPAN'S CURRENT-ACCOUNT BALANCES

Why, when the yen rate was strong from 1977 to early 1979, did the current-account surplus still amount to a total of $27 billion and not deteriorate significantly? Conversely, why didn't the large current-account surpluses from 1981 to 1984 (for a total of over $65 billion) significantly strengthen the yen rate?

These issues can be addressed by looking at microeconomic matters, such as the price elasticity of demand of Japan's exports and imports and at Japan's low profitability and low unit-labor costs (Table 6), and at macroeconomic considerations, concerning the functioning of the mechanism of adjustment in Japan and in its major trading partners (Saxonhouse, 1983).

Empirical work on the Japanese foreign sector has consistently shown that, ceteris paribus, most components of the Japanese merchandise-account balances indeed respond elastically to exchange-rate variations (EPA, 1984; Klein and Bollino, 1984; Moriguchi and Sato, 1982; Onishi, 1983; Shishido, 1981). The degree of responsiveness is greater on the import than the export side, and during yen depreciation rather than appreciation. However, in a general equilibrium context, the adjustment mechanism of Japan's trade balances to exchange-rate variations has been shown to work poorly. By and large, the yen behavior mirrors the U.S. dollar more closely than it does major European currencies.

In principle, currency exchange rates are determined by market conditions, the supply and demand of national currencies. These conditions in turn are determined by capital-account and current-account imbalances. Which imbalances prevail, and precisely what adjusts to what? Under a regime of relatively *fixed* exchange rates and under the conventional adjustment mechanism, capital flows are assumed to finance current-account imbalances. If external financing is inadequate and foreign reserves are low, current-account deficits tend to build up pressure on the exchange rate. In the long run, price and income effects, together with interest-rate movements, should reverse the imbalances. Under a regime of *floating* exchange rates, the adjustment is generally more immediate and at first entirely borne by the currency rate. However, as we all know, in the case of the U.S. dollar—the basic reserve currency—the exchange regime makes little difference. Furthermore, the adjustment mechanism is quite slow in reversing the imbalances. Only in late 1979 did the dollar appreciation take place, after practically four years of depreciation. And only in mid-1985 did the dollar depreciation take place, after practically five years of appreciation. In the 1980–1985 period, trade balances (in heavy deficit) actually tended to adjust to capital-account imbalances (in heavy surplus)—a capital surplus brought about by high interest rates, high rates of return, safe haven, and other considerations.

To some extent due both to microeconomic factors (for example, low price elasticity and high income elasticity of Japan's exports) and to macroeconomic conditions (dealing with Japan's excess saving), a related phenomenon has occurred with the yen. For most of the early 1980s, the U.S. policy blend of loose fiscal and tight monetary policy was mirrored by Japan's relatively loose monetary and tight fiscal policy. This outcome, as we have already seen, has made the U.S. import capital and Japan export it. This in turn has made the dollar scarce and yen abundant (see Figure 7). With time it has also caused substantial injury to U.S. import-competing industries and a considerable amount of sour feelings in the United States toward Japan.

IS THERE A HIDDEN, JUDICIOUS
MARKET PROTECTION IN JAPAN?

No doubt, administrative and technical measures, institutional mechanisms often of an unrecorded type, together with the country's pride in its basically inward-looking culture, make penetration of Japanese markets quite difficult for Western business people. Naturally, there is also much to be added about the so-far heavily regulated Japanese capital markets and about the country's lack of enthusiasm in allowing the yen to be used as an international medium of exchange and store of value. But is there hidden protection in Japan's practice?

It will be worthwhile here to quote extensively the latest EDRC report on Japan, published by the OECD in August 1985. According to the report there are three specific structural features which make penetration of the Japanese market by foreign firms difficult. These include:

> The tendency of large Japanese companies to combine with smaller suppliers into industrial groups which cover a broad range of larger firms' input needs. In other OECD countries, manufactured imports have tended to rise as large firms replace small local suppliers by larger, frequently foreign, suppliers. In Japan, the operation of a local subcontracting system enables large firms to impose very detailed and exacting standards on their local suppliers. Smaller suppliers are required to keep up with changing technologies, sometimes with the active help of their sponsoring large firm. This effective strategy of quasi-vertical integration might reduce the scope for import penetration.

> Throughout the OECD area, the growth of large scale independent distributors, capable of scanning world markets for their product needs, has been a major factor in increasing import penetration. Japan, however, has lagged behind other countries in this respect, and now has more wholesalers and retailers than

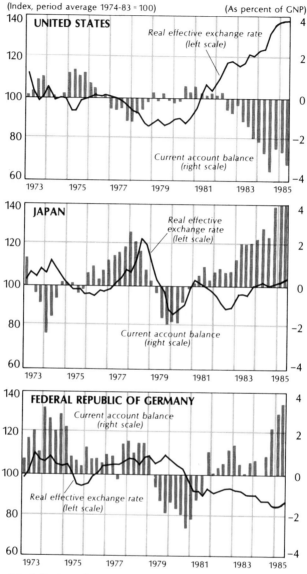

(Index, period average 1974-83 = 100) (As percent of GNP)

¹ Real effective exchange rates are measured by relative normalized unit labor costs.

FIGURE 7. Three major industrial countries: Payments balances on current account, including official transfers, as percent of GNP, and real effective exchange rates. (*Source: I.M.F.*)

the major European countries combined. Foreign firms seeking to sell in Japan therefore have to rely on Japanese partners (who are frequently potential or partial competitors) to distribute their products.

TABLE 6.
Unit Labor Cost in Manufacturing (percentage changes)

	1962–1972	*1972–1982*	*1984*	*1985*
United States	1.8	7.4	0.0	2.4
Japan	3.2	4.1	−4.0	0.6
Germany	3.6	5.2	0.5	0.1
France	2.6	11.0	4.4	3.2
United Kingdom	4.3	14.9	3.3	6.0
Italy	5.5	16.1	8.1	5.4
Average OECD Seven	2.7	8.1	0.4	2.3

Finally, the lack of a real takeover market in Japan rules out the strategy most commonly used by firms elsewhere in entering foreign markets—namely, purchasing a company well-established in that market. In the United States, the number of large takeovers (valued at $100 million or more) increased steadily over the last decade, rising from fourteen in 1975 to 116 in 1982; in Japan, the number of large transfers (exceeding $50 million) has been virtually constant, with only ten such transfers occurring in 1981. . . .

These features of the industrial structure make it costly for foreign firms to operate in Japan, and the standard assumption is that substantial losses are likely to be incurred for almost a decade. Even then, returns are generally not particularly high. The relative absence of direct import competition does not lead to a "soft," overprotected domestic market as might be the case in other countries. For even without the stimulus of strong import competition, intense domestic competition among the major industrial groups to secure leading positions in high growth industries ensures the dynamism of Japanese industry. Indeed, this intense competition may well explain why observed penetration ratios are low despite lower barriers. [OECD/EDRC, 1985e]

Yet something is happening on several fronts: The policy measures announced in May 1984, September 1985 and April 1986 concern the liberalization of yen markets, efforts toward more open domestic markets to foreign penetration, and mild macroeconomic relaxation to promote growth of domestic demand. Independently of all this, it is wrong to punish Japan for its efficiency in production, low wage demand (Table 6), and low profitability (Table 7). Instead, trade partners should encourage Japan to export capital more freely and to dismantle all regulations which limit the use of the yen in international transactions. This would not satisfy those Europeans who claim that "Japan should buy our goods, not our factories."

TABLE 7.
Net Rate of Return (operating surplus as a percentage of net capital stock)

	1960	1970	1975	1980	1984
Germany	16.3	11.0	7.0	8.6	9.9
France	15.3	14.3	9.4	4.8	5.8
Italy	6.8	9.0	0.3	3.6	6.4
United Kingdom	11.4	4.6	1.4	0.7	2.5
European Community	12.9	9.9	5.0	4.8	6.8
United States	7.2	7.5	7.2	6.9	11.4
Japan	2.0	16.5	3.4	2.3	3.7

However, if foreign suppliers could have easier access to Japan's markets and if foreign investors could buy yen-denominated bonds, certificates of deposit, and other instruments more easily, the demand for yen in world markets would drive up its exchange rate. This in turn would render Japanese goods more costly and therefore less competitive on world markets.

To conclude, the feeling remains that, despite trade and financial liberalization progress, the competitive fundamentals between Japan and her major partners will not change as long as macroeconomic policies in the United States and structural rigidities in Europe remain the same.

External Debt and Adjustment in Developing Countries

The difficult policy situations now evolving in the developing world, especially in those LDC countries that are most heavily indebted, stem from: (1) the macroeconomic conditions in OECD countries, characterized by uneven growth, limited market access, and high interest rates; (2) the required structural adjustment in the LDCs themselves during this period of external debt servicing; and (3) the social and political pressures building up in these countries as a direct consequence of declining living standards during the adjustment process (see Figure 8).

WORLD TRADE AND DEVELOPMENT CONDITIONS DO NOT FAVOR LDCs' GROWTH

At present, the developing countries face unfavorable conditions on several fronts. On the *monetary* side there is the continuing pressure on interest rates, a point raised earlier. Most people perceive the level of interest rates, supplemented by the terms and spread of lending above LIBOR as the critical variable in the LDC solvency

(Indices, 1976 = 100)[1]

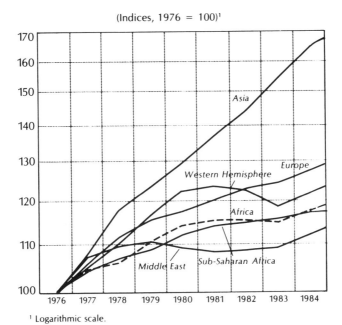

[1] Logarithmic scale.

FIGURE 8. Developing countries: Real GDP by region, 1976–1984. (*Source: I.M.F.*)

equation. It has been computed that any sustained increase of 100 basis points in the level of interest rates increases the debt servicing burden of heavily indebted LDCs by $8–10 billion per year.

On the *trade* side, trends manifested in both 1983 and 1984 were on balance unsatisfactory. In 1985 the situation even worsened. Little improvement is expected in 1986. The evolution of demand on the part of the United States and some other OECD economies where the recovery has been under way was more favorable than in the preceding biennium. Yet, because of barriers erected against LDC exports and the generally poor terms of trade which primary commodities continue to command in world markets, export revenues increased in 1983 by less than $10 billion. Thus, in 1983 a great part of the adjustment fell on imports, which contracted by more than $13 billion with respect to 1982. For the dozen most heavily indebted countries the split of the adjustment fell even more heavily on import (in a ratio of about 3 to 1). In 1985 the growth of export volumes by LDCs was lower than in the previous eighteen months. But the biggest problem came from the price side. Expressed in U.S. dollars, prices of non-oil-commodities products exported by LDCs were down an average of 13–15 percent relative to 1984. In the spring of 1986, under the effect of a strong depreciation of the U.S. dollar, (non-oil) commodity prices have stabilized. For a long time,

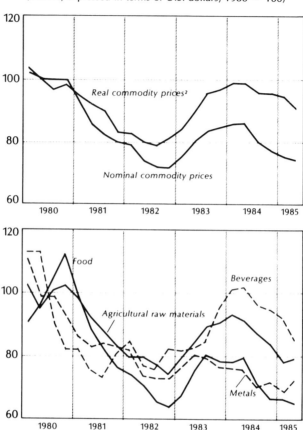

(Indices, expressed in terms of U.S. dollars, 1980 = 100)

[1] For classification of countries, see Appendix IX.
[2] Nominal commodity prices deflated by the UN index of prices of manufactured exports of developed countries.

FIGURE 9. Developing countries: Non-oil primary commodity prices. (*Source: I.M.F.*)

quantity and price trends both reduced the import capacity of primary producing countries. Much lower oil prices have complicated the picture, especially for the high capital absorbing countries like Mexico, Venezuela, Algeria, Indonesia, and Nigeria (see Figure 9).

An increasingly common problem in Third World *finances* is that for the third year in a row some of the debtor countries find themselves in a difficult predicament: net capital inflows have declined sharply. Such is the case for five of the major heavily indebted Latin American countries (Argentina, Brazil, Chile, Mexico, and Venezuela), accompanied by a merchandise trade surplus in 1983 of over $30 billion.

MACROECONOMIC AND STRUCTURAL ADJUSTMENT
IN LDCs IS NEEDED . . .

The rationale of the adjustment policies recommended to indebted LDCs is familiar—and it is a fallacious argument that such an adjustment necessarily and solely reduces living standards and increases social hardship. In any economy, to achieve a trade surplus, domestic spending must be reduced relative to domestic production: income produced domestically has to be greater than income distributed at home. If resources are fully and effectively utilized and output therefore cannot be increased, then achieving a trade surplus must imply cutting domestic spending by lowering living standards. Alternatively, when the economy operates inefficiently, idle resources are available (especially labor) and nonmarket relative prices (especially an overvalued currency) prevail—all well-known features of the typical LDC—elimination of distortions would enable countries to increase domestic output for export and thus achieve a surplus. The produced income would still exceed the distributed one, but living standards would not decline with respect to the period before the adjustment. The matter, therefore, is not *whether* adjustment is causing a deterioration of living standards in LDCs but *whether* delaying such adjustment will deteriorate such standards even more in the future. In this perspective, adjustment is a necessity rather than a choice—but a necessity that, in principle at least, should not compress living standards. On the contrary, it should promote long-term growth.

. . .BUT TRADE AND FINANCIAL FLOWS
HAVE TO SUPPORT LDCs' GROWTH

We all know that the distribution of costs and benefits between lenders and borrowers (a positive-sum game when the lending is voluntary) depends on a number of factors. For example, the real burden of servicing a certain stock of financial liabilities—and, conversely, the real return from lending the corresponding assets—depends on the rate of inflation (which erodes the real value of the debt). It also depends on the rate of exchange of the currencies in which the borrowers' portfolio is denominated, the rate of interest, and (in particular) its spread and terms of maturities. There is no doubt that during the late 1970s financial market conditions—characterized by cheap dollar rates, low real interest rates, and low inflation—favored the borrowers and penalized the lenders. The conditions of the mid-1980s are almost a mirror image: the balance of advantages has definitely tipped in the opposite direction.

From a development viewpoint, aside from political and ethical considerations, one can convincingly argue that a sustained and widespread contraction of financial resources available to LDCs would be contrary to the economic rationale of worldwide resource allocation. Despite the liquidity constraint and obvious macroeconomic mismanagement, one presumption remains: the fundamental comparative advantage of LDCs with respect to the OECD region in the use of capital resources remains strong. Therefore, while it is LDCs' responsibility to improve the economic and institutional environment of their production system, it is the responsibility of our countries to ensure that capital resources keep flowing from the richer to the poorer economies. Historically, the industrialization process of some of our own OECD economies (some of the Mediterranean countries, the United States, and Canada are relevant examples) was partially financed by means of capital inflows.

At the same time, it is important to reiterate that the role of the external sector of LDCs—and the role of the OECD trade policies with respect to them—are crucial in determining the LDCs' ability to service their debt. Since this point is very important and linked to the many issues tossed up in the approach to the new GATT Round, I would like to conclude with a reflection on it. In principle, for any indebted economy, movements in the debt-to-export ratio are broadly accounted for by two factors: (1) the difference between the nominal rate of interest and the rate of growth of export earnings (usually referred to as the *stability condition*) and (2) net financial transfers abroad as percentage of the total debt (the *sufficiency consideration*) (Simonsen, 1984). If the rate of growth of export revenues of indebted countries exceeds the nominal interest rate charged on their loans, additional capital flows to LDCs are not likely to push the debt-to-export ratio to unsustainable levels. In this case current-account deficits can be accommodated. On the other hand, if the interest rate exceeds the rate of growth of export proceeds for any lengthy period of time, an outflow of financial resources from borrowing to lending countries has to take place: LDCs have to accommodate their current-account surpluses, otherwise the debt/export ratio will not be sustained for long. The debt/export ratio is at present extraordinarily high: about 130 percent for all non-oil LDCs, 200 percent for all major heavily indebted LDCs, and 263 percent for the five major Latin American debtors. For the most heavily indebted countries, nominal interest rates are higher than the rate of growth of nominal exports. In other words, the situation is unsustainable and therefore perverse. The LDC debt-export ratio can be reduced only if the relationship between the rate of growth of LDCs' export proceeds and the rate of interest returns to the historical pattern. In other words, the former must exceed the latter (see Table 8).

I would like also to recall that the economic prospects of LDCs depend first and foremost on macroeconomic adjustment in their

TABLE 8.
Non-Oil-Developing Countries: Patterns of Financing
Current-Account Deficits, 1978–1984

	Average		
	1978–1980	*1981*	*1984*
	(in billions of U.S. dollars)		
Current account deficit	75	109	50
Non-debt creating flows	23	27	23
Use of reserves	−10	−5	−13
Net external borrowing	73	103	45
Errors and omissions	−11	−16	−5

own economies, on a more effective role of the market, and on the use of efficient exchange rates. But they are also heavily affected by the macroeconomic conditions and trade policies of the OECD countries. At present, access to OECD markets is severely restricted, especially although not exclusively for the more labor-intensive manufactures and semimanufactures that comprise the exports of major debtor countries. Failure by OECD countries to provide greater and more predictable export markets to LDCs will make the burden of adjustment unnecessarily heavy. It may also lead some of these countries to more of the inward-looking, import-substituting policies to which OECD countries objected so strongly in the past.

The servicing of the debt has also highlighted the problem of access by OECD exports to LDC markets—a problem well at the center of the forthcoming GATT negotiations. Developing countries have to realize that the effective protection on their part by means of tariffs, quotas, and export subsidies (which may have to be given up following the new GATT agreement) is modest when the overvaluation of their exchange rate is taken into account. In the GATT Round it will be necessary to discuss broad trade reforms, especially the question of how the NICs and other medium-income LDCs could graduate to the status of equal trade partners with the North. This would enable them to engage in fair trade as practiced in the OECD context, including the granting of preferential treatment to the least-developed LDCs in an unconditional most-favored-nations format.

Conclusions

The liberal and multilateral trade system established by and among OECD member countries after World War II has come under severe strain during the long recession(s) of the early 1980s. No major

breakdown in the free circulation of goods and services has occurred, though important restrictions have been imposed in critical
sectors such as steel, cars, textiles, footwear, and other basic manufactures. There is also evidence of pending legislation or executive
decisions in a number of countries that could indeed cause certain
important portions of OECD countries' trade to shift from operating
under an MFN principle to operating under a managed environment.
While there may be disagreement on ways and means, and perhaps
even timing of measures to resist protectionism, there is no disagreement on the necessity of halting the erosion of our open multilateral
trade system and of reviving the trade liberalization spirit that prevailed during much of the postwar period. The new GATT Round is
a prerequisite for the current recovery to continue and to strengthen.

The current trend toward unilateral management of trade is due
both to:

1. *Systemic* causes, primarily the tendency of policies to con-
strain the working of the free international trade system to compensate for the rigidities which permeate important aspects of
national economies; and
2. *Conjunctural* causes, related to the high level of unemployment
during the longest recession since World War II and to the
macroeconomic policy blend put into operation to promote the
recovery of economic activity.

It has become easier to blame—and penalize—trade partners
for the consequences of the recession, the overvaluation of a currency, and the cost of the structural rigidities than to promote the
right type of policies for strengthening the recovery and getting rid of
these rigidities. The developing countries are caught in the midst of
the situation. The adjustment process for which we are pressing in
their economies, and which is intrinsically necessary to improve
their performance and to service the debt, has been made more difficult by the policies of our own countries. The new GATT Round is
envisaged to provide support to all that.

But there is something more. Perhaps the most vicious element
in the recent trend toward intervention is the fact that relevant measures distorting or restricting commercial flows increasingly bypass
GATT. The whole array of OMAs, VERs, QIRs, and the like has led to
bilateral arrangements that amount to a great deal of arm-twisting.
Solutions reached among a restricted group of large trading partners
usually tend to discriminate against others. Discrimination, potentially the most serious challenge to our multilateral trading system,
is also loaded with domestic implications. Sectoral trade interventions tend to concern economic activities where producers interests

(both labor and business) are well represented, while consumers' concerns are less prominent. Therefore, because net protection cannot be extended to the entire economy, selective protection amounts to a deceptive form of intervention in income distribution—an activity governments can best carry out by ordinary income redistribution policies. Furthermore, this pattern of trade interventions is often characterized by free mixing of political considerations that have little to do with trade matters.

To put an end to these unfair trade practices will take a lot of political determination and leadership: without them—after all—there is little usefulness to call for yet another round of GATT negotiations.

This paper is contributed by the author in his personal capacity. The paper itself does not imply expression of opinion on the part of the OECD.

References

Abernathy, William et al. (1983) *Industrial Renaissance.* New York: Basic Books.

Albert, Michel and Ball, Jim (1984) *Towards European Economic Recovery in the 1980s.* A report presented to the European Parliament in 1984. Brussels.

Balassa, Bela (ed.) (1973) *European Economic Integration.* Amsterdam: North-Holland.

Boltho, Andrea (ed.) (1982) *The European Economy: Growth and Crisis.* Oxford: Oxford University Press.

Cardiff, B. (1984) Innovation in Europe. Internal Note, January 1984, EEC, DG EFA, quoted in *European Economy* 20 (July):49.

Cline, William (1983) *Trade Policy in the 1980s.* Washington, D.C.: Institute for International Economics.

——— et al. (1978) *Trade Negotiations in the Tokyo Round.* Washington, D.C.: Brookings Institution.

Corden, W. Max (1983) Policy Synthesis. In W. Cline (ed.), *Trade Policies in the 1980s.* Washington, D.C.: Institute for International Economics.

Dunn, R. (1984) *The Many Disappointments of Flexible Exchange Rates.* Princeton Essays in International Finance No. 154. Princeton, N.J.: Princeton University Press.

Economic Planning Agency, Government of Japan (1984) *Proceedings of the EPA Symposium on Economic Interdependence and Flexible Exchange Rates.* Tokyo, February 1984.

Economic Report of the President (1985) Washington, D.C.: Government Printing Office, February.

EEC (1984a) *Annual Economic Report 1984–1985* Brussels, EEC.

EEC (1984b) *European Economy* 20 (July).

EEC (1984c) *European Economy* 21 (September).

General Agreement on Tariffs and Trade (1984) *International Trade 1983/84*, Geneva, September 1984.

Hall, Robert (1982) *Inflation: Causes and Effects.* Chicago: University of Chicago Press.

International Monetary Fund (1985) *World Economic Outlook.* No. 29 spring 1985 with fall 1985 update. Washington, D.C.: IMF.

Klein, Lawrence and Bollino, Andrea (1984) World Recovery Strategies in the 1980s, *Journal of Policy Modeling, Special Issue in Honour of J. Tinbergen* 6(2).

Krueger, Anne O. (1978) *Foreign Trade Regimes and Economic Development: Liberalization Attempts and Consequences.* Cambridge, Mass.: Bollinger.

OECD (1984) *Proceedings of the Symposium on Consumer Policy and International Trade,* 27–29 November, Theme I. Paris: OECD.

OECD (1985a) *Economic Outlook* 38 (December).

OECD (1985b) *Employment Outlook* 3 (September).

OECD (1985c) *Development Co-operation,* 1985 Review by the Chairman of DAC. Paris: OECD.

OECD (1985d) *Costs and Benefits of Protection.* Paris: OECD.

OECD (1985e) *EDRC Report on Japan.* Paris: OECD.

OECD (1986a) *Economic Outlook* 39. Paris: OECD.

OECD (1986) *External Debt of Developing Countries—1985 Survey.* Paris: OECD. In Press.

Onishi, Akira (1983) Project FUGI and the future of ESCAP Countries. In Bert Hickman (ed.), *Global International Economic Models.* New York: North-Holland.

Pechman, J. (ed.) (1983) *Setting National Priorities—The 1984 Budget.* Washington, D.C.: The Brookings Institution.

Saxonhouse, Gay (1983) The Micro- and Macro-economics of Foreign Sales to Japan. In W. Cline (ed.), *Trade Policies in the 1980s.* Washington, D.C.: Institute for International Economics.

Shishido, Shuntaro and Sato, Aideto (1981) Multicountry Dynamic Multipliers Under Fixed and Floating Exchange Rates: An Econometric Analysis, *Journal of Policy Modeling* 3 (3).

Simonsen, M. H. (1984) The Developing Countries Debt Problem. Mimeographed.

Stern, Joseph and Deardorff, Alan (1981) A Disaggregated Model of World

Production and Trade—An Estimate of the Impact of the Tokyo Round, *Journal of Policy Modeling* 3(2).

Stirling, Catherine, and Tochelson, John (1985) *Under Pressure—U.S. Industry and the Challenges of Structural Adjustment.* Boulder, Col.: Westview Press.

Todd, Douglas (1984) Factor Productivity Growth in Four EEC Countries, 1960–81, *European Economy* 20 (July): 69–72.

Tumlir, J. (1984) *Europe's Contribution to World Development.* Prepared for *Jahrestagung der Gesellschaft für Wirtschafts-und Sozialwissenschaften.* Travemünde: Verin für Socialpolitik.

U.S. Congressional Budget Deficit (1984) *Alternative Estimates of U.S. Federal Budget Deficits, 1984–1989.* Washington, D.C.: Government Printing Office.

Whalley, John (1982) An Evaluation of the Tokyo Round Trade Agreement Using General Equilibrium Computational Methods, *Journal of Policy Modeling* 4(3).

PART TWO

INTERNATIONAL COMPETITIVENESS, THE NEW PROTECTIONISM, AND WELFARE

7

The Changing Structure
of U.S. Trade:
Implications for Research
and Policy

WILLIAM H. BRANSON

Introduction

During the past ten to fifteen years the structure of U.S. trade—the commodity and geographical distribution of exports and imports—has changed significantly. These changes have important effects on the pressures on trade policy. Within manufacturing, exports of capital goods and imports of (nonfood, nonauto) consumer goods both doubled (in real terms) from 1973 to 1980 (Branson [1984], p. 50). The labor released from the import-competing sectors tends to be lower-skilled, while the labor needed in the expanding sector tends to be higher-skilled. As shown in Branson (1983b) and Lawrence (1983), the expanding equipment-producing sector is high-technology- and human-capital-intensive, while the contracting sectors tend to use lower technology and to be less skill-intensive.

In addition, the expanding and contracting sectors tend to have different geographical centers within the United States. As Bluestone (1983) shows, within a context of roughly constant total employment in manufacturing from 1973 to 1980, employment contracted by some 10 to 15 percent in the "rust belt" states between Michigan and New York and expanded by an equal amount elsewhere.

The more dissimilar that expanding and contracting sectors are in terms of factor use and geographical location, the higher are ad-

From Princeton University, Princeton, New Jersey, and NBER.

TABLE 1.
U.S. Trade in Manufactures in Constant 1973 Dollars, 1973–1980 ($ billion).

Commodity	1973			1980		
	Exports	Imports	Balance	Exports	Imports	Balance
Chemicals (SITC 5)	5.7	2.5	3.2	14.1	5.6	8.5
Industrial Supplies (SITC 6)	6.8	13.0	−6.2	13.4	20.7	−7.3
Capital Goods (SITC 7)	22.6	11.2	11.4	43.7	22.8	20.9
Consumer Goods (SITC 8)	2.7	7.6	−4.9	6.8	15.2	−7.4
Other Manufactures (SITC 9) (Autos and Arms)	8.7	12.5	−3.8	14.1	21.0	−6.9
Total	46.5	46.8	−0.3	92.1	85.3	6.8

Sources: (1) OECD Data Tape and Commodities Series C for trade data in current dollars. (2) Council of Economic Advisers *Annual Report* (1983) for price indexes as follows: Chemicals and Industrial Materials: Total Goods Deflator, Tables B-7 and 8; Capital Goods: Deflator for Producers' Durable Equipment, Table B-3; Consumer Goods: Deflator for Consumer Expenditure on Durables, Table B-3; Autos: Auto Product Deflator, Tables B-7 and 8.

justment costs likely to be. In an earlier period of rapid growth in *intra*industry trade, these costs were probably lower. In the absence of effective programs of adjustment assistance, relocation, and retraining, rising adjustment costs will bring pressure on trade policy at least to slow the pace of change.

In this paper I briefly summarize research results that suggest the hypothesis of increasing dissimilarity between expanding and contrasting sectors, drawing mainly on the recent papers by Branson (1983b, 1984), Bluestone (1983), and Lawrence (1983).

The Sectoral Structure of Trade

The changing sectoral composition of U.S. trade is illustrated by the data of Table 1, taken from Branson (1984). U.S. trade in manufactures was roughly balanced in 1973 and showed a surplus of $6.8 billion (1973 dollars) in 1980. Over the period, the balance in each category grew in absolute value, indicating the pull on resources from the growing-deficit ones—industrial supplies (such as steel), consumer goods, and autos—to the growing-surplus areas, chemicals and capital goods, particularly electronics and electrical machinery.

The sectors with expanding net exports are identified in most studies as high technology, while the contracting sectors with growing net imports are low technology. The classifications of *Business Week* and Lawrence are shown in Table 2, ordered by the growth rate of sales from 1978 to 1982. (This is the *Business Week* presentation.)

TABLE 2.
Classification of Manufacturing Sectors by *Business Week* and
Robert Z. Lawrence.

Industry	Average Annual Growth Rate of Sales, 1978–1982	Classifications	
		BW	Lawrence
Electronics	16	HT	HT
Information	14	HT	HT
Chemicals	13	B	HT
Energy	13	NR	NR
Drugs	11	HT	HT
Telecommunications	10	HT	HT
Forest products	6	NR	NR
Nonferrous metals	3	NR	K
Steel	2	B	K
Machine tools	1	B	HT
Autos	−2	B	K

Sources: *Business Week* "Industry Outlooks," January 9, 1984; Robert Z. Lawrence (1983).

Business Week uses the categories high technology (HT), natural resources (NR), and basic (B), while Lawrence substitutes capital-intensive (K) for basic. It is clear that the high-technology sectors have experienced relative expansion and the basic or capital-intensive sectors relative contraction. The two industries where the classifications seem to conflict are chemicals and machine tools. Chemicals are a high-technology sector in Lawrence's classification and a basic industry for *Business Week*. For our purposes it is enough to note that the sector has expanding sales and net exports, and it is high technology, if basic. Machine tools make up a small fraction of capital goods; much of the latter is in electronics in the *Business Week* classification. Machine tools also were severely depressed in the 1981–1982 recession. But it may be an example of a high-technology industry where the United States is losing competitive position.

The relation between the technology classification of industries and trade is illustrated by Figure 1, drawn from NSF data. Since the early 1970s, the U.S. trade surplus in products classified as "R&D-intensive" has grown extremely rapidly, as has the deficit on non-R&D-intensive products. This again shows the pull of resources from low-technology to high-technology sectors.

Tables 1 and 2 show that the sectors with expanding net exports are high-technology, while the sectors with expanding net imports are basic or capital-intensive. Figure 1 tends to confirm this relationship; R&D-intensive goods show a growing surplus, and vice versa for non-R&D-intensive goods.

Econometric studies by Branson and Manayios (1977) and

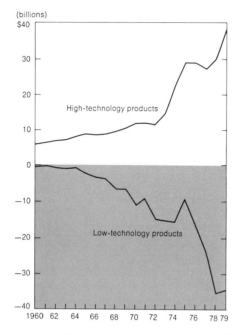

FIGURE 1. U.S. trade balance in high-technology and low-technology goods. (*Source: NSF Science Indicators.*)

Stern and Maskus (1981) have established that U.S. exports are human-capital intensive in production, while U.S. imports are labor-intensive. Human capital and skilled labor are essentially the same thing, as both of those studies showed. This was confirmed indirectly in a recent study by Ott (1983). Studying the characteristics of the capital goods industry, she found that value-added per worker is higher there than in the average "exposed" sector. This is consistent with the expanding capital goods sector having higher-than-average skills and wages.

In summary, the accumulation of evidence from many empirical studies of trade supports the hypothesis that the expanding surpluses and deficits shown in Table 1 pull resources from sectors that are low-technology or basic, not skill-intensive. Resources are pulled toward very different sectors that are high-technology and skill-intensive. This creates a skill mismatch and, in turn, a problem for trade or adjustment policy.

Sectoral Shifts in Employment

The effects of the changing sectoral composition of trade and production on employment are summarized in Table 3. Over the period 1973–1980, total employment in U.S. manufacturing increased slightly, by 0.6 percent. The decomposition of this change into its sources in domestic demand and trade, however, shows a fall of 1.5

TABLE 3.
Changes in Manufacturing Employment, 1973–1980
(percent changes).

Category of Product	Total	Due to U.S. Demand	Due to Trade
Total manufacturing	0.6	−1.5	2.1
Equipment production	13.7	8.5	5.2
High technology	15.7	10.5	5.2
Iron and steel	−14.8	−15.8	1.0
Automobiles	−19.2	−14.9	−4.3

Source: Robert Z. Lawrence, De-industrialization and U.S. International Competitiveness: Domestic and International Forces in U.S. Industrial Performance, 1970–1980, mimeo, Brookings Institution, Washington, D.C., 10/4/82, Table 14.

percent due to domestic demand and an increase of 2.1 percent due to foreign trade. This is consistent with the data of Table 1, which show an increase in the overall trade surplus in manufactures over the same period.

The small increase in total employment is itself the result of a large decrease in employment in basic industries and a slightly larger increase in employment in the overlapping categories of high-technology and equipment-producing industries. This shows the movement of resources in employment terms. The decomposition of the expansion of employment shows that 38 percent of the increase in employment in equipment production and 33 percent in high technology was due to trade. Thus trade made an important contribution to the overall change in the composition of employment in manufacturing during this period.

After 1980, the recessions of 1981 and 1982–1983, with the accompanying rise in real interest rates on the real foreign exchange value of the dollar, reduced employment in manufacturing. Lawrence (1983) shows that the total fell from 20 million in 1980 to 18.9 million in 1982. The decline was larger in the low-technology industries (4.2 percent) than in high-technology industries (2.4 percent). The positive trend from the effects of trade in the latter partially offset the effects of the recession.

It is clear that the changing sectoral composition of trade is having a significant effect on the *sectoral* composition of the demand for labor. The skills of the workers being laid off from the declining sectors are different from those required in the expanding sectors. This is one dimension of the adjustment problem caused by the changing composition of U.S. trade. Table 4, taken from Bluestone (1983), gives an example of the long-run earnings losses that laid-off workers suffer. In the basic industries, six years after they are laid off, workers still face an earnings loss of 12 to 16 percent. However,

TABLE 4.
Long-Term Earnings Losses of Permanently
Displaced Prime-Age Male Workers.

	Average Annual Percentage Loss	
Industry	*First 2 Years*	*Subsequent 4 Years*
Automobiles	43.4	15.8
Steel	46.6	12.6
Meat-packing	23.9	18.1
Aerospace	23.6	14.8
Petroleum refining	12.4	12.5
Women's clothes	13.3	2.1
Electronic components	8.3	4.1
Shoes	11.3	1.5
Toys	16.1	−2.7
TV receivers	0.7	−7.2
Cotton weaving	7.4	−11.4
Flat glass	16.3	16.2
Men's clothing	21.3	8.7
Rubber footwear	32.2	−.9

Source: Louis S. Jacobson, Earnings Losses of Workers Displaced from Manufacturing Industries. In William G. Dewald (ed.), The Impact of International Trade and Investment on Employment. A Conference of the U. S. Department of Labor. (Washington, D.C.: U. S. Government Printing Office, 1978), and Louis S. Jacobson, Earnings Loss Due to Displacement, (Working Paper CRC-385, The Public Research Institute of the Center for Naval Analyses, April 1979), Alexandria, Virginia.

in other low-technology industries such as toys, cotton weaving, and TV receivers, earnings *rise* from 3 to 11 percent after an initial decline. Thus the adjustment problem seems most severe for workers in the highly unionized basic industries. These workers and companies are in the best position to bring pressure on trade policy if adjustment proves too costly.

Geographical Shifts in Employment

The other important dimension of the adjustment problem is geographical. The expanding sectors are in parts of the country different from the contracting sectors. An example of this imbalance is provided in Branson (1983a), which summarizes the characteristics of the hand-held power tool industry. This sector has one of the highest and most rapidly rising growth rates in the capital goods sector. The growth is in the Southeast and Atlantic states in the East and in California. It also seems to be concentrated in relatively large, new plants.

Another example is provided in Table 5, taken from Bluestone

TABLE 5.
Percentage Change in Total Employment by Industrial Sector in Selected States, 1973–1980.

	Mass.	N.Y.	Mich.	Ohio	Ga.	N.C.	Cal.	Texas
Total Manufacturing	6.4	-10.3	-17.3	-11.0	3.3	2.7	20.6	31.5
Durable Mfg.	20.0	-4.8	-19.0	-13.1	7.8	17.2	23.3	43.0
Nondurable Mfg.	-9.6	-15.4	-10.0	-5.9	.9	-4.1	15.1	17.8
SIC 33 Primary Metals	—	-24.4	-27.7	-20.0	—	—	-2.2	27.4
SIC 34 Fabricated Metals	—	-10.0	-22.9	-10.4	4.6	26.3	16.4	29.1
SIC 35 Machinery (excl. Electrical)	42.8	6.3	-7.3	-2.0	36.6	36.8	43.9	77.2
SIC 36 Electrical Equip./Electronic	22.6	-1.1	-14.9	-19.2	30.9	17.1	45.0	88.2
SIC 37 Trans. Equip.	7.8	-12.7	-22.8	-18.6	3.8	101.2	5.8	23.4
SIC 38 Instruments	24.0	4.4	46.1	-3.7	—	—	60.3	43.8
SIC 22 Textile Mill Prod.	-16.7	-34.1	—	—	-8.0	-15.0	—	-26.6
SIC 23 Apparel	-10.0	-22.3	—	-22.3	-3.7	1.8	17.5	8.2
SIC 28 Chemicals	-10.8	-6.5	5.5	9.8	13.4	8.5	16.3	25.6
SIC 314 Footwear	-29.7	—	—	—	—	—	—	—

Source: U.S. Department of Labor, *Employment and Earnings for States and Areas,* 1939–1978, and Supplement 1977–1980. Bulletin 1370-13/1370-15, 1979 and September 1981.

(1983). It shows the percentage changes in employment in manufacturing in selected states by sector. Of Bluestone's sectors, SIC 35–38 are expanding capital goods sectors and SIC 28 is chemicals, SIC 33–34 are contracting basic industries, and SIC 22–23 and SIC 314 are contracting consumer goods sectors, nationally.

The contraction of employment in the rust-belt states of New York, Michigan, and Ohio is evident, as in the expansion in the South and West. Massachusetts and Georgia are interesting cases of large changes in employment composition *within* the state, with contraction in consumer goods and expansion in capital goods. New York, Michigan, and Ohio have shrinking employment in most sectors, with the opposite for North Carolina, California, and Texas.

Thus as the composition of employment by *sector* is changing, as shown in Table 3, so is the *geographical* composition of employment. This creates adjustment problems for communities where plants close as well as for the displaced workers. This is translated into pressure on trade policy due to the concentration of the contracting sectors in the rust-belt states.

U.S. Trade with Developing Countries

During the decade since 1973, the U.S. economy has become increasingly interdependent with the newly industrializing countries (NICs) among the developing countries. These countries have had high investment ratios to GNP, financed mainly by domestic saving but also partly by foreign borrowing. They have invested in manufacturing capacity, importing capital equipment. This increase in international demand for equipment has resulted in an increase of U.S. capital good exports to more than 50 percent of all U.S. manufactures; the twelve NICs enumerated in Branson (1984) absorbed 22 percent of all U.S. capital goods exports in 1981.

In turn, exports of consumer manufactures by the NICs to the OECD countries have expanded rapidly. The NICs provided half of U.S. imports of consumer manufacture (nonfood, nonauto) in 1980, and 40 percent of European imports. As the NICs grew during the 1970s, they imported capital goods from the United States and exported consumer manufactures to the United States.

This pattern of trade has strengthened the interdependence between the U.S. economy and the NICs. United States exports of manufactures are less balanced across commodities than European or Japanese exports, with high shares in the United States for capital goods and chemicals. The NICs are a major market area for these U.S. exports.

The geographical pattern of U.S. trade with the NICs also shows interesting asymmetries. In overall trade in manufactures, the

United States has a large surplus ($12.2 billion in 1980) in trade with the Latin American NICs (Argentina, Brazil, Colombia, Mexico), a small surplus ($2.5 billion) with the ASEAN countries, and a large deficit ($11.3 billion) with the Far Eastern NICs (Hong Kong, South Korea, Taiwan). Thus, the United States exports capital goods to the NICs and imports consumer goods from them, following broad lines of comparative advantage. But the exports are relatively focused on Latin America, mainly Mexico, and imports on the Far Eastern NICs. In Branson (1984) a trade triangle is described, with the United States exporting manufactures, mainly capital goods, to the Latin American NICs, who in turn sell raw materials in the world market. The Far Eastern NICs buy raw materials and sell manufactures, mainly consumer goods, to the United States.

The data presented in Branson (1984) support a view of interdependence between the U.S. economy and the NICs that differs from the relations of Europe or Japan with those countries. The NICs take a high proportion of U.S. and Japanese exports relative to European exports, with the United States relatively concentrated on capital goods and Latin America. The United States is the biggest market for NIC exports of manufactures, particularly consumer goods.

Thus during the period since 1973, growth in the U.S. economy has become increasingly interdependent with growth both in Latin America and among the Asian NICs.

Implications for Research and Policy

The research summarized here has several implications for our understanding of the structural changes in the U.S. economy caused by developments in trade and for policy to cope with these structural changes.

The first implication is that, except for the macrolevel dislocations of 1982–1984 that have been due to a mix of expansionary fiscal and tight monetary policy, at the industry or microlevel the U.S. economy has adjusted flexibly to changing pressures from trade. Resources have been moving from contracting to expanding sectors, with aggregate manufacturing employment actually increasing slightly from 1973 to 1980 or 1981. The expanding sectors generally are higher-technology and higher-productivity than the contracting sectors, so the resource reallocation is likely to increase productivity. Over the same time period, the U.S. trade surplus in manufactures also increased in real terms. Thus until 1981 there was little sign of an underlying problem with structural adjustment in the economy. This suggests that the main source of the recent contraction in manufacturing is macropolicy, not the lack of industrial policy.

A second implication of the research summarized here is a hypothesis for further study. Since the expanding and contracting sectors in the United States are increasingly different, we expect that adjustment costs are rising and that this explains the perception of rising pressure on trade policy. The adjustments to competition described above are costly. Workers lose jobs, and have to move and search for new ones. Towns are faced with plants closing and the tax base shrinking. It is little consolation that growth is simultaneously occurring on the other side of the country. The gains from trade and adjustment go to *all* the consumers/taxpayers in the country; the losses fall on the few who are in the shrinking industries. It can be argued that it is the job of the federal government to minimize the costs of adjustment by using general tax revenue to finance retraining and other *effective* assistance programs. Otherwise the consumers get the gain but the particular workers, unions, and towns take the losses. An effective policy of retraining, job location, and assistance for those who adjust is probably an important part of a policy package to keep the U.S. economy flexible and competitive. Research should be aimed at design of the elements of such a policy.

Finally, the increasing interdependence between the United States and the Latin American and Asian developing countries may have implications for U.S. foreign economic policy. These remain to be spelled out as part of the future research program.

References

Bluestone, B. (1983) Economic Turbulence: Capital Mobility vs. Absorptive Capacity in the U.S. Economy. Paper presented at American Association for the Advancement of Science, Detroit, May 29.

Branson, W. H. (1983a) Data Analysis of U.S. Capital Goods Exports, NBER mimeograph.

——— (1983b) Trade and Structural Adjustment in the U.S. Economy: Response to International Competition. Presented at AEI Conference, September 22–23.

——— (1984) Trade and Structural Interdependence Between the U.S. and the NICs. Presented at Conference on the Global Implication of the Trade Patterns of East and Southeast Asia, Kuala Lumpur, Malaysia, January 4–6, forthcoming as NBER Working Paper No. 1282.

Branson, W. H. and Manayios, N. (1977) Factor Inputs in U.S. Trade, *Journal of International Economics* 7: 111–131.

Lawrence, Robert Z. (1983) Changes in U.S. Industrial Structure: The Role of Global Forces, Secular Trends, and Transitory Cycles. Presented at

Federal Reserve Bank of Kansas City Symposium on Industrial Change and Public Policy, Jackson Hole, Wyoming, August 25–26.

Ott, Attiat F. (1983) Competitive Performance of U.S. Manufacturers. Presented at AEI Conference, September 22–23.

Stern, R. and Maskus, K. (1981) Determinants of the Structure of U.S. Trade, 1958–76, *Journal of International Economics* 11: 207–224.

8

Employment Effects of Japanese and American Protectionism

ROBERT W. STAIGER, ALAN V. DEARDORFF, AND ROBERT M. STERN

Introduction

It has been argued increasingly in recent years that Japan's trade policies are detrimental to the United States. Yet, with only some exceptions,[1] critics are typically unclear about the economic interests which are affected and especially what might happen if existing barriers in Japan were to be removed. In this paper we address the question of which sectors and occupational groups in both Japan and the United States are affected by the existing pattern and possible changes in protection in Japan as well as in the United States. It is our hope that the numerical estimates we provide may help to put the issue of Japanese protection in perspective.

In particular, we find that the greatest effect of both American and—especially—Japanese protection is to protect employment of farm workers in Japan and to antiprotect employment of farm workers in the United States. For almost all combinations of reductions in tariffs and/or NTBs in the two countries that we examine, employment of farm workers falls in Japan and rises in the United States, while employment in most other occupations in the United States declines. Thus, the only group in the United States that would stand

---

From Stanford University, Stanford, California, and the University of Michigan, Ann Arbor, Michigan.

[1] See, for example, Saxonhouse (1983, p. 285) and U.S. Council of Economic Advisers (1984, p. 66) for some analytical judgments about the impact of Japan's agricultural protection which anticipates our main conclusions to be noted below.

to gain employment unambiguously from a reduction in Japanese trade barriers would seem to be workers in U.S. agriculture.

In order to evaluate the employment effects of protection it is necessary to have an analytical and computational framework in which the tariffs, nontariff barriers (NTBs), and input-output relations for Japan, the United States, and many additional countries can be taken into account. Such a framework is provided by the Michigan Model of World Production and Trade, which will be used below. The procedure we follow involves calculating the effects of the hypothetical removal by Japan and the United States individually and jointly of the actual pre-Tokyo Round (1976) tariffs as well as of constructed approximations of the ad valorem equivalents of NTBs covering the period from 1973 to the early 1980s. In each case, the model is solved for changes in production, trade, and other variables of interest. Given the model solution, it is straightforward to calculate the implied changes in employment and thus to assess the extent to which individual sectors and occupational groups are affected.

The remainder of this paper will proceed as follows. In the next section we describe briefly the general structure of the Michigan Model and the data used for computational purposes. We then present a description of the various trade-liberalization scenarios to be explored and explain the solution procedure used to generate the numerical results. These results precede our conclusions, which are contained in the final section.

Description of the Model and Data

The Michigan Model of World Production and Trade was developed originally to analyze the economic effects of the Tokyo Round and has since been used to analyze a variety of other issues, including effects of changes in exchange rates on trade and employment and effects of domestic taxes/subsidies, tariffs, and exchange rates on the structure of protection. Space does not permit a full presentation of the model, but a brief description may be useful for readers not familiar with our work.[2]

The model incorporates supply and demand functions and market-clearing conditions for twenty-two tradeable and seven nontradeable industries in thirty-four countries, plus an aggregate rest-of-world. Supply and demand functions interact on both national and world markets to determine equilibrium prices and quantities traded and produced plus the flexible exchange rates. Labor-demand

---

[2] The model and its various applications are described at length in Deardorff and Stern (1986).

functions determine employment in each industry and country. We abstract from such macroeconomic determinants of aggregate employment as levels of government spending, taxes, and the money stock. Instead, aggregate expenditure is adjusted endogenously to hold aggregate employment constant in each country.[3]

Supply and demand functions are derived from maximization of profit and utility functions. These were selected to permit a rich variety of behavior and to have parameters that could be inferred either from available data or from published econometric estimates. The current version of the model uses a pre–Tokyo Round base of 1976 data on trade, production, and employment for all thirty-four countries, plus tariffs in the industrialized countries. To describe technology, we use the 1972 input-output table for the United States, the 1975 table for Japan, and the 1970 national tables for the EEC members and Brazil. The U.S. table is applied to the remaining industrialized countries and the Brazilian table to the remaining developing countries.[4] Elasticities of capital-labor substitution and import demand used in the model were obtained from the literature.

Our data on tariffs are based on pre–Tokyo Round (1976) levels. These were available at the line-item level of the Brussels Tariff Nomenclature (BTN) and were aggregated using own-country total imports as weights for each of our twenty-two tradeable industries in each country. The tariff rates for Japan and the United States are listed by industry in Table 1.

In the basic version of the model, existing NTBs in developed countries are represented by the fractions of 1976 trade in each sector and country that were covered by any kind of NTB. We then use endogenous tariff-equivalent variables to reduce by that fraction the sensitivity of imports to tariff and other changes. These fractions of NTB coverage were calculated based on data in Murray and Walter (1978), aggregated, concorded, and updated to the later 1970s to reflect restrictions such as in footwear, iron and steel, and television receivers which were in effect at that time. Fractions for textiles and wearing apparel were set equal to shares of imports from nonindustrialized countries. No effort was made to model the particular institutions behind existing NTBs. We have no data on tariffs and NTBs for developing countries, but we do capture elements of their exist-

---

[3] In what follows we disaggregate labor into several skill groups. It would perhaps be preferable in our experiments to hold constant the employment of each skill group in each country as opposed to the aggregate employment of each country. However, data limitations preclude this approach.

[4] We are currently in the process of updating the data base of the model to 1980, introducing more recent input-output tables and processing I-O tables for several additional countries.

TABLE 1.
Pre-Tokyo-Round (1976) Tariffs by Sector in Japan and the
United States (Percent; Weighted by Own-Country Imports)

ISIC	Sector	Japan	United States
1	Agric., forestry, and fish	18.4	2.2
310	Food, beverages, and tobacco	25.4	6.3
321	Textiles	3.3	14.4
322	Wearing apparel	13.8	27.8
323	Leather products	3.0	5.6
324	Footwear	16.4	8.8
331	Wood products	0.3	3.6
332	Furniture and fixtures	7.8	8.1
341	Paper and paper products	2.1	0.5
342	Printing and publ.	0.2	1.1
35A	Chemicals	6.2	3.8
35B	Petroleum and rel. prod.	2.8	1.4
355	Rubber products	1.5	3.6
36A	Nonmetal. min. prod.	0.6	9.1
362	Glass and glass prod.	7.5	10.7
371	Iron and steel	3.3	4.7
372	Nonferrous metals	1.1	1.2
381	Metal products	6.9	7.5
382	Nonelectric mach.	9.1	5.0
383	Electric machinery	7.4	6.6
384	Transport. equip.	6.0	3.3
38A	Misc. manuf.	6.0	7.8
	All industries	6.3	4.5

Source: Based on information provided by the Office of the U.S.
Trade Representative, Washington, D.C.

ing NTBs by modeling a system of import licensing for many of them.

The representation of NTBs in terms of the fractions of trade coverage does not enable us to capture the economic effects that would be experienced if the NTBs themselves were reduced or removed. It would be necessary for this purpose to have direct estimates of the price or quantity effects associated with particular NTBs by sector. Such estimates are very difficult to obtain, however, for a variety of reasons discussed at length in Deardorff and Stern (1985).

In the absence of accurate and reliable estimates, we have constructed "high" and "low" approximations of the ad valorem equivalents of selected NTBs by major sector for Japan and the United States, ranging from 1973 to the early 1980s. These high and low approximations, which are listed in Table 2, were constructed using price differentials between domestic and foreign goods drawn from a variety of sources and some rough guesses based on the NTB trade-

TABLE 2.
Approximations of Selected Ad Valorem Equivalents of NTBs for Japan and the
U.S., Ranging from 1973 to the Early 1980s.

		Japan		United States	
ISIC	Sector	High	Low	High	Low
1	Agric., forestry, and fish	97.0%[a]	27.2%[b]	— %	— %
310	Food, beverages, and tobacco	75.0[b]	16.5[c]	31.9[a]	15.9[b]
321	Textiles	15.0[b]	15.0[d]	17.3[b]	15.0[b]
322	Wearing apparel	18.0[a]	15.0[d]	28.0[a]	15.0[b]
323	Leather products	11.0[b]	3.0[d]	—	—
324	Footwear	11.0[b]	3.0[d]	27.0[b]	—
331	Wood products	25.0[b]	22.0[d]	—	—
332	Furniture and fixtures	—	—	—	—
341	Paper and paper products	—	—	—	—
342	Printing and publ.	—	—	17.2[e]	17.2[e]
35A	Chemicals	17.9[a]	8.1[d]	10.0[b]	5.0[b]
35B	Petroleum and rel. prod.	65.6[a]	27.3[d]	—	—
355	Rubber products	—	—	5.0[b]	—
36A	Nonmetal. min. prod.	10.0[b]	7.5[d]	10.0[b]	5.0[b]
362	Glass and glass prod.	—	—	—	—
371	Iron and steel	—	—	10.0[b]	5.0[b]
372	Nonferrous metals	10.0[b]	—	—	—
381	Metal products	—	—	—	—
382	Nonelectric mach.	9.0[b]	3.0[d]	—	—
383	Electric machinery	9.0[a]	9.0[d]	5.0[b]	—
384	Transport. equip.	10.0[b]	—	10.0[b]	—
38A	Misc. manuf.	—	—	—	—

[a] Estimates used by Brown and Whalley (1980), based on price comparison calculated by Roningen and Yeats (1976).
[b] Guesstimates based on NTB trade coverage indexes for 1976 as reported in Deardorff and Stern (1986) or on reports of informal barriers.
[c] Estimates based on price comparisons for 1979–1980 reported in Bank of Japan (1982).
[d] Estimates based on price comparisons for 1976–1978 reported in Bank of Japan (1979).
[e] Calculated by Morici and Megna (1983) on the basis of U.S. copyright restrictions.

coverage indexes reported in Deardorff and Stern (1986).[5] In the cases of iron and steel and transport equipment, the figures shown are meant to indicate the presence of nontariff restrictions in the

---

[5] As noted in Deardorff and Stern (1985), the use of price differentials may overstate the price effects of existing NTBs especially because of differences in product quality. Instead of using price differentials, Morici and Megna (1983) calculate NTBs by sector for the United States based on the estimated price effects of specific types of NTBs that were susceptible to measurement. These estimates are much lower than those indicated in Table 2, but may themselves be understated because they do not reflect all existing NTBs for the United States. Petri (1984, p. 138) presents estimates of ad valorem tariffs and tariff equivalents of quantitative restrictions for the United States and Japan covering twelve sectors for 1960, 1970, and 1980. Petri's estimates are based on work by Turner (1981) and, with the exception of textiles and apparel for Japan in 1980, are considerably lower than most of our approximations in Table 2. These differences may reflect the fact that Turner focused only on quantitative restrictions and, further, some of his estimates apparently refer to bilateral trade between the United States and Japan.

early 1980s. These various approximations of NTB ad valorem equivalents thus cover a span of years, and even though some of these NTBs were not applicable in all years, we chose nonetheless to assume that they applied throughout the entire period. It is evident from Table 2 that there are substantial differences between the high and low ad valorem approximations, especially for Japan in the agriculture, food, and petroleum sectors. Unfortunately, since we lack methodologically consistent, accurate, and up-to-date information, we have no way of knowing what in fact the correct ad valorem equivalents should be. We decided therefore to use the high ad valorem approximations for computational purposes and to conduct a series of sensitivity tests using various combinations of the high and low approximations.

Since in what follows we will be focusing on the effects of removing tariffs and NTBs and these effects are expected to reflect the pattern of trade, we indicate in Table 3 the values of imports, exports, and net exports by sector for our reference year of 1976 for Japan and the United States. It can be seen that Japan had substantial net imports of agricultural and food products, wood products, petroleum, and nonferrous metals and net exports of textiles, iron and steel, and durable manufactures. The United States had substantial net exports of agricultural products, chemicals, nonelectric machinery, and transportation equipment and net imports of clothing, footwear, petroleum, iron and steel, nonferrous metals, and miscellaneous manufactures. To the extent that particular net importing sectors are subject to relatively high tariffs and/or NTBs, we would expect these sectors to figure importantly in the trade-liberalization experiments that we will describe below.

In determining the effects on employment, we divided the Japanese and U.S. labor force into the following occupational categories: (1) professional, technical, managerial, and administrative; (2) sales and clerical; (3) craftspeople; (4) operatives; (5) nonfarm laborers; (6) farm workers; (7) scientists and engineers; and (8) services. The total employment levels for each category are given in Table 4.

Trade-Liberalization Scenarios and the Solution Procedure

Our choice of trade-liberalization scenarios was dictated by the desire to explore several different aspects of the effects of our measures of protection on Japanese and U.S. employment. In particular, we wish to examine the extent to which Japanese and American employment may be affected by the tariffs and NTBs of these two countries, as well as to explore the employment implications of the mix of these measures. Thus, we have solved the model using five different

TABLE 3.

Value of Imports, Exports, and Net Exports by Sector for Japan and the U.S. in 1976 (billions of dollars)

ISIC	Sector	Japan			United States		
		Imports	Exports	Net Exports	Imports	Exports	Net Exports
1	Agric., forestry, and fish	$ 7.8	$ 0.7	–$ 7.1	$ 8.0	$ 18.0	$10.0
310	Food, beverages, and tobacco	3.3	0.4	–2.9	5.6	5.3	–0.3
321	Textiles	2.7	4.0	1.3	2.0	3.5	1.5
322	Wearing apparel	0.7	0.4	–0.3	3.5	0.5	–3.0
323	Leather products	0.5	0.2	–0.3	0.8	1.0	0.2
324	Footwear	0.1	0.1	—	1.8	0.1	–1.7
331	Wood products	4.1	0.1	–4.0	2.2	2.4	0.2
332	Furniture and fixtures	0.1	0.1	—	0.6	0.3	–0.3
341	Paper and paper products	0.6	0.5	–0.1	3.3	2.8	–0.5
342	Printing and publ.	0.1	0.1	—	0.3	0.7	0.4
35A	Chemicals	2.8	4.3	1.5	5.2	11.5	6.3
35B	Petroleum and rel. prod.	28.3	0.1	–28.2	35.8	4.5	–31.3
355	Rubber products	0.3	1.0	0.7	1.6	0.9	–0.7
36A	Nonmetal. min. prod.	0.5	0.8	0.3	1.1	0.9	–0.2
362	Glass and glass prod.	0.1	0.2	0.1	0.4	0.5	0.1
371	Iron and steel	0.4	11.0	10.6	4.7	2.1	–2.6
372	Nonferrous metals	5.5	0.7	–4.8	5.3	1.8	–3.5
381	Metal products	0.2	2.4	2.2	2.3	2.8	0.5
382	Nonelectric mach.	1.9	8.0	6.1	8.1	21.8	13.7
383	Electric machinery	1.1	9.9	8.8	7.4	8.2	0.8
384	Transport. equip.	0.8	20.2	19.4	16.2	20.3	4.1
38A	Misc. manuf.	2.4	6.6	4.2	11.5	9.3	–2.2
	Total	64.3	71.8	7.5	127.7	119.2	–8.5

Source: United Nations trade tapes.

TABLE 4.
Employment Levels by Occupation for Japan and the U.S., 1976
(thousands of man years)

Occupational Category	Japan	United States
Prof., tech., manag., and admin.	6,143.4	19,295.2
Sales and clerical	15,927.6	24,420.9
Craftspeople	8,589.3	10,401.2
Operatives	8,371.4	13,695.7
Nonfarm laborers	1,881.6	3,583.9
Farm workers	6,369.8	2,747.5
Scientists and engineers	726.6	1,474.5
Services	4,710.3	11,866.2
Total	52,720.0	87,485.1

Source: Adapted from *Population Census of Japan,* 1975, and *U.S. Census of Population,* 1970.

scenarios that are distinguished from one another by the country or countries whose tariffs and NTBs are to be altered.[6]

To explore the employment effects that could be attributed to each country's policies, we first reduced Japanese tariffs to zero, while holding constant Japanese NTBs and U.S. tariffs and NTBs. We then solved the Michigan Model for the resulting changes in employment by sector and occupational group. Thereafter, we reduced Japanese NTBs, holding constant Japanese tariffs and U.S. tariffs and NTBs. Similar experiments were conducted for U.S. tariffs, ceteris paribus, and U.S. NTBs. The final experiment involved complete removal of tariffs and NTBs for both countries jointly.

We make no effort in our choice of trade-liberalization scenarios to account for adjustments in the international structure of protection that might be initiated in response to the unilateral liberalization of Japanese and/or U.S. trade policy. Instead, our computational analysis explores the employment effects of each country's policies within the existing global structure of protection.

Employment Effects of the Removal of Japanese and U.S. Tariffs and NTBs

The sectoral employment effects of each of the five trade-liberaliza-

---

[6] Petri (1984) presents a variety of calculations of the effects of existing protection and hypothetical scenarios of protection based upon a multisectoral computational general equilibrium model that includes the United States, Japan, and rest-of-world. He also calculates the factor content of U.S. and Japanese trade for 1980, based only on labor and physical capital, using the traditional Leontief method and also with reference to assumed appreciation of each country's currency. Although there is some overlap, our work can be distinguished from Petri's because we use a more detailed breakdown of factors and focus explicitly on how these factors may be affected by protection.

tion scenarios for Japan and the United States are given in Table 5. We may first note that the employment effects for Japan of the removal of its NTBs are much greater as compared to the removal of its tariffs. Japanese tariffs and NTBs evidently protect employment in agriculture, wearing apparel, wood products, and petroleum products, and the results of experiments 1 and 2 indicate that employment in these sectors would therefore decline if Japan's tariffs and NTBs were removed. The declines in agricultural employment of 53.1 and 612.4 thousand man-years are especially noteworthy. There are apparently sizable employment increases in food and kindred products, textiles, paper products, chemicals, iron and steel, and durable manufactures. The effects of the removal of Japan's tariffs and NTBs on sectoral employment in the United States are indicated for experiments 1 and 2 in the right-hand columns of Table 5. These results are quite remarkable insofar as they suggest that employment would rise in U.S. agriculture and fall in practically every other sector. The increase in employment of 140.2 thousand man years in U.S. agriculture due to removal of Japanese NTBs is especially noteworthy.

If we consider next the removal of U.S. tariffs and NTBs, as indicated in experiments 3 and 4 in the right-hand columns of Table 5, the employment effects in the United States are greater for NTBs. This corresponds to what we noted above for Japan, but the absolute magnitudes are much smaller than those calculated for Japan.[7] The positive signs indicate that employment would increase, especially in U.S. agriculture, textiles, wood products, paper products, most durable manufactures, and mining. There would be employment declines in wearing apparel, footwear, rubber products, nonmetallic mineral products, transportation equipment, and the remaining nontradeable sectors. The effects of the removal of U.S. tariffs and NTBs on sectoral employment in Japan, shown in experiments 3 and 4 in the left-hand columns of Table 5, are comparatively small but more varied in terms of being positive or negative.

The final experiment reported is the joint removal of tariffs and NTBs. The results are indicated in column 5 in the two sections of Table 5. The negative effects on employment in Japanese agriculture, wearing apparel, wood products, petroleum products, and nontradeables are reinforced, compared to experiments 1 and 2, and the same is true for the positive employment effects. For the United States the

---

[7] There are several reasons why the results for Japan are larger than for the United States: (1) both tariffs and NTBs appear to be higher in Japan than in the U.S.; (2) the skewness of Japan's NTBs toward agriculture brings about larger positive and negative responses across sectors; (3) Japan has higher exports as a percentage of GDP; and (4) the effect of Japan's policies is absorbed by smaller changes in world prices compared to the United States.

largest absolute employment increase is in agriculture, and there are also noteworthy positive effects in leather products, wood products, paper products, and several durable-goods sectors. There are declines in U.S. employment in food products, textiles and wearing apparel, footwear, rubber products, nonmetallic mineral products, iron and steel, miscellaneous manufactures, and most nontradeable sectors.

Let us now consider the employment effects by occupation that might result from the liberalization of Japanese and U.S. trade policies. The details are given in Table 6 for the same set of experiments described above. We have already noted that the effects of removing Japanese NTBs are much greater than for tariffs. It can be seen from experiment 2 in the left-hand section of Table 6 that the removal of Japan's NTBs would reduce the employment of Japanese farm workers by 600 thousand man-years and that the employment of service workers and professional, technical, management, and administrative workers would also decline. The effect of Japanese liberalization on the United States would be to increase the employment of U.S. farm workers and to reduce the employment of all other occupational groups except nonfarm laborers.

If U.S. tariffs and NTBs were removed, as in experiments 3 and 4 in the right-hand columns of Table 6, there would be reductions in the U.S. employment of professional, technical, management, and administrative workers, sales and clerical workers, and service workers. The employment of craftspeople, operatives, nonfarm laborers, farm workers, and scientists and engineers would increase. The effects on Japan shown in the left-hand columns in Table 6 would be comparatively small reductions in the employment of operatives and farm workers and increases in the other occupational categories.

Finally, the joint removal of tariffs and NTBs indicated in experiment 5 would reinforce the reductions in the employment of Japanese farm workers, service workers, and professional, technical, managerial, and administrative workers and reinforce the employment increases in the other categories. In the United States, the employment of farm workers especially, nonfarm laborers, craftspeople, and scientists and engineers would increase and the other categories would decline.

We mentioned in connection with Table 2 that our approximations of the ad valorem equivalents of NTBs for Japan and the United States were subject to an undetermined margin of error. Having used the high values reported in Table 2 in carrying out the trade-liberalization experiments just described, the question arises as to how sensitive our results may be to the ad valorem equivalents chosen. To determine this, we conducted a series of further experiments

TABLE 5.
Changes in Japanese and U.S. Employment by Industry in Each of the Trade-Liberalization Scenarios (thousands of man-years)

ISIC	Barriers Removed Country(ies) Tariff and/or NTB Sector	Changes in Japanese Employment					Changes in United States Employment				
		1 Japan Tariffs	2 Japan NTBs	3 U.S. Tariffs	4 U.S. NTBs	5 Both Tariffs & NTBs	1 Japan Tariffs	2 Japan NTBs	3 U.S. Tariffs	4 U.S. NTBs	5 Both Tariffs & NTBs
1	Agric., forestry, and fish	-53.1	-612.4	-5.3	-7.1	-739.6	14.9	140.2	14.2	29.3	222.7
310	Food, beverages, and tobacco	8.9	111.5	1.3	4.8	138.4	-0.4	-7.5	3.8	-3.9	-8.5
321	Textiles	34.5	252.4	-15.2	-19.2	276.8	-5.0	-33.6	15.9	18.1	-10.5
322	Wearing apparel	-6.5	-15.8	1.7	7.0	-19.4	0.3	-1.2	-18.9	-67.8	-129.2
323	Leather products	0.4	4.7	-0.4	-0.4	4.8	-0.3	-2.4	6.6	9.6	14.8
324	Footwear	-0.2	1.0	0.1	1.1	2.0	0.0	-0.1	-1.3	-15.7	-19.2
331	Wood products	3.9	-15.5	-0.7	-2.7	-10.1	-0.6	2.7	1.0	6.2	9.9
332	Furniture and fixtures	-0.5	2.6	0.2	0.1	2.6	0.0	-0.2	-0.8	1.9	1.5
341	Paper and paper products	2.8	40.0	-0.8	-3.0	42.5	-0.3	-3.0	6.0	9.6	13.8
342	Printing and publ.	0.5	4.0	0.0	-0.1	4.9	-0.1	-1.0	1.0	-1.5	-1.2
35A	Chemicals	-1.2	65.7	-1.8	-0.5	69.8	0.0	-6.0	4.9	2.4	3.4
35B	Petroleum and rel. prod.	-0.5	-129.7	-0.9	-1.2	-140.5	-0.1	-0.2	1.4	4.1	5.0
355	Rubber products	2.6	20.3	0.0	0.4	25.1	-0.4	-3.1	-2.0	-2.2	-7.0

TABLE 5. (Continued)

ISIC	Barriers Removed Country(ies) Tariff and/or NTB Sector	Changes in Japanese Employment					Changes in United States Employment				
		1 Japan Tariffs	2 Japan NTBs	3 U.S. Tariffs	4 U.S. NTBs	5 Both Tariffs & NTBs	1 Japan Tariffs	2 Japan NTBs	3 U.S. Tariffs	4 U.S. NTBs	5 Both Tariffs & NTBs
36A	Nonmetal. min. prod.	1.4	28.8	0.3	0.6	33.8	-0.1	-1.6	-4.0	-3.9	-9.1
362	Glass and glass prod.	0.1	4.8	0.1	0.0	5.4	-0.0	-0.8	-0.1	1.7	1.1
371	Iron and steel	18.8	346.4	-4.5	-3.0	383.9	-0.8	-11.6	3.1	4.2	-3.6
372	Nonferrous metals	1.3	19.1	-1.3	-2.1	18.8	-0.2	-2.1	3.5	7.1	9.5
381	Metal products	-0.7	25.7	1.3	-0.7	27.6	-0.2	-3.8	-3.0	13.3	9.0
382	Nonelectric mach.	9.9	67.9	-3.9	-6.3	74.0	-0.9	-3.5	26.4	41.7	71.4
383	Electric machinery	6.0	39.0	1.2	-0.4	49.4	-0.6	-3.9	6.2	14.3	19.6
384	Transport. equip.	4.4	40.1	1.3	11.3	61.6	-0.2	1.8	5.4	-5.9	4.8
38A	Misc. manuf.	12.7	169.8	10.9	-12.2	195.4	-1.6	-22.2	-14.3	22.8	-13.4
2	Mining and quarrying	0.6	-58.2	-0.8	-1.3	-63.1	-0.6	-3.8	5.8	15.6	17.4
4	Elec., gas, and water	1.0	36.9	-0.2	-0.3	40.3	-0.1	-1.8	-0.5	-1.0	-3.2
5	Construction	-10.1	-43.7	4.0	9.3	-47.6	0.1	-0.1	0.6	-5.7	-5.6
6	Whol. and retail trade	-15.3	-132.0	6.5	11.7	-137.7	-1.9	-18.2	-19.6	-31.8	-73.3
7	Trans., stor., and com.	-1.2	13.9	0.9	1.1	15.8	-0.4	-4.8	-0.3	-0.2	-5.3
8	Fin., ins., and r. est.	-2.7	-35.0	0.5	1.5	-38.1	-0.4	-5.0	-9.7	-15.6	-30.8
9	Com., soc., and per. s.	-17.8	-252.6	5.4	11.4	-276.8	-0.2	-3.3	-31.2	-46.7	-84.0

TABLE 6.
Changes in Japanese and U.S. Employment by Occupation in Each of the Trade-Liberalization Scenarios (thousands of man-years)

Barriers Removed Country(ies) / Tariff and/or NTB Sector / Occupational Group	Changes in Japanese Employment					Changes in United States Employment				
	1 Japan Tariffs	2 Japan NTBs	3 U.S. Tariffs	4 U.S. NTBs	5 Both Tariffs & NTBs	1 Japan Tariffs	2 Japan NTBs	3 U.S. Tariffs	4 U.S. NTBs	5 Both Tariffs & NTBs
Prof., tech., manag., and admin.	-3.13	-50.05	2.16	3.69	-51.48	-1.08	-11.27	-10.30	-12.88	-34.80
Sales and clerical	-1.24	15.71	5.11	8.34	33.05	-2.39	-24.86	-14.29	-20.92	-63.59
Craftspeople	16.55	228.35	4.46	1.94	271.94	-2.13	-20.11	8.58	14.17	2.56
Operatives	44.89	465.28	-9.36	-13.15	531.01	-6.10	-54.36	10.74	2.15	-71.64
Nonfarm laborers	-0.51	1.97	0.73	1.60	3.97	0.12	2.44	1.37	4.11	9.80
Farm workers	-51.93	-600.23	-5.16	-6.92	-724.61	12.43	116.82	11.85	24.38	185.59
Scientists and engineers	1.00	11.04	-0.06	0.11	13.20	-0.27	-2.48	2.83	5.08	6.54
Services	-5.64	-72.08	2.13	4.38	-77.07	-0.59	-6.18	-10.78	-16.09	-34.45

using the low NTB ad valorem equivalents reported in Table 2 and various combinations of the high and low values for the experiment involving joint removal of Japanese and U.S. tariffs and NTBs. While the results of these sensitivity experiments are too detailed to report here, they tended generally to support our findings reported in Tables 5 and 6, even though the numerical magnitudes were reduced in absolute size when lower ad valorem equivalents were used. That is, even with lower or different combinations of NTB equivalents, the joint removal of Japanese and U.S. tariffs and NTBs would lead to significant employment declines in Japanese agriculture especially as well as in wearing apparel, wood products, petroleum products, and the nontradeable sectors, and increases in employment in the industries noted in Table 5. For the United States, the employment increases remain concentrated in agriculture particularly and durable manufactures, and the declines correspond to those indicated in Table 5. The pattern of results for the occupational groups reported in Table 6 was also broadly unchanged when using the low ad valorem equivalents and different combinations of the high and low equivalents.

Among these sensitivity results it should be noted that the effects on agriculture and farm workers continued to stand out, even when we used the low values for NTBs in the agriculture and food sectors alone. Even though this made the NTBs themselves in these sectors quite ordinary, removal of protection continued to cause large effects on employment in agriculture. These effects are presumably due to the quantitative importance of agricultural trade in these countries noted in Table 3.

Conclusion

We began by noting that Japan's trade policies are often criticized, in the United States especially, for being highly restrictive. But it is not generally clear which sectors the critics have in mind and how the existing protection may affect different occupational groups in Japan and the United States. Our purpose in this paper has been to investigate this issue using measures of pre–Tokyo Round tariffs and constructed ad valorem equivalents of NTBs for Japan and the United States. We conducted a series of experiments using the Michigan Model of World Production and Trade in order to determine the employment effects that might result from different scenarios of trade liberalization. We first assumed the removal of Japanese tariffs while holding constant Japanese NTBs and U.S. tariffs and NTBs. We then conducted an experiment assuming the removal of Japanese NTBs, while holding Japanese tariffs and U.S. trade restrictions constant. Two comparable experiments were performed for the United

States. Our final experiment assumed joint removal of each country's tariffs and ad valorem NTB equivalents. Our principal results were as follows:

1. The employment effects of Japan's NTBs appear to be substantially greater than Japanese tariffs. If Japanese NTBs and tariffs were removed there would be a substantial decline in employment, especially in Japanese agriculture.
2. The removal of Japanese tariffs and NTBs would result in an increase in employment in U.S. agriculture and a decline in practically every other sector in the United States.
3. The employment effects of U.S. NTBs also appear greater than for U.S. tariffs, but the absolute magnitudes are much smaller compared to Japan. If U.S. tariffs and NTBs were removed, the employment increases and declines would be spread among a variety of U.S. industries. The effects on sectoral employment would be fairly small and varied.
4. If tariffs and NTBs were removed in both Japan and the United States, the employment effects already noted for Japan are reinforced. U.S. agricultural employment increases noticeably in this experiment, and there is a variety of increases and declines across the other sectors.
5. In terms of occupational groups, the removal of Japanese tariffs and NTBs would result in a sizable decline especially in the employment of Japanese farm workers and service workers. Japanese trade liberalization would increase the employment of U.S. farm workers and reduce the employment of almost all other occupational groups in the United States.
6. If U.S. tariffs and NTBs were removed, there would be increased employment of craftspeople, operatives, nonfarm laborers, farm workers, and scientists and engineers, and declines in the remaining categories. The effects on Japanese employment would be comparatively small.
7. If there were joint removal of tariffs and NTBs in both countries, the occupational results noted for Japan are reinforced. The same is true for the United States except for operatives, which would decline.
8. A series of sensitivity tests was carried out using low values of the ad valorem equivalents of NTBs and combinations of high and low values. While the absolute values of the employment effects were affected, the patterns of these effects remained unchanged for the most part.

It would of course be interesting to determine if our findings would be altered materially if more accurate measures of NTBs were available. The constructed ad valorem equivalents in Table 2 are based on a variety of methods that are not altogether comparable conceptually and may apply to different years in the span from 1973 to the early 1980s. But unless we have misrepresented the sectoral pattern of NTBs in a systematic fashion, our conclusions should be robust. It may therefore come as a surprise to many observers that American farm workers would be the most likely to gain from trade liberalization in Japan and the United States, while for the most part workers in American manufacturing and services are the least likely to gain.

The research underlying this paper was assisted by grants from the Joint Committee on Japanese Studies of the American Council of Learned Societies and the Social Science Research Council and from the Ford Foundation. We are grateful to Gary Saxonhouse for assistance with the data for Japan and for helpful comments on an earlier version of this paper.

References

Bank of Japan (1979) *Showa gō-jū yon-nen-Kokusai bukka hikaku.* Tokyo.

———(1982) *Showa gō-jū nana-nen-Kokusai bukka hikaku.* Tokyo.

Brown, F. and Whalley, J. (1980) General Equilibrium Evaluations of Tariff-Cutting Proposals in the Tokyo Round and Comparisons to More Extensive Liberalization of Trade, *Economic Journal* (December).

Deardorff, A. V. and Stern, R. M. (1985) Methods of Measurement of Non-tariff Barriers, United Nations Conference on Trade and Development, UNCTAD/ST/MD/28. Geneva: United Nations.

———(1986) *The Michigan Model of World Production and Trade: Theory and Applications.* Cambridge, Mass.: MIT Press.

Morici, P. and Megna, L. L. (1983) *U.S. Economic Policies Affecting Industrial Trade: A Quantitative Assessment.* NPA Report 200. Washington, D.C.: National Planning Association.

Murray, T. and Walter, I. (1978) Special and Differential Liberalization of Quantitative Restrictions on Imports from Developing Countries. In L. Perez (ed.), *Trade Policies Toward Developing Countries: The Multilateral Trade Negotiations.* Washington, D.C.: Agency for International Development.

Petri, Peter A. (1984) *Modeling Japanese–American Foreign Trade: A Study of Asymmetric Interdependence.* Cambridge, Mass.: Harvard University Press.

Roningen, V. O. and Yeats, A. J. (1976) Nontariff Distortions of International

Trade: Some Preliminary Empirical Evidence, *Weltwirtschaftliches Archiv* 112 (4): 613–625.

Saxonhouse, Gary R. (1983) The Micro- and Macroeconomics of Foreign Sales to Japan. In William R. Cline (ed.), *Trade Policy in the 1980s.* Washington, D.C.: Institute for International Economics.

Turner, C. G. (1981) *Quantitative Restrictions on the International Trade of the United States and Japan.* Ph.D. Dissertation, Harvard University.

U.S. Council of Economic Advisers (1984) *Economic Report of the President, February 1984.* Washington, D.C.: U.S. Government Printing Office.

9

Labor Market Rigidities and Protectionism

FRANCO SPINELLI

Introduction

The rise of protectionism that has characterized the last ten years has generated different responses among macroeconomists. Some continue to hold valid the traditional microeconomic analysis of the gains from trade which builds upon the concepts of specialization and comparative advantage and shows that free trade represents the policy that leads to the maximization of consumer welfare. In this view, the new protectionism is obviously seen as a counterproductive development.[1] Others have questioned the validity of the traditional analysis of the gains from trade and contend that it ignores, and cannot provide an answer to, various macroeconomic issues present in a world where markets do not adjust smoothly or efficiently. In particular, some of the critics insist that, under real-wage rigidity, employment and balance-of-payments problems cannot be dealt with by traditional monetary, fiscal, and exchange-rate policies but may require a measure of trade protection.[2] The purpose of this

---

From Catholic University, Milan, Italy.

[1] For a general discussion of the issue along these lines see Johnson (1974), Nowzad (1978), Krauss (1978), and Greenaway (1983).

[2] In particular we are referring to the Cambridge Economic Policy Group; its analysis will be described in the section that follows. On the relationship between nominal wage rigidity and protectionism, see Laursen-Metzler (1950), Mundell (1961), Tower (1973), Boyer (1977), Chan (1978), Johansson and Lofgren (1980, 1981), and Eichengreen (1981).

paper is to discuss the relationship between real-wage rigidity and the case for protectionism.[3]

The paper has five major sections. The next section gives a detailed account of the analytical arguments that lie behind the policy suggestions of the forceful and well-established proprotectionism Cambridge Economic Policy Group (CEPG). First, the CEPG rejects the traditional microwelfare theory of the gains from free trade on the grounds that it is static and assumes full employment. Then it builds a macroeconomic model of the real sector of the economy which shows that protectionism *and* real devaluations are equivalent means of stimulating domestic output and eliminating payments imbalances. Finally, once the model is extended to explain domestic prices, and real-wage rigidity is therefore considered, real devaluations are found to be impossible to achieve and protectionism thus emerges as the only viable policy option. "The Debate on the Analysis and Policy Recommendations of the CEPG" provides a critical appraisal of the model of the CEPG. The discussion focuses on the supply side, on the role it assigns to financial markets as well as on the issue of retaliation. The two following sections consider the subsequent work by Eichengreen, which incorporates aggregate supply and wealth effects into the CEPG analysis. Under real-wage rigidity, tariffs on imports are shown to stimulate or *depress* domestic output, depending on the way the tariff revenues are redistributed. The problem with the Eichengreen analysis is that it too ignores the relationship between protectionism, allocative effects, overall employment levels, and the danger of retaliation. The brief "conclusions" summarize the implications of our analysis for the role of protectionism as a policy instrument.

The Cambridge Economic Policy Group:
Unemployment, the Balance of Payments, and
Protectionism

The Cambridge Economic Policy Group has directed the debate on the gains from protectionism away from the traditional microeconomic analysis and stimulated the present macroeconomic debate. This and the fact that, in certain countries, policy making does appear to be influenced by the work of the group explain why, in this paper, we devote particular attention to such work.

For ten years the CEPG has been suggesting that the United Kingdom[4] move away from free trade as a way out of what the CEPG

---

[3] See Brunner and Meltzer (1978, 1982) for earlier analyses of these issues.

[4] In the April 1979 issue of the *Cambridge Economic Policy Review*, the CEPG argues that "many" countries, the United States included, are facing similar problems and should therefore adopt similar policies.

considers that country's basic economic problem. The problem is described as follows:

> The progressive increase in unemployment during the past decade (each peak and trough exceeding each previous one) and the permanent nature of the recession now developing can be displayed in terms of a deterioration which has been taking place in the "full employment" balance of payments. . . .[5]

and

> . . . the decline of United Kingdom industry relative to competitors . . . should be seen as a cumulative, interlocking process, in which a weak balance of trade has caused slow growth of aggregate demand, resulting in low investment and limited opportunities for development of new products and increased productivity. The consequent distortion in competitive power kept the balance of trade weak and perpetuated stagnation of aggregate demand.[6]

In general, these arguments would not justify greater restrictions on trade; in fact, the theoretical literature on optimal intervention has long shown that, even when a country faces a situation similar to that assumed by the CEPG, protectionism does not come out as a first-best solution.[7] However, the CEPG rejects the traditional microwelfare theory of the gains from trade as well as the analysis of optimal intervention on the grounds that

> The . . . theory . . . is a profound obstacle to comprehension of present-day issues because it is an essentially static analysis in which the level of employment in each country is taken as given, thus assuming away the very problem which needs to be solved.[8]

---

[5] *Cambridge Economic Policy Review*, March 1976, p. 8.

[6] *Cambridge Economic Policy Review*, March 1978, p. 4. As Cuthbertson (1979b) recalls, the CEPG estimates of the elasticity of British exports with respect to world trade and of imports with respect to domestic expenditure are 0.8 and 1.1 percent. Furthermore, the two time-trend coefficients (which pick up long-run effects of quality, design, delivery, and service difference) are −0.7 and 2.4 percent per annum, respectively. Together these estimates imply a secular deterioration in the current-accounts balance.

[7] Chacholiades (1978), Lal (1978, 1979), and Greenaway and Milner (1979) all give compact and useful summaries of the main results of the literature on optimal intervention. The details of the analysis are covered in the classical study by Bhagwati (1971). If we abstract from the case of the optimum tariff and from the few other paradoxical situations that international trade theorists have been able to identify (e.g., Metzler's paradox or the case of immiserizing growth), protectionism never turns out to be the first-best solution, no matter what the distortion is.

[8] *Cambridge Economic Policy Review*, April 1979. See also Nield (1979).

The CEPG then reassesses the issue of free trade versus protectionism in a macroeconomic context with a model designed to show that protectionism is the only solution to the balance of payments and unemployment problems. Since this macroeconomic model forms the basis for the policy recommendations of the CEPG, it needs to be examined in detail. The CEPG model has the following basic components:[9]

$$Y = XP + G + X - H \tag{1}$$

$$YI = XP + G + X - \frac{H}{U} \tag{2}$$

$$X = \beta_0[T_x \cdot P/(e \cdot P^*)]^{-\beta_1} \tag{3}$$

$$H = \beta_2 Y[P/(e \cdot P^* \cdot T_h)]^{\beta_3} \tag{4}$$

$$PX = (P \cdot T_x)^{\beta_4} (e \cdot P^*)^{1-\beta_4}, \qquad 0 < \beta_4 < 1 \tag{5}$$

$$PH = (P/T_h)^{\beta_5} (e \cdot P^*)^{1-\beta_5}, \qquad 0 < \beta_5 < 1 \tag{6}$$

Equations (1) and (2) are the real output and real income identities. Y indicates real output, XP private spending, G government spending, X exports, H imports, YI real income, and U the terms of trade. The determinants of exports and imports are given in Eqs. (3) and (4). βs indicate elasticities, P and P^* domestic and world prices, T_x and T_h one-minus subsidies on exports and one-plus tariffs on imports, and e the price of foreign currency.[10] Exports are assumed to depend positively on subsidies and world prices and negatively on domestic prices; imports are assumed to depend positively on domestic output and prices and negatively on world prices and tariffs. Equations (5) and (6) determine the prices of exports and imports in foreign currency and net of subsidies and tariffs. The two prices, which are a weighted average of world and domestic prices, are affected by trade policy. In particular, exporters and foreign producers are supposed to lower (raise) their prices in foreign currency when subsidies and tariffs rise (fall) at home. A related key assumption is that β_4 is greater than β_5; i.e., the price of exports responds more strongly than the price of imports to changes in trade policy.

On the basis of Eqs. (1) through (6), the CEPG computes the terms of trade (U), the balance of trade (B), and the maximum level of output $\tilde{Y}$ that is consistent with equilibrium in the balance of trade. They are:

---

[9] We follow Cripps and Godley (1976). All nonessential variables are ignored.

[10] Subsidies and tariffs are ad valorem.

$$U = \frac{PX}{PH}[11] = T_x^{\beta_4} \cdot T_h^{\beta_5} \cdot [P/(e \cdot P^*)]^{\beta_4 - \beta_5} \tag{7}$$

$$B = X - \frac{H}{U} = \beta_0[T_x \cdot P/(e \cdot P^*)]^{-\beta_1} - \frac{\beta_2 Y[P/(e \cdot P^*)]^{\beta_3 + \beta_5 - \beta_4}}{T_x^{\beta_4} T_h^{\beta_3 + \beta_5}} \tag{8}$$

$$\tilde{Y} = \frac{\beta_0}{\beta_2} \cdot \frac{T_h^{\beta_3 + \beta_5}}{T_x^{\beta_1 - \beta_4}} [P/(e \cdot P^*)]^{-(\beta_1 + \beta_3 - \beta_4 + \beta_5)} \tag{9}$$

In this model, trade-policy changes (i.e., changes in tariff and subsidy rates) affect both the volumes and the prices of imports and exports and protectionism can reequilibrate the balance of trade and stimulate domestic output; the overall elasticity of B and $\tilde{Y}$ with respect to tariffs is $(\beta_1 - \beta_4)$. Furthermore, the nominal exchange rate and the trade-policy variables (i.e., tariff and subsidy rates) enter Eqs. (8) and (9) in a symmetric way, which implies that a real devaluation[12] has the same effects as an appropriate increase in tariffs and subsidies. Thus both an increase in protectionism and a real exchange-rate devaluation should bring about a lasting improvement in the balance of trade as well as in output and employment.[13]

The conclusion that protectionism is the only effective policy instrument follows from the CEPG's theory of inflation,[14] which is needed to complete the model above and is based on the assumptions of mark-up pricing and real-wage *bill* resistance.[15] Under these assumptions, a real devaluation cannot be carried out: any change in e is bound to be offset by a change of the same magnitude in the ratio of domestic to world prices. The reason is the following. A rise in the nominal exchange rate affects the real-wage bill in two ways. First, from the equation for export prices (Eq. [5]) it is clear that a nominal devaluation leads to a higher ratio of export to domestic prices and therefore shifts the income distribution in favor of export profits. Second, because the drop in the foreign-currency price of exports is greater than the drop in the price of imports—β_4 is assumed to be greater than β_5—a nominal devaluation worsens the terms of trade (Eq. [7]), reduces overall disposable income (Eq. [2]), and thereby

---

[11] The price of exports and the price of domestic output are assumed to be the same.

[12] By real devaluation we mean a change in e given P^*/P.

[13] In principle, "the exchange rate, export subsidies, import tariffs, and import quotas can all be potential effective methods in the medium term for increasing the level of output and employment in a balance-of-payments constrained situation" (Cripps and Godley, 1976).

[14] The theory reflects the analysis developed by Kaldor (1973, 1975, 1976).

[15] Real-wage bill resistance means that labor-market conditions lead to a constant ratio of the nominal wage bill to consumer prices.

widens the gap between the target and actual real-wage bills.[16] Real-wage bill resistance and mark-up pricing then translate such a gap into domestic wage and price inflation. Therefore the competitive margins brought about by devaluation are eroded away and no lasting gain in employment is achieved.[17]

In contrast, trade policy is an effective policy instrument both in the short and in the long run. For example, the imposition of (or increase in) tariffs does not lead to any shift in the distribution of income away from wages because tariffs do not affect the price of exports (Eq. [5]). Furthermore, the imposition of tariffs generates a decline in the foreign-currency price of imports and therefore on *improvement* in the terms of trade. Thus, if anything, the actual real-wage bill rises above its target level and there is no reason for a wage-price spiral to be set in motion.[18]

On the basis of this analysis, the CEPG recommends a policy strategy that combines fiscal- and trade-policy measures. Trade policy should be used to stimulate domestic output and remove any balance-of-trade constraints on its growth.[19] Fiscal policy should be set on a path that is both stable and consistent with the balance-of-trade target: i.e., a fiscal rule should be adopted.[20] No active or just stabilizing role is assigned to monetary policy which is seen as having weak and uncertain effects on private expenditure (Cripps and Godley, 1976; Cripps and Fetherson, 1977).[21]

The Debate on the Analysis and Policy Recommendations of the CEPG

The above analysis and policy recommendations have been controversial.[22] Considering the CEPG's rejection of traditional trade theory, Lal (1978, 1979) notes that the relevance of traditional theory is not limited to the cases where the assumptions of perfect markets

---

[16] The workers' target real-wage bill is treated as exogenous. The wage-push component of the inflationary process is seen as a function of the difference between the target and the actual wage bills.

[17] From the equations above it is clear that initially the price of exports falls relative to the price of imports.

[18] The case of the imposition of quotas is even more clear-cut; neither the income distribution nor the terms of trade are affected.

[19] The existence of such a constraint on the growth of output is due to the fact that imports are a function of output. See Eq. (2) above.

[20] We use the term *rule* because of the evident analogy between this policy recommendation for fiscal policy and the Friedmanian recommendation for monetary policy. In both cases there is much emphasis on the need for stability of the policy impulses and in both cases the policy instrument is assigned to the control of the variable—prices in the case of Friedman, the balance of payments in the case of CEPG—believed to be most influenced by the instrument itself. In the next section we

and full employment hold. Indeed, trade theory is often concerned with ranking the effectiveness of alternative policies (including protection) when the perfectly competitive assumptions break down. In particular, even with real-wage rigidity, protection appears to be inferior to various other forms of domestic intervention.

As for the macroeconomic analysis of the CEPG, there are several reasons to believe that it does not adequately support the hypothesis that protectionism creates an expansionary effect.[23] Critics have focused in particular on the supply side of the model. First, because the model has only one good and disregards the interrelationship between profits, productivity, investment, and the balance of trade, the welfare losses due to the departure from free trade are ignored.[24] Second, trade policy leads to an increase in domestic output rather than in its price only if there is a demand-determined level of output and if the labor supply schedule is perfectly horizontal at a given real wage,[25] i.e., if firms are systematically off their labor-demand curves (Blinder [1978], Eichengreen [1979, 1981, 1983]). Third, Eqs. (5) and (6) above are based on the assumptions that (1) trade policy can generate a permanent change in the terms of

---

explain why the CEPG believes that there is a strong, almost one-to-one, relationship between fiscal policy and the balance of payments.

[21] This is not surprising given that, de facto, the model ignores the financial markets. In the section that follows we will come back to this point.

[22] The suggestion that a fiscal rule be adopted follows naturally from the assumption of an *aggregate private* expenditure function which is stable and has a unit marginal propensity to spend. Since this function is not central to our analysis, it is sufficient to note that quite a few studies have raised doubts about it and therefore about the fiscal rule itself. See Worswick (1974), Bispham (1975), Cripps and Godley (1976), Rowan (1976), Higgins (1976), Vines (1976), Blinder (1978), Russell and Wakeman (1978), Greenaway and Milner (1979), Cuthbertson (1979a, b), Chrystal (1979, 1981a, 1981b, 1983), Chrystal and Darnell (1983), Anyadike-Danes (1982, 1983).

[23] A priori, there are reasons to think that, under real-wage rigidity, a country might have to rely on protectionism. First, it is well known that real-wage flexibility is central to the case for free trade, as shown, for example, in Stolper and Samuelson (1941). Second, the macroeconomic literature (Mundell, 1960; Modigliani and Padao-Schioppa, 1978; Argy and Salop, 1979; Branson and Rotemberg, 1980; and Sachs, 1980) has shown that, under real-wage rigidity, a real devaluation may be difficult to achieve. Third, the same literature seems to suggest that, if protectionism is deflationary under nominal wage rigidity, it might turn out to be expansionary under real-wage rigidity.

[24] See Corden, Little, and Scott (1975); Corbet (1977); Batchelor and Minford (1977). At the same time, it is difficult to see how the CEPG can possibly praise tariffs for not raising profits and for stimulating investment spending at the same time (Corbet, 1977; Corden, 1977; Greenaway and Milner, 1979; Scott, 1980; Gould, Mills, and Stewart, 1981).

[25] See Hall (1978), Cuthbertson (1979b), Blinder (1978). Blinder and Hall maintain that what Fetherson and Godley (1978) simulate is not the imposition of quotas but a simple drop in the demand for foreign goods.

trade, (2) causation runs from domestic to world prices,[26] and (3) the prices of domestic goods do not rise with increases in the prices of foreign goods (fixed mark-ups) but importers and exporters respond immediately to foreign price changes (variable mark-ups).[27] The CEPG's analysis of the role of financial markets and monetary policy also appears to be controversial. In fact, even when trade imbalances persist and exchange rates and nominal interest rates remain pegged, demand for and supply of financial assets (which include domestic money and domestic and foreign banks) are assumed to be equal at all times. Rowan (1976), Frenkel (1978), and Blinder (1978) have pointed out that such a continuous equality is unlikely. Thus the CEPG generally ignores the consequences of its proposed strategy on the financial markets and, as a result, it is not clear whether the strategy could be maintained in the medium and long term.

Finally, there is the issue of retaliation. While the CEPG initially acknowledged that retaliation was possible,[28] its model did not incorporate the effects of such retaliation. Recently, however, it was noted that ". . . competition for market shares is now intense and any attempt by one country to steal a march over others is hotly contested. Retaliation, whether in response to devaluation, import controls, or support for domestic industry, now appears all too likely.[29]

Since the CEPG's analysis has not yet satisfactorily specified the determinants of aggregate supply, the role of financial markets,

---

[26] Notice that these two assumptions plus those of mark-up pricing and real-wage resistance imply that domestic prices are completely determined by labor costs and taxes; even world prices do not enter the process.

[27] The empirical evidence the CEPG refers to in its analysis (Coutts, Godley, and Nordhaus, 1977) is limited. See Corden (1977), Batchelor and Minford (1977), Smith (1978), Blinder (1978), Lal (1978), Beenstock and Burns (1979), Scott (1980), Allsopp and Joshi (1980). In their criticism of the assumption that the imposition of tariffs does not lead to higher domestic prices, Batchelor and Minford write "very little published work has been directed at estimating the price response of home producers to profit opportunities which are opened up by increases in import prices. At an aggregate level, some indirect evidence does exist. For example, British producers, faced with similar opportunities in export markets, tend to take up half of any competitive gap in price increases . . . and it has been calculated that price-cost margins in British industry are some 50 percent lower in industries with no significant protection from foreign competition."

[28] *Cambridge Economic Policy Review*, March 1976.

[29] *Cambridge Economic Policy Review*, April 1982. There is no doubt that the level of tariffs advocated by the CEPG has always been very high. According to the April 1980 issue of the *Cambridge Economic Policy Review*, by 1990 tariffs should be as high as 70 percent. Hindley (1977) does alternative calculations of the implicit tariff and comes out with a set of figures ranging between 40 and 400 percent. Batchelor and Minford (1977) maintain that tariffs in excess of 100 percent are necessary to remove a deficit of 3.5 to 4 percent. Scott (1980) says that the CEPG analysis implies a uniform tariff of 50 percent in 1985 and 100 percent in 1990.

or the danger of retaliation, it has not yet been shown that the case for protectionism can be based solely on the assumption of real-wage rigidity.

Real-Wage Rigidity, Flexible Exchange Rates, and the Gains from Protectionism: A Second-Generation Model

The issue of the relationship between real-wage rigidity and the case for protectionism has been investigated further by Eichengreen (1979, 1983). The supply side of his small macroeconomic model, which combines real-wage rigidity and the asset approach to exchange-rate determination, represents the most important departure from the previous analysis of the CEPG and is the key to understanding Eichengreen's overall results. Firms are assumed to be on their demand for labor schedule which implies

$$Y = Y(P/W), \qquad Y' > 0 \tag{10}$$

where again Y indicates real output, P its price, and W nominal wages. The labor supply is perfectly elastic at a fixed real wage, which is defined in terms of consumer prices (PC)

$$w = W/PC \tag{11}$$

and then normalized to one. Consumer prices are a weighted average of domestic and world prices

$$PC = P^\alpha (TeP^*)^{1-\alpha}, \qquad 0 < \alpha < 1 \tag{12}$$

where T is equal to one plus the tariff rate, e is the price of foreign currency, and P^* the price of imports in foreign currency.

Combining the above expressions yields the aggregate supply curve

$$Y = Y[(tT)^{\alpha-1}], \qquad Y' > 0 \tag{13}$$

where $t = eP^*/P$.

Equation (13) is familiar in the literature on real-wage rigidity and implies that more output will be supplied *if* the price of domestic output rises relative to the cost of living.

Economic agents hold domestic (M) and foreign (M^*) currency.[30] Since it is assumed that the exchange rate is never expected to change, the two assets are held in fixed proportion

---

[30] Bonds are ignored. Formally, the model of the CEPG allows for domestic and foreign bonds; de facto, however, because of the assumption of a constant interest rate, it also ignores bonds.

$$\frac{M}{eM^*} = c \qquad (14)$$

where c is constant.

Nominal wealth is defined as

$$NW = M + eM^* \qquad (15)$$

Under the assumption of a balanced budget, M is constant so that the trade account (which alters M^*) and the exchange rate are the only sources of variation in the nominal stock of wealth.[31] One can thus write

$$\dot{M}^* = \left(Y - \frac{E}{P}\right)\left(\frac{P}{eP^*}\right) = \frac{S}{e} \qquad (16)$$

where E and S indicate nominal expenditure and nominal savings. As in the CEPG model, savings are supposed to be zero in the long run. In the short run, however, they are a fraction of the gap between actual wealth and desired wealth, which is a function of income from the sale of domestic product and government transfers R. Formally,

$$S = u[vP(Y + R) - NW] \qquad (17)$$

R will equal the revenue from tariffs

$$R = (T - 1)(1 - \delta)\left[Y - u\left(vY - \frac{M}{P} - tM^*\right)\right] \qquad (18)$$

Finally, demand for output is defined as the sum of domestic and world demand

$$Y = \delta(tT) + X(t), \qquad S', X' > 0 \qquad (19)$$

In contrast to the CEPG model, the presence of supplyside effects implies that t $(=eP^*/P)$ and P now move to clear the markets for goods and assets. By imposing the long-run equilibrium condition $(\dot{M}^* = S = 0)$ the whole system reduced to two equations:

$$Y[(tT)^{\alpha-1}] = \delta(tT)|(1-uv)Y[(tT)^{\alpha-1}] + (1 + c)utM^*| + X(t) \qquad (20)$$

$$0 = \frac{1}{t}u|vY[(tT)^{\alpha-1}] - (1 + c)tM^*| \qquad (21)$$

The two schedules, which give the combinations of t and M^* yielding internal (Eq. [20]) and external (Eq. [21]) equilibrium, are both

---

[31] Tariffs are the only source of revenue, and this is always redistributed to either the general public or firms only.

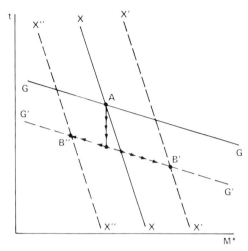

FIGURE 1. Graphical exposition of Eichengreen's model: internal (*G*) and external (*X*) equilibrium schedules.

negatively sloped in the tM^* space (see Figure 1). As t rises, the supply of output falls and demand for it rises; a drop in wealth (a decline in M^*) is required to reestablish equilibrium in the market for goods. Similarly, as t rises, the domestic-currency value of nominal wealth rises above its desired level; a drop in M^* is required to reestablish equilibrium in the market for assets.[32]

After showing that monetary and exchange-rate policies are incapable of stimulating output in this model, Eichengreen considers the effects of trade policy. A higher tariff raises the relative price of foreign goods and stimulates demand for domestic output while at the same time lowering its supply (Eq. [13]). The resulting excess demand for domestic goods can be eliminated through a decline in either M^* or $t(=eP^*/P)$. In Figure 1, the internal equilibrium schedule (*G*) shifts to the left as the tariff is increased. The external equilibrium schedule (*X*) may shift either up or down depending on the relative size of the elasticities of aggregate supply, Y', and the tariff revenue, R', with respect to the terms of trade t. Given R', the lower Y' the smaller the drop in the supply of output due to the imposition of tariffs and the greater the chance of getting a higher overall $P(Y+R)$ sum. In its turn, such higher sum would imply an increased demand for wealth and therefore a set of balance-of-payments surpluses. At the same time, given Y', demand for wealth is

---

[32] Dynamic stability requires that the absolute value of the slope of the internal balance condition be less than the absolute value of the slope of the external balance condition. Examination of the two total differentials in the neighborhood of long-run equilibrium reveals that the stability condition is met.

positively related to R'.[33] Thus, in Figure 1 we could wind up at B' or
B''; in one case there is a balance-of-trade surplus and in the other a
deficit. This analysis also explains why protectionism cannot lead to
a loss of foreign reserves in the model of the CEPG. In fact, the model
assumes that the supply of output is not responsive to changes in the
terms of trade; i.e., it assumes that $Y' = 0$.[34]

Although the effect of trade policy on the balance of payments
depends upon the values of certain behavioral parameters, the output response is policy-determined: output drops or rises depending
on whether the tariff revenues are neutrally redistributed to the
whole private sector via lump-sum subsidies or are passed on to
firms. Consider the situation where tariff revenues are neutrally redistributed. Since it is customary to exclude the Metzler paradox,
the imposition of a tariff is expected to increase tT (= price of imports inclusive of tariffs) and real wages to firms. Thus, although the
demand for domestic output rises, its supply *drops* as the demand
for labor is reduced by higher real wages. In the analysis of the CEPG,
the possibility that protectionism might be deflationary does not
arise because there is not any aggregate supply constraint and output
is entirely demand-determined.

If tariff revenues are redistributed to firms, the Eichengreen
model supports the conclusion that trade policy is expansionary.
Under this assumption, the extra wage costs to firms due to the
imposition of tariffs are exactly offset by the transfer of revenues
from the authorities. T therefore drops out of the aggregate supply
curve, which becomes

$$Y = Y(t^{\alpha-1}).^{35} \tag{13a}$$

Since the ratio eP^*/P declines, the imposition of tariffs reduces

---

[33] A large R' implies an inelastic domestic and foreign demand for output.
Notice that a large marginal propensity to consume improves the likelihood of this
result.

[34] Furthermore, unlike Eichengreen, the CEPG assumes that the marginal propensity to consume is unit even in the short run and that, therefore, R' is high.

[35] The total production subsidy will be $R = (1 - \delta)Ye(T - 1)$ and subsidy per
unit of output $R = (1 - \delta)e(T - 1)$. The supply function becomes

$$Y = Y\left[\frac{P + r}{P^\alpha(TeP^*)^{1-\alpha}}\right]$$

Through successive transformations one obtains (Eq. [13a]).

the real wage seen by firms and therefore both the demand for and the supply of output rise.[36]

Eichengreen Model: Extensions, Modifications, and the Problem of Research Strategy

The short-run impact of trade policy has also been considered by Eichengreen (1983). The short-run scenario is one where real wages adjust slowly to their target level and, as a consequence, real-wage rigidity is not a binding constraint. When trade policy is implemented and the prices of imports and domestic goods rise, the short-run nominal wage stickiness translates into a drop in real wages to firms. Production therefore rises independently of the way tariff revenues are redistributed.[37]

A second extension of the model is to allow the relative demands for domestic and foreign moneys to depend upon the expected rate of change in the exchange rate. Consider the case where a change in trade policy would result in a series of balance-of-trade deficits. If economic agents are rational and trade-account deficits lead to a devaluation in the long run, then there would be an immediate depreciation of the exchange rate and an increase in the domestic currency value of total wealth. This larger stock of wealth increases the excess demand for goods, which requires an even larger improvement in the terms of trade to clear the goods market. Similarly, if trade policy leads to a set of current-account surpluses, the price of foreign currency falls instantaneously and the domestic currency value of the overall stock of wealth declines. These changes yield a smaller increase in the demand for domestic goods. Thus a demand for wealth that is a function of changes in the exchange rate helps generate short-run movements in output which are in the same direction as long-run movements.[38]

Further modifications of the basic model could be considered. For instance, domestic producers could be allowed to have market power in both home and foreign markets. World prices would thus

---

[36] One final point on the comparison between the CEPG and Eichengreen models. In both cases tariffs lead to an improvement in the terms of trade, but the reasons are different. According to the CEPG, foreign producers lower their prices, whereas in the Eichengreen model, domestic prices rise to clear the domestic market for goods.

[37] Of course, in the long run real wages are back to their target level and the results of the previous analysis still apply.

[38] As Eichengreen (1979) points out, a priori one cannot exclude the situation where the instantaneous revaluation of the currency and the effects of changes in wealth on absorption are so large that demand for goods *drops* and a short-run *worsening* in the terms of trade follows. In this case output overshoots its long-run lower level.

affect profits and labor-market utilization.[39] Alternatively, the demand for nominal wealth could be made to depend upon consumer rather than producer prices and the case of a negative stock of foreign wealth—i.e., foreign indebtedness—could also be considered.[40] However, none of the modifications we have mentioned so far leads to rejection of the long-run results that were discussed in the previous section.

The Eichengreen analysis significantly improves on the model of the CEPG by introducing supply constraints, adopting a more general theory of price determination, and allowing for feedbacks between trade flows to the domestic economy via changes in the stock of wealth. However, there is still the question of whether the analysis contains all the key elements needed to satisfactorily settle the issues concerning the short- and long-run effects of trade policy.

According to the CEPG and Eichengreen[41] one has to choose between the standard microwelfare and the macroeconomic approaches to the analysis of protectionism. The fact is, however, that these two approaches are complementary and that any one-good model is inappropriate for analyzing the effects of protectionism. To stress this, it suffices to recall that (1) the fundamental concept of effective protection rests on the distinction between imports and exports and (2) a further distinction between imports, import-competing goods, exports, and nontraded goods is required to consider effective protection in a general equilibrium context.[42] In such a context, protectionism raises the price of imports and therefore shifts demand toward import-competing goods, nontraded goods, and exportables. As a result of foreign competition and higher wages at home, the export sector is crowded out. The drop in employment in this sector can offset the rise in employment elsewhere in the domestic economy. The empirical evidence—see, for instance, the results of the simulations of the general equilibrium Otani model of the Australian economy[43]—supports this analysis.

A second major problem is that there has been little consideration of the effects of protectionism based on nontariff barriers. According to Greenaway (1983),

---

[39] In this situation, the way that aggregate supply responds to foreign prices depends on the relative weight with which these prices enter the determination of firms' profits and consumer prices. On this, see Branson and Rotemberg (1980).

[40] See Boyer (1977).

[41] It should be pointed out that Eichengreen is perfectly aware of the problem.

[42] See GATT (1982). In this context, Greenaway (1983) gives quantitative estimates of the effects of protectionism on consumer welfare.

[43] See Dixon (1979) and Dixon et al. (1983). GATT (1982) also reports that analysis of the actual experience of a number of countries suggests that, on average, some two-thirds of the import duty is shifted onto the export sector.

> Recent developments . . . have resulted in the importance of
> the tariff as an instrument of trade policy being challenged.
> Employment pressures in Western markets in the 1970s have
> been met by widespread protectionist pressures and actions, as
> similar pressures were met in the 1930s. The important qualita-
> tive difference between the two periods is that recently rela-
> tively little use has been made of the tariff. Instead we have
> witnessed a widespread proliferation of non-tariff interven-
> tions—quantitative restrictions, subsidisation and discrimina-
> tory procedures—which have collectively become known as the
> "new protectionism." "New" applies here in both a chronologi-
> cal sense and to distinguish the instruments employed from
> those used in the "old protectionism."

These developments raise the questions of whether (1) real-wage
rigidity provides a rationale for the new protectionism and (2) the
combination of real-wage rigidity and new protectionism alters the
impact of stabilization programs.[44]

A third problem relates to the danger of retaliation. The CEPG
and Eichengreen analyses seem to reflect the belief that retaliation
does not have to be modeled explicitly and that one can simply
modify the results of the standard analysis to reflect potential retaliation. But how meaningful would such a two-step procedure be?

Finally, the literature does not adequately discuss the issues of
why real wages might turn out to be rigid and whether or not one can
rely on the assumption of perfectly constant real wages. Three considerations are in order here. First, if the cause of real-wage rigidity
is to be seen in the pressures of trade unions, then it is not clear why
the adoption of trade policy should translate into higher levels of
employment and output rather than into higher real wages. Second,
even if real-wage rigidity justified the adoption of protectionism by
one country, retaliation could lead to the spread of protectionism to
countries which do not suffer from real-wage rigidity. Third and
most important, as both the literature on real-wage rigidity and Eichengreen (1983) indicate, only under the extreme assumption of
perfect real-wage rigidity do standard fiscal, monetary, and exchange-rate policies turn out to be ineffective in dealing with balance-of-payments and unemployment problems. The question that
has not been addressed so far is what the relationship is between
various degrees of real-wage rigidity and the relative effectiveness of
trade and traditional macroeconomic policies.

---

[44] Since protectionism is basically a substitute for changes in relative prices,
the adjustment processes could be more costly in terms of unemployment. See Tumlir
(1983a, b).

Conclusions

This paper discusses the macroeconomic literature on the relationship between real-wage rigidity and protectionism. The protectionist policy strategy designed by the Cambridge Economic Policy Group is based on (1) the rejection of the traditional trade-theory case against protectionism and (2) a macroeconomic model which implies that trade policy represents the only effective way out of balance of payments and employment problems.

The analysis of the work of the Cambridge Group has indicated several major shortcomings. First, in order to evaluate adequately the issue of free trade versus protectionism, the micro- and macroeconomic approaches have to be combined. Second, the CEPG's model involves an inadequate specification of aggregate supply for an open economy and disregards both the role of financial variables and the danger of retaliation. Thus critics have often argued that the Group has been unable to provide a rigorous analytical case for protectionism.

Subsequent work by Eichengreen has incorporated aggregate supply factors and the role of financial markets. In this analysis, tariffs may stimulate or depress domestic output depending on how tariff revenues are distributed. Despite the improvements in the basic model, the Eichengreen analysis does not fully examine the relationship between real-wage rigidity and the case for protectionism. In particular, there is still no integration of the microeconomic and macroeconomic approaches to analyzing the effects of trade policy and there is no consideration of the danger of retaliation and protection based on nontariff barriers.

I wish to thank Sheetal Chand, Donald Mathieson, Salvatore Schiavo-Campo, George von Furstenberg, and Cliff Wymer for helpful discussions on the topic.

References

Allsopp, C. and Joshi, V. (1980) Alternative Strategies for the U.K., *National Institute Economic Review* 91 (February): 86–103.

Anyadike-Danes, M. (1982) The "New Cambridge" Hypothesis and Fiscal Planning, *Cambridge Economic Policy Review* 8 (April): 33–38.

——(1983) A "Comment" on Chrystal, *Journal of Monetary Economics* 11; 133–135.

Argy, V. and Salop, J. (1979) Price and Output Effects of Monetary and

Fiscal Policy Under Flexible Exchange Rates, *IMF Staff Papers* 26 (June): 224–256.

Batchelor, R. and Minford, P. (1977) Import Controls and Devaluation as Medium-Term Policies, in Corbet et al. (1977), pp. 46–97.

Beenstock, M. and Burns, T. (1979) Exchange Rate Objectives and Macroeconomic Adjustment in the United Kingdom. In R. Mayor (ed.), *Britain's Trade and Exchange-Rate Policy*. London: Heinemann. Pp. 96–122.

Bhagwati, J. N. (1971) The Generalized Theory of Distortions and Welfare. In J. N. Bhagwati et. al. (eds.), *Trade, Balance of Payments and Growth*. Amsterdam: North-Holland. Pp. 69–90.

Bispham, J. A. (1975) The New Cambridge and Monetarist Criticism of "Conventional" Economic Policy-Making, *National Institute Economic Review* 74 (November): 39–55.

Blinder, A. S. (1978) What's New and What's Keynesian in the New Cambridge Keynesianism? In Brunner and Meltzer (1978), pp. 67–86.

Boyer, R. S. (1977) Commercial Policy Under Alternative Exchange Rate Regimes, *Canadian Journal of Economics* 10 (May): 218–232.

Branson, W. H. and Rotemberg, J. J. (1980) International Adjustment with Wage Rigidity, *European Economic Review* 13: 309–332.

Brunner, K. and Meltzer, A. H. (eds.) (1978) *Public Policies in Open Economies*. Amsterdam: North-Holland.

——(1982) *Monetary Regimes and Protectionism*. Amsterdam: North-Holland.

Chacholiades, M. (1978) *International Trade Theory and Policy*. New York: McGraw-Hill.

Chan, K. S. (1978) The Employment Efforts of Tariffs Under a Free Exchange Rate Regime: A Monetary Approach, *Journal of International Economics* 8: 415–423.

Chrystal, K. A. (1979) *Controversies in British Macroeconomics*. Oxford: Philip Allan.

——(1981a) The "New Cambridge" Aggregate Expenditure Function: The Emperor's Old Clothes?, *Journal of Monetary Economics* 7: 395–402.

——(1981b) The New Cambridge Aggregate Expenditure Function: Correction and Confirmation. Discussion Paper, Department of Economics, University of Essex (November).

——(1983) The New Cambridge Aggregate Expenditure Function: A Reply, *Journal of Monetary Economics* 11: 137–138.

Chrystal, K. A. and Darnell, A. C. (1983) The Aggregate Expenditure Function Again. Department of Economics, University of Essex, mimeographed.

Corbet, H. (1977) Britain's Predicament in the Struggle for an Open World Economy. In Corbet et. al. (1977), pp. 1–23.

Corbet, H. et al. (1977) *On How to Cope with Britain's Trade Position.* London: Trade Policy Research Centre.

Corden, W. M. (1971) *The Theory of Protection.* Oxford: Clarendon Press.

——(1977) General Analysis of Import Controls for Balance-of-Payments Purposes. In Corbet et. al. (1977), pp. 24–33.

Corden, W. M., Little, I. M. D., and Scott, M. F. (1975) Import Controls Versus Devaluation and Britain's Economic Prospects. Guest Paper No. 2. London: Trade Policy Research Centre.

Coutts, K., Godley, W. and Nordhaus, W. (1977) *Industrial Pricing in the United Kingdom.* Cambridge, Eng.: Cambridge University Press.

Cripps, F. and Godley, W. (1976) A Formal Analysis of the Cambridge Economic Policy Group Model, *Economica* 43 (November): 335–368.

Cripps, F. and Fetherson, M. (1977) The Role of Monetary Policy in Economic Management, *Cambridge Economic Policy Review* 3 (March): chap. 4.

Cuthbertson, K. (1979a) Demand Management and the "New School": A Comment, *Applied Economics* 11 (March): 71–75.

——(1979b) *Macroeconomic Policy: The New Cambridge, Keynesian and Monetarist Controversies.* New York: Wiley.

Dixon, P. B. (1979) A Skeletal Version of Orani 78: Theory, Data, Computations and Results, Impact Project, Working Paper OP-24, University of Melbourne (June).

Dixon, P. B., Parmenter, B. R., and Powell, A. A. (1983) Trade Liberalization and Labor Market Disruption, Impact Project, Working Paper G-46, Melbourne, University of Melbourne (July).

Eichengreen, B. J. (1979) Protection, Real Wage Resistance and Employment: An Analysis of Some Proposals of the Cambridge Economic Policy Group. Board of Governors of the Federal Reserve System, International Finance Discussion Papers, 150 (September).

——(1981) A Dynamic Model of Tariffs, Output and Employment under Flexible Exchange Rates, *Journal of International Economics* 11: 341–359.

——(1983) Protection, Real Wage Resistance and Employment, *Weltwirtschaftliches Archiv.* 119 (3):429–452.

Fetherson, M. J. and Godley, W. A. H. (1978) New Cambridge Macroeconomics and Global Monetarism: Some Issues in the Conduct of U.K. Economic Policy. In Brunner and Meltzer (1978), pp. 33–66.

Frenkel, J. A. (1978) New Cambridge Macroeconomic and Global Monetarism: A Comment. In Brunner and Meltzer (1978), pp. 91–96.

GATT (1982), *International Trade 1981/82.* Geneva: GATT.

Gould, B., Mills, J. and Stewart, S. (1981) *Monetarism or Prosperity?* London: Macmillan.

Greenaway, D. (1983) *Trade Policy and the New Protectionism.* New York: St. Martin's Press.

Greenaway, D. and Milner, C. (1979) *Protectionism Again . . . ? Causes and Consequences of a Retreat from Freer Trade to Economic Nationalism.* London: Institute of Economic Affairs.

Hall, R. (1978) A Comment on the Fetherson and Godley and Posner Papers. In Brunner and Meltzer (1978), pp. 87–90.

Higgins, C. I. (1976) Some Observations on the Cambridge New School of Economic Policy, *Australian Economic Papers* 15 (December): 201-229.

Hindley, B. (1977) Britain's Economy as Seen by the Cambridge Group. In Corbet et. al. (1977), pp. 34–43.

Johansson, P. O. and Lofgren, K. G. (1980) The Effects of Tariffs and Real Wages on Employment in a Barro-Grossman Model of an Open Economy, *Scandinavian Journal of Economics* 82: 167–183.

———(1981) A Note on Employment Effects of Tariffs in a Small Open Economy, *Weltwirtschaftliches Archiv.* 117: 578–583.

Johnson, H. J. (ed.) (1974) *The New Mercantilism.* Oxford: Basil Blackwell.

Kahn, R. and Posner, M. (1974) Cambridge Economics and the Balance of Payments, *The Times,* London (April 17th and 18th).

Kaldor, N. (1973) Counter Inflation Policy, *The Times,* London, March 13, p. 30.

———(1975) What Is Wrong with Economic Theory, *Quarterly Journal of Economics* 89 (August): 347–357.

———(1976) Inflation and Recession in the World Economy, *Economic Journal* 86 (December):703–714.

Krauss, M. B. (1978) *The New Protectionism: The Welfare State and International Trade.* New York: New York University Press.

Lal, D. (1978) The Wistful Mercantilism of Mr. Dell, *World Economy* 1 (June): 263–277.

Laursen, S. and Metzler, L. A. (1950) Flexible Exchange Rates and the Theory of Employment, *Review of Economics and Statistics* 32 (November): 281–299.

Modigliani, F. and Padao-Schioppa, T. (1978) Management of an Open Economy with "100% Plus" Wage Indexation. *Essays in International Finance* 130. Princeton: Princeton University Press.

Mundell, R. (1960) The Monetary Dynamics of International Adjustment Under Fixed and Flexible Exchange Rates, *Quarterly Journal of Economics* 74 (May): 227–257.

———(1961) Flexible Exchange Rates and Employment Policy, *Canadian Journal of Economics* 27 (November): 509–517.

Nield, R. R. (1979) Managed Trade Between Industrial Countries. In Mayor (ed.), pp. 5–23.

Nowzad, B. (1978) *The Rise in Protectionism.* Washington, D.C.: IMF.

Rowan, D. C. (1976) Godley's Law, Godley's Rule and the New Cambridge Macroeconomics, *BNL Quarterly Review* 29 (June): 151–174.

Russell, T. and Wakeman, L. M. (1978) New Cambridge—Economics Without Markets: A Comment. In Brunner and Meltzer (1978), pp. 95–102.

Sachs, J. (1980) Wages, Flexible Exchange Rates and Macroeconomic Policy, *Quarterly Journal of Economics* 44 (June): 731–747.

Scott, M. F. G. (1980) *The Case Against General Import Restrictions*. London: Trade Policy Research Centre.

Smith, G. W. (1978) Price Determination. In M. Parkin and M. T. Sumner (eds.), *Inflation in the United Kingdom*. Manchester: Manchester University Press. Pp. 93–111.

Stolper, W. F. and Samuelson, P. A. (1941) Protection and Real Wages, *Review of Economic Studies* 9: 58–75.

Tower, E. (1973) Commercial Policy Under Fixed and Flexible Exchange Rates, *Quarterly Journal of Economics* 87 (August): 436–454.

Tumlir, J. (1983a) Trade Policy and Current Economic Problems. In Shadow Open Market Committee, Policy Statement and Position Papers, Graduate School of Management, University of Rochester, Rochester, March 6–7, pp. 47–55.

————(1983b) Statement on Protectionism to SOMC. In Shadow Open Market Committee, Policy Statements and Position Papers, Graduate School of Management, University of Rochester, September 18–19, pp. 53–60.

Vines, D. (1976) Economic Policy for an Open Economy: Resolution of the New School's Elegant Paradoxes, *Australian Economic Papers* 15, 27 (December):207–229.

Worswick, G. N. D. (1974) Influences on the Balance of Payments and Budget Deficit, Letter to *The Times of London*, January 28.

10

United States–Japan Trade Frictions and Competitiveness

TOSHIKO TANGE

Introduction

In recent years Japan has increased its share of manufacturing exports in world markets while the United States has lost its shares in most areas of manufacture. The huge bilateral trade imbalances resulting from these diverse trade performances between the two countries have been a source of intensifying trade frictions and have provoked some protectionist movements. These trends reflect the changing competitive positions of the two countries—a continuous improvement in Japan's competitiveness in international markets and a decline in the U.S. overall competitive position. We are concerned with the relative export competitiveness, which is one of the underlying factors for the recent trade frictions between the two countries.

The relative competitive position of a country in the world market is basically determined by its relative costs, which are in turn associated with its relative export prices vis-à-vis those of other countries. Although both demand and supply factors affect the determination of prices, supply or cost conditions become more important in the long-run analysis of export competitiveness. This paper thus examines the cost competitiveness of Japan's manufacturing exports relative to U.S. exports. Tange (1983) investigated the relationships among export performance, unit costs, and technical

From Kanto Gakuin University, Yokohama, Japan.

change between Japanese and U.S. manufacturing industries over the period 1957–1974. In the face of the changing world, with higher oil prices combined with overall slowdown of productivity growth since 1974 as Denison (1983) points out, we update this line of study for 1975–1981 and compare the present work with the former one.

In this study the unit cost of an industry is determined by using the estimated rates of technical progress, factor price changes, and output growth. Relative cost competitiveness among countries refers to the intercountry differences in the rate of change in unit costs. It is assumed that the wider these differences, the greater would be the differences in exports. Technical progress in this framework is assumed to affect export performance of a country through its effect on costs. This paper assesses how far intercountry differences in the estimated rate of technical progress and the resulting cost advantage are related to intercountry differences in export performance of Japanese and U.S. industries.

Model and Methodology[1]

To examine export competitiveness of Japanese and U.S. manufacturing industries, we assume that their relative exports are related to their relative prices by the following equation:[2]

$$E_j^J/E_j^U = a_j(P_j^J/P_j^U)^{b_j} \tag{1}$$

where E stands for exports, P for output price, b for the elasticity of substitution, and a for a constant. Superscripts J and U denote Japan and the United States, respectively. Subscript j indicates industry.

Prices are subject to the influence of both demand and supply conditions. However, focusing on the supply side of the long-run export price competitiveness, we assume that prices in each country are determined by a mark-up on average cost:[3]

---

[1] This section is based on Tange (1983).

[2] An elasticity-of-substitution framework has been subject to theoretical criticism because of rigid assumptions required for its validity. However, it should be noted that its hypothesis has been supported by several studies. See Leamer and Stern (1970), Kravis and Lipsey (1971), and Richardson (1973).

[3] The relationship between cost and price is explained in the present context by either marginal cost pricing or mark-up pricing. By the former method, which is generally considered to fit the assumption of perfect competition, price is equated to marginal cost at the cost-minimizing or the profit-maximizing output level. By the latter method, which is regarded as more relevant for noncompetitive situations, price is set at the level which adds a mark-up to average cost. In the Cobb–Douglas case of this study, they both amount to the same theory.

$$P_j^I = m_j^I(AC_j^I) \text{ and } P_j^U = m_j^U(AC_j^U) \tag{2}$$

where m is a constant mark-up factor and AC is average costs.

Substituting Eq. (2) into (1), Eq. (1) can be transformed into the following rate of percentage change form:

$$\frac{\dot{E}_j^I}{E_j^I} - \frac{\dot{E}_j^U}{E_j^U} = b_j \left(\frac{\dot{P}_j^I}{P_j^I} - \frac{\dot{P}_j^U}{P_j^U} \right) = b_j \left(\frac{A\dot{C}_j^I}{AC_j^I} - \frac{A\dot{C}_j^U}{AC_j^U} \right). \tag{3}$$

Thus intercountry differences in export performance between the two countries are a function of intercountry differences in the rates of change in average costs.

Now, average costs are derived on the basis of a cost-minimization Cobb–Douglas framework. The Cobb–Douglas production function is written as

$$X_j = A_j e^{\lambda_j t} L_j^{\alpha_j} K_j^{\beta_j} \prod_i X_{ij}^{\gamma_{ij}} \tag{4}$$

where X is gross output (including intermediate products), L is labor input, K is capital input, and X_{ij} is the ith intermediate input used in the production of the jth industry. λ is the rate of Hicks-neutral technical progress. α, β, and γ_i are output elasticities with respect to labor, capital, and the ith intermediate input, respectively.

With inputs priced competitively, the corresponding total costs are defined as

$$C_j = w_j L_j + r_j K_j + \sum_i P_i X_{ij} \tag{5}$$

where C is total costs, w is wage rates, r is the rate of return on capital, and P_i is the price of the ith intermediate input.

Minimizing total costs (Eq. [5]) subject to the production function (Eq. [4]), we obtain the following marginal productivity conditions. Subscript j is deleted for simplification.

$$\frac{\beta}{\alpha} = \frac{rK}{wL} \tag{6}$$

and

$$\frac{\gamma_i}{\alpha} = \frac{P_i X_i}{wL}. \tag{7}$$

The average cost is given by

$$AC = SX^{\frac{1-S}{S}} (Ae^{\lambda t} \alpha^\alpha \beta^\beta \Pi \gamma_i^{\gamma_i})^{\frac{-1}{S}} (w^\alpha r^\beta \Pi P_i^{\gamma_i})^{\frac{1}{S}} \tag{8}$$

where $S = \alpha + \beta + \Sigma \gamma_i$. The rates of percentage change in average cost turn out to be

$$\frac{\dot{AC}}{AC} = \frac{\alpha}{S} \cdot \frac{\dot{w}}{w} + \frac{\beta}{S} \cdot \frac{\dot{r}}{r} + \Sigma \left(\frac{\gamma_i}{S} \cdot \frac{\dot{P}_i}{P_i} \right) + \frac{(1-S)}{S} \cdot \frac{\dot{X}}{X} - \frac{1}{S} \cdot \lambda . \tag{9}$$

Thus the rate of change in average cost is determined by the rates of percentage change in factor prices, output growth, and in the rate of technical progress. It is shown that a higher rate of technical progress may lead to a slower rate of change in unit costs. Technical progress in this sense is observed in a cost-reducing process.

Substituting Eq. (9) into Eq. (3), the hypothesis implied by Eq. (3) is that a country's industry with a higher rate of technical progress relative to the other country may have a slower rate of change in unit costs and may result in a higher rate of export growth. We test the hypothesis by the following cross-section regression (across industries) equation:

$$\dot{E}^J_j/E^J_j - \dot{E}^U_j/E^U_j = c_1 + c_2 (\hat{AC}^J_j/AC^J_j - \hat{AC}^U_j/AC^U_j) + u_j \tag{10}$$

$$\dot{E}^J_j/E^J_j - \dot{E}^U_j/E^U_j = d_1 + d_2 (\hat{\lambda}^J_j - \hat{\lambda}^U_j) + v_j \tag{11}$$

where the symbol $(\wedge)$ over the variables denotes the estimate of the variables; u and v stand for error terms.

To obtain the rate of change in unit cost and the rate of technical progress by industry for both countries we require a time-series estimation of the Cobb–Douglas production function. Adding an error term, e_t, in order to account for technical uncertainties, we have the Cobb–Douglas production function in natural logarithmic form:

$$\ln X_t = \ln A + \lambda t + \alpha \ln L_t + \beta \ln K_t + \Sigma \gamma_i \ln X_{it} + e_t \tag{12}$$

In order to avoid difficulties involved in a direct estimation of Eq. (12), we use the factor shares method by which we can obtain consistent estimates of the coefficients.[4] This is a two-step estimation method: the parameters of the marginal productivity conditions are estimated from the observed factor shares and then the remaining parameters of the production functions are estimated by the ordinary least squares regression method.[5]

---

[4] A direct estimation of this equation may be a questionable method. Explanatory variables, labor, capital, and intermediate inputs tend to be endogenous and hence are not likely to be independent of the error term. In this situation the ordinary least squares estimates may be subject to simultaneous equations bias. Explanatory variables are also not likely to be independent of one another and may cause a problem of multicollinearity.

[5] The following section is based on Klein (1974, pp. 327–333).

The marginal productivity conditions in stochastic form are given by

$$\ln\left(\frac{r_t K_t}{w_t L_t}\right) = \ln\left(\frac{\beta}{\alpha}\right) + \varepsilon_t \tag{13}$$

and

$$\ln\left(\frac{P_{it} X_{it}}{w_t L_t}\right) = \ln\left(\frac{\gamma_i}{\alpha}\right) + \mu_t \tag{14}$$

where ε_t and μ_t are error terms that reflect an incomplete cost-minimization process.

Either Eq. (13) or Eq. (14) has one dependent and one explanatory variable. If we assume error terms have zero expected values, we have the estimates of $\ln(\beta/\alpha)$ and $\ln(\gamma_i/\alpha)$ as the following means:

$$\widehat{\ln\left(\frac{\beta}{\alpha}\right)} = \frac{1}{T} \sum_{t=1}^{T} \ln\left(\frac{r_t K_t}{w_t L_t}\right) \tag{15}$$

and

$$\widehat{\ln\left(\frac{\gamma_i}{\alpha}\right)} = \frac{1}{T} \sum_{t=1}^{T} \ln\left(\frac{P_{it} X_{it}}{w_t L_t}\right) \tag{16}$$

where the sample serves for $t = 1, 2, \ldots, T$. Taking antilogarithms of $\widehat{\ln(\beta/\alpha)}$ and $\widehat{\ln(\gamma_i/\alpha)}$, we have the consistent estimates of β/α and γ_i/α, respectively. The next step is to obtain the estimates of the remaining parameters of the production function. Imposing $\widehat{(\beta/\alpha)}$ and $\widehat{(\gamma_i/\alpha)}$ thus obtained on Eq. (12), we have

$$\ln X_t = \ln A + \lambda t + \alpha[\ln L_t + \widehat{(\beta/\alpha)}\ln K_t + \Sigma\widehat{(\gamma_i/\alpha)}\ln X_{it}] + e_t. \tag{17}$$

$\ln X_t$ is regressed on t and the new variable in parentheses to obtain $\widehat{\ln A}, \widehat{\lambda}$, and $\widehat{\alpha}$. $\widehat{\beta}$ and $\widehat{\gamma_i}$ are estimated as $\widehat{\alpha}$ multiplied by $\widehat{\beta/\alpha}$ and $\widehat{\gamma_i/\alpha}$, respectively. Therefore, $\widehat{\beta}$ and $\widehat{\gamma_i}$ are not subject to any statistical test.

Having obtained the parameter estimates of the Cobb–Douglas production functions by industry, we can calculate the rate of percentage change in unit costs according to Eq. (9).

Empirical Results

Tables 1 and 2 summarize the time-series estimates of the Cobb–Douglas production functions for Japanese and U.S. manufacturing

TABLE 1.
Estimates of the Cobb–Douglas Production Functions—Japan.

Industry	1957–1974						1975–1981					
	λ	α	β	$\Sigma\gamma_i$	constant	$\bar{R}^2$	λ	α	β	$\Sigma\gamma_i$	constant	$\bar{R}^{2a}$
1. Food	—	—	—	—	—	—	0.012 (2.12)	0.071 (3.43)	0.059	0.458	5.188	.965
2. Textiles	0.025 (5.56)	0.126 (11.84)	0.139	0.668	2.208	.997	0.016 (3.52)	0.187 (2.67)	0.084	0.736	1.878	.637
3. Paper Products	0.026 (4.29)	0.118 (14.93)	0.134	0.680	2.318	.999	0.003* (1.38)	0.153 (14.05)	0.121	0.880	0.943	.983^c
4. Chemicals	0.030 (2.94)	0.168 (10.94)	0.236	0.704	0.197	.999^b	0.024 (2.13)	0.154 (2.72)	0.125	0.852	1.227	.935
5. Primary Metals	0.015 (3.72)	0.116 (30.13)	0.136	0.768	0.952	.999	0.006* (1.49)	0.095 (7.33)	0.122	1.066	−0.746	.772
6. Metal Products	0.019 (2.59)	0.193 (18.98)	0.187	0.581	1.867	.999	0.027 (3.77)	0.390 (4.22)	0.072	0.682	0.888	.981
7. Machinery	0.033 (4.45)	0.138 (16.89)	0.204	0.535	3.145	.998	0.054 (3.99)	0.140 (1.96)	0.036	0.364	5.441	.997
8. Electrical Machinery	0.055 (6.41)	0.151 (15.57)	0.161	0.584	2.758	.998	0.053 (3.20)	0.247 (6.27)	0.147	0.713	1.431	.997
9. Transportation Equipment	0.055 (4.57)	0.120 (9.85)	0.122	0.564	4.045	.999	0.033 (3.98)	0.131 (4.86)	0.082	0.484	4.343	.995^d

^{a} $\bar{R}^2$ indicates the coefficient of multiple determination which is adjusted for the degree of freedom. The figures in parentheses are t-statistics. The estimates without asterisks are significant at the 5 percent level and the estimates with an asterisk are significant at the 10-percent level.
^{b} The period covered in the estimation is 1957–1973.
^{c} The period covered in the estimation is 1970–1979.
^{d} The period covered in the estimation is 1970–1981.

TABLE 2.
Estimates of the Cobb–Douglas Production Functions—The United States.

Industry	1957–1974						1975–1981					
	λ	α	β	$\Sigma\gamma_i$	constant	$\bar{R}^2$	λ	α	β	$\Sigma\gamma_i$	constant	$\bar{R}^2$
1. Food	—	—	—	—	—	—	0.019 (4.82)	0.071 (4.07)	0.021	0.781	6.683	.981
2. Textile	0.016 (3.11)	0.229 (5.87)	0.077	0.511	3.409	.987[a]	0.012 (2.85)	0.147 (3.88)	0.023	0.706	6.170	.889[b]
3. Paper Products	0.016 (2.78)	0.204 (4.88)	0.120	0.437	4.089	.992	−0.007* (−1.54)	0.228 (10.37)	0.058	1.165	3.740	.982[c]
4. Chemicals	0.027 (3.50)	0.155 (3.76)	0.157	0.311	5.254	.989	0.023 (3.11)	0.107 (5.67)	0.039	0.619	7.223	.982
5. Primary Metals	−0.005* (−1.48)	0.261 (10.50)	0.098	0.591	2.985	.961	−0.006* (−1.79)	0.229 (11.87)	0.034	1.186	3.523	.962
6. Fabricated Metals	0.007* (1.58)	0.410 (9.72)	0.067	0.588	1.909	.989[a]	0.010 (2.54)	0.231 (8.23)	0.042	0.779	5.295	.953[c]
7. Machinery	0.014 (3.94)	0.341 (12.16)	0.125	0.401	3.479	.993	0.028 (3.27)	0.125 (3.0)	0.024	0.358	8.244	.977
8. Electrical Machinery	0.026 (8.24)	0.290 (14.43)	0.118	0.351	4.338	.996	0.023 (2.10)	0.228 (4.94)	0.035	0.599	6.264	.983
9. Transportation Equipment	0.016 (4.05)	0.292 (9.25)	0.108	0.577	2.946	.975	0.019 (6.47)	0.149 (15.28)	0.023	0.671	6.525	.981

[a] The period covered is 1957–1973.
[b] The period covered is 1970–1981.
[c] The period covered is 1974–1981.

industries, respectively. The choice of industries is determined by availability of data. Nine manufacturing industries are chosen for this study. The periods covered in the estimation are basically 1957–1974 and 1975–1981. However, different periods are used for some industries.[6] The results for the 1957–1974 period are taken from Tange (1983, pp. 322–325). The appendix explains variables and data sources.

All estimates of labor coefficients, α for both Japanese and U.S. industries, are highly significant with positive signs as expected. Most estimates of the rates of technical progress, λ, are also highly significant with positive signs. U.S. primary metals, however, show the negative rates of technical progress for both 1957–1974 and 1975–1981 periods. As for this industry, Kendrick and Grossman (1980), and Gollop and Jorgenson (1980) obtained the negative rates of technical progress for the periods of 1966–1976 and 1966–1973, respectively. These results seem to represent that technical sluggishness has been continuously experienced in the U.S. steel industry during the 1970s as well as the 1960s.

It is shown that the pace of technical change for most industries slowed during the years following the first oil crisis. It is also presented that in all cases but one (the food industry), Japanese industries attained higher rates of technical change relative to the corresponding U.S. industries for both periods on a case-by-case basis. Gollop and Jorgenson (1980) and Kendrick and Grossman (1980) reported the estimates of total factor productivities of U.S. industries. Based on the same method used by Gollop and Jorgenson, Kuroda (1981) estimated the productivity growth of Japanese industries. He pointed out that U.S. productivity growth, on the whole, tended to decline in the late 1960s while Japanese productivity growth rose continuously until 1973. Since their method and periods are different from the present study, their results are not strictly comparable with ours. However, one can say that, taken together, these studies are roughly consistent with ours.

Table 3 reports annual average rates of change in unit costs of Japanese and U.S. manufacturing industries and the determinants of the intercountry differences between them.[7] Unit costs are calculated by using the parameter estimates of the Cobb–Douglas production functions at the industry level, factor prices, and output data. An interperiod comparison for each country shows that unit costs in most industries grew faster for 1975–1981 than those for 1957–1974.

---

[6] Explanations for the different periods covered in the study are given in the footnote of Tables 1 and 2.

[7] The rates of change in variables are estimated by regressing the logarithms of variables on time.

TABLE 3.
The Rates of Change in Unit Costs of Japanese and U.S. Manufacturing Industries and the Determinants of Their Intercountry Differences

Industry	Growth Rates of Unit Costs			Decomposition of Intercountry Differences				
	Japan	U.S.A.	Difference	Wage Effect	Return on Capital Effect	Intermediate Input Price Effect	Output Effect	Technical Progress Effect
1957-1974								
Food	0.0212	—	—	—	—	—	—	—
Textiles	0.0168	0.0105	0.0063	0.0062	0.0037	0.0073	-0.0037	-0.0073
Paper Products	0.0274	0.0180	0.0094	0.0032	0.0068	0.0111	-0.0051	-0.0067
Chemicals	-0.0011	0.0078	-0.0089	0.0109	0.0092	0.0036	-0.0483	0.0158
Primary Metals	0.0095	0.0319	-0.0224	0.0012	0.0040	-0.0044	-0.0041	-0.0192
Metal Products	0.0231	0.0207	0.0024	0.0146	-0.0036	-0.0043	0.0095	-0.0139
Machinery	0.0150	0.0187	-0.0037	0.0046	-0.0014	-0.0006	0.0146	-0.0532
Electrical Machinery	-0.0057	0.0056	-0.0113	0.0046	0.0099	0.0008	0.0018	-0.0282
Transportation Equipment	0.0025	0.0151	-0.0126	0.0	-0.0014	-0.0032	0.0447	-0.0526
1975-1981								
Food	0.0283	0.0478	-0.0195	0.0025	-0.0056	-0.0342	0.0167	0.0011
Textiles	0.0359	0.0534	-0.0175	-0.0001	0.0074	-0.0203	-0.0021	-0.0025
Paper Products	0.0361	0.0752	-0.0391	-0.0039	-0.0073	-0.0314	0.0107	-0.0072
Chemicals	0.0523	0.0658	-0.0135	-0.0021	0.0136	-0.0085	-0.0253	0.0088
Primary Metals	0.0457	0.0948	-0.0491	-0.0107	0.0090	-0.0341	-0.0050	-0.0085
Metal Products	0.0303	0.0692	-0.0389	0.0022	0.0037	-0.0254	-0.0047	-0.0147
Machinery	0.0171	0.0837	-0.0666	-0.0033	-0.0019	-0.0362	0.0204	-0.0455
Electrical Machinery	-0.0191	0.0656	-0.0847	-0.0066	0.0080	-0.0364	-0.0283	-0.0215
Transportation Equipment	0.0309	0.0755	-0.0446	-0.0023	-0.0025	-0.0492	0.0343	-0.0249

Since intercountry differences refer to the percentage changes in the Japanese values less the percentage changes in the U.S. values, negative values shown in the table indicate relatively favorable effects to Japan. That is, Japanese unit costs rose less rapidly than U.S. unit costs. These intercountry differences reveal that some of the U.S. industries such as textiles, paper, and metal products enjoyed favorable cost advantage relative to Japanese industries for the first period, while all U.S. industries lost their relative cost advantage for the second period.

In order to analyze what factors account for these changes in relative cost advantage between Japan and the United States, the intercountry differences in unit-cost changes are decomposed into the weighted rates of changes in factor prices, gross output, and technical progress. It is exhibited that the relative effects of different factors vary among industries and between periods. However, it is shown that as a whole the leading factors to gain Japan's comparative cost advantage for the second period were the technical progress effect, intermediate input price effect, and to a lesser degree the wage effect. Faced with a sudden increase in oil prices in 1973, Japanese firms seem to have adjusted their production method to the new situation by saving their energy consumption and restraining wage increases as well as by keeping relatively high technical progress. All of these factors in turn have contributed to slow their cost increases relative to the U.S. counterparts.

It is important to note that Japanese wage rates by industry rose less rapidly for 1975–1981 than for 1957–1974 while U.S. wage rates grew faster for 1975–1981 than for 1957–1974 (not shown). As a result, Japan's wage rates rose more than U.S. wage rates for 1957–1974, while the relationship was reversed for 1975–1981. This result reveals that, in the face of a substantial rise in oil prices coupled with the declining pace of productivity growth, U.S. wage rates rose more rapidly after the first oil crisis.

We carried out regressions across industries, as formulated in Eqs. (10) and (11), in order to examine the extent to which intercountry differences in export growth between Japanese and U.S. industries can be explained by intercountry differences in unit-cost changes and technical change. The results are shown in Table 4. We found that for both periods the coefficient estimates with respect to relative unit-cost changes were highly significant with negative signs as expected. The findings suggest that the relatively high export growth of Japanese industries is associated with relatively slow increases in their unit costs in comparison with U.S. industries. We obtained the highly significant estimate for the second period in the regression with respect to the relative technical change. This indicates the close relationship between relative export performance and

TABLE 4.
Regressions Explaining Intercountry Differences in Export Growth of Japanese and U.S. Manufacturing Industries

Period	Dependent Variable	Independent Variable			
		Constant	$AC^{\cdot J}/AC^{J} - AC^{\cdot U}/AC^{U}$	$\lambda^{J} - \lambda^{U}$	$\bar{R}^{2}$
1957–1974	$E^{\cdot J}/E^{J} - E^{\cdot U}/E^{U}$	0.107 (9.21)	−3.031 (−2.94)		.521
1975–1981	$E^{\cdot J}/E^{J} - E^{\cdot U}/E^{U}$	−0.066* (−1.73)	−2.494 (−3.06)		.079
1957–1974	$E^{\cdot J}/E^{J} - E^{\cdot U}/E^{U}$	0.094 (3.46)		1.628** (1.27)	.511
1975–1981	$E^{\cdot J}/E^{J} - E^{\cdot U}/E^{U}$	−0.017** (−0.60)		4.568 (2.57)	.412

Note: Estimates without asterisks are significant at the 5 percent level.
* indicates significant at the 10 percent level.
** indicates insignificant at the 10 percent level.

relative technical change for the second period, while this is not the case for the first period.

Additional exercises were performed to supplement the importance of the supply-side variables in each country. We regressed across industries each country's export growth on (a) the rate of percentage change in its unit costs and (b) the rate of its technical progress. The findings are given in Table 5. It is shown that export growth of Japanese industries bears significant correlation with either the technical progress or the cost variable, while in the case of U.S. industries no significant relationship is observed between export performance and either unit-cost change or technical progress. Even in those cases in which U.S. industries demonstrate lower rates of change in average cost for the 1957–1974 period relative to Japanese industries, the resulting cost advantage is not reflected in their export performance. These findings suggest that something continues to be wrong with the linkage between technical progress, cost growth, and export growth for U.S. industries for 1975–1981 as well as for 1957–1974. Similarly, Lawrence (1979) indicates that costs and prices in Japanese export industries grew less rapidly, while those for the United States decreased only slightly, relative to each country's total manufacturing as a whole.

Conclusions

We have been concerned with relative cost competitiveness of Japanese and U.S. manufacturing industries. Our findings can be summarized as follows: Interperiod comparison for each country reveals

TABLE 5.
Regressions Relating Export Growth to Unit-Cost Changes and Technical Change—Japan and the United States

Period	Dependent Variable	Japan Independent Variable				United States Independent Variable			
		Constant	ȦC/AC	λ	R̄²	Constant	ȦC/AC	λ	R̄²
1957–1974	Ė/E	0.238	−3.843		.336	0.101	−1.142**		7.05
		(8.56)	(−2.25)			(3.53)	(−0.72)		
1975–1981	Ė/E	0.231	−2.459		.636	0.094**	0.414**		.129
		(10.52)	(−3.87)			(0.92)	(0.29)		
1957–1974	Ė/E	0.110		2.706	.289	0.058		1.696*	.122
		(2.49)		(2.06)		(2.79)		(1.40)	
1975–1981	Ė/E	0.087		2.902	.755	0.097		1.975**	.082
		(4.90)		(5.06)		(3.60)		(1.31)	

See Table 4 for explanation.

that the pace of technical progress decelerated after the first oil crisis. Intercountry comparison shows that most of the Japanese industries attained higher rates of technical progress than those of the corresponding U.S. counterparts for both periods.

Intercountry differences in manufacturing export growth between the two countries were negatively and significantly correlated with intercountry differences in unit-cost changes. Technical progress was an important determinant of relative export performance for 1975–1981. However, this is not the case for 1957–1974.

For each country, Japanese industries with relatively high rates of technical progress were those with relatively slow growth in costs and those with relatively high rates of export growth. By contrast, U.S. industries did not demonstrate such a close relationship among productivity growth, cost change, and export performance, though in some cases they attained much slower rates of cost change relative to Japanese industries.

It is concluded that productivity growth and cost factors remain influential in determining export performance of the countries for both periods. Important problems with respect to the competitiveness of U.S. industries are not only their lower productivity growth relative to those of Japanese industries, but also the lack of association of their productivity growth and the following cost advantage with their export performance. In the face of the changing surroundings after 1973, it also seems likely that the adjustment mechanism of the Japanese economy works successfully, whereas that of the U.S. economy works poorly.

Taken together, these outcomes suggest that as far as relative competitiveness between Japanese and U.S. manufacturing industries is concerned, a similar tendency is observed between 1957–1974 and 1975–1981 periods. That is, over the entire period Japanese industries continue to be in gaining position while U.S. industries in losing position. It can be said that this situation has been the background of the recent trade frictions between Japan and the United States.

Our analysis has ignored the effect of changes in foreign-exchange rates on the relative export performance. The appreciation of the exchange rate of the yen observed in the 1970s seems to exert unfavorable effects on all Japanese exporters in the same way. Nevertheless, it appears that the relative cost advantage of Japanese exports was strong enough to offset such an unfavorable exchange-rate influence and to expand their exports.

214 T. Tange

References

Bodkin, R. G. and Klein, L. R. (1967) Nonlinear Estimation of Aggregate Production Functions, *Review of Economics and Statistics* 49: 28–44.

Denison, E. F. (1983) The Interruption of Productivity Growth in the United States, *Economic Journal* 93: 56–77.

Gollop, F. M. and Jorgenson, D. W. (1980) U.S. Productivity Growth by Industry. In *New Developments in Productivity Measurement and Analysis* (J. W. Kendrick and B. N. Vaccara, eds.). Chicago: University of Chicago Press.

Kendrick, J. W. and Grossman, E. S. (1980) *Productivity in the United States.* Baltimore: Johns Hopkins University Press.

Klein, L. R. (1974) *A Texbook of Econometrics.* Englewood Cliffs, N.J.: Prentice-Hall.

Kravis, I.B. and Lipsey, R. E. (1971) *Price Competitiveness in World Trade.* New York: Columbia University Press.

Kuroda, M. (1981) Nihon Keizai no Seisansei Suii to Shijo no Performance (Productivity Changes and Market Performance), *Kikan Gendai Keizai* 43: 56–72.

Lawrence, R. Z. (1979) Toward a Better Understanding of Trade Balance Trends: The Cost-Price Puzzle. *Brookings Papers on Economic Activity,* 191–212.

Leamer, E. E. and Stern, R. M. (1970) *Quantitative International Economics.* Chicago: Aldine.

Richardson, J. D. (1973) Beyond (But Back to?) the Elasticity of Substitution in International Trade, *European Economic Review* 4: 381–392.

Tange, T. (1983) Trade Frictions and Productivity Performance—Technological, Price, and Cost Competitiveness of Japan and U.S. Exports, *Journal of Policy Modeling* 5: 313–331.

APPENDIX: VARIABLES AND DATA SOURCES

		Sources	
	Variables	*Japan*	*U.S.A.*
X	Gross output in constant prices (see note below)	4	7
L	Man-hours per year		
	Japan: Persons employed times average hours worked	2,3	
	U.S.A.: Total employee payrolls divided by average wage per man-hour of production workers		8,9
K	Gross capital stock in constant prices	5	10
X_i	The ith intermediate input in constant prices (see note below)	4,6	7–9,11
R	The value of raw materials	4	8,9
wL	Wage income	4	7
w	Wage rate = wL/L		
rK	Nonwage income	4	7
r	The rate of return on capital = rK/K		
E	The value of exports	12	12

Notes. The notes below are mainly applied to the data for 1975–1981. The time-series data on variables except exports are expressed by each country's currency units. Exports which are expressed in millions of U.S. dollars are measured as values of exports, since in the case of the United States, there is no appropriate price index to deflate these values. The data on real variables for Japanese industries are shown in 1975 constant prices and those for U.S. industries in 1972 constant prices.

U.S. gross output in constant prices was estimated as the industrial production indexes multiplied by the base-year gross output in constant prices which were obtained from the 1972 input-output table.

We relied on interpolation and extrapolation techniques to obtain the time series of inter-industry flows of intermediate inputs which are not readily available. The 1970–1975–1980 link input-output tables (expressed in 1980 constant prices) for Japan and the 1967, 1972, and 1977 input-output tables (expressed in current prices) for the United States were chosen as the benchmark tables. Input sectors of origin were aggregated into thirty-four sectors for Japan and thirty-nine sectors for the United States. By the use of these tables we computed the composition coefficients of intermediate inputs within each industry for the benchmark years. The composition coefficients of intermediate inputs for years without input-output tables were estimated by either linear interpolation or linear extrapolation of the benchmark composition coefficients. For some years when the extrapolated composition coefficients showed large negative values, we employed a nonlinear extrapolation method. Finally, the time series of total values of intermediate inputs (in constant prices) used in each industry were multiplied by the respective composition coefficients in each year in order to secure the time series of intermediate inputs disaggregated by industry and by originating input sector.

Sources: For Japan: (1) Bank of Japan, *Price Indexes Annual;* (2) Ministry of International Trade and Industry, *Census of Manufactures;* (3) Ministry of Labor, *Yearbook of Labor Statistics;* (4) Office of the Prime Minister, Economic Planning Agency, *Annual Report on National Accounts;* (5) EPA, *Capital Stock of Private Enterprises, 1965–1983;* (6) EPA, Ministry of Agriculture and Forestry, Ministry of International Trade and Industry, Ministry of Transportation, Ministry of Labor, and Ministry of Construction, *1970–1975–1980 Link Input-Output Tables (Tape).*

For the United States: (7) U.S. Bureau of Economic Analysis, *Survey of Current Business;* (8) U.S. Bureau of the Census, *Annual Survey of Manufactures;* (9) U.S. Bureau of the Census, *United States Census of Manufactures;* (10) U.S. Bureau of Industrial Economics, *1984 U.S. Industrial Outlook;* (11) U.S. Bureau of Labor Statistics, *Producer Prices and Price Indexes.*

For both countries: (12) Organization for Economic Cooperation and Development, *Trade by Commodities.*

11

Aggregate Costs
to the United States
of Tariffs and Quotas
on Imports

DAVID G. TARR AND MORRIS E. MORKRE

Introduction

How much would the U.S. economy gain from removing tariffs and quotas imposed on imports? To answer this question, we have estimated the aggregate costs to the economy resulting from tariffs on all products and also from quotas that existed as of December 1984 on imports in four significant industries: automobiles, textiles, steel, and sugar. The costs to the economy represent the amount by which tariffs and the particular quotas lower real national income. They thus represent the benefits to the U.S. economy that would result from removal of these restrictions. Since there are other quotas that impose costs not included in these figures, the combination of the costs of tariffs and of these quotas provide a conservative estimate of the costs of trade restrictions that existed as of December 1984.[1]

    The aggregate benefits from removing all existing tariffs and the existing quotas studied are estimated to be $9.29 billion per

From Bureau of Economics, Federal Trade Commission, Washington, D.C.

[1] Of course, the trade restrictions in existence evolve over time. Since the publication of our 1984 monograph, the quotas on automobiles have been removed. The monograph necessarily estimated the costs of the tariffs and quotas in existence at the time of its release.

TABLE 1.
Summary Table
Aggregate Costs to the Economy of the Restraints Considered:
Annual Costs and Cumulative Costs Over Four Years* (in billions
of 1984 dollars)**

	Annual Costs	Present Value of Costs over Four Years
Total costs of all tariffs and quotas examined	$9.29	$33.70
All tariffs	7.01	25.41
Quotas, net cost of all esti- mated	2.28	8.29
Automobile "VRA"	1.04	3.76
Sugar quota	0.26	0.95
Textile quota on Hong Kong	0.39	1.41
Steel quota	0.81	2.95
Less: maximum estimated terms-of-trade welfare loss from quota removal	−0.22	−0.78

* Although an aggregate costs-to-consumers estimate is not presented, costs to consumers are greater than the costs to the economy. Thus the costs-to-the-economy estimate may be used as a lower bound estimate of the costs to consumers.
** Due to rounding, the totals may differ from the sum of the entries in the columns relevant to the total.

year.[2] *The benefits over four years have a present value of $33.70 billion.* These estimates, as well as the separate estimates of the costs of tariffs and of the four individual quotas, are summarized in Table 1. (See the last section for details.)

The adjustment costs that would be borne by domestic re- sources if the tariffs and quotas were removed were also estimated. The estimated adjustment costs are compared with the aggregate benefits of removing the restrictions; benefit-adjustment cost com- parisons are also made in three of the four industries in which quo- tas are analyzed and in the context of the multilateral removal of all tariffs.[3]

---

[2] All numbers in this summary are updated to 1984 dollars. The Tarr and Morkre (1984) monograph itself expressed all estimates in 1983 dollars. These num- bers also correct for an error that appeared in the monograph (footnote 6 provides details). Unless otherwise indicated, the source of all the estimates is our 1984 mono- graph with appropriate updating.

[3] In the analysis of the sugar industry, it is assumed that when the quota is removed it is replaced by a direct-subsidy scheme or by a purchase-resale arrange- ment such that domestic growers continue to be guaranteed the minimum level of receipts available under the current domestic price-support program. As a result, there are no adjustment costs borne by domestic resources. See Tarr and Morkre (1984, chap. 4) for a discussion of this issue.

The methodology employed for arriving at an estimate of the aggregate cost of all the restraints takes into account potential problems of interrelatedness and terms-of-trade effects. The estimated costs and benefits to the United States of a multilateral elimination of all tariffs are derived from general equilibrium models. Partial equilibrium analysis is used to determine the effects of removing quotas in the automobile, sugar, and textile industries and of imposing a new quota on the importation of steel. Finally, the expressions *costs to consumers* and *costs to the economy* are used extensively in this paper. These terms are explained in our 1984 monograph (and especially in Morkre and Tarr [1980, chap. 2]).

The following sections examine, in turn, multilateral elimination of all tariffs and import quotas on automobiles, sugar, textiles, and steel. We conclude with a discussion of the aggregate costs and benefits to the economy of the import restraints that are examined.

Multilateral Elimination of All Tariffs

The importance of tariffs as a barrier to international trade has declined during the postwar period as a result of several Multilateral Tariff Negotiation (MTN) rounds. Between 1946 and 1984 the average tariff rate for the United States declined from 10.3 percent to 3.7 percent. The most recent MTN, the Tokyo Round, calls for further cuts in tariff rates phased in over an eight-year period beginning in 1980.

We develop estimates of the welfare effects that would accrue to the United States if all tariffs that remain after the Tokyo Round are reduced to zero. The starting point for these estimates is the work of Brown and Whalley (1980), and Baldwin and Lewis (1978).[4] They adopt a methodology based on multilateral as opposed to unilateral tariff reductions.[5] Full multilateral removal of all tariffs is found to generate a gain in real income for the U.S. economy of at least $7.01 billion per year (Table 2). It is determined from results of a study based on 1973 data, which we have adjusted upward for the growth in nominal GNP.[6]

---

[4] For additional information about the results of the Baldwin and Lewis paper see Baldwin, Mutti, and Richardson (1980).

[5] There is a question of whether unilateral removal of all U.S. tariffs will improve U.S. real income. Because U.S. imports and exports are not an inconsiderable proportion of total world trade, slightly more than 13 percent in 1984, such an action may cause an adverse movement in the terms of trade, the ratio of price of exports to the price of imports. Some empirical results suggest U.S. real income would decline from such an action. In contrast, recent empirical studies of multilateral tariff reductions indicate that U.S. welfare would improve. See, for example, Baldwin, Mutti, and Richardson (1980); Brown and Whalley (1980); and Deardorff and Stern (1983).

TABLE 2.
Tariffs: Benefits to the U.S. of Multilateral Elimination of All Tariffs:
Annual Benefits and Cumulative Benefits Over Four and Twenty
Years (in billions of 1984 dollars)

	Annual Benefits	In Present Value	
		Four Years of Benefits	Twenty Years of Benefits
Gain in national income	7.01	25.41	79.46

Note: The annual stream of gains is assumed to be $7.01 billion per year. Cumulative present value is calculated using a discount rate of 7 percent.

Canceling all tariffs will also affect the pattern of domestic output and employment, and available results indicate that there would be a net adverse effect on domestic firms and workers. Since imports would be cheaper, domestic industries that compete with imports suffer a contraction and this will cause unemployment. Part of this increase in unemployment is offset by new employment opportunities in export industries. Since foreign tariffs are also eliminated, domestic export industries would expand and demand additional workers. The net adverse effect on employment was found to be small, at most $0.38 billion of adjustment costs (Table 3), which is based on Baldwin and Lewis (1978). Thus, considering only the benefits that occur in a single year, the benefit-cost ratio is at least 18 ($7.01/$0.38). For each dollar of adjustment costs the United States stands to gain $18 in real income when all tariffs are eliminated.

A full evaluation of the gains needs to consider the increases in real income in future years. For the first four years after all tariffs are canceled, the present value of the gain in real income is at least $25.41 billion. However, since the adjustment to a zero tariff policy involves a single adaptation by domestic resources, adjustment

TABLE 3.
Tariffs: Adjustment Costs and Annual Gains to
Adjustment Costs Ratio from Multilateral
Elimination of All Tariffs (in 1984 dollars)

Adjustment costs (billions)	0.38
Annual gains per dollar of adjustment costs	$18.45

---

[6] Brown and Whalley (1980). This is a conservative benchmark for the true magnitude of the gain because it is based on a model that includes aggregation bias and uses import demand elasticities that we believe are too low. These points are discussed in Tarr and Morkre (1984, chap. 2, sec. 3). Note that the estimates presented here correct for an error in the adjustment factor used for the growth in nominal GNP between 1973 and 1983 that appeared in Tarr and Morkre (1984, p. 38).

costs remain at $0.38 billion. Therefore, the present value of the net improvement in real income over four years is $25.03 billion.

Automobiles: Quotas on Japanese Imports

In the spring of 1981, the Japanese government announced, after negotiations with U.S. government officials, that it would voluntarily restrain its exports of automobiles to the United States. The action of the Japanese government was taken against a background of falling domestic production and employment in autos and a number of legislative attempts to curb Japanese imports.

The costs to the U.S. economy and the costs to U.S. consumers of this restraint are summarized in Table 4. It can be seen that losses to U.S. consumers and the economy exceed one billion dollars annually. Taken over four years, these numbers are about $4.2 billion and $3.8 billion in present value, respectively. The quota rents obtained by the Japanese are $860 million annually, and U.S. automobile producers are estimated to gain $120 million annually.

There are several reasons to believe that the reported estimates of the costs to consumers and losses to the economy are conservative. First, 1981—a recession year—proved to be the best year to use in estimating the costs of the restrictions. Second, because of a lack of data the apparent markups above list price charged by United States dealers of Japanese cars were ignored. Finally, the exchange-rate adjustments of the base year were taken as representative of the whole restraint experience.[7] As a result, the estimates, such as the estimate of $1.157 billion in annual costs to consumers, can be thought of as conservative estimates. That is, the true costs are at least as large as the numbers in Table 4.

TABLE 4.
Automobiles: Estimate of the Losses to the U.S. Economy ("Deadweight Losses"), Costs to Consumers, Gains to Producers, and Quota Rents Captured by Japanese Producers as a Result of the Voluntary Restraint Agreement on Japanese Automobiles (in millions of 1984 U.S. dollars)

	Annual Costs	In Present Value	
		Four Years of Costs	Twenty Years of Costs
Losses to the U.S. economy	1,037	3,758	11,750
Consumers' losses	1,157	4,195	13,115
U.S. producers' gains	120	436	1,363
Quota rents to Japanese	860	3,118	9,747

TABLE 5.
Automobiles: Annual Costs per Job Protected
by the VRA on Automobiles
(in thousands of 1984 dollars)

Costs to consumers	251.6
Losses to the economy ("dead- weight losses") per job	225.5

In addition to these estimates, the number of jobs protected by the "voluntary restraint agreement" (VRA) is estimated. Using these latter estimates enables calculation of the costs to consumers and to the United States economy for each job protected by the VRA. The annual costs to consumers and to the economy per job protected are $252 thousand and $226 thousand respectively;[8] these results are summarized in Table 5.

A final set of estimates are the cost-benefit ratios. These estimates, which are summarized in Table 6, reveal that for each dollar of earnings losses (by domestic auto workers) saved by the VRA, consumers and the economy would gain over $20 in benefits from its removal.

Sugar

In May 1982 the United States imposed country-by-country quotas on sugar imports. This action was taken to maintain the price of domestic sugar at a level that would eliminate the need for federal government outlays to acquire domestically grown sugar under the sugar price-support program. The world sugar price had fallen sharply in early 1982 because of an increase in world sugar supply, and statutory ceilings on sugar duties and import fees prevented the administration from relying on these instruments to achieve a do-

TABLE 6.
Automobiles: Cost-Benefit Ratios: Costs to
Consumers and Losses to the Economy for
Each Dollar of Earnings Losses Saved by the
VRA

Costs to consumers	$23.90
Losses to economy	$21.41

---

[7] In addition, the analysis was performed under the assumption that producers priced competitively after imports were constrained. If this assumption was not correct (an issue on which we have no evidence one way or the other) there would be additional costs and fewer benefits from retention of the quota.

[8] These costs are *excess* costs to consumers and the economy because they do not include the private costs to the firms involved of producing the output. An analogous argument applies to the textile and steel industries considered in this study.

mestic price that would be high enough to avoid purchases by the government.

Table 7 gives estimates of the long-run welfare effects of the sugar quota. In deriving these estimates we assume the continuation of a domestic price-support program that guarantees minimum receipts to domestic growers. However, we assume that either a direct-subsidy scheme or a purchase-resale arrangement is permitted. While neither of these programs is currently authorized, if trade restrictions were not used to support the domestic price, it seems likely that one or the other would be utilized in order to avoid the heavy costs that would result from the current sugar program, which requires the government to purchase sugar and limits the conditions under which that sugar can be resold.

The results also depend on our estimate of the long-run import-supply price. We estimated the long-run supply price rather than relying on current prices because, as suggested above, the world sugar price is currently depressed by unusually large world sugar supply. The supply price estimate is 15 cents per pound of raw sugar—which substantially exceeds the world price of 7.9 cents in 1983. Therefore, for 1983 and a few years beyond, our welfare-cost estimates are expected to err on the side of understating the true costs.

We estimate that the quota imposes annual costs on consumers of $767 million and annual deadweight losses of $262 million. The deadweight losses are dominated by quota rents of $249 million. The countries with large quotas, the Dominican Republic, Brazil, Australia, and the Philippines, therefore capture sizable windfalls as a result of the U.S. quota.

We also determine the effect on taxpayers of using a quota rather than a price-support program and determine the total costs of the quota to consumers, including the change in taxes paid. Under a

TABLE 7.

Sugar: Estimates of Inefficiency Losses to U.S. Economy ("Deadweight Losses"), Costs to Consumers and Consumers/Taxpayers, and Quota Rents Captured by Foreigners as a Result of Sugar Import Quota (in millions of 1984 dollars)

		In Present Value	
	Annual Costs	Four Years of Costs	Twenty Years of Costs
Losses to U.S. economy and costs to con-sumers/taxpayers	262	951	2,975
Consumers' losses	767	2,779	8,693
Quota rents to for-eigners	249	901	2,819

quota growers receive the minimum level of receipts called for by the price-support program by means of the higher domestic price caused by the quota. We assume that, absent the quota, the government makes payments to growers to assure they receive the same minimum level of receipts. The government payments impose a burden on taxpayers, who are substantially the same people as sugar consumers since sugar is consumed so widely. The introduction of a quota therefore eliminates the need for the government to make payments to growers and results in lower taxes, and the costs of the quota to consumers can be adjusted downward to reflect a reduction in taxes when the quota is imposed. We estimate that the net costs of the quota to consumers and taxpayers combined, or the costs to consumers/taxpayers, is $262 million.

Removing the quota does not reduce domestic sugar output or cause unemployment. The price-support program is assumed to operate to maintain output and employment.

The costs of the sugar quota increase the longer the quota remains in effect. Over four years the present value of the deadweight losses and costs to consumers/taxpayers is $951 million; the present value of the consumer costs is $2.8 billion.

Textiles: Quotas on Hong Kong

The United States has imposed quotas on imports of textile and clothing products for more than twenty-five years. Quotas were first applied in 1957 on imports of Japanese cotton textile products and have since expanded to other textile products and to many other countries. In 1984, the United States imposed import quotas on cotton, manmade fiber, and wool textile products that involved about two dozen exporter countries. The current U.S. restrictions are part of the Multi-Fiber Arrangement (MFA). Under the MFA, the United States has negotiated bilateral agreements that establish individual textile quotas for each restrained country.

Because of the lack of appropriate empirical data, it is not possible to estimate the welfare effects of all the textile import quotas the U.S. has imposed. However, data have been obtained that allow us to evaluate the welfare effects in 1980 of the quotas on nine clothing products made in Hong Kong. While Hong Kong is the largest foreign supplier of textile products to the U.S., accounting for 22 percent of total U.S. textile imports (in 1980), our estimates of the welfare effects of the Hong Kong quotas are only a part of the total cost to the United States of all quotas on textiles.

We find that the annual deadweight losses due to the quotas on the nine Hong Kong clothing products are at least $388 million (Ta-

TABLE 8.
Textiles: Estimates of Inefficiency Losses to U.S. Economy ("Deadweight
Losses"), Costs to Consumers, and Quota Rents Captured by Hong Kong Firms
as a Result of Import Quotas on Hong Kong Textiles (in millions of 1984 dollars)

	Annual Costs	In Present Value	
		Four Years of Costs	Twenty Years of Costs
Losses to U.S. economy	388	1,408	4,402
Consumers' losses	401	1,453	4,545
Quota rents to Hong Kong textile firms	275	998	3,120

ble 8).[9] The major portion of the losses is quota rents, which are $275
million. The costs of the Hong Kong quotas to consumers are $401
million.

While the deadweight losses could be estimated only for the
quotas on imports from Hong Kong, we were able to derive the domestic unemployment effects assuming quotas on the three major
foreign suppliers are eliminated (Hong Kong, South Korea, and Taiwan). In other words, we only find part of the benefits of removing
the quotas on Hong Kong, South Korea, and Taiwan but we calculate
domestic unemployment costs assuming the quotas on all three exporters are lifted. We estimate that 8900 workers would lose their
jobs in domestic clothing factories and textile mills if these quotas
were removed. Thus the costs to the U.S. economy per job protected
are at least $43.7 thousand (Table 9). The costs of adjustment for
8900 unemployed textile workers are $21 million. Therefore the ra-
tio of benefits from removing quotas to adjustment costs is at least 18
(Table 10).

Removing the quotas also increases real income in future years.
Over four years the present value of the net benefit to the U.S. economy is $1387 million.

TABLE 9.
Textiles: Annual Costs per Job Protected by
the Import Quotas on Hong Kong (in
thousands of 1984 dollars)

Costs to consumers	45.1
Losses to the economy ("deadweight losses") per job	43.7

[9] This estimate is based on one of two sets of import-demand elasticities. For
the alternative set of elasticities, larger deadweight losses are predicted. For a discussion of these elasticities see Morkre (1984, App. F).

TABLE 10.
Textiles: Cost-Benefit Ratios: Annual Costs to
Consumers and Losses to the Economy for
Each Dollar of Unemployment Costs Saved by
the Import Quotas on Hong Kong

Costs to consumers	$18.93
Losses to economy	$18.33

Carbon and Alloy Steel Quotas

The domestic steel industry has received some special form of trade protection for eleven out of the past fifteen years.[10] In 1984, the United Steelworkers of America and Bethlehem Steel Corporation petitioned the U.S. International Trade Commission (ITC) for relief from imports under section 201 of the Trade Act of 1974. In that petition they asked for quotas on imports of carbon and alloy steel products so that imports would be at most 15 percent of domestic apparent consumption.[11]

In response to the affirmative decision by the ITC on the petition the president formally rejected protection through the 201 process. However, he directed the United States Trade Representative (USTR) to negotiate voluntary restraint agreements with foreign governments to reduce imports to 18.5 percent of domestic apparent consumption, with semifinished steel excluded from the calculation.

After the president's program was announced, Congress passed, in the Trade and Tariff Act of 1984, a nonbinding "sense of the Congress" that imports should be reduced to between 17 and 20.2 percent of U.S. domestic apparent consumption and authorized the president to negotiate agreements to achieve that goal.[12]

In December the administration announced that agreements had been reached with Japan, Brazil, South Korea, and Spain, and also with South Africa, Mexico, and Australia. The agreement with

---

[10] This is in addition to tariff protection, which in 1984 was about 5.3 percent on steel products.

[11] Also in 1984, there was legislation before Congress (the Fair Trade in Steel Act of 1984) that would utilize quotas to limit imports to 15 percent of domestic apparent consumption. Domestic apparent consumption is defined as domestic shipments plus imports minus exports. If there were no change in domestic inventories, it would equal actual domestic consumption. See Congressional Budget Office (1984) for an analysis of the effects of this legislation.

[12] The 20.2 percent figure is what the president's goal is for imports when semifinished products are included. The bill also provides that continuation of the import relief in any year is contingent on the major steel companies committing "substantially all of their net cash flow from steel operations to reinvestment and modernization of their steel industry." Since most firms are already exceeding this requirement, the latter restraint is not considered onerous.

TABLE 11.
Steel: Estimates of the Losses to Consumers, Costs to the U.S.
Economy, Gains to Producers, and Quota Rents to Foreign
Producers as a Result of an 18.5 Percent Quota on Carbon and
Alloy Steel Products (Excluding Semifinished Products)
(in millions of 1984 dollars)

	Annual Losses	*In Present Value* Four Years of Losses
Consumers' losses	1,145	4,152
Losses to the U.S. economy	813	2,948
Gains to U.S. producers	447	1,588
Quota rents to foreign producers	581	2,105

the European Community[13] will remain in effect, and Canada was not expected to increase its market penetration. The exact level of imports permitted under the new agreements is not known. However, the administration has not changed its goal of restraining imports to 18.5 percent of domestic apparent consumption (excluding semifinished). Thus, this level of restriction is taken as indicative of the level of restraint likely to be achieved; the costs and benefits of this restriction are presented below.

In 1984 dollars, the annual costs to U.S. consumers of the quota are estimated to be $1.145 billion. The annual inefficiency costs to the economy are estimated to be $813 million. The cumulative costs over four years, in present value, of the costs to consumers and the economy are $4.15 billion and $2.95 billion respectively. Part of what U.S. consumers lose is transferred to domestic and foreign producers. U.S. producers gain $447 million per year and foreigners extract $581 million per year in quota rents. These estimates are summarized in Table 11.

In order to obtain some perspective on the quantitative importance of the benefits of the quota in relation to the costs, cost-benefit ratios are provided as well as estimates of the costs of the quota per job protected. For each job protected by this restriction the annual costs to consumers are $115.1 thousand; the annual costs to the economy for each job protected by the quota are $81.7 thousand. These estimates are presented in Table 12. Since Congress has authorized the administration program for at most five years, the benefits

---

[13] Prior to the announcement of the new restrictions, some formal and possibly some informal quantitative restraints on steel imports were already in place. The European Community, Mexico, South Africa, and possibly Japan were already limiting their exports to the United States. The estimates in the monograph are for the additional effects of an 18.5 percent quota, given that these quantitative restraints are already in effect.

TABLE 12.
Steel: Annual Costs to Consumers and to the
U.S. Economy for Each Job Saved by the
Quota on Steel Products (in thousands of 1984
dollars)

Losses to consumers	115.1
Losses to economy	81.7

of the quota are measured by the present value of the deferral of the earnings losses of workers who will be displaced in five years but, without the quota, would otherwise have been displaced immediately. For the purposes of this comparison, the present value of the costs to consumers and losses to the economy are taken over five years. It is found that for every dollar of earnings losses saved by otherwise displaced workers, consumers lose $34.60 and the U.S. economy loses $24.57. The estimates are summarized in Table 13.

Aggregate Costs of All Restraints Examined

The question we are concerned with is the aggregate costs (or dead-weight losses) to the U.S. economy of all import restraints. We have attempted to obtain a conservative estimate of these costs by first obtaining an estimate of the aggregate costs to the U.S. economy of all tariffs and by adding to this the costs of quotas on four significant industries. Methodological issues, addressing why the approach we have adopted is appropriate, are discussed in chapter 1 of our 1984 monograph.

The annual costs of all the tariffs is $7.01 billion. Simply aggregating the estimates of the costs of the four quotas would yield an estimate of $2.50 billion in annual costs. We deduct $0.22 billion from this estimate and obtain $2.28 billion as our estimate of the annual net costs to the economy of the four quotas. The $0.22-billion figure is our upper bound estimate of the welfare losses from a terms-of-trade shift attributable to the removal of the quotas.

Summing the estimate of the annual net costs of the quotas with the estimate of the annual costs of the tariffs yields the result that all the import restraints analyzed cost the economy $9.29 billion annually. Since, in the cases we have examined, the costs to con-

TABLE 13.
Steel: Cost-Benefit Ratios: Costs to Consumers
and Losses to the Economy for Each Dollar of
Earnings Losses Saved by the 18.5 Percent
Quota

Costs to consumers	$34.60
Losses to the economy	$24.57

sumers are greater than the costs to the economy, this value may be taken as a lower bound estimate of the costs to consumers. Moreover, restraints impose ongoing costs on consumers and the economy. That is, these costs will be incurred each year the restraints are in effect. Thus over a four-year period, say, we add to the first-year costs the discounted value of these costs in the next three years and obtain the present value of these costs over four years. Performing this calculation, with a 7 percent discount rate, the present value of the costs to the economy of maintaining these restraints is found to be $33.70 billion. Clearly, if the restraints last beyond four years the present value of the costs would be still higher. These results and the results of the individual studies are summarized in Table 1 above.

Aggregate adjustment costs total $802.2 million in 1984 dollars.[14] Thus, for each dollar of adjustment costs saved by the restraints in the aggregate, $42 are lost to the economy in four years. Adjustment costs are a one-time cost. The benefits to consumers and the economy continue year after year, however. Therefore benefit-cost calculation beyond four years would result in higher benefit-cost ratios.

The estimate of the aggregate costs to the economy is a conservative one: i.e., the true costs are at least as great as those indicated. Tarr and Morkre (1984, chap. 1) explain some of the most important reasons why the estimate is conservative. For example: the losses to the economy from "rent-seeking" are ignored; not all quotas have been quantified; and a maximum estimate for the terms-of-trade loss has been utilized. Moreover, a reading of the monograph itself will reveal the many cases in which parameter choices (such as elasticity estimates) and methodological decisions were made that resulted in lower estimates of the costs. For this reason the reader should regard the estimates of the costs of the trade restraints, such as $34 billion in costs to the economy over four years, as conservative estimates.

This paper is based on our monograph, Tarr and Morkre (1984). The views expressed do not necessarily reflect those of the Federal Trade Commission or its individual commissioners. The authors would like to acknowledge the assistance of Keith Anderson and Richard Higgins of the Federal Trade Commission and all others who were acknowledged in our monograph; in addition, we are indebted to Thomas Bayard of the Ford Foundation regarding the terms-of-trade adjustment analysis.

The Federal Trade Commission is charged with enforcement of the nation's antitrust and consumer protection laws. Through its enforcement of

---

[14] This derives from $246.9 million in automobiles, $149.5 million in steel, $21.2 million in textiles, and $384.6 million from multilateral elimination of tariffs.

these laws, the FTC attempts to provide consumers with the benefits of a competitive and efficiently functioning economy. The FTC is concerned about restrictions on imports because they limit competition in the affected markets and as a result consumers pay higher prices for the goods and services involved. Over the past few years the FTC's Bureau of Economics has published several staff reports that estimate the effects of import restrictions. In addition, the FTC has prepared submissions to other Federal agencies, including the International Trade Commission, analyzing the effects of petitions that would increase import barriers.

References

Baldwin, Robert E. and Lewis, Wayne E. (1978) U.S. Tariff Effects on Trade and Employment in Detailed SIC Industries. In W. G. Dewald (ed.), *The Impact of International Trade and Investment on Employment*, A Conference on the Department of Labor Research Results. Washington, D.C.: U.S. Government Printing Office. Pp. 241–264.

Baldwin, Robert E., Mutti, John H., and Richardson, J. David (1980) Welfare Effects on the United States of a Significant Multilateral Tariff Reduction, *Journal of International Economics* 10: 405–423.

Brown, Fred and Whalley, John (1980) General Equilibrium Evaluations of Tariff-Cutting Proposals in the Tokyo Round and Comparisons with More Extensive Liberalisation of World Trade, *Economic Journal* 90: 838–866.

Congressional Budget Office (1984) *The Effect of Import Quotas on the Steel Industry*. U.S. Congress.

Deardorff, Alan V. and Stern, Robert M. (1983) The Economic Effects of Complete Elimination of Post-Tokyo Round Tariffs. In W. R. Cline (ed.), *Trade Policy in the 1980s*. Cambridge, Mass.: MIT Press. Pp. 673–710.

Morkre, Morris E. (1984) *Import Quotas on Textiles: The Welfare Effects of United States Restrictions on Hong Kong*. Bureau of Economics Staff Report to the Federal Trade Commission. Washington, D.C.: U.S. Government Printing Office.

Morkre, Morris E. and Tarr, David G. (1980) *Effects of Restrictions on United States Imports: Five Case Studies and Theory*. Bureau of Economics Staff Report to the Federal Trade Commission. Washington, D.C.: U.S. Government Printing Office.

Tarr, David G. and Morkre, Morris E. (1984) *Aggregate Costs to the United States of Tariffs and Quotas on Imports: General Tariff Cuts and Removal of Quotas on Automobiles, Steel, Sugar, and Textiles*. Bureau of Economics Staff Report to the Federal Trade Commission. Washington, D.C.: U.S. Government Printing Office.

PART THREE

INDUSTRIAL POLICY AND INDUSTRY STUDIES

12

Industrial Policy and Trade Distortion

RICHARD N. COOPER

U.S. industry these days feels under siege from foreign competitors and points to rising shares of imports in its home market and falling shares of U.S. exports in world markets. Attention has been drawn to a host of foreign practices that apparently help to explain the increased competition from foreigners, ranging from specific export promotional tactics and specific import prohibitions to broadly drawn industrial policies and industrial targeting that allegedly provide impetus to foreign exports and simultaneously discourage imports from the United States and elsewhere. These practices in one variant or another have been discovered to be widespread, being used not only by other industrial countries but by less developed countries as well, particularly the newly industrialized countries such as Korea and Brazil. But Japan is held up as the main culprit, not so much because its practices are more extensive than those in other countries but because they are somewhat mysterious and lost behind Japanese reticence and linguistic ambiguity, and above all because Japan has emerged as the most successful competitor in a number of industries in which Americans have hitherto considered themselves unrivaled. It is foreign success rather than the practices themselves—which in many cases have existed for many years and in some cases have actually diminished in importance—which has given rise to such widespread concern and has led to calls for U.S. action ranging from retaliation to emulation.

From Harvard University, Cambridge, Massachusetts.

This paper addresses these American concerns about what have come to be called "unfair trade practices" from the perspective of public policy. What response should the U.S. government make to these foreign practices and their alleged impact on the foreign trade—and even the industrial viability—of the United States?

With respect to the future viability of American industry, the view has been expressed that the theory of comparative advantage which provides the intellectual underpinnings for a liberal trade policy is fundamentally misleading, since it takes comparative advantage as given, whereas in fact it is determined by government policy. In particular, it is claimed that the country that gets the head start in a period of rapid technical change is likely to develop a "comparative advantage" in the product in question. Government actions that lead to early development thus determine comparative advantage.

The paper will take up the objectives and instruments of industrial policy in several other countries, focusing on Japan. It will then inquire into governmental influences on the American economy and its structure of trade, which on close inspection turn out to be more pervasive than most Americans think and have some unexpected twists. The paper then addresses the "making" of comparative advantage by government policy, and finally turns to various alternative approaches to U.S. policy for dealing with the pervasive influence of governments on the composition of output and trade, both in a cooperative framework and by acting on its own.

Macroeconomic Context

Before we turn to these matters, it is important to address a fundamental analytical error that underlies much of even informed discussion with respect to so-called unfair trade practices and other policy distortions to international trade. That is the supposition that the overall trade balance, and lying behind that economic growth and employment, is determined or strongly influenced by the foreign practices that are typically singled out for admiration or condemnation; i.e., by policies or practices that limit particular imports or promote particular exports. This error is an example of the "fallacy of composition," whereby summing up a number of separate actions, each with well-defined effect (enlarging the Japanese import quota on citrus will surely lead to larger Japanese imports of citrus products) will not in fact have the expected overall effect. Concretely, the Japanese could remove every policy measure and alter every practice foreigners point to as restricting imports, and the consequences would not involve a reduction in the large Japanese trade surplus and might not even result in an overall increase in Japanese imports.

The reason is that a country's balance of trade in goods and services is determined by the difference between national saving and national investment, and it is only insofar as actions influence savings and investment that they can influence the trade balance:

$$X - M = S + (T - G) - I$$

Here the difference between exports (X) and imports (M) equals net foreign investment (unilateral transfers are neglected), and net foreign investment in turn must equal the difference between national saving (= private sector saving [S] plus the government operating surplus [$T - G$]) and national investment (I). This relationship is an accounting identity, from the definition of the concepts in the national accounts; decisions that affect one of these aggregates automatically must affect one or more others in a consistent way.

This relationship is of fundamental importance in assessing overall trade performance. While lifting the Japanese citrus quota will almost certainly raise Japan's imports of citrus and will probably raise overall Japanese imports (but by less than the increase in citrus imports), it would not reduce the large Japanese trade surplus except insofar as lifting the quota affected national savings and/or investment: probably not at all, or only negligibly. Given a large savings–investment imbalance, a rise in one particular import will be offset by a decline in other imports and/or a rise in exports. Paradoxically, it is even conceivable that a stripping away of all Japan's protective practices[1] would lead to a *rise* in the trade surplus rather than a decline, if the sudden import competition reduced Japanese investment more than it reduced saving; but since "saving" includes corporate earnings, it could equally plausibly reduce the trade surplus by reducing corporate profits but at the same time stimulate corporate investment in order to survive in the new, more competitive environment. The point is that to assess the overall impact one must look beyond the commodities immediately affected by the change in policy, whether it be import restriction or export promotion.

The significance of this in the present context is that since 1981 the United States has had a rapidly growing trade deficit, whereas Japan and several European countries have developed large surpluses. This trend in overall imbalances has had a strong influence on the rise in import shares in the U.S. market and the decline in U.S. export shares mentioned at the outset, and correspondingly on

---

[1] I use the term *practices* since much difficulty in import penetration in Japan is due, in my judgment, less to governmental policy than to deeply ingrained purchasing practices by Japanese firms and midlevel ministry officials.

the competitive pressures felt by American firms. But they arise from overall macroeconomic developments, not from "unfair trade practices," however many of those there might be. It is of course unrealistic to expect industries affected by severe foreign competition at home or abroad to sort out the macroeconomic influences from the specific foreign (or domestic) policies affecting the industry or commodity in question. But for purposes of addressing policy it is essential to make this distinction; failure to do so is bound to lead to frustration, since even a vigorous use of the wrong instruments will not achieve the desired objective.

In 1984 the United States ran a current-account deficit of $95 billion, or 2.6 percent of GNP, a record high. Gross private savings were 18.4 percent of GNP, also a record high since 1945. Gross investment was 17.4 percent of GNP, typical for a boom year. But the deficit on governmental account (including state and local governments) was 3.4 percent of GNP, down from 1983 but nearly a historic high, excluding the Second World War. Under these circumstances, the United States was bound to have a large trade deficit. Paradoxically, additional investment stimulated by additional tax concessions to investment, frequently urged by the business community as a means to become more competitive internationally, would actually worsen the trade balance during the period of investment, both by increasing investment and by increasing the budget deficit.

An analogous development occurred in Japan. Private savings and investment rates have been considerably higher in Japan than in the United States over the past three decades, and on average roughly equal to one another until 1975. Investment fell sharply then and has since remained low by Japanese standards. Japan greatly extended its social welfare programs in the early 1970s, and that combined with an economic slowdown produced large government deficits, reaching over 4 percent of GNP in 1979. Since then it has been Japanese policy to reduce the budget deficit; but private savings have remained in excess of investment, so a large current-account surplus emerged in 1981, and by 1984 it had reached nearly 3 percent of GNP.

How can these movements in savings and investment, inclusive of government, get translated into trade surpluses or deficits? A simple version of the answer is that the excess private savings of Japan, to the extent it could not be satisfied by claims on government (resulting from the budget deficit) sought investment abroad. This in turn put downward pressure on the yen, which depreciated and made Japanese goods more competitive in world markets. In the United States, in contrast, a combination of government deficit and private investment in excess of private savings strengthened interest rates and thereby attracted capital from abroad, thus leading to appreciation of the dollar and worsening the competitive position of American products both at home and abroad. So the main mechanism of equilibration was the exchange rate. Under a system of fixed exchange rates this pressure of a desired increase in net private savings cannot weaken the currency, so it reduces income (causes a recession) to the point at which the reduced savings, the increased budget deficit (due to lower tax revenue), and the improvement in the current-account balance (due to lower imports) preserve the equality between net national savings and net foreign investment. The recession may also put downward pressure on wages and prices and improve international competitiveness in that way.

Either way, the link between the overall trade position and overall savings–investment behavior is inescapable, and no fiddling around with particular trade policies or practices will get around it. For instance, the occasional call for a U.S. import surcharge would improve the trade balance mainly through the increased revenue to the government (reducing the dissaving by the government), and the increased investment that some proponents want it to stimulate would undermine even that improvement if the investment were not accompanied by higher private savings.

Of course, from the perspective of an individual industry these macroeconomic developments seem unimportant relative to the industry-specific policies of countries; and it is true that such policies can strongly influence the commodity structure and geographic direction of trade. But the industry perspective is myopic; in assessing the impact of industrial policy on trade as a whole, it is crucial to take into account the macroeconomic environment.

Industrial Policy in Japan and Elsewhere

"Industrial policy" has no well-defined boundaries, and at its broadest we can take it to mean any government policies that affect the structure of output, or, slightly more narrowly, any government policies whose intended purpose is to affect the structure of output. But perhaps the best way to characterize industrial policy of the type that concerns many Americans now is to discuss briefly but concretely the policies of the country that is seen to be most threatening: Japan.

This task is somewhat more difficult than it might seem, since Japanese policies have changed substantially over the past twenty-five years, and some of the measures most frequently cited in fact belong largely to the past. Japanese industrial policy will be described here in the three phases frequently cited by Japanese analysts: end of postwar price control (1952) to the early 1960s, aimed at establishing the base for a modern industrial economy; 1960–1972, following elimination of foreign-exchange controls, aimed at excelling in exports; and 1972 to the present, aimed at shifting the structure of the Japanese economy from capital-intensive to knowledge-intensive activities.[2] The dividing lines between these periods are of course somewhat artificial, and some continuity of both policies and problems can be found during the past forty years, but over the period substantial changes in both policy orientation and instruments of policy occurred.

THE FIFTIES

In the early 1950s the Japanese desired to build a modern industrial society, drawing insofar as possible on the strengths they already had, which included a skilled workforce in steelmaking, shipbuilding, and optics (for binoculars) built up during World War II. Strong government guidance in modernization had been part of Japanese history during the previous eighty years, and it was turned to again. Crucial industries were identified, forecasts of demand were made, and the industries were encouraged to invest accordingly. A rationalization program was begun for steel in 1951. Special industry promotion laws were passed for synthetic fibers (1953), petrochemicals (1955), machinery (1956), synthetic rubber (1957), electronics (1957), and aircraft (1958). Assembly of automobiles was made a priority in Japan in 1952 (Warnecke, p. 127). The occupation-imposed Antimonopoly Act was amended in 1953 to permit the formation of "recession" and "rationalization" cartels with government approval in order to prevent cut-throat price competition and to induce orderly reduction in capacity during periods of slack demand (such as immediately following the Korean War, when the revisions were passed). The Export and Import Trading Act was also passed in 1953, permitting cartels to fix prices and to limit imports. By 1971 there were 195 legally recognized cartels under the Export and Import Trading Act, 13 under the Antimonopoly Act, and 23 under separate legislation pertaining to the machinery, electronics, and fertilizer industries (Yamamura, p. 82), a decline in number by about 20 percent from the mid-1960s (Caves and Uekusa, p. 148).

It was during this period too that the Fiscal Investment and Loan Program (FILP) was created, whereby postal savings accounts (historically an important depository of household savings) and public pension reserve funds were channeled into a series of trust funds (about forty today) for the promotion of public policy. These trust

---

[2] The following description is a blend from several sources: Namiki in Warnecke, U.S.–Japan Trade Study Group, Yakushiji in Aoki, Yamamura, and interviews with MITI officials.

funds include the Japan Development Bank (JDB) and the Export-Import Bank of Japan.

Investment by the favored industries was encouraged by special tax incentives and by loans from JDB. Japanese industry drew 13 percent of its external financing from JDB in 1952–1955, and another 15 percent from other FILP programs (these figures had declined to 4 and 10 percent, respectively, by 1971–1975). Four key selected industries—electric power, shipping, coal, and steel—got 24 percent of their external financing from JDB and another 13 percent from other FILP programs in 1952–1955 (Noguchi in Yamamura, p. 131). So this government finance was a key instrument of policy; moreover, a JDB loan often provided a signal for lending (at commercial terms) by the quantitatively more important private banks, on the grounds that the favored firms were likely to involve lower risk than other business loans.

Finally, foreign-exchange control existed throughout this first period, and import licences were used to further the industrial policy. For instance, foreign cars were more durable and commodious than domestic cars, and as the taxi industry revived and thrived its demand for foreign cars rose (including for used cars from American forces resident in Japan). Purchase of such cars was limited under foreign-exchange regulations in 1951, imports were liberalized in 1952 but sharply tightened again in early 1954 and a "buy domestic" campaign was started with the taxicab companies. Japanese production with improved quality required foreign technology. MITI in 1952 promulgated guidelines for auto-assembly licensing agreements which inter alia stipulated that after a specified period of time eleven key auto parts had to be produced in Japan (Yakushiji in Aoki, pp. 278–281). Foreign-exchange regulations were used to limit imports in many other industries as well and to shape the development of each favored industry.

THE SIXTIES

Although Japan recognized the importance of exports from as early as 1949, when export promotion was adopted as MITI's main goal, the 1950s can be characterized principally as a period of import substitution, as Japan began to produce more sophisticated products that permitted a reduction in imports of these products. In 1960 there was a major trade- and foreign-exchange liberalization, associated with pressure from the United States and Europe to move toward currency convertibility and to accept fully the obligations of the General Agreement on Tariffs and Trade (GATT), which Japan had joined in 1955 preparatory to Japan's admission to the Organization of Economic Cooperation and Development (OECD), the club of industrialized countries, in 1964. This move eliminated exchange controls and general use of overt import restrictions as a major instrument of industrial policy, although some approved cartels continued to limit imports, presumably with MITI knowledge. The relative importance of the JDB also declined sharply as the private banks became both stronger and more assertive.

A consequence of the liberalization of foreign-exchange regulations and of the growing strength of sources of domestic credit in Japan is that MITI had to rely more on moral suasion, less on directives. It did not always work. An effort to pass a new law supporting selected industries unexpectedly failed due to domestic opposition in the early 1960s, and in 1965–1966 the Sumitomo steel company flouted MITI's administrative guidance to cut back steel production. The growth of independent banks inhibited the development of "national champions" in Japan, since each bank wanted to have within its "family" of firms a representative from each major industry. The degree of competitiveness among major Japanese banks and firms, and the difficulty it sometimes poses for government, was already encountered in 1955 when a MITI plan to create a single small, inexpensive people's car (along the lines of Volkswagen) to open the mass market was leaked to the press (Japan's press is more competitive and more aggressive than that in the United States) and created a storm of protest from the actual and would-be automakers. The plan was abandoned and vigorous competition developed among Japan's automakers.

A general policy can continue in the face of even major exceptions and derogations. But it is also likely that such exceptions remind the officials, if they need reminding, that there are distinct limits to their authority, and they therefore influence what MITI calls for, and what industry calls on MITI to call for if the industry is not unanimous. It is not true, as foreigners are sometimes led to believe, that Japanese business leaders are unwilling to take risks on their own and to stand out from the crowd.

By the 1960s steel and shipbuilding were commercial successes and relative emphasis shifted to encouragement of the machine tool industry, which, like steel, and on the basis of close observation of the American economy, was seen to be a prerequisite for a modern industrial economy. It continued to get tax breaks, modest subsidies, and favored procurement.

THE SEVENTIES

In the early 1970s there was a marked shift in Japanese policy in a number of respects. The Japanese public had become restless about growing pollution, about the inadequate welfare system, and even about the fact that they had to pay much higher prices for some Japanese products than Japan's overseas customers did (television sets, especially, became a local cause celèbre). Moreover, MITI and other officials became concerned about the rapid growth of Japan's imports of oil, even before the oil shock of late 1973. In response to general public pressure, Japan adopted in 1972 a much more generous social security system and introduced stiff pollution standards. In response to the dollar crisis of 1971–1972, Japan took a number of steps to liberalize imports, to liberalize direct investment inflows, and to monitor exports with the object of restraining too rapid growth. Japan also eliminated its "buy only Japanese" policy with respect to government procurement, and loans under FILP were made subject to Diet approval, something that had not been required before 1972 and which greatly reduced their flexibility as an instrument of industrial policy.

Looking to the future, MITI emphasized the growing importance of "knowledge-intensive" industries and encouraged Japanese industry to move in that direction. The Agency for Industrial Science and Technology (AIST) was created within MITI to finance research projects in ceramics, computers, seabed mining, and flexible computer-aided manufacturing systems. The criteria for AIST support are that the item in question is not yet on the commercial market and that the research effort would be too large or too risky for private firms to undertake alone. An early success was a desalination process that was later commercialized by private firms and sold in the Middle East. MITI in 1983 had a total R&D budget of about $250 million, which was divided between MITI's own fifteen laboratories and support for R&D by private firms, compared with about $10 billion in total spent annually by Japanese firms on research and development.

The most heavily publicized cases of government R&D support concern the VLSI (very large-scale integrated circuit) project started in 1976, on which some $120 million in conditional loans (repayable only if there was commercial success) was made by the government between 1976 and 1979; and government support of a so-called fifth-generation computer in the early 1980s. But there are sources of support of high-technology industries other than research grants and conditional loans. Since 1978 the National Aeronautics and Space Development Agency has given preference in its procurement to satellites with high local content, which now exceeds 60 percent. However, Japan's semiconductor market "can be said today [1984] to be completely open to American-owned companies" (U.S.–Japan Trade Study Group, p. 54).

Japan does not only help the products of the future. Since 1978 it has had a program to "restructure" Japanese industries that are depressed, for whatever reason. Firms accounting for two-thirds of a depressed industry's output can petition the government for a restructuring plan that involves an agreed reduction in capacity, with loan guarantees and tax benefits accruing to firms that scrap capacity under the plan. In mid-1984 there were twenty-two officially designated industries, of which five (paper, ethylene, compound fertilizer, polyolefins, and PVC resin) had formed legal cartels to restrict output and price competition (U.S.–Japan Trade Study Group, p. 64). This represents a substantial decline in the use of cartels from twenty years earlier. In addition, FILP support for Japanese industry is proportionately very much less than it used to be, and the government-loan-rate differential below market rates dropped from around 3 percent in the early 1960s to about one percent in the early 1980s (Noguchi in Yamamura, p. 137). In general, Japanese government involvement in determining industrial structure is far less than it once was—in part because the two instruments of foreign-exchange licensing and credit control are now unavailable for disciplining large firms. But it continues to provide hortatory guidance in MITI's "Visions" and other government pronouncements and to back these up with direct or indirect funding on a modest scale, and with directed government procurement.

EUROPE

Other countries have industrial policies that are similar to those in Japan, and that are generally more extensive. For example, Britain, France, and Italy all have had organizations analogous to JDB that channel publicly raised funds to private enterprises. All provide tax breaks to encourage investment in general and favored investment (by industry and by region) in particular. All have extensive state-owned industrial enterprises, something that is rare in Japan, that receive periodic infusions of new equity capital, which is difficult to distinguish from subsidies when the firms are running operating losses. All have given extensive support to their steel and textile industries to consolidate operations and to scrap obsolete capital. Britain, France, and Germany have also provided government support to cushion declining demand in their shipbuilding industries. In the high-technology area, all have provided extensive government funding and preferred government procurement in aerospace, computers, and telecommunications (for a survey of actions, see Carmoy in Warnecke). For instance, national Post, Telephone, and Telegraph (PTT) organizations in these countries rarely procure foreign-made equipment; the same is true of national power companies with respect to heavy electrical-generating equipment.

Newly industrializing countries also have adopted strong industrial policies, apart from the traditional technique of restricting imports that compete with the production of favored industries. Korea has, at least in one area, adopted a novel incentive: Koreans who work on contract engineering and construction projects in the Middle East have been exempt from the draft and given priority in public housing when they return home (Warnecke, p. 133).

Observations on Industrial Policies

The purpose of this sketchy survey is to illustrate how widespread are the uses of "industrial policies" and how diverse are the instruments of support that governments may use. They raise the question of how such extensive interference with market forces can be reconciled with a liberal trading system predicated on the mutual gains that flow from reliance on comparative advantage to determine each country's structure of output and trade, with certain acknowledged exceptions having mainly to do with national security.

In particular, the discovery that foreign governments intervene extensively in national economic development even at the sectoral level, and that these interventions may impinge on the market for American products both at home and abroad, has recently led to a number of stated or implied recommendations for U.S. policy (see, e.g., LICIT and Magaziner and Reich). The U.S. government, it is suggested, should:

1. Insist that other countries give up the practices which allegedly represent "unfair competition" for American firms;
2. Adopt measures similar to foreign actions that are deemed to have been successful—e.g., create a revived Reconstruction Finance Corporation modeled on the Japan Development Fund;
3. Raise import barriers to goods enjoying "unfair competition," sometimes only after (1) has failed or as a threat to encourage foreign compliance with (1); and
4. Match the foreign competitive measures in third-country markets (e.g., through generous Exim Bank financing) and/or restrict unrelated imports into the United States from countries engaging in unfair competition in third markets.

Before we turn to policy issues for the United States, however, several remarks should be made about the overall economic impact of these industrial policies.

First, most of them are not new, and have been around for a long time, so whatever real stimulus they provide should have been adjusted to by adaptation elsewhere in the economic system. France, Italy, and Japan among major countries began extensive industrial policies in the early 1950s. Britain launched on this course in earnest in the mid-1960s. Indeed, if anything, the impact of industrial policies has been declining in Japan in recent years, and the Thatcher government in Britain has attempted to reduce that country's sectoral policies in the early 1980s.

Second, in many cases a costly quid pro quo is exacted for government support of a firm or industry, especially in terms of loss of freedom or flexibility over decisions regarding employment, plant closings, new investment, and diversification. This loss of freedom and flexibility is directly or indirectly cost-increasing. Such factors are typically not allowed in the reckoning as negative unfair competition, a partial offset to the aids that are received.

Third, it is often forgotten that the United States, while not having an industrial policy as such, nonetheless has many measures which directly or indirectly assist American business. These are sufficiently extensive and variegated to warrant extensive treatment in a moment.

Fourth, it should not be forgotten that measures which discriminate in favor of certain firms or industries by that very fact discriminate *against* other firms or industries. In economics there are only rarely opportunities for a "free lunch," and someone has to pay for the special aids that are granted to others. This is an important analytical point and will be discussed further below.

The U.S. government has had, and continues to have, extensive sectoral involvement in the U.S. economy. For example, in the nineteenth century it gave land grants to the railroads, and more recently it has constructed a vast highway system to open up areas of the country and provide cheap inland transport. It provides cheap, underpriced water to irrigate Arizona and California farms, producing the citrus that growers complain about being unable to sell "fairly" to the Japanese and Europeans. It has extensive R&D programs for the Department of Defense and for the National Aeronautics and Space Administration that generate such commercially valuable spinoffs as jet engines, helicopters, and the Boeing 747 (see Nelson et al.). It is true that Europeans and Japanese exaggerate the quantitative importance of the commercial impact of defense R&D, but most American analysis of foreign government policies is also qualitative, leaving the impression of greater quantitative importance than is generally warranted. Extensive charitable deductions under the U.S. tax system permit the United States to provide higher education to a much larger percentage of the labor force than the Europeans could afford with their tax-supported systems and in "unfair competition" with the private universities of Japan.

It is perhaps useful to address more systematically government subsidies and other policies that influence American exports, since the U.S. government engages in a host of actions that influence the competitiveness of American exports, ranging from direct actions to encourage exports through activities to stimulate production and general support for business activity to actions that by discouraging certain industries lead indirectly to encouragement of others. The following list proceeds from the most direct form of export encouragement to less direct forms (this list is adapted from Cooper in Warnecke).

1. Economic and military assistance to less developed countries, tied to the procurement of American goods. In this case the U.S. government in effect buys the American goods and gives them away, or lends them on very easy terms. Foreign aid represents an extreme form of export subsidization, but it is accepted as contributing to economic development or national security, and the importing countries in this case would be unlikely to hold the United States accountable for unfair import competition or to impose countervailing duties. But third countries may lose export orders because of foreign aid shipments tied to U.S. procurement. The subsidization of American exports would cease if foreign aid grants and loans were freely usable for the purchase of goods and services anywhere, as is the case with loans from the World Bank. U.S. foreign assistance and military credit sales amounted to about $15.5 billion dollars in 1982, or about 4.5 percent of total U.S. exports of goods and services.

2. Under U.S. tax laws until 1984, corporations that derived at least 95 percent of their gross receipts from exports could qualify as domestic international sales corporations (DISC) and could defer payment of corporate profits tax until dividends were remitted to the parent corporation. This provision, which cost in excess of $1 billion in annual revenue forgone in the mid-1970s, amounted to an interest-free loan from the government for expenditures involved in the promotion of exports. The subsidy element—about $60 million a year—was thought to be much less than the forgone revenues, since the taxes would have eventually to be paid. In fact, in the 1984 tax act that eliminated the DISC and permitted in its place the Foreign Trade Corporation, many of the unpaid taxes were waived, so the interest-free loan turned out ex post facto to be a direct subsidy.

3. U.S. government subsidizes both the construction and operation of merchant vessels under U.S. registry. Construction subsidies do not increase exports since such subsidies are available only to purchases by U.S.-flag companies, but of course

operating subsidies to shipping make it easier for Americans to export shipping services. Both programs are long standing, and in the mid-1970s the operating subsidy amounted to around $200 million a year. Ship construction and shipping services generally involve heavy government involvement throughout the world.

4. The Export-Import Bank provides medium-term credit for American exports. For a number of years the interest rates were below market rates, so a direct subsidy was involved. More recently, the bank has tried to keep its lending rates above its borrowing rates by enough to cover its operating costs, except when necessary to meet foreign competition. The subsidy to American exports is thus now the more subtle (and smaller) one that arises from the use of U.S. government credit in borrowing in the capital market plus the absence of a requirement to pay dividends on the bank's capital.

5. Until 1973 the Commodity Credit Corporation (CCC) gave substantial subsidies to U.S. exports of many agricultural products, the counterpart of a system of high domestic price supports combined with the view that in the absence of agricultural policy the United States would be a substantial exporter of agricultural products, expecially grains, cotton, tobacco, etc. The high price supports stimulated output, so the program also involved limitations on acreage. This system was reinstituted on a lesser scale in the early 1980s. It is difficult to say whether agricultural exports would be larger or smaller than they would have been in the absence of the government support program, since the support prices and the acreage controls could be expected to have opposite effects on farm production.

6. Investment in plant and equipment in the United States enjoys a 10 to 25 percent investment tax credit. The credit in effect lowers the cost of domestic investment by that amount and thus stimulates the productive capacity of the economy. The credit operates for all investment, however, so it is not obvious whether on balance exports or imports are stimulated more by the tax credit. The first-round effects of increased production and income could go either way. The major long-run effect of the investment tax credit is to make American industry somewhat more capital-intensive than it would be without the credit, both in each industry taken separately and in its overall industrial structure. In addition, since 1981 there have been extremely generous write-off provisions for the depreciation of new investment. These provisions have a similar effect to the investment tax credit.

Depletion allowances for oil and other minerals have the

effect of stimulating domestic production of such products and thus serve to reduce imports or to increase exports of these products. Until 1975 this tax privilege was available to American-owned mineral investment anywhere in the world, but now it is limited to production in the United States.

7. There are many areas of direct government expenditure for activities that support business enterprise. Examples are federal spending, net of user charges, for airports and air traffic control, for dredging rivers and harbors, and for providing postal service. Government funds by the billions have been devoted to development of water resources, which provide both cheap hydroelectric power in the areas covered by them and cheap water for irrigation in the southwestern part of the country, resulting in a great stimulation of agricultural output there. In addition, the Rural Electrification Administration has subsidized the electrification of the rural parts of the American economy for nearly fifty years, at low interest rates, thus making farming somewhat less costly than it would otherwise be.

8. Price controls on domestically produced natural gas cheapen energy for Americans with access to the price-controlled gas and hence provide "subsidies" (but not revenue-reducing ones) for American exports as well as for domestic sales of products that require gas to be used in their production. In 1985 some, but not all, gas price controls were removed, so this "subsidy" will diminish in importance over time. For nearly a decade before 1981 U.S. oil prices were also held below world market prices, with similar effect.

9. Government expenditures on research and development help to cover the initial cost of new economic activities that often later lead to exports. The classic example is agriculture research, which has been financed by government for over a century and has led to vast improvements in the productivity of American agriculture and to improvements in the quality of agricultural products. Sometimes too, large export sales are a distant by-product of military research development and development expenditures, as was the case with the jet engine. Currently the government is spending substantial sums on research and development in the energy sector, both on nuclear power and on such possibilities as liquefaction of coal. To the extent that the last proves to be economically feasible, it may augment future exports of American coal.

10. Extensive government purchases sometimes lead to the development of products that are highly competitive in world markets by helping private firms spread their own research and development costs as well as other overhead expenditures over

a larger number of sales. The list of products here in principle
is a long one, but the point is quantitatively important in relatively few industries, such as military equipment, avionics,
some kinds of telecommunications equipment, and ground
tracking stations for satellites.

11. The most pervasive influences, and quantitatively probably the
most important stimulus to exports of particular goods, but also
the least obvious, is the host of government regulations on U.S.
production which have been introduced to improve the working environment or the natural environment. Such items as
effluent controls, safety regulations, minimum-wage legislation, and restrictions on child labor can have a profound effect
on the competitiveness of particular industries, and hence on
the relative competitiveness of other industries less directly
affected. Since most observers would not mention such government actions in a list of export "subsidies"—and indeed they
do not normally give rise to a loss of government revenue except where the government occasionally incurs some of the
costs, for example, of antipollution actions—it is worthwhile
to trace through the influence on exports of one of these regulations, the minimum wage. The key assumptions in this analysis
are that over time balance is maintained in international payments, for example by movements in the exchange rate of the
dollar, and that the government takes whatever steps are necessary to assure full employment of the labor force. So we are
looking here for the *sectoral* effects, the relative stimulation or
retardation of production in particular sectors of the economy
that arise from the regulation in question.

The minimum wage, if set high enough to exceed the wages
that would otherwise be paid in some industries, reduces the
international competitiveness of those industries by raising
their costs. The industry will find it more difficult to compete
with products from abroad. Imports will rise, and restoration of
equilibrium in the balance of payments will require some depreciation of the dollar relative to what it would otherwise be.
The depreciation, in turn, will increase the competitiveness of
all sectors where wages are not influenced by the minimum
wage. Put more concretely, it is likely in the United States that
the minimum wage discourages the production of apparel
(which is displaced to some extent by imports) and encourages
the production and export of machinery. Thus in an indirect
fashion, via adjustment of the exchange rate, the export of machinery is "subsidized" (but again not in a fashion that reduces
revenue to the government). A similar argument holds, mutatis
mutandi, for other government regulations. For example, meet-

ing required safety standards will raise costs more in some industries than in others, and via adjustments in the exchange rate will increase the competitiveness of industries or firms whose costs for safety have increased least. (See Kalt for a finding that environmental regulations have had a discernible effect on the composition of U.S. trade.)

So the influence of government actions on international competitiveness is pervasive, but it may also be so indirect as to be difficult to trace in detail with any confidence. It may nonetheless be substantial, even when it flows from actions aimed at objectives quite different from a desire to stimulate exports.

The United States shares a special characteristic with a few other countries such as Canada, Australia, and West Germany: namely, the federal structure of its government. The federal government accounts for only about one-third of total government expenditures in the United States and for about one-fifth of total civilian government employment. For the most part, the influence of state and local governments on the structure of production and costs falls into categories (7) and (11) in the foregoing list: expenditures that support business enterprise in a general way and regulation on the conditions of production or marketing. In addition, local governments sometimes support particular firms in the form of cheap land, low utility rates, or cheap credit. Starting in the 1950s a number of localities used their privilege of floating tax-exempt securities to provide cheap credit to new firms through the issue of so-called industrial development bonds, a practice that continues. The business-promoting activities of state and local governments are not of course aimed at encouraging exports from the United States, but rather from the particular state or locality to the rest of the United States, and only incidentally to other countries.

We saw above in the case of the minimum wage that a measure which has a negative impact on one industry indirectly affects others positively. The same point works in the opposite direction as well. Discrimination in favor of certain firms or industries automatically involves discrimination against firms and industries that are not specially favored. If subsidies or tax breaks or below-market credits are given to favored firms, others have to make up the difference by paying more taxes or more for credit than would be true in the absence of the discriminatory measures. And the currency will appreciate to the extent that exports are stimulated, thus putting others at a disadvantage with respect to foreign competition. When Japan allows the formation of cartels in periods of recession or for industrial restructuring, the impact of which is to hold domestic prices above what they would otherwise be, it is a negative action for those that buy from the cartel. Where consumers are made to bear the additional cost, as in the notorious color-television case, exports are not adversely affected. But when the cartel raises the price of steel or industrial chemicals or machinery or a host of other products, increased costs emerge for the downstream purchasers. (Of course, for domestic prices to remain above world market prices some form of import restriction must exist.) It may also be true, as Yamamura points out, that the possibility of creating recession cartels has generated higher capacity than otherwise would occur by removing from investing firms some of the risk of a major downturn in the market, and that this excess capacity in turn encourages exports at something below average cost. In that event, the yen will be stronger, and cartelization will put other firms at a disadvantage for that reason too. These points are generally neglected by those who criticize the unfair trade practices of Japan and other countries.

A similar argument applies to required procurement of domestic products. An enduring and justified complaint of the American heavy electrical-generating equipment industry is that potential purchasers in other major industrial countries buy exclusively domestic products, regardless of cost. This is true especially in Europe, where electricity supply is typically provided by public authorities, but it is even true in Japan, which like the United States has extensive private utilities. In contrast, the American market for heavy generating and transmission equipment is relatively open, and perhaps one-fifth of U.S. purchases are from abroad, mainly Japan. However, the requirement by foreign utilities to buy domestic in general will raise the costs of generating electricity there, and those costs must be either subsidized by the government or passed on to consumers, including industrial consumers. So while U.S. heavy-electrical-equipment industry suffers from this practice, the rest of American industry in general benefits by virtue of paying lower electricity charges than their foreign competitors must. Similar arguments apply to the requirement in some countries that computers be purchased locally. Over time, unless the local computers are competitive in quality and price, the (mostly state-owned) enterprises that are burdened by this obligation will suffer in competitiveness.

We can now return to a point raised at the outset: Can comparative advantage be made? Of course it can. In a tradition going back at least to Frank Taussig, it has been recognized that comparative advantage is determined not only by a country's natural endowments but also by its social and political and educational systems.[3] It is

---

[3] Taussig (1927, pp. 57–58) pointed to Germany's well-trained chemists and lab assistants as the basis for that country's comparative advantage in chemical dyes and other chemical products.

determined by the quality as well as the quantity of its labor force, by the motivation of its workers, and by their willingness to work diligently. Insofar as government provides for inland transport, education, efficient banking and other financial transactions, these too can influence comparative advantage, as can the long list of items discussed above for the United States, especially the regulatory environment. It would be absurd to pretend otherwise and to treat each geographic area as a tabula rasa with natural endowments but with no social or political system.

That is perhaps not what is meant when people talk about "making" comparative advantage rather than "finding" it. Rather, they may have in mind permanent cost advantages that are generated by a head start or by extensive production of a particular product. If important and durable economies arise from "learning by doing," then "doing" can give an advantage, however it is brought about, as analyzed by Krugman. However, two points should be kept in mind before rushing headlong to do many things in the interests of reaping the learning-by-doing cost advantages that they may engender. First, undertaking production which is not at once profitable in order to reap the advantages of learning by doing represents an investment, and to undertake any investment on the supposition of future positive rates of return is not sufficient. It will be a good investment only if the yield on the investment is at least as high as that on alternative investments. If on analysis that seems to be the case, then—as with any new investment opportunity—many parties may simultaneously want to undertake it, and that would not necessarily be a bad thing.

Second, "decisive" cost advantages for a given product or product group achieved by learning by doing turn out to be remarkably transient in many instances, given the large number of products that have had their commercial introduction in the United States but the production of which has subsequently been relocated abroad. Evidently there are cost factors that eventually overwhelm the cost advantages achieved even by a relatively long head start in production and the learning-by-doing gains thus achieved. There remains the possibility, however, that other countries do not recognize these two points and that they therefore undertake government support for activities which turn out to be bad investments, but which in the meantime create competition for otherwise successful American firms. What if anything should be done about it?

Possible Policy Directions

The problems posed above have been around for a long time. What we now call industrial policy goes back, in the strictly commercial arena, at least to the time of the early eighteenth century, when France tried (successfully) to create a high-quality porcelain industry in competition with the Saxon industry in Dresden. The effort in textiles is even older, as when in the early seventeenth century England attempted (unsuccessfully) to start a finished-textile industry in competition with the Flemish cities by prohibiting the export of wool.

EXISTING ARRANGEMENTS

The General Agreement on Tariffs and Trade of 1947 dealt with the problem of subsidies and international trade by suggesting (in Article 16) that export subsidies on manufactured goods (note the exclusion of primary products) should generally be eschewed and permits contracting parties to impose countervailing duties when such subsidies cause material injury. (In addition, Article 19 provides a general escape clause from GATT commitments, permitting countries to reimpose tariffs, but only on a nondiscriminatory basis, whenever a domestic industry is subject to substantial injury by imports.) A GATT working party attempted in 1960 to define more precisely what export subsidies were. In the mid-1970s the United States introduced its "traffic light" proposal, distinguishing between subsidies that were prohibited (red), subsidies that were clearly permitted (green), and subsidies that were potentially troublesome and were subject to consultation and possible countervailing action when they cause injury to some other contracting party to the GATT (yellow). This proposal was not adopted in the form in which it was presented, but it provided a framework for the Code on Subsidies and Countervailing Duties that was adopted in 1979 as part of the Tokyo Round of multilateral trade negotiations.

The 1979 code prohibits export subsidies except on certain primary products and except by developing countries. Code signatories undertake not to use such subsidies (Article 9), and their use creates a rebuttable presumption of adverse effects. They are thus subject to countervailing duties without an injury test, but subject to international approval. The code also provides, in its annex, an illustrative list of export subsidies, which goes a long way toward defining them. The code acknowledges the widespread use of, and permits, many other subsidies, but signatories recognize that these can hurt the trade interests of other countries and they therefore "seek to avoid causing such effects through the use of subsidies." In evaluating the use of subsidies in pursuit of domestic economic objectives, signatory countries are to "weigh . . . possible adverse effects on trade" (Article 11). If other countries are injured by such subsidies, they can countervail the subsidies in question (see Appendixes 1 and 2 for the relevant code articles and the illustrative list of export subsidies).

This general language leaves a very large area for interpretation, not to mention the cracks and overlaps in the illustrative list of prohibited subsidies. U.S. practice is gravitating toward an interpretation that requires a domestic subsidy to provide a "special favor" to a firm or industry before it is countervailable under U.S. law. That is to say, the United States tries to rule out as countervailable subsidies such broad legislative favors as accelerated depreciation, investment tax credits, research and development tax credits, and so on. Thus a domestic subsidy is countervailable if it causes material injury to an American industry through stimulated exports and if the subsidy is selective rather than general in its impact on the foreign firm or industry.

On the whole, the approach embodied in the GATT code and in evolving U.S. practice seems very sensible. Export subsidies are prohibited, and other subsidies are permitted but are countervailable if they are selective and if there is injury to another party. But several practical problems remain. First, on this track we must await sharper definition of the distinction between selective and general subsidies on a case-by-case basis. Second, during the period in which this sharper definition is taking place, the possibility exists for harassing imports by bringing test cases, and creating uncertainties whenever there is a preliminary finding of subsidy through "suspension of liquidation," under which an importer is put on notice that a higher duty may have to be paid at some subsequent date, but the importer does not know what the duty will be. Third, there is no assurance that other countries will move in the same direction as the United States in their interpretation of the distinction between selective and general subsidies. The United States tends to be the most active country in developing the case law, perhaps because other countries have less formal mechanisms for restricting imports if they choose to.

In their detailed study of treatment of subsidies to international trade, Hufbauer and Erb suggest that the list of prohibited export subsidies needs to be tightened and that the distinction between general and specific subsidies needs to be substantially clarified. But they basically accept the existing framework. Their most novel suggestion is in the area for remedies to subsidies, where they propose the countervailing *subsidy,* to be financed by an internationally approved import duty on goods coming from the country providing the offending subsidy (Hufbauer and Erb, p. 129). The advantage of a countervailing subsidy as opposed to a countervailing duty is that it permits the injured country to continue to sell in third markets and even in the home market of the subsidizing country. Its obvious disadvantage is that it would affect fourth-country competitors, who now would have to compete with two subsidizing countries, and that might engender a race toward subsidies. It would perhaps ultimately lead to a "disarmament" negotiation to remove the subsidies, as happened during the late 1970s and early 1980s with respect to official export credits, thereby reducing the distortions to international trade. But once subsidies are introduced, eliminating them is a prolonged, difficult, and often not wholly successful process as the effort to get consensus on official export credit restraint also illustrates.

THREE ALTERNATIVE CRITERIA

A major difficulty with public debate in this area is that it mixes three quite different criteria in assessing subsidies: distortions to resource allocation, fairness or equity, and injury. It is reasonable to conjecture that if there were no injury the issues of fairness and distortion would not arise in the practical world of policy, although academic economists would be concerned with the misallocative effects of distorting subsidies. However, when injury does arise, the three different criteria tend to be commingled, yet each points to a rather different solution.

Subsidies, domestic or export, induce distortions in the allocation of resources and hence should be eliminated or offset in the interest of economic efficiency except in those cases where the subsidy is itself designed appropriately to offset some other distortion, such as an externality of some kind. This is the principle that underlies the prohibition on export subsidies and the permissible imposition of a countervailing duty. As pointed out above, however, the countervailing duty cannot undo the distortion with respect to competition in third markets. A plan to eliminate all of the distortions introduced by government action would be a counsel of perfection given the extensive government intervention in modern economies enumerated above. It would even be difficult against all selective subsidies, which would invariably be justified on grounds of correcting a distortion in capital or labor markets, or as exploiting an externality, or on national security grounds, or in extreme cases as necessary to ensure domestic peace and political harmony. Governments are likely to abandon their extensive array of domestic subsidies only when they come to deem the costs, defined broadly, to be greater than the rewards.

Emphasis on equity or fairness leads to a second approach to policy, which would be to harmonize domestic measures among countries. If an activity has positive externalities or national-security value, that attribute is presumably not limited to a particular country. Most countries are concerned about having substantial local production of the staple food, perhaps of steel, perhaps of small arms, and increasingly of electronics on grounds of national security. Nations can negotiate broad ground rules on what is and is not acceptable. That would offer one concrete meaning to the otherwise obscure phrase, providing "a level playing field." The rules would be permissive rather than obligatory, but they would also be limiting, in that countries could not subsidize beyond what was agreed. The United States tried in the Tokyo Round to negotiate a more detailed elaboration of acceptable but possibly troublesome subsidies, but the result was the less-specific code described above. However, the United States could try again to negotiate greater international agreement on domestic subsidies that are permissible and on subsidies that are sufficiently potentially troublesome that they should be avoided. Inevitably such a negotiation would have to be on a conditional MFN basis, as the subsidies code was, since the interests of more than ninety GATT members are too diverse to permit any meaningful harmonization among all of them. By general consensus, developing countries are held to a lesser standard than are the fully industrialized countries, although the extent to which the standard should be relaxed is still a matter of considerable and continuing dispute.

Negotiation on harmonization of subsidies would be a cooperative approach. If other countries decline to cooperate willingly, the United States could approach the matter unilaterally. One way to do this is through the notion of "reciprocity" as embodied in Senator Danforth's telecommunications bill. This bill is motivated by the fact that Japanese and major European markets in telecommunications equipment are effectively closed to American (and other foreign) sellers, since most of this procurement is undertaken by government-owned (PTT) monopolies. Danforth's bill would require other countries to open their individual markets to imports of U.S. telecommunications equipment within three years under the threat of a sharp increase in U.S. tariffs on telecommunications products coming from them, from roughly 8 percent today to about 35 percent. The underlying principle is that the terms of access should be the same in each product field, telecommunications in this case, and that the United States should persuade others to adopt U.S. practices—which with the recent breakup of AT&T, means relatively open procurement by private telecommunications companies in the United States. In the absence of foreign adoption of U.S. practice, the United States will greatly reduce their access to the U.S. market.

There are two problems with this as a general approach. First, it does not address the question of exports of third countries. (That is perhaps not a major problem in telecommunications; indeed, the

United States continued to hold 38 percent of the world market in telecommunications products in 1982, compared with only 11 percent for Japan despite its alleged export prowess.) Second, success flowing from the threat embodied in the Danforth bill is likely to vary from country to country. Japan has a large stake in the U.S. market. France, whose practices are if anything even more exclusive than Japan's, does not. Japan might comply in its negotiations with the United States, Britain and Germany might comply partially, and France might not comply at all. The result at the end of three years would be that the United States would have to have different levels of restriction on products from each of these countries and value-added criteria to prevent geographic arbitrage among them. The issue is even more complicated when one allows for the difference between national ownership and location of production through foreign subsidiaries. Thus new distortions would be introduced into international trade, the discrimination implied would represent a sharp break with the most-favored-nation principle embodied in the GATT, and the consequence would be much closer surveillance over imports, with correspondingly greater opportunities for threats and harassment. These developments would not be in the overall U.S. interest.

A second unilateral approach toward a "level playing field," or more accurately toward reducing the protectionist mischief that can be done under that label, would be to introduce a uniform tariff of, say, 10 percent on all U.S. imports of manufactures, against a presumed entitlement of zero, combined with a stipulation that any industry wanting protection above that level would bear an exceptional burden of proof to show that it was substantially injured by a substantial foreign subsidy, one that was well above 10 percent, except in the case of prohibited subsidies. By imposing a levy on all imports of manufactures, the uncertainty that foreign exporters now face with respect to U.S. administrative law in the area of subsidies and countervailing duties could be greatly reduced. The disadvantage of this kind of measure, of course, is that it imposes a burden on all consumers of imports and also directly and indirectly reduces the competitiveness of U.S. exports, mitigated only in part by giving drawbacks of the duty on their imported inputs. Also, over time it might be difficult to sustain the principle that the 10 percent duty covered most foreign subsidies, against an asserted entitlement of no duty.

The third major approach shifts the emphasis to injury and away from the subsidies as such except for the clearly prohibited subsidies. It recognizes that government influence is pervasive and of long standing, and that in many ways such influence has been absorbed into the existing prices and economic structure. It focuses instead on large changes in government policy and the injury that such changes may cause. This approach would call for prior notification of all major changes in government policy and gradualism in the implementation of these changes. When gradualism is not followed, it would permit degressive (that is, gradually phased-out) relief to the injured party, with a view to encouraging ultimate adjustment to the new situation. Procedures would be necessary for discussing new policies and for considering measures that would achieve the same objective with smaller external impact. They would cover any major change in policy with external repercussions on particular industries and would have the objective of modifying the proposed action so as to reduce the imposition of costs on other countries. A gradual introduction of the new measures, like the multiyear staging of tariff reductions, is one way to reduce the costs of adjustment. The principles involved here cover subsidization of domestic production that competes with imports as well as subsidization of exports.

Instead of calling for harmonization of policies, an exacting requirement in a world of independent nation-states, this approach calls for extensive prior consultation on any industrial policy changes that are likely to cause injury, with a view to avoiding those changes but also with a view toward mitigating any injury that does occur.

Variants of the harmonization approach and the approach emphasizing injury are not incompatible with one another. It would be possible to emphasize injury as the main strategy while still negotiating with other countries to reduce the discrepancies among their industrial policies. But extreme harmonization would not be necessary.

ADVICE TO THE UNITED STATES

In framing U.S. policy, it is necessary to consider what is in the best interest of the United States, given its capabilities and limitations. The United States cannot favor particular industries secretly; that is not consistent with the way American government operates. Should it do so openly? My answer would be that open support for particular industries should be given only if a strong public-policy case can be made for such support on its merits: either on grounds of national security or if strong and demonstrable externalities are engendered by such support. This approach, while sounding blandly obvious, in fact has strong implications with respect to some of the proposals that have been made. For example, the Labor Industry Coalition for International Trade has complained of closed markets in other industrial countries for electric-power-generating equipment, in contrast to imports by the United States that on occasion have reached

20 percent of U.S. purchases. This, they contend, is unfair (see LICIT, pp. 79–82). But under the present regime the United States is not losing any of the economies of scale that it might otherwise obtain. In fact, the U.S. share of world exports actually rose between 1965 and 1980, from 5 to 10 percent. In addition, Americans presumably get lower-cost power by permitting import competition. Power is an important input into industry. It is possible, for instance, that part of the difficulties of aluminum refiners in Japan is due to preferred Japanese procurement of domestic electric-generating equipment. While it would certainly be desirable to be able to sell U.S. equipment in France and Japan, it is not obviously in the U.S. interest to stop purchases from those countries even if they decline to open their markets to U.S. equipment, and indeed the existing regime may on balance even favor U.S. industry as a whole. We simply do not know about the general equilibrium effects.

Furthermore, U.S. actions should not be motivated by arguments that rest on the fallacy of composition—that is, that the action would generate employment or improve the overall trade balance. Except in the short run, employment and the overall trade balance are determined by the macroeconomic conditions of each economy, not by particular trade policies.

In short, the United States should look at other countries (1) for practices that are illegal under GATT and its codes and (2) for policy measures that may have useful application in the United States. But in the end the United States should adopt measures that are best for the United States in the institutional setting of the United States, not just because they seem to have worked well abroad. Many actions by foreign governments have been costly and largely unsuccessful; those that have been successful would not necessarily or generally be successful in the American context. The United States could adopt many of the practices of Europe or Japan, but it would be unwise to do so. In particular, Americans should have to make a specially strong case for discriminatory treatment in favor of any particular industry. It is much easier for foreign countries to "pick winners" because they observe successful new industries in the United States. How would the U.S. government pick the industries of the future? To what experience could Americans turn? Instead, the United States relies on private rewards to thousands of firms and individuals, each making a guess as to which activities will be winners in the future. Most will be wrong. Some will be right.

But what kind of position does this leave the United States in with respect to bargaining with other countries on their practices? Might it not be desirable for the United States to introduce Danforth-style reciprocity or in other ways to threaten to close U.S. markets with a view to getting foreign countries to open theirs? Here we must recognize limitations of the United States. The American government cannot bargain subtly in the economic arena, and it has always found it difficult to back away from a publicly stated and argued position introduced for bargaining reasons but not fully acknowledged as such. Many Americans will believe the arguments that have been advanced. In short, a pluralistic, open society cannot bluff. It simply cannot carry it off. Foreigners will be skeptical of any non-serious threat, and once domestic political support has been built for the threat, the threat becomes serious but ceases to be a bluff. For this reason the United States should threaten actions only when it is clearly willing to undertake them. And in general it should be willing to undertake them only if they are in its best interests, not simply as a bargaining tactic.

It is true that the ambiguity surrounding decision making within the United States, and particularly the relationship between the president and the Congress when it comes to trade matters, is sometimes helpful in bargaining with foreigners, since foreigners can never be certain that Congress will not take the upper hand and move in a way which puts them at a disadvantage. This uncertainty is a reality of American politics, and it can sometimes be used successfully in the bargaining context. But it is rather different from the bluff of a poker player.

If other countries continue to be recalcitrant in pursuing practices that the United States considers unacceptable, should the United States retaliate as a demonstration that it is willing to take action hurtful to the other country, even if it is also hurtful to the United States? As suggested above, the general answer to this question is negative. However, it cannot absolutely be ruled out, if the action has a reasonable prospect of inducing a change in behavior by the other country that is beneficial to the United States. But this prospect is so heavily conditioned on the exact manner, timing, and context of the threatened retaliatory action that general rules are not likely to be helpful. It is a case where "playing it by ear" is preferable to playing by score or, to mix metaphors, by recipe. That is where the art of diplomacy comes into the economic arena.

References

Aoki, Masahiko (ed.) (1984) *The Economic Analysis of the Japanese Firm.* Amsterdam: Elsevier.

Caves, Richard E. and Uekusa, Masu (1976) *Industrial Organization in Japan.* Washington, D.C.: The Brookings Institution.

Cline, William R. (1982) *Reciprocity: A New Approach to World Trade Policy?* Washington, D.C.: Institute for International Economics.

———(ed.) (1983) *Trade Policy for the 1980s*. Washington, D.C.: Institute for International Economics.

Hufbauer, Gary Clyde and Erb, Joanna (1984) *Subsidies in International Trade*. Washington, D.C.: Institute for International Economics.

Jacquemin, Alexis (ed.) (1984) *European Industry: Public Policy and Corporate Strategy*. Oxford: Clarendon Press.

Kalt, Joseph P. (1985) The Impact of Domestic Regulatory Policies on International Competitiveness. Cambridge, Mass.: HIER Discussion Paper No. 1141, mimeographed.

Krugman, Paul (1985) Notes on Trade in the Presence of Dynamic Scale Economies. Cambridge, Mass. Mimeographed.

Labor-Industry Coalition for International Trade (1983) *International Trade, Industrial Policies, and the Future of American Industry*. Washington, D.C.: LICIT.

Magaziner, Ira C. and Reich, Robert B. (1983) *Minding America's Business*. New York: Vintage.

Ministry of International Trade and Industry (1980) *The Vision of MITI Policies in the 1980s*. Tokyo: MITI.

Nelson, Richard R. (ed.) (1982) *Government and Technical Progress: A Cross-Industry Analysis*. New York: Pergamon.

Patrick, Hugh and Rosovsky, Henry (eds.) (1976) *Asia's New Giant*. Washington, D.C.: The Brookings Institution.

Taussig, Frank W. (1927) *International Trade*. New York: Macmillan.

U.S.–Japan Trade Study Group (1984) *Progress Report: 1984*. Tokyo.

Warnecke, Steven J. (ed.) (1978) *International Trade and Industrial Policies*. London: Macmillan.

Yamamura, Kozo (ed.) (1982) *Policy and Trade Issues of the Japanese Economy*. Seattle: University of Washington Press.

APPENDIX 1
KEY ARTICLES PERTAINING TO SUBSIDIES IN THE 1979 CODE ON SUBSIDIES AND COUNTERVAILING DUTIES

Article 8   Subsidies—General Provisions

1. Signatories recognize that subsidies are used by governments to promote important objectives of social and economic policy. Signatories also recognize that subsidies may cause adverse effects to the interests of other signatories.
2. Signatories agree not to use export subsidies in a manner inconsistent with the provisions of this Agreement.
3. Signatories further agree that they shall seek to avoid causing, through the use of any subsidy:
   (a) injury to the domestic industry of another signatory,

(b) nullification or impairment of the benefits accruing directly or indirectly to another signatory under the General Agreement, or

(c) serious prejudice to the interests of another signatory.

4. The adverse effects to the interests of another signatory required to demonstrate nullification or impairment or serious prejudice may arise through

(a) the effects of the subsidized imports in the domestic market of the importing signatory,

(b) the effects of the subsidy in displacing or impeding the imports of like products into the market of the subsidizing country, or

(c) the effects of the subsidized exports in displacing the exports of like products of another signatory from a third country market.

Article 9   Export Subsidies on Products Other Than Certain Primary Products

1. Signatories shall not grant export subsidies on products other than certain primary products.

2. The practices listed in points (a) to (l) in the Annex are illustrative of export subsidies.

Article 10   Export Subsidies on Certain Primary Products

1. In accordance with the provisions of Article XVI:3 of the General Agreement, signatories agree not to grant directly or indirectly any export subsidy on certain primary products in a manner which results in the signatory granting such subsidy having more than an equitable share of world export trade in such product, account being taken of the shares of the signatories in trade in the product concerned during a previous representative period, and any special factors which may have affected or may be affecting trade in such product.

2. For purposes of Article XVI:3 of the General Agreement and paragraph 1 above:

(a) "more than equitable share of world export trade" shall include any case in which the effect of an export subsidy granted by a signatory is to displace the exports of another signatory bearing in mind the developments on world markets;

(b) with regard to new markets traditional patterns of supply of the product concerned to the world market, region or country, in which the new market is situated shall be taken into account in determining "equitable share of world export trade";

(c) "a previous representative period" shall normally be the three most recent calendar years in which normal market conditions existed.

3. Signatories further agree not to grant export subsidies on exports of certain primary products to a particular market in a manner which results in prices materially below those of other suppliers to the same market.

Article 11   Subsidies Other Than Export Subsidies

1. Signatories recognize that subsidies other than export subsidies are widely used as important instruments for the promotion of social and economic policy objectives and do not intend to restrict the right of signatories to use such subsidies to achieve these and other important policy objectives which they consider desirable. Signatories note that among such objectives are:

(a) the elimination of industrial, economic and social disadvantages of specific regions,

(b) to facilitate the restructuring, under socially acceptable conditions, of certain sectors, especially where this has become necessary by reason of changes in trade and economic policies, including international agreements resulting in lower barriers to trade,

(c) generally to sustain employment and to encourage re-training and change in employment,

(d) to encourage research and development programmes, especially in the field of high-technology industries,

(e) the implementation of economic programmes and policies to promote the economic and social development of developing countries,

(f) redeployment of industry in order to avoid congestion and environmental problems.

2. Signatories recognize, however, that subsidies other than export subsidies, certain objectives and possible form of which are described, respectively, in paragraphs 1 and 3 of this Article, may cause or threaten to cause injury to a domestic industry of another signatory or serious prejudice to the interests of another signatory or may nullify or impair benefits accruing to another signatory under the General Agreement, in particular where such subsidies would adversely affect the conditions of normal competition. Signatories shall therefore seek to avoid causing such effects through the use of subsidies. In particular, signatories, when drawing up their policies and practices in this field, in addition to evaluating the essential internal objectives to be achieved, shall also weigh, as far as practicable,

taking account of the nature of the particular case, possible adverse effects on trade. They shall also consider the conditions of world trade, production (e.g. price, capacity utilization etc.) and supply in the product concerned.

3. Signatories recognize that the objectives mentioned in paragraph 1 above may be achieved, *inter alia*, by means of subsidies granted with the aim of giving an advantage to certain enterprises. Examples of possible forms of such subsidies are: government financing of commercial enterprises, including grants, loans or guarantees; government provision or government financed provision of utility, supply distribution and other operational or support services or facilities; government financing of research and development programmes; fiscal incentives; and government subscription to, or provision of, equity capital. Signatories note that the above form of subsidies are normally granted either regionally or by sector. The enumeration of forms of subsidies set out above is illustrative and non-exhaustive, and reflects these currently granted by a number of signatories to this Agreement. Signatories recognize, nevertheless, that the enumeration of forms of subsidies set out above should be reviewed periodically and that this should be done, through consultations, in conformity with the spirit of Article XVI:5 of the General Agreement.

4. Signatories recognize further that, without prejudice to their rights under this Agreement, nothing in paragraphs 1–3 above and in particular the enumeration of forms of subsidies creates, in itself, any basis for action under the General Agreement, as interpreted by this Agreement.

APPENDIX 2
ANNEX ILLUSTRATIVE LIST OF EXPORT SUBSIDIES

(a) The provision by governments of direct subsidies to a firm or an industry contingent upon export performance.

(b) Currency retention schemes or any similar practices which involve a bonus on exports.

(c) Internal transport and freight charges on export shipments, provided or mandated by governments, on terms more favourable than for domestic shipments.

(d) The delivery by governments or their agencies of imported or domestic products or services for use in the production of exported goods, on terms or conditions more favourable than for delivery of like or directly competitive products or services for use in the production of goods for domestic consumption, if (in the case of products) such terms or conditions are more favourable than those commercially available on world markets to their exporters.

(e) The full or partial exemption, remission, or deferral specifically related to exports, of direct taxes or social welfare charges paid or payable by industrial or commercial enterprises.

(f) The allowance of special deductions directly related to exports or export performance, over and above those granted in respect to production for domestic consumption, in the calculation of the base on which direct taxes are charged.

(g) The exemption or remission in respect of the production and distribution of exported products, of indirect taxes in excess of those levied in respect of the production and distribution of like products when sold for domestic consumption.

(h) The exemption, remission or deferral of prior stage cumulative indirect taxes on goods or services used in the production of exported products in excess of the exemption remission or deferral of like prior stage cumulative indirect taxes on goods or services used in the production of like products when sold for domestic consumption; provided, however, that prior stage cumulative indirect taxes may be exempted, remitted or deferred on exported products even when not exempted, remitted or deferred on like products when sold for domestic consumption, if the prior stage cumulative indirect taxes are levied on goods that are physically incorporated (making normal allowance for waste) in the exported product.

(i) The remission or drawback of import charges in excess of those levied on imported goods that are physically incorporated (making normal allowance for waste) in the exported product; provided, however, that in particular cases a firm may use a quantity of home market goods equal to, and having the same quality and characteristics as, the imported goods as a substitute for them in order to benefit from this provision if the import and the corresponding export operations both occur within a reasonable time period, normally not to exceed two years.

(j) The provision by governments (or special institutions controlled by governments) of export credit guarantees or insurance programmes, of insurance or guarantee programmes against increases in the costs of exported products or of exchange risk programmes, at premium rates, which are manifestly inadequate to cover the long-term operating costs and losses of the programmes.

(k) The grant by governments (or special institutions controlled by and or acting under the authority of governments) of export credits at rates below those which they actually have to pay for the funds so employed (or would have to pay if they borrowed on international capital markets in order to obtain funds of the same maturity and denominated in the same currency as the export credit), or the payment by them of all or part of the costs incurred by exporters or financial institutions in obtaining credits, in so far as they are used to secure a material advantage in the field of export credit terms.

Provided, however, that if a signatory is a party to an international undertaking on official export credits to which at least twelve original signatories to this Agreement are parties as of 1 January 1979 (or a successor undertaking which has been adopted by those original signatories), or if in practice a signatory applies the interest rates provisions of the relevant undertaking, an export credit practice which is in conformity with those provisions shall not be considered an export subsidy prohibited by this Agreement.

(l) Any other charge on the public account constituting an export subsidy in the sense of Article XVI of the General Agreement.

13

Targeted Industrial Policies: Theory and Evidence

PAUL R. KRUGMAN

As the economic recovery of 1982–1985 slows, we are beginning to hear once again from the advocates of industrial policy. The proposals of these advocates include general incentives for capital formation, R&D, retraining of labor, and so on; but they also usually involve "targeting" of industries thought to be of particular importance. By targeting I mean an effort to change the allocation of investment (as opposed to its overall level) so as to favor particular industries in which the private market is believed to underinvest. There may be other concepts of targeted industrial policy, but the question of the government's role in the allocation of investment is surely the most important and controversial one.

The key question in evaluating calls for a policy of industrial targeting is, of course, how we decide which industries are to be targeted. Many advocates of targeting are, to put it bluntly, slippery on this point. They call for a coherent industrial strategy backed by new government institutions but do not define the substance of that strategy. Presumably the details are to be worked out later. Yet there is a wide range of opinion about which industries should be targeted and very little agreement about the criteria to be used to settle these disputes. If we can agree in advance, in more or less academic forums, on criteria for selecting target industries, it may be reasonable to expect government agencies to fill in the seven-digit detail. If we cannot devise such criteria, the prospects for success are slim; the

From the Massachusetts Institute of Technology, Cambridge, Massachusetts.

problem of criteria for targeting is a deep one—and deep analysis is not something that government agencies do well.

The case for a targeted industrial policy therefore stands or falls on the issue of criteria for selection. Can we devise criteria for choosing targets that will by and large pick the right industries? If we can, can we devise an institutional framework that will actually act on these criteria and not degenerate into a system of political payoffs? The answers I will suggest are not encouraging. Most criteria for targeting suggested by the advocates of industrial policy are poorly thought out and would lead to counterproductive policies. While there are more sophisticated criteria suggested by economic theory, we do not know enough to turn the theoretical models into policy prescriptions. Indeed, we find it hard to tell whether industrial policies have been successful even after the fact. Given this lack of clear guidelines, it is very naïve to suppose that government agencies can somehow intuit their way to appropriate policies.

This paper is in two main parts. The first part is a discussion of criteria for selecting target industries. It begins with an analysis of "popular" criteria advanced in publications aimed at a large audience, then turns to more sophisticated criteria suggested by economic theory. The second part examines the other side of the coin, the evaluation of actual industrial policies. It discusses the difficulties in determining, even after the fact, whether an industrial policy "worked." These problems are then illustrated with two examples, the steel industry and the semiconductor industry.

Criteria for Industrial Targeting

Even a skeptical discussion of targeted industrial policies should admit at the outset that there is no question that an optimal policy of industrial targeting would be beneficial. Markets are not perfect, and the numerous market failures and distortions in the real world surely lead to too little investment in some industries, too much in others. The question is, which ones? Markets are not perfect, but they are probably not so imperfect that random interventions are liable to improve on them.

Unfortunately, most discussions of industrial targeting are vague about what we should target. There is a good deal of emphasis on the importance of detailed study of industries, but even the most detailed study will not help us formulate policy if we do not know what we are looking for. There is also frequent assertion of the need for a coherent strategy—but a coherent, wrong-headed strategy may be worse than no strategy at all.

The absence of clear criteria for choosing targets makes discussion difficult. What I will try to do in this section is to analyze criteria that are explicit in some discussions and implicit in many others. These criteria fall into two groups. First are what I will call "popular" criteria. These are criteria which are frequently advanced in books and articles aimed at a large audience rather than at professional economists. The criteria that I have found most often in this literature are high value-added per worker, linkage to the rest of the economy, the prospect of future international competitiveness, and targeting by foreign governments. From an economist's perspective, all of these criteria are badly flawed. It is possible to show by both abstract "thought experiments" and by concrete example that an industrial strategy that uses any of these criteria to choose target industries is likely to reduce economic growth, not promote it.

While the public debate on industrial policy is dominated by these simplistic criteria, however, there is also an economist's case for targeting. This case emphasizes the role of targeting in the face of imperfect markets, resulting in particular from economies of scale, externalities, and the incentive-distorting effects of the government policies. These concepts furnish a valid basis for targeting—*if* the theoretical concepts can be turned into measurable factors in practice, and *if* one believes that the machinery of industrial policy will actually work in the way we intend.

Popular Criteria for Industrial Targeting

Most writing about industrial policy is vague about the content of such a policy. Any attempt to analyze specific ideas is therefore risky. The analyst who isolates a particular concept and criticizes it is likely to be told that he or she is oversimplifying. Yet there must be some specific concepts in the minds of the advocates of industrial targeting. My own readings of recent discussions suggest that the most important criteria envisioned by advocates of industrial targeting are the following:

1. **High Value-Added per Worker.** Some authors have pointed to the wide range of value-added per worker across industries and suggested that countries can raise their national income—to some extent at other countries' expense—by deliberately shifting their economic structure into the high value-added industries.
2. **Linkage Industries.** Many authors have also suggested that there is a special payoff to investment in "linkage" industries, such as steel and semiconductors, whose outputs are used as inputs by other industries.
3. **Future Competitiveness.** It is often argued that the government has a valuable role to play in targeting industries in which a

country is not currently competitive on world markets but in which it will be or can be made to be competitive in the future.

4. Responding to Other Governments. A final argument which has become very popular is that industrial targeting must be used to counter other governments' industrial policies lest our country's industrial structure become determined by other countries' targeting.

HIGH VALUE-ADDED PER WORKER

In their admirably clear tract on industrial policy, *Minding America's Business*, Magaziner and Reich (1982) immediately lay out their basic criteria for industrial targeting:

> We suggest that U.S. companies and the government develop a coherent and coordinated industrial policy whose aim is to raise the real income of our citizens by improving the pattern of our investments rather than by focusing only on aggregate investment levels. Our country's real income can rise only if (1) its labor and capital increasingly flow toward businesses that add greater value per employee and (2) we maintain a position in these businesses that is superior to that of our international competitors.[1]

Leaving on one side the issue of competitiveness, to which we return below, this passage clearly states two features of the proposed policy: a reliance on reallocation of investment rather than an increased flow, and direction of investment toward sectors with high value-added per worker.

There is great plausibility to the idea that reallocation of workers into high value-added sectors will raise national income. There is a wide range of value-added even among quite aggregate groups of industries. Other things being equal, a higher share of workers in the high value-added industries would mean higher national income per capita.

But would other things be equal? The crucial question to ask is *why* there is so much variation among industries in value-added per worker. Why does labor not move into the high value-added sectors without special encouragement? The answer, of course, is that by and large high output per worker reflects high input per worker: large quantities of capital, extensive training and education. Sending garment workers to a refinery does not by itself make them as productive as the existing refinery workers—you also have to equip each of them with several hundred thousand dollars' worth of capi-

---

[1] Magaziner and Reich (1982), p. 4.

tal equipment. Sectors with high value-added per worker generally have low value-added per unit of capital or per skilled worker.[2]

Suppose that the government were to follow a policy of encouraging investment in high value-added sectors—that is, sectors with high ratios of physical and human capital to labor—without at the same time increasing the overall rate of investment. It is easy to pursue a "thought experiment" to see the consequences. Since the capital-labor ratio in high value-added industries is higher than in low value-added industries, a given amount of investment would employ fewer people. Employment growth would slow and unemployment would rise. At the same time, since the capital-output ratio is also higher in high value-added industries, the rate of economic growth would actually be reduced. This may seem paradoxical, since output per worker would be rising more rapidly than before, but the paradox is resolved by the fact that the slowdown in employment growth would more than offset the rise in productivity growth.

Over time, if they are allowed to operate, market forces would tend to correct some of these effects. Rising unemployment would put downward pressure on real wages, and lower real wages would lead firms to move toward more labor-intensive techniques. In the long run, employment would be restored, with more workers in high value-added sectors but lower productivity in each sector—and probably lower output per worker in the economy as a whole. At least some advocates of high value-added targeting, however, would try to prevent this adjustment:

> As a national strategy, the substitution of lower real relative wages for productivity improvements would eventually make America a relatively poor country, albeit one with a healthy balance of payments. Accordingly, a rational industrial policy should encourage firms to invest in productivity improvements and increased output rather than reduce real wages.[3]

In other words, as unemployment rose, real wages would be sustained through government legislation or less formal suasion.

In short, a strategy of encouraging investment in industries with high value-added per worker appears, in our thought experiment, to have very poor results: slower growth and rising unemployment. But would it actually work out that way in practice? As it happens, there is abundant experience with this kind of policy. For

---

[2] For example, the chemical industry has a value-added per worker more than three times that in textiles, but its capital-labor ratio is also more than three times as high. (Numbers from *Statistical Abstract of the United States*).

[3] Magaziner and Reich (1982), p. 339.

much of the postwar period, encouragement of capital-intensive, high value-added industries was a key element of development strategy in many less-developed countries. It is generally acknowledged now that such policies were misguided. They tended to produce "dualistic" economies, divided between high-wage, capital-intensive but economically inefficient favored sectors and a low-wage, high unemployment residual sector.[4] The success stories of the less-developed world have been exactly those countries that, instead of prematurely developing their capital-intensive industries, exploited their comparative advantage to export labor-intensive products. Thus the proposal to foster high value-added industry amounts to a suggestion that we adopt a strategy which looks like a bad idea in theory and has worked poorly in practice as well.

LINKAGES

A second frequently advanced criterion for industrial targeting is that special encouragement should be given to industries which are important "linkage" sectors in the sense that their output is in turn used as an input by a number of other industries. A representative view on this is that of Eleanor Hadley, who writes in explaining the success of Japanese industrial policy that:

> Japanese target industries have been selected not only for their own importance but for their ramifying effect on other industries. For example, steel was chosen because, in an industrial economy, steel is the basic building block. Have cheap, good-quality steel, and the products made of it—ships, automobiles, rails, locomotives, heavy electrical equipment—will enjoy a price advantage.[5]

Similar views recur through much of the industrial policy literature. Magaziner and Reich offer a view identical to Hadley's; Mueller and Moore (1982) similarly argue for a need to target "basic industries, such as steel, which have important multiplier consequences throughout the economy."

On the surface, the idea of a special significance to the production of linkage industries seems highly plausible. If capital and labor are used to produce a final good—say dishwashers—then that is all they produce. If they are instead used to produce steel, the steel can in turn be used to produce many different items. So it is natural to

---

[4] See, for example, Little, Scitovsky, and Scott (1975).

[5] Hadley (1983), p. 6.

suppose that, other things equal, it is more productive to allocate more capital and labor to steel.

On reflection, however, the argument is not so clear. Saying that steel is used in many industries conveys the impression of multiple returns to output. But while steel is used in many industries, a particular ingot of steel is used only once. A linkage of industry's products can be made to sound like "catalysts" for the rest of the economy, but unlike a real catalyst steel does not get to be reused many times.

What does formal economic theory have to say? In textbook economic models, the fact that some industries are inputs into other industries is not in and of itself a source of market failure. In the absence of other distorting factors, the market will in theory produce exactly the appropriate amount of investment in linkage industries.

These textbook models, in which all "marginal whatnots" are equal, are of course poor approximations of reality, and it could easily be that the ways in which the world is different from the models do make extra investment in linkage industries desirable. For example, there could be external economies in the linkage sector. But it is equally possible to conceive of cases in which it is the final goods sectors that should be encouraged—e.g., if they are more labor-intensive and unemployment is a problem.

The point is that the fact that an industry provides inputs into other industries does not in and of itself mean that markets underinvest in the industry. There may be market failures that do make it desirable to promote a linkage industry, but the fact that an industry provides inputs to the rest of the economy gives us no help in deciding whether or not it should be targeted.

FUTURE COMPETITIVENESS

Some proponents of industrial policy have realized that the differences of criteria for selection of targets represent a problem. An answer proposed by some, such as Diebold (1980), is the criterion of eventual international competitiveness. Adams (1983) argues that restricting targeting to industries that can eventually become competitive on world markets is a relatively hard-nosed criterion for selection:

> The criterion of present or future competitiveness on world markets . . . is a difficult market test. If the industry can meet that test, we can presume that resources are being allocated efficiently . . . [but the] world-market test must be applied with a

dynamic view since industries presently in need of assistance may ultimately be competitive.[6]

There is a strong appeal to the notion that an industry is worth supporting if it will eventually be able to stand on its own feet in the face of international competition. We know that this is not a toothless criterion: many industries have received protection and support without ever becoming self-sustaining. (Indeed, there may well be industries deserving of support which would fail to pass the test, as discussed below.) The criterion of eventual competitiveness also has an honorable intellectual lineage, having been propounded by no less an economist than John Stuart Mill.

But it is a fallacious criterion. There are at least two ways in which an industry might meet the criterion of eventual competitiveness, yet in fact not be a proper candidate for targeting.

The most obvious way in which an industry might meet the criterion of eventual competitiveness is if comparative advantage is shifting in the industry's direction for reasons independent of industrial policy. Suppose, for example, that a country has a small capital stock but a very high savings rate. Over time, as the country accumulates capital, its comparative advantage will shift toward capital-intensive industries, simply as a result of market forces. In the economist's imaginary world of perfect markets, the shift in industrial structure would occur at exactly the right rate. In the real world, the pace is bound to be wrong; but there is no presumption that markets are too sluggish—they could equally well move too quickly.[7]

The important point is that in our example—meant of course to be suggestive of postwar Japan—targeting of capital-intensive industries will meet the criterion of eventual competitiveness, regardless of whether or not it actually promotes economic growth. It may be desirable to accelerate the movement into more capital-intensive industries, or it may not—it depends on the precise nature of capital market imperfections. Certainly it is possible to build an industry too soon. Singapore is now building personal computers; should it have tried to develop a computer industry in 1965? Adjusting too fast is as economically irrational as not adjusting at all.

Our first case, then, is where the eventual competitiveness of an industry essentially happens for reasons independent of industrial policy, something that some have called the case of the "pseudo

---

[6] Adams (1983), p. 413.

[7] An interesting point in this connection is that "growth stocks," whose value depends on anticipated future rather than current earnings, have historically been bad investments. This suggests that financial markets tend if anything to lay too much stress on future as opposed to present returns.

infant industry." A second case arises when industrial targeting is responsible for eventual competitiveness, but at excessive cost. Suppose that there is an industry with worldwide excess capacity and little new investment. By subsidizing the cost of capital, a country could induce its firms to resume investing, building more modern, capital-intensive plants than their competitors. These plants might well have lower operating costs than those in other countries, so that even after the capital subsidy is ended the targeted industry will be able to export and operate at higher-capacity utilization than other countries' industries. Yet in the absence of any other special reason for supporting the industry, such as technological spillovers, the social rate of return on investment in an industry with excess capacity is bound to be quite low. Again, that is not an argument drawn out of thin air; as argued below, the apparent success of Japanese industrial policy in steel may be partly of this kind.

The last example stressed subsidy of capital. It is also possible that by subsidizing the acquisition of knowledge in an industry— either by subsidizing R&D or by protecting an industry while it moves down the learning curve—industrial targeting can sometimes create industries which are self-sustaining thereafter. As with a subsidy to capital, the eventual competitiveness does not show that the policy was justified. There is an enormous literature on the infant-industry issue, which boils down to this: having the industry grow up healthy is not enough; its existence must generate enough extra national income to compensate for the initial cost. Suppose for example that a costly subsidy program creates an industry which is competitive, but not by a wide margin, so that it would be nearly as cheap to import the industry's products. Then the policy meets the criterion of eventual competitiveness but was nonetheless a mistake.

What these examples demonstrate is that eventual competitiveness is not a useful guide to selecting targets. No doubt there are industries which will eventually be competitive that should be targeted; there are also without question future competitive sectors that should not be targeted, and for that matter there are sectors worth supporting that will never be able to stand on their own feet. Unfortunately, knowing that an industry will or might become competitive tells us nothing about whether it should be promoted.

RESPONSE TO FOREIGN TARGETING

One of the most influential arguments for industry targeting is that it must be used to counter foreign competition. On this argument, our criterion for selection of industries ought to be essentially defensive. We should support industries that have been targeted by foreign governments in order to avoid letting our industrial structure be determined as the "obverse of other countries' industrial policies." There is great appeal to the idea that the policies of foreign governments should not be allowed to distort our industrial structure. As one recent report argues:

> [The] concept that the U.S. must reduce production in any sector—such as steel, automobiles, or semiconductors—as a result of decisions taken by foreign governments, is tantamount to resigning ourselves to having our economy shaped by the policies of others rather than by the impersonal operation of the market place. Our adherence to a "laissez faire" philosophy under these conditions would mean that the structure of American industry would be determined, not by market forces, but by the industrial policies of other governments.[8]

Should the United States, then, fight fire with fire—meet targeting with countertargeting? We probably will, but like our other popular criteria, this one does not stand up too well under analysis.

The problem is that in economics two wrongs do not make a right. A distortionary foreign policy may reduce U.S. welfare,[9] but countering it with an equivalent U.S. policy will often merely make things worse.

Suppose, for example, that foreign countries subsidize exports of an agricultural commodity, say wheat. This is undeniably a distorting policy, and since the United States exports wheat, it lowers the price of U.S. exports and reduces our national income. Yet a program of countersubsidy by the United States would depress prices still further, compounding the damages. Here the plausible idea of meeting foreign targeting turns out to be a very bad criterion. The example is, of course, not hypothetical: this is exactly what happened.

The response of advocates of a policy of meeting foreign competition would presumably be that wheat is a bad example. Foreign industrial targeting should not be matched in a mindless fashion, but only when it threatens key sectors.

But what defines a key industry? If we can find criteria which make an industry particularly crucial, then we should target that industry regardless of whether other countries choose to target it. If the industry does not meet their criteria, foreign targeting gives no reason to change our judgment.

---

[8] Labor-Industry Coalition for International Trade (1983), p. 15.

[9] Or it may increase our welfare. If Colombia were to subsidize its coffee exports, this would distort the international trading pattern—but in a way that benefits us. One economist remarked that when the U.S. government determined that European governments were subsidizing their exports of steel to the United States the appropriate response should have been to send a note of thanks.

In practice, an industrial policy aimed at meeting foreign competition would probably lead to government encouragement of investment precisely where the returns to investment are depressed by the targeting of other governments. A case in point is steel. Steel is almost universally regarded as an industry worth targeting, and partly as a result is an industry with low returns. In meeting foreign policies, the United States would thus be targeting an industry where the market returns are bound to be low. The only justification would be if there were other reasons to target steel. As already suggested and argued at greater length below, this is a dubious proposition.

In general, meeting foreign industrial policy seems to be almost a recipe for picking sectors where there is excess capacity and low returns.

CONCLUSIONS

We have examined four popular criteria for selecting targeted industries and found them wanting. These criteria are not straw men. They are criteria proposed by some of the best-known advocates of industrial targeting and are at least as sophisticated as the ideas that shape most public debate.

Of the four criteria, two would probably be quite disastrously counterproductive. Targeting of high value-added industries is both in theory and in practice a recipe for slower growth and higher unemployment; defensive targeting to meet foreign policies will often be a way of ensuring that investment is funneled into areas with excess capacity and depressed rates of return. The other criteria, linkages and future competitiveness, are less obviously destructive; but they are not likely to be beneficial, either.

I am sure that some advocates of industrial targeting will deny that they have in mind anything as simplistic as the concepts just described. The proponents of these criteria, however, do not think they are being simplistic. And when the time to choose industrial targets comes, it will be a break with all past experience if the criteria for selection are more sophisticated than these.

Nonetheless, it is possible to suggest some more sophisticated criteria for targeting which might be used to carry out a successful industrial policy. I find it hard to believe that they can serve as useful guides for policy, but in fairness they ought to be described.

More Sophisticated Criteria

Only the most die-hard believer in the functioning of free markets would deny that a government planner with sufficient information and freedom of action could increase national income by targeting certain industries. The idealized model in which free markets lead to a perfectly efficient outcome relies on extreme assumptions, particularly about returns to scale and the ability of firms to capture fully all the benefits of their activities. Since these assumptions are visibly violated, there clearly exists a set of government policies—including activities we would describe as industrial targeting—that could raise national income.

The problem is that knowing that a useful industrial policy exists does not necessarily help us implement it. To be helpful, an advocate of industrial targeting must be able to describe operational criteria for choosing target industries. This task may not be hopeless, but it is not simple. What I will do is analyze the way three types of deviations from the idealized competitive model might give rise to a case for targeting and discuss the difficulties in formulating actual policies on the basis of existing knowledge.

ECONOMIES OF SCALE
AND IMPERFECT COMPETITION

The most obvious failing of conventional economic models is their assumption of constant returns to scale and the associated assumption of perfect competition. In the view of most businesspeople and many economists, the norm—at least in manufacturing—is some degree of increasing returns and a more-or-less oligopolistic market structure. Of particular importance for many discussions of industrial policy are "dynamic" economies of scale, resulting both from the role of R&D and from the experience curve.

It makes a great deal of difference whether these economies of scale are internal or external to firms. For example, does each firm in the industry have its own experience curve, or is there an industry experience curve that reflects output nationwide (or worldwide)? The case where the economies of scale are largely at the level of the industry rather than the firm is quite different from the case of firm-specific scale economies, and it is dealt with below.

In the case of internal economies of scale, the starting point for a discussion of policy is the realization that markets will not be perfectly competitive. An industry will consist of a small group of firms, or if it consists of many firms they will be producing differentiated products. Prices will be above marginal costs; firms will often act strategically, taking actions aimed at influencing the decisions of other firms. The range of possible behavior, and of response to government policies, is much wider than in the standard competitive model.

In the United States the traditional concern of government has been with protecting consumers from the exercise of market power by firms. The response has been antitrust and, in cases of very powerful scale economies, regulation. Only with the growing importance of trade has focus shifted to the protection or promotion of domestic firms against foreign competitors. There is definitely room for activist policy here, but deciding what to do is not straightforward. Theoretical models can be devised in which an industry with economies of scale should be targeted, but others can be devised in which it should not.

Let us begin by sketching out one sort of situation in which targeting might be advantageous. Suppose there is an industry in which there are only two serious competitors, a U.S. and a Japanese firm, and that each firm knows that its costs will fall sharply as it gains experience. Each firm will tend to follow a "Boston Consulting Group" strategy, initially setting its prices low in order to move down the experience curve. If it could, each firm would like to convince the other that it will follow a very aggressive policy, to encourage its competitor to pull back, but the firms may have no credible way of making such a commitment.

In this context, a targeted industrial policy could serve the purpose of helping domestic firms play their strategic game. A government subsidy, for example, could make credible the intention of the domestic firm to pursue an aggressive pricing policy, deterring its competitor. The withdrawal of the competitor could raise profits by more than the amount of the subsidy, in effect transferring monopoly rents from foreigners to domestic residents. Thus there is at least the possibility of a successful predatory industrial policy.[10]

Unfortunately for policymakers, small variations in the situation could reverse the conclusion. Suppose for example that there are not one but several U.S. firms, and that the industry concerned is one in which we are a net exporter. Then it still might be the case that an output subsidy could benefit the United States by deterring foreign competition. But it could also be the case—and this becomes more likely, the more U.S. firms there are—that the opposite is true. In competing with each other, U.S. firms may be setting their export prices too low and investing too much for their own collective good; their collective profits might be improved if they could be induced to pull back. This is the classical argument for exploitation of market power in trade: you should raise the price of your exports, not lower it.

Which of these stories is right? The answer surely varies across industries. To act with any hope of success would require a deep

---

[10] This analysis is based loosely on Brander and Spencer (1982) as well as on Krugman (1983).

study of each industry in question—a deeper study than any that has ever been carried out.

EXTERNAL ECONOMIES

Even in textbook analyses, external economies are acknowledged to be a justification for government intervention. If the output of firms generates experience useful to other firms, or if the results of one firm's research and development can be "reverse engineered" by other firms to improve their own technology, then there is a clear opening for government action. The question becomes one of political economy: can the government act with enough wisdom to do more good than harm?

The obvious examples of external economies are in innovative industries. Developers of new products or processes cannot help conveying valuable information to competitors. Even if some details of an innovation can for a time be closely held—for example, a manufacturing process—the simple knowledge that something can be done is often highly valuable to competitors.

Some discussions of industrial targeting also seem to suggest that there are external economies in the relationships between innovative industries and their customers. Such a view appears to be the implicit model in this recent statement by the Semiconductor Industry Association: "The U.S. advantage in semiconductors has . . . enabled the U.S. to maintain a competitive lead in most other high technology fields."[11]

Presumably the idea is that close proximity to suppliers makes it easier for the users of the high-technology products to pick up ideas that are "in the air," enabling them to keep abreast of and exploit the latest advances in technology. The case for believing in important interindustry externalities of this sort does not seem as compelling as the case for intraindustry externalities, but there are doubtless some examples.

Externalities are clearly important in innovative industries. If that were the whole story, these externalities would mean that firms underinvest in technology and would provide a clear case for government subsidy of R&D and promotion of industries on the early part of their learning curve. Unfortunately, this is not the whole story. Recent theorizing on competition in innovative industries has suggested that there are some other reasons why firms may *overinvest* in technology.[12] There are two main reasons. First, there may be wasteful duplication of research. There may be six firms trying to

---

[11] Semiconductor Industry Association (1983), p. 1.
[12] See Dasgupta and Stiglitz (1980).

develop a process when there should only be two or three. An R&D subsidy would encourage each firm to invest more, but it would also encourage entry, encouraging further duplication of work. Second, established firms may try to use heavy investment in R&D to deter potential competitors. This may lead them to develop technologies "too soon," leading to a situation where the social returns to more R&D are actually quite low.

For these reasons, a simple policy of subsidizing high-technology industries is not necessarily a good idea. In principle one could devise a better policy, one that combines some subsidy elements with industry restructuring to reduce the number of firms, encourage them to do joint research, and the like. It is possible that Japanese industrial policies actually do in some degree approach this model. All one can say from a U.S. perspective is that to select targeted industries successfully, back them with subsidies, restructure them, and do all this in an objective way would require that government officials show a depth of understanding and subtlety of action unprecedented in U.S. history—and do it on a routine basis.

OTHER GOVERNMENT POLICIES

It is arguable that the most important reason the idealized model of a competitive economy is wrong is that we in fact have a large, intrusive government. The government imposes taxes and regulations that are not neutral across industries; it offers unemployment insurance and imposes minimum wages; it protects declining industries and bails out firms in trouble. All of these actions distort incentives in the market.

It is a familiar proposition from the literature on economic development that distortions due to government action may make other offsetting government actions desirable. For example, protection of imports can lead to an overvalued exchange rate, which in turn may imply that export subsidies can raise national income. Similarly, if the government tends to promote or protect labor-intensive sectors it may be able to undo some of the damage by simultaneously promoting capital-intensive projects.

In general, however, the appropriate response to government-induced distortions is to try to minimize them, not to target particular industries in which the country underinvests. The interaction of the tax system with inflation during the 1970s probably led the United States to invest too much in housing, too little in plant and equipment; surely the right response was reform of the tax system, not targeting of particular capital-intensive industries.

It is sometimes argued that existing government policies, though not explicitly targeted, do have differential effects across industries and that this means that we should respond with targeted offsetting policies. The answer, however, probably is that we should respond with policy reforms that are also not explicitly targeted, even though they too may in fact differentially favor certain sectors.

CONCLUSIONS

There is a theoretical case for industrial targeting. A time may come when economists are sufficiently knowledgeable to make concrete policy recommendations based on that theoretical case. As it stands now, however, the theory does not look very operational. If we must have a targeted industrial policy, it would probably be best to target the high-technology industries, which have both important dynamic-scale economies and important externalities. But we have no assurance that this is actually the right policy. There are arguments, and not outlandish ones, suggesting that targeting of these industries might well lower national income.

Evaluating Targeted Policies

There is no lack of experience with targeted industrial policies. Japan, of course, has pursued a policy of targeting throughout the postwar period. France has also made fairly consistent efforts to target particular industries. Other countries, including Germany, Britain, and indeed the United States, have at times targeted individual sectors. One might be inclined, then, to sweep aside the theoretical discussion of the previous part of this paper with a call for a look at the evidence. What has worked in practice?

Unfortunately, this is not so simple as it seems. In the first place, simply ascertaining what a country's industrial policies have been is often quite difficult. In the modern world, governments rarely use clean, transparent tools like flat subsidies or tariffs to promote targeted industries. Instead they use a variety of hard-to-measure instruments—tax incentives, credit allocation, procurement policies, recession cartels, red-tape barriers to imports, and so on. The extent of effective targeting is not only hard for observers to ascertain; it is a fair bet that even the officials administering the programs do not know how much support they are providing.

Above and beyond this difficulty is the problem of evaluation. Even if we are sure that a country did in fact target a particular industry, there is no simple way to tell whether that policy raised national income. The issue of evaluation is similar to the problem of selecting targets in the first place, and is similarly difficult.

The plan of this part of the paper is to review the problem of evaluating targeted industrial policy, then illustrate the difficulties

TABLE 1.
Quantifiable Factors in Japan's Faster Productivity
Growth

		Japan	U.S.
Net saving as percent of GDP, 1974–1980		19.5	6.5
Rate of growth of employment, 1973–1980		0.7	2.1
Full-time school enrollment (%)			
Ages 15–19:	1960	39.4	64.1
	1975	76.3	72.0
Ages 20–24:	1960	4.8	12.1
	1975	14.5	21.6

Sources: OECD, *Main Economic Indicators, Historical Statistics* and U.S. Bureau of the Census, *Social Indicators III.*

with brief discussions of the two most famous cases of industrial targeting: the Japanese successes, real or alleged, in steel and semiconductors.

The Problem of Evaluation

Most studies of industrial policy do not worry explicitly about the problem of evaluating a policy's success. The attitude of most authors seems to be that they will recognize success or failure when they see it. In practice, this usually leads to evaluation based on one of two criteria: the overall success of economies whose governments use targeted industrial policies or the eventual competitiveness of targeted industries.

The argument from overall success in its basic form is the statement that "Japan has a targeted industrial policy and Japan has a high growth rate, so Japanese-style targeting must work." I may be accused of caricaturing the position of advocates of targeted policies, but in fact this is the main argument of many advocates of targeting: "How did Japan manage for 20 years to have real per annum growth of 10 percent? Inasmuch as no one else has achieved that, it strikes me that something other than market forces is an element in explaining it."[13]

The problem with the argument from overall success is that industrial policy is only one of many ways in which countries differ. Table 1 shows, for example, some readily quantifiable reasons for the disparity between U.S. and Japanese rates of productivity growth

---

[13] Eleanor Hadley, quoted in *High Technology* (1983), p. 20.

during the 1970s. Japan had a far higher savings rate than did the United States, together with a much lower rate of growth in employment; thus, capital per employee rose much more rapidly in Japan than in the United States. At the same time, Japan was rapidly accumulating human capital, as indicated by the growing proportion of highly skilled workers.

There is no lack of possible explanations of Japan's rapid productivity growth and no reason to assume that everything Japan does contributes to that growth. Japan's agricultural policy almost surely is a drain on the economy, yet the economy has performed well. It is entirely possible that Japanese industrial policy has also been unproductive or counterproductive but has been outweighed by favorable factors. Argument from aggregates does not work; only an examination of the specifics of targeting can be used to evaluate its effectiveness.

But what specifics should be examined? In practice, most authors end up using the criterion of eventual competitiveness. If a targeted industry ended up as an effective competitor on world markets, the policy is judged a success. Japanese steel and semiconductors are held up as examples of success based on the growth in Japanese market share rather than on any careful calculation of costs and benefits. As we have already pointed out, however, eventual competitiveness does not necessarily provide any justification for industrial targeting, and it also is no evidence that targeting was a good idea. It may instead either reflect forces that had nothing to do with industrial policy or represent a victory achieved at excessive cost.

In order to evaluate targeted industrial policies, we must make a careful analysis based on the same criteria we would use to select industrial targets. In particular: Did the policy give domestic firms a useful strategic advantage? Did it generate valuable external economies? Did it offset a distortion caused by other government policies? Hardest of all to determine, were these benefits worth the cost?

The Success That Wasn't: The Case of Steel

If the United States ever does adopt a strategy of industrial targeting, it is almost inevitable that steel will be one of the chosen industries. Japan's rapid emergence as a massive exporter of steel in the 1960s and early 1970s is still the most widely cited example of successful industrial policy (although semiconductors have recently begun to share the honor). The decline of the U.S. industry is correspondingly held up as an example of the adverse consequences of the lack of a U.S. response. In terms of the "popular" criteria for choosing a target examined in the first part of this paper, steel has everything: high value-added per worker, thanks to its capital intensity; linkages, due to its status as a basic material; in the Japanese case, eventual competitiveness on world markets; and in the case of the United States, the fact that at least some of the industry's problems could be attributed to foreign targeting.

But we have seen that these are not valid criteria. Looking at the industry's experience more critically suggests a quite different conclusion. Remarkably, this most famous of successes for industrial targeting was no success at all.

BACKGROUND ON THE STEEL INDUSTRY, 1960–1980[14]

To understand the dynamics of competition in the steel industry requires an appreciation of four factors: the "maturity" of steelmaking technology, the internationalization of raw-material supply, the persistent differential between U.S. and Japanese employment costs, and the unexpectedly slow growth in demand after 1973. These factors, more than industrial policy, determined the basic outline of shifting market positions.

The technology of making steel is a "mature" one: it is fairly standardized and not changing too rapidly. As a result, the most advanced nations do not have a significant technological advantage over only moderately advanced countries. From the 1950s on, new steel plants in Japan, Europe, and the United States have all been roughly comparable in their labor and materials efficiency. More recently, advanced developing countries such as Korea have also shown their ability to borrow this technology.

It should be noted, however, that while new plants have been roughly comparable in different countries, there is a strong vintage effect: new plants have higher labor productivity than older plants. This is important in explaining relative U.S. and Japanese productivity performance.

There was a time when the world distribution of steelmaking was largely determined by the location of raw materials. Steel production was located on top of coalfields which were not too far from sources of iron ore. By 1960, however, the advantages of traditional locations had evaporated. On one hand, traditional raw-material sources were becoming increasingly worked out. On the other hand, falling ocean transportation costs made it possible to exploit new sources, such as Brazilian iron ore and Australian coal. The result was to turn steel into a "footloose" industry: any coastal location with a good harbor would do. The critical determinants of location became the costs of capital and labor.

---

[14] This exposition is based on Crandall (1981).

In spite of the rapid rise in real wages in Japan over the past twenty years, the compensation of U.S. steelworkers has consistently been far higher than those of their Japanese counterparts. In the mid-1960s U.S. steelworkers received wages and benefits about six times those of Japanese workers; in 1981 they still received about twice as much. During the 1960s the major reason for this differential was the higher level of U.S. wages in general, which in turn reflected general U.S. economic advantages: superiority in high-technology industries, a higher level of capital per worker, greater self-sufficiency in natural resources. As these advantages have narrowed, the differential in the steel industry has been sustained through a sharp rise in the wages of U.S. steelworkers relative to the U.S. manufacturing average, from 38 percent above the average in 1967 to a 71 percent premium in 1977.[15] (It is curious though perhaps not surprising that many discussions of the competitive problems of the U.S. steel industry—such as that of Magaziner and Reich—do not even mention the exercise of market power by the steelworkers as a possible source of difficulty.)

Finally, the state of the steel industry in all countries has been powerfully conditioned by the slow growth in consumption since 1973. From 1968 to 1973 world steel output grew at an annual rate of 5.7 percent; after 1973 the combination of higher energy prices and slower growth in industrial countries brought a sharp slowdown, even before the worldwide recession of recent years. From 1973 to 1978 world output of steel rose at an annual rate of only 0.5 percent.

MARKET FORCES AND STEEL COMPETITION

Before proceeding to analyze the role of industrial policy, it is worth asking what the effect of these factors would have been if there had been no government intervention. Otherwise we may be attributing to MITI developments that would have happened in any case.

The first critical point is that by the early 1960s the Japanese steel industry would have had a competitive advantage over the U.S. industry even if the Japanese government had kept hands off. The same technological "book of blueprints" was available to both countries; access to raw materials was no longer a crucial factor; and labor costs were much higher in the United States. Capital was becoming steadily more available in Japan, thanks to a high savings rate. Quite independent of industrial targeting, Japan was gaining a comparative advantage in steel while the United States was losing one.

Given this underlying shift, the rational investment strategies of the two industries were quite different. Japanese firms naturally

---

[15] Data on steelworker compensation from Crandall (1981).

built new, "greenfield" plants. U.S. firms could have built such plants but could not have made them pay, since their labor costs would still have been far higher than those of their Japanese competitors. The rational strategy—in terms of long-run profit maximization, not just short-term advantage—would have been to invest only to maintain existing capacity or to take advantage of special opportunities to add capacity cheaply through "roundout" additions at existing sites. (The "greenfield" plants built in the United States during the 1960s yielded a disappointing rate of return.)[16]

Because of its increasing relative proportion of newer plants, the Japanese industry eventually was bound to outstrip the United States in labor productivity. This would not have been a sign of failure on the part of either U.S. workers or managers, simply a reflection of the newer vintage of the Japanese plants. The United States could keep up, but only at excessive capital cost. The productivity of capital is as important an economic consideration as the productivity of labor.

Finally, with the sharp slowdown of world demand after 1973 there would have been excess capacity in the steel industry whatever the policies of government. In this excess-capacity environment the plants that stayed open would be newer plants with lower operating costs: in other words, Japanese capacity utilization would be higher than that of U.S. firms.

What should be clear from this exposition is that the broad picture in U.S.–Japanese steel competition is not too different from what it would have been without Japanese targeting. This is not to deny a role to MITI, but we should not overstress its importance.

JAPAN'S TARGETING OF STEEL

From the 1950s to the early 1970s steel was a targeted industry in Japan. This meant doing several things. First, and probably most important, the Japanese steel industry became a favored claimant in a rationed capital market in which interest rates were below market-clearing levels—an important if hard-to-measure subsidy. Second, the industry received tax breaks. Third, the industry received some subsidies and low-interest loans, although these were relatively unimportant. The combined effect was basically to give Japan's steel industry a low cost of borrowed capital. At the same time, the assurance that in recessions the industry's profits would be protected by cartelization probably made firms more willing to risk having excess capacity.

The result was that from the mid-1960s through the early

---

[16] Magaziner and Reich (1982), p. 161.

TABLE 2.
Financing of Japanese Steel Investment

Retained earnings as % of net investment, 1967–1971	1.5
Long-term debt as % of capital employed	
1964	46.1
1971	67.7
Rate of return in steel, 1971	10.7
Rate of return, all Japanese manufacturing, 1971	17.5

Sources: International Iron and Steel Institute, *Financing Steel Investment,* 1961–1971, and OECD, *Profits and Rates of Return,* 1979.

1970s, the period of most rapid growth, the Japanese industry had a distinctive pattern of financing and rates of return, shown in Table 2. Investment was overwhelmingly financed by the issue of debt, hardly at all out of retained earnings. The rate of return was well below the average for Japanese manufacturing.

The eventual return on this investment was even lower than this table suggests. After 1973 the growth of world steel demand fell off sharply, and Japanese steel production peaked in this year. Although Japanese firms have low operating costs and have thus managed to maintain higher rates of capacity utilization than their competitors, steel prices have been low enough that profits have been low—certainly not high enough to have made investing in steel profitable. In fact, little new investment has taken place since 1973. It is only thanks to the prevalence of low-interest loans and the capital gains from subsequent inflation that the Japanese steel industry has remained solvent. To caricature the Japanese industry's position, in the 1970s the steel companies were willing to operate the capital-intensive plants the government built for them.

DID TARGETING OF STEEL HELP JAPAN?

The crucial question now becomes Was targeting of steel a wise policy? Did it in fact raise Japan's growth rate?

On the test of market returns, the targeting of steel does not look at all like a good idea. Because of the unexpected steel glut of the 1970s, the heavy investments in steel in the period 1965–1972 turned out to yield very low rates of return. By encouraging these investments, targeting funneled resources into a sector with low private rates of return. Only if social rates of return were much higher than private rates can the policy be justified.

The most common reason advanced why there may have been extra social returns is steel's role as a linkage industry. This is the justification offered by Hadley (1983) and Magaziner and Reich (1982); it is also suggested by some professional economists, including Adams (1983). But, as we have seen, linkages by themselves do not create a divergence between social and private rates of return. A true market failure is required.

As we have argued, targeting can create strategic advantages that enable domestic firms to capture rents from foreign competitors. In this case, however, with a depressed world industry, there were no rents to capture.

It is also possible for a targeted industry to generate useful technological externalities. But the mature technology of steelmaking makes such externalities unlikely; indeed, the U.S. and Japanese industries seem to have had rough technological parity from 1960 on.

If there is another argument for the usefulness of Japan's targeting of steel, it is not prominent in the literature. Heresy though it may seem, it is hard to avoid the conclusion that the most famous of industrial policy successes was no success at all. It encouraged Japanese industry to invest in an activity with low returns and generated no visible side benefits.

SHOULD THE UNITED STATES HAVE TARGETED STEEL?

If the United States had targeted steel in the 1960s and 1970s, the results would have been similar to the Japanese results, but even less favorable. The United States could have built new "greenfield" plants as productive as Japan's, but because of higher U.S. labor costs they would have had lower capacity utilization and lower profit rates than Japan's. In other words, the private rate of return on any targeted investment in the U.S. steel industry would have been low indeed.

Arguments for extra social returns in steel in the United States are similar to those for extra returns in Japan, and are similarly dubious. The one exception we might make is an argument rarely mentioned. There *is* a market failure in steel: the market power of the steelworkers. This provides a possible though risky justification for intervention. Because steelworker wages are above their free-market levels, it makes sense to offset this distortion by subsidizing the steel industry's labor costs. The problem is of course that this might only encourage wages to go still higher. Ideally the government could strike a bargain: employment subsidies in return for wage restraint. The problem is that politically such a bargain is almost inconceivable.

CONCLUSIONS

The experience of the steel industry is usually cited as an example of the favorable consequences of industrial targeting in Japan and the unfavorable consequences of U.S. inaction. In fact it is a poor example. Japanese targeting was probably not crucial in determining the course of U.S.–Japanese competition, and to the extent it was effective it probably reduced Japanese national income.

The Success That May Have Been: Semiconductors

In recent years, the semiconductor industry has acquired much of the aura once associated with steel as a symbol of national economic prowess. As was once the case with steel, a semiconductor industry is something possessed only by the most advanced countries; like steel, semiconductors are an input into other advanced industries; like steel, semiconductors are closely connected with a country's military potential. In the 1950s, a national presence in steel was a political must for every country that could afford it; in the 1980s and 1990s semiconductors will play much the same role.

More important for our economic analysis is the indisputable fact that the semiconductor industry is about as far as one can get from the classical model of a perfect market.

BACKGROUND ON THE SEMICONDUCTOR INDUSTRY

The key feature of the semiconductor industry is its extremely rapid pace of technological change. The real cost of a given amount of computing capacity is cut in half every few years. This means a very short product cycle, which in turn has two major consequences: strong dynamic-scale economies and important external economies.

The shortness of the product cycle makes dynamic-scale economies important in two ways. First, the costs of R&D cannot be amortized over many years' production. As a result R&D is a large part of a firm's cost, and the per-unit cost depends strongly on a firm's sales. Second, because product cycles do not last very long, firms are always in the early, steep part of the experience curve. So for each individual firm, average costs fall quite sharply with cumulative output.

In addition to the dynamic-scale economies at the level of the firm are additional, external economies that spill over between firms. Some of these spillovers seem to operate through personal contact—hence the high-tech clusters of Route 128 and Silicon Valley. Others operate through the possibility of "reverse engineering" or more general forms of imitation and may apply at a national or even a world level.

DETERMINANTS OF INTERNATIONAL COMPETITION

In an industry with strong dynamic-scale economies, international competition is somewhat more complex than in conventional models of international trade. There is an important element of simple comparative advantage, but history and market access can also be crucial. And the importance of the experience curve makes it normal for shifts in market position to occur suddenly rather than gradually.

Comparative advantage in high-technology industries is largely determined by access to human capital of the right kind. The countries and regions that have done well in high-technology competition are those with relatively abundant supplies of highly educated workers. Labor costs in production are not as important as the ability to maintain close links between production and R&D, so as to keep abreast of changing technology.

As Table 3 suggests, a once-overwhelming U.S. lead in highly educated labor has been narrowed over time by other countries, especially Japan. Even in the absence of industrial targeting by other countries this would lead us to expect some reduction of U.S. market share in high-technology industries, including semiconductors.

How would this fall in market share come about in the absence of targeting? One recent study has argued that in the absence of targeting the process would be gradual:

> In an open market American firms would lose market share slowly when Japanese production began . . . the overall pattern of trade in a range of semiconductor products in an open market should see American producers losing market share slowly to Japanese producers but retaining a permanent market position based on their initial advantage.[17]

This argument is, however, almost surely wrong, because of the importance of the experience curve. The basic situation in high-technology industries is that Japan is acquiring a comparative advantage in areas in which U.S. firms have historically had dominant market shares. U.S. firms thus have the initial advantage of greater cumulative experience, but Japanese firms have lower input costs. It makes no sense in this situation for Japanese firms to try to increase their market share gradually across the board, since this would fail to overcome the U.S. advantage in experience. Instead, the natural strategy of a Japanese firm—regardless of whether or not the government is involved—is one of rapid penetration of a narrow market

---

[17] Borrus, Millstein, and Zysman (1982), p. 147.

TABLE 3.
Human Capital Indicators for High-Technology Industries

	Japan	U.S.
Scientists and engineers engaged in R&D per 10,000 workers		
1970	33.4	63.6
1978	49.4	58.3
Electrical engineering graduates per 1,000,000		
1970	133	85
1977	185	66

Sources: National Science Board, *Science Indicators* (1980) and Borrus, Millstein, and Zysman (1982).

segment. This involves aggressive pricing to gain market share and move down the learning curve. Thus "surges" involving a Japanese willingness to take initial losses and a rapid increase in Japanese market share in a narrow product line are probably endemic to the process of Japanese catch-up to the United States.

This is not to say that targeted industrial policies could not also play a role. Subsidies to R&D could obviously promote a particular industry. More subtly, a protected domestic market could serve as a springboard for exports. By providing a secure base, a protected domestic market can encourage domestic firms to invest in R&D and to move down the learning curve while at the same time deterring foreign competition from doing the same. This can lead to a larger market share for domestic firms even in unprotected markets. The allegation of the U.S. semiconductor industry is that a combination of subsidies and the advantage of a protected domestic market, rather than market forces, have led to the rapid growth in Japanese semiconductor exports.

JAPANESE TARGETING OF SEMICONDUCTORS

Japan's targeting of semiconductors contains one well-documented but probably not-too-important element—government-subsidized, collaborative research—and one disputed but possibly crucial element—closure of the domestic market. Several major studies have alleged that these two policies in conjunction have been the prime cause of Japanese success,[18] but it remains possible that policy was actually a minor factor.

The undisputed part of Japanese policy has been the encour-

---

[18] Borrus, Millstein, and Zysman (1982) and Semiconductor Industry Association (1983).

agement of joint research projects supported by government subsidy of which the best known is the Very Large Scale Integration (VLSI) program. Relative to the size of the industry, the subsidies do not appear to have been very large. The Semiconductor Industry Association estimates a total subsidy of $507 million from 1976 to 1982— about $75 million per year. At the same time, Japanese sales of integrated circuits in 1981 were valued at nearly $3 billion.[19] So the extent of subsidy by itself was almost certainly not enough to give Japanese firms a decisive advantage. More uncertain is whether encouragement of joint research and market sharing allowed Japanese firms to avoid duplicative research, thus making their R&D more efficient than that of U.S. competitors. U.S. industry executives tend to be doubtful about this. In general, the allegations of predatory Japanese targeting focus less on subsidized research than on the effects of a closed domestic market.

Until the mid-1970s Japan had overt protection of its semiconductor industry, through tariffs and quantitative restrictions. After dismantling of these barriers, however, the share of imports in Japanese consumption did not rise. Indeed, it showed a downward trend during the period 1975–1982, except for a temporary reversal following the massive appreciation of the yen in 1978. The argument of U.S. critics has been that the structure of the Japanese industry allows de facto closure of the market through informal guidance without any explicit controls on imports.

The key feature of Japan's industry structure is that the major producers of semiconductors are also the major consumers. These firms are not, however, vertically integrated in the usual sense of the term. Each firm sells most of its output on the open market while buying most of its semiconductors from other firms. It is argued, however, that these are really not arm's-length transactions. In effect, Japanese firms may be colluding to buy only from each other, with this collusion promoted by discreet guidance from MITI.

Is this really the case? The prime piece of evidence usually cited is the low share of imports in the Japanese market. Although U.S. semiconductor firms make about two-thirds of the world's integrated circuits, they account for only about a sixth of the Japanese market. One might point out, however, that a similar though less striking disparity exists between Japan's share of the world and U.S. markets: Japan accounts for nearly 30 percent of the world integrated circuit production but only 12 percent of U.S. consumption.[20] Japan does run a substantial surplus in semiconductor trade with the

---

[19] Subsidy figure from Semiconductor Industry Association, sales figure from Borrus, Millstein, and Zysman.

[20] Figures from *Business Week*, May 23, 1983.

United States, but this need not be taken to demonstrate protection. More significant but less objective is anecdotal evidence of a "buy-Japanese" mentality among Japanese firms. Whether this represents a hidden official policy is much less clear.

In any case, is the combination of subsidy and market closure the basic explanation of Japan's rising market share in semiconductors, particularly its leading position in memories? Probably not. As we have argued, a rising Japanese market share in high-technology industries generally would be happening in any case, and the rapid penetration of narrow market sectors is exactly what we would expect. Government policy may have helped determine that memories rather than some other type of product were the market segment selected, but the general character of what has happened probably has little to do with official targeting.

WAS JAPANESE POLICY A SUCCESS?

To the extent that Japanese industrial policy has been responsible for the growth of the semiconductor industry, was that policy a success? The basic criteria for success would be either (1) capture of substantial rents from U.S. firms or (2) external economies benefiting other industries. In both cases the returns are not yet in.

The rents from semiconductor targeting, if there will be any, lie in the future. Although numbers are not available, it seems clear that Japan's export of 64K RAMs has not yet earned a return sufficient to justify the investment. The large Japanese market share was won through a price war that led to substantial losses for U.S. firms and is unlikely to have been marked by Japanese profits. There has been no sustained breathing space for the Japanese to exploit their market dominance, since a similar costly battle for the 256K RAM is now looming. If there are to be big profits for the Japanese firms, they still lie several years in the future.

The external economies from semiconductor production are also yet to be seen. It is often asserted that a country which has a decisive advantage in production of semiconductors will thereby gain a comparable advantage in "downstream" products such as computers, but there is no solid evidence that this is true. The United States is far from being out of the semiconductor business and retains leadership in many other high-technology areas. Thus it will be years before the alleged adverse effects of Japanese targeting on U.S. economic performance become clearly visible.

CONCLUSIONS

In contrast to the fairly clear case of steel, the effects of industrial targeting in semiconductors are enveloped in fog. We do not know clearly the extent to which the industry was really targeted; we do not know how important the targeting was in international competition; and we do not know whether the policies of the Japanese government, whatever they were, raised or lowered Japanese national income.

Semiconductors are a classic example of a nonclassical industry. Nearly every market failure one can think of is present. So if any sector is suitable for government intervention, this is the one. Yet it is unclear whether the government intervention which has taken place was either crucial for the industry or beneficial from a national point of view.

General Conclusions

The advocates of industrial targeting generally claim that targeting has worked in other countries and is a major reason for better economic performance abroad than in the United States. While the discussion just presented is far from a conclusive rejection of this assertion, it certainly raises questions.

The crucial point is that evaluating the success of targeted industrial policies is a very difficult task. Most authors do not realize this. They go into painstaking detail on the technology and history of an industry, then become sloppy and casual when they come to the truly difficult task of economic evaluation.

We have examined briefly two industries in which most people believe that targeted industrial policy scored major successes. In one case, that of steel, it is hard to find any reason to call the policy a success—unless one reverts to the view that because Japan is a successful economy, everything Japan did must have been well conceived. In the other case, semiconductors, we are not sure what Japanese policy was—and the payoffs to that policy, whatever it was, are still matters of the uncertain future.

Prospects for Successful Industrial Targeting

It would be foolhardy to say that there is no case for a targeted industrial policy. Market imperfections are legion. Given sufficient information, enough power, and enough freedom from political pressures, a MITI-type agency might make a significant contribution to national income. But in the real world, the prospects for such gains are poor. We have noted a series of negative points:

> The most commonly cited criteria in popular discussions of targeting—criteria' at least as sophisticated as the criteria likely to govern actual targeting—are misconceived, in some cases disastrously so.

While there is a valid case for targeting grounded in economic theory, the theoretical basis is too complex and ambiguous to be useful, given the current state of knowledge.

We are not easily able to evaluate the costs and benefits of industrial targeting even after the fact. In spite of the huge literature on industrial policy, the criteria generally used for evaluation are crude and can easily be misleading.

There are no clear-cut cases of successful industrial targeting. Of the two most famous examples, Japanese targeting of steel probably reduced national income, while the returns are not yet in on Japan's targeting of semiconductors.

In some respects this paper has loaded the dice in favor of targeting. The examples surveyed were the apparent successes, not the obvious failures: steel and semiconductors, not synfuels and the Concorde. Yet the verdict still has to be that there is very little support for the idea that industrial targeting is a desirable policy.

It is already clear from congressional hearings and popular discussion what the elements of a U.S. program of industrial targeting are likely to be. The key element will probably be a "development bank" that will provide low-interest loans and loan guarantees to favored firms. These firms will mostly be of two types. First will be firms in "mature, linkage industries"—in other words, the troubled, high-wage, unionized, politically powerful traditional heavy industries. The second will be "key emerging industries"—in other words, the glamorous and prestigious high-technology areas. Whatever the intentions, in the U.S. political system it is inevitable that political factors will weigh heavily on the choice of favored firms.

It is hard to believe that such a policy will accelerate U.S. economic growth. Its direct effect will probably be to slow growth and raise unemployment. More important, the easy answer of targeting will help postpone our coming to grips with the real sources of disappointing U.S. performance.

This chapter is a revised version of a paper originally published in *Industrial Change and Public Policy*, Federal Reserve Bank of Kansas City, 1983.

References

Adams, F. G. (1983) Criteria for U.S. Industrial Policy Strategies. In F. G. Adams and L. R. Klein (eds.), *Industrial Policies for Growth and Competitiveness.* Lexington, Mass.: Lexington Books.

Borrus, M., Millstein, J., and Zysman, J. (1982) *International Competition in Advanced Industrial Sectors: Trade and Development in the Semiconductor Industry.* Washington, D.C.: U.S. Government Printing Office.

Brander, J. and Spencer, B. (1982) Strategic Commitment with R&D. Kingston, Ont.: Queen's University. Mimeographed.

Crandall, R. W. (1981) *The U.S. Steel Industry in Recurrent Crisis.* Washington, D.C.: Brookings Institution.

Dasgupta, P., and Stiglitz, J. (1980) Uncertainty, Industrial Structure, and the Speed of R&D, *Bell Journal of Economics,* (Spring): 1–28.

Diebold, W. (1980) *Industrial Policy as an International Issue.* New York: McGraw-Hill.

Hadley, E. M. (1983) The Secret of Japan's Success, *Challenge* 26 (May/June): 4–10.

International Iron and Steel Institute (1974) *Financing Steel Investment, 1961–1971.*

Labor-Industry Coalition for International Trade (1983) *International Trade, Industrial Policies, and the U.S. Economy.*

Little, I., Scitovsky, T., and Scott, M. (1975) *Industry and Trade in Some Developing Countries.* Oxford: Oxford University Press.

Magaziner, I. and Reich, R. (1982) *Minding America's Business.* New York: Vintage Books.

Mueller, R. E. and Moore, D. H. (1982) America's Blind Spot: Industrial Policy, *Challenge* 24 (Jan./Feb.): 5–13.

National Science Board (1980) *Science Indicators.* Washington, D.C.: U.S. Government Printing Office.

Organization for Economic Cooperation and Development (1979) *Profits and Rates of Return.* Paris: OECD.

Semiconductor Industry Association (1983) *The Effect of Government Targeting on World Semiconductor Competition.* Washington, D.C.

14

Comparative Advantage and Possible Trade Restrictions in High-Technology Products

MORDECHAI E. KREININ

Introduction

Concern about deterioration of the U.S. leadership in high-technology products emanates in large measure from the decline in the country's overall competitive position and trade performance, and from the alleged stagnation of the "traditional" heavy industries. Will high-technology industries go the way of steel and autos? Can they be relied upon to remain a mainstay of the American economy?

One indicator of the country's competitive position is the changes in the unit-labor costs. Table 1 shows that in the decade since 1973, U.S. labor cost in manufacturing (measured both on national currency and on U.S. dollar basis) rose faster than its counterparts in Japan and Germany. When measured on U.S. dollar basis (namely, allowing for changes in the exchange value of the dollar), U.S. unit-labor cost also rose faster than those of France, Canada, and Italy. But these averages, as well as the overall trade performance, conceal substantial differences among industries and cannot be generalized to describe the position of any subset of industries.

Next, automobiles and steel represent special cases, where the deterioration of the U.S. competitive position is attributable in no small measure to high unit-labor costs relative to the U.S. national manufacturing average. In sharp contrast, unit-labor cost in the Japanese auto and steel industries advanced in tandem with the Japanese

---

From Michigan State University, East Lansing, Michigan.

TABLE 1.
Annual Rate of Change in Unit-Labor Cost in Manufacturing
1973–1984

Country	National currency basis	U.S. dollar basis
United States	6.7	6.7
Japan	0.8	3.1
Germany	4.1	4.4
France	10.0	4.5
United Kingdom	13.4	9.2
Canada	9.2	6.3
Italy	15.0	4.8

Source: Bureau of Labor Statistics, *International Comparisons of Productivity and Labor Cost Trends,* June 1985.

national manufacturing average; and to some extent the same holds true for Germany.[1] The conditions in autos and steel are not necessarily replicated in the high-technology industries.

Nor can the massive trade deficits in 1983–1985 be used as an indicator of the situation in the high-technology sector. For the most part the deficits find their root in certain macroeconomic causes. These include first the "excessively high" exchange value of the dollar during 1981–1985. In turn that may be due to high real-interest rates in the United States (relative to foreign countries as well as to the United States' own historical standard), caused by the monetary and fiscal policies mix; to the attraction of funds to a country that is generally perceived as a "safe haven"; and to reduced foreign lending by American banks. Second, the more rapid economic recovery in the United States than abroad increased imports of goods and services more than exports. And, finally, the huge external debt of Latin American countries, traditional customers of the United States, forced upon them belt-tightening measures that sharply curtailed their imports. In this context it ought to be remembered that if the less-developed countries (LDCs) are to service and repay their external debt, the creditor (industrial) countries would have to sustain sizable trade deficits with them to make such repayment possible.

No inference can be drawn from the overall trade position to the competitive health of the high-technology industries. Those need to be examined in their own right. This paper assesses the changing U.S. competitive position in this sector and examines the reasons for these changes. It then inquires into the desirability of using strategic trade policy to promote the American interest and improve U.S. welfare. Is it in the interest of the United States to

---

[1] For details see Kreinin (1984).

negotiate with the European Community and Japan mutual restrictions on market access in high-technology products?

What Are High-Technology Industries?

There exists no universally accepted definition of high-technology industries or products. Most scholars and government agencies define the high-technology sector in terms of factor inputs rather than output: either the proportion of scientists and engineers in the labor force or the research and development (R&D) intensity of production. There are serious problems with these proxies, the main one being that they identify a set of industries at a given point in time. As such they may overlook changes that occur when innovative industries become less dynamic, or conversely when industries advance in their technological sophistication. The rate of technological diffusion is an important determinant of the question How long will a high-technology industry remain high-technology? (Soete and Turner, 1984, and literature cited therein). And that rate varies greatly between industries.

Despite this and other problems the input criteria are used extensively for identifying the high-technology industries, partly for lack of a better alternative. Thus the U.S. Department of Commerce (1983)[2] identifies high-technology industries by the simultaneous presence of two characteristics: (1) above-average level of scientific and engineering skills, or alternatively high R&D efforts relative to value added and (2) a rapid rate of technological development. These criteria yield the following list of industries:

Aircraft and parts

Computers and office equipment

Electrical equipment and components

Optical and medical instruments

Drugs and medicines

Plastic and synthetic materials

Engines and turbines

Agricultural chemicals

Professional and scientific instruments

Industrial chemicals

---

[2] That study presents a wealth of data and statistical tabulations that are used in this chapter.

TABLE 2A.
U.S. Producers' Shipments, Exports, Imports, and Trade
Surplus in High-Technology Manufacturers, 1974 and
1981 (in billion dollars)

Year	U.S. producer's shipments	U.S. trade[a]		
		Exports	Imports	Export surplus
1974	126.6	21.5	9.5	12.0
1981	291.9	58.5	32.2	26.3

[a] Based on trade data reported on an SIC, not SITC, basis.
Source: Lester Davis, Technology Intensity of U.S. Output and Trade. Washington, D.C.: U.S. Department of Commerce, Office of Trade and Investments Analysis, July 1982, Appendix tables 3 and 4.

In 1980 these high-technology industries spent on R&D a percent of value-added that was triple the average for the entire manufacturing sector, while the share of scientists and engineers in the labor force of these industries is more than double the national average.

Most industrial and trade classifications are too aggregative to pinpoint the high-technology subcategories. Moreover, several sources of data are used in this paper; they are drawn from different classifications that do not always concur with each other: Information on international trade is based on the SITC, or alternatively on highly aggregative GATT categories; data on U.S. production and costs are based on the SIC, or alternatively on input-output tables; and production data for other countries are based on the UN ISIC. The concordance between the various classifications is not precise at the level of disaggregation needed to zero in on the high-technology industries, hence the occasional inconsistency between some of the tabulations.

The High-Technology Sector in the United States

Tables 2A and 2B show the relative size of the high-technology sector in the American economy. With shipments approximating $300 billion in 1981, that sector constitutes about 14 percent of total manufacturing shipments. However, it formed 32 percent of total manufacturing exports and only 19 percent of imports, generating an export surplus of about $26 billion. The rate of growth in labor productivity in this sector in the 1970s was 5.6 percent.

In 1980 the high-technology industries represented 5 percent of total employment (compared to 20 percent in all manufacturing) but accounted for more than 25 percent of total scientific and technical manpower, and for more than 60 percent of private industrial R&D expenditures. About half the benefits from all R&D were retained in

TABLE 2B.
High-Technology Share of U.S. Manufacturers'
Shipments, Exports, and Imports[a] (in percent)

Year	High-technology share of total manufacturers		
	shipments	Exports	Imports
1974	13.2	29.3	13.0
1981	13.9	32.2	18.8

[a] Based on trade data reported on an SIC, not SITC, basis.

Source: Lester Davis, Technology Intensity of U.S. Output and Trade. Washington, D.C.: U.S. Department of Commerce, Office of Trade and Investments Analysis, July 1982, Appendix tables 3 and 4.

the manufacturing sector, while the remaining half was gained by the nonmanufacturing sectors. If one adds interindustry spillover within the manufacturing sector itself, it is apparent that R&D has significant external benefits.

Although this country spends more on R&D than any other industrial country, the trend in the 1970s was unfavorable to the United States. Between 1964 and 1979 the share of R&D expenditures in GDP declined from 3.1 to 2.4 percent in the United States. By contrast, it rose from 1.5 to 2.0 percent in Japan and from 1.4 to 2.3 percent in Germany. The numbers of scientists and engineers employed in R&D grew by 18 percent in the United States, compared to 59 and 48 percent in Japan and Germany respectively.

In addition, because high schools in Japan and the major European countries place great emphasis on mathematical and scientific literacy, workers in these countries have a stronger background in technological matters than do U.S. workers.

These developments, coupled with the growth of the high-technology sector, have produced a shortage of certain scientific and engineering skills in the United States. This is documented in the following statement:

> As a result of these trends, during the 1970's, the U.S. labor market was characterized by shortages of personnel in several high technology specialties. Most prominent among the shortages or tight labor market conditions reported during this period were those for all types of computer specialists. This reflected the burgeoning applications of computers and their related servicing industries throughout the economy. Similar situations were reported for electronic specialists and chemical, electrical, and industrial engineers.
>
> The increases in salary levels in the private sector, which re-

*sulted from a tight labor market, seriously affected recruitment
of instructors for U.S. engineering school faculties (currently,
there are 1,600 vacancies) and for the U.S. armed forces (where
pay scales did not keep up with the private sector). These increases also contributed to a sharp drop in the number of engineering Ph.D. candidates. [U.S. Department of Commerce, 1983,
p. 25]*

A productive factor that is critical to the development of high-technology industries is in short supply, and its supply elasticity (which
depends on university training) is low at least in the short and intermediate run. This conclusion has important policy implications to
be addressed in a later section.

Competitive Performance of the U.S.
High-Technology Sector

Within the manufacturing sector, the United States continues to
maintain a strong competitive edge in high-technology industries.
But that lead appears to be weakening, and the range of products in
which this country has a distinct advantage is narrowing. Two types
of evidence will be presented in support of this proposition: trends
in international trade flows and the behavior of domestic cost and
prices.

INTERNATIONAL TRADE PERFORMANCE

Table 3 presents trade statistics for eleven highly aggregative manufacturing industries (a classification used in the GATT tabulations)
and for all manufacturing, for 1973, 1982, 1983, and 1984. The 1983
and 1984 data can be viewed as a "survival test," showing differential industry performance under the severe strains of: overvalued
dollar, decline of imports into traditional U.S. markets, and the
faster economic recovery in the United States relative to that of foreign countries. Moreover, given what can be projected for 1985, the
1984 data are likely to be representative of that year as well.

Because the classification is highly aggregative it is not possible
to isolate the high-technology industries. Each category contains
both high- and low-technology products. For example, *"chemicals"*
include drugs, medicines, and industrial chemicals, which are high-
technology, as well as soaps and detergents, which are not. Nevertheless, there is a concentration of high-technology products in the
first four categories, while the remaining seven categories are heavily
laden with middle- and low-technology industries.

U.S. trade balance in manufacturing deteriorated somewhat between 1973 and 1982 (bottom of Table 3). Yet the categories contain-

ing many high-technology industries performed well, showing vastly increased surpluses during this period. But the high-technology categories did not escape the sharp deterioration that occurred in 1983. The total manufacturing deficit rose from $8 billion to $33 billion—an increase of $21 billion. Most of that was accounted for by a decline in the surplus of the four high-technology categories, especially in the various machinery items. Their surpluses declined further in 1984. Yet these were the only surplus categories in the large deficit year, 1984.

Similar trends are reflected in changes in the country's shares in world exports (Table 4). Between 1973 and 1984 the U.S. export share in aircraft and in certain machinery items declined, but it has increased in computers, power-generating machinery, and chemicals. Japan's share in machinery and the EC share in aircraft rose markedly, while the Community lost market share in certain machinery items and in chemicals.

Further disaggregation of the data, with a focus on high-technology products as defined by the Commerce Department, also suggests that the U.S. lead, while still strong, is narrowing. A substantial portion of the U.S. high-technology surplus is attributed to aircraft, computers, and certain chemicals. In the other high-technology industries (such as machinery), that lead is eroding; it is being challenged by the Japanese advance. Even in the main lead items, a future Japanese challenge is looming in computers, and a present European challenge exists in wide-bodied jet aircraft. These conclusions were obtained by the U.S. Commerce Department (1983, Statistical Appendix, Tables 5, 12, and 23) from analysis of global market shares as well as from indexes of revealed comparative advantage of the ten high-technology industries.

With respect to future trends, the U.S. aircraft industry is likely to face greater competition from the European consortium Airbus Industrie, while the computer and semiconductor industries are likely to face greater competition from Japan. In other high-technology areas, such as fiber optics (electrical equipment), biotechnology (drugs and medicines), and robotics, the commanding U.S. lead may also be eroded by competition from its trading partners.

DOMESTIC COST-PRICE BEHAVIOR

Although international trade performance has long been used as an indicator of comparative advantage, such evidence must be supplemented by information on domestic costs and prices. Comparative statistics on trade performance reflect the effects of exchange-rate changes and trade barriers as well as of the country's underlying comparative advantage. In contrast, the domestic cost measures

TABLE 3.
U.S. Trade Flows in Eleven Manufacturing Categories—Selected Years ($ billions)

A. High-technology Industrial Categories

	X	M	Balance
Chemicals			
1973	6	3	3
1982	22	12	10
1983	21	13	8
1984	24	16	8
Machinery for specialized industries			
1973	8	3	5
1982	24	12	12
1983	18	11	7
1984	19	17	2
Office and telecommunication equipment			
1973	4	2	2
1982	17	12	5
1983	19	17	2
1984	23	25	-2

B. Other industries

	X	M	Balance
Iron and steel			
1973	1	3	-2
1982	2	10	-8
1983	1	7	-6
1984	1	12	-11
Other semimanufactures			
1973	2	4	-2
1982	6	11	-5
1983	6	12	-6
1984	6	16	-10
Road motor vehicles			
1973	6	10	-4
1982	14	32	-18
1983	14	37	-23
1984	17	48	-31

C. Total manufacturers

	X	M	Balance
1973	43	43	0
1982	138	146	-8
1983	131	164	-33
1984	141	225	-84

TABLE 3 (*Continued*).

U.S. Trade Flows in Eleven Manufacturing Categories—Selected Years ($ billions)

A. High-technology Industrial Categories	X	M	Balance	B. Other industries	X	M	Balance
Other machinery and tr. equipment				*Household appliances*			
1973	11	6	5	1973	1	3	−2
1982	40	19	21	1982	3	10	−7
1983	38	22	16	1983	2	11	−9
1984	38	30	8	1984	3	16	−13
Of Which				*Textiles*			
				1973	1	1	0
				1982	3	3	0
				1983	2	3	−1
				1984	2	5	−3
Power-generating machinery				*Clothing*			
1973	3	2	1	1973	0	2	−2
1982	10	5	5	1982	1	9	−8
1983	9	6	3	1983	1	10	−9
1984	10	9	1	1984	1	15	−14
Aircraft and aircraft engines				*Other consumer goods*			
1973	5	1	4	1973	2	4	−2
1982	16	4	12	1982	7	17	−10
1983	14	3	11	1983	6	19	−13
1984	13	5	8	1984	6	25	−19

Source: GATT *International Trade*, various issues, appendix tables.

TABLE 4.
Shares (in Percent) of the U.S., EC (10), Japan, EFTA, and Canada in Their
Combined World Exports of Selected Commodity Categories

Year	U.S.	Japan	EC(10)	EFTA	Canada	Total
All manufacturing						
1973	15.5	12.3	57.7	10.2	4.3	100
1979	15.3	13.1	58.0	9.9	3.7	100
1981	17.7	16.9	52.0	9.2	4.1	100
1983	16.3	17.6	51.7	9.4	5.0	100
1984	16.6	19.1	49.4	9.2	5.7	100
Chemicals						
1973	17.2	6.2	64.7	9.6	2.2	100
1979	17.8	5.9	64.4	9.0	2.6	100
1981	20.3	6.4	60.8	8.9	3.7	100
1983	18.0	6.7	62.5	9.3	3.5	100
1984	19.0	7.0	61.4	9.0	3.6	100
Machinery for specialized industries						
1973	18.9	7.2	60.8	11.0	2.1	100
1979	18.5	10.2	58.1	10.9	2.3	100
1981	22.9	13.7	51.3	10.3	2.6	100
1983	17.9	14.8	53.2	11.0	2.6	100
1984	18.1	16.1	51.6	11.3	2.9	100
Office and telecommunication equipment						
1973	27.6	13.4	48.4	6.9	3.7	100
1979	27.1	16.8	46.3	6.7	3.2	100
1981	30.4	20.7	40.7	5.8	2.6	100
1983	32.1	23.0	37.0	5.3	2.6	100
1984	31.6	26.1	34.1	4.6	3.6	100
Power-generating machinery						
1973	21.6	9.6	52.9	10.1	5.8	100
1979	19.9	12.7	53.5	9.5	4.3	100
1981	23.9	16.5	47.3	8.1	4.2	100
1983	22.6	16.4	45.6	9.3	5.6	100
1984	23.2	19.3	42.2	8.7	6.6	100
Aircraft and aircraft engines						
1973	60.5	0.5	32.6	0.6	5.8	100
1979	50.4	0.4	44.9	1.7	2.6	100
1981	48.7	0.4	46.6	1.2	3.1	100
1983	49.0	0.6	45.3	1.6	3.5	100
1984	44.7	0.4	49.6	1.8	3.5	100

Source: Computed from GATT tabulations.

highlight the country's comparative advantage in high-technology products without regard to exchange-rate changes. As such they offer a better guide to long-run trends in the country's trade position (once equilibrium exchange rate is restored).

Comparative advantage is determined by the *internal ranking* of industries from the lowest to the highest cost per unit of output (Kreinin, 1983). As a proxy for a ranking of *all* industries, production costs in the high-technology industries can be compared with the average cost for all manufacturing. Although it is desirable to cover all production costs, data availability restricts the analysis to labor cost, so that capital and other costs are omitted.

Table 5 compares 1981 labor cost in the high-technology industries with the national manufacturing average.[3] Labor production cost has two components: labor productivity, proxied in the table by value-added per employee, and compensation of employees. The ratio of the latter to the former is labor compensation per dollar of value added, which is the proxy for labor cost per unit of output. These three ratios are shown (in that order) in the three right-hand columns of Table 5, where all figures are on an annual basis.

For all high-techology industries combined, the value-added per employee ($52,620 per year) far exceeds that for all manufacturing ($41,330 per year). Compensation per employee ($26,170 per year) is also above that for all manufacturing ($22,510 per year) but by a proportionately smaller amount. As a result, labor compensation per unit of value added ($0.5) in the high-technology sector is less than the national manufacturing average ($0.55). Note that the differential would have been higher had the high-technology sector itself been excluded from the all-manufacturing average. The fact that labor production cost in the high-technology sector is less than the national manufacturing average (primarily because of relatively high productivity) indicates the existence of U.S. comparative advantage in that sector.

Turning to the individual industries that make up the high-technology sector, it is seen that the degree of comparative advantage varies a great deal among these industries. It is highest (labor costs are lowest) in chemicals, computers, and scientific instruments, where value-added per employee is particularly high by national standards. It is low in certain machinery items, where the Japanese appear to capture a rising share of world markets. Finally, there are four industries in which U.S. comparative advantage, as measured by relative labor cost, has eroded. In two of them (ordnance and guided missiles), government is the main customer, and the U.S. technological lead is vast. Hence the high labor cost may not be reflected in trade flows in the foreseeable future. In the case of telecommunication equipment (and to some extent electronic components), the high U.S. labor costs may soon be reflected in adverse market shares. This trend may be accelerated by the breakup of AT&T, which opened the U.S. market to foreign suppliers of equip-

---

[3] A similar approach was employed in Kreinin (1984). That article spells out the limitations of this approach. In a more complete analysis it is desirable to examine trends over time in these costs.

TABLE 5.

U.S. Labor Production Costs in High-Technology Industries and All Manufacturing, 1981

High-technology industry	SIC category	Value added (million dollars)	Compensation (million dollars)	Employees (thousands)	Value added per employee[a] (thousand dollars)	Compensation per employee[a] (thousand dollars)	Labor Compensation per dollar of value added
Industrial inorganic chemicals	281	9273.6	3410.4	114.0	81.35	29.92	0.37
Plastics materials, synthetics	282	10210.6	4211.9	147.0	69.46	28.65	0.41
Drugs and medicinals	283	14879.4	4508.8	169.7	87.68	26.57	0.30
Industrial organic chemicals	286	16229.0	4821.1	147.5	110.03	32.69	0.30
Agricultural chemicals	287	6217.4	1401.4	55.5	112.03	25.3	0.23
Ordnance and accessories	348	3083.1	2006.1	80.1	38.49	25.05	0.65
Engines and turbines	351	7381.6	3909.3	125.6	58.77	31.13	0.53
Office and computing machines	357	21173.5	9798.0	387.5	54.64	25.29	0.46
Electrical distributing equipment	361	4827.2	2483.3	116.7	41.36	21.28	0.51
Electrical industrial apparatus	362	8559.2	4652.4	209.6	40.84	22.20	0.54
Radio, TV receiving equipment	365	3728.1	1613.7	78.5	47.49	20.56	0.43
Telecommunications equipment	366	24983.9	14947.7	574.4	43.50	26.02	0.60
Electronic components	367	18536.7	10387.7	503.5	36.82	20.63	0.56
Aircraft and parts	372	28144.4	18466.9	581.4	48.41	31.76	0.66
Guided missiles, space vehicles	376	8210.5	5400.5	152.2	53.95	35.49	0.66
Measuring, controlling devices	382	9180.1	5014.3	226.9	40.46	22.10	0.55
Medical instruments	384	5698.7	2595.0	136.9	41.63	18.96	0.46
ALL HIGH-TECHNOLOGY INDUSTRIES		200317.0	99628.8	3807	52.62	26.17	0.50
ALL MANUFACTURERS		837506.5	456214.8	20264	41.33	22.51	0.55
For comparative purposes:							
Blast furnace, basic steel products	331	24662.6	17519.9	477.4	51.66	36.70	0.71
Motor vehicles	371	34841.2	22790.2	695.6	50.09	32.76	0.65

[a] In thousands of dollars per year.

Source: U.S. Census of Manufacturers, annual survey.

ment, while foreign markets (except Japan, with which the United States has a special agreement) remain closed to foreign competition, under the control of government procurement policies.

A fourth high-cost industry is aircraft, the single largest high-technology industry in terms of value-added: productivity is lower than the average of the high-technology sector (although it is higher than "all manufacturing"), and the compensation rate is well above the average. As a result, labor compensation per unit of value-added is 0.66—the highest of all high-technology industries and far above the national manufacturing average. This condition was sustainable only as long as the United States had a global monopoly in aircraft production, or as long as the American companies employed unique technology not available elsewhere. Both these conditions are now disappearing. The above statistic can be viewed as an early warning signal: Unless a new generation of technology is developed and introduced, or certain wage concessions are made,[4] the industry will be exposed to a serious threat from the European consortium.

To attain cross-country comparability it is necessary to use United Nations and OECD statistical publications. Because the data are more aggregative, no industry breakdown is provided. For the entire high-technology sector, labor compensation per unit of value added was 0.33 in Japan (1980) compared to 0.35 for all manufacturing. The respective figures for the United Kingdom (1981) were 0.48 and 0.47, and in Germany (1981) 0.46 and 0.46. In 1981 neither the United Kingdom nor Germany had a comparative labor-cost advantage in the high-technology sector (relative to their own respective position in all manufacturing), although they may have such an advantage in specific industries such as office equipment or drugs. On the other hand, Japan shows an overall labor-cost advantage in the high-technology sector, particularly in certain machinery items.

A major caveat attached to this entire approach arises from the product-cycle theory of the commodity composition of trade: labor production costs are far less important in the case of newly developed products than when production becomes standardized. For industries on the cutting edge of technology, the labor-cost comparison *understates* the degree of U.S. comparative advantages. Once such technology becomes available to foreign competitors, that advantage is likely to be eroded, and unit-labor costs become an important guide to future performance.

---

[4] Limited wage concessions were granted in 1984, when the industry negotiated a two-tier wage contract: Newly hired workers will receive significantly lower wage rates than present workers. The impact of this provision on average wage rate in the industry, which would depend on the rate of employment turnover, remains to be seen.

CONCLUSION

A lead in technology-intensive products is important to the United
States in terms of its trade position, growth potential, and employment, and because of the high-wage and low-pollution characteristics of these industries. While still strong, that lead is narrowing.
Both the trade performance and the domestic cost data suggest the
oncoming of a strong European challenge in jet aircraft and a strong
Japanese challenge in various machinery items. Additionally, possible Japanese competition in advance computers is indicated by their
industrial policy. Unless the trend is reversed, the U.S. competitive
edge will continue to decline, although it will certainly not disappear. Also, as foreign countries play catch-up in technology the
United States is being gradually squeezed into the upper part of the
scale in terms of the technological sophistication of the goods it
produces.

Before examining the policy implications of these changes, it is
necessary to inquire into the reasons for the decline in the U.S.
position. One obvious cause is the natural evolution of other industrial countries as they upgrade their technological sophistication,
drawing in part on technologies that have already been developed.
The United States as the technological leader must advance faster to
stay ahead, and its lead will be increasingly confined to a narrower
and more sophisticated range of products. But popular discussion
points a finger to industrial policy and targeting in Japan (and perhaps in France) as the main reason of the erosion in the U.S. position. After examining this argument, we shall turn to a more traditional explanation—changes in factor endowments.

Industrial Policy

There is a serious debate in the United States about the efficacy of
industrial policy pursued in other countries. Particular attention is
focused on the targeting of industries by the Japanese Ministry for
Trade and Industry (MITI). That agency is said to select specific
industries for promotion and development and to offer the following
types of assistance and incentives:

Financing for modernization, development, and investments

Other direct grants and loans

Cartel formation through exemption from antitrust laws

Trade restrictions and government procurement

Tax incentives

Joint private-government ventures and encouragement of international joint ventures

French policy, known as indicative planning, offers similar incentives to foster specific industries, but with less effective results.

It is widely argued that by pinpointing industries to be developed with governmental assistance, the MITI was highly instrumental in the development of capital-intensive industries such as autos and steel. It is now similarly engaged in encouraging knowledge-intensive industries. Government outlays (in a variety of forms) for promoting the computer industry have been estimated at $1 billion over a five-year period, while $0.5 billion has been allocated for the aerospace program over a similar period (Eckelmann and Davis, 1983).

In addition to direct and indirect assistance, the Japanese government is said to play a critical role in identifying the industries to be promoted and in government–industry coordination of investment as well as research and development efforts. The government also plays a crucial role in limiting certain imports, in controlling the import of technology into Japan, and in improving the imported technology and adapting it to Japanese needs.

So successful are Japanese industrial policies said to be that certain writers have advocated the adoption of similar measures by the United States (Thurow, 1983), and the clamor for such policies has reached the stage of proposed legislation by a congressional subcommittee (Subcommittee on Banking, Financing, and Urban Affairs, 1983).

But the burden of professional opinion seriously questions the effectiveness of industrial policy in managing industrial adjustment. In a now-famous paper, Charles Schultz (1983) argues and documents four central propositions: (1) There is no evidence to support the much-feared deindustrialization of the United States. Apart from the well-known trouble spots such as steel, the U.S. manufacturing sector performs well (in terms of output, employment, and productivity) relative to that of other industrial countries. (2) The success of Japan is not a result of MITI industrial policy. Rather it is due to a high level of savings and investment coupled with strong and creative entrepreneurship on the part of the private sector. MITI may have provided some direction, but has also made some serious targeting errors. The best microeconomic decisions were made by market forces within a stable macroeconomic environment provided by the government. (3) The U.S. government lacks the analytical ability to pick winners and losers. (4) The American system is ill suited for a centralized targeting policy and for making critical choices among firms and regions on the basis of economic criteria rather than political pressures.

Likewise, in a series of studies Gary Saxonhouse (1983a,b; 1984) maintains that the impact of Japanese industrial policy has been minimal at best. Following are selected conclusions of his studies:

1. Japan gives less formal aid to its high-technology sectors than do the governments of most other industrialized economies.
2. There are no significant quotas and tariffs on high-technology products coming into Japan. Japanese protection is concentrated on agricultural products and by doing so works against Japanese high-technology interests.
3. High-technology sectors receive smaller subsidies from the Japanese government than is the case in the United States and Europe. Likewise tax rates in Japan are far less discriminatory between sectors than is true in the other industrialized economies.
4. Whatever signals the Japanese government may be sending to the private sector as to what might be promising new areas of development evoke resource responses that seem modest by comparison with the performance of the equity markets in the United States. Japanese government cooperative research and development projects are a partial substitute for what is achieved in the United States as a by-product of well-functioning markets for experienced scientific and engineering manpower.
5. The American government sponsors vastly more research and development than does the Japanese government but the raison d'être of much of this research is basic science and national security considerations. Examination of individual programs suggests that regardless of national security or basic science auspices, American government programs in high technology, which have commercial and international competitive ends in mind, are at least as large in the United States as in Japan. U.S. government-sponsored research in the defense areas has vast commercial application.

MITI is shown to play mainly the role of a catalyst and coordinator. It indicates or signals areas of interest but has no power to induce firms to follow that lead. Its coordinating activity is directed mainly at the avoidance of duplication in research efforts.

Conclusions 4 and 5 require further elaboration.[5] It is often claimed that targeting policy has placed Japan ahead of the United States in its ability to draw resources first to the capital-intensive and now to the knowledge-intensive sectors. Since in the United

---

[5] Based on Saxonhouse (1983a,b; 1984).

States this role is performed by the capital markets, there exists a market failure that requires rectification by government policy. But in fact the opposite appears to be the case. There is no "market failure" in the U.S. capital markets. Rather, they had great success in concentrating large resources in promising but risky ventures on the technological frontiers. To some extent Japanese industrial policy is designed to offset market failure in the Japanese capital market.

Second, in the United States the diffusion of useful research results across firms is possible because of the high degree of professional orientation among scientists and engineers employed in private industry. This pattern has developed because of the common theoretical background of university-trained R&D staff, which not only facilitates communication but also creates labor-market incentives for communicating effectively with R&D workers at other firms.

By contrast, in Japan most advanced managerial and scientific training is done under firm auspices. Advanced degrees are less common in Japanese facilities, and the right mix of skills and information is obtained by using foreign consultants on a temporary basis. Skills specific to the firm's needs are developed and there is little emphasis on turning out well-rounded scientists.

As a result there is a faster and more effective diffusion of R&D results among U.S. firms. But that diffusion has an international side effect: It makes probable the leakage of at least some of this information to foreign firms. The leakage of such data is facilitated by sophisticated information-gathering programs sponsored by the Japanese government and firms. Japan has benefited from much overseas R&D through the following channels: American professional association meetings, American technological consultants, American professional journals, Japanese firm-sponsored graduate students sitting in American graduate research facilities; and more directly from technology held by the American government. Unless it is classified, the results of the very large amount of contract research sponsored by the American government are available globally on demand. Patents resulting from contract research have been held by the American government and characteristically have been licensed at a fixed rate to all comers. The U.S. government finds it difficult even to prevent the illegal leakage of classified technology to the Soviet Union. By contrast, in Japan the results of the relatively small amount of corporate research funded by the Japanese government have been generally held privately. Because of the language barrier, Japanese technical publications are not usually accessible to American scientists.

However, the importance of these differential practices is likely to diminish. As the Japanese catch up with much of American technology and find themselves on the technological frontier, they will have to develop their own inventions. Also, in the 1980s U.S. technology policy has become more protectionistic. Rather than belonging to the public, patents now developed under American government grants or contracts belong to the grantors or to contracting companies that use federal funds to develop new technologies. Moreover, unless a specific government waiver is obtained, the right to sell or use a government patent is limited only to firms manufacturing substantially in the United States. At the same time Japanese technology policy is becoming less protectionistic (see, for example, *Wall Street Journal*, 1984).

Conclusions similar to Saxonhouse's were reached by other students of the subject. Both Lawrence (1983) and Krugman (1984) find that industrial policies of foreign governments did not inflict serious harm on the United States. Yet there is also support for the contrary view, expressed by the Department of Commerce, that Japanese industrial policy is propelling that country toward technological leadership. After reviewing the pro-and-con evidence, it can be concluded that: (1) Foreign and particularly Japanese advance in the high-technology area would have taken place with or without industrial targeting. It can be explained by changes in relative factor endowments (see next section). (2) Industrial policy served as a catalyst to private efforts and had the effect of speeding up the process that would have occurred anyway but perhaps at a slower pace.

Changes in Factor Endowments

Traditional theory, originally expounded by Heckscher and Ohlin and later extended by numerous authors, explains a country's trade mix in terms of its factor endowments. A country would specialize in, and export, those commodities whose manufacture uses intensively its relatively abundant factors and import commodities whose manufacture uses intensively its relatively scarce factors.

RELATIVE CAPITAL ENDOWMENT, 1963–1975

On this theory, past Japanese advance in capital-intensive industries such as steel and autos can be explained by massive capital formation in that country. As shown in Table 6, Japan's share of global capital resources doubled between 1963 and 1975, while the U.S. share declined sharply and the share of two main European countries declined slightly. The United States also experienced a decline in the share of skilled labor. But apart from that there were only small changes in the share of labor commanded by various countries. The implication is that there has been a rise in the capital/labor endowment ratio in Japan and a corresponding decline in the United

TABLE 6.
Shares in World Resources (in percent)

		Capital	Skilled labor	Semi-skilled labor	Arable land
United States	1963	41.9	29.7	18.3	27.4
	1975	33.4	26.3	19.1	29.3
Japan	1963	7.1	7.8	12.6	0.9
	1975	14.7	8.6	12.3	0.8
Germany	1963	9.1	7.1	6.8	1.3
	1975	8.3	6.6	5.9	1.1
France	1963	7.1	6.6	5.3	3.2
	1975	7.9	6.2	4.5	2.6
United Kingdom	1963	5.6	7.0	6.5	1.1
	1975	4.9	6.4	5.3	1.0

Source: Harry P. Bowen, Changes in the International Distribution of Resources and Their Impact on U.S. Comparative Advantage, *Review of Economics and Statistics* (August 1983), Table 3, p. 405.

States, and that explains the Japanese success in capital-intensive industries. This was supplemented by aggressive and rapid penetration of selected segments of foreign markets by Japanese firms.

RELATIVE KNOWLEDGE ENDOWMENT, 1963–1980

Similar changes in factor endowments, unfavorable to the United States, have taken place in the area of technology. The United States experienced a significant decline, and other countries a significant increase, in respective share of the global endowment of scientists and R&D efforts. This is shown first in terms of rates of growth between 1963 and 1980 (Table 7). The United States is the only major country where the proportion of R&D scientists in the labor

TABLE 7.
Rate of Resource Growth, 1963–1980, Relative to Total Labor Force

	Capital	R&D Scientists
United States	1.4	−1.1
Japan	8.3	5.1
Germany	3.0	5.6
United Kingdom	3.3	5.6
France	4.9	1.9
Canada	2.0	1.1
NICs	6.2	—

Source: Mutti and Morici (1983), Table 3.

TABLE 8.
Relative Resource Endowments, 1963 and 1980 (Each Country's Endowment as a Percent of World Total)[a]

	Year	Capital	Skilled labor	Semi-skilled labor	Unskilled labor	Arable land	R&D scientist
United States	1963	41.9	29.4	18.3	0.60	27.4	62.5
	1980	33.6	27.7	19.1	0.19	29.3	50.7
Canada	1963	3.8	2.5	1.7	0.06	6.5	1.6
	1980	3.9	2.9	2.1	0.03	6.1	1.8
France	1963	7.1	6.6	5.3	0.11	3.2	6.1
	1980	7.5	6.0	3.9	0.06	2.6	6.0
Germany	1963	9.1	7.1	6.8	0.14	1.3	7.5
	1980	7.7	6.9	5.5	0.08	1.1	10.0
Japan	1963	7.1	7.8	12.6	0.30	0.9	16.2
	1980	15.5	8.7	11.5	0.25	0.8	23.0
United Kingdom	1963	5.6	7.0	6.5	0.14	1.1	6.1
	1980	4.5	5.1	4.9	0.07	1.0	8.5

[a] Computed from a set of 34 countries, which in 1980 accounted for over 85 percent of gross domestic product among market economies.
Source: Mutti and Morici (1983).

force has declined. In Japan and Germany that proportion has increased significantly.

As a result of these differential growth rates, the share of the United States in the world endowment of capital declined from 42 to 34 percent and its share in the global endowment of R&D scientists fell from 63 to 51 percent between 1963 and 1980 (Table 8). Similarly, there was a decline in the relative number of scientists and engineers engaged in R&D. The corresponding shares of Japan, the United Kingdom, and Germany increased markedly. Over the same period the level of R&D expenditures in other industrial countries rose relative to the United States. The level of that effort in Japan, Germany, and France combined was only 18 percent of that in the United States in 1964 and 57 percent in 1979. In 1980 the ratio of R&D expenditures to GNP in Germany and Japan was almost at the level of that in the United States.

RELATIVE KNOWLEDGE ENDOWMENT, 1963–1983[6]

There is evidence that these trends continued into the 1980s. Between 1963 and 1983 real expenditures on all R&D performed by

---

[6] This subsection is based on Levy and Terleckyj (1985). See also National Science Foundation (1983).

industry rose at an annual rate of 2.7 percent in the United States, 4.7 percent in seven major European countries,[7] and 10.2 percent in Japan. (Note that the proportion of government-funded R&D done in private firms is much higher in the United States than elsewhere.) Likewise, the number of R&D scientists grew at 2.5 percent per year in the United States, 3.8 percent in Europe, and 6.7 percent in Japan.

While real R&D expenditures in Europe and Japan grew consistently over the period, their growth in the United States has been rather uneven. Following a 7.2 percent annual growth from 1963 to 1969, the growth rate plummeted to 1.5 percent between 1969 and 1975 and then rose to 6.1 percent between 1975 and 1983. Even the last figure falls far short of the Japanese advance.

Finally, in an interesting regression analysis, Levy and Terleckyj (1985) demonstrate that government-funded industrial R&D influences private R&D in the United States; and that foreign (mainly Japanese) R&D has been positively associated with industrial R&D efforts in the United States, and possibly it has stimulated them. Conversely, U.S. R&D outlays appear to have influenced R&D outlays in Europe and Japan. But there is no indication of positive cross effects among the latter two areas.

SUMMARY

Because R&D scientists and capital in Japan expanded faster than the other factors, the endowment ratio of capital (both physical and human) to labor increased substantially relative to the United States. In Germany and the United Kingdom the endowment ratio of human capital to other factors also increased. These changes in relative factor endowments go a long way toward explaining the improvement of the foreign competitive position in high-technology products relative to the United States.

Two other reasons for the decline in the U.S. technological lead are cited by Mutti and Morici: rising foreign income levels and market size, and the rapid transfer of technology to foreign countries.

> As income levels in Europe and Japan have grown, the U.S. market has become less unique in terms of its large sales potential over which initial product development costs can spread. . . . There has been a contraction in the length of time necessary for products to become standardized enough to allow production to spread outside the United States. In other words, technology is being rapidly transferred to other countries, mak-

---

[7] The United Kingdom, France, Germany, Italy, the Netherlands, Sweden, and Switzerland.

ing the U.S. competitive advantage in any given high-technol-
ogy product short lived. [Mutti and Morici, 1983]

In sum, the increased competitive strength of Japan and Europe
in high-technology products can be explained by changes in relative
factor endowments and other market forces. Industrial policy in
other countries hastened the pace of these developments; it was not
their root cause.

We next address the question whether the decline in U.S. technological competitiveness requires a policy response by the government.

Strategic Trade Policy—Theoretical Considerations

In a perfectly competitive environment, the only possible justifica-
tions for trade intervention by the government are the following:

1. Imposition of an optimum tariff on imported goods designed to
   improve the terms of trade, or of a tax on imported capital,
   designed to improve the terms of borrowing;
2. Infant-industry protection, but only if a direct subsidy is not
   feasible;
3. Possible offset to domestic distortion, but only when domestic
   measures are not available.

These reasons have not been considered important enough to justify
a drastic departure from the U.S. traditional stance of free trade.

In recent years economists redirected their attention to oligopolistic markets, where the number of firms producing a product and
making independent decisions is very small. This has become
known as a *strategic* environment. The main feature distinguishing
it from a competitive environment is the emergence and persistence
of economic profits. *Strategic trade policy* is a term coined to describe measures that can shift the equilibrium generated by oligopolistic interchange.

In oligopolistic markets nations compete for their share of
global economic profits. One main objective of strategic trade policy
is to enable "our" firms or government to capture a bigger share of
these profits than would be the case without the policy. "Our" share
of global oligopoly profits can be increased by expanding the market
share of U.S. firms. In the case of export industries, an export subsidy (or in its absence, a subsidy for R&D) would enable "our" oligopolistic firms to capture a larger share of the export markets. If the
resulting increase in their economic profits exceeds the cost of the
subsidy, the policy improves "our" national welfare, albeit at the

expense of others. In the case of imported products produced by foreign oligopolists, the imposition of a tariff enables "our" oligopolists to expand their market share. The resulting increase in economic profits of "our" firms plus the rise in government tariff revenue enhances national economic welfare. The nature of these policies will be explained with the help of simple diagrams. The explanation draws heavily on the work of Brander and Spencer (1984a,b). The literature is surveyed in Grossman and Richardson (1985).

In the simplest case assume that "we" import a product produced by a foreign monopolist. There are no domestic producers of that product, so that the foreign monopolist is in fact a global monopolist. He is assumed to produce at constant cost conditions, so that the marginal cost (MC) curve is horizontal.

Figure 1 depicts the profit-maximizing position of the monopolist selling in "our" market, where D represents the demand in our market for the foreign-produced product and MR is the resulting marginal revenue curve. The intersection of MC and MR determines the quantity Q that "we" import from the foreign monopolist. Price P is charged, and the excess of P over MC is economic profit per unit of output. Total economic profit extracted from our market by the foreign monopolist is the shaded area. A specific import tariff would raise the MC curve to MC^t, reduce the quantity imported from Q to Q^t, and increase the price to the consumers from P to P^t. Foreign monopoly profit declines to the rectangular area bounded by points MC^t, P^t, a, b. However, because of the decline in quantity, not all the change in foreign monopoly profit is appropriated by "our" government. Rather, that area is the rectangle bounded by points MC, MC^t, c, b. The loss in consumer surplus is represented by area P, P^t, a, d.

In the case described in Figure 1, the policy intervention is beneficial because the foreign monopoly profit appropriated by the government exceeds the loss to domestic consumers.[8] The optimal tariff is the level that maximizes the difference between the gain in government revenue and the loss to the domestic consumers. Since that varies with the shape of the demand curve, knowledge of the demand elasticity is needed to determine the level of tariff. Similar information on the shape and level of the marginal cost curve (which is not necessarily horizontal) is also required. Figure 2 and an attendant explanation repeat the analysis for the case of a rising MC curve and an ad valorem tariff.

In a reverse case, assume that "our" firm is the global monopolist with a constant MC curve, exporting to foreign countries (in

---

[8] Changes that occur in the foreign market as a result of the shrinkage of sales in our market are of no concern here.

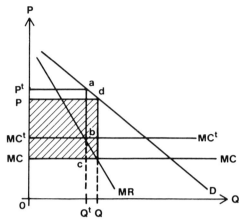

FIGURE 1. Foreign monopolist selling in "our" market: A tariff reduces foreign monopoly profits.

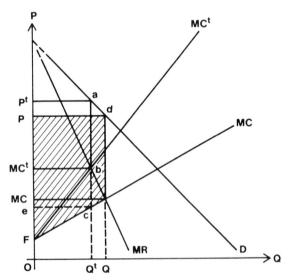

FIGURE 2. A foreign monopolist selling in "our" market under an ad valorem tariff and a rising MC curve. Total profit of the foreign monopolist, extracted from "our" consumers, is the shaded area (integrating over the MC curve). A 100 percent tariff raises the marginal cost from *MC* to *MCᵗ*. Equilibrium quantity declines from *Q* to *Qᵗ* while price rises from *P* to *Pᵗ*. Monopoly profit extracted from our consumers declines from the shaded area to the area bounded by *F, Pᵗ, a, b*. But because of decline in quantity, not all of the difference is captured as "our" government revenue. Rather, government tariff revenue is the rectangular area bounded by *MCᵗ, e, b, c*, while consumer surplus declines by area, *P, Pᵗ, a, d*. As long as the tariff revenue to "our" government exceeds the loss to "our" consumers, the policy is beneficial. Knowledge of the demand elasticity and the cost structure is required to determine the desirability of the policy.

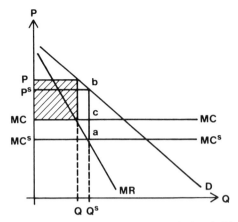

FIGURE 3. A domestic monopolist selling abroad: A subsidy increases domestic monopoly profits.

which there are no local producers), and that the local and foreign markets are segregated. This is shown in Figure 3, where D is foreign demand, MR is marginal revenue from foreign sales, and the intersection between MC and MR determines the profit-maximizing quantity of exports, Q. Price is set at P, and monopoly profit per unit is the difference between P and MC along the price axis. Total monopoly profits extracted from foreigners is the shaded area. A specific export subsidy (government subsidy of X dollars per unit of output) to the local monopoly firm lowers its marginal costs to MC^s, reduces the export price from P to P^s (in other words, "our" terms of trade deteriorate) and raises quantity to Q^s. Economic profit appropriated from foreign markets increases to the rectangular area bounded by points MC^s, P^s, a, b. The subsidy cost to the government is the rectangular area bounded by MC, MC^s, a, c. It is smaller than the gain in monopoly profit. The difference between the gain in monopoly profit and the cost of the subsidy is the net gain to the country. Its size depends on the shape of the demand curve. Again, information on the cost structure and the demand elasticity is needed to determine the optimal size of the subsidy—the subsidy that would maximize the excess of appropriated profits over the subsidy cost. Figure 4 presents the more complex case of a rising MC curve and an ad valorem (50 percent) subsidy.

Since GATT's rules prohibit an export subsidy, its place can be taken by subsidy for research and development. Because it applies to all output rather than just to exports, the cost of that subsidy could be higher. But against the greater cost there are two benefits: First, the price to the domestic consumers declines. Second, the R&D has external spillover effects, as well as the "learning by doing" effect. In

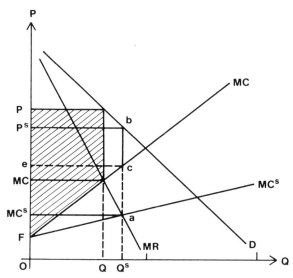

FIGURE 4. A domestic global monopolist selling abroad under an ad valorem subsidy and a rising MC curve. The original profit extracted from foreign consumers is the shaded area. An export subsidy lowers the marginal cost (only with respect to foreign sales) from *MC* to *MCˢ*. Exports rise from *Q* to *Qˢ* while the export price declines from *P* to *Pˢ* (foreign consumers benefit from our subsidy, and our terms of trade deteriorate). Monopoly profits of the domestic firm rise to the area bounded by *F, Pˢ, a, b*. The subsidy cost to the government is the area bounded by *a, c, e, MCˢ*. As long as the increase in profit is greater than the cost of the subsidy, it pays to subsidize exports. Information on the cost structure and demand elasticity is needed to determine the desirability of the policy.

a sense much R&D is a public good, where a private innovator does not fully appropriate the benefits of his or her discovery. Hence, without a subsidy too little R&D will be conducted by the private sector.

Here lies a composite rationale for subsidizing R&D: It enables domestic firms to capture a larger share of the world market and thereby appropriate a larger share of global profits; and it produces positive domestic externalities. Note that much of the private R&D is conducted by oligopolies that realize economic profit, and a government subsidy supplements such private spending. However, effective policy requires substantial information about firms' costs, demand, and the extent of domestic spillovers.

These simple examples generalize to other situations. Suppose a domestic and a foreign firm (such as Boeing and the European Airbus Industrie) compete in a third market. If the government of one of the countries provides export or R&D subsidies to its domestic firm, this producer may be able to capture a larger share of the world market and increase its profit net of the subsidy. Thus, the country could gain in terms of income and employment. The reason for this outcome is that the government's action is credible to the foreign competitor, so the foreign firm reduces its output in view of the reduced costs of its competitor.

However, such governmental policy risks retaliation by other countries, possibly resulting in international economic disorder if not chaos. All countries could then lose. For this reason a negotiated *cooperative* approach to the division of global economic rents is preferable to a noncooperative approach. But a cooperative approach that determines the level of subsidization opens the way to cheating, often witnessed in such situations.

Other extensions of the analysis include its applicability to oligopolistic markets and to cases where firms enjoy increasing returns to scale or benefit from "learning by doing." In the latter cases protection of domestic markets and promotion of export markets can reduce per unit costs, thereby saving resources.

This analysis, which suggests that there is room for beneficial policy intervention in oligopolistic markets, is subject to serious limitations that considerably weaken the case for intervention, especially as it applies to the high-technology sector. Those limitations will be considered next.

Limitations of the Oligopoly Analysis

EXISTENCE OF OLIGOPOLY PROFITS

The foregoing argument for policy intervention rests on the existence of global oligopoly profits to be appropriated. Yet many high-technology industries cannot be categorized as oligopolistic. Data on the four-firm concentration ratios for four-digit SIC industries in the U.S. high-technology sector are summarized in the frequency distribution in Table 9. Only in twenty-four out of sixty industries do the largest four firms account for more than half their respective markets. In thirty-six industries the market share of the largest four firms is under 50 percent. Clearly the degree of monopoly power and hence the level of monopoly profit varies greatly between industries in this sector. At times even one industry has an oligopolistic subsector (mainframe computers) and competitive subsectors (microcomputers). Moreover, ease of entry and hence persistence of monopoly profits varies a great deal. Much of oligopoly profits is highly transitory and exists only until technology is diffused and/or entry of new firms occurs. As an example we contrast two industries:

Aircraft: highly oligopolistic; difficult entry

Semiconductors: competitive, easy entry

TABLE 9.
Frequency Distribution of Four-Firm Concentration
Ratios Among Four-Digit SIC High-Technology
Industries

Four-firm concentration ratio (Percent)	Number of four-digit high-technology industries
Above 70	6
50–69	18
30–49	28
Under 30	8
Total	60

Source: Based on the U.S. Census of Manufacturing.

Although no concentration ratios are presented for foreign countries, there exist variations in the degree of monopoly power across countries.

Any optimal strategic trade intervention would have to be limited to the concentrated industries. It would require the policymaker to differentiate between industries and trading partner. This means the demise of the MFN even in pretense. It also means that *discretion* would have to be substituted for *rules* in the conduct of U.S. policy. This opens the door to a great deal of unproductive rent-seeking activity in the United States, where groups and industries seek protection or subsidies through lobbying and bloc voting (Baldwin, 1984, and literature cited therein). The desirability of encouraging these activities is at best questionable.

Such a policy would be a complex enterprise. And the difficulty is compounded by our inability to measure economic profit as distinguished from accounting profits. One indication of the existence of economic profits (losses) is movement of resources into (out of) the industry. But this is an ex post indicator rather than an ex ante measure.

A final complication arises from the existence of labor-market distortions in some of the concentrated industries. It was shown in Table 5 that labor production cost in the aircraft industry is well above the national average. Yet it is not clear that such a high-wage industry should receive a government subsidy to offset a labor-market distortion.

R&D

The second, related rationale for policy intervention is positive externalities associated with R&D. Yet it is not clear that the capital markets do not account for spillover effects. Moreover, R&D intensity varies greatly among high-technology industries, as the sample

TABLE 10.
R&D Intensity in Selected Industries

Industry	Expenditures on R&D as a percent of value-added, 1980
Drugs and medicine	22
Office, computing, accounting machines	33
Communication equipment	16
Electrical equipment	15
Aerospace and missiles	46
Instruments	13
Chemicals except drugs	8

Source: Department of Commerce (1983), Table 6.

in Table 10 demonstrates. There are also variations by the degree of "learning by doing" and by the level of external benefits or spillover derived. These variables are not even susceptible to measurement. Again, the complexity of the task rules out a rationally developed trade policy.

FACTOR INPUTS IN FIXED SUPPLY

It was shown above that certain scientific and engineering talents are a scarce resource, commonly used in all high-technology industries. It is also inelastic in supply. Any form of protection or subsidy to certain oligopolistic industries in the high-technology sector would enable them to draw the scarce resource from the nonsubsidized oligopolistic industries. The latter would have to contract. The profit-shifting gains from targeting any one industry are dissipated by the profit-shifting losses of other industries in the high-technology sector (Dixit and Grossman, 1984). For example, if a certain scientific skill is used in both the aircraft and computer industries, a subsidy to the first industry would cause the second one to contract. Profits captured by the aircraft industry could be matched by profits lost to the computer industry.

In the event that the two types of industries are symmetrical in all respects, the optimal policy is free trade. If they are not symmetrical, the government could subsidize those industries that are most able to appropriate foreign oligopoly profit. Alternatively, there is some scope for successful industry promotion when the supply of scientists can respond to its rate of return, or when other factors can be substituted for scientists in the production of high-technology goods. Nevertheless, given the lead time needed to train scientists and engineers, the capacity constraints in universities, and the very limited substitutability of other factors for scientists, the potential benefits from targeting individual industries are clearly exaggerated when viewed in a general-equilibrium context.

NEED FOR INFORMATION

A sensible strategic policy requires a rather exacting and elaborate set of information, such as demand elasticities, economic profits, cost structure, cost of R&D, slope of the learning curve, spillover effects of R&D, degree and types of scale economies, and potential number of competitors. Also needed is knowledge of firms' behavior and their response to government policy and to announcements by competitors. This type of information is not available in the present state of the art.

RETALIATION

Strategic policy attempts to improve "our" situation at the expense of others by appropriating global profits. What is gained by one country is lost to another. As such, the policy invites retaliation, and a process of mutual retaliation can be harmful to all. This indicates the superiority of a cooperative approach to the distribution of profit, provided that a mechanism can be devised to enforce and verify agreements so as to avoid cheating.

REDISTRIBUTION

As shown in Figure 1, domestic and foreign consumers may have to pay a higher price to enable "our" firms to capture foreign monopoly profits. Such redistribution may not be socially acceptable.

MULTINATIONAL CORPORATIONS

A key requirement for the strategic trade policies is that "our" firms and projects be distinguishable from "theirs." Yet many firms are transnationally owned, and many projects are joint ventures by firms with different nationalities. Trade policies that redistribute profits toward some favored project, or toward some favored firm, would fail to aid "us" significantly unless our residents have disproportionate shares in the favored projects or firms.

DISCRETION VERSUS RULES

A move of trade policy from a set of rules to discretionary measures invites unproductive "rent-seeking" activity on the part of companies and industries, as each attempts to elicit policies that would benefit it.

SUMMARY

Given these and other limitations, the suitability of U.S. strategic trade policy in the high-technology sector is highly questionable. Nevertheless it may be desirable to monitor the high-technology trade flows and to tighten and monitor proprietary rules for R&D results.

Analysis of Trade Patterns

Is it a worthwhile objective for the United States to negotiate with Japan and the EEC *mutual* restrictions on market access in high-technology products? The United States has a trade surplus in such products with all areas except Japan.

Canada and the developing countries would not be directly affected by a mutual three-way agreement for market restrictions. Indeed, restricting any of the three major markets will divert exports to these other areas (such as the LDCs) and intensify competition there. From that the United States can only lose: more than half its surplus is with areas to which the restricted exports would be diverted. The same is true for Japan, but not for Europe. Europe would benefit the most from such diversions.

Moreover, the nature of this trade varies greatly from one product to another. This is shown in Table 11, which presents a trade matrix for each of five high-technology industries at an aggregative level (GATT's grouping).

It is noted that in all five high-technology categories there is either a two-way or three-way competition in third markets. In the case of chemicals, it is mainly between the United States and Europe, while in sophisticated machinery it is mainly a three-way competition. The United States has the largest stake in these markets and may lose most from intensified competition there.

Centering attention on intra-U.S.–Europe–Japan trade, we note a U.S. surplus with both Europe and Japan in chemicals and aircraft and a U.S. surplus with Europe and a deficit or balance with Japan in machinery items.

Further disaggregation of the data for 1981 (not presented here) shows even greater variations among product categories. In drugs, plastics, agricultural chemicals, and aircraft the main competition in third markets is between the United States and the European Community. In telecommunications equipment it is a three-way competition, with Japan being a major actor in the United States, Europe, and third markets. The interest of each of the "big-three" trading areas differs from one industry to another.

TABLE 11.
Trade Matrices for 1983 (billion dollars, FOB)

Importer/ exporter	U.S.	EC(10)	Japan
Chemicals			
U.S.	—	4.7	1.5
EC	5.4	38.6	1.0
Japan	2.8	1.7	—
EFTA	0.9	7.7	0.2
Canada	2.7	0.6	0.2
Other	9.6	21.0	5.3
Machinery for specialized industries			
U.S.	—	4.2	2.6
EC	3.3	19.5	1.2
Japan	0.8	0.6	—
EFTA	0.4	6.4	0.2
Canada	3.7	0.5	0.2
Other	9.8	23.1	10.8
Office and telecommunication equipment			
U.S.	—	1.5	5.9
EC	6.4	11.4	2.5
Japan	1.4	0.1	—
EFTA	0.7	2.5	0.4
Canada	2.0	0.1	0.2
Other	8.6	6.4	4.7
Aircraft and aircraft engines			
U.S.	—	2.0	0.1
EC	3.5	6.1	0.0
Japan	1.5	0.2	—
EFTA	1.2	0.5	0.0
Canada	0.8	0.1	0.0
Other	6.9	4.1	0.1
Power-generating machines			
U.S.	—	1.1	1.4
EC	1.7	6.9	0.5
Japan	0.5	0.1	—
EFTA	0.3	1.9	0.1
Canada	2.6	0.2	0.1
Other	4.4	8.6	4.7
All manufacturers			
U.S.	—	33.1	42.0
EC	28.8	200.6	17.2
Japan	9.7	5.2	—
EFTA	4.9	46.6	3.6
Canada	29.4	3.7	3.6
Other	58.0	124.1	73.6

Source: GATT International Trade 1983–1984 appendix tables.

Conclusions

There exists a vast diversity among industries that belong to the high-technology sector when judged by the criteria relevant for strategic trade policy:

Some industries are dominated by multinationals, while others consist mainly of national firms.

Some industries are highly oligopolistic in terms of the numbers of firms and/or ease of entry, while others are competitive.

Some industries suffer from excessively high labor costs, while others do not.

Some products have a substantial "captive" governmental market, while others do not.

Certain oligopolistic high-technology industries use common factor inputs that are fixed or inelastic in supply, so that expansion of one industry may mean contraction of another.

In some industries R&D expenditures approach half of value-added, while in others that share is only a quarter.

Some industries are on the cutting edge of modern technology, while the technology of others is on the verge of being standardized and diffused.

Industries vary in the degree of scale economies, in the shape of their "learning curve," and in the degree of externalities attached to their inventions and innovations.

Industries differ in their cost conditions, profit margins, demand elasticities, and perceived responses of competitors to any policy measures.

Industries vary in the domestic and international rate of diffusion of their technology.

Industries vary in the location (third markets or not) and nature of the three-way competition, and the relative strength of each of the three main competitors. Also, in some cases new players from the NICs may enter once technology becomes standardized.

Industries exhibit significant variations in the X/M ratios (trade in each product category is not unidirectional), and hence may require differential approaches to trade policy.

The interest of the United States, the EC, and Japan differs from one industry to another.

How will different industries be affected by the existence of free trade between the EC and EFTA?

Given these and other differences this question arises: Should the high-technology industries be treated as one sector for the purpose of trade policy? The industries included in this sector are so diverse in terms of all criteria relevant to trade policy that they cannot be the subject of one uniform policy. In fact, some high-technology industries have more in common with certain middle-technology industries than they do with other high-technology industries. Any negotiations would have to be conducted on an industry-by-industry basis. A special trade policy for the high-technology sector makes little sense in view of this diversity.

Yet the technological lead of the United States is being gradually narrowed, as Japan and Europe play catch-up. Does that not call for some policy measure? The answer takes us back to the one characteristic that these industries have in common—high human capital input—and to the fundamental reason for the erosion in the U.S. position: underlying resource shifts and diffusion of knowledge.

It is the root cause of the problem that needs to be addressed by U.S. policy. Once before in recent history the United States faced a serious technological challenge: the post-sputnik race with the Soviet Union. The U.S. response was a monumental shift in factor endowment toward the acquisition of knowledge and human capital. That was accomplished through:

Support, encouragement, and promotion of mathematics and science education at the high school level. It has the effect of improving the technological sophistication of the labor force and of preparing high school graduates to enter scientific and engineering curricula at the college level.

Massive government support for science and engineering at the college and postgraduate level.

Large government support for university research in science and engineering, not unlike the land-grant policy for agriculture.

The impact of the post-sputnik efforts has now been dissipated and the policy itself has waned. If this study leads to any policy conclusions with respect to the high-technology sector (viewed as one sector), it is the need to restore the old policies so as to increase the human capital of the United States relative to other factors. Internal policies to encourage savings and investments would also be desirable. International trade policy, if it is called for at all, must be approached on an industry-by-industry basis.

This paper is based on a more detailed report prepared for the National Science Foundation. The author is grateful to the NSF for financial support, and to Professor Carl Davidson for helpful comments on an earlier draft.

References

Baldwin, R. (1984) Incentives and Rent Seeking: Trade Policy and Subsidization. Mimeographed, University of Wisconsin.

Brander, J., and Spencer, B. (1984a) Tariff Protection and Imperfect Competition. In *Monopolistic Competition in International Trade* (H. Kierzkowski, ed.). Oxford: Oxford University Press.

——— (1984b) Export Subsidies and International Market Share Rivalry. Working Paper no. 1404, Cambridge Mass., National Bureau of Economic Research.

Dixit A., and Grossman G. (1984) Targeted Export Promotion with Several Oligopolistic Industries. Discussion paper in Economics no. 71, Princeton University Woodrow Wilson School of Public and International Affairs.

Eckelmann, R., and Davis, L. (1983) Japanese Industrial Policies and the Development of High Technology Industries: Computers and Aircraft. Washington, D.C.: U.S. Department of Commerce, Office of Trade and Investment Analysis, February. Mimeographed.

Grossman G., and Richardson D. (1985) Strategic Trade Policy: A Survey of Issues and Early Analysis, Princeton University, *Special Papers in International Economics*, no. 15.

Kreinin, M. E. (1983) *International Economics: A Policy Approach*, 4th ed. New York: Harcourt Brace Jovanovich. Chap. 11.

——— (1984) Wage Competitiveness in the U.S. Auto and Steel Industries. *Contemporary Policy Issues* (Journal of the Western Economic Association) (January): 39–50.

Krugman, P. (1984) U.S. Response to Foreign Industrial Targeting, *Brookings Papers on Economic Activity*. Washington, D.C.: Brookings Institution.

Lawrence, R. (1983) Is Trade Deindustrializing America? *Brookings Papers on Economic Activity*, I. Washington, D.C.: Brookings Institution.

Levy, D., and Terleckyj, N. (1985) Trends in Industrial R&D Activities in the U.S., Europe and Japan, 1963–1983. Paper presented at an NBER Conference on Productivity and Growth in the U.S. and Japan. Cambridge, Mass., August.

Mutti, J. and Morici, P. (1983) *Changing Pattern of U.S. Industrial Activity and Comparative Advantage*. National Planning Association, NSF, Science Indicators, Washington, D.C.

Saxonhouse, G. (1983a) Tampering with Comparative Advantage in Japan? Statement before the International Trade Commission, November, Washington, D.C.

——— (1983b) Statement on Japanese Government Policies before the Joint Economic Committee, U.S. Congress, November.

——— (1984) High Technology, Government Policy, and Evolving Comparative Advantage in Goods and Services: Biotechnology in Japan and the United States. Mimeographed. Ann Arbor, University of Michigan, Discussion Paper 130. March.

Schultz, C. (1983) Industrial Policy: A Dissent. *The Brookings Review* I (Fall): 3–12.

Soete, L. and Turner, R. (1984) Technology Diffusion and the Rate of Technological Change, *Economic Journal* (Sept.): 612–623.

Spencer, B., and Brander, J. (1983) International R&D Rivalry and Industrial Strategy, *Review of Economic Studies* 50: 707–722.

Subcommittee on Banking, Financing, and Urban Affairs, U.S. House of Representatives (1983) *Forging an Industrial Competitiveness Strategy.* November.

Thurow, L. (1983) The Case for Industrial Policies. Cambridge, Mass.: MIT. Mimeographed. November.

U.S. Department of Commerce (1983) An Assessment of U.S. Competitiveness in High Technology Industries. February. Washington, D.C.: International Trade Commission.

Wall Street Journal (1984) Japanese to Share Military Know-How with the U.S., August 15, p. 32.

15

Automobile Prices and Protection: The U.S.–Japan Trade Restraint

ROBERT C. FEENSTRA

Introduction

A prominent feature of recent U.S. trade policy has been the restraint on automobile imports from Japan. Beginning in April 1981, this "voluntary export restraint" (VER) has limited Japanese auto sales to 1.68 million annually. The restraint was supposed to expire in March 1984, but instead, under U.S. pressure the ceiling was raised to 1.85 million and extended for another year. Most recently the limit has been set at 2.3 million annually for April 1985–March 1987. This trade arrangement is a particularly important example of the "new protectionism" since the auto industry was initially denied tariff protection under the escape-clause provision of the General Agreement on Tariffs and Trade (GATT). Thus, the rules for international safeguards embodied in the GATT were bypassed in favor of the VER.

The effect of the trade restraint on import and domestic auto prices has been the subject of recent debate in the United States. A study by Wharton Econometrics (1983) reports that from 1980 to 1982 the rise in average new-car selling prices was $2600 and that $1000 of this amount was due to the VER.[1] On the other hand, U.S.

From Columbia University, New York, New York.

[1] Wharton Econometric Forecasting Associates (1983). In Wharton Motor Vehicle Service *Special Analysis: The Japanese Quota* (January 1983) the price rise due to the VER is reported more precisely as $851 for imported autos over the period 1980 to 1982 and $324 for domestic autos.

automotive producers have pointed out that the consumer price index of the Bureau of Labor Statistics (BLS) has increased by an annual average of 4.3 percent for autos over 1981–1984, compared with 4.7 percent for all items.[2] It should be noted that the BLS price index corrects for quality changes in automobiles, such as the addition of greater size, improved engine features, and so forth. Thus, an upgrading of car models and a corresponding rise in price will not be reflected in that index. This is a very significant correction since the trade restraint has led to an upgrading of Japanese models, as observed by Feenstra (1984) during its first year.[3]

In this paper we shall examine the effect of the trade restraint on automobile prices and quality upgrading for both Japanese imports and American small cars. Summarizing our results, from April 1981 to April 1985 the suggested retail prices of all Japanese models increased by 24 percent, or about 5 percent per year. We find that two-thirds of this amount can be explained by the upgrading of individual models. In dollar terms, import prices have risen due to upgrading by some $200 each year, giving a $1,000 rise by 1985. This upgrading may benefit consumers who would purchase a luxury import in any case, since they now have more models to choose from, but harms consumers who desire the basic imports.

In addition to the quality upgrading, there has been a second consumer cost of the VER. When the trade restraint began, in April 1981, the Japanese yen was at one of it strongest levels in recent history. Immediately thereafter the yen started its well-known depreciation against the dollar. This exchange-rate movement would normally lead to lower prices for Japanese imports, but because of the trade restraint was not reflected in reduced import prices for autos. We conclude that a second cost of the VER was to prevent the yen depreciation from being passed on to American consumers in terms of lower auto prices.

Turning to U.S. autos, we investigate the price and quality upgrading of subcompact and compact models. From April 1981 to April 1984, we find a 9.1 percent rise in the suggested retail price, or 3 percent per year. A fraction of this amount is due to model upgrading. These figures can be interpreted in two ways. On one hand, if the yen depreciation had led to lower import prices without the VER, then we expect that U.S. auto prices would have been lower,

---

[2] These are seasonally unadjusted figures, average from March 1981 to March 1984. The BLS producer price index for autos rose by an annual average of 4.1 percent over the same period.

[3] The quality upgrading can be considered a consequence of the VER since it applies to the *number* of autos imported. If instead the trade restraint applied to the *value* of imports, as with a tariff, then we would not expect producers to shift toward the higher-price, higher-quality models.

too.[4] This point is underscored by noting that in the two years just prior to the VER, the domestic auto industry experienced some of its largest price increases ever—22 percent and 17 percent respectively for U.S. small cars over 1979–1980 and 1980–1981. Thus, while the recent increase in U.S. small-car prices has been moderate at 3 percent per year, we should recognize that the historically high prices of 1981 have been maintained. Without the protection provided by the trade restraint, import and domestic auto prices would have been lower.

On the other hand, since the actual rise in U.S. auto prices has been moderate, it follows that the recent surge in profits of domestic automakers cannot be attributed to price increases, but instead must be explained by volume increases and various cost reductions. Since the VER has led to less price competition in the U.S. market, domestic companies have been able to earn record profits from the volume increases and cost reductions rather than lowering prices for consumers.

From 1984 to 1985 the export restraint on passenger autos was raised by 24.3 percent, from 1.85 to 2.3 million. This extension was made amid renewed protectionist sentiment in the U.S. Congress but was not formally requested by the United States. Our data show that the loosening of the restraint has not been sufficient to lower import prices or reverse the quality upgrading. Import prices over 1984–1985 rose by 7 percent, with 3 percent of this amount due to upgrading. Thus, further liberalization of the trade restraint is needed to bring benefits to U.S. consumers. The extent to which such liberalization can occur depends on political pressures within the United States and Japan.

Recent Experience in the U.S. Auto Industry

On May 1, 1981, the Japanese government announced a three-year system of VERs on the export of passenger cars to the U.S. market. For the period April 1981–March 1982 these exports would not exceed 1.68 million, while for the second year (April 1982–March 1983) the export ceiling would be raised according to the growth in the U.S. market. At the end of the second year a decision about whether to extend the export restraint for a third year would be made. In addition to these limits there was provision for 82,500 exports of certain utility vehicles (such as the Subaru Brat, Toyota Land Cruiser and van) and 70,000 exports to Puerto Rico, bringing the total exports to 1,832,500 units. This limit was not increased for

---

[4] The impact of the VER on U.S. domestic car prices is examined in greater detail in Crandall (1984).

the second year of the restraint (since the U.S. market did not grow) and was also applied for the third year. For the fourth year, April 1984–March 1985, the ceilings on passenger cars, utility vehicles, and exports to Puerto Rico were increased by 10 percent. Most recently the export limit on passenger cars was raised from 1.85 to 2.3 million annually for April 1985–March 1987.

These actions were made against a background of falling production and high unemployment in U.S. autos, along with several legislative attempts to curb imports. For example, in early 1981 Senators Danforth and Bentsen introduced a bill (S.396) to impose quotas on the import of automobiles from Japan of 1.6 million units during 1981–1983. Indeed, this bill was scheduled for markup (line-by-line revision) in the Senate Finance Committee on May 12, and no doubt contributed to the specific action taken by the Japanese. Other bills included more stringent import quotas and domestic content requirements that specify the minimum content of American parts for autos sold in the United States. Supported by the UAW, the domestic content bill passed the House of Representatives in 1982 and 1983 (HR.5133 [1982] and HR.1234 [1983]) and was introduced into the U.S. Senate in 1984 (S.707).

An earlier legislative action was the petition for import relief by the UAW in June 1980, made to the U.S. International Trade Commission (ITC). In August 1980 the commission received a petition for similar import relief from Ford. Following rules established in the GATT, a recommendation for relief can be given only if the "increased imports of an article are a substantial cause of serious injury, or threat thereof, to the domestic industry." The U.S. trade law defines the term *substantial cause* as "a cause which is important and not less than any other cause." The ITC determined that, while imports of autos into the United States had increased and the domestic industry was in fact injured, the recession in the United States was a greater cause of injury than the increased imports.[5] Accordingly, import relief was not given. It was also found that the shift in consumer preferences toward small, fuel-efficient autos (due in part to rising gasoline prices) was an important cause of injury, but less important than the recessionary conditions.

In Table 1 we present background data for the auto industry during the period to which the VER applies. In April 1980–March 1981, the year immediately preceding the VER, U.S. production and employment were at depressed levels while the Japanese market share of 21.2 percent was a historic high. From the second row we see that U.S. production has picked up in the most recent year while

---

[5] United States International Trade Commission (1980) *Certain Motor Vehicles and Certain Chassis and Bodies Therefor.* Publication 1110 (December).

TABLE 1.
New Passenger Automobiles

	1979	Apr 80– Mar 81	Apr 81– Mar 82	Apr 82– Mar 83	Apr 83– Mar 84
Japanese Imports (1,000)	1,617	2,012	1,833.3	1,831.2	1,851.7
U.S. Production[a] (1,000)	8,419	6,220	5,602	5,274	7,594
U.S. Consumption[b] (1,000)	10,530	9,491	8,679	8,869	10,727
Japan Imports/U.S. Consumption (%)	15.4	21.2	21.1	20.5	17.3
Employment[c] (1,000)	904	705	698	650	744
U.S. Production/ Employment (%)	9.3	8.8	8.0	8.1	10.2

[a] For May–April periods, except 1979 calendar year.
[b] Retail sales of domestic production for May–April period (except 1979 calendar year) plus total imports.
[c] Average employment for May–April periods (except 1979 calendar year) in SIC 3711, *Motor Vehicles and Car Bodies*, plus SIC 3714, *Motor Vehicle Parts and Accessories.*

Source: Bureau of Labor Statistics, *Employment and Earnings and Supplement,* various issues. United States International Trade Commission, *The U.S. Automobile Industry: Monthly Report on Selected Economic Issues,* various issues.
Revised and updated from Feenstra (1984).

U.S. consumption began increasing in April 1982–March 1983. The rise in total consumption has led to a drop in the Japanese market share. Employment has also increased, though this occurs more slowly than the rise in production: as shown in the final row, the number of cars produced per worker has increased from 8.1 to 10.2 recently. The rise in the average product of labor is in part a normal occurrence during the upswing of a business cycle and also reflects new investment and production techniques in the auto industry.

To determine the impact of the VER on prices, a sample of Japanese import and American small (i.e., subcompact and compact) models was taken from *Automotive News Market Data Books* for 1979–1985 (only Japanese data were collected for 1985). The sample covers the base version (i.e., without options) of every model available in each year with the exception of utility vehicles and station wagons.[6] In addition to the suggested retail price in March or April of each year, data were obtained on the quantity sold and model length, width, weight, horsepower, type of transmission, and whether the base version had power steering, power brakes, or air conditioning. In the section "Estimation of Product Quality" below,

---

[6] For Japanese models, import quantities include both station wagon and non-wagon quantities (such as Toyota Corolla sedan plus wagon), whereas only the price and quality characteristics of nonwagon imports were obtained.

we shall use these characteristics to estimate the quality of car models. In the following sections we shall report our results for Japanese imports and American small autos, respectively.

Before turning to our results, we should note several qualifications. By using suggested retail prices we are ignoring additional dealer markups faced by consumers, which have been substantial in recent years. To this extent our price data give an underestimate of the consumer cost of the VER. In addition, we are ignoring model options which are not provided as standard equipment but which a consumer must purchase to obtain a car. Anecdotal evidence suggests that such "required options" have been frequently used in the purchase of some recent Japanese models. Data on this practice are not available, however, and we consider only the quality upgrading that has occurred on the base versions (i.e., without options) of each model.

Price and Quality of Japanese Imports

In Table 2 we show information for Japanese imports over 1979–1985. The unit values shown in the first row are a weighted average of suggested retail prices of base models, using the quantities sold as weights. The prices for 1981 were those in effect on April 8, just prior to the announcement of the export restraint. Accordingly, we shall treat 1981 as our base year for comparisons.[7] The unit values show a rise of 29 percent, from \$6,211 in 1981 to \$8,038 in 1985. However, this rise includes both the effect of increasing prices for individual models and the shift in quantity demanded toward higher-priced models. A more appropriate measure of the overall price increase is to construct a price index using constant weights between each two years (see "Price and Quality Indexes," below). Reported in the second row, this price index shows an increase of 24 percent in suggested retail prices between 1981 and 1985, or about 5 percent per year.

The variety of Japanese models offered was quite stable over the period, with new models introduced only recently. The qualities of individual models, however, were upgraded throughout the period of the trade restraint. In the second-last row of Table 2 we report the unit quality of imports, measured as a weighted average across models (as computed in "Estimation of Product Quality"). In the

---

[7] If Japanese producers anticipated the export restraint, then the price rise and quality upgrading over 1980–1981 may also be attributed to the export restraint. This hypothesis is considered in Feenstra (1985) and finds some statistical support. The interested reader is invited to revise the index number calculations in Table 2 using 1980 as the base year.

TABLE 2.
Sample of Japanese Imported Automobiles

	1979	1980	1981	1982	1983	1984	1985
Unit Value	4,946	5,175	6,211	6,834	7,069	7,518	8,038
(% change)	—	(4.6)	(20.0)	(10.0)	(3.4)	(6.4)	(6.9)
Price Index	80.8	83.5	100.0	107.8	109.5	115.8	123.9
(% change)	—	(3.3)	(19.8)	(7.8)	(1.6)	(5.8)	(6.9)
No. of Models	21	24	24	24	26	29	31
New Models	—	3	0	0[a]	4[a]	4	3
Unit Quality	5,072	5,161	5,504	5,875	6,239	6,462	6,674
(% change)	—	(1.8)	(6.6)	(6.7)	(6.2)	(3.6)	(3.3)
Quality Index	93.2	93.9	100.0	104.9	109.3	112.9	116.6
(% change)	—	(0.8)	(6.4)	(4.9)	(4.2)	(3.3)	(3.3)

[a] In 1982–1983 the Datsun Sentra, Pulsar, and Stanza replaced the 210, 310, and 510, respectively, and are not counted as new models.

Obtained from *Automotive News,* Market data book issue, 1979–1984.

final row we report the quality index, constructed using constant weights between each two years (see "Price and Quality Indexes"). The quality index shows a rise of 17 percent over 1981–1985, compared with 24 percent for suggested retail prices. Thus, *two-thirds of the rise in import prices can be explained by the upgrading of individual models.*

The dollar increase in quality can be computed through multiplying the change in the quality index times $6,211, the 1981 base price. This gives a quality rise of about $200 per import each year, leading to a $1,000 increase by 1985. The quality upgrading has a consumer cost that varies across individuals. The upgrading may benefit consumers who would purchase a luxury import in any case, since they now have more models to choose from, but harms those who desire the basic models.

It is perhaps surprising that much of the price rise in imports can be attributed to quality upgrading. We would normally expect the trade restraint to have a further upward effect on prices, independent of quality, by creating an artificial shortage. We shall now argue that the VER has had such an upward effect on prices by preventing movements in the dollar/yen exchange rate from being passed through in import prices.

In Figure 1 we show the quarterly dollar/yen exchange rate over the past several years (relative to 1981, 01 = 100). This exchange rate has been multiplied by the Japanese consumer price index, giving a rough indication of what the U.S. price of Japanese autos would have been under free trade. In the first quarter of 1981 the yen was at one

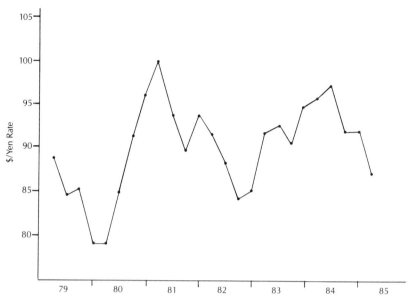

FIGURE 1. Dollar/yen exchange rate times Japanese consumer price index *(Source: IMF,* International Financial Statistics, *various issues.)*

of its strongest levels in recent history, having appreciated 21 percent from the previous year. Indeed, this appreciation corresponds very closely to the 20 percent rise in Japanese auto prices from 1980 to 1981 (see Table 2). Immediately after the VER was in place the yen began its depreciation against the dollar, due in part to high U.S. interest rates. The greatest depreciation is obtained by comparing first quarter 1981 to third quarter 1982. Since 1983 the yen depreciation has partially reversed itself, but the effective exchange rate remains below its first-quarter-1981 peak.

Based on this exchange-rate behavior, we expect that without the VER Japanese auto prices would have *fallen* after 1981. This prediction is reinforced by noting that in the year just before the VER, the 21 percent appreciation of the yen corresponded to a nearly equal rise in imported auto prices. It is logical to expect that the reversal in the yen movement would have led to some fall in imported auto prices. However, in the presence of the artificial shortage created by the trade restraint, no such decline in auto prices has occurred. *We conclude that a further impact of the trade restraint was to prevent the yen depreciation from being passed on to American consumers through lower imported auto prices. This consumer cost is in addition to the quality upgrading of import models that occurred.*

TABLE 3.
Sample of American Small Autos

	1979	1980	1981	1982	1983	1984
Unit Value	4,186	5,067	5,915	6,446	6,581	6,781
(% change)	—	(21.0)	(16.7)	(9.0)	(2.1)	(3.0)
Price Index	70.1	85.6	100.0	107.5	107.3	109.1
(% change)	—	(22.1)	(16.8)	(7.5)	(−0.2)	(1.7)
No. of Models	24	22	23	27	33	34
New Models	—	1	7	4	4[a]	7
Unit Quality	4,195	4,132	4,183	4,351	4,497	4,563
(% change)	—	(−1.5)	(1.2)	(4.0)	(3.4)	(1.5)
Quality Index	98.3	97.8	100.0	102.1	103.4	103.8
(% change)	—	(−0.5)	(2.2)	(2.1)	(1.3)	(0.4)

[a] In 1983 the Dodge 400 and Chrysler LeBaron were down-sized from earlier models and are not counted as new.
Source: Obtained from *Automotive News,* Market data book issue, 1979–1984.

Price and Quality of American Small Autos

In Table 3 we report the price and quality data for U.S. subcompact and compact models. The unit value, constructed as a weighted average of suggested retail prices of base models, shows a rise of 14.6 percent from 1981 to 1984. However, a considerable portion of this rise is due to a demand shift toward larger models. The index of suggested retail prices, constructed using constant weights between each two years, increases by only 9.1 percent from 1981 to 1984, or 3 percent per year—less than the rise in the overall consumer price index over that period. We also see that there has been an active introduction of new models and expiring of old. Some quality upgrading of U.S. models has occurred, though less than the amount of the price rise. In the final row of Table 3 we report an increase of 3.8 percent in the quality index from 1981 to 1984, which is slightly less than half of the rise in the price index.

It is also of importance that in the two years just before the trade restraint began, U.S. small-car prices rose very substantially—22.1 percent and 16.8 percent respectively over 1979–1980 and 1980–1981. This compares with a rise in all consumer prices of 13.5 percent and 10.4 percent respectively over the same periods. Thus, while the increase in U.S. small-car prices since 1981 has been moderate at 3 percent per year, we can alternatively interpret the evidence as saying that the historically high prices of 1981 have simply been maintained. This view corresponds with our discussion of the dollar/yen exchange rate and import prices. In the absence of the VER, we expect that the yen depreciation would have led to lower import prices. This would have created greater price competition on domestic producers, and some lowering of U.S. auto prices too. Instead, the trade restraint has insulated the U.S. industry from movements in the dollar/yen exchange rate, thereby permitting the high prices of 1981 to be maintained.

However, we should also recognize that the surge in profits of U.S. automakers cannot be attributed to recent price increases for small cars, since these increases have been moderate. Evidence on the extent of the profit turnaround is as follows:

Profit Rate (Profits/Sales Revenue)

	1982	1983	1984
American Motors	−6.4%	−4.5	0.4
Chrysler Corporation	1.7%	5.3	12.2
Ford Motor Company	−1.8%	4.2	5.6
General Motors	1.6%	5.0	5.4
Industry Average	−0.3%	4.5	6.3

Source: Automotive News, various issues.

Substantial losses were recorded in the automobile industry in 1981, with some producers continuing to show losses in 1982. All companies were able to begin earning profits in 1983, though American Motors did not reach this point until the fourth quarter of that year. The profits earned by companies during 1984 broke all previous records, totaling $9.8 billion as compared with $6.3 billion in 1983.

The profit surge of U.S. automakers can be explained by a variety of factors. The volume expansion as the demand for cars has increased (see Table 1) will lower average costs due to economies of scale and raise profits. Direct cost reductions have also been achieved as fewer workers are rehired coming out of the recession and the average product of labor increases (Table 1). U.S. firms have reported that the breakeven volume for profitability has been reduced in each company, reflecting a decrease in fixed costs. In addition, a number of recent U.S. models have proved very popular among consumers. Last, it should be noted that a portion of U.S. automakers' profits are obtained from truck sales, which have been protected by a 25 percent tariff since 1980.

While the cost reductions in U.S. industry indicate that some adjustment to potential competition has taken place, consumers have not yet benefited from this adjustment. The trade restraint has led to less price competition in the U.S. market, enabling domestic companies to earn record profits from volume increases and cost reductions rather than lowering prices. Compared with a tariff, the VER gives greater market power to domestic producers since the supply of Japanese imports is constrained in quantity. The recent experience in U.S. autos appears to be an important example of the exercise of market power under a quantitative trade restraint, with U.S. firms increasing their profits in response to higher demand and reduced costs but not lowering consumer prices.

Estimation of Product Quality

For each of the Japanese and U.S. small-car models, data were collected on the suggested retail price of base versions (i.e., without options), quantity sold, and various characteristics. The characteristics will be used as a measure of quality upgrading, using the statistical technique of hedonic regressions. The basic reference on this technique is Griliches (1971).

JAPANESE HEDONIC REGRESSIONS

In Table 4 we show the results of regressing the logarithm of Japanese model price on the various characteristics. Over the 179 models in 1979–1985 we are able to explain 93 percent of the variation in price ($R^2 = 0.925$ in the first column). The coefficients of each characteristic can be given a precise interpretation: the coefficient of 0.37 for width, for example, indicates that an increase in width of one foot would raise the estimated price by 37 percent. The transmission variable takes the value of unity if the model has a five-speed or automatic transmission as standard equipment and zero otherwise; the coefficient of 0.14 indicates that this feature raises the estimated price by 14 percent. The presence of air conditioning as standard equipment raised the estimated price by 15 percent. In the final regression we have omitted weight and power-brake variables since these estimated coefficients when included were highly insignificant (with standard errors nearly twice the coefficient size). Omitting these variables has only a slight effect on the other coefficients (see below).

It can be noticed that the length variable has a negative (but insignificant) coefficient, which is unexpected. This may be due to multicollinearity with other characteristics or misspecification of the equation. Aside from the negative sign on length, the 1979–1985 regression appears to fit rather well. We have included dummy variables for the various years, equaling unity in that year and zero otherwise. Except for 1980 the estimated coefficients of the year dummies are highly significant. The estimate of 0.212 in 1985, for example, indicates that 21.2 percent of the (unweighted) price rise from 1979 to 1985 is *not* explained by any change in characteristics. Thus the year coefficients can be interpreted as the quality-adjusted price rise.

TABLE 4.
Japanese Hedonic Regressions.
Dependent Variable: Japanese Auto Price (Logarithm)

Period	1979–1984	1979–1981	1982–1983	1984–1985
Obs.	179	69	50	60
R^2	0.925	0.901	0.929	0.923
SSR	1.675	0.626	0.368	0.560
Intercept	6.25*	5.73*	7.45*	6.06*
	(0.44)	(0.67)	(0.88)	(0.88)
Length (feet)	−0.018	−0.057	−0.066	0.015
	(0.016)	(0.031)	(0.039)	(0.024)
Width (feet)	0.37*	0.56*	0.28	0.37*
	(0.096)	(0.16)	(0.21)	(0.17)
Horsepower (100 HP)	0.71*	0.83*	0.79*	0.61*
	(0.056)	(0.11)	(0.13)	(0.090)
Dummy Variables				
Transmission	0.14*	0.12*	0.18*	0.16*
(5-speed or auto)	(0.021)	(0.031)	(0.047)	(0.043)
Power Steering	0.056*	0.027	0.047	0.088*
	(0.025)	(0.057)	(0.044)	(0.040)
Air Conditioning	0.15*	0.20*	0.18*	0.13*
	(0.030)	(0.065)	(0.062)	(0.050)
Year 1980	0.012	0.0030		
	(0.030)	(0.031)		
Year 1981	0.124*	0.118*		
	(0.031)	(0.033)		
Year 1982	0.160*			
	(0.032)			
Year 1983	0.140*		−0.015	
	(0.032)		(0.027)	
Year 1984	0.180*			
	(0.032)			
Year 1985	0.212*			0.32
	(0.032)			(0.028)

* Significant at 95 percent level. Standard errors are in parentheses.

A measure of quality is obtained by computing the predicted
price from the hedonic regression not including the portion explained by the year dummies. This calculation is repeated for each
year, obtaining a measure of model quality for each model. The unit
quality reported in the second-last row of Table 2 is a weighted
average across models, using the quantities sold that year as weights
(for 1985 we use the 1984 quantities as weights). The quality index

reported in the last row of Table 2 is computed with constant weights between each two years, as described in "Price and Quality Indexes."

It is clear that our measure of quality is sensitive to the estimated coefficients of the year dummies, since these coefficients measure the quality-adjusted price rise. We checked the sensitivity of these coefficients to the model specification by reestimating the 1979–1985 regression, while omitting each time one of the following variables: length, width, weight, and horsepower. Below we report the range of point estimates for the year coefficients obtained from these regressions:

Year Dummy	Coefficient Range
1980	0.0094–0.0161
1981	0.111–0.128
1982	0.147–0.171
1983	0.140–0.162
1984	0.180–0.206
1985	0.212–0.237

By comparing these coefficient ranges with the estimates and standard errors in Table 4 (first column), several results are obtained. First, the coefficient ranges are not more than one standard error away from the Table 4 estimates. This means that the estimates in Table 4 (first column) are not very sensitive to the specification of the regression, which gives us confidence in using these estimates. The insensitivity of the coefficients is explained by high multicollinearity of the data. Second, it can be noted that for 1983–1985 the year estimates in Table 4 are at the lower end of the coefficient ranges. This suggests that we may be underestimating the quality-adjusted price rise in these years. However, the upper end of the coefficient ranges in 1983–1985 are obtained when the width and horsepower variables are omitted. Since these variables are highly significant when included, we shall not regard the upper end of the coefficient ranges for 1983–1985 as accurate estimates. Instead, we shall continue to use the point estimates of the year dummies obtained from the Table 4 regression (first column) when estimating product quality.

In Table 4 we also show the Japanese regression for selected pairs of years. A test for coefficient stability of the quality characteristics can be made by separately estimating the regression for each year, obtaining the unrestricted cumulative SSR of 1.335. The restricted SSR with equal coefficients in 1979–1985 is 1.675, as shown in the first column of Table 4. The F-statistic for testing coefficient

stability is computed as 0.92, with 36 and 130 degrees of freedom.[8]
The 95-percent level of the F-distribution is 1.50, so we can accept
the null hypothesis of equal coefficients for the characteristics in
each year. Accordingly, we used the 1979–1985 regression to estimate product quality.

AMERICAN HEDONIC REGRESSIONS

In Table 5 we report the results of regressing the logarithm of U.S.
small-car prices (i.e., subcompact and compact models) on the various characteristics for 1979–1984 and selected pairs of years. In
comparison with the Japanese regressions the fits are not as good,
which is seen especially from the R^2 values for the two-year regressions. The length variable now has a significantly positive coefficient, while weight has a negative coefficient (significant only at the
90-percent level). The width variable was omitted from the final
regressions since it was highly insignificant when included (with a
standard error four times its coefficient size). We also checked the
sensitivity of the year coefficients by reestimating the 1979–1984
regression while omitting each time one of the following variables:
length, width, weight, and horsepower. For each year dummy, the
resulting coefficient range from these regressions was within one
standard error (plus or minus) of the point estimates in Table 5 (first
column). It follows that the 1979–1984 estimates in Table 5 are not
sensitive to the specification of the regression.

When the American and Japanese data are pooled over 1979–
1984, the length coefficient drops to 0.0016 (significant at the 90-
percent level) while the width coefficient is highly insignificant. In
the pooled regression we have equal coefficients for all quality characteristics but allow different year dummies for American and Japanese models. The SSR of the pooled regression is 3.45, compared
with 2.24 from adding the SSR of the separate national regressions.
The F-statistic for testing whether the American and Japanese regressions have equal coefficients for the quality characteristics is computed as 18.8, with 8 and 179 degrees of freedom.[9] This compares
with a 95-percent level for the F-distribution of 1.94, so we soundly

---

[8] The F-statistic is computed as $[(1.675-1.335)/36]/(1.335/130) = 0.92$, where
six quality characteristics appear in the regression of each year giving $6 \times 6 = 36$
restrictions in the 1979–1985 regression. The yearly regressions have a total of 7×7
$= 49$ coefficients, giving $179 - 49 = 130$ degrees of freedom for the unrestricted SSR.

[9] The F-statistic is computed as $[(3.45-2.24)/8]/(2.24/279) = 18.8$, where the
coefficients of eight quality characteristics are restricted to be equal in the pooled
regression. The separate American and Japanese regressions have a total of 307 coefficients, giving $307 - 28 = 279$ degrees of freedom.

TABLE 5.
American Hedonic Regressions
Dependent Variable: American Small-Auto Price (logarithm)

Period	1979–1984	1979–1980	1981–1982	1983–1984
Obs.	163	46	50	67
R^2	0.879	0.618	0.652	0.859
SSR	0.958	0.300	0.239	0.266
Intercept	7.77*	8.09*	7.94*	8.14*
	(0.13)	(0.24)	(0.21)	(0.22)
Length (feet)	0.040*	0.025	0.061*	0.0078
	(0.013)	(0.024)	(0.019)	(0.023)
Weight (tons)	−0.13	−0.11	−0.21	0.30*
	(0.077)	(0.15)	(0.12)	(0.14)
Horsepower	0.14*	0.013	0.10	0.12
(100 HP)	(0.062)	(0.138)	(0.16)	(0.070)
Dummy Variables				
Transmission	0.14*	—[a]	—[a]	0.10*
(5-speed or auto)	(0.050)			(.045)
Power Steering	0.11*	0.11*	0.051	0.13*
	(0.022)	(0.049)	(0.040)	(0.027)
Power Brakes	0.091*	—[a]	0.12*	0.081*
	(0.017)		(0.025)	(0.021)
Air Conditioning	0.51*	—[a]	—[a]	0.45*
	(0.060)			(0.055)
Year 1980	0.198*	0.192*		
	(0.024)	(0.027)		
Year 1981	0.350*			
	(0.025)			
Year 1982	0.408*		0.061*	
	(0.025)		(0.022)	
Year 1983	0.388*			
	(0.026)			
Year 1984	0.417*			0.032
	(0.026)			(0.017)

* Significant at 95-percent level. Standard errors are in parentheses.
[a] Indicates that no model had this variable as standard equipment.

reject the hypothesis of equal coefficients for the quality characteristics across the national regressions.

In Table 5 we also report the American hedonic regressions for selected pairs of years. A test for coefficient stability of the quality characteristics is performed by separately estimating the regression for each year, obtaining the unrestricted cumulative SSR of 0.697.

The restricted SSR with equal coefficients for the quality characteristics in 1979–1984 is 0.958, as shown in the first column of Table 5. The F-statistic for testing coefficient stability is computed as 1.87, with 25 and 125 degrees of freedom.[10] The 95-percent level of the F-distribution is 1.61, so we initially reject the hypotheses of equal coefficients for the quality characteristics in each year.

To investigate stability more closely, we performed an F-test for equal coefficients of the characteristics in each *pair* of years, with the results:

Years	F-statistic	Degrees of Freedom
1979–1980	1.54	4, 36
1980–1981	3.15	4, 34
1981–1982	1.39	5, 38
1982–1983	0.86	5, 46
1983–1984	0.82	7, 51

The only pair of years in which we reject the hypotheses of equal coefficients is 1980–1981, where the F-statistic of 3.15 exceeds the 95-percent level of the F-distribution given by 2.65. In all other pairs of years we accept the null hypothesis of equal coefficients for the characteristics. In view of these results we decided to use the 1979–1984 regression, shown in the first column of Table 5, to compute product quality.

One explanation for the unstable hedonic regression over 1980–1981 may be the consumer response to gasoline-price changes. Ohta and Griliches (1983) examine in detail the stability of hedonic regressions for U.S. used autos during 1970–1981 and find that the regression coefficients change between April and October 1979 if gasoline costs are not taken into account. They also propose a correction for the change in gasoline prices, so that the estimated regression is stable.[11]

When examining coefficient stability, Ohta and Griliches use both the conventional F-test and a weaker Bayesian criterion due to Leamer (1978). Leamer's test is derived on the assumption of diffuse

---

[10] The F-statistic is computed as $[(0.958—0.697)/25]/(0.697/125) = 1.87$. The number of quality characteristics appearing in the yearly regressions differs, because in some years no model has a particular characteristic such as air conditioning. The total number of estimated coefficients in the yearly regressions is 38, while the 1979–1984 regression has 13, giving $38 - 13 = 25$ restrictions and $163 - 38 = 125$ degrees of freedom for the unrestricted SSR.

[11] In Feenstra (1984) gas mileage was included in the hedonic regressions for 1980–1981. It had a negative coefficient for the Japanese import and American small-car regressions and a positive coefficient for American large cars. The former result led us not to include this variable in the present study.

priors, and the critical level for the F-statistic is then computed as $L_B = (n - k)(n^{q/n} - 1)/q$. In this expression k is the number of parameters in the unrestricted regression, q is the number of parameters restricted by the null hypothesis, and n is the number of observations. For testing coefficient stability of the quality characteristics over 1979–1984, the critical level $L_B = 5.92$, compared with the observed F-statistic of 1.87 reported above.[12] Thus, according to Leamer's test we can accept the hypothesis of equal coefficients for the characteristics in each year. This reinforces our decision to use the 1979–1984 regression to compute product quality. The calculation of quality is the same as that reported above for the Japanese models.

Price and Quality Indexes

The price and quality indexes reported in Tables 2 and 3 are computed with constant weights between each pair of years. Specifically, between each two years the Laspeyres and Paasche price indexes were computed, where the former uses the first-period quantities as weights and the latter uses the second-period quantities. The Fisher Ideal index was then computed as the geometric mean (square root of the product) of the Laspeyres and Paasche indexes. This method is recommended in Diewert (1976).[13] The same calculation was performed for model qualities where these were obtained as the predicted price from the hedonic regressions *not* including the contribution of that year's dummy variable. The Fisher Ideal indexes for price and quality were separately computed for Japanese and American models, as reported in Tables 2 and 3.

When new models are introduced, as occurred in our sample, the calculation of the price and quality indexes is affected. Since the Paasche index uses second-period quantities as weights, we need to include a hypothetical price and quality for the year before the model first appears. This problem also arises with the Laspeyres index when a model is dropped: in this case the calculation requires a hypothetical price and quality for the year after the model last appeared. Fortunately, our use of hedonic regressions permits a natural solution to this "new goods" problem. In any year when a model is not available, we can predict its hypothetical price and quality from the hedonic regression by using its actual characteristics in the next, or previous, year (depending on whether a model is

---

[12] The critical level is computed as $L_B = (163 - 38)[163^{(25/163)} - 1]/25 = 5.92$. See also footnote 10.

[13] It can be noted that the Laspeyres and Paasche indexes in our sample differed by less than 1 percent for each pair of years, so forming the Fisher Ideal index was a minor modification.

being added or dropped). Of course, in a year when a model is not available its quantity sold is zero.

This methodology allows us to construct the price and quality indexes while the range of models offered changes. According to this approach, a new model would show a fall in its price the first year it is available if the actual price charged is *below* that predicted by the hedonic regression. This is because the predicted price is used as its hypothetical price in the year before it was first available. This price fall would affect the value of the Paasche price index. Since the *quality* of a model is always computed as a predicted price from the hedonic regressions (not including the contribution of that year's dummy variable), a new model will always show a constant quality between the year before and the first year it is available. Even though the quality is constant, the existence of this new model will still affect the value of the Paasche quality index by having a slight tendency to make the quality index itself constant. The statements we have made for a Paasche index apply to the Laspeyres index when a model is dropped.

Conclusions

The VER has imposed several costs on U.S. consumers. First, the substantial depreciation of the yen after 1981 was not passed through in lower imported auto prices, as would be expected without the trade restraint. This represents a loss to all purchasers of Japanese or competing domestic models. In addition, there has been a significant quality upgrading of import models, amounting to $200 per import each year. This upgrading may benefit consumers who would purchase a luxury import in any case, since they now have more models to choose from, but harms those who desire the basic models.

For U.S. small cars, we found a 9.1 percent increase in the suggested retail prices from 1981 to 1984, or 3 percent per year. While this increase is moderate, we must also recognize that U.S. small-car prices rose rapidly just prior to the VER and that these high prices have been maintained. The recent profit surge of U.S. producers should be attributed to volume increases and various cost reductions. While the cost reductions indicate that some adjustment to potential competition has taken place within the U.S. industry, consumers have not yet benefited from this adjustment. The VER has led to less price competition in the U.S. market, enabling domestic companies to earn record profits from the volume increases and cost reduction rather than lowering prices.

From 1984 to 1985 the export restraint on passenger autos was raised by 24.3 percent, from 1.85 to 2.3 million. This extension was made amid renewed protectionist sentiment in the U.S. Congress but was not formally requested by the United States. Our data show that the loosening of the restraint has not been sufficient to lower import prices or reverse the quality upgrading. Import prices over 1984–1985 rose by 7 percent, with 3 percent of this amount due to upgrading. Thus, further liberalization of the trade restraint is needed to bring benefits to U.S. consumers. The extent to which such liberalization can occur depends on political pressures within the United States and Japan.

Financial support from the Ford Foundation is gratefully acknowledged.

References

Automotive News Market Data Book (1979–1984) Detroit: Automotive News.

Crandall, Robert W. (1984) Import Quotas and the Automobile Industry: The Costs of Protectionism, *The Brookings Review.* Summer.

Diewert, W. Erwin (1976) Exact and Superlative Index Numbers, *Journal of Econometrics* 4: 115–145.

Feenstra, Robert C. (1984) Voluntary Export Restraint in U.S. Autos, 1980–81: Quality, Employment, and Welfare Effects. In Robert Baldwin and Anne Krueger (eds.), *The Structure and Evolution of Recent U.S. Trade Policy.* Chicago: University of Chicago Press.

——— (1985) Quality Change Under Trade Restraints: Theory and Evidence from Japanese Autos. Discussion Paper No. 298. Columbia University, New York. June.

Griliches, Zvi (1971) Hedonic Price Indexes for Automobiles: An Econometric Analysis of Quality Change. In Zvi Griliches (ed.), *Price Indexes and Quality Change.* Cambridge, Mass.: Harvard University Press.

Leamer, Edward E. (1978) *Specification Searches: Ad Hoc Inference with Non-Experimental Data.* New York: Wiley.

Lindert, Peter H., and Kindleberger, Charles P. (1982) *International Economics.* Homewood, Ill.: Richard D. Irwin.

Ohta, Makota, and Griliches, Zvi (1983) Automobile Prices and Quality: Did the Gasoline Price Increase Change Consumer Tastes in the U.S.? NBER Working Paper No. 1211 (October), Cambridge, Massachusetts.

Wharton Econometric Forecasting Associates (1983) *Impact of Local Content Legislation on U.S. and World Economies.* July, Philadelphia, Pennsylvania.

16

Protectionism in the Steel Industry: A Historical Perspective

WILLIAM T. HOGAN

The trend toward protection in the steel industry on a worldwide basis developed with the increase in steel trade which grew steadily after 1950 and accelerated rapidly from the middle 1960s to the present. In 1950, with a number of companies in many countries recovering from the ravages of World War II, relatively little steel was available for export, since most of the production was desperately needed at home. In that year, some 20 million metric tons were exported throughout the world, which amounted to 10.7 percent of total global production. By 1970, steel exports increased to 117 million metric tons, or approximately 20 percent of a much expanded world steel production. In 1974, during the worldwide boom, exports of steel were 169.8 million tons, or 24 percent of world production. From that time to the present, exports remained relatively stable with a slight increase to 173 million tons in 1983, or 26.1 percent of world production. Table 1 gives world production, total exports, and the percentage they represent for selected years.

The increase in exports is due primarily to the growth of capacity in the industrialized nations, which in many instances was well above domestic needs. In the most recent years, a number of countries in the Third World have built steel industries which also export considerable tonnage.

The Japanese increased their steelmaking potential and production in the 1960s and the 1970s. Output in 1960 was 22 million

From Fordham University, New York, New York.

TABLE 1.
World Steel Production, Exports, and the
Percentage Exports Represent of World Steel
Production
(millions of metric tons of raw steel)

Year	Exports*	World Steel Production	Export Percentage
1950	20.5	192.0	10.7
1955	34.0	270.5	12.6
1960	52.7	345.5	15.3
1965	78.5	457.0	17.2
1970	117.4	595.3	19.7
1974	169.8	708.7	24.0
1980	171.8	716.0	24.0
1983	173.0	663.0	26.1

* In terms of exports, the figures represent a raw-steel
equivalent.

Source: International Iron and Steel Institute, *World
Steel in Figures.* Brussels, 1985.

metric tons. By 1970 it had risen to 93 million and reached its peak
of 119 million in 1973. By 1978 Japanese steelmaking capɑ ity had
risen somewhat beyond 145 million tons.

A decision was made in the 1960s to increase steel-industry
output not only to satisfy the Japanese market but also to supply a
significant portion of the world steel market. In a number of years in
the last two decades, Japan has exported as much as 50 percent of its
steel output, most of it in terms of steel products; however, a very
significant portion was in terms of such products made of steel as
automobiles and ships. In the early 1980s, the Japanese automobile
industry exported about 55 percent of its output. Production from
1980 to 1983 averaged 11 million vehicles with exports averaging
slightly under 6 million vehicles per year. This involved the export
of several million tons of steel in the automobiles.

The European Economic Community (EEC) expanded capacity
and production to allow for a significant tonnage of exports, although the figure was not nearly as high as that of the Japanese. In
some years, however, as much as 25 percent of the production of a
number of countries was exported, as output increased from 29 million tons for the Community in 1950 to 155 million in 1974, a better
than fivefold advance. There was a brisk trade among the members of
the Community as well as substantial exports outside. The leading
exporters in terms of percentage are Belgium and Luxembourg,
which consistently export some 70 percent of their steel, much of
which goes to EEC countries. These two countries do not consider
shipments to the EEC as exports since they regard it as a market
common to all of the members.

The extra capacity over and above domestic needs in both Japan and Western Europe forced both areas to look for export outlets. Virtually all of the world was considered a potential market. However, the principal target was the United States. Export tonnage began to flow to the United States in large amounts in the middle 1960s, reaching 10.3 million net tons in 1965, of which 4.7 million came from Japan and 4.2 million from the EEC. The 1965 tonnage represented a sharp increase from 6.4 million tons imported the year before. The basic reason for this was the labor negotiations which took place in 1965 with the possible threat of a strike. As a consequence, steel consumers hedged against this possibility and imported large tonnages. In 1966 and 1967, despite the fact that there were no negotiations between management and the steelworkers' union, imports continued to increase, although somewhat modestly. In the first year they were 10.7 million tons and in the second 11.4 million tons. Then came 1968, a negotiating year, and the relations between the labor union and the steel industry were somewhat stormy—offering the strong possibility of a strike. To protect themselves, steel customers, remembering a four-month strike in 1959, ordered heavily from foreign producers. The extent of their orders brought imports to an all-time high of 18 million tons, a sizable increase over the previous year.

As early as 1966 steel producers in the United States sought some protection against what they considered extensive and unrestricted imports of steel. The first attempt was a temporary tariff that was abandoned in favor of a quota on steel imports. Hearings on legislation to set a quota were held in June 1968. Both the steel industry and the steelworkers' union testified in favor of some type of quota. However, the hearings were terminated when the Japanese and the Europeans offered to establish voluntary restraints on the amount of steel they would send to the United States. The restraints took the form of a total import figure for 1969 on a worldwide basis of 14 million net tons. The Japanese portion was 5.75 million, or 41 percent, and the same was allotted to the members of the EEC, which at that time were six since the United Kingdom had not yet joined the Community. An attempt was made in 1968 to include the United Kingdom in the arrangement but it was unsuccessful.

The agreement made between governments was to extend for three years with a 5 percent increase in imports for the second and third years. Thus, in 1969, it would be 14 million tons; in 1970, 14.7 million tons; and in 1971, slightly in excess of 15.4 million tons. Both the Japanese and the Europeans stated their intention to maintain the same product mix insofar as they were able.

As a result of the voluntary restraint agreement, imports to the United States in 1969 dropped to 14 million tons and, although an increase to 14.7 million would have been allowed, in 1970, imports dropped again to 13.4 million tons, which was 1.3 million tons less than the allotted quota. There was a decided shift to higher-priced items as well as an increase in the prices of imported steel as exporters to the United States took advantage of the quota to raise some prices. Specifically, the 18 million tons imported in 1968 represented a total cost of $1.976 billion. In 1970, with imports down to 13.4 million tons, a sharp drop indeed, the cost was $1.967 billion, virtually equal to that of 1968.

In 1971, worldwide steel demand fell and production of raw steel declined from 419 million metric tons to 396 million. This triggered more export activity on the part of the Europeans and the Japanese. The year's allotment was to have been 15.4 million tons, according to the voluntary restraint agreement. However, by October 1971 imports exceeded this figure, rising to 15.5 million tons. Technically speaking, it was maintained by the exporters that the Americans had violated the quota agreement when the Nixon administration placed a 10 percent surcharge on all imports into the United States as of August 15, 1971. The foreign producers argued that the quota agreement entered into in late 1968 contained an understanding that during the three-year period no tariff or mandatory quota of any kind would be levied against steel. This was technically correct. However, the exporters of steel to the United States had exceeded the quota for the year before the surcharge was announced, since orders for October were taken several months prior to that date.

In 1971, imports reached a record 18.3 million tons, and negotiations were held to renew the quota for three more years. These were concluded in 1972 with an accord reached easily with the Japanese and after much difficulty with the Europeans. Such circumstances were not surprising since the Europeans had seven nations and many companies involved, whereas the Japanese were one nation with relatively few steel companies.

The second agreement on voluntary restraints entered into in 1972 was short-lived because of the worldwide boom in steel that took place in 1973 and 1974. Steel demand increased sharply and consumers the world over were anxious to get steel wherever they could, and thus quotas were abandoned without much question and world steel trade attained a new record.

In 1975, there was a sharp drop in steel activity, due in part to the increase in petroleum prices, which diverted sizable funds to the purchase of energy. As a consequence, steel in the industrialized world was not in great demand, and production fell by 20 percent in the United States, 19 percent in the EEC, and 14 percent in Japan. Consequently the steel industries in both Japan and the EEC looked to exports to bolster their lagging demand. Again, the United States was the principal target, particularly since the voluntary restraint agreements that were terminated in 1974 were not reinstated. Thus, the U.S. market was, with the exception of some restraints on specialty steel, completely open until the trigger-price mechanism was adopted in 1978.

European Restraints on Imports

In 1972, because of shipments of steel products from Japan to European countries both inside and outside the EEC, action was taken to limit and monitor shipments of the major Japanese steel producers to the Common Market. The original term was for one year, 1972, and the quota amounted to 1,267,000 net tons. This was subsequently extended for two additional years, and the quota increased to 1,344,000 tons. The increase for the two years was occasioned by the entrance of Denmark and Ireland into the Common Market on January 1, 1973. The effect of this quota can be seen from the following figures. In 1971, the Japanese exported 2.2 million tons of steel to nine countries of the current Common Market. In 1972, this figure was reduced to 1,700,000 tons. In subsequent years, there were further reductions, with 1974 resulting in a 1,200,000-million-metric-ton figure. At this point, the quota was discontinued.

As indicated, 1975 was a depressed year, and with import restrictions abandoned in the Common Market the Japanese increased their shipments significantly. In fact, in the first seven months, the imports were the equivalent of the preceding year. The Europeans viewed this with alarm and asked the Japanese to adopt an orderly marketing agreement that would restrict imports to the EEC. This was approved in December 1975 and reinstated the previous quota, which limited the six major steel producers in Japan to 1,344,000 net tons per year. It is interesting to note that the Japanese cut their exports for the last three months of 1975 dramatically. This arrangement is still in force.

In order to further limit imports, the EEC has adopted a quota system for all countries outside its borders. These quotas have been in force for several years with a number of countries. As of June 1984, bilateral agreements were entered into with ten countries in addition to Japan. Four others, the three Scandinavian countries and Austria, had arrangements based on reciprocity. Table 2 lists the countries as well as the quotas and the actual tonnage sent into the EEC by the various countries in 1983.

The same quantities were in force in 1984. In addition, there was a trigger-price system of sorts that forbade exporters to the Common Market to sell at a price less than 6 percent below the Common Market list price. Countries with which there was no agreement were

TABLE 2.

	Quantities laid down in the arrangements	Net tonnages delivered[1]
Spain	754,000	954,212
Australia	393,750	57,221
South Korea	218,000	76,464
Japan	Special understanding which refers to an agreement reached within the industry	113,185
Brazil (pig iron)	245,000	116,203
South Africa	292,500	183,241
Czechoslovakia	665,265	577,343
Poland	406,675	279,669
Romania	385,310	131,698
Bulgaria	273,200	160,299
Hungary	358,950	263,545
Sweden	Quantities not laid	161,660
Finland	down in the	907,803
Austria	arrangements (but	990,288
Norway	based on reciprocity)	560,003

[1] Provisional figures, the BLEU having not yet provided definitive statistics.
Source: Official Journal of the European Communities, September 1984.

required to charge the list price on their exports to the Common Market.

Imports to Japan

Until quite recently, Japanese imports were insignificant in relation to their exports and the total consumption of steel. For example, in 1976, the Japanese exported 37 million metric tons and imported less than 200,000 tons. In 1977, 35 million tons were exported and imports were less than 250,000 tons. In recent years, however, imports have increased significantly, as Table 3 indicates.

The fact that the figures are given in crude steel equivalent indicates that the actual products shipped into Japan represent less

TABLE 3.
Japanese Steel Imports: 1979–1984
(thousands of metric tons crude steel equiv.)

1979	1,612
1980	1,273
1981	1,646
1982	2,135
1983	2,914
1984	4,242

Source: Japan Iron and Steel Federation, *Monthly Report of Iron and Steel Statistics,* June 1985.

tonnage. A good average would be 80 percent of the crude steel equivalent. Thus, in 1984 actual products shipped into Japan would be about 3.4 million tons, or approximately 5 percent of the total market.

The Japanese have no quotas on steel imports. However, the recent increase in imports, particularly from South Korea, has caused great concern among the Japanese steel producers who view with alarm the increased capacity in South Korea and the probability that more steel will be sent to Japan.

Trigger Prices in the United States

The drop in production in 1975 from the record output in 1974, although drastic, was considered temporary, and the industry in both Japan and Western Europe looked for a recovery in the following year. This in fact took place, as output in both Japan and Western Europe recovered somewhat in 1976. In the EEC, it rose from a low of 126 million metric tons to 135 million, and in Japan it rose from a low of 102 million tons to 107 million. Prices firmed up somewhat in Western Europe, and as a consequence there was not the urge to export a great deal of steel. The EEC exports to the United States amounted to 3.2 million net tons in 1976, while Japan maintained the high figure of 8 million tons, a significant increase over the 5.2-million-ton figure of 1975. Total imports into the United States in 1975 were 12 million tons, a drop of some 4 million from 1974, reflecting the decline in U.S. demand.

In 1977, the EEC, wishing to regain its customers, pushed exports to the United States to 6.8 million tons, more than double the preceding year, while Japan witnessed a slight decline to 7.8 million tons. Competition for the U.S. market was keen as total imports reached a record 19.3 million net tons. The Japanese and the EEC countries concentrated heavily on the American market, since it was the most lucrative in terms of price and offered a substantial amount of tonnage. In 1977, imported steel came predominantly from Japan and the EEC, with these locations accounting for 14.6 million tons out of the 19.3 million tons. Canada contributed 1.9 million with the next largest amount, 0.8 million tons, coming from South Korea.

The market in the United States was in shambles in 1977 and early 1978, and two integrated steel companies were in such financial difficulties that one, Alan Wood Steel Company, actually closed its doors, while another, Youngstown Sheet & Tube, had to be absorbed by Jones & Laughlin. Further, profits in 1977 for the entire industry virtually disappeared. Total net income for some 95 percent of the industry amounted to $22.3 million on sales of approximately $40 billion, or less than one-tenth of 1 percent. This figure would have dropped further had Alan Wood's losses been included, but since they had gone out of business, the losses were not registered. It should be noted that Bethlehem Steel wrote off over $400 million of its assets, and this contributed to the very low earnings figure for the industry.

Under these circumstances, the steel industry made a strong appeal to the Carter administration in late 1977 for import relief, and the administration responded with what was termed a "comprehensive program for the steel industry." One of its principal recommendations was to institute a "trigger-price" mechanism that required the Department of the Treasury to "set up a system of trigger prices based on the full cost of production, including appropriate capital charges, of steel mill products by the most efficient foreign steel producers [then considered to be the Japanese], which would be used as a basis for monitoring imports of steel into the United States for initiating accelerated antidumping investigations with respect to imports priced below the trigger prices."[1] This system was designed to provide "a basis for initiating antidumping investigations without any prior industry complaints." The trigger prices were based on cost data provided by the Japanese producers plus freight to the United States, plus a minimal profit, and were to be adjusted quarterly. Thus, if steel were shipped below the trigger price, it automatically touched off an investigation to ascertain whether or not the producer of that steel was dumping. The program was put into effect in May 1978 in order to allow the trading partners of the United States an opportunity to produce and ship steel that had been ordered. This resulted in an unprecedented influx of 7.2 million tons in the first four months of 1978, which helped bring the total for that year to a record 21.1 million net tons. The trigger price was welcomed by the U.S. producers and also benefited the importers.

In 1977, the U.S. market was a jungle. With deep price-cutting prevalent, these low prices resulted in losses for everyone concerned, and many Europeans could sustain such losses only because they were either government owned or government subsidized. The advent of the trigger price restored some semblance of order to the U.S. market and became an integral part of the sales policy of importers.

The system was sustained through 1978 and 1979. However, in 1980, worldwide conditions, particularly those in the EEC, had deteriorated to such an extent that devices were employed to circumvent the trigger price, and United States Steel Corporation filed anti-

---

[1] U.S. Steel Industry Task Force, *A Comprehensive Program for the Steel Industry*. Report to the President, Washington, D.C., December 13, 1985, p. 13.

dumping suits against the Europeans which prompted the U.S. government to suspend the trigger-price mechanism.

At a summit conference in Italy in 1980, President Carter was asked to have these suits withdrawn and reinstate an improved trigger-price mechanism. This was finally agreed to in October, when the suits were dropped and the trigger-price system restored.

In 1981, the steel producers in the EEC appealed to the U.S. government to adjust the trigger-price mechanism to allow them greater access to the market. They maintained that the trigger price was above the actual domestic price level in the United States and made it extremely difficult for importers to sell steel. Many companies in Europe openly challenged the trigger price by shipping steel at a price well below it, while others asked for preclearance—which, in fact, was permission to undersell the trigger price once it could be proved that the seller's costs were low enough to allow this. These requests were denied by the Commerce Department, and in November 1981 the department brought action against five countries (Brazil, Romania, France, Belgium, and South Africa) for trade violations with respect to hot-rolled sheets and plates. In spite of these actions, a number of Western European steel producers continued to ship steel into the United States at prices considerably below the trigger price. As a consequence a number of antidumping suits were filed. By mid-January 1982, some ninety-two of these suits had been filed with the International Trade Commission and, for all practical purposes, the trigger-price system was dead.

In late 1982, in order to forestall antidumping and countervailing duty suits filed by the U.S. steel producers, a voluntary restraint agreement was concluded with the EEC that would limit most of their heavy-tonnage steel products to between 5 percent and 6 percent of the American market. In addition, there were a number of products not included that were called consultation products, meaning that, if the tonnage imported under these categories surged beyond a certain level, investigations would be undertaken. This agreement was scheduled to last until December 1985.

President Reagan's Quota Plan

In 1984, with steel imports growing constantly during the year and threatening to reach new highs, a good deal of pressure was exerted by the industry to control the size of import tonnage. Bethlehem Steel and the United Steelworkers filed a petition with the International Trade Commission in January to limit steel imports to 15 percent of the American market. This petition was granted partially by the International Trade Commission in terms of the products listed. Pipe and tubes were excluded from any restraints, while restrictions were placed on other products. President Reagan saw fit to reject this proposal; however, the administration came up with one of its own which would restrict imports to 18.5 percent of the American market, plus 1.7 million tons of semifinished steel. This was the goal and was to be negotiated with countries around the world. The individual steel companies were not involved in negotiations since this was a government-to-government affair.

In negotiating with the various countries, it appears that the 18.5 percent will not be realized. The figure will probably be closer to 22 percent, including the semifinished steel. For example, in negotiating with the Japanese, the approach of the trade representative from the United States was to grant them 5.3 percent of the American market. The Japanese wanted 6.4 percent and a settlement was made at 5.8 percent thus allowing more than was originally calculated. The negotiations with South Korea indicated in the beginning that their share was to be 1.4 percent. The South Koreans wanted 2.3 percent; the final settlement was at 1.9 percent.

The Canadians contended that they should not be restricted since they did not dump into the United States, and their principal companies that exported to the United States were not subsidized. Therefore, they saw no reason why they should be under a quota and in its place agreed to exercise some restraint so that their exports would not surge to new heights. This seems to be an arrangement that will stand.

In terms of the Europeans, an agreement that resembled the 1982 pact was negotiated. However, it did include most of the consultation products in the actual quota. Their share of the U.S. market would be approximately 6 percent.

By the end of December 1985, the successes of the total plan had not yet been established, since imports in 1985 were not much less than those in 1984, which was an all-time record of 26 million tons. For the full year 1985, they totaled 24.3 million tons, the second highest tonnage in history. There is, however, some hope that in 1986 the restraints will be applied, since agreements arrived at with various countries called for them to license exports to the United States and to license only the amount agreed on. Thus, it is quite conceivable that there will be a reduction in 1986.

The agreement is to last through 1989 to grant the steel companies in the United States sufficient time to introduce new equipment and replace what is left of the old equipment. This is in progress at the present time, and in 1989 the industry in the United States will be in a better competitive position. The overall agreement ruled out antidumping or countervailing duty suits except in the case of semifinished steel. It should be noted that when the plan was first proposed in 1984, there was a considerable split in the administration.

TABLE 4.
Steel Production in Third World Countries
for 1984
(in million metric tons)

China	43.4
Brazil	18.4
South Korea	13.0
India	10.3
Mexico	7.5
North Korea	6.5
Taiwan	5.0
Venezuela	2.7
Argentina	2.6

Source: International Iron and Steel Institute, *World Steel in Figures.* Brussels, 1985.

A number of cabinet members were entirely opposed to any restrictions, while others were in favor of them and their arguments carried. It was stated in a number of quarters in Washington that the restraints would lead to an increase in prices that would cost the American public several billion dollars. The contrary has been true. During the latter part of 1984 and 1985, not only were there no increases in price, but prices actually deteriorated by as much as 20 percent to 30 percent. Import restraints will have very little if any effect on prices as long as the market remains sluggish. Prices will only increase when there is an improvement in the demand for steel.

Third World

In the early 1970s there was relatively little steel production in the Third World. In 1975, its output was approximately 60 million tons. Since that time, contrary to the trend in the industrialized world, which has seen the steel industry decline, the Third World has increased its capacity by more than 100 percent. In 1984, production from the Third World, including China, was approximately 120 million tons or double that of ten years earlier. There are some nine countries capable of producing more than 2 million tons of steel, as Table 4 indicates.

Some of the Third World countries exported significant portions of their steel production. South Korea exported 5.7 million metric tons, Brazil 5.1 million, and Taiwan 2.1 million tons. Lesser amounts came from other countries such as India, Venezuela, and Mexico. China with its huge population required virtually all of its production at home. In fact, in 1984 it imported approximately 8 million tons from Japan, as well as significant amounts from other countries. Figures are not available on North Korea, although estimates indicate that very little of its steel production is exported.

TABLE 5.
Steel Exports to the United States
from Selected Third World Countries:
1980 and 1984

Country	1980	1984
South Korea	1,000,000	2,200,000
Brazil	500,000	1,500,000
Argentina	18,000	300,000
Mexico	67,000	800,000
Taiwan	86,000	160,000

Source: American Iron and Steel Institute, *Statistical Yearbook,* 1984.

The growth in Third World production has been concentrated in a relatively few countries. In 1975, China accounted for some 26.5 million tons of raw steel output. As indicated, by 1984 this had risen to 43.4 million. Over the same period South Korea increased its output from 2 million tons to 13 million. Taiwan rose from 1 million tons to 5 million. Brazil increased from 8.4 million to 18.4 million tons, Mexico from 5.3 million to 7.5 million, and Venezuela from 1.1 million to 2.7 million. As indicated, the principal exporters are Brazil, South Korea, and Taiwan, and much of this tonnage has been directed to the market in the United States. Table 5 indicates the growth in exports to the United States from selected Third World countries from 1980 and 1984. In general, the Third World increased its exports to the United States over the five-year period by well over 100 percent. In fact, in 1983, after the Europeans had signed an agreement to restrict exports to the United States, a number of countries in the Common Market complained that the tonnage they relinquished had been appropriated by the Third World countries so that there was a slight increase in total imports to the United States, despite the European quota.

The Third World countries, particularly Brazil and South Korea, have come to rely heavily on the U.S. market for their exports and will continue to do so in the years ahead. Under President Reagan's plan to restrict imports, both Brazil and South Korea have been awarded significant tonnages. If the American market reaches 100 million tons, South Korea will export 1.9 million tons and Brazil approximately 1 million tons. However, in the case of Brazil, the vast portion of its exports will be in semifinished slabs. Brazil has constructed a steel mill at Tubarao dedicated to the production of semifinished steel and capable of producing 3 million tons. In the first ten months of 1985 some 720,000 tons of semifinished steel were exported from Brazil to the United States. Most of this was concentrated in the newly formed California Steel Company, which is 25 percent owned by the Brazilian Iron Ore Company.

TABLE 6.
Import Penetration for Steel Markets in Selected Countries
(in percents)

Country	1975	1976	1977	1978	1979	1980	1981	1982	1983	19
United States	13.5	14.1	17.8	18.2	15.2	16.3	19.1	21.8	20.5	2€
Canada	13.0	11.1	12.1	11.5	14.5	10.6	22.7	12.8	N.A.	N.
Japan	0.4	0.2	0.3	0.4	1.4	1.1	2.3	3.4	4.9	E
EEC	7.4	10.0	10.9	7.0	7.2	10.3	7.1	10.1	9.9	7

Note: Compiled from production import and export figures for the countries mentioned.

From the foregoing it is evident that the steel industry in most lands throughout the world enjoys some type of protection. This is a fact of life, and it is very doubtful that the situation will be changed in the next few years. In fact, it may intensify, particularly since demand for steel will be considerably short of the available supply for at least three to four years. Should there be a better balance between supply and demand, this would have a decided impact in lowering the protection that is now prevalent among steel producers.

In terms of import penetration, the United States is by far the hardest hit among the industrialized countries. Japan, on the other hand, has suffered the least damage from imports, as Table 6 indicates.

There is no doubt that the countries which have steel industries, be these large or small, want to see them thrive as much as possible, and are therefore unlikely to allow them to be either destroyed or considerably damaged by imports.

References

American Iron and Steel Institute (1984) *Statistical Yearbook.*

Hogan, W. T. (1971) *Economic History of the Iron and Steel Industry in the United States.* Lexington, Mass.: Lexington Books. 5 volumes.

——— (1984) *Steel in the United States: Restructuring to Compete.* Lexington, Mass.: Lexington Books.

International Iron and Steel Institute (1985) *World Steel in Figures.* Brussels.

Japan Iron and Steel Federation (1985) *Monthly Report of Iron and Steel Statistics.* June.

U.S. Steel Industry Task Force (1985) A Comprehensive Program for the Steel Industry. Report to the President. Washington, D.C., December 13.

PART FOUR

MONETARY POLICY, EXCHANGE RATES, AND THE NEW PROTECTIONISM

17

Protectionism and the Misaligned Dollar: The Case for Monetary Coordination

RONALD I. McKINNON

Without international monetary coordination, sharp exchange-rate fluctuations are inevitable. Each national fiat money has no intrinsic value other than what the issuing government manages to establish. Thus, under floating exchange rates where countries are not obligated to follow a common monetary policy, international investors become very nervous. Portfolio managers must continually guess which fiat currency (including both bonds and transactions balances) will provide the best *future* combination of interest yield, convenience, and low-price inflation.

Any political or economic "news"—say, an election or a new assessment of growth in the Gross National Product—might be sufficient for investors to switch their preference from currency A to currency B (Frenkel and Mussa, 1980, 1985). Because asset markets clear much faster than goods markets, A's exchange rate will then depreciate beyond its long-run equilibrium—i.e., overshoot until regressive expectations set in and restore portfolio balance. But this stabilizing speculative element is weak because national monetary policies remain so uncertain vis-à-vis each other.

Since floating began in the early 1970s, unexpectedly large changes in real exchange rates (deviations from purchasing-power parity) have generated protectionist pressure—more in the form of quotas and other nontariff barriers (NTBs) rather than tariffs. A quota tends to insulate domestic prices of the protected good from contin-

From Stanford University, Stanford, California.

ual changes in foreign competitive pressure arising from currency misalignments, whereas a tariff (unless prohibitive) does not.

Superimposed on these large changes in *relative* currency values were two great worldwide inflations in the 1970s and unexpectedly sharp deflation in the early 1980s. This cyclical instability in the world economy further increases the incentives of individual nation-states to intervene to protect domestic producers in industry and agriculture.

Consequently, a stable international monetary standard is necessary if free trade in goods and services is to be preserved. Putting the matter into historical perspective, the surprisingly rapid progress of the GATT in the 1950s and 1960s in reducing trade restrictions now seems to have been made possible by the 1945 Bretton Woods agreement that committed the industrial countries to maintain "approved" par values for their exchange rates. In principle, these par values were to be easily adjustable, but in practice they were not. In fact, the system evolved into a fixed-rate dollar standard in which American monetary policy was imposed on other countries in a manner that fairly successfully stabilized the common (dollar) price level in terms of internationally tradeable goods.

Can an international monetary system with exchange rates more stable than those prevailing over the past decade and a half, and less violent cyclical fluctuations of inflation and deflation, be reestablished? Much hinges on how financial policy in the center country, the United States, is conducted. Consider first the immediate problem of the misaligned dollar.

Dollar Overvaluation in the Early 1980s

Nobody can deny the great protectionist pressure that developed in the United States in the early 1980s. Nor, from 1981 through most of 1985, is there doubt that the extraordinary appreciation of the dollar against European currencies—and to a lesser extent against the Japanese yen—was the major force behind the protectionist momentum. From the overvalued dollar America developed symptoms of a dual economy: buoyant output in the nontradeable sectors such as services of all kinds and military procurement and depression in agriculture, mining, and most of civilian manufacturing open to foreign competition.

However, increased protectionism would have been no solution at all. Reneging on the long-standing American commitment to maintain free international trade would invite foreign retaliation and undermine the economic basis for the postwar prosperity of the industrial world. In addition, restricting imports entering the United States—while international financial pressure in favor of the dollar remains unchanged—would reduce American demand for foreign currency and drive the dollar up further. American exporters would then be doubly hurt: through the higher dollar on the one hand and because of higher dollar prices of importable inputs on the other.

But to thwart protectionism, the continual tendency toward financial imbalance between the United States and the industrial countries of Western Europe and Japan must be righted. The large U.S. fiscal deficit is commonly (and correctly) blamed for much of the trade deficit—but it cannot explain why the dollar exchange rate got so far out of line. I hypothesize that monetary coordination among the United States, the European bloc, and Japan is the only practical way of first correcting dollar over- (or under-) valuation and then preserving longer-run price and exchange-rate stability.

The Fiscal Conundrum

However, the most common explanation of why the dollar became overvalued points to fiscal rather than misplaced monetary policy.

Huge budget deficits, which the Federal Reserve refused to monetize, increased interest rates on dollar assets in real terms—after future American price inflation is discounted. As capital was attracted from abroad in the early 1980s, the dollar was bid up in the foreign exchanges and "overshot" its long-run equilibrium until expected dollar depreciation offset the relatively high yields on U.S. government bonds and corporate securities. In the meantime, the unduly appreciated dollar depressed American exports and stimulated imports.

This conventional argument sees a monotonic chain of causation: from budget deficits to interest rates to the dollar-exchange rate to the trade deficit. It originated in 1981 when U.S. interest rates rose sharply—in response to projected Reagan budget deficits and monetary tightness by the Federal Reserve—and the dollar also rose strongly in the foreign exchanges. The implication is that the U.S. fiscal deficit must be largely eliminated before the dollar's overvaluation can be overcome.

The alternative view, developed below, suggests that monetary policy may be assigned to stabilize the exchange rate in the face of substantial shifts in fiscal policy. Trade deficits would still develop to match budget deficits even if the nominal exchange rate does not jump and "overshoot." One must distinguish the investment-savings imbalance (which determines the trade deficit) from whatever the exchange-rate regime happens to be.

For example, suppose the United States had been on a fixed nominal exchange rate when the large budgetary deficits began to develop. Then a deficit in U.S. trade, of the same order of magnitude we currently observe, would still have evolved—perhaps even earlier. The American business downturn of 1982 would have been less severe if the U.S. Federal Reserve System had been obligated to have less tight money in order to prevent the dollar from appreciating so precipitately. With better-maintained domestic income, American imports would have been higher in the 1982–1983 period.

Note also that the great depreciation of the dollar from March 1985 to March 1986, from 260 yen (3.4 deutsche marks) to 175 yen (2.3 deutsche marks) per dollar, began before there was any clear improvement, or prospect for improvement, in the U.S. fiscal deficit. Instead, the fall was "engineered" (as discussed more below) by having very high money growth in the United States compared to relatively tight monetary policies in Germany and Japan.

The fundamental point is that, when capital is internationally mobile with a domestic imbalance between saving and investment, nations will readily develop deficits or surpluses in the current account of the balance of payments under fixed exchange rates—as, say, under the late-nineteenth-century gold standard. At the present time, for example, the U.S. trade deficit will remain very large as long as the government fiscal deficit continues to force expenditures above income by creating a deficiency in saving throughout the American economy. A better-aligned (lower-valued) dollar would, however, ameliorate the depression in American tradeable goods industries even if it would not do much to correct the trade deficit per se. This greater international competitiveness would allow U.S. gross exports to increase, although net exports need not change much as long as the U.S. fiscal deficit remains high.

That there is no necessary relationship between fiscal deficits and movements in nominal exchange rates can be seen from another angle. After all, few would claim that the large dollar depreciations of the 1970s were caused by American budgetary surpluses. Indeed, the U.S. ran fiscal deficits, albeit much smaller, in those years. The large fiscal deficits in France after Mitterand came into power in 1981 seemed to weaken the franc rather than strengthen it.

Furthermore, no monotonic or otherwise stable relationships seem to exist between nominal interest rates and a currency's strength in the foreign exchanges. Indeed, much of the extraordinary rise in the dollar-exchange rate from mid-1984 to the first quarter of 1985 has been associated with *falling* U.S. interest rates. Specifically, from August 1984 to February 1985 American interest rates fell 2 to 3 percentage points relative to those in Germany while the dollar was rising from 2.88 to 3.25 marks.

Although interest rates remain important, expectations of future political safety, price inflation, and other sources of future exchange-rate movements often dominate the portfolio preferences of international investors. The gnomes of Zurich, Luxembourg, and Singapore continually look for the safest haven (currency) in which to place their internationally liquid assets.

Suppose the American government moved seriously toward cutting expenditures. U.S. interest rates would fall immediately in anticipation of lower future fiscal deficits, and this effect by itself would tend to depress the dollar in the foreign exchanges. Against this, people might expect that the resulting reduction in the projected national debt would lessen the chances of price inflation in the distant future. Similarly, other taxes on the holders of dollar assets become less likely. The United States could then seem like an even safer haven for international capital.

Because of these opposing considerations, even resolute action by the American government to eliminate its unsustainable fiscal deficit need not bring the dollar down in the foreign-exchange markets—although it probably would. (The one dramatic exception is a general withholding tax on interest and dividend income including that from all those American securities owned by foreigners. That certainly would bring the dollar down.) At best, fiscal policy is a blunt instrument, subject to long delays and uncertainties, for influencing the exchange rate.

Enter Monetary Policy

In contrast, monetary policy is immediately flexible and can be made to influence the exchange rate unambiguously. From the nineteenth-century gold standard to the fixed exchange rates of the 1950s and 1960s under the old Bretton Woods agreement, examples abound of countries successfully subordinating their monetary policies to maintain a fixed exchange rate with some other stable money. Central banks can react quickly to international shifts in the demand for the money they issue.

In the asymmetrical Bretton Woods system, countries other than the United States were directly responsible for maintaining their exchange rates within 1 percent of either side of their formal dollar parities. For example, from 1950 to 1970, the Bank of Japan kept the yen within three-quarters of 1 percent of 360 yen to the dollar by raising yen interest rates and contracting when international payments were in deficit, and expanding the yen money supply when the Japanese currency tended to appreciate. Japanese monetary policy, based on this fixed-exchange-rate rule, led to stable yen prices for the broad range of internationally traded goods and contributed to Japan's extraordinary postwar recovery.

Similarly, in these same two prosperous decades, European governments generally subordinated their monetary policies to preserve stable exchange rates for long periods—with small, infrequent adjustments in their dollar parities. Only Britain continually resisted the necessary internationalization of its domestic monetary policy with consequent balance-of-payments deficits and numerous "sterling crises" throughout the 1950s and 1960s. And Britain had the least successful domestic growth and foreign-trade performances of any Western European economy.

The Flaw in Bretton Woods

But the Bretton Woods system had an inherent weakness. The monetary policy of the center country, the United States, was insufficiently guided by any exchange rate or other international obligation of its own. Even the American commitment to a weak form of gold convertibility, itself inadequate, had eroded by the late 1960s.

Consequently, in 1970–1973 the international system of fixed exchange rates broke down when the United States increased U.S. money growth despite the fact that the dollar was under obvious downward pressure in the foreign exchanges. Mistakenly, in 1971 President Nixon forced the other governments to let the dollar be devalued rather than contract the U.S. money supply. Private investors took this as a signal to reduce their holding of dollar assets in favor of foreign currencies—forcing further depreciations of the dollar in 1972–1973, as shown in Figure 1.

The resulting great inflation in the dollar prices of goods and services in the 1970s (Table 1) was aggravated by another unwarranted depreciation of the dollar in 1977–1979. Foreign governments became loath to bend their monetary policies to reestablish fixed dollar parities with what they then saw to be a chronically depreciating international currency.

Responding firmly, albeit belatedly, to domestic price inflation, the U.S. Federal Reserve System tightened its monetary control procedures in October 1979. But international confidence in the dollar was not restored until the election of a more conservative president in late 1980. The remarkable shift in portfolio preferences back into dollar assets, and the great dollar appreciation of 1981–1982, surprised everyone. In response to this clear signal from the foreign exchanges that U.S. monetary policy was now too tight, the Fed did not loosen up soon enough. The result was the sharp deflation and depression of 1982.

That changes in the dollar exchange rate are an excellent leading indicator of inflation or deflation to come within the American economy is clearly shown in Figure 2. Although spread out for more than two years, the lagged impact of a change in the exchange rate on the American Wholesale Price Index (WPI) seems to peak after five

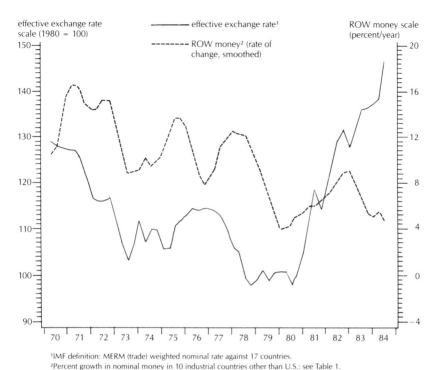

FIGURE 1. U.S. effective exchange rate and the rest of the world money (quarterly observations).

quarters. Thus Figure 2 plots current changes in the WPI against changes in the dollar exchange rate five quarters earlier. Since floating exchange rates began in the early 1970s, the negative correlation is easily visible and quite remarkable: −0.528 with the unsmoothed quarterly data and −0.817 when smoothed with a five-quarter moving average.

Tradeable goods are heavily represented in the WPI and that index is naturally more sensitive to exchange-rate changes. But even the U.S. GNP deflator (not shown in Figure 2), with its large component of nontradeable services, is sensitive, with exchange-rate effects peaking after eight quarters (McKinnon, 1985). Thus one can see that having the Fed key on the dollar exchange rate is quite consistent with its most basic objective: to stabilize the domestic U.S. price level.

Although threatening to undermine the American free-trade ethic, the overvaluation of the dollar in the early 1980s had one significant advantage. The international concern over chronic American inflation is now largely dissipated. Indeed, Germany, Japan, and the United States now have low-price inflation (Table 1). Thus 1986

TABLE 1.

Price Inflation in Tradeable Goods, Eleven Industrial Countries (percentage change in annual averages of WPIs)

	Belgium	Canada	France	Germany	Italy	Japan	Nether-lands	Sweden	Switzer-land	United Kingdom	United States	World Average	Rest of World[a]
(Weights: GNP 1964)	(.0132)	(.0394)	(.0778)	(.0892)	(.0494)	(.0681)	(.0144)	(.0167)	(.0113)	(.0796)	(.5408)		
1958	-4.4	0.4	5.1	-0.5	-1.7	-6.5	-1.3	4.3	-3.2	0.8	1.5	0.68	-0.30
1959	-0.3	0.8	7.2	-0.8	-2.9	0.9	0.2	0.9	-1.6	0.3	0.2	0.57	1.00
1960	1.2	0.2	3.5	1.3	0.8	1.1	0.0	4.1	0.6	1.3	0.2	0.81	1.54
1961	-0.2	0.2	3.0	1.5	0.0	1.1	-0.2	2.2	0.2	2.6	-0.4	0.47	1.50
1962	0.8	1.1	0.6	0.9	3.2	-1.6	0.3	4.7	3.3	2.3	0.2	0.64	1.16
1963	2.5	1.3	2.9	0.5	5.3	1.6	2.4	2.9	3.9	1.0	-0.4	0.72	2.03
1964	4.7	0.9	3.5	1.0	3.0	0.4	6.1	3.4	1.3	3.1	0.2	1.15	2.27
1965	1.1	1.3	0.7	2.5	1.8	0.7	3.0	5.2	0.6	3.5	2.0	1.98	1.95
1966	2.1	2.9	2.8	1.7	1.5	2.4	5.0	6.4	1.9	2.9	3.4	3.02	2.57
1967	-0.9	1.9	-0.9	-1.0	-0.2	1.7	1.0	4.3	0.3	3.1	0.2	0.45	0.75
1968	0.2	2.2	-1.7	-0.7	0.6	1.0	1.9	2.0	0.1	4.1	2.4	1.68	0.83
1969	5.0	3.7	10.7	1.9	3.6	2.0	-2.5	3.5	2.8	3.7	3.9	3.99	4.09
1970	4.7	2.4	7.5	5.0	7.4	3.7	4.6	6.8	4.2	7.1	3.6	4.54	5.65
1971	-0.5	2.0	2.1	4.3	3.3	-0.8	4.5	3.2	2.1	9.1	3.3	2.94	2.67
1972	4.0	4.3	4.7	2.5	4.1	0.8	5.1	4.6	3.6	5.3	4.4	3.74	3.24

TABLE 1. (Continued)

	Belgium	Canada	France	Germany	Italy	Japan	Nether-lands	Sweden	Switzer-land	United Kingdom	United States	World Average	Rest of World[a]
(Weights: GNP 1977)	(.0172)	(.0487)	(.0885)	(.1122)	(.0471)	(.1404)	(.0228)	(.0195)	(.0148)	(.0572)	(.4316)		
1973	12.4	11.2	14.7	6.6	17.2	15.8	6.9	10.3	10.7	7.4	13.1	12.42	11.91
1974	16.8	19.1	29.1	13.5	40.8	31.4	9.6	25.3	16.2	22.6	18.8	22.00	24.43
1975	1.2	11.2	-5.7	4.6	8.5	3.0	6.7	6.4	-2.3	22.2	9.3	6.93	5.12
1976	7.1	5.1	7.4	3.7	23.8	5.0	7.8	9.0	-0.7	17.3	4.6	6.58	8.09
1977	2.4	7.9	5.6	2.7	16.6	1.9	5.8	9.2	0.3	19.8	6.1	6.35	6.55
1978	-1.9	9.3	4.3	1.2	8.4	-2.5	1.3	7.6	-3.4	9.1	7.8	4.99	2.86
1979	6.3	14.4	13.3	4.8	15.5	7.3	2.7	12.5	3.8	12.2	12.5	10.73	9.39
1980	5.8	13.5	8.8	7.5	20.1	17.8	8.2	13.9	5.1	16.3	14.0	13.33	12.82
1981	8.2	10.1	11.0	7.7	16.6	1.7	9.2	11.6	5.8	10.6	9.0	8.50	8.13
1982	7.7	6.0	11.1	5.8	13.9	1.8	6.6	12.6	2.6	8.6	2.1	4.80	6.85
1983	5.2	3.5	11.0	1.5	10.5	-2.2	1.8	11.2	0.5	5.5	1.3[b]	2.73	3.82
1984	7.4	4.1	13.3	2.9	10.4	-0.2	4.2	7.9	3.3	6.2	2.4	3.98	5.18

[a] United States excluded
[b] Preliminary

Source: IMF, International Financial Statistics, 1984 Yearbook and July 1985, line 63, wholesale price indices including finished goods and primary products.

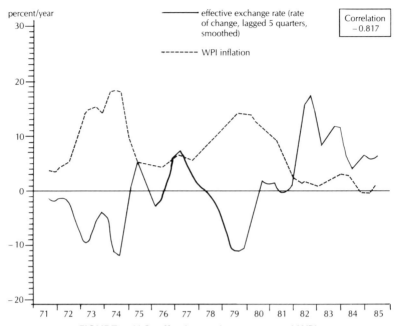

FIGURE 2. U.S. effective exchange rate and WPI.

is a good time to negotiate a new agreement for stabilizing exchange rates—at a much lower foreign-exchange value for the dollar—while keeping international price inflation close to zero.

For any new exchange-rate agreement to be successful, however, the flaw in the old one must be corrected. In cooperation with other central banks, the U.S. Federal Reserve System must give exchange-rate stability more weight in the future conduct of American monetary policy. Speculative pressure is now too great for Japan or European countries to stabilize dollar-exchange rates on their own; many have tried (and failed) to do so in recent years—particularly in the turbulent months of late 1984 and early 1985 when the dollar became so extremely overvalued.

A New Monetary Order for the 1980s

Assume now that in making American monetary policy the Federal Reserve System abandons its traditional insular approach, which virtually ignores the foreign exchanges. By some miracle, suppose that the Bank of Japan, the Bundesbank (representing the European bloc), and the Fed all agree to coordinate their monetary policies to achieve exchange stability.

How could such a system be efficiently managed to nudge the dollar down in the foreign exchanges without significant inflationary consequences? Once this transition is completed, how can fixed exchange rates and stable prices be maintained?

Announcement effects are as important as the fact of monetary cooperation itself. To harness the market's expectations in favor of the new exchange-rate regime, the three central banks must spell out what they intend to do in a consistent fashion. Only then will the required adjustments in national monetary policies turn out to be minimal.

So what should the triumvirate announce? The new monetary order would have four essential elements:

1. Explicit target zones for the yen/dollar and mark/dollar exchange rates;
2. A commitment to adjust domestic monetary policies symmetrically among the three countries to achieve these targets;
3. Rules for restrained but decisive direct interventions to correct "disorderly conditions" in the foreign exchanges; and
4. Joint management of aggregate money growth within the triumvirate in order to stabilize their common price level in the longer run.

Let us discuss each in turn.

Target Zones for Exchange Rates

Exchange-rate targets would be designed (and announced) to achieve a rough purchasing-power parity among the three countries, taking their current stable price levels as benchmarks. Illustrative calculations suggest that about 2.3 marks and 200 yen to the dollar— far under today's market quotations—approximate what the triumvirate should strive for.

[*Warning:* We have to understand that these exchange-rate targets are designed to align national price levels, *not* to correct bilateral—or multilateral—trade deficits or surpluses. Even if the dollar were nudged down so that the American price level became better aligned with those of Germany and Japan, the large U.S. fiscal deficit would still stimulate excessive consumption and leave a large U.S. trade deficit, albeit one that was somewhat smaller.]

Because of the current substantial difference in interest rates between the United States and the other two countries, a broad 10 percent band should be established around these two central rates. To illustrate, the dollar could be targeted to stay within a range of 2.20 and 2.40 marks and within 190 to 210 yen.

If the dollar was outside these ranges when agreement was first reached these target zones would be necessarily "soft" (Williamson, 1985). That is, the participating central banks would not be committed to achieve them immediately. In particular, any massive official intervention in the foreign exchanges to push rates in the desired direction would be ruled out.

Nevertheless, the targets are real enough. The gnomes would clearly understand the direction in which the central banks were pushing. In view of the misinformation and confusion that now prevail in the exchange markets, a clear official declaration of exchange-rate goals would allow private expectations to coalesce in support—provided that the accompanying program of monetary adjustment was credible.

Mutual Monetary Adjustment

Among the three countries, monetary adjustments would take place symmetrically for as long as the relevant exchange rate was outside its target zone—whether weeks, months, or years. When the dollar exchange rate is above its target zones, the Fed should expand the money supply and reduce interest rates while the Bundesbank and Bank of Japan contract symmetrically. (And act conversely if the dollar were ever to fall below its target range.) In this way, the total "world" money supply will remain roughly constant, but relative amounts of constituent currencies will fluctuate to meet the demand for them.

For example, suppose that the current mark/dollar exchange rate is 2.80, that the Fed's normal long-term annual growth rate for M1 is between 4 and 6 percent, and that the Bundesbank's normal growth in what it calls "central bank" money is also between 4 and 6 percent. Then the Fed would be publicly committed to increase its money growth above 6 percent (possibly reducing interest rates), while the Bundesbank kept its money growth below 4 percent (possibly raising interest rates), until the mark/dollar rate fell below 2.4 marks and into its target zone.

To be successful in changing traders' expectations to push the mark/dollar exchange rate in the desired direction, this commitment to mutual monetary adjustment must be unambiguous. To avoid adverse expectations, other potentially conflicting rules need to be jettisoned.

For example, the surprisingly sharp rise of the dollar within two weeks in February 1985 from 3.2 to about 3.47 DM was due at least in part to an apparent conflict in the U.S. Federal Reserve System's immediate monetary objectives. In November and again in December 1984, the Fed cut the discount rate and embarked on much faster money growth; it correctly noted that such expansion was warranted because (among other factors) the dollar at 3.0 marks was grossly overvalued even then. And for November, December, and January, growth in U.S. M1 spurted to more than 11 percent, measured on an annual basis.

However, in January the Fed then published—as required by the U.S. Congress—its money-growth targets for all of 1985. A normal 4 to 7 percent growth range for M1 during 1985 was announced. Unfortunately, this published money growth target now conflicted with the higher money growth actually taking place in early 1985. In February and March, actual M1 was far above the cone of "permissible" levels officially published.

The market came to expect that the Fed would have to contract to get M1 back on its "normal" path. In anticipation, U.S. interest rates rose sharply in February 1985 and drove the dollar up further in the foreign exchanges. This surge into dollar assets assumed panic proportions when Fed Chairman Volcker, testifying before Congress on February 20, suggested that the Fed would end the progressively easier credit policy adopted in late 1984.

Clearly, the Fed should have made clear that monetary ease would continue indefinitely and that lower long-term growth in M1 would not be resumed until the dollar had fallen into its target zone.

Fortunately, the Fed did persist with a higher rate of domestic monetary expansion—about 12 percent per year through 1985—as if it were keying on the dollar exchange without admitting it. Finally, on July 16, 1985, in its midyear report to the U.S. Congress, the Fed officially abandoned its old 1985 target of 4 to 7 percent money and "rebased" the money supply at its new higher level. It then respecified domestic money growth to be 3 to 8 percent, from this now higher base, for the remainder of 1985.

Even without the dollar exchange rate as an official target, this massive additional monetary expansion undoubtedly helped prevent the dollar from increasing further. By mid-August 1985 it had fallen back to 2.8 DM—still considerably overvalued, and about where it was the year before. But the effect on the exchange rate was lessened because the Fed's stated intentions were somewhat ambiguous about how far it might like to push the dollar down.

The credibility of this unusual seeming attempt by the Fed to key on the exchange rate was further undermined by the absence of any agreement on how foreign central banks would react. Those countries with weak currencies—most particularly the European bloc—should have reduced their money growth below normal when the Fed undertook its unusual expansion in 1985. Downward pressure on the dollar would then come from both sides.

If, instead, the German and Japanese central banks behaved

perversely by expanding in tandem with the Fed in 1985, the private markets would have no assurance that the dollar would be successfully pushed down. Not knowing what the other central banks were going to do, private speculators were less likely to support the Fed's actions by anticipating dollar depreciation. Not until September, 1985 did the main central banks jointly announce their intention to drive the dollar down. They had, considerable success.

Clearly, monetary adjustments by one central bank are much more likely to succeed in influencing the exchange rate if the market knows that the other two are supporting it. Thus one can see the great value of a formal, well-publicized international agreement on the format for monetary coordination.

Official Intervention in the Foreign Exchanges

The fact, or even the possibility, of direct official intervention in foreign exchanges captures newspaper headlines. As the American government agonizes over what to do about the exchange rate, the immediate focus is on whether or not the Federal Reserve Bank of New York—in consultation with the U.S. Treasury and the Federal Reserve System—should intervene as a buyer or seller of foreign exchange.

On March 8, 1985, the Federal Reserve Bank of New York announced it had intervened to buy deutsche marks seven times between August and January in relatively modest (for this huge market) amounts of one or two hundred million dollars in each case. The European and Japanese central banks were known to intervene more often, and more heavily, over the same period. As usual, the Fed refused to reveal the details of its more recent and substantially heavier interventions in February and early March 1985.

But this emphasis on direct intervention is misplaced, and so is some of the secrecy that veils the precise goals of these interventions.

With the integration of the American, European, and Japanese capital markets, gross stocks of private financial claims on—and liabilities to—foreigners tend to dwarf official exchange reserves. For example, by the end of 1983 private Japanese claims on foreigners were about ten times as high as official exchange reserves; with the further Japanese financial liberalization in 1984 these gross private claims again increased. In financially open European economies like those of Germany and Britain, the ratios of gross private claims on foreigners to official exchange reserves are even greater than in the Japanese case.

The upshot is that exchange reserves are too small for direct government intervention to have a significant impact on the huge internationally mobile private holdings of stocks and bonds. Indeed, ample evidence in 1984–1985 suggests that official attempts to intervene in the absence of monetary coordination, and without influencing the adverse expectations of private traders, did wash out for all practical purposes. For stabilizing the exchange rate, official intervention will be ineffective *unless* it is accompanied by a supporting monetary policy. And these mutual monetary adjustments—as described above—need not require direct intervention in the foreign exchanges.

That said, there remains a limited role for direct official intervention to correct disorderly conditions in exchange markets over a short period such as one trading day.

Having posted target zones for exchange rates (according to our hypothetical monetary agreement), the triumvirate of central banks could treat as "disorderly" any substantial exchange-rate movement away from these official targets. For example, if the target is 2.1 to 2.3 DM/dollar and the rate suddenly moves from 2.8 to 3.0 or more, the market is disorderly: the movement is both large and in the wrong direction.

Indeed, such a perverse movement indicates that private traders are not properly informed of official intentions—or that the official exchange-rate targets lack credibility. To reaffirm the central banks' objective of guiding exchange rates into their target zones, some stabilizing intervention is warranted.

To be both limited in magnitude and decisive in result, any such intervention should be reinforced by discrete monetary adjustments beyond previous measures. This is most easily accomplished by ensuring that interventions in the foreign exchanges are *symmetrically unsterilized* in their impact on each country's monetary base.

For example, to prevent the dollar from increasing further, suppose the Bundesbank (in consultation with the Fed) purchases 200 million dollars worth of marks in the open foreign-exchange market. They could agree that the Bundesbank would retire those marks from circulation while the Fed contracted the American monetary base by 200 million dollars. Consequently, interest rates would likely rise in Germany and fall in the United States, thus helping to drive the dollar down.

This is powerful medicine. If the distribution of monetary base between the two countries is affected, even modest official exchange interventions have great leverage—as private traders will quickly realize.

Need Dollar Depreciation Be Inflationary?

Suppose the dollar exchange rate is pushed down into the target zones suggested above. Is it possible to avoid reigniting the kind of rapid price inflation associated with the depreciating dollar of the unhappy 1970s?

Yes, because of the inherent symmetry in the above proposal for monetary coordination. When the Fed expands, the other principal central banks contract below normal growth—and vice versa. The result is no unusual growth in the monetary base for the system as a whole even as the dollar is pushed down to its purchasing-power parity.

The great dollar depreciations of the 1970s were associated with increased monetary growth in the United States coupled with sometimes explosive monetary growth in Europe and Japan, as shown in Table 2. The reason for this loss of monetary control abroad was due to foreign central banks' not very successfully resisting having their own currencies appreciate when international portfolio preferences had shifted sharply away from dollar assets. Through direct interventions to buy dollars and sell their own money, or through equivalent domestic monetary expansions to reduce interest rates, they lost monetary control.[1]

This fundamental asymmetry in the world dollar standard, where other central banks react to the dollar exchange rate but the Fed usually does not, is seen in Figure 3. For 1971 through 1985, one can see the strong negative correlation between percent changes in money growth in the rest of the industrial world (ROW) and percent changes in the dollar exchange rate. With unsmoothed individual quarterly observations, the simple correlation is −0.305, as shown in the upper panel, whereas the correlation becomes stronger at −0.620 if a five-quarter moving average is used—as shown in the lower panel of Figure 3.

The system went askew in the 1970s because the U.S. Federal Reserve System failed to contract when international demand unexpectedly shifted into foreign currencies at a time when the dollar was not overvalued—at least not by today's standards. Because the principal player, the Fed, was not playing the game correctly, the other central banks were simply overwhelmed.

Accidental or not, the great increase in "world" money growth in the 1970s had a strong inflationary impact on the prices of internationally tradeable goods, whether manufactures or primary com-

---

[1] For a more complete description of how the international money multiplier works, see R. McKinnon, Currency Substitution and Instability in the World Dollar Standard, *American Economic Review* 72 (30) (June 1982).

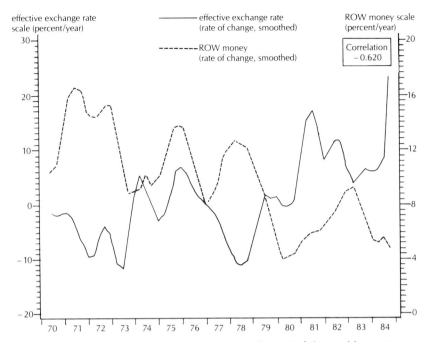

FIGURE 3. U.S. effective exchange rate and the rest of the world money.

modities. And all the major industrial economies experienced this price inflation (Table 1)—particularly those like the United States whose currencies had depreciated relative to the others. Undoubtedly, these foreign monetary repercussions help explain why fluctuations in the dollar exchange rate display the strong (lagged) effects on the American price level shown in Figure 2.

Through mid-September 1985, however, the situation was quite different. The dollar was truly overvalued by any reasonable standard. The portfolio pressure in the foreign exchanges was strongly in favor of dollar assets, which increases the derived demand for U.S. base money. The situation was one of price stability— indeed, one of undue deflationary pressure in those sectors of the American economy that must compete on world markets.

In these circumstances, it would be relatively safe to increase monetary expansion in the United States to drive the dollar down— and dangerous not to. But as long as the Fed remains expansionary, the other central banks must agree to maintain tight money during the transitional correction in the dollar exchange rate. Once exchange rates were aligned, the three central banks would, ideally, have also agreed to manage their joint money supply to stabilize the

TABLE 2.
Money Growth in Domestic Currencies, 11 Industrial Countries (percentage change in annual averages of M1)

	Belgium	Canada	France	Germany	Italy	Japan	Netherlands	Sweden	Switzerland	United Kingdom	United States	World Average	Rest of World[a]
(Weights: GNP 1964)	(.0132)	(.0394)	(.0778)	(.0892)	(.0494)	(.0681)	(.0144)	(.0167)	(.0113)	(.0796)	(.5408)		
1956	2.9	-1.2	10.3	7.2	8.5	16.4	-3.7	7.4	6.0	1.0	1.1	3.78	6.94
1957	-0.1	4.0	8.6	12.1	6.3	4.1	-2.0	3.4	1.8	2.7	-0.6	2.43	6.01
1958	5.8	12.8	6.4	13.1	9.9	12.8	11.9	1.6	9.2	3.0	4.3	6.47	9.04
1959	3.2	-3.2	11.4	11.8	14.0	16.5	4.5	18.0	6.1	4.6	0.1	4.53	9.74
1960	1.9	5.1	13.0	6.8	13.5	19.1	6.7	-1.2	10.2	-0.8	-0.4	3.72	8.58
1961	7.7	12.4	15.5	14.8	15.7	19.0	7.7	10.7	8.1	3.2	2.9	7.39	12.68
1962	7.2	3.3	18.1	6.6	18.6	17.1	7.5	5.6	16.6	4.4	2.1	6.18	10.99
1963	9.8	5.9	16.7	7.4	16.9	26.3	9.8	8.1	8.9	0.3	2.8	6.86	11.65
1964	5.6	5.1	10.3	8.3	6.7	16.8	8.5	7.7	0.2	5.0	4.1	6.16	8.59
1965	7.4	6.3	9.0	8.9	13.4	16.8	10.9	6.4	12.8	2.7	4.3	6.59	9.30
1966	6.7	7.0	8.9	4.5	15.1	16.3	7.2	9.9	3.1	2.6	4.6	6.31	8.33
1967	4.7	9.5	6.2	3.3	13.6	13.4	7.0	9.8	6.0	3.2	3.9	5.49	7.37
1968	6.8	4.4	5.5	7.6	13.4	14.6	8.8	-1.8	11.5	6.0	7.0	7.51	8.12
1969	2.3	6.9	6.1	8.2	15.0	18.4	9.4	2.0	9.5	0.4	5.9	7.00	8.30
1970	-2.5	2.4	-1.3	6.4	21.7	18.3	10.6	7.3	9.8	6.4	3.8	5.80	8.15
1971	10.3	12.7	13.7	12.0	22.9	25.5	16.7	9.0	18.2	11.8	6.8	12.45	16.74
1972	15.0	14.3	13.0	13.6	18.0	22.0	17.7	11.8	13.4	13.1	7.1	12.21	16.10

TABLE 2. (Continued)

	Belgium	Canada	France	Germany	Italy	Japan	Netherlands	Sweden	Switzerland	United Kingdom	United States	World Average	Rest of World[a]
(Weights: GNP 1977)	(.0172)	(.0487)	(.0885)	(.1122)	(.0471)	(.1404)	(.0228)	(.0195)	(.0148)	(.0572)	(.4316)		
1973	9.8	14.5	9.9	5.8	21.1	26.2	7.4	9.6	-1.0	8.6	7.3	11.06	13.91
1974	6.8	9.3	12.6	6.0	16.6	13.1	3.1	16.3	-1.7	4.8	5.0	7.78	9.88
1975	12.4	13.8	9.9	13.8	8.3	10.3	18.7	15.2	2.4	15.6	4.7	8.83	11.96
1976	9.6	8.0	15.0	10.4	20.5	14.2	11.8	14.0	7.3	13.8	5.7	9.91	13.10
1977	8.0	8.4	7.5	8.3	19.8	7.0	14.3	8.3	4.7	14.4	7.6	8.72	9.57
1978	6.7	10.0	11.2	13.4	23.7	10.8	5.3	13.6	12.7	20.1	8.2	10.99	13.11
1979	3.5	6.9	12.2	7.4	23.9	9.9	2.7	12.7	7.8	11.5	7.7	9.23	10.39
1980	-0.2	6.3	8.0	2.4	15.9	0.8	4.2	21.1	-5.4	4.9	6.2	5.53	5.01
1981	3.6	4.3	12.3	1.2	11.1	3.7	2.6	12.0	-0.9	10.0	7.2	6.50	5.96
1982	3.4	2.0	14.9	3.5	9.9	7.1	4.9	9.8	3.1	8.3	6.5	6.96	7.31
1983	5.0	10.2	12.1	10.3	17.3	3.0	10.6	11.4	7.6	13.4	11.1	10.1	9.48
1984	3.3	2.3	8.2[b]	3.3	8.4[b]	2.9	4.1	2.4[b]	2.5[b]	14.9[b]	6.9	6.08	5.45

[a] United States excluded

[b] Preliminary

Source: Federal Reserve Bank of St. Louis, International Economic Conditions (June and August 1985)

common price level into the indefinite future.[2] Then private expectations would be favorable, and the unfortunate inflationary experience of the 1970s need not be repeated.

Of course, even if the dollar depreciates under these controlled circumstances, there will be a one-time increase in the dollar prices of tradeable goods and a simultaneous decrease in their prices when measured in marks or yen. But this change in relative prices is necessary to rescue unprotected American farmers, manufacturers, and miners from heavy taxation imposed on them by the dollar's overvaluation and to prevent an outbreak of protectionism in the United States.

After this once-and-for-all correction in the dollar exchange rate, the principal central banks would begin their regular program of ongoing coordination. Nominal exchange rates would be kept within their preassigned bands, and the common international price level would be better stabilized into the indefinite future. Governments could then more realistically negotiate new rounds of the General Agreement on Tariff and Trade (GATT) to remove NTBs—many of which developed in the era of floating exchange rates—and the modest remaining tariff barriers. With a sufficiently stable international price level, even the difficult job of liberalizing trade in agricultural products would be more likely to succeed.

Addendum

After this paper was completed, on the weekend of September 21–22, 1985, a major exchange-rate agreement was announced among the finance ministers and central bank heads of the five principal industrial countries: Britain, France, Germany, Japan, and the United States. Their stated intention was to undertake strong financial measures (not spelled out) to drive the dollar down. The announcement effect was quite dramatic—the dollar fell by more than 10 percent over two trading days. That a better alignment for the dollar exchange rate has now become an objective of official policy is a major step forward in the preservation of free international trade.

On the other hand, it is far from clear that the officials involved

---

[2] This paper has not dealt with the precise definition of monetary targets for the three countries that would secure price stability in the longer run. This subject is treated in McKinnon (1984), chap. 5. Such a monetary program would avoid sharp changes in the collective money supply while gearing its long-term growth to maintain a stable purchasing power over a common, broad basket of internationally tradeable goods.

have worked out a sufficiently coordinated program of mutual and symmetrical monetary adjustment (as sketched above) to sustain a better alignment of exchange rates and preserve price stability into the future. No details of a monetary program were released at the September meeting.

Rather, the emphasis seemed to be on massive official interventions in the foreign-exchange markets—which, however big, will tend to wash out unless the market views such interventions as harbingers of monetary adjustment to come.

Similarly, the agreement hinted that the Europeans and Japanese would cut taxes. But, as suggested above, the exchange-rate effects of such fiscal adjustments by themselves are ambiguous.

Whether a coherent program of monetary coordination successfully evolves remains to be seen. However, the signs now in early 1986 seem more favorable than I had previously dared hope.

Throughout 1985, the three principal central banks had in fact supported the intentions of American, Japanese, and European officials to drive the dollar down. Growth in U.S. M1 was a relatively expansionary 12 percent, whereas German and Japanese M1 growth was much more restrained—about 5.5 percent. Equally important, the governor of the Bank of Japan formally announced on October 24, 1985 that, in order to keep the yen down in the foreign-exchange markets, Japanese money growth would be restricted for the rest of the year.

The result of these several actions was an engineered fall in the dollar from as much as 3.4 DM and 260 yen in February 1985 to about 2.45 marks and 200 yen by December. These nominal rates are much closer to any reasonable estimate of purchasing-power parity.

However, the exchange system is not yet secured by a well-understood international agreement on future monetary coordination. If, for example, the dollar were to begin falling sharply to much below its purchasing-power parity, the three central banks should be prepared to quickly reverse roles: the Federal Reserve should tighten up as the Bundesbank and Bank of Japan both undertook monetary ease. Then one could rest better assured that the principle of symmetrical monetary coordination had finally been accepted.

Additional empirical and theoretical support for the proposals advanced in this paper can be found in the author's book *An International Standard for Monetary Stabilization*, Washington, D.C., Institute for International Economics and Cambridge, Mass.: M.I.T. Press, 1984.

I would like to thank Kenichi Ohno for his great help in preparing this paper.

References

Frenkel, Jacob and Mussa, Michael (1980) The Efficiency of the Foreign Exchange Market and Measures of Turbulence, *American Economic Review* 70 (May).

—— (1985) Asset Markets, Exchange Rates, and the Balance of Payments. In R. Jones and P. Kenen, *Handbook of International Economics*, vol. 2, chap. 13. Amsterdam: North-Holland.

McKinnon, Ronald I. (1974) A New Tripartite Monetary Agreement or a Limping Dollar Standard? Princeton *Essays in International Finance* No. 106, Princeton, N.J.

—— (1982) Currency Substitution and Instability in the World Dollar Standard, *American Economic Review* 72 (June).

—— (1984) *An International Standard for Monetary Stabilization.* Washington, D.C.: Institute for International Economics.

—— (1985) The Dollar Exchange Rate as a Leading Indicator for American Monetary Policy. Stanford University (unpublished).

Williamson, John (1985) *The Exchange Rate System.* Washington, D.C.: Institute for International Economics.

18

Average Protection and Economic Policy

MICHAEL MUSSA

Introduction

Between the summer of 1980 and early 1985, the foreign-exchange value of the U.S. dollar, measured on a multilateral trade-weighted basis, appreciated by nearly 90 percent. Corrected for movements in national price levels, the real appreciation of the U.S. dollar over this period amounted to almost 80 percent. During this same period, the U.S. current account moved from a small surplus to a deficit equal to about 3 percent of U.S. GNP—the largest such deficit in at least this century. As the U.S. dollar has strengthened and the U.S. current account has deteriorated, pressures for protectionist measures have mounted. Actions to provide at least temporary protection to the U.S. auto and steel industries were adopted in the early 1980s. Recent proposals to provide renewed or increased protection to the shoe and textile industries in the U.S. were forestalled only by a presidential veto. Many proposals for increased protection of trade-sensitive industries enjoy wide support in the U.S. Congress, reflecting the serious problems afflicting a wide range of both exporting and import-competing industries in the United States.

Protectionist measures, such as import tariffs and quotas, affect the domestic relative prices of the products of different industries and shift the allocation of resources among these industries. Such measures can benefit firms and workers in specific industries that

From the Graduate School of Business, University of Chicago, Chicago, Illinois.

face foreign competition; and much of the pressure for particular protectionist measures usually comes from domestic industries likely to benefit directly from these measures. The broader appeal of protectionism, however, probably derives from the generally fallacious notion that it is possible to protect all of domestic industry from foreign competition, or more generally that it is possible to provide a positive average level of protection for domestic industry. The fundamental fallacy in the simplistic version of this notion is the implicit assumption that restricting some categories of imports has no offsetting effects on other imports or on exports. If trade were always balanced, this implicit and intuitively appealing assumption would always necessarily be false. Balanced trade means that the value of a country's imports equals the value of its exports. With balanced trade, measures that reduce the value of imports of some goods must induce some combination of exactly offsetting increases in the value of imports of other goods and reductions in the value of exports.[1] Hence, with balanced trade, it is not possible to provide a positive (or negative) average level of protection for domestic industry.[2]

The issue of the average level of protection of domestic industry becomes more complicated when trade need not always be balanced, as generally it need not be in a world of capital mobility. The purpose of this chapter is to analyze this more complicated issue. In this analysis, a critical distinction is made between results that may apply in the short run and results that must hold in the long run. In the short run, a variety of policies (including protectionist policies) may affect a country's trade balance. Policies that enlarge a trade surplus or reduce a trade deficit may be viewed as providing positive average protection for the country's tradable-goods industries. Conversely, policies that reduce a trade surplus or enlarge a trade deficit may be viewed as providing negative average protection for domestic tradable-goods industries. In the long run, however, leaving aside gifts of foreign aid, the present discounted value of a country's trade-

---

[1] This is a generalized version of Lerner's (1933) symmetry theorem which states that (under balanced trade) an across-the-board, ad valorem import tariff is equivalent to an across-the-board, ad valorem export tax. Both the import tariff and the export tax are ad valorem taxes on international trade that raise the domestic relative price of all imports in terms of all exports. These two equivalent taxes on trade reduce the volume of trade, both exports and imports, in exactly the same way and to exactly the same extent. Either of these two equivalent taxes provides positive protection to domestic import-competing industries and negative protection to domestic export industries. Neither provides positive (or negative) average protection to all domestic industries.

[2] In addition to not protecting domestic industry on average, protectionist commercial policies also generally have well-known harmful effects from distorting the allocation of resources for both producers and consumers.

balance surplus must equal its initial net foreign indebtedness.[3] Hence, positive average protection for domestic tradable-goods industries during one period generally implies negative average protection for these industries in some earlier or subsequent period.

A key assumption that is maintained throughout the analysis of the short-run and long-run effects of commercial policies on the average level of protection is that such policies affect only the distribution of resources among different productive activities, and not the aggregate supply or level of employment of productive resources. Commercial policies such as import tariffs and quotas or export incentives affect the domestic relative prices of products entering into international trade in comparison with the relative prices of those products prevailing in foreign markets. Such policies will normally affect the distribution of resources among different activities in the tradable-goods sector of the economy (export industries and import-competing industries) and perhaps also between the tradable- and nontradable-goods sectors. There is no general reason to presume, however, that policies that affect relative prices will have any systematic effect on the aggregate supplies or levels of employment of broad classes or factors of production such as labor and capital.[4]

The assumption that commercial policies do not affect aggregate supplies or employment levels for factors of production implies that such policies cannot induce expansion (or contraction) of all domestic industries. Analysis of the effect of commercial policies on the average level of protection, therefore, focuses on the effects of these policies on the distribution of resources between tradable and nontradable goods industries. A trade surplus (and hence positive average level of protection for tradable-goods industries) means that a country is producing more tradable goods than it is consuming. To achieve this result it is usually necessary to shift resources from the

---

[3] Suppose that all payment imbalances must be financed by flows of interest-bearing assets. Then, the rate of accumulation of such assets, vis-à-vis the rest of the world, is equal to the current-account balance which, in turn, is equal to the trade balance plus interest received on the existing net asset position. The solution of this simple differential equation (subject to the usual boundary condition that in the limit the stock of net foreign assets grows more slowly than the interest factor) implies that the present discounted value of the trade surplus must equal initial net foreign indebtedness. In other words, the value of a country's future trade surpluses must pay the interest and principal on its initial foreign debt. This condition can be appropriately modified to take account of transfers (gifts to or from foreigners) and holdings of non-interest-bearing assets such as gold.

[4] Commercial policies might affect long-run labor supply by influencing the labor leisure trade-off. There is no general presumption, however, that protectionist policies tend to expand labor supply or that such an effect is welfare improving if it occurs. There is also no general presumption that commercial policies are useful in a business-cycle context; see Kimbrough (1984) for an analysis.

nontradable- to the tradable-goods sector, relative to the distribution of resources that would prevail with balanced trade.[5] Since commercial policies generally affect relative prices among different tradable goods (exports, imports, and import-competing goods) rather than relative prices between tradables and nontradables, there is no general presumption that commercial policies will have powerful effects on the trade balance and hence on the average level of protection for the tradable-goods sector. In contrast, fiscal and monetary policy often have temporary (and subsequently reversed) effects on the trade balance and on the average level of protection of the tradable-goods sector. An expansionary fiscal policy will tend to induce a temporary excess of national spending over national income and a corresponding trade deficit which implies temporary negative average protection for the tradable-goods sector. The effects of an expansionary monetary policy depend critically on the exchange-rate regime. Under a fixed exchange-rate regime, the short-run effect is likely to be a temporary trade deficit and hence temporary negative average protection for the tradable-goods sector. Under a floating exchange-rate regime, the short-run effect of monetary expansion is likely to be a depreciation of the real exchange rate that induces a temporary trade surplus and temporary positive average protection for the tradable-goods sector. These issues will be examined in order after first discussing the effects of commercial policies on the average level of protection.

Commercial Policy and Average Protection

A country's trade balance is in surplus (or deficit) when the value of its exports exceeds (or is less than) the value of its imports. When the trade balance is in surplus, more domestic resources are devoted to production of tradable goods for export than implicitly are freed from domestic tradable-goods production by imports of foreign products. Thus, a trade surplus is generally associated with an expansion of the tradable-goods sector of the economy, relative to its size under balanced trade. In this sense, it may be said that a trade surplus implies a positive average level of protection for the tradable-goods sector of the economy. (Under the assumption that aggregate supplies and employment levels of productive resources are not

---

[5] Commercial policies and other policies could induce the tradable-goods sector to expand (or contract) at the expense of the nontradable-goods sector without generating a trade surplus (or deficit). For purposes of the present discussion, however, this possibility will be ignored. Generation of a trade surplus (or deficit) will be treated as synonymous with expansion (or contraction) of the tradable-goods sector relative to the size of the economy. Caution is required in interpreting this chapter when this assumption is not at least approximately correct.

affected, this positive average level of protection for the tradable-goods sector comes at the expense of the nontradable-goods sector, leaving zero average protection for all of domestic industry.) Conversely, a trade-balance deficit is associated with a negative average level of protection for the tradable-goods sector—fewer domestic resources are devoted to the production of exports than are implicitly freed from domestic production of import-competing products, and these additional resources for tradable-goods production are obtained from the nontradable-goods sector of the economy.

It is commonly believed that tariffs, import quotas, export subsidies, and other commercial policies have systematic and permanent effects on the trade balance and hence on the average level of protection of the tradable-goods sector. For example, it is widely believed that imposition of an import tariff permanently improves the trade balance because it discourages imports. This intuitively appealing view of the long-run effects of an import tariff on the trade balance, however, is mistaken. An import tariff generally reduces the long-run volume of trade, both imports and exports, with no long-run effect on the trade balance. The same is true for other types of commercial policies.

These policies affect the domestic relative prices of tradable goods and thereby induce shifts in patterns of domestic production and consumption of these goods. In the long run, however, commercial policies will not generally affect the difference between the value of domestic output and the level of domestic spending. Such an effect would be essential to a long-run impact on the trade balance because the trade balance is necessarily the excess of the value of domestic output over domestic spending. This view of the trade balance is associated with the literature on the "absorption approach" to analysis of the balance of payments.[6] This approach emphasizes the logically necessary conclusion that an excess of the value of exports over the value of imports must imply an exactly equal excess of the value of domestic production over the level of domestic spending. In the long run, there is no reason to presume that policies that affect domestic relative prices of tradable goods would affect the relationship between the value of domestic output and the level of domestic spending.

Theoretical arguments have been advanced for why commercial policies may have short-run effects on the trade balance and, by implication, on the average level of protection of the tradable-goods sector. For example, for a country that maintains a fixed exchange rate, imposition of an import tariff will generally raise domestic

---

[6] For a discussion of the absorption approach, see Alexander (1952) and Johnson (1958).

nominal prices of imported goods, raise the long-run equilibrium value of the domestic price level, and raise the long-run equilibrium value of the domestic nominal money supply. If the domestic credit component of the domestic money supply is held constant, there will need to be an inflow of foreign exchange in order to satisfy the increase in the long-run equilibrium of domestic money demand. Absent international capital mobility, a short-run trade balance surplus is necessary to bring about this inflow of foreign exchange. The short-run excess of the value of domestic output over domestic spending associated with this short-run trade surplus may be induced either by the direct effect of reduced real money balances (because of the increase in the domestic price level) on desired hoarding or by the effect of higher domestic interest rates on desired domestic spending. As domestic money balances rise to their new long-run equilibrium level the incentive for hoarding or the level of domestic interest rates declines to the level consistent with balance in the trade account.[7]

Interestingly, an export tax that has the same long-run effects on resource allocation as an import tariff has the opposite short-run effect on the trade balance. The export tax reduces domestic nominal prices of export goods, reduces the long-run equilibrium value of the domestic price level, and reduces the long-run equilibrium value of the domestic money supply. To achieve the required reduction in the actual money supply, holding its domestic credit component constant, there must be a short-run outflow of foreign exchange and an associated trade-balance deficit. Thus, under the assumptions of this analysis, an export tax provides temporary negative average protection for the tradable-goods sector; whereas an import tariff provides temporary positive average protection for this sector. Neither policy, however, provides permanent positive or negative average protection for the tradable-goods sector. Only temporary trade surpluses or deficits are needed to adjust the money supply to the new long-run equilibrium level implied by these policies.

In theory, temporary commercial policies can have temporary effects on the trade balance and hence on the average level of protection of the tradable-goods sector. The logical basis for such effects is illustrated by the case of a temporary import tariff. Imposition of a tariff that is expected to be temporary raises the cost of consumption during the period when the tariff is in effect relative to the cost of consumption after the tariff is removed. Under plausible assumptions, such a change in the relative price of consumption in different time periods should discourage consumption during the period

---

[7] For a formal analysis of the effects of tariffs on the balance of payments in a monetary framework, see Mussa (1974 and 1976).

when the tariff is in effect and encourage consumption subsequently. Because of this effect on the intertemporal pattern of desired spending, the temporary tariff should stimulate an initial trade-balance surplus that will later be offset by a trade-balance deficit.[8] Thus, the temporary tariff provides positive average protection to the tradable-goods sector initially, and it subsequently provides negative average protection to this sector. Other temporary commercial policies that affect intertemporal relative prices of spending in different periods should, by the same logic, have temporary, self-reversing effects on the trade balance and on the average level of protection of the tradable-goods sector.

The Trade Balance and Average Protection Over Time

There is an important general reason why commercial policies and other policies should have only temporary, and usually self-reversing, effects on the trade balance and hence on the average level of protection of the tradable-goods sector. Every country is subject to an intertemporal budget constraint with respect to its foreign trade which generally requires that trade surpluses at one point in time be offset by earlier or later trade deficits. If trade imbalances are financed by flows of non-interest-bearing reserves, then we would generally expect that a trade surplus leading to a reserve inflow would be offset, sooner or later, by a trade deficit of equal magnitude. The only circumstance in which this offset would not occur would be if the country wished to add to its stock of non-interest-bearing reserves.

If, as is now typically the case, trade imbalances are financed by flows of interest-bearing assets, then it is necessary to account for the accumulated interest on asset flows used to finance trade imbalances. A temporary trade surplus implies accumulation of a stock of net claims on the rest of the world (or a reduction in the stock of foreign claims on domestic residents). If this increase in net foreign assets is later eliminated by an excess of domestic spending over domestic income, the implied trade deficit must exceed the initial trade surplus by the amount of the interest accumulated on this increase in net foreign assets. Alternatively, suppose that the increase in net foreign assets is not dissipated by a subsequent excess of spending over income. In this case, to hold constant the increase in net foreign assets, it is necessary to increase spending relative to the value of domestic product permanently by the amount of the

---

[8] This channel through which temporary commercial policies may influence the trade balance has been emphasized by Svennsson and Razin (1983).

interest flow on the increase in net foreign assets. This means that a temporary trade surplus is offset by a permanent trade deficit equal to the interest earnings on the assets accumulated as a consequence of the trade surplus.

It is possible, of course, for a country to have a temporary trade surplus and corresponding positive average level of protection for the tradable-goods sector that is not subsequently offset by a trade deficit and corresponding negative average level of protection for the tradable-goods sector. The simplest way to achieve this is to make gifts to other countries, for example, through foreign aid. Even without tying aid to purchases of exports of the donor country, the effect of aid must be to finance an excess of exports over imports for the donor country (relative to what would have occurred in the absence of aid). Alternatively, a country could run a temporary trade surplus and add permanently to its holding of non-interest-bearing reserves or could acquire interest-bearing assets and never spend either the interest on or principal value of these assets. Such practices are basically another means of making unrequited gifts to the rest of the world.

This principle applies not only to commercial policies but also to any policies that might be used, deliberately or inadvertently, to affect the trade balance and hence the average level of protection of the tradable-goods sector. Aside from making gifts to the rest of the world, there is no effective means to provide permanent positive average protection to the tradable-goods sector. Positive average protection provided at one time must be offset by negative average protection at some other time.

Fiscal Policy and Average Protection

Commercial policies are probably not the principal means by which positive or negative average protection is provided on a temporary basis to the tradable-goods sector. Any policy that affects the trade balance has, by definition, an effect on the average level of protection. The most important policies that have such effects are usually macroeconomic policies that influence levels of domestic spending and domestic income and also frequently the difference between domestic spending and domestic income.

Fiscal policy is often suggested to have important effects on the trade balance.[9] When private saving and investment are held constant, an increase in the government's fiscal deficit implies an increase in domestic spending relative to domestic income and hence an increase in the trade deficit or a reduction in the trade surplus. Of course, if private saving increased one-for-one with an increase in the government deficit, as suggested by the Ricardian proposition, government deficits would have no direct effect on the trade balance. However, there is a variety of reasons why private savings might not show such a response to government deficits, leaving a channel through which government deficits would affect the trade balance.[10]

The mechanism through which fiscal policy affects the average level of protection of the tradable-goods sector is often described as follows. Consider an expansionary fiscal policy that increases the general level of domestic spending for both tradable and nontradable goods. The increased demand for tradable goods can be absorbed, at constant relative prices, by increased imports and diminished exports. To clear the market for nontradable goods, however, it is necessary to raise the relative price of nontradable goods in terms of tradable goods. This relative price change encourages a shift of domestic resources away from tradable-goods production and toward nontradable-goods production. This relative price change and resource shift constitute negative average protection for the tradable-goods sector.

Monetary Policy and Average Protection Under Fixed Rates

The effect of monetary policy on the average level of protection of the tradable-goods sector depends on the nature of the nominal exchange-rate regime. Consider first a country that maintains a fixed exchange rate. If the government does not use trade restrictions or impose foreign-exchange controls for balance-of-payments purposes, then maintenance of a fixed nominal exchange rate constrains the size of the domestic money supply to the level determined by the

---

[9] The empirical relationship between the fiscal deficit and the trade balance is likely to be complicated by the business cycle. In the United States, the trade balance tends to improve during a recession because domestic demand for imports falls more than foreign demand for U.S. exports. The fiscal deficit usually tends to worsen during a recession because tax revenues fall while government spending rises. The business cycle therefore tends to create positive correlation between the trade balance and the fiscal deficit. This offsets the negative correlation predicted by the notion that a government fiscal deficit contributes to an excess of national spending over national income.

[10] Recently, Frenkel and Razin (1986), building on the work of Blanchard (1983), have developed formal models that provide a rationale for this property based on the assumption of finite-lived individuals. See Buiter (1984) for a different but related approach to these issues.

long-run demand to hold domestic money. An attempt to sustain a domestic money supply different from this level will lead, through a variety of mechanisms, to gains or losses of foreign-exchange reserves that ultimately compel either adjustment of the domestic money supply to its long-run equilibrium level or a change in the exchange rate.[11] In the shorter run, however, there may be latitude to expand or contract the domestic credit component of the money supply without immediately suffering a completely offsetting change in the foreign-exchange reserve component of the money supply.

Suppose that such a country, which is initially in a position of balance-of-payments equilibrium, decides to expand the domestic credit component of its money supply. Domestic demand will be stimulated. If financial capital is not perfectly mobile vis-à-vis international capital markets, domestic interest rates may decline. Under the pressure of greater domestic demand, domestic prices and wages may be pushed upward. The trade balance will move into deficit. This deficit will be financed by an outflow of foreign-exchange reserves resulting from official intervention in support of the fixed exchange rate. By definition, this trade deficit implies negative average protection for the tradable-goods sector of the economy. Domestic producers of tradable goods (both export- and import-competing firms) have difficulty raising the prices of their products to meet higher domestic factor costs because they face foreign competitors who have not experienced the same increased costs. Domestic producers of nontradable goods do not face such competition, and they tend to expand at the expense of producers of tradable goods. This is a situation where negative average protection is inflicted on the tradable-goods sector because of an "overvalued" exchange rate; that is, an exchange rate that is so high that it must be supported by official intervention.

If the loss of foreign-exchange reserves is not sterilized, then the domestic money supply will gradually decline toward its sustainable, long-run equilibrium level. The trade deficit will gradually disappear. The overvaluation of the exchange rate will gradually be eliminated. The average level of protection of producers of tradable goods will gradually rise toward zero. The government, however, may engage in sterilized intervention under which losses in foreign-exchange reserves are offset by expansions of the domestic credit component of the money supply, with the result that the domestic money supply is held above its sustainable, long-run equilibrium

---

[11] This principle is emphasized especially in the monetary approach to balance-of-payments analysis. For a recent survey of the relevant literature, see Frenkel and Mussa (1985).

level. Alternatively, the government may obtain the foreign exchange it requires for intervention by borrowing in world capital markets. In either case, the government is sustaining an overvalued exchange rate by financing an excess of spending over income. As would normally be expected of an expansionary fiscal policy, this generates a trade deficit and negative average protection for the tradable goods sector.

In the longer run, this policy is not sustainable. The government will run out of reserves or exhaust its foreign borrowing capacity. When or before this happens, the government may decide to devalue its exchange rate. If the devaluation is sufficiently large, and the domestic credit component of the money supply is not allowed to expand subsequent to devaluation, then a temporary surplus in the balance of payments should be generated. In this situation, the exchange rate will be temporarily undervalued, the trade balance will be in surplus, and positive average protection will be afforded to the tradable-goods sector. The foreign-exchange inflows associated with the balance-of-payments surplus will, over time, restore the reserves lost or repay the foreign borrowings undertaken during the period overvaluation of the exchange rate. Negative average protection for the tradable-goods sector during the period of overvaluation will be offset by positive average protection during the period of undervaluation.

Rather than devaluing, a government might attempt to sustain its nominal exchange rate by imposing trade restrictions. A general import tariff, for example, would raise domestic nominal prices of imported and import-competing goods, the general domestic price level, and presumably the long-run equilibrium level of demand for domestic money. An import tariff that raised the long-run equilibrium level of money demand to the size of the actual money supply would validate the existing exchange rate and stem the foreign-exchange outflow. Imposition of such a tariff, however, would not mean continuation of negative average protection for the tradable-goods sector, as existed during the period of temporary overvaluation. As previously discussed, an import tariff under conditions of balanced trade generally implies neither positive nor negative average protection for the tradable goods sector, but only a shift of resources from export-competing to import-competing industries. However, if the government wished to recover reserves lost or repay debts incurred during the period of overvaluation, it would have to find some means of generating a temporary balance-of-payments surplus. During the period of this surplus, positive average protection would be afforded to the tradable-goods sector that would offset the negative average protection imposed during the period of exchange-rate overvaluation.

Floating Exchange Rates and Protection

Under a floating exchange-rate regime, the average level of protection of the tradable-goods sector is affected by the market forces that determine the exchange rate. The "asset market approach" to exchange rates emphasizes that expectations of future economic events and economic policies, as well as current events and policies, influence the exchange rate and the current account. Presentation and analysis of a formal model that explicates these complex dynamic linkages are beyond the scope of the present chapter.[12] However, it is useful to summarize the main elements and implications of such a model.

First, the trade balance is affected by the value of the real exchange rate. The real exchange rate is defined as the nominal exchange rate adjusted for the ratio of domestic prices to foreign prices. It represents the relative price of the composite of domestic goods in terms of the composite of foreign goods. An increase in this relative price worsens the trade balance because it encourages both domestic and foreign residents to shift their purchases from domestic to foreign goods.

Second, the long-run equilibrium value of the real exchange rate may be thought of as the value of the real exchange rate that would maintain current-account balance on average in the long run. This long-run equilibrium value of the real exchange rate is not necessarily constant. Changes in technology or tastes may alter the relative price of domestic goods in terms of foreign goods that is consistent with longer-run equilibrium in the world economy. Relevant changes in technology include changes that affect the overall growth rates of different countries, as well as changes that affect the efficiency of production in different industries. Changes in tastes include changes in the desired distribution of domestic and foreign spending across different goods, and changes in desired levels of spending relative to income (and associated changes in long-run equilibrium patterns of net foreign asset holdings). At any moment of time, the current long-run equilibrium value of the real exchange rate reflects current expectations concerning present and future patterns of technology and tastes that are relevant for determining the value of the real exchange rate that would, on average, achieve balance in the current account.

Third, the long-run equilibrium value of the nominal exchange rate reflects the long-run equilibrium value of the real exchange rate and the long-run equilibrium values of the domestic and foreign

---

[12] A model that incorporates the essential elements described in this section is presented in Mussa (1985).

nominal price levels. The long-run equilibrium values of nominal price levels are influenced by present and expected future levels of domestic and foreign money demand and supply. An increase in expected future levels of the domestic money supply, holding all other factors constant, raises the long-run equilibrium value of the domestic price level and depreciates to an equal extent the long-run equilibrium value of domestic money in terms of foreign money. The long-run equilibrium value of the real exchange rate, however, is not affected by this decline in the long-run equilibrium value of the nominal exchange rate.

Fourth, nominal exchange rates under a floating-rate system are rapidly adjusting variables that respond very rapidly to changes in actual economic conditions and changes in expectations of future economic conditions. In contrast, national price levels, at least in moderate inflation countries, are relatively slowly adjusting variables, in comparison with the adjustment speeds exhibited by exchange rates, stock prices, and other asset prices determined in highly organized markets. This difference in speeds of adjustment of the nominal exchange rate and of nominal national price levels creates latitude for divergences between the current nominal and real exchange rates and their respective long-run equilibrium values. Associated with such divergences there may be other "disequilibrium phenomena," including deviations of output and employment levels from their natural equilibrium values. When there is a sudden change in current or expected future economic conditions, the nominal exchange rate responds immediately to this change. The real exchange rate moves along with the nominal exchange rate because national price levels adjust more slowly to changes in actual and expected economic conditions. Hence, the real exchange rate moves both in response to information that alters the long-run equilibrium value of the real exchange rate and in response to information that leaves the long-run equilibrium value of the real exchange rate unchanged but alters the long-run equilibrium nominal exchange rate. Indeed, the nominal exchange rate may show a magnified short-run response to alterations in its long-run equilibrium value because of sluggishness in the adjustment of national price levels.[13] This magnified response of the nominal exchange rate will be translated into a similar response of the real exchange rate.

With these ideas in mind, consider an economy that is in full equilibrium before an unexpected increase in the domestic money supply that is perceived as permanent once it occurs. Suppose, for simplicity, that before this increase in the money supply, the actual

---

[13] This is the "overshooting" phenomenon described by Dornbusch (1976).

and expected inflation rates in the home country and in the rest of the world were zero, and no change was expected in the exchange rate between domestic money and the money of the rest of the world. If we assume that money is neutral in the long run, the unexpected, permanent increase in the domestic money supply implies a proportionate increase in the long-run equilibrium values of all prices measured in terms of domestic money, including the price of foreign exchange. Because of the sluggishness of adjustment of many domestic prices, however, the general price level does not immediately rise to its new long-run equilibrium level, but rather remains initially very close to its level before the money-supply increase. To maintain equilibrium in the domestic money market in the face of an increase in the domestic money supply, with the domestic price level essentially unchanged, domestic interest rates must fall. (Alternatively, domestic output might expand and increase the demand for domestic money, but this possibility will be ignored in the present discussion.)

The exchange rate, in contrast to the domestic price level, should respond immediately to the increase in the domestic money supply. Indeed, the foreign-exchange value of domestic money may fall more initially than the decline in its long-run equilibrium value. This is because the decline in the domestic interest rate, with interest rates in the rest of the world unchanged, implies that there should be a forward premium on domestic money in order to maintain the international interest arbitrage condition. This forward premium on domestic money should correspond, at least approximately, to the expected rate of appreciation of domestic money in the foreign-exchange market. In order for there to be the expectation of appreciation in the foreign-exchange value of domestic money, its initial foreign-exchange value after the money-supply increase should be below its new long-run equilibrium value. Thus, the initial depreciation of the foreign-exchange value of domestic money in response to the money-supply increase should "overshoot" the required long-run depreciation.

The initial decline in the nominal foreign-exchange value of domestic money, with little change in the general level of domestic prices, implies a corresponding decline in the real exchange rate. In other words, the initial effect of the unexpected increase in the domestic money supply is to decrease the relative price of domestic goods in terms of foreign goods. This relative price change should shift demand toward domestic goods and away from foreign goods. In particular, the tradable-goods sector of the domestic economy should be encouraged to expand because domestically produced exports have become cheaper to foreign purchasers while imports should face a harder time competing with domestically produced import substitutes.

The trade balance, in this situation, is subject to two conflicting forces. On the one hand, the reduction in the relative price of domestic goods in terms of foreign goods and the consequent shift of demand toward domestic goods tends to improve the trade balance. On the other hand, the reduction in domestic nominal and real interest rates tends to stimulate an increase in domestic spending relative to income which implies a deterioration of the trade balance. It is assumed that the first of these effects dominates over the second and that the trade balance improves. This is consistent with the plausible notion that depreciation of the real exchange rate tends to improve the trade balance and to provide positive average protection for the tradable-goods sector of the economy.

It is noteworthy that an expansionary domestic monetary disturbance under a floating exchange-rate regime is assumed to induce an initial improvement of the trade balance; whereas such a policy change is assumed to worsen the trade balance initially under a fixed-rate regime. This difference is related to Mundell's analysis of the "reverse transmission" of monetary disturbances under floating exchange-rate regimes in the presence of international capital mobility.[14] In Mundell's analysis which assumes rigidity of national price levels, domestic monetary expansion allows for an expansion of domestic output and a reduction of the domestic nominal interest rate. With international capital mobility (and no expected change in exchange rates) the foreign nominal interest rate must fall to match the decline in the domestic nominal interest rate. To maintain equilibrium in the foreign money market with a constant foreign money supply and price level, foreign output must decline. The foreign-exchange value of domestic money must decline by enough to generate a trade imbalance (a surplus for the home country and corresponding deficit for the foreign country) that rationalizes the changes in domestic and foreign output. Thus, Mundell's analysis of "reverse transmission" implies that domestic monetary expansion under a floating exchange-rate regime induces a trade surplus for the home country.

The positive average protection that is provided to the tradable-goods sector as a consequence of an unanticipated increase in the domestic money supply is only temporary. Gradually, the domestic price level rises in response to the increase in the money supply and to the temporary economic situation that this money supply increase generates. At the same time that the domestic price level is rising,

---

[14] See Mundell (1968), chapter 18.

the excess depreciation of the exchange rate is being corrected and the foreign-exchange value of domestic money is rising toward its new long-run equilibrium. These two factors both contribute to an increase in the real exchange rate, that is, to a rise in the relative price of domestic goods in terms of foreign goods. This appreciation of the real exchange rate erodes the positive average protection provided to the tradable-goods sector by the initial depreciation of the real exchange rate. In addition, assets acquired as a consequence of the trade surpluses associated with the temporary depreciation of the real exchange rate will ultimately lead to trade deficits associated with expenditure of the interest and principal on these assets. Thus, the positive average protection of the tradable-goods sector generated by an unanticipated increase in the money supply will later be offset by negative average protection for this sector of the economy.

Under the same assumptions, the same conclusions apply for any unanticipated upward shift in the path of the domestic money supply, relative to its previously anticipated path. Since the domestic price level is relatively slow to adjust, such an expansionary monetary disturbance is felt in a temporary depreciation of the real exchange rate that provides temporary positive protection to the tradable-goods sector of the economy. This temporary positive average protection for the tradable-goods sector is gradually eroded by appreciation of the real exchange rate because of higher domestic inflation and correction of excessive depreciation of the nominal exchange rate. Later, negative average protection of the tradable-goods sector occurs during the process of working off the foreign assets acquired during the period of positive average protection. By symmetry, these conclusions apply in reverse to any unanticipated downward shift in the path of the domestic money supply relative to its previously anticipated path. Such a disturbance initially induces negative average protection for the tradable-goods sector which is gradually eroded and ultimately reversed.

Conclusion

The main conclusions of this chapter may be summarized as follows. The popularity of protectionist commercial policies probably derives partly from the misapprehension that such policies typically provide not only protection for particular domestic industries but also positive average protection for domestic industry. Absent a capacity to affect aggregate supplies or employment levels of factors of production, however, such policies can only affect the distribution of resources among different industries. Still, a concept of positive or negative average protection might be defined in terms of effects on the size of the tradable-goods sector relative to the total resources available to the economy. Since a trade surplus implies that more tradable goods are produced domestically than are consumed domestically, it is natural to associate such a surplus with positive average protection for the tradable-goods sector. Conversely, a trade deficit is naturally associated with negative average protection for the tradable-goods sector.

Commercial policies affect primarily relative prices among tradable goods (exports, imports, and import-competing goods). Hence, these policies should affect primarily the distribution of resources within the tradable-goods sector of the economy. A tariff on imports of specific categories of foreign goods, for example, shifts domestic resources toward production of domestic substitutes for these foreign goods and away from domestic production of exportables or of other import-competing goods. It is also possible that commercial policies would have some marginal impact on the distribution of resources between the tradable- and nontradable-goods sectors of the economy. There is, however, no general presumption that commercial policies should have powerful effects on the trade balance and hence on the average level of protection of the tradable-goods sector. The country's intertemporal budget constraint with respect to its international trade implies that any temporary effects of commercial policies on the trade balance should be reversed in the longer term.

An expansionary fiscal policy that stimulates an excess of national spending over national income should worsen the trade balance and hence implies negative average protection for the tradable goods sector. This effect, however, is temporary. In the longer term, repayment of foreign debts incurred to finance fiscal expansion (or replenishment of assets sold to foreigners) will require trade surpluses that imply positive average protection for the tradable-goods sector.

The effects of an expansionary monetary policy on average protection depend importantly on the exchange-rate regime. Under a fixed-rate regime, the short-run result of an expansionary monetary policy is likely to be temporary negative average protection for the tradable-goods sector. Domestic inflation will force up costs for domestic producers of tradable goods relative to their foreign competitors, and a trade deficit will be financed by a loss of reserves. To restore lost reserves there will need to be either a subsequent tightening of monetary policy or a devaluation. In either case, reserve accumulation normally implies a trade surplus and hence positive average protection for the tradable-goods sector that offsets the negative average protection initially created by the monetary expansion.

Under a floating exchange-rate regime, an unanticipated monetary expansion is likely to induce a sharp depreciation of the real exchange rate that improves the trade balance and implies initial positive average protection for the tradable-goods sector. Over time, however, the real exchange rate will appreciate, and eventual dissi-pation of the foreign assets acquired during the period of trade sur-pluses implies trade deficits and hence negative average protection for the tradable-goods sector.

The general message that emerges from this analysis is that policies that induce trade surpluses or deficits can provide positive or negative average protection to the tradable-goods sector of the economy, in the sense that they induce this sector to expand or contract relative to the size of the economy. Such positive or nega-tive average protection, however, is necessarily temporary and self-reversing. The inflow of foreign assets (or reduction in foreign debts) associated with a trade surplus and a positive average level of pro-tection in one period must generally be offset by an outflow of for-eign assets (or increase in foreign debts) associated with a trade deficit and negative average level of protection in some earlier or subsequent period.

References

Alexander, S. S. (1952) Effects of Devaluation on the Trade Balance, Interna-tional Monetary Fund *Staff Papers* 2: 263–278.

Blanchard, O. (1983) Debt, Deficits and Finite Horizons, *Journal of Political Economy* 93: 223–247.

Buiter, W. H. (1984) Fiscal Policy in Open Interdependent Economies, Dis-cussion Paper No. 28, Centre for Economic Policy Research, London, England.

Dornbusch, R. (1976) Expectations and Exchange Rate Dynamics, *Journal of Political Economy* 84: 1161–1176.

Frenkel, J., and Mussa, M. (1985) Asset Markets, Exchange Rates and the Balance of Payments. Chapter 14 in the *Handbook of International Economics*, vol. II, edited by R. Jones and P. Kenen. Amsterdam: North Holland, pp. 680–747.

Frenkel, J., and Razin, A. (1986) Fiscal Policies in the World Economy, *Journal of Political Economy*, forthcoming.

Johnson, H. G. (1958) Towards a General Theory of the Balance of Payments. In *International Trade and Economic Growth*, edited by H. G. John-son. Cambridge: Harvard Univ. Press, pp. 153–168.

Kimbrough, K. (1984) Commercial Policy and Aggregate Employment under Rational Expectations, *Quarterly Journal of Economics* 99: 567–586.

Lerner, A. P. (1933) The Symmetry between Import and Export Taxes, *Economica* 3: 308–313.

Mundell, R. A. (1968) Capital Mobility and Stabilization Policy under Fixed and Flexible Exchange Rates. In *International Economics,* edited by R. A. Mundell. New York: Macmillan, pp. 250–271.

Mussa, M. L. (1974) A Monetary Approach to Balance of Payments Analysis, *Journal of Money, Credit and Banking* 6: 333–351.

Mussa, M. L. (1976) Tariffs and the Balance of Payments. In *The Monetary Approach to the Balance of Payments,* edited by J. A. Frenkel and H. G. Johnson. London: Allen & Unwin, pp. 187–221.

Mussa, M. L. (1985) The Theory of Exchange Rate Determination. In *Exchange Rate Theory and Practice,* edited by J. F. O. Bilson and R. C. Marston. Chicago: Univ. of Chicago Press (for the National Bureau of Economic Research), pp. 13–58.

Svennsson, L., and Razin, A. (1983) Trade Taxes and the Current Account, *Economic Letters* 13: 55–57.

19

Foreign Exchange Intervention as an Alternative to Protectionism

JOHN F. O. BILSON

Introduction

The success of an international monetary system is often discussed in terms of performance of two parity conditions. The purchasing-power parity condition states that the exchange rate adjusts to offset differences in inflation rates. The uncovered interest-rate parity condition states that national interest-rate differentials should reflect the expected rate of change in the exchange rate, which, through purchasing-power parity, should reflect the inflation-rate differential.

By either of these standards, the system of floating exchange rates that evolved out of the ashes of the Bretton Woods system has performed poorly. Because of the volatility of nominal exchange rates, the terms of trade between major trading partners has been subject to large and sustained swings. For example, the IMF's index of relative export unit values for the United States has risen by 44 percent between 1980 and 1984. This increase has been associated with a record current-account deficit for the United States and with considerable economic distress in U.S. export- and import-competing industries.

Similar problems exist on the capital-account side. In 1981 the average yield on three-month Eurodollar deposits was around 17 percent. This rate compares with the 12 percent average yield on deutsche marks and the 8 percent yield on Japanese yen. Adjusting

From The University of Chicago, Chicago, Illinois, and the National Bureau of Economic Research.

for the average inflation rate in 1981 (U.S. 10 percent, West Germany 6 percent, Japan 5 percent), the real interest rates were 7 percent in the United States, 6 percent in West Germany, and 3 percent in Japan. The high yield on U.S. dollars did not reflect any market perception that the dollar was overvalued in 1981. To the contrary, the dollar strengthened throughout this period, and reports in the financial press typically associated high U.S. interest rates as a factor supporting the dollar's advance.

There is, of course, a relationship between the failure of the purchasing-power parity and interest-rate parity conditions. Rudiger Dornbusch first described this relationship in his influential paper on exchange-rate dynamics (Dornbusch, 1976). In the Dornbusch model, a system of fixed exchange rates will maintain purchasing-power parity by coordinating the monetary policies of the member countries. However, with flexible exchange rates, interest rates are determined by domestic conditions and the exchange rate must overshoot the PPP level to maintain capital-market equilibrium.

For example, assume an initial equilibrium at purchasing-power parity and introduce a 5 percent nominal interest-rate differential between the home (U.S.) and foreign (Europe) countries. Assume that the exchange rate adjusts toward the parity value at a rate of 20 percent per year. With risk neutrality, the dollar would consequently have to appreciate immediately by 25 percent to induce an expected depreciation of 5 percent per year. The mechanism by which this appreciation takes place is straightforward. At the initial equilibrium, Europeans would like to invest in dollars to take advantage of the higher yield. Since the current account is fixed in the short run, there can be no net capital exports from the United States. Hence the incipient capital flow causes an appreciation of the exchange rate. With risk neutrality, this appreciation will continue until the incipient demand for U.S. assets is eliminated.

The introduction of risk aversion into this model probably accentuates the volatility of the system. Risk analysis has shown that the least risky asset for a resident of a country is a short-term instrument denominated in the currency of that country. A Eurodollar deposit is low-risk for an American investor but high-risk for European or Japanese investors. To induce the latter to invest in U.S. instruments, the expected yield must exceed the yield on a local instrument by an amount that is sufficient to compensate for the risk. Risk segments the national capital markets and results in interest rates that are predominantly determined by local conditions. In Bilson (1985) I demonstrate that risk aversion increases the volatility of both exchange rates and interest-rate differentials.

The Dornbusch model and its extensions have demonstrated that the instability of financial prices that has occurred over the past decade is a direct result of the system of floating exchange rates. While stable and coordinated monetary and fiscal policies would lessen this instability, it remains the case that, for a given set of policies, deviations from purchasing-power and uncovered interest-rate parity will be greater under flexible exchange rates.

The main purpose of this paper is to propose an intervention strategy that would stabilize exchange rates around their parity values and would stabilize interest-rate differentials at levels approximately equal to differences in inflation rates. In the next section, I will summarize the main features of the European Monetary System (EMS) and discuss the modifications to the EMS that would be necessary if the system were to be extended to the major currencies. In the following section, I will describe the technical details of the intervention strategy and I will simulate its performance over the floating-rate period. The results offer convincing evidence that it is possible to create an intervention strategy that is both profitable and stabilizing.

The European Monetary System Model

In the EMS, each currency has a declared parity value against the European Currency Unit and each member country is obligated to intervene to ensure that its currency does not rise or fall outside a range around the parity value. While the EMS has been successful in reducing the volatility of the European cross-rates, the structure has a number of undesirable features.

The first problem is that the parity values are stated in nominal terms. Since the EMS includes countries with different inflation rates, periodic realignments against the ECU are necessary to prevent the high-inflation countries from losing competitiveness against the low-inflation countries. There have been eleven such realignments since the start of the system. Realignments, or devaluations, are discrete changes in exchange rates that offer foreign exchange speculators the possibility of extremely large returns. While the high-inflation countries, particularly France and Italy, have capital controls that have prevented capital flight in the period before realignments, a properly functioning monetary system should have parities that are continually and gradually adjusting to differences in national inflation rates.

The second problem with the EMS is the on/off nature of the intervention strategy. As long as the currency remains within the band, there should be no intervention. When the currency hits the border, the country is meant to intervene in a quantity sufficient to keep the currency within the band. Since the resources of the central bank are limited, this do-or-die strategy may occasionally fail. A better strategy would be a linear intervention rule in which the quantity of intervention is proportional to the deviation of the currency's value from the parity value. Hence a 5 percent deviation could result in an intervention of $10 million, a 10 percent deviation in $20 million, and so on. If the 10 percent deviation were reversed to 5 percent, the central bank would take profits on the $10-million secondary intervention. If the currency returned to parity, the central bank would take profits on the first intervention and maintain a neutral position. With a linear intervention rule, the central bank would be continually intervening in the market in a predictable way.

The third problem with the EMS is the ECU itself. Within the European Monetary System it is reasonable to have a central basket currency as the stabilizing anchor. Within a world monetary system, a more sophisticated multicurrency-based strategy is called for. At one time, the deutsche mark may be overvalued against the dollar and undervalued against the yen. In this case, the optimal strategy would be to borrow in Japanese yen and invest in dollars. Given the set of parities and the national interest rates, there is an optimal portfolio which determines the position that should be taken in each currency. Within this sytem, there is no need for a central currency, be it the SDR or the dollar, against which the other currencies should be fixed.

The fourth problem with the EMS lies in its political dimension. The EMS is an international agreement that requires the national governments to take certain actions to ensure that their currencies stay within the band. With a linear intervention strategy, it would be necessary for the positions in all currencies to be determined simultaneously. Furthermore, the position taken in a given currency might be unrelated to its own circumstances. For example, if all currencies were at their parity values and British interest rates were 10 percent above German rates, it would be optimal to borrow in deutsche marks and lend in sterling. While the Bank of England would probably appreciate the downward pressure on British rates, it would be unreasonable to assume that political capital could be made in Germany from a policy that would tend to cause interest rates to rise. Furthermore, a politically based solution would have to exclude Switzerland, which is prohibited by its constitution from joining international agreements of the EMS variety.

In a world monetary system the intervention should be undertaken by an exchange stabilization fund (ESF), which could be either a part of the International Monetary Fund or an independent international agency. The member countries would each contribute capital to the fund. In a recent Japanese proposal (Hosomi, 1985), suggested capital contributions were to be $100 million for the United States and $50 million for Japan and West Germany. While these figures

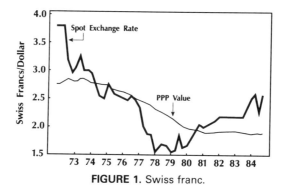

FIGURE 1. Swiss franc.

may appear small relative to the size of the foreign exchange market, the ESF would be able to extend its resources by borrowing additional amounts in overvalued currencies. It is also possible that private-sector funds could also be raised to supplement the resources provided by the government entities.

The role of the ESF would be to publish parity values for the main currencies and to determine an appropriate portfolio of financial instruments. The general trading strategy would be to borrow in currencies that are overvalued relative to the parity values and bear a low-interest yield. Funds borrowed would be invested in high-yielding, undervalued currencies. In the next section, the details of this intervention strategy will be outlined. The concluding section will discuss the stabilizing effects of the strategy on exchange rates and interest rates.

The Intervention Strategy

Figures 1 to 4 illustrate the relationship between a purchasing-power parity measure and the actual exchange rate for the four major currencies. The purchasing-power parity is defined in Eq. (1):

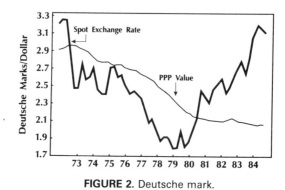

FIGURE 2. Deutsche mark.

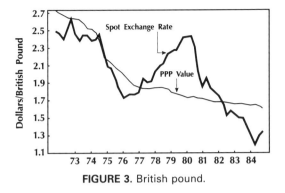

FIGURE 3. British pound.

$$PPP(*/\$) = k(*) \, (CPI(*)/CPI(US)). \tag{1}$$

The CPI indexes are taken from International Financial Statistics; the base year for the indices is 1980. The $k(*)$ consequently represents an estimate of the parity exchange rate for 1980. The values are estimated to minimize the variance of the divergence between the actual rate and the parity over the sample period ranging from the third quarter of 1972 to the second quarter of 1985. The estimated 1980 parity values are:

	PPP($/)*	*PPP($/*)*
Swiss franc	1.9944	.5014
Deutsche mark	2.1541	.4642
Japanese yen ($\times$100)	2.4843	.4025
British pound	0.5852	1.7088

Over time, these values are adjusted by the ratio of the consumer price indexes.

There is certainly room for disagreement concerning both the base values for the parities and the choice of the consumer price

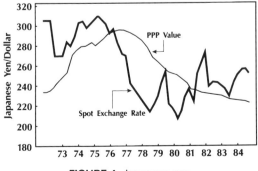

FIGURE 4. Japanese yen.

indexes for the adjustment over time. Other alternatives for the adjustment include the deflator for gross domestic product or the ratio
of the money supplies. In other research I have found that the choice
of a base parity and of the adjustment factor do not have a substantial
influence on the results of strategy.

The reason for this result may be explained by reference to
Figures 1 to 4. In all cases, the actual exchange rate exhibits erratic
fluctuations around the stable parity line. As the actual rate moves
above the line, the ESF would begin to sell dollars. If price moved
back toward the parity, it would purchase the dollars back. Hence
short-term movements lead to buy-low/sell-high interventions that
are profitable independent of the choice of the parity. In addition,
most of the alternative parity measures exhibit similar trends over
the sample period.

In order for the strategy to work, there must be a predictable
tendency for the change in the actual exchange rate to be related to
the deviation of the actual rate from the parity value. For the linear
intervention rule, a model that encompasses this tendency is described in Eq. (2):

$$s_{t+1} - s_t = \alpha \, (\text{PPP}_t - s_t) + u_{t+1} \tag{2}$$

In this equation, s_t represents the log of the exchange rate in period t,
PPP_t is the log of the parity value, α is an adjustment parameter
measuring the rate at which the actual rate converges to the parity
value, and u_t is a residual.

It would be possible to modify Eq. (2) in order to allow for
nonlinear intervention rules. One alternative that appears to work is
to introduce the cubed value of the parity deviation as an additional
independent variable. This is equivalent to assuming that the adjustment parameter, α, is a function of the square of the parity deviation.

$$\alpha = \alpha_0 + \alpha_1 \, (\text{PPP}_t - s_t)^2 \tag{3}$$

Since the α_1 parameter is typically positive, the addition of Eq. (3) to
Eq. (2) results in the expectation that the adjustment velocity will be
more rapid if the deviation from the parity is large.

The adjustment to parity represents the commodity-market
side of the intervention strategy. It is now necessary to consider the
capital-market side. The floating-rate system has also resulted in
wide fluctuations in nominal and real interest-rate differentials.
Many of the problems that can be traced to the system, including the
third-world, agricultural, and banking-debt crises, can be attributed
directly to large, unanticipated movements in interest rates. Movements in real interest rates have direct effects on the economy, and

they also influence foreign exchange rates by attracting capital toward markets with high real interest rates.

We begin by defining the real interest-rate differential as:

$$x_t = f_t - s_t - E_t (PPP_{t+1} - PPP_t) \qquad (4)$$

In Eq. (4), f_t is the log of the three-month forward exchange rate. The term $f_t - s_t$ is the three-month forward premium on the currency that is equal, through the covered interest-rate parity condition, to the nominal interest-rate differential. The second term represents the expected differential rate of inflation. Hence x_t is the real interest-rate differential.

In order to implement this approach, estimates of the expected inflation-rate differential must be formed. I assume that market participants form their expectations of future inflation by considering both the current interest-rate differential and the current inflation. Specifically, forecasts are based upon the equation

$$PPP_{t+1} - PPP_t = \phi(f_t - s_t) + (1 - \phi)(PPP_t - PPP_{t-1}) + v_{t+1} \qquad (5)$$

This equation may be considered as a composite forecast of the inflation-rate differential. The weight, ϕ, was estimated by Zellner's seemingly unrelated regression procedure over the period from 1972Q3 to 1985Q2. In order to increase the precision of the estimate, the weighting factor was constrained to be the same for all the four countries in the sample. The resulting estimate of ϕ was .5016 and the estimated standard error was .047. On the basis of these results, I assume that the expected differential rate of inflation is equal to half of the current interest-rate differential and half of the current inflation-rate differential.

Using this assumption, Eq. (4) can be restated as

$$x_t = .5(f_t - s_t - (PPP_t - PPP_{t-1})). \qquad (6)$$

While this approach may be simplistic, it has the virtue that the real interest rate is easy to compute. Take the nominal differential (10 percent), deduct the inflation-rate differential (5 percent), and the real differential is half of the difference (2.5 percent).

It remains to be seen, however, whether this measure of the real rate differential has a predictable impact on the exchange rate. The idea is that a high real interest rate attracts capital and hence causes the exchange rate to appreciate. If this view is correct, then the β parameter in Eq. (7) should be negative.

$$s_{t+1} - s_t = \alpha(PPP_t - s_t) + \beta(f_t - s_t - (PPP_t - PPP_{t-1})) + u_{t+1} \qquad (7)$$

Equation (7) was estimated using quarterly data over the period from 1972Q2 to 1985Q3. In order to allow for the lagged PPP term and the future spot rate in the dependent period, the estimation sample period runs from 1972Q3 to 1985Q2. The two coefficients were constrained to be the same for each currency, and constant terms were suppressed. The system of equations was estimated using Zellner's seemingly unrelated regression procedure.

$$s_{t+1} - s_t = .0466(PPP_t - s_t) - .2458(f_t - s_t - (PPP_t - PPP_{t-1})) + u_{t+1} \quad (8)$$
$$\phantom{s_{t+1} - s_t = }(.0254) (.2450)$$

	Standard Error	Durbin-Watson
Swiss franc	.0726	1.7133
Deutsche mark	.0645	1.6485
Japanese yen	.0558	1.5525
British pound	.0514	1.3556

Correlation Matrix				
	SF	DM	JY	BP
SF	1			
DM	.85	1		
JY	.68	.59	1	
BP	.53	.58	.45	1

While they are not highly significant, both of the coefficients are of the expected sign. The model predicts that approximately 5 percent of the deviation from purchasing-power parity will be eliminated through the exchange rate over a single quarter. (It is reasonable to assume that prices will also adjust to eliminate divergences from parity, but that is another story.) A favorable real interest-rate differential is associated with an appreciating exchange rate, but this effect is small and uncertain.

The variables in Eq. (8) help predict the expected change in the exchange rate. The expected return from sterilized foreign-exchange intervention is equal to the logarithmic difference between the expected future spot rate and the forward exchange rate.

$$E(r_t) = E(s_{t+1}) - f_t \quad (9)$$

The expected return can be decomposed into the expected appreciation of the currency against the dollar, $E(s_{t+1}) - s_t$, and the forward premium or discount, $f_t - s_t$. These two terms are equivalent to the expected appreciation and the dividend yield on a stock. Because of the unpredictable nature of exchange rates, the variation in the expected return is dominated by the variation in the forward premium or discount. Since the forward premium is equal to the difference in nominal interest rates, the basic intervention strategy involves borrowing in low-yielding currencies and lending in high-yielding currencies. This activity will lead directly to a convergence in nominal interest rates and, since interest-rate movements are an important source of exchange-rate instability, to greater stability in exchange rates.

To define the strategy more explicitly, we solve a mean-variance portfolio allocation problem (see Bilson, 1984). Expected utility is defined to be positively related to expected profits and negatively related to the variance of profits.

$$E(U) = E(r)^t q - (1/2\lambda)q^t \Omega q \qquad (10)$$

In this equation, q is a vector whose typical element is the dollar value of the position in a particular currency. Ω is the covariance matrix of the forecast errors, and λ is a risk-aversion parameter that determines the scale of the position. (The superscript t represents the transpose of the vector.)

The elements of q are chosen to maximize expected utility. The solution to the optimization problem is:

$$q = \lambda \Omega^{-1} E(r) \qquad (11)$$

The positions taken in a currency are generally positively related to the expected return and negatively related to the variance of the return. For illustrative purposes, the factor of proportionality is set equal to $100. This value results in a level of risk comparable to equities if the capital base is assumed to be $1000. This information is of value in assessing the leverage of the portfolio.

The positions described in Table 1 have a number of interesting characteristics. The net dollar position is typically small relative to the positions in the other currencies. For the most part, the program borrowed in dollars in the period from 1972 to 1977, invested in dollars from late 1977 to 1984, and then borrowed for the remainder of the period. This pattern basically matches the periods of dollar strength and weakness over the floating-rate period. Among the European currencies, the program borrowed in low-yielding Swiss francs in order to invest in higher-yielding European currencies. The largest positions occurred in 1973Q4 and 1974Q1, when the Japanese yen was at a 30 percent annualized discount against the dollar.

The main question that we are interested in is the contribution of the program to the stability of the international monetary system. The first approach that we shall adopt toward this question is based on the Friedman–Telser approach, which relates the profitability of the intervention strategy to the contribution to stability. Following

TABLE 1.
Summary of Positions Taken
(Values in U.S. Dollars)

Date	SF	DM	JY	BP	US
72:3	215	−840	333	727	−435
72:4	595	−894	−206	782	−275
73:1	1303	−2258	−743	1462	235
73:2	−1402	463	131	865	−57
73:3	−192	−599	−208	1493	−493
73:4	−3315	121	5644	482	−2932
74:1	−1205	−1247	3480	1171	−2199
74:2	700	−972	−267	433	106
74:3	−187	−542	421	890	−582
74:4	−603	−739	682	1649	−988
75:1	−138	−637	224	779	−227
75:2	−24	−532	102	423	30
75:3	−900	−391	1741	313	−762
75:4	−603	−224	454	936	−563
76:1	−887	−296	1032	762	−611
76:2	−1011	−131	232	1722	−812
76:3	−1027	−625	67	3128	−1542
76:4	−586	−466	−51	1989	−884
77:1	−37	−472	105	671	−266
77:2	513	−727	−582	702	93
77:3	−103	−206	−283	354	239
77:4	37	−226	−683	−46	872
78:1	−535	−68	−338	477	464
78:2	−133	−342	−1281	1322	435
78:3	−1036	259	−1067	1514	330
78:4	−639	−39	−1237	998	918
79:1	−1386	456	260	238	431
79:2	−1471	670	−210	799	211
79:3	−462	20	−66	−263	771
79:4	−928	9	39	548	330
80:1	−954	−182	741	−46	441
80:2	−1120	395	737	377	−389
80:3	−1342	585	459	−45	343
80:4	−245	281	−485	−818	1268
81:1	−916	1267	−442	−686	778
81:2	−85	969	−1177	−1081	1375
81:3	270	313	−1420	−95	932
81:4	−459	688	−794	44	521
82:1	−1032	767	132	−318	450
82:2	−1470	1277	306	−692	577
82:3	−1348	1122	375	−69	−79
82:4	−1093	831	254	−102	109
83:1	−513	199	−16	220	109
83:2	−558	505	−82	30	104
83:3	−849	673	12	288	−125
83:4	−854	887	−306	269	4
84:1	−871	696	−211	324	61
84:2	−530	593	−464	116	285
84:3	−852	759	−333	688	−262
84:4	−148	233	−452	863	−495
85:1	−1534	1223	−414	1397	−672
85:2	−750	735	−81	759	−662

this approach, if a system is profitable, it contributes to the stability of the system. In Table 2, the actual and expected profits generated by the portfolio are described.

The third column in Table 2 describes the evolution of a $1000 investment over the sample period. By the end of the period, the initial investment had appreciated to a value of over $5000. This rate of capital appreciation compares favorably with the return on traditional investments. For example, $1000 invested in market portfolios of equities in 1972 would have appreciated to the following values for each of the major markets.

Exchange Stabilization Fund (1984)	$4645
United States	$1488
United Kingdom	$1399
Japanese yen	$3686
West Germany	$1489

The equity returns are based upon the IMF indexes of industrial share prices. These indexes exclude appreciation as a result of the payment of dividends. Since the ESF appreciation excludes the payment of interest on the base capital, both calculations are underestimates of the true appreciation. Despite the difficulties in making this type of comparison, it is clear that the ESF appreciation is far greater than the appreciation of the United States, United Kingdom, and West Germany equity markets and that the ESF portfolio also dominates the Japanese equity market.

The series are also roughly comparable in terms of their absolute risk. The largest declines in value over a one-year period are around 20 percent for both the equity portfolios and the ESF portfolio. The standard deviation of the ESF fund may be slightly larger than the standard deviation of the equity portfolios, but this is due to the fact that the ESF returns are skewed toward abnormally large returns. The average loss over the sample period was 3.7 percent, with a standard deviation of 2.9 percent; the average gain was 7.7 percent, with a standard deviation of 6.6 percent. The ESF portfolio consequently has desirable risk characteristics.

While the absolute risk of the portfolio is important for some purposes, the financial risk of the portfolio is more appropriately measured by the correlation of the returns with the market. Since the ESF portfolio consists predominantly of spreads across currencies, and since the portfolio can be either long or short, there is no reason to expect that the portfolio returns would be correlated with a particular market. However, since the portfolio tends to borrow in low-yielding currencies and invests in high-yielding currencies, the beta

TABLE 2.
Actual and Expected Profits
(Values in U.S. Dollars)

Date	Expected Profit	Actual Profit	Cumulative Capital
72:2			1000
72:3	15	-13	987
72:4	15	9	996
73:1	77	-128	868
73:2	39	13	880
73:3	36	56	929
73:4	558	289	1197
74:1	257	160	1389
74:2	11	56	1467
74:3	18	-64	1373
74:4	59	81	1484
75:1	15	-57	1400
75:2	7	42	1458
75:3	57	-24	1423
75:4	21	-51	1351
76:1	35	-35	1303
76:2	57	-63	1221
76:3	163	140	1392
76:4	65	99	1530
77:1	8	0	1530
77:2	14	30	1576
77:3	6	-28	1532
77:4	20	-42	1468
78:1	21	-16	1444
78:2	61	-37	1391
78:3	85	192	1658
78:4	79	184	1963
79:1	39	7	1976
79:2	48	-24	1929
79:3	19	22	1971
79:4	29	143	2253
80:1	36	-10	2231
80:2	20	57	2358
80:3	30	83	2554
80:4	37	87	2776
81:1	35	40	2887
81:2	61	175	3392
81:3	39	-15	3341
81:4	21	87	3632
82:1	19	86	3944
82:2	40	31	4067
82:3	21	20	4148
82:4	15	42	4322
83:1	5	8	4357
83:2	5	-11	4309
83:3	10	-4	4292
83:4	15	28	4412
84:1	14	17	4487
84:2	11	0	4487
84:3	20	-36	4325
84:4	17	74	4645
85:1	66	71	4975
85:2	20	40	5174

Note: Cumulative capital = $K_t = K_{t-1}(1 + \pi_t/1000)$ where π_t equals actual profits.

of the ESF portfolio will tend to be negative to the extent that increases in interest rates are associated with declining stock prices. In fact, the largest declines in equity values occurred in 1973 and 1974 because of the rise in oil prices. This was the period of the largest expected and actual returns on the ESF portfolio.

The preceding analysis suggests that the ESF portfolio has desirable risk and return characteristics. The question remains whether investment in the portfolio would contribute to the stability of the foreign exchange market. Since this is a counterfactual question, it is not possible to provide a definitive or statistically based answer. Some comments are, however, in order.

To begin with, it is important to stress that the intervention implicit in the portfolio-selection rule is of the sterilized variety. The ESF portfolio borrows and lends in different currencies, but it does not alter the quantity of money outstanding in any currency. The primary effect is consequently on interest rates rather than exchange rates. To the extent that the ESF activities alter the demand for debt denominated in the different currencies, the intervention should result in interest-rate differentials that are more closely correlated with inflation-rate differentials. The extent of the influence depends upon the size of the fund's assets and on the extent to which the fund's activities influence the decisions of other investment managers.

As far as the exchange rate is concerned, the purchasing-power parity component of the trading strategy does encourage investments in undervalued currencies and borrowings in overvalued currencies. In the short term, the current account may be considered as fixed so that the immediate effect of an implicit capital-account surplus will be to exert upward pressure on the exchange rate. In the longer term, the inflow of investment capital should cause interest rates to decline and the demand for money to increase. Hence, although the causal relationships are not precise, there is a reasonable presumption that the portfolio-intervention strategy will also stabilize exchange rates around the purchasing-power parity level.

The main purpose of the ESF portfilio is not to stabilize the market by the use of its own market power but to create a model portfolio that will influence the decisions of other managers in the investment community. If managers become aware that portfolio intervention strategies offer a good risk/return tradeoff relative to conventional investments, they may become more willing to undertake activities that will result in a greater degree of capital-market integration. This tendency could be reinforced by partially directing monetary policy toward the achievement of the ESF funds objectives.

Conclusion

Many studies have shown that changes in exchange rates are unpredictable. This is a characteristic that exchange rates share with other asset prices. In this paper I have attempted to demonstrate that the unpredictable nature of exchange rates does not preclude the formulation of a successful intervention strategy. The strategy I have proposed appears to be superior to conventional instruments as an investment, and it also has a direct effect on the stability of nominal interest-rate differentials. To the extent that the variability of interest-rate differentials has been a source of instability in exchange rates, it is possible that the intervention strategy would also stabilize exchange rates.

The problems with the post–Bretton Woods monetary system are associated with the instability of both interest-rate differentials and exchange rates. The demands for protection from foreign competition are also related both to interest rates and exchange rates. The intervention program outlined in this paper is an attempt to reduce the demand for protectionist legislation by reducing the instability of the international financial markets. Intervention strategies do not constitute fundamental reforms of the system since they impose no constraint on the monetary independence of the participating countries. Perhaps for this reason, these strategies may be easier to implement. And if they are successful, the strategies may remove the need for fundamental reforms.

Summary

The system of floating exchange rates that has evolved during the past decade has been a source of instability in international capital and commodity markets. Economic entities who have been adversely affected by the system have reasonably sought protection from foreign competition through demands for tariffs, quotas, and other barriers to trade. Apart from the inherent inefficiencies and inequities of these types of protectionist measures, it is unlikely that legislative efforts can adjust rapidly enough to counter the volatility of exchange rates. Furthermore, the probability is that previous protectionist measures will be retained after the rationale for them has been removed. The protectionist path consequently leads to a progressive deterioration in world trade.

The alternative to protectionism is a structured program of intervention designed to ensure greater stability of exchange rates and interest rates. The European Monetary System has been a qualified success in stabilizing the exchange rates between the currencies of the members of the European Monetary System. It has consequently been worthwhile to examine the feasibility of extending the EMS framework to a World Monetary System linking the prices of the four major currencies—the dollar, yen, mark, and pound. In this paper I have discussed the main features of a world stabilization fund and traced the hypothetical performance of the fund over the floating-rate system. The evidence suggests that such a fund would be both profitable and stabilizing.

The views expressed are solely the responsibility of the author.

References

Bilson, John F. O. (1984) Purchasing Power Parity as a Trading Strategy, *Journal of Finance* 39 (July): 714–722.

——— (1985) Macroeconomic Stability and Flexible Exchange Rates, *American Economic Review* 75 (May): 62–67.

Dornbusch, Rudiger (1976) Expectations and Exchange Rate Dynamics, *Journal of Political Economy* 84 (December): 1161–1176.

Friedman, Milton (1953) The Case for Flexible Exchange Rates. *Essays in Positive Economics*. Chicago: University of Chicago Press, pp. 157–203.

Hosomi, Takashi (1985) Towards a More Stable International Monetary System, *Japan Center for International Finance*, pp. 1–35.

Telser, Lester (1959) A Theory of Speculation Relating Profitability and Stability, *Review of Economics and Statistics* 41: 295–301.

20

Dollar Variability, the New Protectionism, Trade and Financial Performance

JOSEPH ASCHHEIM, MARTIN J. BAILEY,
AND GEORGE S. TAVLAS

> Let us remember that the uncertainty created by unpegged exchange rates is almost always smaller and far less harmful than the uncertainty that stems from incorrectly pegged exchange rates.
>
> Fritz Machlup,
> The Alignment of Foreign Exchange Rates (1972), p. 94

Recent years have featured the strengthening of the dollar in the face of a combination of U.S. budget deficits with huge U.S. trade-account and current-account deficits. Along with a robust recovery from a severe recession, there has been a moderation of domestic inflation, a global dollar appreciation, and an intensification of domestic pressures for U.S. protectionism against other countries, mirroring similar pressures elsewhere. Whether the new protectionism is due, partly or wholly, to the strengthening of the dollar under exchange-rate flexibility is a vexing question. We address this question in what follows.

As a first step we consider the links between budget deficits and external payments. "Protectionism Revived" examines dollar appreciation as a rationale for the revival of protectionism. The next section analyzes the compatibility of dollar appreciation with massive deficit financing, followed by an examination of empirical

From the George Washington University, Washington, D.C.; the University of Maryland, College Park, Maryland, and U.S. Department of State; and the International Monetary Fund, Washington, D.C.

results regarding the impact of exchange-rate variability upon trade performance in the Big Seven industrial countries. We then explore the influence of exchange-rate variability on global financial performance and consider the interaction of U.S. competitiveness with dollar floating before summarizing our results. In brief, we find that flexible exchange rates automatically move so as to maintain the American competitive position in the world economy, even in the face of fiscal deficits at home and abroad.

Budget Deficits and International Payments

A major issue with regard to U.S. budget deficits has been the question whether they raise interest rates. Whatever the final outcome of the controversy, recent work indicates that even if there is a significant impact of budget deficits on nominal interest rates, there may be no significant effect of budget deficits on real interest rates (Galli and Masera, 1983). Moreover, in an open-economy framework, the strength of the dollar vis-à-vis other national currencies reflects trade and capital movements within the worldwide network of commerce and finance.[1]

Thus, contemporary U.S. economic policy aimed at combating stagflation has had a dual effect of (1) attracting capital from the rest of the world that finances an excess of imports over exports, moderating domestic inflationary pressures, and (2) expanding the availability of loanable funds for U.S. domestic investment, thereby offsetting the crowding-out that cyclical budget deficits would otherwise exert. This twofold effect is the reverse of the beggar-my-neighbor policy of devaluation as a technique of stimulating economic recovery from recession or depression, particularly associated with the depression of the 1930s. Rather than a beggar-my-neighbor policy of devaluation, an enrich-my-neighbor policy of upvaluation has transformed the process of U.S. economic recovery into an engine of *global* economic recovery. Global recovery has been stimulated by rising U.S. imports, along with mounting capital inflows, from the rest of the world.

In current public discussion of the effects of large U.S. budget deficits, it is often taken for granted that such deficits represent a drain on private saving, reducing net national saving, bidding-up real interest rates, crowding-out productive investment, and slowing growth. Abroad, such propositions are used to suggest that U.S. deficits harm foreign economic growth (by attracting saving to the

---

[1] See Pearce (1983) for an overview of the main approaches to exchange-rate determination.

United States at the expense of other countries) and worsen the international debt crisis (by increasing the debt-servicing burden).

While these conclusions follow logically from the standard Keynesian analytic framework predominant in the postwar years, they have been challenged by a "new classical" doctrine that takes a different view of private-sector saving behavior.[2] According to this doctrine, households take into account and make provision for such future taxes by increasing their current saving to offset the government's borrowing. Assuming such "super rational" behavior, the impact of financial markets upon increased government borrowing is offset by greater private saving, and real interest rates and investment are unaffected. Only the level of government spending affects private spending; taxation and government borrowing are equivalent in their effects on net national saving, interest rates, and investment.

This doctrine (sometimes referred to as the Ricardian Equivalence Theorem) is subject to two caveats.[3] First, the deficits must not be so large in relation to the rate of increase in nominal GNP that interest-bearing government debt would grow forever relative to the size of the economy. Second, even if deficits do not depress net saving and capital formation, a larger interest-bearing debt does impose a "dead weight" burden on the economy due to the distorting economic effects of higher taxes required to make interest payments.

Insofar as capital imports from abroad contribute to holding down the dead weight burden on the domestic economy, they facilitate the financing of budget deficits. Recognition of the importance of this point—in terms of the potential for providing massive foreign financing through capital imports—became evident in the Reagan administration within its first year in office. In December 1981, William Niskanen, a member of President Reagan's Council of Economic Advisors, maintained (see Haberler, 1982) that U.S. interest rates, rather than being much affected by domestic budget deficits, are primarily determined by international capital markets. A rise in U.S. interest rates will attract capital from abroad. Hence, U.S. budget deficits will largely be financed by capital imports, which will counteract any crowding-out of domestic private investment.

In the spring of 1982, Niskanen's viewpoint was met with skepticism by Gottfried Haberler. Haberler (1982) then recalled that in 1977 and 1978 current-account deficits of $14 billion had frightened both policymakers and financial markets and were widely viewed as the cause of dollar depreciation. He expressly deplored as a sad spectacle the richest country in the world importing capital to fi-

---

[2] For a recent discussion see Kormendi (1983).

[3] We are indebted to G. Paul Balabanis for pointing out to us these considerations.

nance budget deficits on a massive scale. He predicted that there would ensue an outcry of indignation coupled with a variety of defensive and retaliatory measures against the U.S. economy. He then firmly averred that the system of managed floating of the major currencies would endure. He therefore ruled out a restoration of the Bretton Woods system of "stable but adjustable" exchange rates, let alone the gold standard. The merit of this prediction is enhanced by subsequent confirmation of the compatibility between substantial capital imports and dollar appreciation under exchange-rate flexibility. We return to the significance of this confirmation in "Dollar Floating with Large Government Deficits," below.

Protectionism Revived

The decade beginning the post–Bretton Woods era has been characterized (Kindleberger, 1978, p. 16) as "a new world order after the breakdown of the dollar system—if it has in fact broken down." Among the world's national currencies, the predominant position of the dollar has been reaffirmed since the great American recession of the early 1980s as the dollar has appreciated.

Since the termination of fixed parities under the Bretton Woods system, the spot (market) rate of exchange has displayed movements of wide variability. Yet, however volatile exchange-rate behavior has turned out to be, the decade of the 1970s can be characterized as one of dollar depreciation (Schmidt, 1979; Cohen, 1981), whereas the period of 1980–1984 was marked by dollar appreciation.

So long as currency depreciation is the perceived tendency, the quest for protectionism that domestic industries and groups may voice is arguably moderated by the general realization that currency depreciation enhances the international competitive position of the economy concerned. Hence, even in the face of mass unemployment, the protectionist-minded may defer to the recognition that currency depreciation stimulates both exporting and import-competing industries. Conversely, when currency appreciation is the perceived tendency, the international competitive position of the strengthening-currency country undergoes erosion.

Erosion of a competitive position draws attention to particular industries and income groups in which the clustering of economic adversity (whether cyclical or secular) is pronounced. Even as recovery convincingly proceeds, the concomitant experience of currency appreciation provides political ammunition to the protectionist-minded. A prima facie case for adopting autarkic policy measures stems from a weakened competitive position of both exporting and import-competing industries.

Such is the analytical underpinning of the beggar-my-neighbor-

policy approach. Involving a chain reaction of competitive devaluations in a global-depression setting, this policy depiction has typi-
fied macroeconomic thinking since Keynes's *General Theory*. It was
largely as an antidote to the perceived tendency of global economic
contraction to trigger retaliation via devaluation that the fixity of
parities emerged as the centerpiece of the Bretton Woods system.

The experience of the American recovery of 1983–1984 negates
the Keynesian beggar-my-neighbor approach of countercontrac-
tionary exchange-rate policy. The vigor and robustness of the recovery are embodied in, as well as illustrated by, not only a lowered
unemployment rate but also a simultaneous upsurge in the number
of jobs.[4] The net growth in job opportunities the American economy
has created over the last decade has been most impressive when
recognizing that this period (1974–1983) included the two severest
energy dislocations of modern times as well as the deepest recession
of the last half-century.[5]

A domestic by-product of dollar appreciation, in the context of
recovery from the severest recession in half a century, has been a
drive for a new American protectionism. The new protectionism
combines diverse strands. One of these is a multiplicity of nontariff
trade-restrictive measures. A second is a campaign in support of a
new industrial policy. A third is a politicizing of trade policy by
favoritism toward selected countries. A fourth is the phenomenon of
exchange-rate protection. We consider each in turn.

Under the impact of diverse domestic and foreign pressures,
complex political compromises have resulted in an increasing variety of nontariff trade measures. Such measures as quotas, price trig-
gers, domestic-content rules, and the like are targeted to favor particular industries and income groups. The close focusing of nontariff
trade measures has the political advantage of concealing the price-
raising effects of protectionism while responding to the outcry for
adjustment assistance to clusterings of economic adversity. A systematic review (Baldwin, 1982) of the rationale for such nontariff
trade measures points to the prevalence of conditions under which
these measures frequently fail to accomplish their purported objective and to the consequent pressure from the aided sectors for more
help—that is, for further protection. Perceptive and penetrating as
such critical analysis of the inefficiency of the new trade policy has

---

[4] During the first three years of the latest recovery, about 8.5 million new jobs
had been created.

[5] From 1973 to 1983, almost 18 million new jobs were created in the United
States. By comparison, during the same period OECD lost 1.5 million jobs; see OECD
(1984). As of this writing (November 1985), employment in the United States has risen
since late 1982 by more than triple the gain in the United Kingdom, roughly twice the
rise in Japan, and contrasts with declines in West Germany, Italy, and France.

been, it is essentially oriented to the trade or commercial side. What we seek to consider further is the monetary aspect of this new protectionism: i.e., the nexus between dollar appreciation under flexible exchange rates and the new protectionism.

In the face of an onslaught of foreign competition, there has also emerged a new political coalition of economically powerful personalities mounting a campaign for the adoption by the U.S. government of an industrial policy. Central to this policy is the national involvement of governmental decision making in picking among rival firms the winners- and losers-to-be, respectively—those to be favored or disfavored by discretionary measures that would be federally determined and applied.

Advocates of industrial policy have posited a foreign-trade rationale for their policy orientation. They regard American firms as increasingly failing to meet growing industrial competition from abroad. More fundamentally, they envisage industrial policy as a manifestation of democracy itself, not quite as an economic ideal but as an alternative preferable to either outright protectionism or to a drift toward "lemon socialism" (Thurow, 1984). It is left ambiguous, however, whether all socialism is "lemon," and whether central economic planning is the ultimate implication of an industrial policy that is distinct from "lemon socialism." In any event, a robust economic expansion and dollar appreciation in a regimen of free convertibility with floating exchange rates are about as far a cry from "America drifting toward lemon socialism" (whether national socialism or international socialism) as can be conjured.

In contrast, a more challenging facet of the new protectionism is the emergence of instances of subordination of U.S. trade policy to what are perceived as needs of foreign policy. Newly highlighted (Bhagwati, 1984) cases in point are: the 1984 Caribbean Basin Recovery Act providing favored, one-way preferences on a select group of products and to a select group of countries in one region; the movement since 1981 toward a U.S.–Israel Free Trade Area; and recent discussions between the United States and Canada aiming at a bilateral and sectoral program for a free trade area. We are thereby warned (Bhagwati, 1984) of a new tendency to supplant *multilateralism* with *bilateralism* after the liberalization of world trade in the decades of the 1950s and 1960s under the impact of the General Agreement on Tariffs and Trade (GATT). On strong theoretical grounds we are thereby also alerted to the danger of trade diversion supplanting trade creation that the replacement of multilateralism with bilateralism poses (Bhagwati, 1984).

In the meantime, while well-grounded, concern over the replacement of multilateralism with bilateralism is not negated by the surge in U.S. demand for imports across the board. Trade liberalization on a bilateral and sectoral basis, if pursued actively long enough, merges into a multilateralizing approach. In other words, granting the second-best character of the bilateral and sectoral approach, its replication, if sustained, transforms bilateralism into multilateralism. Without our thereby condoning departures from multilateralism, an eventual proliferation of bilateralism might on balance be liberalizing, rather than constraining, world trade.

The extraordinary magnitude of U.S. trade deficits reflects a veritable flood of both manufactured and agricultural imports from developing, as well as developed, economies. In turn, the surge in U.S. demand for imports stimulates other-country exports and helps their recovery while boosting their interest rates just as it boosts U.S. rates. Furthermore, insofar as U.S. interest rates attract foreign investors (Wojnilower, 1983), a net drain on foreign capital markets can occur only through an enlarged current-account deficit in the U.S. balance of payments. (Without that, an inflow of foreign capital would necessarily be offset by an outflow of capital.) Such an enlarged deficit can, of course, result from appreciation of the dollar. When it does, U.S. imports are further stimulated, additionally enhancing economic recovery abroad at the same time that foreign interest rates rise. In short, if the U.S. deficit were raising interest rates in other countries, that result could obtain only in step with a boost to recovery in those countries. Accordingly, under exchange-rate flexibility, the mobility of international capital flows interacts both rationally and functionally[6] with interest-rate differentials that are price-level-adjusted.

Within a flexible exchange-rate system, the level of the exchange rate is a by-product of fiscal and monetary policies interacting with protection policies in different countries. In this context, the concept of exchange-rate protection has been advanced (e.g., Corden, 1985) as implying attempted manipulation of the exchange rate in order to increase the profitability of export and import-competing industries at the expense of nontradeable industries. Such manipulation would also generate a current-account surplus (or a smaller deficit) while simultaneously augmenting the volume of lending, or reducing the volume of borrowing, abroad. Thus in a floating exchange-rate system with significant intervention in the foreign-exchange market, intervention to moderate an appreciation is usually intended to provide some exchange-rate protection. In contrast to exchange-rate protection, ordinary protection involves favoring one part of the tradeable sector over others, without neces-

---

[6] On functionality see, for example, Aschheim and Park (1976), McKinnon (1979), Murphy (1979), and Cohen (1981).

sarily altering the current account and the level of lending or borrowing abroad.

The appeal of exchange-rate protection is apt to be a tempting one at a time when an exponent of comparative advantage as the bedrock of world trade pronounces the economic policies of the Reagan administration as yielding a 50 percent overvaluation of the U.S. dollar (Samuelson, 1985; see also Marris, 1984). Even for a government that does not entirely share such an exchange-rate assessment, it may be difficult to withstand the temptation to resort to exchange-rate protection in the face of persistently huge fiscal deficits. A related contentious question is whether possible resort to exchange-rate protection can be rendered cost-effective, even if not downright counterproductive. The significance of the latter question is enhanced by the possibility that the international trading climate may coalesce a sizable number of major trading partners to exert pressure on an ally so as to implement exchange-rate protection. A case in point is the unloading by the United States and ten allied nations of $10 billion on foreign-exchange markets between January 21 and March 1, 1985, one of the largest coordinated interventions against the dollar since the advent of floating in 1973 (Federal Reserve Bank of New York, 1985). Though some dollar depreciation ensued, a partial reappreciation followed. Whether moderate intervention is sufficient to reverse the course of a currency remains an open question.

At this writing the chief financial officials of the United States, West Germany, the United Kingdom, France, and Japan concluded an agreement in New York on September 22, 1985, to cooperate toward lowering the value of the U.S. dollar by concerted intervention in the foreign-exchange market. This agreement was reached in a open bid to head off a proliferation of moves toward protectionism in America. It thus appears that the largely free floating of the dollar characteristic of the period of dollar appreciation during 1980–1984 has since early 1985 been compromised as a concession to protectionist pressures and the attendant risks of a world trade war.

Dollar Floating with Large Government Deficits

With an eye to the future, we assume that U.S. government budget deficits will remain very large throughout the 1980s.[7] Suppose further that, despite at best mixed evidence, a significant effect of fiscal deficits on interest rates exists. In turn, such an effect on interest rates depends upon a positive effect of deficits (that is, of debt-

---

[7] As of this writing, official projections of U.S. fiscal budget deficits are above $150 billion annually over the next several years.

financed tax cuts) on consumption or a negative effect on net national saving—i.e., that the decline in public saving is not offset by a concurrent rise in private saving. This effect on consumption stimulates a slack economy and hastens the recovery. More rapid recovery and expansion are associated with rising interest rates.

Has, however, the recent policy mix in the United States been retarding recovery abroad, especially in Western Europe? Certainly such was the gist (DeGrauwe and Fratianni, 1983) of the European critique of U.S. financial policy voiced by Messrs. François Mitterand, Helmut Schmidt, Valerie Giscard d'Estaing, Denis Healey, and others. The essential point analytically invalidating this high-level European critique is the shift in exchange-rate regime from fixed rates to floating. A U.S. policy mix of fiscal looseness and monetary restraint would be contractionary for Europe if European currencies were pegged to the dollar. A policy of monetary restraint in the United States temporarily raises real interest rates in the American economy, thereby stimulating capital inflow from Europe. But because of the fixity of exchange rates, U.S. demand for European goods and services is not stimulated as it would be if the dollar were allowed to appreciate.

In contrast, consider the same financial-policy mix under floating exchange rates. An expansionary fiscal policy and a restrictive monetary policy in the United States engender an appreciation of the dollar vis-à-vis European currencies. The dollar appreciation enlarges the U.S. current-account deficit and augments the stimulus of demand for European goods and services beyond what the fixity of exchange rates would permit. This contrast between fixed and floating exchange rates is dramatized by the enormity of both the current-account and especially the trade-account deficit that the "Reagan–Volcker policy mix" has evinced under the floating exchange-rate regime of "Regan–Treasury" vintage.

It emerges from our foregoing analysis that even in the face of the new protectionism, the fiscal-monetary policy mix that supports the recent U.S. recovery amid a modest domestic inflation has constituted the proving ground for the analytical (as well as political) reconciliation between Keynesian fiscalism and Chicago monetarism. Under open-market determination of relative currency values, exchange-rate *variability* has proved to be the safety valve of U.S. economic expansion as a catalyst of world economic recovery.

It has been ascribed (Tobin, 1984, p. 102) to "pure serendipity" that the Reagan administration timed a classic Keynesian antirecessionary fiscal policy to coincide with a contracyclical change in monetary policy in late 1982. Less charitably, the fiscal-monetary policy mix of the Reagan administration has been reproached abroad for lending aid and comfort to the dark forces of protectionism via the prodigious dollar appreciation ascribed to this mix, which in turn affords the pretext of the erosion of U.S. export competitiveness. But the compromising of global trade liberalization is arguably a modest price for the rest of the world to have had to pay for U.S. adherence to floating exchange rates in the presence of as great a stimulus to world trade as the U.S. payments account exerted during the recent great recession.

Exchange-Rate Variability and Trade Performance

The theory of "optimum currency areas," so named by Robert Mundell (1961) in his seminal contribution, focuses on the choice between fixed and flexible exchange rates in the framework of economic characteristics of the countries or regions under consideration. The question of what constitutes optimality of currency areas is part of the more general question of the optimality of exchange-rate regimes (Tower and Willet, 1976). Alternatively stated, whether the formation of a currency area is desirable will depend essentially on what type of exchange-rate system will be adopted if the currency area is not formed.

Accordingly, the quest for an optimum exchange-rate system calls for the stipulation of a criterion (or of criteria) by which the effects of exchange-rate variability can be evaluated. At least two criteria can be identified. One is to assess the impact of exchange-rate variability on international trade flows. A second is to assess the impact of exchange-rate variability on the performance of foreign-exchange markets.

In terms of the first criterion, the crucial issue is whether exchange-rate volatility reduces the volume and/or distorts the pattern of world trade. Perhaps the most serious drawback that has been ascribed to exchange-rate variability is its influence upon the international trading climate. Fluctuations of exchange rates engender swings in international competitiveness and, correspondingly, in employment levels of import-competing and export industries. In this regard, the U.S. unemployment problem in the early 1980s has at least partly been attributed to the appreciation of the dollar (e.g., Corden, 1985), which, in turn, has been adduced as a rationale for the clamor for sectoral protection. Moreover, it has been suggested that the net global effect of exchange-rate variability is protectionist: protective measures are more readily imposed than dismantled and, once imposed, acquire an entrenched constituency. Insofar as such an overall net effect on a global scale obtains, it might be discernible in reduced levels of particular countries' volume of international trade. In what follows, we investigate whether such a tendency exists.

Recent time-series studies dealing with the effects of exchange-rate variability on trade flows have yielded mixed results. For example, in a study investigating the impact of exchange-rate uncertainty on twenty-two manufacturing and primary-product sectors in Brazil, Coes (1981) found that nominal exchange-rate volatility has had a negative and highly significant impact on export volumes. Similarly, in a study dealing with Germany and the United States, Akhtar and Hilton (1984a) found that nominal exchange-rate variability reduced the export volumes of manufactured goods for both countries and that "the link between variability and trade has become stronger in recent years" (p. 15). Cushman (1983) used real exchange-rate variability in his estimation of fourteen bilateral trade flows (all involving the United States or the Federal Republic of Germany) among industrial countries and found a significant negative effect on trade quantities arising from that variability in six of these cases. However, an extension of Cushman's work by the research department of the IMF (1984) covering exports from the seven largest industrial countries—Canada, France, Germany, Italy, Japan, the United Kingdom, and the United States—to each of the other six (for a total of forty-two estimated equations) produced only two cases where the coefficient on exchange-rate variability was negative and statistically significant.[8]

Despite the mixed results from time-series studies, much policy discussion in international forums has proceeded as though a negative association between exchange-rate variability and industrial-country trade has been firmly established. For example, a recent report produced by the Group of Twenty-Four (1985), which represents all of the Third World nations in the IMF, and a companion document produced for the Group of Ten (1985) by its deputies argue that the present floating exchange-rate system has not lived up to expectations. A main weakness cited by both reports is that volatile exchange rates have "discouraged" trade (Group of Twenty-Four, 1985, p. 19; Group of Ten, 1985, p. 9).

This section presents further evidence on the determinants of real exports of the Big Seven OECD countries. In order to examine whether exchange-rate variability has exerted an impact on trade flows since the advent of floating, we estimated regressions for each of the following countries—Canada, France, Germany, Italy, Japan, the United Kingdom, and the United States. The regressions, using quarterly data, cover the interval 1973:I through 1984:III, the last

---

[8] Cross-sectional studies have for the most part supported the view that exchange-rate variability affects the pattern, but not the volume, of trade. For overviews of the cross-sectional literature see Farrell, DeRosa, and McCown (1983), IMF (1984, p. 20), and Thursby and Thursby (1985, pp. 154–158).

quarter for which all the relevant data were available at the time of writing. We chose to begin our study with 1973:I for two reasons: (1) That date corresponds to the time of the formal abandonment of the Bretton Woods regime of fixed exchange rates and (2) since several major nations had begun to allow their currencies to float in foreign-exchange markets several years earlier, the choice of 1973:I as the beginning of our estimation period allowed us to incorporate lagged values on exchange-rate variability in the regressions. The estimated regressions are of the following form:

$$\log X_i = \log a_1 + a_2 \log Y + a_3 \log RP_i + a_4 \log OP + a_5 V_i + e_i \quad (1)$$

where X_i is the volume of exports of country i, Y is real GDP of industrial trading-partner nations, RP_i is a measure of relative prices of traded goods of country i to those of its trading partners, OP represents real export earnings of oil-producing countries, V is ex-change-rate variability. The residual e is assumed to be a random error term with Gauss–Markov properties.

The formulation of proxies for each of these independent variables entails potential problems. Economic theory suggests that income in trading-partner countries should be a determinant of a nation's exports. Quarterly GDP (GNP) data for thirteen OECD nations are available for the period under study here.[9] Similar data for LDCs are not available. Turning first to the developed countries, for each of the seven countries whose trade we study we constructed a series for aggregate real GDP of the other twelve OECD nations for which quarterly data are available over the estimation period as our industrial-country-income variable, Y. The aggregation of national GDP series necessitates their conversion to a common currency—in our case, U.S. dollars. During the period of investigation, however, the foreign-exchange value of the U.S. dollar underwent considerable fluctuation, and we want to ensure that our results are not influenced by the particular exchange-rate level chosen for the dollar. Hence, two series on Y for each country were constructed. In one series, Y was valued at third-quarter-1980 exchange rates for the dollar (a time of a "low" dollar). In the other series, Y was determined on the basis of fourth-quarter-1984 exchange rates (a time of a "high" dollar).

Previous empirical studies dealing with the determinants of industrial-country exports have not considered the impact of oil exporters' earnings on those exports. However, since 1973, both oil

---

[9] The countries for which quarterly data on real GDP are available over the estimation period are Australia, Austria, Canada, Finland, France, Germany, Italy, Japan, Norway, Sweden, Switzerland, the United Kingdom, and the United States. In 1982, these thirteen countries accounted for 91.9 percent of total real OECD GDP.

producers' export earnings and their importance as export markets for industrial nations have increased greatly. Therefore, we wish to include them in our study. For these countries, however, we posit that it is their ability to purchase industrial-nation exports with their own export earnings—rather than the volume of their GDPs—that determines their purchases of developed-country goods. (That is, we assume that these countries' imports are determined by foreign-exchange availability rather than income.) Hence, we use the dollar value of the export earnings of oil-producing countries (as defined by the IMF) deflated by the dollar-denominated export-unit-value indexes of the industrial nations taken as a whole to represent the real purchasing power of oil exporters as it pertains to the exports of the developed nations. We treat developed-nation and oil-producing trading partners separately since the two groups of countries may well have different import elasticities with respect to "income."

The series on relative prices, RP, should, in theory, be the ratio of export prices of country i to those of its major trading partners. While export-price (unit-value) indexes for each of the Big Seven exist on a quarterly basis (and were used as the numerators of our relative-price ratios), such indexes do not exist for the OECD as a whole (let alone the OECD less each of the Big Seven). One possible proxy for an aggregate (across countries) export-price series would be an aggregate wholesale-price index. Even here, however, such a series for the OECD as a whole does not exist on a quarterly basis, to our knowledge. Another possible proxy is the OECDwide consumer price index, which does exist on a quarterly basis although its correlation with the OECD WPI is by no means one-to-one. We tried two price indexes as denominators for the relative-price terms in our equations: the OECD CPI (our variable of choice) and the U.S. WPI (as a proxy for the OECD WPI). For most of the countries, the former variable produced statistically significant results; for the remainder, the latter did. Our choice of variables is discussed in the notes to Table 1.

In order to capture the impacts of changes in the overall movement of a currency's exchange rate on a country's exports, we used the nominal effective rates for the currencies of the Big Seven countries published by Morgan Guaranty Bank. Since we are interested here in the volatility of exchange rates (rather than whether they are rising or falling around a trend), we have selected the absolute value of the quarter-to-quarter percentage change in the nominal effective exchange rate as our measure of exchange-rate volatility.[10] Thus, the

---

[10] While most studies use the standard deviation of the exchange rate as a measure of instability, the issue of a suitable measure of instability has been the subject of debate. See Rana (1981; 1984) and Brodsky (1984).

measure of variability used is:

$$V_{i,t} = (E_{i,t} - E_{i,t-1})/E_{i,t-1} \qquad (2)$$

where $V_{i,t}$ is the absolute value of the percentage change in the nominal trade-weighted exchange rate, E, of country i. In the results reported below, $V_{i,t}$ is entered into the equations in both current-period form and as an eight-period, second-degree polynomial-distributed-lag over quarters t through $t - 7$. The latter formulation was used in order to capture possible delayed responses of exports to exchange-rate variability.

With regard to the other regressors used, our intention was to avoid excessive manipulation of lag structures that could give the impression of having employed search procedures. Accordingly, for most of the countries we used Y, RP, and OP in current-period form. The exceptions are: (1) the RP term in the Japanese and the U.K. equations appears as a second-degree, eight-quarter polynomial-distributed lag, and (2) the oil-earnings' term in the Japanese and U.S. equations appears with a one-period lag. The oil-earnings' term was insignificant and therefore dropped from the equations for Canada, while the RP term was insignificant and dropped from the equations for Italy.

The regression results are reported in Table 1. Two sets of equations—(1a) and (1b), and (2a) and (2b)—are reported for each country. In equation set (1), the exchange-rate volatility variable is entered in its current-period form, while equation set (2) includes the eight-quarter polynomial-distributed lag on exchange-rate volatility. Equations with the letter a calculate aggregate developed-country trading-partner real GDP on the basis of the 1980:III bilateral exchange rates between the U.S. dollar and the currencies of the other OECD countries while in equations with the letter b the 1984:IV bilateral exchange rates are used. All variables except exchange-rate volatility are in terms of logarithms. (As noted above, the volatility variable is the absolute value of a percentage change.) A serial-correlation correction was performed on the equations for each country except the United Kingdom. (No autocorrelation correction of the U.K. equations was necessary.) A nonparametric test for the presence of seasonality (assuming stability) using the Kruskal–Wallis statistic was performed on real exports for each country and for real oil revenues. All the export series displayed evidence of seasonality at the 0.1-percent level; so these data were seasonally adjusted using the X-11 ARIMA technique. The data used in constructing the OECD GDP variable had already been seasonally adjusted. The explained variance of the regressions in Table 1 for

TABLE 1.
Regression Results: Effects of Exchange-Rate Variability on Exports of the Big Seven Countries

Country	Equation	Constant	Real OECD GDP 1980 Exch. Rate	1984 Exch. Rate	Relative Prices	Real Oil Revenues	Exchange-Rate Variability Current Period	Lagged	Rho	Summary Statistics R²	DW	SER
Canada	(1a)	−5.74 (−4.3)	1.40 (7.7)		−0.57 (−3.2)		−0.001 (−0.2)		0.54 (4.0)	.936	2.10	.040
	(1b)	−5.00 (−4.2)		1.34 (8.0)	−0.54 (−3.0)		−0.001 (−0.1)		0.53 (3.8)	.937	2.09	.040
	(2a)	−5.97 (−4.3)	1.43 (7.5)		−0.56 (−2.9)			−0.005 (−0.02)	0.55 (3.9)	.934	2.12	.041
	(2b)	−5.20 (−4.1)		1.37 (7.7)	−0.53 (−2.8)			−0.0003 (−0.01)	0.54 (3.8)	.974	2.10	.040
France	(1a)	−8.20 (−11.5)	1.76 (17.1)		−0.04 (−2.1)	0.07 (5.1)	0.10 (0.7)		0.34 (2.3)	.990	1.88	.015
	(1b)	−7.18 (−10.2)		1.67 (15.9)	−0.04 (−2.0)	0.07 (5.1)	0.10 (0.7)		0.37 (2.5)	.989	1.87	.016
	(2a)	−8.22 (−9.3)	1.76 (14.0)		−0.04 (−1.8)	0.07 (4.8)		0.22 (0.3)	0.32 (2.1)	.990	1.89	.016
	(2b)	−7.15 (−8.2)		1.66 (12.9)	−0.04 (−1.6)	0.07 (4.8)		0.15 (0.2)	0.35 (2.3)	.990	1.87	.016
Germany	(1a)	−9.17 (−4.8)	1.92 (7.1)		−0.11 (−2.0)	0.06 (1.8)	.09 (0.4)		0.75 (7.2)	.964	1.99	.027
	(1b)	−7.63 (−4.4)		1.76 (6.9)	−0.09 (−1.7)	0.06 (2.1)	.11 (0.4)		0.73 (6.8)	.963	1.95	.028
	(2a)	−9.33 (−4.9)	1.94 (7.1)		−0.10 (−1.7)	0.05 (1.5)		1.50 (0.7)	0.71 (4.9)	.963	2.02	.028
	(2b)	−7.88 (−4.6)		1.79 (7.1)	−0.08 (−1.4)	0.06 (1.8)		1.79 (0.8)	0.60 (4.5)	.962	1.99	.028
Italy	(1a)	−8.94 (−6.5)	1.84 (10.0)			0.07 (1.7)	0.14 (0.3)		0.39 (2.6)	.895	2.06	.058
	(1b)	−7.79 (−6.2)		1.74 (10.0)		0.08 (1.9)	0.13 (0.3)		0.38 (2.6)	.894	2.06	.058
	(2a)	−11.03 (−6.2)	2.11 (9.0)			0.04 (0.8)		3.00 (1.8)	0.38 (2.5)	.898	2.09	.057

	Eq									R^2	D-W	SE
	(2b)	−9.67 (−5.9)		1.99 (8.9)		0.04 (1.0)		2.92 (1.7)	0.37 (2.5)	.897	2.09	.058
Japan	(1a)	−9.83 (−7.7)	2.00 (11.4)		−1.06 (−7.4)	0.22 (8.7)			0.50 (3.5)	.989	1.86	.029
	(1b)	−8.53 (−7.6)		1.89 (11.9)	−1.05 (−7.7)	0.23 (9.4)	−0.16 (−1.1)		0.4 (3.2)	.989	1.84	.029
	(2a)	−9.76 (−3.5)	1.99 (4.9)		−1.06 (−3.9)	0.22 (7.8)		0.01 (0.004)	0.52 (3.4)	.988	1.83	.031
	(2b)	−8.44 (−3.3)		1.88 (5.1)	−1.06 (−4.0)	0.23 (8.5)	−0.16 (−1.1)	0.002 (0.001)	0.49 (3.1)	.988	1.81	.030
UK	(1a)	−4.02 (−7.3)	1.17 (15.9)		−0.10 (−1.5)	0.06 (3.3)				.927	1.89	.031
	(1b)	−3.33 (−6.6)		1.11 (15.9)	−0.09 (−1.3)	0.06 (3.5)	0.28 (1.3)			.927	1.91	.031
	(2a)	−3.98 (−6.8)	1.16 (14.6)		−0.10 (−1.5)	0.06 (2.6)		0.78 (0.8)		.922	1.92	.032
	(2b)	−3.31 (−6.1)		1.11 (14.5)	−0.09 (−1.3)	0.06 (2.9)	0.30 (1.4)	0.70 (0.7)		.922	1.93	.032
US	(1a)	−7.86 (−3.5)	1.83 (5.5)		−0.18 (−3.4)	0.03 (1.1)			0.76 (6.9)	.942	1.91	.030
	(1b)	−5.90 (−2.9)		1.66 (5.1)	−0.18 (−3.2)	0.04 (1.2)	0.33 (1.0)		0.78 (7.4)	.941	1.91	.030
	(2a)	−8.01 (−4.0)	1.86 (6.1)		−0.19 (−3.9)	0.04 (1.3)		−1.09 (−0.8)	0.70 (5.8)	.944	1.92	.029
	(2b)	−5.99 (−3.2)		1.68 (5.6)	−0.18 (−3.6)	0.04 (1.4)	0.30 (1.0)	−1.14 (−0.8)	0.72 (6.2)	.942	1.92	.030

Notes: Dependent variable is volume of exports.

Real OECD GDP is real GDP in national currency terms for 13 countries converted to U.S. dollars at 1980:III and 1984:IV exchange rates.

The relative-price variable for France, Germany, Italy, and the United States is the nation's export-unit-value index divided by the OECD CPI. For Canada, Japan, and the United Kingdom it is the nation's export-unit-value index divided by the U.S. WPI. For Japan and the United Kingdom the relative-price series were constructed by using an eight-period second-degree polynomial-distributed lag.

Real oil revenues are the dollar value of export earnings of oil-exporting countries divided by the dollar-unit-value index of industrial country exports. For Japan and the United States real oil revenues are lagged one period.

Exchange-rate variability is the absolute value of the percent change of the country's nominal effective exchange rate.

The source of the nominal effective exchange rate is the Morgan Guaranty Bank. The source of all other variables is the IFS.

First-order serial correlation corrections were performed using a maximum likelihood technique.

each country is well above .90 except for Italy, where it is slightly below .90.

The regressions show that the major determinant of real exports for each of the Big Seven OECD countries is real economic activity in the remainder of the OECD. The results also indicate that the coefficients on real GDP are not significantly affected by changing the set of exchange rates used to aggregate national GDPs—compare equations (a) with (b)—or by changing our choice of proxy for exchange-rate volatility from the current-period to the lagged form—compare equation sets (1) with (2). The coefficients on real OECD GDP range from a low of 1.11 for the United Kingdom (Eqs. [1b] and [2b]) to a high of 2.11 for Italy (Eq. [2b]). For each country, the coefficients on real GDP are slightly higher when that variable is calculated on the basis of 1980 exchange rates (a procedure that gives greater weight to the non-U.S. OECD nations in aggregating GDPs).

As previously noted, relative prices were not found to exert an influence on real exports from Italy. For the other major European countries, relative prices exert a small impact, with coefficients ranging from $-.04$ in France to about $-.10$ in both Germany and the United Kingdom. Relative prices are a more important determinant of real exports of the non-European countries, with the strongest impact found in the Japanese equations.

The impact of real oil revenues on real exports was found to be very similar among the European countries, with coefficients ranging from .04 to .08; significant in nearly all cases. The Japanese equations have the highest coefficients (about .22); the U.S. equations have coefficients of around .04 and fall short of significance. As noted, we found no significant impact of real oil revenues on Canadian exports. That failure probably reflects that nation's dependence on the United States as its primary export market. (Since 1973, more than 60 percent of Canadian exports have been sent to the United States; the figure reached 73 percent in 1984.)

The equations indicate that exchange-rate variability has not exerted a negative and significant impact on real exports of any of the Big Seven countries. This finding holds whether exchange-rate variability is used in current-period form or in its distributed-lag form. In the case of the current-period formulation, negative coefficients were obtained in the Canadian and the Japanese equations. For both countries, however, the t-statistics are insignificant. (The largest absolute value occurs in both the Japanese equations, where the t-statistics are 1.1.) In the case of the distributed-lag form of the exchange-rate variability term, negative coefficients were found in the Canadian and the U.S. equations. Again, they are insignificant in both instances. (The largest absolute value of the t-statistics is in the U.S. equations, where it is 0.8.) In most of the other equations, the coefficients on the exchange-rate variability terms are positive and insignificant; the exception is Italy, where it is positive and significant. In addition to the findings reported above, we tried a one-period lag on exchange-rate variability and four-period and twelve-period polynomial-distributed lags. In no instance did we find a negative and significant coefficient on the exchange-rate variability term.[11]

Exchange-Rate Variability and Financial Performance

Our second suggested criterion for assessing exchange-rate-regime optimality is analytically separable from the first, albeit empirically intertwined with it. Alongside the concern about the impact of exchange-rate variability upon international trade flows has arisen the contention that short- and intermediate-term fluctuations of exchange rates may result in a misalignment of such rates.

Misalignment of exchange rates, in common with any perceived misalignment, is in the eye of the beholder. Whatever misalignment of exchange rates might have occurred since the move to more flexible exchange rates at the beginning of the 1970s, it has not prevented the extent of the subsequent expansion and diversification of world trade. Moreover, the perceiver of a misaligned exchange rate, under floating with freely convertible currencies, can avail himself of the open market for exchange-rate determination. By opting for participation, the perceiver of a misaligned exchange rate can test and thereby attempt to capitalize upon the opportunity to engage in open-market exchange transactions while at the same time contributing to the realignment process that might rectify the assumed misalignment.

By contrast, in a regime of fixed exchange rates, the perceiver of a misaligned exchange rate is "stuck" with that fixed parity for so long as it remains there. It was indeed the intertia, procrastination, and aversion to making official changes of fixed parities, in adjusting exchange rates to changed supply-demand conditions in the foreign-exchange market, that proved the undoing of the regime of fixed parities embodied in the Bretton Woods system (Murphy, 1985). The demise of Bretton Woods constitutes suggestive evidence that exchange-rate misalignment not only was present under a fixed-exchange-rate system but may have contributed to that system's ultimate undoing.

Claims of currency overvaluation or undervaluation that have found expression since the advent of floating imply open profit opportunities to those with confidence in such claims. Thus, the for-

---

[11] These results are available from the authors upon request.

eign-exchange market under floating is an open forum for "putting your money where your mouth is" in the wake of overvaluation and undervaluation assertions that market observers (and others) are free to make and/or test.

The foreign-exchange market, as a quintessential financial market, is in principle analogous to the stock and bond markets as well as to other markets for financial claims. Divisions of opinions as between bulls and bears (i.e., differences of assessment of market prices as expressing overvaluation or undervaluation of particular shares of stock) are part and parcel—indeed, not intending a pun, the stock in trade—of the speculative drive that stock-exchange transactions can reflect. The notion that floating exchange rates lead to currency misalignment is itself subject to open-market verification. The foreign-exchange market under floating provides a focal outlet for the interaction among the respective holders of various shades of opinion as to the "correct" value of currencies in terms of each other. The variability of exchange rates thus constitutes an ongoing open-market discovery and reconciliation process between rival assessments of the "true" worth of currencies that are mutually convertible at whatever rates the traffic will bear.

Whether the impact of exchange-rate volatility on the performance of the foreign-exchange market itself is stabilizing or destabilizing is the focus of both ongoing analysis and institutional evolution. Since the advent of floating, the condition of purchasing-power parity has been honored in the breach; oscillations of exchange rates have greatly exceeded the variation in relative commodity prices. In cognizance of this failure of the transnational price-arbitrage condition, the financial asset-market approach was advanced, arguing for the efficiency of financial markets as against the apparent sluggishness of price adjustment in commodity markets (Bilson, 1985). An important component of this analysis has been a model (Dornbusch, 1976) of exchange-rate dynamics incorporating an "overshooting" effect in which sluggish price adjustment in the real-goods markets results in increased variability of interest rates and exchange rates. The theoretical importance attributed to this effect is that it suggests the volatility of the floating-rate system as being due to inherent differences between commodity and financial markets rather than to irrational practices of market participants.

In turn, as another of the pioneers of the theory of optimum currency areas, McKinnon has combined that literature with the more recent asset-adjustment approach to exchange-rate determination. In particular, he argues that discrete jumps in the spot exchange rate can exceed, in percentage terms, immediate changes in the domestic supply of (or demand for) money or in domestic interest rates. According to McKinnon, overshooting occurs in that the initial effect of a monetary expansion on the exchange rate exceeds "the ultimate effect" (McKinnon, 1979, p. 192). He has further contended that speculation in the foreign-exchange market per se is stabilizing, but that the instability of the floating-rate system is due to "insufficient speculation." McKinnon's theme has been reaffirmed by the contrast drawn by Bilson (1985) between fixed- and floating-rate systems. Under fixed rates, financial shocks are spread globally with interest rates being internationally linked by a tendency to interest-rate parity. In contrast, under floating exchange rates, interest rates are dominated by domestic conditions, and movements in the exchange rate are primarily determined by nonspeculative activity. Bilson maintains that an alleged lack of speculative activity, especially activity based upon longer-range fundamentals, may be an important factor of global monetary instability.

Undeniably, the control mechanism of fixed exchange rates that the Bretton Woods system embodied did not endure. It can be taken for granted that the use of exchange controls to fix exchange rates would not be seriously considered by major trading nations. Alternatively, a return to a system like Bretton Woods would require an act of faith that the causes of its breakdown were not endemic to a regime of fixed exchange rates in a multicurrency world. Instead, the institutional framework of floating rates is growing more innovative and adaptable.

The internationalization of financial markets and the proliferation of futures markets have come to include both spot and forward trading in foreign exchange. Thus, interspatial and intertemporal arbitrage transactions in foreign exchange have included the broadening, over both space and time, of currency markets as a consequence of the same set of forces that have transformed banking into a global activity. These forces include competition, deregulation, and telecommunications technology. Hence, the limiting of foreign-exchange risks by hedging and options trading is facilitated and enhanced globally.

Such globalization of currency convertibility suggests that an ongoing interaction between trade flows and capital movements is forging a financial interdependence network based upon flexible exchange rates as a transmission mechanism from money supply to money income.[12] With this evolutionary process unfolding, it appears premature now to declare, following McKinnon (1984), floating exchange rates a failure. After all, the free determination of share prices in the stock market has still not been pronounced a failure despite the fact that on Wall Street there did occur a stock market

---

[12] On the variable exchange rate as a transmission mechanism see, e.g., Cobham (1984).

boom and there did ensue a stock market crash. Certainly no serious proposal of doing away with share-price variability, let alone abolishing the stock market, has been deduced from the proven possibility of a stock market crash. Consider the dollar in the same light. The 1980 to early 1985 boom in the dollar's exchange rate has been viewed by some (e.g., Marris, 1985) as auguring a hard landing for the dollar. Though private-sector trading has not thus far engendered a dollar crash, it is an open question whether managed floating by the collusive action of the financial authorities of the leading industrial nations, determined to "bring down" the value of the dollar, might not yield a dollar crash. Even if it does, that would hardly be a basis for pronouncing the floating dollar a final failure.

Versus the verdict of floating exchange rates as a failure, a counterview still under trial is (Murphy, 1985, p. 72) that "a high degree of exchange rate responsiveness to market pressures is . . . an important safeguard against delaying real economic adjustments too long." Protectionism is a delaying, or even blocking, device aimed to obstruct real economic adjustments to changes in international competitiveness. The very strength of the protectionist outburst attests to the antagonism against changes in international competitiveness deriving from exchange-rate sensitivity to market pressures. That is perhaps the most concrete disadvantage of the floating-rate regime. Yet the volume of trade has not been reduced by exchange-rate variability; indeed, world trade has expanded rapidly since 1971. Thus we conclude that the main result of the floating-rate regime has been that necessary readjustments have been facilitated; the world economy has become more flexible in real, as well as in financial, terms.

Maintaining Competitiveness Through Dollar Variability

What results from our consideration of the relationship between flexible exchange rates and the new protectionism can now be generalized from the case of a rising dollar to that of a declining dollar. The search for a subterfuge for protectionism is adaptable to a declining dollar as well as to a rising one. In the case of a declining dollar (Schmidt, 1979), the excuse for import restrictions would be that of reducing the supply of dollars to the rest of the world so as to prop up the international dollar value.[13] The outcome, in terms of diminishing the gains from trade by curtailing the benefits from the international division of labor, would be analogous to the outcome

---

[13] For reference to an alarming acceleration in the pace of protectionist intervention beginning in 1977 see Krauss (1978).

of import restrictions when imposed to reduce the loss of export competitiveness in the case of a rising dollar. In other words, it is the *variability* of exchange rates in both directions, and not only in the case of the appreciating dollar, that can be (and has been) put to protectionist use, once a retreat from the discipline of the international division of labor is unleashed.

Next, consider the view (Krugman, 1983) that exchange-rate variations will not produce an equilibrium adjustment in the balance of payments. Specifically, in the case of the rising dollar, it is the notion (Buiter and Miller, 1982) that the dollar upsurge is only a transitory gain: in the long run, it is averred, the exchange rate will revert to purchasing-power parity. Yet, contrary to this view, flexible exchange rates (Korteweg, 1980) actually bring about an equilibrium adjustment in the balance of payments, as evidenced in changed prices of U.S. goods and services relative to foreign goods and services, as well as in capital movements. No amount of overvaluation- or undervaluation-labeling of exchange-rate movements can detract from the actual equilibration that the balance of payments (in both current and capital accounts) undergoes under the impact of exchange-rate variability.

The foregoing conclusion confirms the proposition (Schmidt, 1979) that, in the case of the United States in particular, under exchange-rate variability, the balance of payments does not really matter. Exchange-rate targeting is therefore, even if not unfeasible, redundant and hence unwarranted. Globally the dollar is a reserve currency and other countries, accordingly, either peg their currencies to it or float their currencies against it. In either case, the United States is, in effect, relieved of paying its way in the world: the United States does not need to worry about borrowing abroad excessively so long as it maintains no exchange controls or import restrictions. The characterization of U.S. policy as "benign neglect" (by Kindleberger, 1985, and by Zolotas, 1985) is a misnomer and a contradiction in terms, in that sustained and protracted negligence is hardly benign. The point is that exchange-rate flexibility promotes commercial and financial adjustments by economic agents, both at home and abroad, in response to relative supply-demand shifts in the foreign-exchange market. Such adjustments are the antithesis of neglect, whether benign or malign. As previously noted (Corden, 1985), in a flexible exchange-rate system, the level of the exchange rate is but a by-product of the mix of monetary and fiscal policies interacting with protection policies of different countries.

Thus, it is only the misperception of exchange-rate flexibility as a rationalization (rather than a rationale) for protectionism—old or new—that may pose a serious danger. The danger is that policymakers will apply trade and/or payments restrictions, triggering retreat from optimization of the international division of labor. We conclude that flexible exchange rates automatically move so as to maintain a country's competitive position in the world economy. They evidently have in the case of the United States amid the severest recession in half a century. A more robust recovery could hardly have been asked for; and a more clear-cut reversal of a beggar-my-neighbor policy could hardly have been proffered.

Summary and Conclusions

This essay has considered whether contemporary U.S. protectionism has been stimulated by dollar appreciation under flexible exchange rates. We find that dollar appreciation no more justifies protectionism than does dollar depreciation. There is evidence that support for protectionism has existed under both appreciating and depreciating exchange-rate movements. Specifically, the support for the new protectionism emerged in the 1970s—a period of dollar depreciation.

In contrast, the period 1980–1984 has combined dollar appreciation with rising external deficits. This combination has had a number of consequences. (1) In place of a beggar-my-neighbor policy of devaluation in association with a severe recession, the American economy has experienced an enrich-my-neighbor policy of upvaluation. (2) Exchange-rate flexibility has acted as an adjustment mechanism equilibrating the U.S. balance of payments while contributing to both the U.S. and global recoveries. (3) The vigor of the U.S. recovery is evidence that an optimizing reallocation of resources was implemented in response to the interaction of trade and capital movements under floating exchange rates. (4) Exchange-rate variability does not seem to have impeded the growth and diversification of world trade. (5) By comparison to a regime of fixed parities, floating exchange rates appear to be more conducive to a global clearing of foreign-exchange markets as an automatic payments-adjustment mechanism. Finally, (6) official collusive intervention by the leading industrial nations since 1985 implies a coordinated policy of exchange-rate protection for the dollar in a concerted endeavor to head off a world trade war.

We are grateful to Dominick Salvatore for stimulation and helpful comments.

References

Akhtar, M. A. and Hilton, R. S. (1984a) Effects of Exchange Rate Uncertainty on German and U.S. Trade, *Federal Reserve Bank of New York Quarterly Review* 1: 7–16.

——— (1984b) Exchange Rate Uncertainty and International Trade: Some Conceptual Issues and New Estimates for Germany and the United States. Federal Reserve Bank of New York Research Paper.

Aschheim, J. and Park, Y. S. (1976) *Artificial Currency Units: The Formation of Functional Currency Areas.* Essays in International Finance No. 114. Princeton, N.J.: Princeton University, International Finance Section.

Baldwin, R. E. (1982) *The Inefficiency of Trade Policy.* Essays in International Finance No. 150. Princeton, N.J.: Princeton University, International Finance Section.

Batten, D. S. and Ott, M. (1983) Five Common Myths About Floating Exchange Rates, *Federal Reserve Bank of St. Louis Review* 65: 5–15.

Bhagwati, J. N. (1984) Letting Politics Mandate Trade Policy, *New York Times* (September 9):F3.

Bilson, J. F. O. (1985) Macroeconomic Stability and Flexible Exchange Rates, *American Economic Review* 2: 62–67.

Blanchard, O. and Dornbusch, R. (1984) U.S. Deficits, the Dollar and Europe, *Banca Nazionale del Lavoro Quarterly Review* 148: 89–113.

Brodsky, D. A. (1984) Fixed Versus Flexible Exchange Rates and the Measurement of Exchange Rate Instability, *Journal of International Economics* 16: 295–306.

Buiter, W. H. and Miller, M. H. (1982) Real Exchange Rate Overshooting and the Output Cost of Bringing Down Inflation, *European Economic Review* (May/June): 85–123.

Cobham, D. (1984) Convergence, Divergence and Realignment in British Macroeconomics, *Banca Nazionale del Lavoro Quarterly Review* 149: 159–176.

Coes, D. V. (1981) The Crawling Peg and Exchange Rate Uncertainty. In *Exchange Rate Rules: The Theory, Performance and Prospects of the Crawling Peg* (John Williamson, ed.). New York: St. Martin's. Pp. 113-136.

Cohen, B. J. (1981) *The European Monetary System: An Outsider's View,* Essays in International Finance No. 142. Princeton, N.J.: Princeton University, International Finance Section.

Corden, W. M. (1985) Protection, the Exchange Rate, and Macroeconomic Policy, *Finance & Development* 2: 17–19.

Cushman, D. (1983) The Effects of Real Exchange Rate Risk on International Trade, *Journal of International Economics* 15: 45–63.

DeGrauwe, P. and Fratianni, M. (1983) U.S. Economic Policies: Are They a Burden of the Rest of the World?, *Economic Notes* 3: 69–85.

Dornbusch, R. (1976) Expectations and Exchange Rate Dynamics, *Journal of Political Economy* 84: 1161–1176.

Farrell, V. S., DeRosa, D. A., and McCown, T. A. (1983) Effects of Exchange Rate Variability on International Trade and Other Economic Variables: A Review of the Literature. Washington, D.C.: Federal Reserve Board Staff Studies No. 130.

Federal Reserve Bank of New York (1985) Treasury and Federal Reserve Foreign Exchange Operations, *Quarterly Review* 2: 58–59.

Galli, G. and Masera, R. S. (1983) Real Rates of Interest and Public Sector Deficits: An Empirical Investigation, *Economic Notes* 3: 5–41.

Group of Ten (1985) The Functioning of the International Monetary System. Report by the Deputies of the Group of Ten (June).

Group of Twenty-Four (1985) The Functioning and Improvement of the International Monetary System. Report of the Deputies (August 30).

Haberler, G. (1982) Inflation and Incomes Policy, *Economic Notes* 2: 20–46.

International Monetary Fund (1984) Exchange Rate Volatility and World Trade. Washington, D.C.: Occasional Paper No. 28.

Kindleberger, C. P. (1978) *Government and International Trade.* Essays in International Finance No. 129. Princeton, N.J.: Princeton University, International Finance Section.

——— (1985) The Dollar Yesterday, Today, and Tomorrow, *Banca Nazionale del Lavoro Quarterly Review* 155: 295–308.

Kormendi, R. C. (1983) Government Debt, Government Spending, and Private Sector Behavior, *American Economic Review* 2: 994–1010.

Korteweg, P. (1980) *Exchange-Rate Policy, Monetary Policy, and Real Exchange-Rate Variability.* Essays in International Finance No. 140. Princeton, N.J.: Princeton University, International Finance Section.

Krauss, M. B. (1978) *The New Protectionism: The Welfare State and International Trade.* New York: New York University Press.

Krugman, P. R. (1983) International Aspects of U.S. Monetary and Fiscal Policy. In *The Economics of Large Government Deficits.* Boston: Federal Reserve Bank of Boston. Pp. 112–133.

Machlup, F. (1972) *The Alignment of Foreign Exchange Rates: The First Horowitz Lectures.* New York: Praeger.

Marris, S. N. (1984) *Managing the World Economy: Will We Ever Learn?* Essays in International Finance No. 155. Princeton, N.J.: Princeton University, International Finance Section.

——— (1985) The Decline and Fall of the Dollar: Some Policy Issues, *Brookings Papers on Economic Activity* 1: 237–244.

McKinnon, R. I. (1979) *Money in International Exchange: The Convertible Currency System.* New York: Oxford University Press.

——— (1984) *Why Floating Exchange Rates Fail.* Discussion Paper No. 42. Rome: Bank of Italy.

Murphy, J. C. (1979) *The International Monetary System: Beyond the First Stage of Reform.* Washington, D.C.: American Enterprise Institute.

—— (1985) Reflections on the Exchange Rate System, *American Economic Review* 2: 68–73.

OECD (1984) Employment Outlook. Paris: OECD (September).

Pearce, D. K. (1983) Alternative Views of Exchange-Rate Determination, *Federal Reserve Bank of Kansas City Economic Review* (February): 16–30.

Rana, P. B. (1981) Exchange Rate Risk Under Generalized Floating: Eight Asian Countries, *Journal of International Economics* 11: 459–466.

—— (1984) Fixed Versus Flexible Exchange Rates and Measurement of Exchange Rate Instability: Comment, *Journal of International Economics* 16: 307–310.

Samuelson, P. A. (1985) Curing the Trade Imbalance: Where Iacocca and Common Sense Err, *New York Times* (September 15):F3.

Schmidt, W. E. (1979) *The U.S. Balance of Payments and the Sinking Dollar.* New York: New York University Press.

Thurow, L. (1984) *Should America Adopt an Industrial Policy?* Burkett Miller Distinguished Lecture. Chattanooga, Tenn.: Center for Economic Education, University of Tennessee.

Thursby, M. C. and Thursby, J. G. (1985) The Uncertainty Effects of Floating Exchange Rates: Empirical Evidence on International Trade Flows. In *Exchange Rates, Trade, and the U.S. Economy* (S. W. Arndt, R. J. Sweeney, and T. D. Willett, eds.). Cambridge, Mass.: American Enterprise Institute/Ballinger. Pp. 153–165.

Tobin, J. (1984) Unemployment in the 1980s: Macroeconomic Diagnosis and Prescription. In *Unemployment and Growth* (A. J. Pierre, ed.). New York: Council of Foreign Relations. Pp. 79–112.

Wojnilower, A. M. (1983) Discussion of Implications of the Government Deficit for U.S. Capital Formation. In *The Economics of Large Government Deficits.* Boston: Federal Reserve Bank of Boston. Pp. 99–111.

Zolotas, X. (1985) *The Unruly International Monetary System.* Papers and Lectures 51. Athens: Bank of Greece.

21

The Dollar's Borrowed Strength

OTMAR EMMINGER

Turning Point for the Dollar?

The unbalanced American external position has sometimes been compared to the famous Tower of Pisa: obviously leaning but unexpectedly stable. But some correction of the extravagant U.S. external deficit, and with it of the dollar, will sooner or later become inevitable. It may well be, it is even likely, that the peak which the dollar reached at the end of February 1985 has been its turning point toward a definitely lower level. The risk of a sharp fall of the dollar, with its possible impact on American inflation and interest rates, is a threat to the U.S. economy. As such a sharp fall could have disturbing effects on world trade, it might also be embarrassing for the rest of the world. I shall try to show that a "soft landing" for the dollar is still more likely than the widely feared "collapse." Before turning to the prospects for the future, however, I shall try to explain why the dollar has remained so strong for so long, and what its effects have been.

Over recent years *the exchange rate of the dollar has become by far the most important price in the world economy* (ten years ago this role would have been attributed to the oil price). It has an enormous impact both on the American economy and on the rest of the world. The overly high dollar has changed—some would say distorted—the structure of world trade and of major economies, begin-

Former President, Deutsche Bundesbank.

ning with the American economy. It has been itself the result of a staggering shift in the regional structure of international capital movements with the result that the United States, the richest country in the world, has been attracting capital imports that, on a net basis, have been much more than double the total capital imports into the Third World; and the United States has recently financed more than a quarter of its total capital needs from foreign sources. Taking all together, it has been the largest imbalance the world economy has seen for a long time.

My thesis will be that, contrary to some official views on both sides of the Atlantic, the impact of the high dollar has been, on balance, rather favorable for the Europeans—despite some inherent risks and dangers—while the negative effects have fallen more on the American economy. Thus the high dollar has become more and more an American problem.

The prolonged strength of the dollar has been not only the most important, but also the most overexplained—and maybe least understood—economic event of our time. At first sight it has been a paradoxical phenomenon: What for every other currency would be a cause of weakness—huge budget and trade deficits—seemed to drive the dollar higher and higher. And often the dollar got an upward push in the markets when the American money stock M_1 rose disproportionately for a few weeks. All this tallies perfectly with the definition of a paradox, which according to Webster's Dictionary is "a statement that is seemingly contradictory or opposed to common sense, yet is perhaps true."

A bewildering number of different explanations have been offered for this paradoxical and unique phenomenon. They range from vague political and psychological generalities, like

> a strong country has a strong currency; the strong dollar is a vote of confidence for the United States and against Europe; the political and social stability of the United States attract money from all over the world (safe-haven argument); the dollar will remain strong as long as Republicans rule in the White House ("Reagan bonus"); there is no real alternative to the dollar for foreign investors, etc.

to a number of very diverse economic explanations, like

> high interest rates in the United States; the impressive decline of inflation in the United States since 1981; the high profit potential of the American economy in general; the superior performance of the American economy, especially the contrast between the strong and flexible American economy and the "sclerotic" European economies; the American tax benefits for profits and new investment; the use of the dollar as the world's

main trading and financing currency, which is allegedly creating a growing demand for dollars; the urgent demand for dollars by highly-indebted countries (as if they had surpluses in Dmark or Yen which they could convert into dollars!); or—to use President Reagan's recent explanation—the fact that America's trading partners have not caught up with the U.S. recovery (which places the responsibility for the strong dollar plainly on the "weaker" industrial countries).

There can be no doubt that the overriding influence on the exchange rate of the dollar is *capital flows*, which have completely overwhelmed the influences of the trade and current-account balances. The crucial questions are: Who are the chief foreign investors in dollar assets? What are their main motivations? This is a very wide and complex field.

But before venturing into some nebulous generalities, one should rather take a glance at the actual composition of the American capital balance. This look at the actual facts shows some astonishing results, which disprove a number of oversimplified one-sided explanations. The most important examples are the following:

Between 1982 and 1984, when the American capital balance vis-à-vis the rest of the world improved by a staggering $90 billion (net),[1] the total inflow of foreign money (gross) into the United States increased hardly at all. The net improvement in the capital balance was largely accounted for by a sharp drop in American private lending abroad (from $108 billion in 1982 to $13 billion in 1984). Only a part of this tremendous drop can be explained by reduced bank lending due to the international debt crisis.

A look at the facts also shows that the high dollar has been supported much more by capital flows from Japan than by those from Europe; and Japan cannot possibly be characterized as suffering from anything similar to "Eurosclerosis" or from a lower economic performance or profit potential than the United States.

Moreover, a factual analysis of the motivations should not overlook the fact that in 1984 the flow of foreign funds into dollar assets was strongly promoted by several actions of the Ameri-

---

[1] This is an approximation, derived from the deterioration of the American payments deficit on current account from $9 billion in 1982 to about $100 billion in 1984. The absolute figures for this deficit (and the corresponding net capital imports) are a little uncertain; but the magnitude of the huge change since 1982 cannot be doubted.

can administration, notably the abolition of the 30 percent withholding tax for foreigners as well as the American–Japanese agreement on the liberalization of the Japanese capital market. The suspension of the withholding tax may not have been a bad decision, but it was taken at the wrong time. For a foreign observer it is difficult to understand why the American side voluntarily increased the disturbing payments imbalance at a moment when its impact was beginning to fall so heavily on the American economy.

The "Fundamental Factors" and the Dollar

Over the last few years, most forecasts about the dollar have turned out to be wrong. Even those who strongly believe in dollar strength for general political and psychological reasons, irrespective of interest rate and trade developments, have sometimes got their forecasts wrong. Thus, several U.S. government officials forecast near the end of 1983 that the dollar had probably reached its peak and was likely to show a moderate decline in 1984. In actual fact, the dollar rose in the course of 1984 by 15 percent against the deutsche mark and 12 percent against a weighted basket of major currencies.

There are good economic reasons for this unpredictability. The dollar is unpredictable mainly because of its dependence on a multitude of very diverse capital flows, with a variety of motivations—for example foreign purchases of American bonds and shares, direct investment in the United States, investment of official exchange reserves in dollar assets, but also borrowing abroad by American companies, foreign lending by American banks, capital flight from weak countries, and, for short-term exaggerations, on speculation, and so forth. Paul Volcker once said this dependence of the dollar on a variety of different capital flows makes the dollar trend a "Russian roulette."

Some of the forces behind these capital flows are of a fundamental and longer-lasting nature: e.g., large structural differences in interest rates and earnings prospects or fundamental differences in political and economic stability between the United States and other countries. Thus it would be wrong to include among the so-called fundamentals only the conventional factors, namely inflation differences and trade and current-account trends. In the case of the dollar, more than for any other currency, some deep-seated influences on capital flows are certainly fundamentals, too; and at present they are more powerful than the so-called traditional fundamentals.

If one takes account of the fundamentals in the American capital balance, one could perhaps say that the high dollar is not overvalued—because in a pure market sense it is not. But that does not alter

the fact that the exchange rate of the dollar is "distorted" or misaligned, if measured against cost and price relationships, and that
this misalignment has an enormous impact on competitive positions
and on trade. The fact that the fundamental factors of the American
capital balance have overpowered other fundamental factors is one
of the major problems of the present international exchange-rate
system. The distortion in the competitive positions has become a
source of dangerous protectionist pressures. And it is, of course, an
anomaly that the wealthiest country in the world is, on a net basis,
borrowing abroad on an unprecedented scale.

We sometimes hear that the predominance of capital movements over other fundamentals is a new phenomenon and that it has
made traditional textbook wisdom and former experience obsolete.
How short are people's memories! Already in the early 1960s the
dollar's position was dominated by capital flows for a number of
years. At that time America put up the best performance as concerns
price stability and ran surpluses in its payments balance on current
account. And yet it suffered such great capital outflows and gold
losses that in 1963–1964 an interest-rate equalization tax on certain
capital exports was introduced (and maintained until 1973). There
was, however, a fundamental difference from the present situation:
In the early 1960s America was *the* low-interest-rate country of the
world; today it is *a structural high-interest-rate country.* This has
reversed the signs of the problem.

The fact that the exchange rate of the dollar is more dominated
by capital movements than that of any other currency puts the dollar
in a class by itself. This is reinforced by the unique position of the
dollar as the world's chief reserve and intervention currency, and as
the dominating currency in the international financial markets. The
United States does not have, as a rule, a financing problem for its
payments deficits—in contrast to practically all other countries.
Therefore the United States can afford—or up to now has believed it
can afford—the luxury of a passive balance-of-payments strategy
(i.e., of "benign neglect").

All this means that the rules for exchange-rate policies, adjustment and financing of payments deficits, and also for intervention in
the exchange markets can be very different for the dollar as compared with all other currencies. The dollar is the only currency for
which it can be said with certainty that under conditions of capital
mobility it can function only as a fully floating currency; any fixed
dollar rate, or even a mere target zone for the dollar, would sooner or
later be toppled by the enormous amount of highly liquid and volatile dollar holdings in the world and by irresistible capital flows. As
experience has shown, other major currencies can function fairly
well in a regional system with firm but readily adjustable parities,

especially when—as in the European Monetary System—the mutual payments relations are determined more by a very large volume of trade and service transactions than by capital transactions.

The Driving Forces Behind the Capital Flows

I have already emphasized that the dependence of the dollar on a variety of capital flows makes its future prospects nearly unpredictable. The only thing we can predict with any confidence is that the present payments imbalance and exchange-rate distortions are not sustainable forever. However, nobody can predict *when* the inevitable turnaround will come—or, if it has already started, how far it will go. Nor is it as yet foreseeable whether it will be forced upon the United States from abroad—e.g., by a decline of confidence on the part of foreign investors—or whether the United States will itself be lowering its need for foreign funds—e.g., by cutting its budget deficit or by sliding into a recession, with a consequent significant decline in dollar interest rates. It is even possible that both factors may play their part—with a loss of confidence triggering action on the budget deficit.

To gain at least some idea about the sustainability (or otherwise) of the present constellation we have to look more closely into what has happened up to now. If we measure the net capital imports of the United States by the payments deficit on current account, we see an increase from $9 billion in 1982 to $42 billion in 1983 and to over $100 billion in 1984.[2] What have been the driving forces behind this staggering increase? Are they likely to persist? There are some schools of thought which believe they can give clear-cut answers—very contradictory answers. Some are very optimistic, others very pessimistic for the dollar.

The *dollar pessimists* believe that the dollar is on the brink of collapse because the huge current-account deficit is unsustainable or because American interest rates are bound to go down with the threat of a recession, and above all because a very large part of the capital flows into the dollar is in their view "hot money" and very unreliable.

The *dollar optimists* believe that the dollar will remain high for a long time to come. In their view its value is mainly determined by confidence in the political and economic stability of the United States and by the superior performance and earning power of its economy. Some very vocal advocates of this view (such as Professor

---

[2] Even if the current-account deficits were actually lower by annual amounts of $10 to $15 billion (because not all invisible income was recorded), the upsurge from 1982 to 1984 would still be staggering.

TABLE 1.
Capital Balance of the United States
($ billion)

	1982	1983	1984
Net balance of capital movements:			
Direct investment	+18.2	+6.6	+18.0
Portfolio investment	+5.3	+10.4	+30.4
Enterprise sector	+4.2	−6.6	+10.6
Banks	−45.1	+19.4	+23.2
U.S. government	−5.4	−4.5	−5.1
Statistical discrepancy (unrecorded net inflows)	+32.8	+11.5	+24.7
Balance on official reserve transactions	+2.0	−4.0	+0.2
Total (equal to balance on current account)	−8.1	−40.8	−101.5

Source: U.S. Department of Commerce (+ sign equals inflow).

Giersch, president of the Kiel Institute of World Economics) emphasize in particular the contrast between the high flexibility and technological lead of the American economy versus the rigidity and alleged technological lagging behind of the European economies (what they call "Eurosclerosis"). In their view, this difference between the United States and Europe will keep the dollar high irrespective of interest-rate movements or current-account deficits. This view is often called the "portfolio theory" of the dollar. Mr. McNamar, former Deputy Secretary of the U.S. Treasury, recently defined this portfolio theory as follows: "Exchange rate movements are a function of investment preferences at a country level. . . . I believe the dollar's strength reflects, not some temporary interest rate or trade balance factor, but a fundamental *relative* improvement in U.S. economic policies, performance and prospects *compared* to the other reserve countries."[3]

Which of these mutually exclusive opinions is right: the optimistic or the pessimistic one? In my view both are misleading, because both take partial aspects as an explanation for the whole. This shows up clearly when we look more closely at the actual composition and development of the American capital balance (see Table 1).

First, by far the largest change between 1982 and 1984 was the decline in foreign lending by American banks, from $111 billion in 1982 to nearly zero in 1984. This would by itself explain the net

---

[3] At the Davos Symposium, Davos, Switzerland, February 2, 1985.

improvement of the American capital balance over this period! Even if we take this enormous change on the credit side of the American banks together with the changes in their liabilities to foreigners, the turnaround of the American banks from being net lenders to net borrowers from abroad is still by far the largest change in the capital balance between 1982 (amounted to $68 billion) and 1984. Apart from the effect of the international debt crisis on bank lending, there have also been other constraints on foreign lending by American banks, and probably a lower demand for dollar credit on the part of other industrial countries. Where does this leave the portfolio theory, which tries to explain everything by the decisions and preferences of *foreign investors?*

Second, among the recorded capital inflows, a fast-growing part was due to borrowing abroad by American corporations, mostly at medium term in the Euromarkets. For the foreign lenders, it certainly could be counted among dollar-portfolio movements. But the initiative has been on the American side, and these transactions were certainly not carried out irrespective of the interest-rate differentials.

Third, for those who plead that the overriding attraction has been the dynamism and the higher earning power of American business, the statistics hold a disappointment in store. For this high earning power should chiefly be reflected in foreign purchases of American stock and foreign direct investment in the United States. Both items together were, however, hardly higher in 1984 than in 1982 and contributed relatively little to the financing of the enormous increase in the American current-account deficit. They constituted in 1984 about one-fourth of the total recorded inflows of private capital (and less than one-fifth if the nonspecified inflows of the "statistical discrepancy" are added). After all, since the middle of 1983 the American stock exchange has performed less well than the Japanese and some European stock exchanges.

Fourth, if we look at the geographical sources of capital flows to the United States it is clear that the higher earning power of American business is only one among several factors, and not even the most important one. Contrary to a generally held opinion, it is not mainly Europe from which capital has been pulled to the United States. This capital has come from all over the world, and the main supplier has recently been Japan—which, after all, is not suffering from "Eurosclerosis"! Japan had during 1984 a stupendous net long-term capital outflow of no less than $49 billion of which, according to Mr. Ogata, deputy governor of the Bank of Japan, $29 billion was Japanese investment in foreign securities, mostly dollar bonds, while foreign borrowing in Japan amounted to $14 billion. There can be no doubt that a major motivation for these huge capital flows was the difference between the high American and the much lower Japanese interest rates—buttressed by an underlying confidence that the dollar, if a turnaround were to come, would fall only moderately.

Summing up some major characteristics of the American capital balance over the three years 1982 to 1984:

It is evident that the huge increase in *net* capital inflows is a multivariant phenomenon which cannot be satisfactorily explained by one single factor.

A major part of the increase in the *net* capital inflow has been due to initiatives on the American side, as evidenced by the sharp drop in foreign lending by American banks, by the increased borrowing abroad of American corporations, and by actions of the American administration which have facilitated the inflow of capital.

High American interest rates have clearly played a big role, while other contributions have come from confidence considerations (including the safe-haven motive) as well as from attractive after-tax earnings prospects in the American economy (without which the high nominal interest rates could not have been sustained for so long). I would say: the crucial factors as concerns foreign investors have been interest rates and confidence, and often a combination of the two.

There is no denying the fact that there exists a sharp contrast between America and Europe as concerns economic and financial flexibility, wage and other rigidities, etc. But this difference seems at present to be largely compensated for by the distorted exchange rates: witness the unusually high profitability of many European export-oriented industries, a phenomenon equally apparent in Japan.

As a general impression from an analysis of the American capital balance, I would conclude that some of these movements, and in particular the retrenchment of American bank lending abroad, are unlikely to continue indefinitely in similar magnitudes. The increasing net dollar-asset position in the world may also lead to a certain saturation point in the global addiction to the dollar. Japanese pension funds and insurance companies are reported to be near the limits that they are permitted to hold in foreign securities.

The Role of Interest Rates

At any rate, even in the opinion of adherents of the classical portfolio theory, "relative changes in interest rate differentials are clearly
one element influencing exchange markets," although "they cannot
explain the dollar's persistent strength."[4] It is a moot point whether
one has to look primarily toward nominal interest-rate differentials
or whether real-interest-rate differentials are the decisive influence
on interest-rate-oriented capital flows. In my view, the major factor
in this field are nominal differences in interest rates together with
exchange-rate expectations and possible tax advantages. But even if
"anticipated relative after-tax *real* rates of return" are chosen as the
decisive influence,[5] movements in nominal interest rates play a role,
if all other things (relative inflation and taxes) remain equal.

At the beginning of 1985 the interest advantage for dollar assets
over yen and deutsche mark assets was still between 3 and 4 percentage points. This would be enough to set a wholesale exodus of capital to the United States in march, at least from those countries which
enjoy freedom of capital movements, were it not for the exchange-
rate risk. As is well known, the exchange-rate risk for the dollar
against the deutsche mark and the yen was rated much lower at the
beginning of 1985 than at the beginning or in the middle of 1984.
Thus one has always to look at *interest rate differentials combined
with the anticipated exchange risk.* This can, of course, lead to a self-
fulfilling prophecy (or a bootstrap phenomenon): a more favorable
anticipation of future dollar rates can make an existing interest-rate
differential more attractive and lead to higher capital inflows, thus
confirming the more favorable forecast. In 1984 there were some
other important developments which boosted capital flows into the
dollar, even at lower interest-rate differentials. One factor was the
liberalization and internationalization of the Japanese financial markets. The American–Japanese agreement of May 1984 seems to have
contributed, at least in its initial stage, mainly to the opening of the
Japanese capital market to foreign borrowers and to a considerable
upsurge of capital exports from Japan to the United States. Thus, it
*clearly boosted the dollar and depressed the yen exchange rate, very
much against its intended purpose.* Another factor was the abolition
of the American withholding tax on interest earned by foreigners.
This has made foreign investment in American securities more attractive, even at a lower interest-rate difference. A tax-free 10 percent yield may be more attractive than a taxable 12 percent yield.

---

[4] R. T. McNamar, Deputy Secretary of the Treasury, speech before the National
Foreign Trade Council, New York, January 30, 1985, page 8.

[5] See McNamar, page 8.

It is obvious that interest-rate differentials alone cannot explain every movement of the dollar, particularly over shorter periods. But this is even more true of the portfolio theory or the more dogmatic view of the unmitigated dollar optimists. Both do not take account of the major role played by the drastic change in the external position of the American banks and only partly of the increased foreign borrowing by American corporations. And what has really changed since mid-1984 in the after-tax real rate of return in favor of dollar assets? Have the earnings prospects of American business significantly improved since then relative to Japan or Europe? If anything, it has been the reverse. The modest capital inflows in the form of direct investment and foreign purchases of American stocks seem to confirm that in early 1985 the dollar was delicately poised—perhaps already at the peak of its market valuation.

But when all is said, it is still true that interest-rate differentials in favor of dollar assets, especially if they are combined with optimistic exchange-rate expectations, can have a significant influence on capital flows and the exchange rate of the dollar. This raises some fundamental questions. Is the present interest-rate differential in favor of dollar assets a true indicator of underlying differences in long-term profitability? Is it true, as some American experts claim, that it helps to steer the world's savings to the most productive uses? Here some doubts are in place. For the historically high American interest rates are mainly due to government policies and interferences. One such factor is the high structural budget deficit. Is it a productive use of foreign capital if it helps finance—directly or indirectly—such a structural budget deficit? Another distortion results from the American tax system, and here not only from the general tax deductibility of interest payments but also from the overgenerous tax advantages for new investment which have been so much enlarged by the 1982 tax act.[6] This has created an insensitivity of business, housebuilding, and consumers to high interest rates, which has inevitably held the equilibrium level of interest rates high. Thus, the change of the United States from a former low-interest country to the structural high-interest country of today is to some extent an artificial phenomenon and does not necessarily reflect a significantly higher pretax profit potential. The conclusion that the present tax advantages for American business are artificially high is underlined by the fact that the recent Treasury proposals for a "fairer" tax system envisaged a partial elimination of these tax features. The present American tax system may make the United States a structural high-interest-rate

---

[6] According to a study by a Washington institute, the average tax rate on business profits from new investment has plummeted from 33 percent in 1980 to 4.7 percent in 1984.

country for a long time ahead. Will this perhaps force other industrial countries to enter into competition with the United States in the
tax field?

Another fundamental question has been raised with regard to
the role of free capital movements in such a distorted scenario. The
misalignment of the dollar has already provoked very dangerous
protectionist pressures. Some have asked: Would it not be better to
put some restrictions on these unbalancing capital flows and thus
help preserve free trade in goods? An interest-equalization tax (on
the model of the U.S. tax of 1964) or outright capital export controls
have been suggested. The West German and British authorities have
definitely rejected such ideas. The Japanese have—inadvertently!—
even opened the door wider for capital outflows by their policy of
financial liberalization, thus involuntarily depressing the yen
against the dollar and increasing the dangerous trade and payments
imbalance.

A more rational answer to the existing international imbalance
would, of course, be an attempt to come to grips with the underlying
causes of the acute capital shortage in the United States and the large
interest-rate differentials. Needless to say that *this would presup-
pose a change in the American policy mix toward a less expansive
budgetary policy* and also a revision of the *American tax system*,
which is keeping the equilibrium interest rate artificially high.

WHY NONINFLATIONARY MONETARY POLICIES
ARE NOT ENOUGH

The experience of the last two years has convincingly demonstrated
that it is not enough for the leading countries to pursue "sound
noninflationary policies" in order to attain a stable and well-bal-
anced system of exchange rates. Such a convergence toward noninflationary policies was actually reached in 1983 between the United
States, Japan, and West Germany. But nonetheless the disturbing
misalignment of the dollar against these other currencies even increased. The convergence toward noninflationary policies must also
be supported by a sound relationship in the fiscal-monetary policy
mixes and in interest rates. *Only in this way can we hope to achieve
a more rational and also more stable exchange-rate structure.*

There are at present great contrasts in budgetary policies between America on the one side, Japan and a number of European
countries on the other side. There are also large differences between
them as concerns the impact of taxation on the equilibrium interest-
rate level. It has sometimes been suggested that a better balance
could be promoted by deliberately relaxing fiscal and tightening
monetary policies in some European countries. But that would mean

absorbing even more capital resources for budget deficits and making capital even more scarce worldwide.

There can be no doubt that the main responsibility for getting out of the uncomfortable exchange-rate trap lies with American fiscal policy. After all, the United States is at present clearly living beyond its means and is "becoming addicted to a large flow of capital from abroad" (Paul Volcker)—with the danger of heavy withdrawal pains should this capital inflow diminish abruptly. Moreover, this continuous piling up of external debt represents a heavy mortgage on the future.

Of course, some European countries could also make a contribution *by strengthening the profitability of business investment* and thus making it less sensitive to relatively high interest rates. This might lead to a smaller outflow of capital to the United States and provide support for European currencies. Would this mean following President Reagan's recent advice that the other industrial countries should "catch up with the U.S. recovery" in order to get more balanced exchange rates? Not entirely. For he probably wanted to suggest (like other high American officials) that Europeans should pursue a more expansionary budget policy. This might, however, be counterproductive. The only sensible contribution on the European side would, in my view, be a better climate and better conditions for business investment, including a more flexible wage and labor system.

At least up to March 1985, the American capital gap was being *overfinanced* by the large net inflow of foreign capital (together with the virtual stop of American lending abroad). This overfinancing was reflected in the constant upward pressure on the dollar. Thus, from the point of view of the external equilibrium, American interest rates were too high. In some recent remarks,[7] Paul Volcker seemed to imply that one could not risk any relaxation because of the need to attract sufficient foreign capital. This would not, however, justify maintaining interest rates at a level where *excessive* capital inflows keep the dollar excessively high. The external current-account deficit is more or less identical with the domestic capital gap. Finding the right level of interest rates, consonant with the real need for foreign capital inflows and without endangering the domestic equilibrium, is certainly a high-wire act. But at a time when the exaggerated level of the dollar constitutes a major risk for the American economy—including the risk of being pushed into irreversible protectionist mistakes—*monetary policy should perhaps look more than before toward the exchange rate as an indicator.*

---

[7] Before the domestic monetary policy subcommittee of the House Banking Committee, February 26, 1985.

Future Prospects

If we want to get some idea about what lies immediately ahead, we would have to make assumptions concerning budgetary policy, economic activity, inflation performance, and interest rates in the United States in 1985 and 1986. I want rather to concentrate on *interest rates*, as one of several elements of the future scenario, in which the other elements may be reflected. Is it worthwhile to speculate on the likely development of American interest rates? Forecasts for them since the middle of 1984 have been wrong at least as often as forecasts for the dollar. I will nevertheless risk a forecast by repeating one which I made in a speech in Washington in September 1984, shortly before the recent general downward movement of American interest rates began. I think that between now and the end of 1985, American interest rates are more likely to go farther down than up (with the usual short-term fluctuations up and down) unless the American economy, against all the odds, were to bounce back strongly in 1985. Why are they likely to decline? First, because of the softening in the American economy. Second, because American wage costs and prices are likely to rise only moderately, in future too, and far less than previously expected. Third, because I count on the psychological effect of budget-cutting measures for 1986 and beyond—not the least important reason!

Interest rates in other countries are likely to follow suit, but probably only in part, so that the interest-rate differential may shrink. But a slight reduction in present differentials does not necessarily portend an immediate, abrupt fall in the dollar. We should not forget that interest rates are not the only relevant factor, but that taxation, evaluation of exchange risk, and general confidence factors all play their part in foreign investment. If American interest rates go down in connection with a convincing cut in the budget deficit, this may increase foreign confidence in the United States so much that the dollar may remain strong despite lower interest-rate spreads. But a significant budget cut would probably also slow down the American economy—at least temporarily—and reduce business profits. Thus, the dollar may decline not only because of lower interest rates but also because the American profit situation will no longer look as attractive as before. This would be even more likely if the proposed tax reform were to reduce some of the overgenerous tax benefits for American corporations.

Soft Landing or Abrupt Fall of the Dollar?

If we think about the coming turnaround of the dollar we encounter another problem. Will the readjustment to a more normal level (which might already have started) come through a "soft landing"—

a gentle decline—or through a precipitous fall, with inevitable overshooting?

The outcome is very important both for the U.S. economy and
for the rest of the world. As Paul Volcker once said, a dollar collapse
triggered by a loss of foreign confidence would open a Pandora's box
of economic problems for the United States. It could drive up the
inflation rate and might upset my optimistic forecast about American interest rates. On the other hand, it would help the American
economy to get out of its foreign-trade impasse, although it would
probably take quite some time before the American trade and current-account balance showed a significantly better picture.

For the rest of the world, an overly abrupt fall in the dollar
would upset a lot of trade and competitive relationships. On the
other hand, it would give other industrial countries a greater leeway
for monetary policy, and it would lessen protectionist dangers. For
the highly indebted Third World countries, the net outcome would
mainly depend on the impact on dollar interest rates, dollar commodity prices, and on U.S. economic activity.

I would say that in the short run, an abrupt and exaggerated fall
in the dollar would involve more difficulties and problems than
advantages. Therefore I do not subscribe to the view that the best
news for the world economy would be a lower dollar. It very much
depends on the way in which it were to come about. It has rightly
been said (by, among others, Mr. Leutwiler, former president of the
Swiss National Bank and former chairman of the BIS) that the longer
the distorted dollar value and the huge one-sided capital flows last,
the larger the potential for an exaggerated fall becomes. But there are
also some reasons for expecting a "soft landing": there is, first, the
unexpectedly low inflation rate in the United States and the international confidence in the American central bank. Second, since other
countries will be greatly interested, too, in "softening" an eventual
dollar adjustment, they would probably help by lowering their own
interest rates (which they could do without any great risk if and
when a dollar fall provides them with lower import prices and lower
pressure of export demand). Third, there is still the possibility that
the U.S. Congress will finally agree on a confidence-inspiring cut in
the budget deficit for 1986 and beyond. If the "addiction to foreign
capital" (Volcker) were thus lessened, the adjustment of the dollar
would certainly proceed more smoothly.

We have repeatedly heard from American government officials
that "the U.S. has no plan aimed at coping with a possible steep
plunge in the dollar's value" (Donald Regan). But plan or no plan,
indirectly it is, of course, largely American fiscal and monetary policies which will be decisive when the turnaround comes.

How far could intervention in the exchange markets contribute to an orderly retreat of the dollar? This is a controversial subject, particularly in America. I believe that intervention, especially if it is a concerted action on both sides of the Atlantic, could soften the movement and smooth out erratic exaggerations. Intervention in the exchange markets is certainly a secondary matter compared with appropriate fiscal and monetary policies. Nevertheless, it might have been useful if American authorities had accumulated some foreign-exchange reserves in time, so as to be prepared for future contingencies (and it may be profitable, too). Just a side remark: It is utterly misleading to refer to the huge volume of transactions in the foreign-exchange markets—a *daily* volume of up to $100 billion has been indicated for the New York market alone—in order to make central bank interventions of $1 to $2 billion look ridiculous. What is essential for comparison is not the gross volume of interbank trading but the *net* amount of purchases or sales of dollars in the market. Speculators who are at the same time hedging their positions have no lasting influence. Although these net amounts can also rise to several billion dollars a day, there are situations of overbought or oversold currencies where even a few hundred million dollars can have a significant smoothing effect.

The Dollar—Increasingly an American Problem

Which side has suffered the most from the excessive dollar value? In my view, it has been the American economy:

Through the distortion of its competitive position in the world and the consequent distortions in its whole economic structure which have led to a split-level economy;[8]

Through the accumulation of an enormous external debt which will not only make the United States a net debtor country but whose increasing interest burden will weigh on the American current account for a long time ahead;

Because of the drag it exercises on current economic activity in the United States. It is strange that Americans are only now beginning to realize that, by depressing profits in large sectors of the economy and deflecting a lot of demand abroad, the high dollar in conjunction with the huge trade deficit has not only contributed to the present softening in the American economy but also has compromised future growth prospects by lowering investment in a significant part of industry.

---

[8] This distortion is not diminished by the fact that perhaps less than half of the overall deterioration of the American trade balance can be attributed to the strong dollar.

To be sure, the high dollar has also involved advantages: it has in 1983–1984 helped to prevent an overheating of the American economy by deflecting demand abroad; it has kept the inflation rate down in America, and it has given an impetus to rationalize and to increase productivity. It is also true that the large net inflow of foreign capital has alleviated the pressure which the financing of the budget deficit would otherwise have exercised on the domestic financial markets and thus has prevented a still higher interest-rate level and a squeezing out of private investment. Prof. Feldstein once wrote that as long as we have the high budget deficit, it is more of an advantage than a disadvantage to have large capital inflows and a high dollar. But over time—and with the increasing misalignment of the dollar—the balance has clearly shifted to the disadvantage of the American economy.

It is nearly the reverse for the rest of the world: in the past, one could complain that the high dollar, and the high American interest rates behind it, forced overly high interest rates on the rest of the world and thus curbed its economic recovery. But this no longer holds entirely true. In countries with good domestic stability, like Japan, West Germany, and some others, monetary policy and interest rates have been largely (although not entirely) uncoupled from the high dollar since about the beginning of 1984. The price-raising effect of the high dollar on import prices has partly been offset by the fall in the dollar prices of commodities (including oil) and partly been absorbed by lower domestic cost increases (so that in Germany and Japan the domestic inflation rate could be kept around 2.5 percent).

Much more important is the stimulus which the combination of the American domestic expansion together with the strong dollar has exerted on the European economies. This is reflected not only in the strong increase of European exports to North America (by over 30 percent in dollar terms in 1984), but also in the indirect effects of the American expansion on important European markets. This external stimulus came just at the right time, when domestic demand in Europe was languishing,[9] partly because of restrictive fiscal policies, partly for other reasons. An expansionary stimulus which did not increase indebtedness was what Europe needed in 1983–1984, also in order to be able to carry through the budgetary improvements so badly needed for structural reasons.

Thus, for a number of industrial countries the benefits to their exports, and to their whole economic activity, arising from the

---

[9] Domestic demand in real terms increased in Western Europe by only 1 percent in 1983 and 2 percent in 1984, as compared to 4.6 percent and 8.75 percent in the United States.

strong American expansion and the high dollar, have clearly outweighed the negative influence on their monetary policies. They
have learned to live with a strong dollar. Even France was able to
enjoy a continuous lowering of its interest rates over the last few
months.[10] If Britain in January 1985 had the opposite experience, it
was only partly attributable to the high dollar and more to a combination of several specific British problems. Finally, the strong dollar,
by keeping the deutsche mark down, has contributed to the longest
period of exchange-rate stability in the European Monetary System
since it was set up in 1979.

This rather positive evaluation of the effects of the high dollar
on Europe should, however, not let us overlook some possible future
costs and risks. Should, for instance, the dollar bounce back from the
sharp drop that began in March 1985, a breaking point may be
reached where the disturbing effects on European prices and monetary policies, but also a likely negative reaction of American trade
policy, might more than outweigh the advantages. Another risk is a
further abrupt fall of the dollar, the possible effects of which I have
briefly described above. But even if there should be a "soft landing"
of the dollar, we cannot neglect the costs, both in America and in
Europe, involved in the restructuring of industries, which in Europe
have too heavily leaned on the exchange-rate advantage or in the
United States have been too much depressed by a prolonged period
of misalignment.

Thus the strength of the dollar has been no unmixed blessing
for Europe. The main drawback and risk is of a too abrupt fall, for
which Europe is not well prepared. For America, however, it has
already for some time now been a major problem. Some time ago, a
well-known American magazine carried the headline "The dollar, a
source of pride and problems." Over time the problems have gained
the upper hand.

Americans will sooner or later become aware of the fact that the
huge external deficit and the exchange rate of the dollar are very
acute problems for the American economy. They are, at least in part,
the consequence of the excessive budget deficit. Maybe the pressure
arising from the external imbalance will help to get the domestic
imbalance under control.

I remember that about a dozen years ago a high U.S. official said
to the Europeans: "The dollar is our currency, but your problem!" I
have the impression that now the dollar has returned home as a
problem of the United States. This is particularly true if we not only
consider the present problems but also look ahead to the somber

---

[10] Raymond Barre, the former French prime minister, recently even praised the
high dollar!

eventualities of the future. That the U.S. administration has now recognized this has been confirmed by the agreement of the Group of Five of September 1985, which came about at the urgent request of the American side.

This is a revised version of Otmar Emminger, "The Dollar's Borrowed Strength," Occasional Paper No. 19, New York: The Group of Thirty, April 1985.

PART FIVE

THE NEW PROTECTIONISM
AND
ECONOMIC DEVELOPMENT

22

The Demand for Protection Against Exports of Newly Industrializing Countries

MICHAEL MICHAELY

Introduction

"Newly industrializing countries" have always existed: the chain of industrialization has been continuous. Germany became a newly industrialized country when England was an "old," established industrial economy. At the turn of the century, to mention another example, Sweden was a newly industrialized country. And, needless to say, Japan is a relatively recent addition to the list of industrialized countries. Yet in recent years the term *newly industrializing* came to refer to a whole group, and to insinuate some measure of surprise: countries which were presumed to belong to one category—that of primary-producing economies—have broken the class barrier and joined the well-established category of industrial economies. To economic observers, this is a source of gratification. But in the "old," developed economies this transformation is often regarded as a threat—a point of view that tends to lead to protectionist measures aimed specifically against the exports of the group concerned. It is this conceived threat that will be analyzed in the present paper.

Expansion of NIC Exports

The group of newly industrializing countries (NICs) has no legal definition. But it is most commonly meant to include the following

From the Hebrew University of Jerusalem, Jerusalem, Israel.

countries: Brazil, Hong Kong, Korea (South), Mexico, Singapore, and Taiwan.[1] It usually does not refer to another group, which preceded the NICs by roughly a decade in its process of industrialization—particularly in expansion of manufactured exports: Greece, Ireland, Israel, Spain, and Yugoslavia. In the case of the latter group, the process of industrialization, and in particular its implications for the established industrial world, somehow escaped particular attention—a point in contrast which will be mentioned later.

Table 1 records the expansion of industrial exports of the group of NICs between 1965 and 1980. Column (1) presents the absolute values of these exports in the two years, at current prices, whereas column (2) shows the percentage of these exports in the total exports of goods in each of the countries concerned.

It may be seen that in each of those countries, industrial exports grew over the fifteen-year period from 1965 to 1980 at a very dramatic pace. In aggregate for the group of the five countries, these exports grew from 1.8 to 58.4 billion dollars. In real terms, taking into account a roughly threefold increase in prices during the period, this is an increase of about tenfold. Even more significant, for the purpose at hand, is the structural change in the countries' exports: in all but Hong Kong, in which these exports had constituted the overwhelming majority of exports all along, the share of industrial exports in the country's total exports increased substantially over the period.[2]

This has meant also a substantial expansion of these exports in relationship to magnitudes of relevant economic variables in the developed countries (DCs)—the "old," established industrial economies. As a ratio of aggregate imports of the DCs, industrial exports of the group of NICs increased from 1 percent in 1965 to 4 percent in 1980. As a ratio of aggregate income of the DCs, the exports concerned increased over the period from 0.1 percent to 0.8 percent. Impressive though this change is, the absolute ratios at the end of the period observed (1980) are still rather low: 4 percent of total imports, or less than 1 percent of total income, would probably not normally assign the variable under investigation great importance.[3] The fact

---

[1] Information for Taiwan for the last decade is missing, unfortunately, from standard international data sources. This country will, therefore, not be covered in the quantitative analysis of the paper.

[2] It is the combination of a reasonably large absolute size of exports and rapidly expanding industrial exports, in both absolute level and share in aggregate exports, that probably classifies an economy into the NIC category. Had size been disregarded, several other countries (such as Jamaica or Costa Rica) would belong to this group. Borderline cases are probably those of the Philippines and Uruguay, which might have been added to this group.

[3] These are comparisons designed to give a proper perspective. But, to prevent misunderstandings, it should be emphasized that not all the industrial exports of the

TABLE 1.
Industrial Exports of Newly Industrializing Countries

Country	Value (in Million Dollars, Current Prices) (1)		Percentage of Country's Aggregate Exports of Goods (2)	
	1965	1980	1965	1980
Brazil	134	7,770	8.4	38.6
Hong Kong	1,069	18,344	93.5	96.5
Korea	104	15,758	59.4	89.8
Mexico	179	6,062	16.4	39.6
Singapore	338	10,463	34.5	54.0

Source: Data from UN, Yearbook of International Trade Statistics, various issues.

that the exports concerned did provoke particular attention in the developed economies, leading to rather strong negative reactions and specific protectionist measures, should therefore indicate that these exports possess attributes that enhance some impacts beyond what would be expected from sheer size. In other words, the increase of industrial exports from the NICs to the DCs, rapid though it was, constituted only a small fraction of the increase of industrial exports of developed countries to one another. Is there, then, a specific attribute of the industrial exports of the NICs, distinguishing it from exports of DCs, that would make it particularly likely to be considered a threat?

Factor Intensities of Exports

Origins of trade are commonly and conveniently classified into two primary sources: differences in factor proportions among countries and factor intensities of goods, leading to the trade of the "Heckscher–Ohlin" type; and product differentiation of basically similar goods which, in conjunction with some differences in tastes, leads to the trade in "Linder"-type goods. The more countries differ in factor scarcities, the more predominant will be the share of trade of the first type in their aggregate bilateral trade; while the more similar their per capita income levels, the larger will be the share of trade of the

---

NICs were sold to the DCs. Hence the ratios of exports of the NICs to the DCs to the latter's imports and income would be lower than those shown, although not radically different. It is estimated that in 1981 imports of manufactures from all LDCs constituted 2 percent of the total use of manufactured goods in the highly developed countries. See Balassa (1984), Table 3.

second category.[4] In addition, trade will arise out of temporary (albeit, often, very important) origins: delays in sharing information, and in particular in transfer of technological knowledge, are most important among such sources of trade.

Less-developed economies and highly developed economies differ largely from each other, as groups, in their relative scarcity of factors; and trade between a country belonging to one group and a country belonging to the other may thus be expected to originate predominantly from differences in factor proportions. The majority of LDC exports to DCs is most clearly of this nature: it consists of the exports of primary goods or chemical products in which countries obtain comparative advantages by the simple availability of specific natural resources, soil, and climate. But the exports of manufactured goods from a less-developed to a highly developed economy may also be expected to derive largely from the relative abundance of certain factors. Specifically, it is the abundance of unskilled or little-skilled labor that would grant the less-developed economy its advantage. In trade among highly developed economies, on the other hand—economies roughly similar to each other in income levels and factor proportions—exchange of Linder-type goods may be expected to form the major part.

If this is true, a demand for specific discrimination in DCs against imports of manufacturers from LDCs may be foreseen. These are imports that lead to a more substantial impact, per unit of trade, on displacement of factors in the importing country and on income distribution in it. Specifically, labor is liable to be affected adversely and is hence likely to raise stronger objections to these imports than, on average, to imports of equal size from highly developed trade partners.

A thorough empirical investigation of the attributes of trade would be beyond the confines of the present paper. But partial evidence will be offered in verification of the presumed nature of manufactured exports by the NICs.

Data on ratios of capital to labor in individual manufacturing industries (classified at the three-digit level of the SITC) are provided in the well-known study of G. Hufbauer (1970). Along with them, the study offers also data on the wages per man-year of work in each industry. These data are derived from U.S. input-output ratios; they refer to roughly the start year (1965) of the period of expansion under consideration. Their use for all countries, as well as for later periods, is justified as long as the ranking of industries, in the measures under consideration, does not vary among countries and over

---

[4] For some of the fundamental analysis of the distinction of sources of trade, see Lancaster (1980) and Helpman (1981).

time. Sufficient evidence exists to suggest that the first condition—resemblance among countries of rankings of industries by factor intensities—is indeed by and large fulfilled. On the other hand, no data of a similar nature exist from which it could be inferred that rankings have not changed *over time*. But it may be assumed that over relatively short periods (fifteen years) the rankings have not indeed changed in a manner radical enough to invalidate the inferences derived from the use of unchanged magnitudes.

Based on these data, the average factor content and wages per man-year were calculated for the baskets of manufactured exports of highly developed economies and for the aggregate of the five NICs, for 1965 and 1980. The results are presented in Table 2.

It appears that in 1965, at the start of the period under consideration, the attributes of exports of the NICs were indeed very substantially different from those of the exports of DCs—and in the expected direction. In relation to the DCs, manufactured exports of the NICs were highly labor-intensive (the labor-to-capital ratio being more than twice as high in exports of the former as of the latter) and particularly intensive in low-skill labor—a fact indicated by the very large spread in the average wage levels in the two baskets. By 1980, both gaps became substantially smaller but were obviously still there. This, indeed, should be expected: the further a newly industrializing country develops, the less may the factor-scarcity differentials between it and a developed economy be expected to be, and the smaller the differences in factor intensities of representative export baskets of the two.

The most salient fact, however, is that even toward the end of the period under consideration, a substantial degree of differentials in factor intensities existed between exports of the highly developed economies (and presumably, though not inevitably, manufacturing of these goods for the local market as well) and exports of the NICs. This, it has been argued above, provides a source of demand for protection in the former against exports of the latter.

Nature of Exported Goods

Another source of potential discrimination against exports of the NICs may be the nature of the goods they export. This is necessarily related to the factor content of the goods, but is nevertheless a separate argument. Once more, only rough evidence may be suggested here, rather than a thorough investigation of the nature of goods.

A readily available measure of differences is the classification of the exports of manufactures into two broad categories: "machinery and equipment" and "other manufactures." The latter are, presumably, mostly final consumption goods, whereas the former repre-

TABLE 2.
Attributes of Exports of Manufactures by Developed Countries and by NICs
(in thousand dollars)

	Capital Per Man		Wages Per Man-Year	
	1965	1980	1965	1980
Highly developed countries	16,013	13,938	6,335	6,030
Newly industrializing countries	7,030	10,766	4,635	5,624

Source: Export structure—data from Yearbook of International Trade Statistics; capital intensity and wages—from Hufbauer (1970), Table A-2.

sent a high proportion of capital goods purchased by producers. It may be presumed that protection against imports of consumption goods tends to be relatively high, for reasons which essentially explain the very existence and prevalence of protection: the interests of consumers are diffused and weakly represented, whereas interests of domestic producers of the goods are narrowly concentrated, well-defined, and effectively represented. In imports of capital goods, on the other hand, the potential users are themselves local producers with well-defined constituency and interests. Barriers against such imports tend, hence, to be relatively lower.

If newly emerging industrial exporters tend, as a rule, to export relatively heavily goods of one category or the other, a source of discrimination in protection would exist. Indeed, a consistent association of the proportions of the two categories in total exports of manufacturing with the level of development is to be found. This is demonstrated in Table 3.

Comparing both LDCs as a whole and, specifically, the NICs with the highly developed economies, the pattern that emerges is similar to that found earlier—namely, of radical differences in the starting year, 1965, which narrowed down substantially by 1980, the end year. In 1965, the share of "other manufactures" in total exports

TABLE 3.
Share of Major Categories in Exports of Manufactures (Percent)

	Machinery and Equipment		Other Manufactures	
	1965	1980	1965	1980
Highly developed countries	45.0	48.1	55.0	51.9
Less developed countries	12.7	25.1	87.3	74.9
NICs				
Brazil	21.4	43.4	78.6	56.6
Hong Kong	7.3	18.1	92.7	81.9
Korea	5.2	21.9	94.8	78.1
Mexico	7.9	48.2	92.1	51.8
Singapore	30.4	48.9	69.6	51.1

Source: Data from the World Bank, World Tables, 3rd ed.

of manufactures was, in all LDCs and in almost all of the specific NICs, drastically higher than in the developed economies. Manufactures of textiles were certainly a most important component of these exports. In 1980, a difference in the same direction still existed, but it was significantly smaller. In fact, in three of the five NICs surveyed—Brazil, Mexico, and Singapore—the share of machinery and equipment was by 1980 practically the same as in the highly developed economies. The change in Mexico, from 1965 to 1980, was particularly dramatic.[5]

It may be inferred that this attribute of the nature of exported goods has probably been a source of a tendency to discriminate against exports of manufactures by newly emerging manufacturers, but that this factor was of substantially less importance toward the end of the period under consideration than at its beginning.

Still another factor that must be contributing to the demand for barriers against imports from NICs is that the latter countries' ability to retaliate is highly constrained. This is due to two largely interrelated reasons. First, the countries under consideration already maintain, by and large, and have maintained all along, a relatively high level of protection of their own. Beyond lending some legitimacy to the demand by others to discriminate against exports of these countries, it would probably imply that each of the countries has already established trade barriers that it would be reluctant to exceed. This ties in with the second factor, namely, the structure of *imports* of the countries involved. Largely due to the level and structure of protection, easily replaceable imports constitute only a minor part of the countries' aggregate imports. The major import components are capital goods, food and raw materials, and, most often, oil. Of these, capital goods and some of the food are imported overwhelmingly from the highly developed countries. But imposition of import barriers on these goods—as well, of course, as on the other components, which are imported from LDCs—would face a forbidding opposition for the reasons elaborated earlier. Hence, the likelihood of retaliation by the NICs is small enough to be, most probably, ignored in the contemplation by the highly industrialized countries of specific restrictions on imports from the NICs.

Finally, the general macroeconomic context should be taken

---

[5] Generally, an increasing share of machinery and equipment in the total exports of manufactures is a clear attribute of development. With few exceptions, this appears in both cross-section and time-series comparisons, in the last two decades. This relationship holds, though, primarily for semi-industrial countries, and ceases to be generally valid once a high level of development is reached. Among highly developed economies, the only country in which the share under consideration increased substantially throughout the last twenty years is Japan—the country with the highest rate of development and industrialization in this group.

into consideration. Manufactured exports of the NICs have expanded primarily over a period in which the contraction of activities due to foreign competition is highly visible and particularly objectionable. This may explain, at least in part, the contrast between the relative calm with which the expansion of manufactured exports of the then newly emerging exporters—Spain, Greece, etc.—was accepted during the 1960s and the resentment with which exports of NICs of the later vintage have been met, particularly during the last decade.

Future Demand for Protection

It is thus found that the following elements may be contributing to the demand for protection, in the highly developed world, against the manufactured exports of the NICs: the factor content of the latter—specifically, its relative intensity in unskilled and semiskilled labor; the nature of the exported goods; the absence of retaliatory power of the NICs; and the context of a relatively stagnant world economy, suffering from high unemployment, which the expansion of manufactured exports of the NICs has had to face.

An attempt to predict the future course of demand for the protection under consideration would thus involve presumptions about anticipated developments of these elements. Here the emerging picture is probably not entirely dark.

To start with, as the NICs keep developing, relative factor scarcities in them must gradually approach those of the highly developed economies. In particular, the abundance of unskilled and semiskilled labor must be reduced. As a result, the factor content of goods exported by the NICs would become more similar to that of the DCs, leading to a lesser impact of this trade on factor displacement and income distribution. We have seen, earlier, that such tendency has indeed already been manifested over the period surveyed (1965–1980). Its future extension would appear most likely.

A very similar prediction is suggested for the development of the share of capital goods in manufactured exports of the NICs. In this instance, even more, a rapid approach of the position of NICs to that of the DCs has already been observed—to the degree, we recall, that countries like Brazil or Mexico now resemble highly developed economies in that aspect. This difference in composition of the exports of manufactures is most likely to gradually lose much of its significance as a source of discriminatory treatment of the exports of NICs.

The future course of growth of the highly developed world is a matter of sheer guess. Whether a turning point from the general downward slide that started in 1973 is at hand is a subject for speculation. This part of the assessment of the future course of protection must thus be left open; it can only be pointed out that the way it actually turns will have a major impact on protection in general and on barriers on imports from the NICs in particular.

Finally, a factor that seems most likely to lower the demand for protection is the fact that existing protection in the DCs, while slowing down the process of adjustment, could not have prevented it altogether. Contraction, in the importing countries, of activities competing with exports of the NICs has been taking place, and seems most likely to proceed, gradually, in future years. As an illustration, Table 4 describes import competition and the domestic activity in the United States in two sectors, textiles and clothing, which are most often mentioned in the context of U.S. protection against imports from the NICs. It is clear that, whatever the trade barriers, a radical transformation and adjustment must have taken place in the United States over the last generation, changing significantly the size and the role of the two activities in the American economy. Employment in the textiles industry declined substantially in absolute size. In the clothing industry the size of employment has fluctuated with no general trend, but in relative terms it has still exhibited a persistent decline. Recalling that *within* the United States a massive geographic migration of these activities took place, this information certainly yields a pattern of substantial restructuring. While figures such as those of Table 4 are often cited as justification for protection by its proponents, these data point out clearly the declining weight and diminishing role of the protected sectors. The smaller the size of the potentially protected sector, the lower naturally should be the demand and pressure for protection. Thus, recent clamor for further protection and impending new legislation in this direction notwithstanding, a longer-term *reduction* of trade barriers against imports of textiles and clothing may be anticipated.

If a prediction may be ventured, hence, it is that the demand for protection in the highly developed economies against exports of the NICs should be gradually diminishing—particularly if general world growth is resumed. In time, the present NICs will be exporting a range of goods substantially different from what it is at present. Their present exports will then be provided by other countries—the future NICs—whose identity could only be guessed. But for the latter, the main market will still be that of the present DCs. And in this market, it may be assumed, protection of the specific activities concerned will be weaker, due to the continuous process of adjustment. All around, thus, manufactured exports of newly emerging industrial countries may be expected to face in the future a more welcoming reception in the highly developed world than they do today.

TABLE 4.
Textiles and Clothing: Domestic Activity and Imports in the United States

	Gross Output (in m. Dollars Current Prices) (1)	Imports (in m. Dollars Current Prices) (2)	Employment (Millions of Employed) (3)	Ratio of Imports to Output [=(2)/(1)](%) (4)	Ratio of Output [(1)] to U.S. GNP (%) (5)	Share of Employment [(3)] in Aggregate U.S. Employment (%) (6)
			A. TEXTILES			
1950	4,600	321	1,201	7.0	1.62	2.00
1955	4,409	359	984	8.1	1.11	1.56
1960	4,764	550	835	11.5	.95	1.27
1965	6,465	799	827	12.4	.94	1.16
1970	8,473	1,135	975	13.4	.86	1.24
1975	10,088	1,234	868	12.2	.66	1.01
1980	14,908	2,541	848	17.0	.58	.85
1983	17,517	3,274	744	18.7	.54	.73
			B. CLOTHING			
1950	3,622	58	1,066	1.6	1.27	1.78
1955	4,332	116	1,077	2.7	1.09	1.70
1960	5,070	293	1,098	5.8	1.01	1.67
1965	6,713	543	1,207	8.1	.98	1.70
1970	8,951	1,269	1,364	14.2	.91	1.73
1975	11,204	2,551	1,243	22.8	.73	1.45
1980	16,267	6,945	1,264	42.7	.63	1.27
1983	20,138	10,421	1,164	51.7	.62	1.15

Source: Gross output: unpublished data, National Income and Wealth Division, U.S. Department of Commerce; imports: UN *Yearbook of International Trade Statistics* and *Commodity Trade Statistics;* employment: ILO *Yearbook of Labor Statistics.*

References

Balassa, B. (1984) Trends in International Trade in Manufactured Goods and Structural Change in the Industrial Countries. World Bank Staff Working Papers, No. 611.

Helpman, E. (1981) International Trade in the Presence of Product Differentiation, Economies of Scale and Monopolistic Competition: A Chamberlin–Heckscher–Ohlin Approach, *Journal of International Economies* 2: 305–340.

Hufbauer, G. C. (1970) The Impact of National Characteristics and Technology on the Commodity Composition of Trade in Manufactured Goods. In *The Technology Factor in International Trade* (R. Vernon, ed.). New York: Columbia University Press, for the National Bureau of Economic Research, pp. 145–231.

Lancaster, K. (1980) Intra-Industry Trade under Perfect Monopolistic Competition, *Journal of International Economics* 10: 151–175.

23

The Extent and the Cost of Protection in Developed–Developing-Country Trade

BELA BALASSA AND CONSTANTINE MICHALOPOULOS

Introduction

The focus of this paper is the measures of protection applied to trade between developed and developing countries. This choice reflects concern with the adverse repercussions of recently imposed protectionist measures in the two groups of countries as well as the increasing importance of mutual trade for their national economies.

The paper analyzes the extent and the cost of protection in developed and in developing countries, with special attention to measures affecting trade between the two groups of countries. The first section reviews the tariff and nontariff measures applied by the developed countries and provides empirical evidence on the cost of protection in these countries. We then examine the use of protective measures in the developing countries and indicate the resulting cost to their national economies. In conclusion we briefly indicate the policy implications of the findings.

Protection in the Developed Countries

TARIFF PROTECTION

The successes of the postwar period with tariff disarmament in the developed countries are well known and do not require detailed discussion. While the original purpose had been to undo the damage resulting from the competitive imposition of import duties during the 1930s, tariffs in the major developed countries were reduced

From the Johns Hopkins University, Baltimore, Maryland; and the World Bank, Washington, D.C.

below predepression levels by the end of the 1950s. These reductions, undertaken on an item-by-item basis, were followed by across-the-board tariff reductions in the framework of the Dillon Round (1960–1961), the Kennedy Round (1964–1967), and the Tokyo Round (1974–1977) of trade negotiations.

Taken together, in the course of the Dillon, Kennedy, and Tokyo Round negotiations, tariffs on manufactured goods imported by the developed countries were lowered, on the average, by nearly two-thirds. Table 1 shows that post–Tokyo Round tariff levels in major developed countries averaged 6 to 7 percent for finished manufactures and were even lower for semimanufactures and raw materials. Apart from overall reductions, the procedure applied in the Tokyo Round also lessened the dispersion of tariffs as higher tariff rates were cut proportionately more than lower rates.

The question arises, however, if the remaining tariffs bear disproportionately on products imported from the developing countries. There are two aspects to this question. First, whether tariffs on products of interest to developing countries are higher (or lower) at each level of processing; second, whether there is tariff escalation that affects developing-country exports of manufactures.

Table 1 shows that manufactured products of interest to the developing countries are in general subject to higher tariffs than products on the same level of fabrication originating in the developed countries. Thus, post–Tokyo Round tariffs on all imports of semimanufactures and finished manufactures, and on such imports from developing countries, respectively, average 4.9 and 8.7 percent in the United States, 6.0 and 6.7 in the European Common Market, and 5.4 and 6.8 percent in Japan (Table 1).

Furthermore, there is evidence of tariff escalation. Thus, post–Tokyo Round average tariffs on raw materials, semimanufactures, and finished manufactures are 0.2, 3.0, and 5.7 percent for the United States; 0.2, 4.2, and 6.9 percent for the European Common Market; and 0.5, 4.6, and 6.0 percent for Japan (Table 1).[1]

The cited averages pertain to all processing chains, several of which have little relevance for most developing countries. Such is the case in particular for petroleum-based products and for metal products, where processing is highly capital-intensive and requires a considerable degree of technological sophistication that is found only in developing countries at higher levels of industrialization.

---

[1] The table reports import-weighted tariff averages that are relevant for comparisons of overall tariff averages and tariffs on products exported by the developing countries. As noted in Balassa and Balassa (1984), unweighted tariff averages show a similar pattern of escalation. At the same time, unweighted averages are higher than the weighted averages as the latter are reduced by reason of the fact that high (low) tariffs that discourage (encourage) imports are given low (high) weights.

TABLE 1.
Post–Tokyo Round Tariff Averages in the Major Developed Countries

	Tariffs on Total Imports			Tariffs on Imports from LDCs
Raw Materials	*Semimanufactures*	*Finished Manufactures*	*Semi- and Finished Manufactures*	*Semi- and Finished Manufactures*
United States	0.2	3.0	5.7	4.9	8.7
European Common Market	0.2	4.2	6.9	6.0	6.7
Japan	0.5	4.6	6.0	5.4	6.8

Source: General Agreement on Tariffs and Trade, *The Tokyo Round of Multilateral Trade Negotiations,* II—Supplementary Report (January 1980): 33–37.

Excluding these products would raise the extent of tariff escalation even further.

Table 2 provides data on average tariffs in the developed countries for products in eleven processing chains that are of interest to developing countries and, among them, to countries at lower levels of industrial development. The raw materials in question weigh heavily in the exports of the countries concerned, and the processing of these materials is frequently within their technical competence. Also, with the major exception of paper, processing is not a highly capital-intensive activity.

It is apparent that, except for wood, tariffs escalate in all cases. But this exception is more apparent than real, since the major input into furniture is semimanufactured wood that has lower tariffs. And the overall importance of tariff escalation is indicated by the fact that the products in question account for 47 percent of the exports of nonfuel primary and semiprocessed products from the developing to the developed countries but for only 11 percent of manufactured exports. At the same time, the data reported in Table 2 exclude textiles and clothing, iron and steel, and footwear, where there is also tariff escalation but where quantitative import restrictions tend to be the effective barrier to developed-country markets.

Escalation of tariffs can cause effective rates of protection to exceed nominal rates by a substantial margin. At the same time, for developing-country producers, the relevant consideration is the protection of the processing margin (value-added), or effective protection, rather than the nominal tariffs levied on individual products.

Data provided in an earlier paper by Yeats (1974) permit estimating effective rates in the post–Tokyo Round situation for three semimanufactured products: processed cocoa (15.8 percent), leather (13.5 percent), and vegetable oil (70.2 percent). In the cases considered, the ratio of effective to nominal tariffs ranges from 3.2 (leather) to 8.7 (vegetable oil); the differences in the ratios are explained largely by interindustry differences in the share of value-added in output.[2]

Such protection tends to discriminate against industrial processing in these countries and, in particular, in countries at lower levels of industrial development. Other things being equal, a 20 percent effective rate of protection in developed countries means that firms engaged in processing in a developing country would have to compress their processing margin (value-added) by 25 percent in order to compete with processing activities in the developed coun-

---

[2] The Tokyo Round did little to reduce the extent of tariff escalation; the ratios of effective to nominal protection are similar to those calculated by Yeats (1974) for the post–Kennedy Round situation.

TABLE 2.
Pre– and Post–Tokyo Round Tariffs for Twelve Processing Chains

Stage of Processing	Product Description	Tariff Rate[a]		1981 Developing Countries Exports to Industrial Countries[b] (US$ millions)
		Pre-Tokyo	Post-Tokyo	
1	Fish, crustaceans, and molluscs	4.3	3.5	1,145
2	Fish, crustaceans, and molluscs, prepared	6.1	5.5	580
1	Vegetables, fresh or dried	13.3	8.9	1,291
2	Vegetables, prepared	18.8	12.4	20
1	Fruit, fresh, dried	6.0	4.8	2,409
2	Fruit, provisionally preserved	14.5	12.2	2,474
3	Fruit, prepared	19.5	16.6	1,321
1	Coffee	10.0	6.8	4,385
2	Processed coffee	13.3	9.4	288
1	Cocoa beans	4.2	2.6	994
2	Processed cocoa	6.7	4.3	433
3	Chocolate products	15.0	11.8	43
1	Oil seeds and flour	2.7	2.7	579
2	Fixed vegetable oils	8.5	8.1	1,374
1	Unmanufactured tobacco	56.1	55.8	1,117
2	Manufactured tobacco	82.2	81.8	39
1	Natural rubber	2.8	2.3	2,045
2	Semimanufactured rubber (unvulcanized)	4.6	2.9	3
3	Rubber articles	7.9	6.7	390

Stage of Processing	Product Description	Tariff Rate[a] Pre-Tokyo	Tariff Rate[a] Post-Tokyo	1981 Developing Countries Exports to Industrial Countries[b] (US$ millions)
1	Raw hides and skins	1.4	0.0	144
2	Semimanufactured leather	4.2	4.2	437
3	Travel goods, handbags etc.	8.5	8.5	1,082
4	Manufactured articles of leather	9.3	8.2	748
1	Vegetable textiles yarns (excluding hemp)	4.0	2.9	150
2	Twine, rope and articles; sacks and bags	5.6	4.7	203
3	Jute fabrics	9.1	8.3	73
1	Silk yarn, not for retail sale	2.6	2.6	38
2	Silk fabric	5.6	5.3	176
1	Semimanufactured wood	2.6	1.8	1,241
2	Wood panels	10.8	9.2	744
3	Wood articles	6.9	4.1	524
4	Furniture	8.1	6.6	681
	TOTAL			27,171
	MEMORANDUM ITEMS			
	Total Manufactures			57,910
	Textiles, Footwear, Iron and Steel			23,373
	Manufactured Exports Subject to Tariff Escalation (except textiles, footwear, iron and steel)			6,490
	Total Nonfuel Primary			43,792
	Nonfuel Primary Subject to Tariff Escalation			20,681

[a] Unweighted average of the tariffs actually facing developing-country exports (i.e., Generalized System of Preference, Most-Favoured-Nation, other special preferential rates, etc.) in the market of EEC, Japan, Australia, New Zealand, Canada, Austria, Switzerland, Finland, Norway, and Sweden.

[b] Includes exports to the United States, Japan, and the EEC.

Source: Alexander J. Yeats, The Influence of Trade and Commercial Barriers on the Industrial Processing of Natural Resources, World Development 9(5)(May 1981): 485–494 and World Bank Trade Data System.

tries. With some of the costs of processing, including the cost of capital, not being compressible, tariff escalation in the developed countries thus puts industrial processing in the developing countries at a considerable disadvantage.

NONTARIFF BARRIERS

Parallel with reductions in tariffs, quantitative import restrictions were liberalized during the 1950s in Western Europe, where these restrictions had been applied largely for balance-of-payments purposes after World War II. Import liberalization also proceeded, albeit at a slower rate, in Japan—where restrictions had been employed on balance-of-payments as well as on infant-industry grounds, although a number of products remained subject to quantitative import restrictions until the early 1970s. Finally, the United States continued with its broadly liberal trade policy and abandoned the American selling-price provisions on coal-tar-based chemicals but imposed limitations on the imports of Japanese cotton textiles.

Agriculture was an exception to the process of import liberalization during the postwar period. In fact, apart from the United States (a large net exporter of food and feeding stuffs), agricultural protection in the developed countries was reinforced after 1960. The European Community has encouraged high-cost production by setting high domestic prices in the framework of the Common Agricultural Policy, thereby turning an import surplus in major foods into an export surplus. Also, with higher wages raising domestic production costs, agricultural protection has intensified in Japan.

Increased use has been made of nontariff protection in manufacturing industries as well. The developed countries have generally refrained from applying the GATT safeguard clause; they have relied instead on so-called voluntary export restraints and orderly marketing arrangements to limit imports.

Measures of nontariff protection on textiles and clothing apply exclusively to developing-country exporters. Thus, while the Long-Term Arrangement Regarding Cotton Textiles (1962) was originally aimed largely at Japan, its successor, the Multifiber Arrangement (1979), limits the imports of textiles and clothing from the developing countries. And whereas the MFA earlier permitted annual import growth of 6 percent in volume, in the course of its subsequent renewals and reinterpretations it has become increasingly restrictive. While Japan is not party to the MFA, there is evidence of informal limitations on the imports of textiles and clothing from the developing countries.

Japan severely limits the importation of footwear from all sources, whereas several of the larger European countries restrict footwear imports from the developing countries alone. Finally, during the 1970s, the United States limited the imports of nonrubber footwear from Korea and Taiwan (China) and the International Trade Commission has again recommended the imposition of restrictions on the importation of footwear.

Since the early 1970s, nontariff measures have also assumed increased importance for steel. In the United States there are formal and informal limitations on the importation of carbon and specialty steel from Japan, from the European Community, and from several developing countries; the Community restricts imports from Japan and from developing countries; and informal measures limit steel imports from Korea into Japan.

France and Italy have long restricted automobile imports from Japan. In recent years they have been joined by Belgium, Germany, and the United Kingdom. In turn, the United States negotiated limitations on the imports of automobiles from Japan in 1981 but let the agreement expire in early 1985.

In the electronics industry, the European Community has imposed limitations on the imports of several products from Japan and, to a lesser extent, Korea and Taiwan. In turn, the United States has eliminated earlier restrictions on the importation of color television sets. Finally, informal barriers limit the importation of telecommunication equipment into Japan.

Table 3 shows the extent of nontariff barriers applied by the major developed countries following recent increases in these barriers. The table provides information on the use of nontariff measures affecting imports from the other developed countries, from the developing countries, and from all countries taken together, in the United States, the European Common Market, and Japan, based on a joint World Bank–UNCTAD research effort.

Nontariff barriers have been defined to include all transparent border measures that directly or indirectly limit imports. Quantitative import restrictions and so-called voluntary export restraints limit imports directly. In turn, variable import levies that equalize domestic and import prices, minimum price requirements for imports, voluntary export price agreements, as well as tariff quotas involving the imposition of higher duties above a predetermined import quantity, have an indirect effect on imports.

Table 3 shows the share of imports subject to nontariff measures, calculated by using world trade weights. The use of world trade weights allows for differences in the relative importance of individual tariff items in international trade while abstracting from the idiosyncracies of national protection. In contrast, calculating for a particular country the percentage share of own imports subject to restrictions is equivalent to using own imports as weights, which

TABLE 3.

Relative Shares of Imports Subject to Nontariff Measures, May 1985 (World Trade Weighted)[a]

	Nonfuel Products	Agriculture	Manufacturing	Textiles and Clothing	Footwear	Iron and Steel	Electrical Machinery	Transport Equipment	Rest of Manufacturing
UNITED STATES									
Imports from									
all countries[b]	6.4	11.5	5.6	47.8	0.1	21.8	0.0	0.0	0.4
industrial countries	3.4	11.7	2.7	25.5	0.0	24.6	0.0	0.0	0.0
developing countries	12.9	11.8	14.4	65.3	0.1	4.5	0.0	0.0	1.9
EUROPEAN COMMUNITY									
Imports from									
all countries[b]	13.9	37.8	10.1	42.4	10.2	37.9	4.2	3.9	3.8
industrial countries	10.5	46.7	5.7	13.6	0.3	33.7	3.1	3.8	2.6
developing countries	21.8	27.5	21.4	65.2	12.5	28.9	4.7	4.6	5.3
JAPAN									
Imports from									
all countries[b]	9.6	33.8	5.4	14.0	39.6	0.0	0.0	0.0	6.0
industrial countries	9.5	35.7	5.5	14.0	34.3	0.0	0.0	0.0	7.1
developing countries	10.5	30.2	5.4	14.2	42.2	0.0	0.0	0.0	1.9

[a] The data collected by Nogues, Olechowski, and Winters for 1983 have been adjusted for the termination of the U.S.–Japanese automotive agreement. Other changes in protection occurring between 1983 and 1985 have been relatively minor.
[b] All countries include the socialist countries of Eastern Europe, hence the overall average does not necessarily lie between average for imports from the industrial and from the developing countries.

Source: Julio J. Nogues, Andrzej Olechowski, and L. Alan Winters, The Establishment of Non-tariff Barriers to Industrial Countries' Imports. World Bank Department Research Department Discussion Paper No. 115 (January 1985) and the sources cited therein.

means that the more restrictive the measure the lower its weight in the calculations; in the extreme, prohibitive tariffs have zero weight.[3] Also, calculating the percentage share of tariff items has the disadvantage that it gives equal weight to all items, even though they may vary in importance to a considerable extent.[4]

Table 3 reports nontariff barriers for nonfuel imports and, within this total, for agricultural and for manufactured imports; it further disaggregates manufactured goods into textiles and clothing, footwear, iron and steel, electrical machinery, transport equipment, and other manufactures. Fuels have not been included because the nontariff measures applied do not appear to aim at protecting the domestic production of competing fuels.

The results are indicative of the high protection of EEC and Japanese agriculture, where most commodities competing with domestic production encounter nontariff barriers. With protection applying chiefly to temperate-zone products, these barriers affect a somewhat higher proportion of agricultural imports from developed than developing-country suppliers. The proportions are about the same in the case of the United States, where the extent of nontariff barriers of agricultural products is relatively low.

In the United States and the European Community, nontariff barriers on manufactured imports discriminate to a considerable extent against developing-country exporters. This discrimination is largely due to the restrictions imposed on developing-country exports of textiles and clothing in the framework of the Multifiber Arrangement (MFA). As noted above, Japan is not party to the MFA but is said to use informal measures to limit its imports of textiles and clothing from the developing countries; in fact, as shown below, its imports have been growing at a lower rate and account for a smaller proportion of domestic consumption than in the United States and the European Common Market.

The data reported in Table 3 do not include other border measures that could, but may not, be used with protective effect, such as antidumping and countervailing duties, price monitoring, and investigations of alleged practices that may give rise to the imposition of such duties and automatic import authorizations. There is some

---

[3] For example, France limits the imports of automobiles from Japan to 3 percent of domestic sales while, for several years, the United States restricted imports from Japan to about 20 percent of domestic sales. Correspondingly, the own-import ratio was substantially lower in France than in the United States, even though nontariff measures were much more restrictive in the first case than in the second.

[4] At the same time, to the extent that all, or most, countries apply quantitative import restrictions to the same commodities, for example textiles, their share in world trade will be lowered, thereby affecting the world trade-weighted average of nontariff measures.

TABLE 4.
Relative Shares of Nontariff Measures and Other Border Measures
(all products less fuels; all countries; world trade weighted)

	Nontariff Measures[a] (1)	Other Border Measures[b] (2)	Sum of Columns (1) and (2) (3)[c]
European Community	13.9	11.6	21.0
United States	6.4	3.4	9.5
Japan	9.6	0.0	9.6

[a] See Table 3.
[b] Countervailing and antidumping duties, price surveillance, price investigation, quantity surveillance, and automatic licensing.
[c] The figures in this column are less than the sum of those in the columns reported because some trade flows face several barriers.
Source: See Table 3.

evidence that these practices have been applied in certain circumstances in lieu of safeguards and with both the intent and effect of protecting domestic industry rather than simply offsetting distortions introduced by the exporter (Finger, Hall, and Nelson, 1982). Their use has also increased since the late 1970s (Nogues, Olechowski, and Winters, 1985).

Nevertheless, given the legitimate role that such practices can play in trade, they have to be treated differently from other nontariff measures. Thus, rather than eliminating the measures themselves, one should assure that they are not used for protective purposes.

As an illustration, the nontariff measures reported in Table 3, as well as the other border measures just described, are reported in Table 4. It should be noted, however, that for lack of information, the data on other border measures do not include Japan.

The data reported in Table 3 and 4 do not include health and safety measures and technical standards that may be used with a protective intent.[5] Nor do the data comprise various informal measures that are prevalent in countries which rely to a considerable extent on administrative discretion rather than on codified rules to limit imports. Finally, the data are limited to trade-related measures with the exclusion of domestic measures (e.g., producer subsidies and regional development measures) that bear on trade indirectly through their effect on domestic production.

Despite increasing barriers to trade, the share of imports from the developing countries in the consumption of manufactured goods

---

[5] The only country covered in the paper for which such information is available is Japan. According to UNCTAD, health and safety measures and technical standards pertain to 48 percent of Japan's imports from industrial countries and to 17 percent of its imports from developing countries. See UNCTAD, *Problems of Protectionism and Structural Adjustment*, Report by the Secretariat, Part I: Restrictions to Trade and Structural Adjustment TD/B/1039, January 28, 1985, Table 2.

TABLE 5.
Relative Importance of Manufactured Imports from
Developing Countries

	Import-Consumption Ratio (in current prices)			
	1973	*1978*	*1981*	*1983*
UNITED STATES				
Iron and steel	0.6	0.9	1.4	2.3
Chemicals	0.4	0.5	0.6	0.9
Other semimanufactures	0.9	1.5	1.7	1.9
Engineering products	0.7	1.3	2.0	2.6
Textiles	1.8	1.6	2.3	2.2
Clothing	5.6	11.3	14.0	15.1
Other consumer goods	1.9	3.7	4.8	5.2
All manufactures	1.1	1.8	2.4	3.0
EUROPEAN COMMON MARKET				
Iron and steel	0.4	0.4	0.6	0.7
Chemicals	0.5	0.6	0.8	1.1
Other semimanufactures	1.3	2.5	1.9	2.3
Engineering products	0.3	0.9	1.3	1.4
Textiles	2.6	3.7	4.1	4.4
Clothing	5.7	11.4	16.4	16.0
Other consumer goods	1.1	1.6	2.9	3.1
All manufactures	0.9	1.6	2.0	2.1
JAPAN				
Iron and steel	0.2	0.3	1.0	1.6
Chemicals	0.3	0.5	0.8	0.9
Other semimanufactures	1.0	0.9	0.9	0.9
Engineering products	0.2	0.3	0.5	0.4
Textiles	2.2	2.3	2.1	1.9
Clothing	7.6	7.4	8.9	8.2
Other consumer goods	0.8	1.1	1.3	1.5
All manufactures	0.7	0.8	0.9	1.0

Source: GATT, *International Trade;* United Nations, *Yearbook of Industrial Statistics;* and OECD, *Indicators of Industrial Activity,* various years.

by the major developed countries continued to rise during the last decade. Table 5 shows the relationship between manufactured imports from the developing countries and the consumption of manufactured products, defined as production plus imports less exports, in the United States, the European Community, and Japan. Information is provided on the developing-countries' market shares in the years 1973, 1978, 1981, and 1983.

There are no signs of a slowdown in the growth of the developing-countries' share in industrial countries' markets except for the group of other semimanufactures, which are heavily weighted by natural-resource products, and for the category of textiles and clothing, where the MFA has become increasingly restrictive. At the same time, until recently, the import shares of textiles and clothing continued to rise, reflecting the upgrading of products exported by the developing countries in the face of limitations imposed on increases in volume. Furthermore, developing-country exporters increasingly shifted to the exportation of products that did not encounter barriers such as engineering goods and iron and steel, which later has subsequently become subject to restrictions.

The data further show that differences between the United States and the European Community, on the one hand, and Japan, on the other, were increasing over time as far as the share of imports from developing countries in their domestic consumption is concerned. Thus, while this share was 1.1 percent in the United States, 0.9 percent in the Common Market, and 0.7 percent in Japan in 1973, the corresponding shares were 3.0, 2.1, and 1.0 percent in 1983.

It appears, then, that although Japan is not a party to the MFA and has few formal barriers to imports from the developing countries (the major exception being footwear), it has increasingly lagged behind the other major developed countries in importing manufactured goods from the developing countries. Yet, with its rapid economic growth and the accumulation of physical and human capital, Japan has approached the other developed countries in terms of factor endowments and thus one would have expected it to resemble their import pattern more closely. The fact that the opposite has happened may be taken as an indication of the use of informal measures of protection against developing-country exports in Japan.

Note finally that, while increased protection through nontariff measures in developed-country markets has been accompanied by increased penetration of developing-country exports in these markets, this should not be interpreted to mean that such protection would not have involved an economic cost in the developed countries or would not have adversely affected developing countries. It rather means that protection has been concentrated in particular sectors and that developing countries have been able to alleviate its impact on their foreign-exchange earnings through export diversification and product upgrading.

THE COST OF PROTECTION

Apart from its adverse effects on foreign exporters, import protection imposes a cost on the domestic economy. Earlier estimates of the cost of protection in the developed countries were generally low, rarely attaining 1 percent of the gross national product. These estimates, however, failed to consider the losses involved in forgoing the exploitation of economies of scale in protected markets. Taking account of economies of scale, it has recently been estimated that

TABLE 6.
Effects of Some Major VERs In Developed Countries[a]

		Clothing		Automobiles	Steel
		USA 1980	EC 1980	USA 1984	USA 1985
(1)	Increased payments on imported goods, $ million	988	1,050	1,778	1,530
(2)	Loss of consumer surplus, $ million	408	289[b]	229	455
(3)	Resource cost of producing the additional quantity domestically, $ million	113	70	185	7
(4)	Cost to the national economy in the protecting country (welfare cost), $ million, (1) + (2) + (3)	1,509	1,409	2,192	1,992
(5)	Jobs saved through protection, thousands	8.9	11.3	45.0	28.0
(6)	Welfare cost per job saved, $ thousand, (4)/(5)	169.6	124.7	48.7	71.1
(7)	Average labor compensation, $ thousand, (annual)	12.6	13.5	38.1	42.4
(8)	Ratio of welfare cost to average compensation, (6)/(7)	13.5	9.2	1.3	1.7
(9)	Lost revenues for exporters, $ million	9,328	7,460	6,050	1,508
(10)	Ratio of increased payments on imported goods to lost revenues for exporters, (1)/(9)	0.11	0.14	0.29	1.01

[a] U.S. dollar estimates are evaluated at current prices for the years indicated.
[b] Foregone tariff revenues, due to the quota introduction, are not included.

Source: Orsalia K. Kalantzopoulos, The Cost of Voluntary Export Restraints for Selected Industries in the U.S. and the EC. Washington, D.C.: World Bank.

protection has reduced potential output by about 10 percent in Canada (Harris, 1983, p. 115). Further losses are incurred in the event of the use of voluntary export restraints, which involve an income transfer to foreign exporters.

Table 6 reports available estimates on the welfare cost of voluntary export restraints, which have come into increased use in recent years. This cost consists of the loss of consumer surplus, the resource cost of producing the additional quantity domestically, and increased payments on imported goods as exporters charge higher prices for the limited quantity they sell. It has been calculated for clothing in the United States and the European Community and for automobiles and steel in the United States.

Rows (1) to (4) of the table show the components of the cost of protection, as well as its total, for the industries in question. Row (5) further indicates the number of jobs saved in the protected industries on the assumption that labor productivity is not affected thereby. In turn, row (6) shows the welfare cost per job saved in the industries in question.

While the data refer to different years, this will hardly affect the results since prices changed little during the period. Thus, it is apparent that the welfare cost of saving a job is considerably higher in the clothing industry than in the case of automobiles and steel.

Data on the ratio of the welfare cost to average labor compensation, reported in row (8), are directly comparable across industries, since the numerator as well as the denominator of the ratio are expressed in the prices of the same year. The results show that this ratio was 13.5 in the United States and 9.2 in the EEC clothing industry while it was 11.3 in the U.S. automobile industry and 1.7 in the U.S. steel industry.

The welfare cost of saving a job in the protected industries thus exceeds the wages paid in these industries by a considerable margin, with the differences being by far the highest in the case of clothing, where the import limitations pertain to products originating in developing countries. The cost to the consumer, including higher prices for domestic products resulting from protection, exceeds even this figure. Nor do the estimates take account of job losses in other industries that are discriminated against by protection.

At the same time, while higher prices paid on imports represent a transfer to foreign suppliers, the volume of their exports is adversely affected by the protectionist measures applied. As shown in row (10) of Table 6, the transfer implicit in the higher prices paid to exporters compensated for hardly more than one-tenth of the loss in revenues owing to the reduced volume of exports. The corresponding ratio was 0.14 for automobiles; it was 1 for steel, where higher prices apparently offset for the loss in export volume.

Although similar calculations have not been made for agricultural products, comparisons of domestic and world market prices provide an indication of the relative costs of protection in various markets, although world market prices would rise if protection measures were dismantled. The calculations reported in Table 7 pertain to the 1978–1980 average, that is, before the rise in the value of the U.S. dollar had distorted international price relationships.

The cost of protecting domestic agriculture is indicated by the high ratio of domestic to world market prices in the European Community and Japan. In both cases, domestic prices exceeded world market prices by approximately one-half for wheat. In the Community the price differential exceeded 100 percent for maize; comparable data for Japan are not available. By contrast, domestic prices were slightly below world market prices for both wheat and maize in the United States.

The domestic prices of beef and veal were especially high in

TABLE 7.
Nominal Protection Coefficients for
Agricultural Products, 1978–1980[a]

	US	EEC	Japan
Wheat	0.90	1.52	1.49
Maize	0.85	2.10	n.a.
Beef and veal	0.81	1.36	2.41[b]
Lamb and sheep	1.10	1.48	n.a.
Sugar	1.48	1.76	1.59

[a] The nominal protection coefficient is the ratio of
domestic to world market prices.
[b] Data provided by the Australia–Japan Research
Center, Australia National University, Canberra,
Australia.
Source: U.S. Department of Agriculture.

Japan, exceeding the international price two to three times. In the
EEC, the price differential surpassed one-third for beef and veal and
approached one-half in the case of lamb and sheep. In the United
States, domestic prices were slightly below world market prices for
beef and veal and slightly above the prices for lamb and sheep.

While the United States protects the domestic production of
sugar, the excess of domestic over world market prices for this commodity was greater in the EEC and Japan than in the United States.
This situation has continued despite the overvaluation of the dollar.
Also, the EEC countries have subsidized their sugar exports, with the
subsidy reaching 1.2 billion in 1984. Over the last eight years, the
Common Market exported 38 million tons of sugar as domestic output rose from 10.8 to 13.3 million tons and consumption declined.
During the same period, U.S. sugar imports declined from 6 to 3
million tons (*The Economist*, August 10, 1985).

In conclusion, it should be emphasized that, apart from the
measured cost imposed on the national economy, the protection of
noncompetitive, low-productivity sectors has unfavorable long-term
effects on the developed countries by postponing adjustment as well
as the upgrading of labor. Nontariff barriers have particularly adverse effects by reducing competition, introducing discriminatory practices, and keeping out new entrants which frequently are
developing countries. In particular, the Multifiber Arrangement
has perverse effects in encouraging the upgrading of products in
the developing countries while considerations of comparative
advantage would call for such upgrading to occur in the developed
countries.

Finally, high protection involves the misallocation of new additions to the capital stock. This is because, apart from safeguarding
existing firms, protection provides an inducement for new investments in sectors where the developed countries have a comparative

disadvantage. Correspondingly, less capital is available to high-skill, high-technology industries where these countries possess important advantages. Ultimately, then, protection unfavorably affects economic growth in the developed countries as well as in their trading partners among developing countries.

Protection in the Developing Countries

THE EXTENT OF IMPORT PROTECTION

Comparable estimates on the level of protection and the share of imports subject to quantitative import restrictions are available for relatively few developing countries. At the same time, available information indicates that the scope of nontariff measures is much greater, and levels of protection are both higher and show greater variation, in these countries than in the developed countries.

Studies by Balassa and Associates (1971), Bhagwati (1978), Krueger (1978), and Balassa and Associates (1982) showed considerable differences in the trade regimes of the developing countries during the 1960s. These differences pertained to the protection of the manufacturing sector and the consequent bias against primary activities (in particular, agriculture) as well as to the extent of the bias against exports. The countries in question may be divided into three groups on the basis of the policies applied during this period.

The first group included Argentina, Brazil, Chile, Pakistan, and the Philippines, all of which highly protected their manufacturing industries, discriminated against primary production, and biased the system of incentives against exports. In these countries, the average net effective protection of the manufacturing sector, reflecting adjustment for the overvaluation of the exchange rate associated with protection, ranged between 40 and 150 percent.

The countries of the second group, including Colombia, Israel, and Mexico, had considerably lower levels of industrial protection. Also, the extent of discrimination against primary activities was less than in the countries of the first group. Nonetheless, there was substantial bias against manufactured exports, with value-added obtainable in domestic markets exceeding that obtainable in exporting by 40 to 90 percent compared with 120 to 320 percent in the first group.

Finally, in Korea, Singapore, and Malaysia, there was little discrimination against manufactured exports, with the excess of value-added obtainable in domestic markets over that obtainable in export markets ranging from 6 to 26 percent. The same conclusion applies to the primary exports of the countries of this group that did not discriminate against primary activities.

More recent estimates are available for several of these countries. They show little change in relative incentives to manufacturing and to primary production in the case of Korea. At the same time, reforms undertaken in the second half of the 1960s reduced, to a lesser or greater extent, the protection of manufacturing activities and discrimination against the primary sector in Brazil, Colombia, Mexico, and the Philippines. In turn, changes in the opposite direction occurred in Malaysia (Roger, 1985).

On the whole, however, while several developing countries had liberalized their trade regimes in the late 1960s, trade policies in most of these countries discriminate in favor of import substitution and against exports, and there is considerable dispersion in the effective protection provided to various economic activities. Also, in several large Latin American countries protection was increased again in response to the external shocks of the post-1973 period.

THE COST OF PROTECTION

The cost of protection in developing countries can be rather high. Estimates for several of the countries cited above showed this cost to equal 9.5 percent of GNP in Brazil, 6.2 percent in Chile, 6.2 percent in Pakistan, 3.7 percent in the Philippines, and 2.5 percent in Mexico during the 1960s (Balassa and Associates, 1971).

These results were obtained in a partial equilibrium framework and do not allow for the losses of economies of scale in protected domestic markets. Subsequently, De Melo estimated the cost of protection for Colombia in a general equilibrium framework, incorporating intermediate products, nontraded goods, as well as substitution among products and among primary factors (De Melo, 1978). Excluding land reallocation within agriculture and postulating an optimal export tax for coffee, the cost of protection was estimated at 11.0 percent of GNP, assuming labor to be fully employed, and 15.8 percent, assuming that additional supplies of labor are available at a constant real wage.

De Melo's results are considerably higher than the estimates made in a partial equilibrium framework, even though Colombia was in the middle range among developing countries in terms of levels of protection. Thus, De Melo estimated effective protection to average 25 percent in the Colombian manufacturing sector, without an exchange-rate adjustment, while the comparable result in the Balassa study was 35 percent.

It would appear, then, that the estimates obtained in a partial equilibrium framework understate the cost of protection. Part of the reason is that estimates made in this framework do not allow for the fact that the cost of protection rises with the dispersion of interindustry rates of protection (Nugent, 1974, pp. 62–63). Yet the dispersion of protection rates is much greater in developing than in developed countries and, within the former group, in highly protected rather than less-protected economies.

PROTECTION AND ECONOMIC GROWTH

Protection has traditionally been justified on the grounds that it will enable industries to grow up and eventually to confront foreign competition. The assumptions underlying this infant-industry argument is that protection is required on a temporary basis to offset the costs firms incur upon undertaking a new productive activity that will not be fully recouped by the firm itself but by the industry as a whole. This is because the firms initially entering upon a new activity will generate so-called externalities through labor training and technological improvements.

While these changes are supposed to permit productivity to increase more rapidly in protected infant industries of the developing countries than in the developed countries, the evidence suggests that protection has rather retarded productivity growth. Thus, in the early postwar period, the protected Latin American countries experienced virtually no increase in productivity (Bruton, 1967).

Also, in the 1960–1973 period, incremental capital-output ratios were the highest in Chile (5.5) and India (5.7), which had by far the highest protection levels. In turn, these ratios were the lowest in Singapore (1.8) and Korea (2.1), which had the lowest levels of protection. Finally, incremental capital-output ratios declined in countries such as Brazil (from 3.8 in 1960–1966 to 2.1 in 1966-1973) that reduced their levels of protection during the latter part of the period (Balassa and Associates, 1982, p. 3).

High incremental capital-output ratios reflect slow productivity growth under protection, which tends to discourage exports, as production in the confines of domestic markets limits the exploitation of economies of scale, capacity utilization, and technological improvements, thereby aggravating the adverse effects of inefficient resource allocation. By contrast, in national economies where protection levels are low, exports are encouraged, permitting the exploitation of economies of scale and higher-capacity utilization, with the carrot and the stick of competition in foreign markets providing inducements for technological change.

The above considerations may explain the observed positive correlation between exports and economic growth. This was first shown by Michalopoulos and Jay (1973) in a cross-section production-function type relationship, with exports added to the conventional explanatory variables of capital and labor. Subsequently, Feder (1983) found that the use of primary factors in export production, rather than in producing nonexport products, entailed a 1.8 percentage-point difference in economic growth rates during the 1964–1973 period in a group of thirty-one semi-industrial countries.

These results relate to a period of rapid expansion in the world economy. The question was raised if they would also apply following the deterioration of world market conditions as a result of increases in petroleum prices and the slowdown of economic growth in the developed countries after 1973. This question has been answered in the affirmative in studies by Krueger and Michalopoulos (1985) and by Balassa (1984).

Krueger and Michalopoulos (1985) showed that the average rate of growth of both exports and GNP was higher for outward-oriented developing economies with relatively balanced trade incentives than for inward-oriented developing countries characterized by high protection during the 1960–1973 period of high world economic growth as well as during the 1973–1981 period of external shocks. Balassa further showed that while the external shocks of the latter period entailed a greater economic cost for outward-oriented countries, which had a larger trade share relative to GNP, the excess cost was offset severalfold through more rapid economic growth in these countries than in inward-oriented economies (Balassa, 1984). Differences in growth performance, in turn, were attributed to differences in the adjustment policies applied in response to external shocks.

In subsequent research the trade policies applied at the beginning of this period of external shocks and policy responses to external shocks was introduced simultaneously in a cross-section investigation of forty-three developing countries in the 1973-1979 period (Balassa, 1985). The trade policies applied at the beginning of the period have been represented by an index of trade orientation estimated as deviations of actual from hypothetical values of per capita exports, the latter having been derived in a regression equation that includes per capita incomes, population, and the ratio of mineral exports to the gross national product as explanatory variables. In turn, alternative policy responses to external shocks have been represented by relating the balance-of-payments effects of export promotion, import substitution, and additional net external financing to the balance-of-payment effects of external shocks.

The results show that initial trade orientation as well as the character of policy responses to external shocks importantly affected rates of economic growth in the 1973–1979 period. Thus, GNP growth rates differed by 1.0 percentage point between countries in the upper and in the lower quartiles of the distribution in terms of their trade orientation in 1973. There was further a 1.2 percentage-point difference in GNP growth rates between countries in the upper and the lower quartiles of the distribution in terms of reliance on export promotion, as against import substitution and additional net external financing, in response to the external shocks of the 1973–1978 period.

The results are cumulative, indicating that both the initial trade orientation and the choice of adjustment policies in response to external shocks importantly contributed to economic growth during the period under review. In fact, these two factors explain a large proportion of intercountry differences in GNP growth rates, which averaged 5.0 percent in the forty-three developing countries under consideration during the 1973–1979 period, with an upper quartile of 6.5 percent and a lower quartile of 3.3 percent.

Conclusions and Policy Implications

The review of protection in developed countries showed that, on the average, trade barriers tend to be higher on agricultural products than on manufactures and within manufacturing tend to be concentrated in a few sectors. By contrast, developing countries protect manufacturing industries more than agriculture, and their barriers are both more widespread and more variable.

Nontariff barriers are more important than tariffs in inhibiting trade between developed and developing countries; nevertheless, because of their escalation, tariffs continue to restrain access to developed-country markets in certain manufactured products. At the same time, with some important exceptions such as high-technology products, the developed-countries' nontariff barriers tend to be more prevalent, and their tariffs tend to be higher, on products of interest to developing countries than on their trade with each other.

It was further shown that the developed countries pay a large cost for maintaining employment in a few manufacturing sectors through protection. At the same time, such calculations underestimate the long-term costs of protection. This is because protection tends to slow down technological progress and leads to the misallocation of new investment.

The analysis of the cost of protection in developing countries focused primarily on the fact that countries with liberal trade regimes tend to grow faster and withstand better adverse developments in the international economy. The reason for their superior performance lies primarily in the lower degree of economic distortions and the greater flexibility associated with their trade regimes, which provide similar incentives to production for domestic and for foreign markets as well as to industry and agriculture.

Despite increasing protection in recent years, the extent of market penetration by developing countries in developed-country markets has risen, as has overall trade interdependence between the two groups of countries. This increased interdependence, in turn, raises the opportunity for mutually advantageous trade liberalization that can promote structural adjustment and stimulate long-term growth in both developed and developing countries.

Multilateral trade negotiations in the framework of the GATT provide an appropriate—indeed, the only—avenue for significant trade liberalization. Such negotiations would need to encompass all items of importance to trade between developed and developing countries in manufactures, agriculture, and services, and include both tariff and nontariff barriers. All developing countries and (especially) the NICs need to be active participants in such negotiations and be prepared to offer a certain degree of reciprocity consistent with their level of development.[6]

The authors alone are responsible for the contents of this paper that should not be interpreted to reflect the views of the World Bank.

References

Balassa, Bela (1984) Adjustment Policies in Developing Countries: A Reassessment, *World Development* 12(9): 955–972.

―――― (1985) Exports, Policy Choices, and Economic Growth in Developing Countries After the 1973 Oil Shock, *Journal of Development Economics* 18(1): 23–36.

Balassa, Bela and Associates (1971) *The Structure of Protection in Developing Countries*. Baltimore: Johns Hopkins University Press.

―――― (1982) *Development Strategies in Semi-Industrial Economies*. A World Bank Research Publication. Baltimore: Johns Hopkins University Press.

Balassa, Bela, and Balassa, Carol (1984) Industrial Protection in the Developed Countries, *The World Economy* 7(2): 179–186.

Bhagwati, Jagdish N. (1978) *Anatomy and Consequences of Exchange Control Regimes*. Cambridge, Mass.: Ballinger. Pp. 19–78.

Bruton, H. J. (1967) Productivity Growth in Latin America, *American Economic Review* 57: 1099–1116.

De Melo, Jaime (1978) Estimating the Costs of Protection: A General Equilibrium Approach, *Quarterly Journal of Economics* 92(2): 209–226.

―――――――――――

[6] A companion paper by the authors, "Liberalizing Trade between Developed and Developing Countries," examines the objectives, scope, and modalities of multilateral trade liberalization between developed and developing countries.

Feder, Gershon (1983) On Exports and Economic Growth, *Journal of Development Economics* 12(1): 59–73.

Finger, J. M., Hall, H. K., and Nelson, D. R. (1982) The Political Economy of Administered Protection, *American Economic Review* 72(3): 452–466.

Harris, R. G., with Cox, D. (1983) *Trade, Industrial Policy and Canadian Manufacturing*. Toronto: Ontario Economic Council.

———— (1978) *Liberalization Attempts and Consequences*. Cambridge, Mass.: Ballinger.

Krueger, Anne O. and Michalopoulos, C. (1985) Developing-Country Trade Policies and The International Economic System. In Ernest M. Preeg, ed., *Hard Bargaining Ahead: U.S. Trade Policy and Developing Countries*. Overseas Development Council, U.S.–Third World Policy Perspectives No. 4. New Brunswick, N.J.: Transaction Books. Pp. 39–57.

Michalopoulos, Constantine and Jay, Keith (1973) Growth of Exports and Income in the Developing World: A Neoclassical View, AID Discussion Paper No. 28. Washington, D.C.: Agency for International Development.

Nogues, Julio J., Olechowski, Andrzej, and Winters, L. Alan (1985) The Establishment of Non-Tariff Barriers to Industrial Countries' Imports. World Bank Development Research Department Discussion Paper No. 115. January.

Nugent, Jeffrey B. (1974) *Economic Integration in Central America: Empirical Investigations*. Baltimore: Johns Hopkins University Press.

Roger, Neil (1985) Trade Policy Regimes in Developing Countries. Washington, D.C.: World Bank. Mimeographed.

Yeats, Alexander J. (1974) Effective Tariff Protection in the United States, the European Economic Community, and Japan, *The Quarterly Review of Economics and Business* 14(2): 41–50.

24

Developing Countries and Reform of the World Trading System

CARLOS F. DIAZ-ALEJANDRO
AND GERALD K. HELLEINER

Introduction

Over the past thirty-five years changes in international politics, in the character of international economic activity, and in the behavior of both private corporations and sovereign governments have rendered increasingly salient some of the limitations in the original GATT and have generated new problems for it. The GATT, originally the central institutional pillar of the postwar international trading system (a role it performed remarkably well), has gradually become less effective and less credible. Its effectiveness and credibility are particularly challenged at present by the developing countries.

The GATT was constructed at a time when a major world war had just ended and memories of the protectionist and discriminatory practices of the 1930s were fresh—a time of unusual and worldwide commitment to the building of a more stable, efficient, and equitable international order. In the trade sphere, the vision of the architects of the new order was of a more liberal and nondiscriminatory system within which independent and equally treated partners would trade in open and competitive markets. Macroeconomic events were to be more effectively managed than previously, it was hoped, by governments imbued with a new confidence in their capacity to maintain full employment. The international financial dimensions of these

From Columbia University, New York, New York; and University of Toronto, Toronto, Ontario, Canada.

macroeconomic aspirations were to be supported by the new International Monetary Fund.

The original norms and expectations of the GATT's founders were breached in many spheres but nowhere more than in terms of the rise of preferential and discriminatory trading areas and arrangements.

A particularly severe blow to nondiscriminatory principles was the negotiation, under GATT auspices, of discriminatory quotas against "low-cost" suppliers of textiles and textile products. Originally negotiated on a short-term basis for cotton textiles over twenty years ago, they have since been greatly extended in time and in product and country coverage. The Multi-Fiber Arrangement (MFA), the successor to the original short-term cotton agreement, continues to legitimize some of the most egregious of the discriminatory practices of the industrialized countries and constitutes a standing repudiation of the GATT's purported first principle of nondiscrimination. It has been enormously harmful to the GATT's image and credibility—particularly, of course, among developing countries.

The multilateral and nondiscriminatory aspirations implicit in the GATT were also confounded in the arrangements within the European Economic Community (EEC), and between it and many of its trading partners. No less contrary to the nondiscrimination principles of the GATT, although probably of relatively small overall significance, is the multilaterally agreed system of tariff preferences granted by industrialized countries since the early 1960s on semiprocessed, processed, and manufactured products from developing countries. Only about two-thirds of world trade is now estimated to take place on the basis of nondiscriminatory (most-favored-nation) tariffs that are equally available to all under firm and contractual commitments in the GATT.

Also damaging to the status and credibility of established multilateral institutions like the GATT was the increasing resort to international codes and agreements of a much less than universal character. In such areas as capital liberalization, the terms of export credit, and the appropriate conduct of transnational companies, the Western industrialized countries negotiated their own codes or agreements within their Organization for Economic Co-operation and Development (OECD) without waiting for more universal accommodations to be reached. Even within the GATT, some of the codes governing nontariff measures negotiated during the Tokyo Round are applied, contrary to previous principle and practice, only to the exports of some countries; eligibility for benefits is conditional upon signature of the codes.

In recent years there has been a quantum leap in the extent to which industrialized countries have employed nontraditional (i.e., nontariff) measures to restrain imports. Many of these measures are neither specifically authorized nor explicitly forbidden by the GATT. The most visible of these much-discussed measures of "new protectionism" are so-called voluntary export restraints and orderly marketing agreements (similar in type to the MFA). These are bilaterally negotiated against the threat of unilateral imposition of restrictions by the importing countries, and they are thus inherently discriminatory. It is widely feared that such arrangements, now applied to footwear, electronics, steel, motor vehicles, textiles and clothing, and agriculture—sectors which together constitute close to half the total value of world trade—will gradually intrude upon more and more segments of international exchange. Particularly vulnerable to these new instruments of protectionism are the newly expanding manufactured exports of the developing countries.

A variety of other new nontariff measures have also been increasingly deployed. These include local content requirements; government procurement policies; laws concerning standards; variable levies on imports; and subsidies for local production under the terms of "industrial," "regional," or other national policies. Administrative discretion, complexity, and obscurity have substituted in these measures for the relative simplicity and automaticity of the import tariff. With these highly contingent and lawyer-intensive protectionist instruments inevitably also comes discrimination among trading partners. Where complexity and discretion take over from simple rules, the weaker firms and countries invariable lose most.

Recently, moreover, pressures arising from serious worldwide macroeconomic dislocation have been added to the deteriorating environment for world trade and investment created by changing politico-economic circumstances and declining respect for the previously agreed (GATT) norms. These macroeconomic difficulties not only have had direct effects upon world trade but have also generated sharp new pressures for protectionism to save jobs from competitive imports. The smaller industrialized countries and the developing countries, while typically highly vulnerable to events in the world economy, have rarely been able to exert much influence upon them. In the current difficult times, as in previous such periods, the weakest have been hit the hardest.

This is not the place to address the need for global economic expansion, better support for those hardest hit by recent external shocks, backup for the international financial system, or the specific measures that might best serve these requirements. While these issues are bound to arise in discussions among trade ministers, they are not the designated responsibilities of the GATT. The problem before the trading community is that world trade and the GATT-based system of international trading rules and principles are themselves in greater jeopardy now than at any time since the GATT's creation.

The immediate task must be to prevent any further deterioration in world trade and to arrest the dangerous downward slide into bilateralism, ad hoc protectionism, and the flouting of multilaterally agreed norms. Uncertainties as to market access are prejudicial to investment, debt management, and the prospects both for adjustment to the current difficult circumstances in the developing countries and their eventual recovery. Current discriminatory practices and demands for "reciprocity" are reminiscent of the bullying tactics and retaliatory practices of the 1930s, the very circumstances that led to the creation of the GATT in the first place. The only immediately available means is to enjoin renewed adherence to the principles of the original GATT system to the maximum extent possible. This would not only restore some predictability and order to a dangerously disorderly scene, but would also rebuild the GATT's credibility both among the contracting parties themselves and in the rest of the world, which still looks to the GATT as the center of the trading system.

The key principles that must govern attempts to make the current system function effectively and augment the existing apparatus are time-honored: nondiscrimination, transparency, and predictability. It is also crucially important that the effort should be multilateral and lead to a genuinely multilateral system.

Our discussion presents an agenda for both short-run and longer-run reform in the world trading system, with particular attention devoted to the needs and concerns of the developing countries. We begin, in the next section, with a review of the arguments for freer trade with developing countries. Following that we argue for building reform efforts upon the existing GATT system. "Foreign Investment, Trade in Services, and Developing Countries" considers the case for new initiatives in services and investment. "Other Key Areas for Negotiation" canvasses other prime areas for diplomatic initiative in the trade sphere. Then we consider means for negotiating a new trade order. Finally we focus on reforms requiring immediate attention.

The Case for Freer Trade with Developing Countries

The postwar international economic order was on the whole created by and for the victorious industrialized powers. Africa, Asia, and the Caribbean were still mostly under colonial rule and were largely absent at the creation of the IMF, the World Bank, and the GATT. Latin American countries and India participated actively in some conferences, including that at Havana which framed the stillborn ITO (International Trade Organization), but their arguments found few echoes in the institutions that later emerged during the 1950s and 1960s. Bargaining at the GATT was dominated by countries seeking access to large industrial markets and offering reciprocity in kind; less developed countries (LDCs) until recently remained passive spectators of this process. While the rules of the tariff bargaining game showed little concern for LDC interests, the great postwar expansion nevertheless resulted in new trade opportunities for many Third World countries. Their exports grew at rates faster than during the dismal interwar period, and their export bills became more diversified, both as to products and geographical destinations. Some of the LDCs benefiting from trade expansion were simply lucky, but many others worked hard at generating a supply of exportable goods suitable for expanding international demand.

For some years after the war many LDCs, remembering interwar circumstances and wishing to promote their infant industries, preferred to provide incentives to boost production for sale in domestic markets rather than for export. This "import-substitution" strategy quickly ran into difficulties, particularly in countries with small markets. Beginning in the 1960s, leading LDCs began to redress the imbalance between incentives for domestic and foreign sales—i.e., between import substitution and export expansion.

As exports responded, imports of machinery, raw materials, and intermediate goods expanded, allowing faster growth rates of gross national product. Indeed, for the 1960s and 1970s there is a well-established empirical regularity showing a close link between export growth and output growth for all but the poorest of the LDCs. In the latter countries, while other influences like the weather, the availability of aid, and the development of skills and infrastructure have been of relatively greater importance, exports are also major determinants of their capacity to import and, consequently, to grow. LDC export earnings are thus the means to obtain, typically from industrialized countries, key development inputs that would be very expensive to produce at home. Expanding export earnings are also crucial for the smooth management of LDC external debt and for the attraction of fresh foreign loans and investments. Northern protectionism that blocks LDC export earnings strikes not only at the heart of their development efforts but also threatens the normal functioning of international capital markets.

The LDCs therefore have a strong interest in an international environment that offers expanding trade opportunities. Most of them have much to gain from further liberalization of their own foreign-trade regimes as well. At the same time, such a process of liberalization is a delicate one in which both substance and style matter a great deal. In recent years some industrialized countries have been pressing LDCs, particularly the newly industrializing countries (NICs), to reduce further their barriers against imports of commodities, services, and direct foreign investment, suggesting that unless the LDCs go along with such demands, the industrialized countries may shut their markets to LDC goods. At the same time that LDCs are pressed to import more goods and services, they are urged to cut back on some of their export promotion policies, this despite their large net deficits on manufactured-goods trade with industrialized countries. Not surprisingly, LDCs, particularly those heavily in debt, have regarded these proposals as misguided.

It is important to analyze demands for "reciprocity" from the LDCs, both in general and with particular reference to the NICs. International-trade theory emphasizes that a country's gains from trade do not depend on "reciprocity" (defined in the GATT sense) from its trade partners. The founding fathers of the GATT were, of course, well aware that national gains could be achieved by unilateral reductions of trade barriers. The mumbo jumbo on reciprocity was a then politically clever device to enlist within each country the support of mercantilists wanting to export more against the protectionists wanting to import less. An argument could be made for reciprocal reduction and binding of trade barriers so as to avoid the temptation to each country of using import or export restrictions to improve its terms of trade. Such restrictions could easily lead to trade wars after which every country would end up worse off.

It is very doubtful that this is what today's shouting about lack of LDC "reciprocity" is all about. When the conditionality of application of new GATT codes on subsidies and countervailing duties is already seen by many—and certainly by all the developing countries—as an important retreat by the industrialized countries from the first GATT principle of *unconditional* nondiscrimination, further talk of "reciprocity" seems rather more like bullying, a style hardly conducive to fruitful negotiation.

Moreover, the increasingly insistent emphasis on problems presented by LDCs' import policies seems not only disproportionate but also at odds with the long-term trends in their policies. As noted earlier, many LDCs began some time ago to turn away from excessive emphasis on import substitution and toward export promotion. The elimination of the bias against exports could have been achieved by the rapid abolition of all import barriers and the unification of exchange rates. Most of the present-day NICs, plagued by macroeconomic and balance-of-payments disequilibria that are much less tractable than those sporadically affecting industrialized countries, opted instead for a package of measures that included export subsidies (offsetting some of the effects of overvalued currencies), export guidelines of various sorts, steadier and more realistic exchange rates, plus an elimination of the most extreme import restrictions. Foreign investors operating within LDCs, who had in earlier years received direct and indirect subsidies in their sales to the local market, were now nudged into exporting, often receiving further subsidies. (It is worth recalling that when foreign investors sold mainly within LDCs, the prevailing northern advice was that a good investment climate called for generous LDC subsidies to transnational enterprises.)

In many LDCs, balance-of-payments difficulties caused by post-1973 exogenous shocks halted the virtuous circle of higher export earnings and further relaxation of import controls which in turn had reinforced their export orientation. As a result, complex foreign-trade systems combining import restrictions and export subsidies were frozen into place. Present incentive systems are uneven and, from the national viewpoint of many LDCs, probably still far from optimal. However, it is doubtful that, in many LDCs, average incentives to exporters now exceed those to firms engaged in production for the domestic market. It is also clear that few LDCs have recently been piling up foreign-exchange reserves or growing faster than their record for the last twenty years. Most LDCs today have long shopping lists for northern goods, purchases that must be shelved due to a lack of foreign exchange. It is also well known that the servicing of the LDCs' external debt, especially following the unexpected increase in interest rates and severe recession of the early 1980s, today takes up a very large share of their foreign-exchange earnings.

Under present circumstances, therefore, a lowering of import restrictions and elimination of export subsidies by LDCs to accommodate demands from some industrialized countries are likely to lead to further balance-of-payments troubles and a decline in LDC economic activity. Thus such actions are more likely to lead to a decline than an expansion in LDC imports from the North. The most effective means of expanding northern exports to the South is now, as it has always been, for the North to import more goods from the South.

The mercantilistic spasm seizing industrialized countries, and particularly the United States during the 1980s, presents more immediate dangers to northern interests than just lagging exports. To give a concrete example, a heavily indebted country like Brazil is being denied the means for a smooth servicing of its external liabilities. Not only are its steel and shoe exports challenged as "artificially" competitive but exports of sun-intensive orange juice and chickens are also decried as resulting from unfair subsidies. Even sugar, which Brazil has been exporting for about four centuries, is shut out by quotas in the U.S. and driven out of traditional markets by (in this case) truly dumped European sugar. Eurocurrency spreads and credit availability are closely linked to the export outlook, and external recession and protectionism have not helped Brazil's efforts to roll over its debt, not to mention its search for additional finance at a reasonable cost. If slow growth and northern protectionism persist, and particularly if recession recurs, no one should be scandalized if official Brazilian voices (and those from many other LDCs) call much more energetically for a satisfactory recontracting of external obligations. The case can be made, after all, that the financial rules of the game should be no less flexible than those regarding trade.

Postwar trade expansion benefited on the whole both industrialized and developing countries, and contributed to less unpleasant international relations than those of 1919–1939. But there *are* gaps and flaws in international arrangements for trade and finance. The GATT has never overcome some of its birth defects, and Keynes' "lusty twins" (the IMF and the World Bank) are themselves undergoing a difficult menopause. The present U.S. proposals to extend the GATT into some services are misguided in timing, style, and substance. They may, however, at least highlight the long-run need to reform the GATT–Bretton Woods system and, in particular, to reconsider the possible advantages of elements in the original ITO proposal, an issue raised by the LDCs over ten years ago. We now turn to a discussion of these matters.

Building Upon the GATT

The challenge today is to identify the most glaring gaps and weaknesses in the present international trading order and to pinpoint those principles embodied in the GATT—above all, those of nondiscrimination, predictability, and transparency—that appear most worthy of preservation in the short and the long run.

To the founding fathers of the GATT, the principle of nondiscriminatory multilateral trade, embodied in the unconditional most-favored-nation clause, was as important as the search for a freer international flow of commodities. The motivation was not merely, or even mainly, consideration of economic efficiency. Rather, it was the product of memories of international political frictions generated before World War II by the discriminatory preferential arrangements enforced by imperial powers and other countries aspiring to hegemonic preeminence. In the view of many historians, the scramble for preferential trading arrangements and the exclusion of rivals from both sources of raw materials and promising markets contributed to the tensions that led to both world wars. In particular, emerging commercial powers, latecomers to both industrialization and colonial empires, were not easily integrated into trading and financial networks.

These lessons maintain their relevance in the 1980s. They should strongly discourage departures from the broad principle of nondiscrimination in commodity trade except for transitional preferences for LDCs (further discussed below) and customs unions formed by those countries. Neither economic theory nor common sense favors the adoption of fresh discriminatory practices by industrialized countries in commodity trade. Existing arrangements, such as the European Economic Community, present a difficult obstacle to the search for nondiscrimination. While it may not be feasible to eliminate such arrangements, their discriminatory scope could at least be frozen.

It was the intention of those who framed both the GATT and the ITO to devise trading rules that would allow a maximum of *predictability* regarding the openness of foreign markets, in order to stimulate long-term investments. Naturally, no nation will be able to commit itself to maintain the same degree of openness to trade under all circumstances, so allowances were made for escape clauses, such as Article XIX in the GATT. The intention, however, was to make the adoption of any departure from commitments as *transparent* as possible so it could be subjected to international review and surveillance. These principles of predictability and transparency maintain their attractiveness, even if, particularly during the last decade, they have been honored more in the breach than in practice. Their attractiveness rests not just in the inducement they provide for efficient trade expansion, but also in the contribution they make to the creation of an atmosphere of fair play among competing economic agents, an atmosphere without which political pressures could arise, again leading to trade wars.

A structural weakness of the GATT, making it difficult to enforce the key principles of nondiscrimination, predictability, and transparency, stems from its birth as a treaty rather than an institution, as the ITO would have been. The professional staff in the GATT secretariat is very limited, a small fraction of the numbers working in the IMF and the World Bank. The small staff of the GATT, however able, can neither engage in vigorous multilateral surveillance of departures from its rules nor participate actively in dispute settlement, much less maintain detailed inventories on nontariff barriers (a task more effectively carried out in recent years by the UNCTAD staff). The GATT has thus emerged as a forum for negotiations rather than as an impartial and active referee of trade disputes. This has made trade-negotiation outcomes in the GATT very vulnerable to the whims and pressures of the large trading nations and blocs. For this and other reasons noted earlier, it has often been described by the developing countries as a "rich man's club." A reformed GATT, to be credible to the weaker trading units of the world, would have to have sufficient resources to permit its secretariat to engage in interpretation, surveillance, and enforcement of trade rules.

A GATT with adequate staff and authority could play a crucial role in settling disputes concerning unfair trade-related subsidies and dumping. Such matters might be better handled by the accretion of decisions within a strong GATT, guided by its present charter, than by the writing of detailed new codes. In fact, unless GATT is infused with a new vision neither present in the Tokyo Round nor evident in the present climate of reciprocity demands in the United States and defensive protectionism in Europe and Japan, new codes may simply further erode the principle of nondiscrimination. It is important, therefore, that before broad extensions of the GATT into new areas are undertaken, its authority, credibility, and basic principles—all now in very great jeopardy—first be restored.

When the process of reform is viewed over, say, a ten-year horizon, several areas covered in the ITO charter and other issues thrust forth by international economic events over the last four decades emerge as natural candidates for further rule making. Such rule making should be seen in the context of a new and broader trade organization built around the core of a restored GATT. Two such areas, highlighted by recent U.S. proposals, are trade in services and direct foreign investment.

Foreign Investment, Trade in Services, and Developing Countries

It is best at the outset to recognize explicitly the links between international trade and international investment and the inevitable implications of national policies for both. The international trading patterns of the future are determined by today's investment decisions; and, conversely, international investment decisions today are governed to a substantial degree by expectations as to the openness or restrictiveness of trading opportunities in the future. Both private firms and national governments engage in practices that are restrictive of others' trading and investment possibilities. National policies respecting rights of establishment, national treatment of foreign firms once established, and the international flow of goods, services, data, and factors of production are all obviously matters for independent sovereign judgment. The rights and obligations of private firms in the national and international economic arena are large and complex topics on which governments are bound to take divergent views. The object must nevertheless be to seek international accommodation and consensus among sovereign governments so that at least the *international* rules of the trading and investment game are subject to certain agreed principles, however small in number, which are understood and, to the maximum extent possible, accepted by all.

It has been noted that few services were included in the original GATT rules. Some were regarded as involving national security concerns (e.g., telecommunications); others were at that time heavily controlled by nations who wanted no constraints on their freedom of action (e.g., shipping, which LDCs wanted included under GATT rules). Statistically speaking, international trade in "services" is by now of significant global proportions and has been growing at a much more rapid rate than goods trade in recent years. The industrialized countries, particularly the United States, are substantial and growing net exporters of services of both the factor and nonfactor sort, while the developing-countries' net deficits in services continue to grow. But this category, a catchall for that international exchange which is clearly not commodity trade, is so all-inclusive as to be nearly meaningless for interpretation.

International service flows, even leaving aside those generated by labor and capital located outside their own countries, are a heterogeneous and little-studied category. Some are closely connected to commodity flows, others are not. Many involve a high degree of intrusiveness into local cultures and even sovereignty, or at least are so perceived by various countries. Coastal shipping, radio and television, domestic air traffic, local telephones and telegraphs are some of the service activities many countries regard as out of bounds for foreign economic agents. Insurance, banking, and data flows, which figure prominently in the United States' push for the extension of GATT into services, are also so regarded by many countries.

Many of these activities and concerns are at the very core of national development strategies and are intimately related to policies on technology (both imported and domestic) and foreign investment. Indeed, if countries were to be given an all-or-nothing choice between a closed economy and one open not just to commodity trade but to all services and factor movements as well, many would choose to pass up the gains from commodity trade rather than allow foreigners to run such "commanding heights" as their banking, shipping, and insurance sectors, as they often did during pre–World War II days. To many, the thrust by the current U.S. administration to place these matters upon the GATT agenda seems tantamount to launching an effort to dismantle various screening and control measures painstakingly constructed over the postwar period—not only in LDCs but also in many industrialized countries—in order to rein in burgeoning U.S.-based and other transnationals. Nor is the irony of the rising northern clamor for the vetting and control of the *out-*

ward flow of technology and foreign investment from industrialized countries lost on the bemused LDC assessors of the new northern policy thrusts.

While the origins of the U.S. push for GATT involvement in international trade in services seem to lie primarily in the finance and telecommunications sectors, it is possible to interpret it, as many do, as an attempt much more generally to "open up" the markets of the GATT contracting parties to the direct foreign investment and other activities of transnational corporations. In this scenario, access for developing-countries' goods in the markets of the rich may in future be traded off under legitimate GATT auspices, instead of via bilateral diplomatic pressure, against improved access for industrialized-countries' "services" and investment in the LDCs.

In this context, it is important to note that there have been important related international negotiations under way for many years in non-GATT arenas. These include the effort to construct a code of conduct for transnational corporations in the UN Center for Transnational Corporations, UNCTAD's work on the drafting of a code for the transfer of technology (and the principles and rules governing restrictive business practices), and the latter's work relating to shipping and insurance. These activities, which presumably are not considered by the United States to be proceeding in a satisfactory direction, do not appear to figure in the new trading and investment order that is being so assiduously promoted by the United States in the GATT.

Transnational corporations have been very much involved in the postwar boom in international trade. In the ITO charter, attention was given to possible restrictive business practices, an issue also stressed by LDCs and smaller industrialized countries in recent years. Scholars have also remarked on the lack of international antitrust rules and, more generally, on the lack of internationally agreed rules of the game with respect to international factor flows of capital and labor. A broad reform agenda should certainly include a "GATT for investment" as well as a "GATT for migration." Unfortunately, the U.S. proposals do not seem to be offered in this broad spirit; rather they are widely viewed as seeking to open doors for U.S. direct investment in specific areas, and in a manner that almost seems to regard other countries' culture and sovereignty as mere nontariff barriers.

When an appropriately broad approach is taken, explosive issues are thrust upon the table: if Tokyo is to be made just like home for U.S. lawyers and bankers, why not have Texas give "national treatment" to Mexican maids? Will New York City be opened up fully to Indian doctors and South Korean construction crews? Which services and factor flows, in short, are to be "opened up," and what principles are to be followed in those decisions?

A key consideration should be that the creation of new rules for services must not involve a retreat from established GATT principles applicable to commodity trade. It is conceivable that the consensus already reached on the benefits of multilateral commodity trade will not be reached either on services or on capital or labor flows, so that the number of nations willing to commit themselves to freer rules in those new arenas will be smaller even than the GATT "club" (to which many developing countries, like Mexico, still do not belong). Failure to join any such new clubs should not impinge on the principles of nondiscrimination, predictability, and transparency already accepted, at least in theory, for commodity trade. In other words, while new services codes may not involve unconditional most-favored-nation clauses, because of culture-specific and politically potent notions as to the appropriate character of "reciprocity," no nation should see its fundamental GATT rights in the area of commodity trade threatened for not wishing to adhere to the new codes.

The appeal of new codes will, of course, depend on their attractiveness to various types of countries, and on how balances between rights and obligations are struck. A "GATT for investment," for example, should involve more than just an opening of doors. It should seek as well to clarify issues of jurisdiction and extraterritoriality (issues recently illustrated by disputes over the participation of European-based U.S. subsidiaries in the construction of the Soviet pipeline). It should also be responsive to the concerns of LDCs and small industrialized countries regarding restrictive business practices engaged in by transnational corporations, especially in the transfer of technology. Balance in overall coverage will also be important to some countries. The provision of greater security for direct foreign investors would be more easily granted, in some cases, if accompanied by codes giving greater security to migrants, a matter historically neglected in international economic relations but of growing importance.

In sum, the specific proposals being advanced by the United States to expand the purview of the GATT are inadequate if they are to constitute a longer-term approach to the problems of the world's trading regime such as is now required and is implicit in the liberal rhetoric of the U.S. administration itself. The addition of services and investment to the present GATT seems a dubious and unhelpful way to begin to restore strength and credibility to a dangerously rickety trading system. Reforming GATT and other international agencies charged with the making and interpretation of rules for trade and financial flows will be a delicate and careful process.

Other Key Areas for Negotiation

LDC PREFERENCES AND "GRADUATION"

GATT has recognized the principle of special treatment for developing countries, most notably in the Generalized System of Preferences. While the net gains to NICs from such departures from nondiscrimination are moot, the least-developed countries could stand to benefit from the maintenance and expansion of such preferences. A broad reform and extension of the GATT should not only involve a reaffirmation of special treatment for developing countries but also tackle the difficult issue of how NICs and other relatively advanced LDCs should gradually be expected to accept the rules for commodity trade that are applicable to industrialized countries, including their granting of preferences to the least-developed countries in an unconditional most-favored-nation fashion. In return, the NICs might at least expect to be "graduated" (along with the rest of the developing countries) from such openly discriminatory arrangements against them as the MFA.

Viewed in a long-term perspective, "graduation" becomes a legitimate and important issue, both for the system as a whole and for the possible graduates. For reasons of their own national welfare, NICs will eventually want to liberalize their import regimes further, rationalize their export promotion schemes, and become dues-paying members of the inner club in which trade rules are written and interpreted. Other LDCs, with smaller domestic markets but relatively high per capita incomes, may also seek to be on the "inside" of international rule-making, hoping to obtain greater predictability in their access to external markets.

LDCs have much to gain from resisting the lure of discriminatory special trading (or financial) relationships, which typically are sold to them by larger and richer economies as being aimed at other "exotic and unfair" trading blocs, but which historically have frequently ended up limiting both the economic and political development of the weaker countries. The gradual but complete incorporation of the "new Germanys" and "new Japans" into the trading order and the provision of a minimum of economic security for independent small countries are necessary conditions for international stability.

PRIMARY COMMODITIES

The Havana charter of the ITO contained provisions for international commodity agreements which balanced the interests of consuming and producing countries. Those provisions promised an improvement over the shaky interwar performance of highly imperfect primary commodity markets while addressing issues such as security and freedom of access to commodities and raw materials that had created political frictions during the interwar years. Oil and soybean export embargoes and large fluctuations in commodity prices, especially since the early 1970s, are reminders that these issues are far from obsolete. LDCs, of course, have for many years pressed for international commodity agreements. Considerable energies went into the attempt in the 1970s to construct an Integrated Program for Commodities featuring the Common Fund for the buttressing of international commodity agreements. Very little has emerged, however, from all these inputs. In the meantime food and fuel-exporting countries have (more or less) on their own adopted their own market-stabilization arrangements. In the early 1980s other commodity prices plunged to their lowest real values in over thirty years. A comprehensive code covering commodities, food, and fuel would therefore be a desirable aim for an expanded GATT. Such a code would have to balance concerns about stability of prices and expansion of supplies. Within such a framework it may also be possible to tackle the stubborn problem of agricultural protectionism, often defended on the grounds of "national security."

MACROECONOMIC COORDINATION IN THE NORTH AND DEVELOPING COUNTRIES

Events of the 1970s and early 1980s have demonstrated how macroeconomic turbulence can seriously impinge not just on trade but also on the rules guiding it. Unemployment and exchange-rate overvaluation (both often caused by tight monetary policies) generate pressures for protectionism and create uncertainty about future adherence to the trading rules. Recession and protectionism in the North hamper the smooth servicing of the external debt of LDCs, threatening the stability of the international financial system. At present, the international coordination of decisions regarding macroeconomic stability, trade, and financial flows is at best loose. LDCs and small industrial countries seriously affected by the macroeconomic and trade decisions of the leading countries of the world economy have few responsive forums where these issues can be discussed multilaterally. Bankers, insisting on the punctual servicing of LDC debts, appear to have little contact with the authorities in their own countries which are responsible for limiting LDC exports. At present, there is no international authority capable of calling attention to and helping to correct such inconsistencies and anomalies. These considerations indicate the need for closer coordination between a stronger and reformed GATT/ITO and institutions such as the IMF

and the World Bank. Such coordination could both deter protectionism in industrialized countries and smooth the way for the eventual
possible "graduation" of the NICs. Broad reforms in the functioning
of the IMF and World Bank—no less important to the developing
countries, and probably more so, than to those in the trading system—are also now appropriate. There is an obvious economic logic
to the developing countries' declared preference for moving negotiations on international monetary and financial reform forward in parallel with trade negotiations. But IMF and World Bank reform is too
long a story for this paper.

STATE TRADING AND DEVELOPING COUNTRIES

The original ITO contemplated not only the active participation of
socialist countries in the international trading system but also substantial state trading by market economies. Rules covering "planned
trade" and state enterprises were not worked out in detail, and such
a task would indeed be formidable. Nevertheless, state trading,
which is already of wider significance than is generally realized, and
the accommodation of "planned trade" deserve priority in a long-
term reform agenda. This is not just because the participation of
socialist countries in a rule-oriented trading system appears to be a
desirable goal but also because many LDCs, and even industrialized
countries, may in the future give greater importance then they already do to commodity trade carried out by state enterprises. It is in
the interests of all, not least those of countries which themselves do
not conduct much trade through state enterprises, to bring this expanding trade within the GATT-based system. In this, as in many
other issues, transparency will be crucial to an atmosphere of fairness, and the implementation of transparency will require a strong
trade secretariat.

Negotiating a New Trade Order

Skeptics may doubt that the many complex items placed on such a
reform agenda could be successfully negotiated in a world composed
of over 150 heterogeneous nation states. It could be a profound mistake, however, to think only in terms of agreements on a region-by-
region basis or among those with which it might in the first instance
be a little easier to agree. The temptations of that route must be
resisted, lest the multilateral system to which the world must eventually turn be set back for years or even decades and the world risk
degeneration into a period of trade blocs, spheres of influence, bilateral unpleasantnesses, and possible anarchy. It is dangerous for the
world to be divided into separate political and/or economic blocs

within which different "club rules" apply but between which there are no agreed rules. While some amount of bloc formation is inevitable and even desirable, world order depends upon a minimum degree of recognition of and adherence to universal norms. The United Nations system is the expression of this universally felt need and, for all its faults, if it were not there, it would be necessary to create a new equivalent.

In the sphere of international economic events and policies, the UN has many different instruments, of which the GATT, which is formally nothing more than a contract among some of its members, is only one. The formal membership of the GATT is, in fact, far less than that of the entire United Nations. Its membership nevertheless includes many centrally planned economies and many developing countries which, although they do not formally belong to the GATT, participate in its "regime" on a de facto basis. Other trade issues are regularly considered within the UN Conference on Trade and Development, the UN Center on Transnational Corporations, and other bodies. It will be important to seek to involve all of the interested and capable parts of the multilateral system, in whatever ways are most appropriate, in any effort to restore and rebuild the trading order.

The task of negotiating a new world trading order is far from impossible. One may note some recent encouraging precedents. A draft treaty acceptable to almost all nations was produced by the UN Conference on the Law of the Sea. Negotiations during the 1970s on international monetary reform established a system of indirect representation so that a Committee of Twenty could carry out discussions on questions ultimately involving a much larger number of countries. In the proposed trade negotiations it may be necessary—on efficiency grounds—to devise some such means of achieving representation without full participation.

In the negotiating process, North–South polarization may be avoided by the emergence of new coalitions cutting across such categories. In particular, an association of "middle" countries, including both NICs and the smaller industrialized countries, could play an important role in balancing the bargaining power of the largest trading units. It should be a major objective of these nations in particular, but as well of all concerned with the longer-run survival of a credible, efficient, and equitable system of global economic exchange, to set in motion a process through which these "gaps," possible reforms, and other requirements of the global trading and financial system can be systematically and holistically addressed. For trade, one might easily imagine another representative Committee of Twenty, perhaps reporting to a joint GATT/UNCTAD committee, or perhaps working to a precise timetable geared to a world conference in international trade, a second Havana. Others have suggested such a process for the broader questions of finance as well as trade, and an eventual "New Bretton Woods." The mechanics are not for us to detail. What matters is that such a process or processes be discussed and launched as soon as possible.

Some Reforms Requiring Immediate Attention

While the launching of a longer-term negotiating process leading to a more complete and updated global trading and financial order is clearly required in the near future, there are pressing trade matters that require immediate attention. The most important immediate issue before the GATT is unfinished business from the Tokyo Round of multilateral trade negotiations. That is the question of the terms of a revised "safeguard" clause that would be both effective and equitable and thus prevent (or at least greatly reduce) the total evasion of the GATT to which importing countries have increasingly resorted in recent years. Indeed, the object must be generally to bring the growing range of nontariff, trade-restricting measures, both formal and informal, under international surveillance and to subject them to multilaterally agreed rules and procedures. Quotas, voluntary restraints, orderly marketing agreements, and the like must be reined in before they bolt away with the whole system and themselves become the norm. Until this is achieved, there can be little hope of arresting the continuing process of "rot" in the international trading framework.

It is therefore fundamental to the restoration of the credibility of the GATT that a satisfactory safeguard mechanism quickly be agreed on. Its principal elements must include arrangements for detailed international monitoring and surveillance of trade-restricting safeguard measures and related adjustment, together with equitable procedures for dispute settlement; specific and strict time limits and phasing-down procedures; strictly defined and internationally sanctioned objective criteria, based on economic principles, for the circumstances, scope, and terms of their use; with the onus of proof of the need for such measures resting upon the importing country. (The "serious injury" that authorizes safeguard action in the current Article XIX has never been defined, so it is in fact still unilaterally determined by the importing country on its own terms.)

If the traditional GATT principles are to be honored, safeguard action should be permissible only on a nondiscriminatory basis, unless discrimination—say, in favor of the poorest countries—is itself multilaterally agreed. Some industrialized countries' insistence upon the right to selectivity (a more innocuous-sounding word than *discrimination*) has been at the root of the failure so far to achieve a new safeguard agreement; it must be said that some exporters are willing to acquiesce in discriminatory arrangements in order to protect their own future market shares. The principle of nondiscrimination is so fundamental to a well-functioning world trading system that it *must* be retained, and deviations therefrom—actual or proposed—systematically rejected. Only temporary derogations, in narrowly defined and strictly timebound circumstances, should ever be tolerated; and, even then, only if the maintenance of trading "order"—the return to *some* set of agreed rules—absolutely requires it. Agreement on a revised safeguard system should logically be followed by a negotiated "winding down" and "phasing out" of voluntary restraint and orderly marketing agreements that do not meet its terms, not the least of which must be the Multi-Fiber Arrangement.

The GATT codes on nontariff measures, laboriously constructed during the Tokyo Round, have not as yet shown much sign of meeting the high expectations held by many commentators at the time of their agreement. Ambiguities (sometimes deliberate) and uncertainties abound in their carefully negotiated texts, and there is as yet little sign of the promised accumulation of "case law" that would help to resolve them. While a strengthened GATT secretariat may ultimately be the most important element in a workable system of codes, a more positive immediate approach might be to resolve remaining ambiguities such as the precise meaning of the "material injury" that authorizes antidumping and countervailing duties, an agreed means of establishing a causal link between "injury" and imports, and a universally agreed basis for measuring the extent of export subsidies in different countries and circumstances and appropriate offsetting duties. Such agreements should accompany renewed efforts to bolster the development of open, efficient, and impartial dispute-settlement procedures, without which the existing system of trading rules, even with the new codes, is likely to generate outcomes consistently biased against the smallest and weakest partners.

It is also crucial to stop, and seek to reverse, the process through which the new GATT codes have encouraged further erosion of the principle of *unconditional nondiscrimination* in trade. Reciprocity is now being demanded of countries before they are to be treated in accordance with the terms of the codes on subsidies and countervailing duties and government procurement. This conditionality of their nondiscriminatory treatment is contrary to the first, most fundamental, article of the GATT; and, in the case of the developing countries, also contradicts Part IV, which expressly states that the developed-country contracting parties do not expect reciprocity from LDCs in return for provision of access to their markets. Without early return to first principles in these respects, the developing countries seem unlikely to join in efforts to bolster the GATT-based codes.

Whatever else is done, it is vital, at a time of increasing resort to opaque, contingent, and discretionary instruments of trade policy, to increase the *transparency* of international trade-restricting practices. The visibility and predictability of the GATT-"bound" import tariff were major advantages of that particular trade-policy instrument, advantages that are perhaps only now being fully appreciated. The GATT, the UNCTAD, and the IMF all seek to monitor trade-restrictive practices in their own ways. A way must urgently be found regularly and systematically to collect and publicly disseminate information concerning the new instruments of trade policy—their extent, incidence, effects, and changes, country-by-country, over time. Discriminatory practices should be particularly sought out and publicized in the light of their uniquely damaging effects upon the system.

Developing countries and certain industrialized countries, notably Canada, have long protested the effects of *escalation in tariffs* and other trade barriers upon their exports of semiprocessed and processed primary products. Since demand elasticities typically rise with the level of processing of the final product, the trade in semiprocessed and processed products displaced by these escalating barriers is potentially very great. Surely a start could at last be made toward the phased deescalation of trade barriers in the primary product sector.

The history of declared *"standstills"* on trade barriers has not been a very impressive one. A 1963 GATT Program of Action declared that "no new tariff or non-tariff barriers should be erected by industrialized countries against the export trade of any less-developed country in the products identified as of particular interest to the less-developed countries . . . particularly . . . barriers of a discriminatory nature." The OECD members have, since then, also made solemn pledges not to expand their trade barriers.

Declarations committing future governments are obviously subject to reviews and reinterpretations. Nevertheless, if ever there was a time when it would be helpful to have a credible announcement of a firm political commitment to hold the line against further protectionism, at least against the developing countries and preferably more generally, it is in the debt-ridden, nervous, and depressed second half of the 1980s.

Conclusion

Thirty-five years after its inception, and following a period of dramatic changes in the international economy, the functioning of the

GATT is in need of major reconsideration. Rather than beginning on a selective series of fresh new tasks, as some now suggest, the most important current requirement, particularly at a time of great international disorder and trade uncertainty and growing disrespect for existing trading principles and rules, is the restoration of the credibility and authority of the established but now weakened GATT-based system.

The case for a more liberal trading order is as powerful as it ever was; yet the world is in grave jeopardy of sliding back into the discredited mercantilist practices of earlier periods. The basic principles of nondiscrimination, predictability, and transparency are fundamental to an efficient and equitable trading order, and it is crucial to pursue them in a fully multilateral manner. The pressure from some quarters to add new elements to the GATT should be seen as an opportunity for a longer-run review of the entire international framework for the conduct of world trade in goods and services and in international flows of capital and labor. Parallel changes and recent severe stresses in the international monetary and financial arena suggest that a fundamental review of international institutional machinery is appropriate there as well. The evident links between trade and financial policies would seem to call for an overall review of the entire GATT–Bretton Woods system. A process for the conduct of such a holistic review should be set in motion as soon as possible.

In the meantime, there are urgent requirements that the GATT should immediately address, the most important of which are the negotiation of a revised safeguard clause and the phasing out of all trade-restricting measures not consistent with it; the sharpening up of existing GATT codes and arresting of the tendency toward conditionality in the application of GATT norms; the development of instruments to increase greatly the transparency of international restraints on trade; measures to reduce the continuing escalation of trade barriers with levels of processing; and the proclamation of an effective standstill on trade barriers against the products of developing countries.

This paper is an updated and shortened version of the authors' *Handmaiden in Distress: World Trade in the 1980s* jointly published in 1982 by the North–South Institute, Ottawa; Overseas Development Council, Washington, D.C.; and Overseas Development Institute, London. Professor Diaz-Alejandro's tragic death in July 1985 put an untimely end to the authors' plans for joint revision. Professor Helleiner takes full responsibility for the changes that have been made.

25

Policy Implications of International Creditworthiness in Trade-Gap and Savings-Gap Economies

GERSHON FEDER AND LILY V. UY

Introduction

The recent debt crisis and the simultaneous reduction in commercial banks' lending to less-developed countries have focused attention on the issue of creditworthiness in the international financial arena. During the years following the first oil crisis, the role of international commercial lenders increased substantially as providers of development finance to a large group of less-developed countries. It has been shown that creditworthiness considerations affect significantly the lending decisions of commercial lenders (Feder and Ross, 1982), and it follows therefore that continued access to funds from such lenders depends on the borrowing countries' ability to maintain or improve their creditworthiness.

Most of the less-developed countries are expected to remain net borrowers in the next two decades if their economic growth is to continue at a reasonable rate. Given the limited scope for expansion of multilateral and bilateral lending, economic growth for many countries will depend in part on their ability to attract foreign capital in the form of investments or loans. Creditworthiness is therefore an important factor in facilitating growth for such countries, and it is reasonable to expect that effects of various policies and growth objectives on creditworthiness will be considered by policymakers. In order to make such considerations practical, creditworthiness needs

From the World Bank, Washington, D.C.

to be defined in quantitative terms, and its relation to various economic variables needs to be explicitly defined.

The present paper utilizes an empirical measure of creditworthiness based on bankers' perceptions to estimate the effect of various variables hypothesized to influence assessments of countries' debt-servicing capacity. The data pertain to a cross section of countries within the period 1979–1983. Such estimates necessarily employ a *ceteris paribus* assumption, which prevents a realistic assessment of the effects generated by policy changes. The second part of the paper therefore develops a dynamic simulation model of a hypothetical average economy. The simulations allow analysis of changes in macroeconomic variables and creditworthiness over time within a system that maintains accounting identities and behavioral constraints. Several changes in policy variables are considered which highlight the importance of export expansion. The latter is, of course, an often-suggested policy objective, but the present paper demonstrates its effectiveness in terms of a somewhat nonstandard criterion.

The Empirical Model

The purpose of the analysis in this section is to identify variables and indicators that significantly affect creditworthiness as perceived by international lenders and to estimate their weight. As done in earlier studies, the analysis assumes a reduced-form equation

$$CW = f(X) \qquad (1)$$

where CW is a measure of creditworthiness and X is a set of variables and indicators related to debt-servicing capacity of borrowing countries. The present analysis improves upon previous work by utilizing a direct measure of creditworthiness of borrowing countries as reported by bankers involved in international lending. Earlier works utilized proxivariables related to creditworthiness such as risk premiums (Sargen, 1977; Feder and Just, 1977, 1980) or volume of credit (Kapur, 1977; Eaton and Gersovitz, 1981).

The direct measure of country creditworthiness is published every six months by the banking and investment journal *Institutional Investor* on the basis of a survey conducted among bankers in several scores of international financial institutions. This creditworthiness ranking is within the interval (0,100) and can therefore be interpreted as a probability (see the discussion in Feder and Ross, 1982). In order to make the formulation of the model compatible with the underlying assumptions of ordinary least squares, a logistic transformation is employed. Suppose that the creditworthiness ranking as reported by *Institutional Investor* (say R) is related to the vector of relevant indicators (**X**) by the following functional form:

$$R = e^{\beta'X+\varepsilon}/[1 + e^{\beta'X+\varepsilon}] \qquad (2)$$

where β is a vector of parameters (weights) and ε is a normally distributed random variable with mean zero. Note that if **X** is an indicator positively related to creditworthiness, it will have a positive β parameter.

From Eq. (2) one can obtain:

$$R^* \equiv \ln[R/(1 - R)] = \beta'X + \varepsilon \qquad (3)$$

where R^* is the logit of R. Equation (3) is a straightforward linear regression equation that will be estimated once the vector **X** is defined. The variables and indicators reviewed below are derived from earlier studies or from discussions of variables usually considered by lenders in their country-risk analysis (e.g., Goodman, 1978; Feder, Just, and Ross, 1981).

EXPLANATORY VARIABLES

Debt/GNP. This is a standard measure of a country's degree of indebtedness. The total stock of debt is compared to the flow of national resources from which the debt is to be serviced. The higher the ratio of debt to GNP, the higher the burden of debt and the lower creditworthiness.

International Reserves/Imports. The main purpose of holding foreign-exchange reserves in developing countries is to safeguard the short-term import capacity of the economy in the face of fluctuations in foreign-exchange receipts. Drawing down reserves is a flexible means of finance in that it can be exercised at the sole discretion of the government and can be activated immediately. The larger reserves are relative to imports, the more reserves are available also to service external debt, making it less likely that the government would defer such payments. Therefore a higher reserve/import ratio is expected to lead to higher creditworthiness ranking.

Average Exports Growth Rate. Since exports are the main source of foreign-exchange inflows for most developing countries, their ability to finance both imports and debt-service payments (the main claimants of foreign exchange) depends on export performance. Countries with high growth rates for exports are expected to enjoy better creditworthiness rankings.

Average GDP Growth Rate. The growth of GDP is a measure of the economy's overall economic performance, and as such it is probably a factor affecting lenders' assessment of the country's creditworthiness. A stagnant economy is less likely to be able to repay its debt if an unfavorable balance-of-payments situation develops. High-growth countries are therefore expected to be more creditworthy, *ceteris paribus*.

Terms of Trade. The ratio of export prices to import prices, starting from a common base year, provides some measure of the relative deterioration (or improvement) of the country's terms of trade (and hence the change in its balance-of-payments position) in comparison to the other countries in the sample.

Export Vulnerability to External Shocks. As mentioned earlier, exports are the most important source of foreign exchange. It is reasonable to expect that countries with volatile exports will be subject to more frequent liquidity crisis when their exports are at the bottom of a cyclical movement. It follows that countries with volatile exports may be viewed as less creditworthy.[1] There are a number of ways to measure export volatility. One simple procedure is to measure the extent to which export revenues are concentrated in very few commodities (say three). The more concentrated exports are, the higher is the risk that a change in world markets may have a major effect on export revenues of the economy.

GNP Per Capita. The level of per capita income is a standard summary measure of the wealth of the country, its level of development, and in a sense an indication of the government's ability to muster additional resources to solve an impending balance-of-payments crisis without having to disrupt debt-service payments. A higher level of GNP per capita may imply a higher level of nonessential consumption that provides the government with more flexibility in releasing resources for debt-service payments. As argued in Feder, Just, and Ross (1981) a relative measure of per capita income rather than absolute value is required in simulation models, and we therefore measure the per capita income relative to sample mean in the respective year.

---

[1] Eaton and Gersovitz (1981) raise a counterargument: countries with more volatile exports are more frequently in need of borrowing to smooth their consumption path and will therefore be induced to maintain a positive record on debt servicing. The debate can be resolved only empirically.

Oil Exporter Dummy Variable. In view of the special advantageous situation oil exporters have enjoyed since 1973, it is hypothesized that a country which is a substantial oil exporter will have a better credit ranking, *ceteris paribus*. Obviously, a high degree of concentration is a characteristic of all major oil exporters, but this negative effect is already reflected in the export-vulnerability index mentioned above.

Political-"Risk" Dummy Variable. Political factors play an important role in country-risk assessment. However, the definition and practical specification of political risks in quantitative analysis are problems with no straightforward solution. One such model, referred to in Overholt (1982, p. 46), uses weights given to different factors such as leadership and type of regime, yielding a political stability score. It would be beyond the scope of the present study to replicate such a model, and the merits of the effort are slim since the simulation model would necessarily have to ignore political aspects. It was therefore considered more appropriate to construct a simple dummy variable to indicate countries where there is an adverse external or internal political situation such as military conflict (e.g., Iran–Iraq), internal insurgency (El Salvador), violent change of regime, and so on. Countries experiencing such phenomena are hypothesized to be viewed as bad risks, *ceteris paribus*, and the coefficient of the political-risk dummy variable should be negative.

Debt-Service Difficulties Dummy Variable. Several countries in the sample have experienced debt-servicing difficulties in parts of the period covered by the study. It is quite clear that when a country is known to have debt-service difficulties with respect to some of its creditors, other creditors are alarmed and the credit rating is likely to fall. For this reason a dummy variable was incorporated in the analysis indicating the countries (and periods) when a debt-service difficulty was known to have occurred. It is expected that the coefficient of this variable will be negative.

Estimation

The data set covers eight periods of six months each between the second half of 1979 and the first half of 1983. Fifty-five countries are included, but a number of observations were not complete due to missing data, thus the total number of country-period observations is 405. The results of estimating Eq. (3) are presented in columns (1) and (2) of Table 1. All parameters are statistically significant and have the expected sign. The goodness of fit ($R^2 = .7$) is quite satisfactory.

TABLE 1.
Estimation Results

Variable	(1) Parameter	(2) t-value	(3) Elasticity
Constant	−1.0007	5.071	—
Debt/GNP	−.4225	3.271	−.0868
International reserves/imports	.0659	6.593	.1031
Average exports growth	1.8844	3.727	.0442
Average GDP growth	10.3643	7.629	.2643
Terms of trade	.2583	2.233	.1219
Export-vulnerability index	−.6286	2.884	−.2238
Relative GNP per capita	.3650	9.973	.1825
Oil-exporter dummy	.3975	5.183	n.a.
Political-risk dummy	−.2005	3.072	n.a.
Debt-service-difficulty dummy	−.3245	3.271	n.a.
R^2	.700		
Number of observations	405		

The parameters are not dimension-free and therefore their absolute magnitude cannot be taken as an indication of their relative importance. One can calculate, however, from Eq. (2) the elasticity of the creditworthiness ranking with respect to each of the indicators:

$$\frac{\Delta R}{R} \cdot \frac{X_i}{\Delta X_i} = \beta_i \cdot X_i(1 - R) \qquad (4)$$

Evaluating at the midpoint $R = .5$, and using the sample means values[2] of the various X_i, the resulting estimates of the elasticities are presented in column (3) of Table 1.

It is apparent that the elasticities are generally low (none exceeds .25 in absolute value), reflecting the fact that many variables enter risk-assessment considerations. This result, however, should be qualified by the observation that the elasticities are only meaningful in a *ceteris paribus* sense, which cannot hold in reality, as changes in any one variable are necessarily accompanied by changes in other variables. For instance, an improvement in the terms of trade would also be reflected in higher export growth and possibly a change in the export-vulnerability ratio and in the volume of accumulated reserves. Another deficiency of the calculated elasticities is the fact that they reflect an instantaneous (short-run) effect of the respective variables on creditworthiness ignoring the dynamic implications of changes. These qualifications suggest that proper assessment of the effect of changes (and especially policy-induced

---

[2] Elasticities cannot be calculated in the case of the dummy variables.

changes) in economic variables on creditworthiness perceptions should be carried within a framework of a macroeconomic model of the whole economy. This will be performed in the next section. In the remainder of this section we investigate hypotheses regarding the evolution of creditworthiness assessments over time within the period covered by the study.

The impact of changes in the dummy variables is quite substantial, in absolute terms. An adverse political development can imply a five-percentage-point reduction in the creditworthiness ranking. A rescheduling request may produce an eight-percentage-point reduction in the creditworthiness ranking, and a major oil discovery will bring up the ranking by ten percentage points.[3]

The estimates reported in Table 1 assume that the parameters of Eq. (3) are fixed over time within the four years spanning the study period. However, it is quite conceivable that the deepening of the world recession following the second oil shock produced a secular deterioration in creditworthiness perceptions for all countries, such that for a given set of economic indicators for any country the creditworthiness ranking is lower toward the end of the study period. This hypothesis can be tested easily by adding a set of time-specific dummy variables to the regression equation.[4] The results are presented in Table 2. Comparing these results with Table 1, it is observed that all parameters except for the constant are practically unchanged. The constant term is considerably smaller in absolute terms. The time-dummy variables confirm a gradual deterioration in creditworthiness perceptions over time, although the shift is statistically significant only from the second half of 1981 onward.

The next step is to relax the assumption that all parameters other than the constant term are fixed over time. Since it is quite cumbersome to include time-shift parameters for all periods (implying seventy additional coefficients) and given that column (1) of Table 2 indicates a rough grouping of two subperiods (periods 1–4 and 5–8), an estimate was obtained by breaking the sample appropriately into two subsamples. The estimates are presented in columns (2) and (3) of Table 2, and it is apparent that some parameters changed considerably over time. The formal Chow test shows that the two regressions are significantly different (F value 2.78). Most noticeable is the decline in the weight attached to debt-servicing difficulties and the increase in the weight attached to export vulnerability. Incorporating the time-shift effects for these two variables and

---

[3] All calculations based on an initial rank of .5.

[4] The dummy variable for the first period (second half of 1979) is omitted to avoid multicollinearity. All other time-dummy coefficients are therefore estimates of deviation relative to the first time period.

TABLE 2.
Time Effects on Estimated Coefficients

Variable	Time Dummies (1)	First Subperiod (2)	Second Subperiod (3)	Final Version (4)	
Constant	−.6923 (3.310)	−.8675 (2.863)	−1.0242 (3.859)	−.9524 (4.952)	
Debt/GNP	−.4839 (3.788)	−.5525 (3.008)	−.4186 (2.342)	−.5008 (3.959)	
International reserves/imports	.0598 (6.006)	.0443 (3.373)	.0749 (5.003)	.0586 (5.959)	
Average export growth	1.9232 (3.879)	1.7038 (2.523)	2.2133 (2.986)	1.9794 (4.025)	
Average GDP growth	10.1536 (7.609)	9.1986 (4.895)	10.7543 (5.676)	9.9382 (7.514)	
Terms of trade	.1928 (1.686)	.2848 (1.379)	.1724 (1.072)	.2279 (2.021)	
Export-vulnerability index	−.5815 (2.715)	−.3115 (1.049)	−.8199 (2.640)	−.3476 (1.587)	$- .3963 T_2$ (5.017)
Relative GNP/capita	.3625 (10.073)	.3826 (7.508)	.3341 (6.480)	.3585 (10.054)	
Oil-exporter dummy	.4072 (5.417)	.3492 (3.373)	.4570 (3.947)	.3916 (5.230)	
Political-risk dummy	−.1819 (2.785)	−.2518 (2.560)	−.1106 (1.288)	−.1705 (1.672)	
Debt-service-difficulty dummy	−.3125 (3.381)	−.5893 (4.205)	−.1694 (1.378)	−.5425 (3.928)	$+ .3682 T_2$ (2.058)
Time dummies: D_2	−.1464 (1.319)				
D_3	−.1262 (1.132)				
D_4	−.1485 (1.349)				
D_5	−.2617 (2.408)				
D_6	−.3371 (3.097)				
D_7	−.3380 (3.137)				
D_8	−.4269 (3.967)				
R^2	.7175	.7133	.7189	.7185	
Number of observations	405	190	215	405	

reestimation of the model using the complete sample produced statistically significant shift effects—column (4) of Table 2. The Chow test now indicates that one cannot reject the hypothesis that once the differences in the parameters of export vulnerability and debt-servicing difficulty indicators are accounted for, there is no difference between the parameters of the model over time.

A possible explanation of the change in lenders' views regarding the implications of debt-servicing difficulties is that the uncertainty and apprehension following the first few cases of debt-servicing difficulties was somewhat reduced due to the fact that rescheduling agreements were being reached, with the borrowers agreeing to IMF-recommended reforms. No actual losses were incurred.

The increased importance of export vulnerability is probably a result of the adverse development in many commodity prices due to the deepening recessions that were more damaging to countries with higher export concentration.

The Simulation Model

A proper assessment of the effects of different policy-induced changes requires a dynamic model of the economy that can reflect the interrelationships between various macroeconomic variables and external borrowing. One simple model that was used extensively in literature on the role of external capital and growth is the two-gap model. Earlier studies of the dynamics of indebtedness (e.g., Ohlin, 1966; King, 1968; Feder, 1980) utilized models of this type, and in the present section a somewhat more detailed model will be developed. The model assumes that growth is constrained by the shortage of foreign exchange to finance imports under the trade-gap case and by the shortage of resources to finance the investments under the savings-gap case. In each case, the different policy-induced changes for two LDC groups (the oil exporters and the oil importers) will be discussed separately.

We start with a description of model variables and parameters:

VARIABLES[5]

Q = gross domestic product (GDP)

C = aggregate consumption

I = gross domestic investment

I_d = domestic production of capital goods

---

[5] All variables are in real terms and have a time dimension. It is omitted here for simplicity. A dot over a variable denotes the rate of change over time.

M_k = imports of capital goods

M_c = imports of consumption goods

M_m = imports of raw materials

M = total imports of goods and nonfactor services

X = exports of goods and nonfactor services

B = total outstanding debts

A = loan-amortization payments

R = international reserves

PARAMETERS

α = incremental (local) capital/output ratio

β = incremental (foreign) capital/output ratio

r = reserves/imports ratio

i = rate of interest on external debt

i_0 = rate of interest on reserve holdings

g = desired rate of growth of GDP

ε = rate of growth of exports

c = marginal propensity to consume

m_m = raw material requirement per unit of GDP

m_c = proportion of imports of consumption to goods relative to total consumption

p = rate of growth of population

a = rate of debt amortization

v = export vulnerability ratio

Q_0 = GDP at year zero

C_0 = total consumption at year zero

B_0 = debt at year zero

X_0 = exports at year zero

P_0 = population at year zero

BASIC MODEL EQUATIONS AND IDENTITIES

Resources–Uses Identity

$$Q + M - X = C + I \qquad (5)$$

Balance-of-Payments Identity[6]

$$M - X + \dot{R} = \dot{B} + i_0 \cdot R - iB \tag{6}$$

Production Function[7]

$$\dot{Q} = \min \left(\frac{I_d}{\alpha} ; \frac{M_k}{\beta} \right) \tag{7}$$

Raw Materials Requirements[8]

$$M_m = m_m \cdot Q \tag{8}$$

Reserve Requirements

$$R = rM \tag{9}$$

Consumption Imports Requirements

$$M_c = m_c \cdot C \tag{10}$$

Growth Plan

$$\dot{Q} = g \cdot Q \tag{11}$$

Efficiency Constraints

$$\beta \cdot I_d = \alpha \cdot M_k \tag{12}$$

Population Growth

$$P = P_0 \cdot e^{pt} \tag{13}$$

Definitional Equations

$$M = M_c + M_k + M_m \tag{14}$$

$$I = I_d + M_k \tag{15}$$

For the purpose of analyzing the impact of changes in variables

---

[6] The assumption that a fixed interest rate applies to all external debt is adopted as a simplification.

[7] The assumption of constant ICOR is a common simplification in models dealing with growth and foreign resources—e.g., Alter, 1961; Avramovic et al., 1964; King, 1968; Chenery and Strout, 1966; and McKinnon, 1964. The latter assumes the same equation as Eq. (7) above.

[8] See McKinnon, 1964.

related to the credit ratings of the borrowing countries, two alternative specifications are used for closing the model.

Trade-Gap Situation

$$X(t) = X_0 \cdot e^{\varepsilon t} \tag{16}$$

Savings-Gap Situation

$$C(t) = C_0 + c \cdot [Q(t) - Q_0] \tag{17}$$

The system of Eqs. (5)–(16) can be solved for all endogenous variables, and in particular for $B(t)$ and $C(t)$, in terms of model parameters and time (t), under a trade-gap specification while Eqs. (5)–(15) and (17) are solved for all variables under a savings-gap specification. No constraints are imposed on the extent of borrowing, assuming that the growth target and other policy variables are set so as to comply with upper-bound constraints on the availability of foreign funds. By definition the savings levels implied by the solution are feasible under a trade-gap situation.

Trade-Gap Situation. To determine the amount of foreign exchange required to fill the export-import gap, a consumption function which is endogenous in the model is obtained by manipulating Eqs. (5)–(16), yielding

$$C(t) = [(1 + m_m - \alpha g)Q_0 e^{gt} - X_0 e^{\varepsilon t}]/(1 - m_c) \tag{18}$$

$$\dot{B}(t) - iB(t) = \{\beta g + m_m + m_c[1 - (\alpha + \beta)]g\}[1 + r(g - i_0)]$$
$$(1 - m_c)^{-1}Q_0 e^{gt} - [1 + m_c r(\varepsilon - i_0)](1 - m_c)^{-1}X_0 e^{\varepsilon t}$$
$$\equiv \theta e^{gt} - \phi e^{\varepsilon t}. \tag{19}$$

Where θ and ϕ depend on parameters only, integrating Eq. (19) from zero to t yields

$$B(t) = B_0 e^{it} + \theta(g - i)^{-1}(e^{gt} - e^{it}) - \phi(\varepsilon - i)^{-1}(e^{\varepsilon t} - e^{it}) \tag{20}$$

Obviously debt grows over time, at least in the earlier time interval. The eventual decline of debt is conditioned on ϕ being positive and sufficiently large relative to θ and B_0. Since this paper considers a time span $(t \leq 15)$ that is relatively short in the context of a debt-growth model, these conditions are not developed explicitly.

Savings-Gap Situation. Under an effective savings-gap situation, the determination of the resources requirements necessitates that an exports function be first derived from the given system of Eqs. (5)–(15) and (17), yielding

$$X(t) = [1 + m_m - \alpha \cdot g - (1 - m_c) \cdot c] \cdot Q_0 e^{gt}$$
$$- (1 - m_c) \cdot (C_0 - c \cdot Q_0) \tag{21}$$

$$\dot{B}(t) - iB(t) = (1 - m_c \cdot i_0 r) \cdot (C_0 - c \cdot Q_0)$$
$$- [(1 - c) - (\alpha + \beta)g - r(g - i_0)$$
$$\cdot (g + m_m + m_c)] \cdot Q_0 e^{gt}$$
$$\equiv \mu - \eta \cdot e^{gt} \tag{22}$$

Integrating Eq. (22) from 0 to t yields

$$B(t) = B_0 \cdot e^{it} + \frac{\mu}{i} \cdot (e^{it} - i) - \frac{\eta}{g \cdot i} \cdot (e^{gt} - e^{it}) \tag{23}$$

As in Eq. (20), debt grows over time, but it will decline eventually if η is sufficiently large.

Application of the Model

Given initial values and other parameter values the model simulates the evolution over time of a hypothetical economy. Specifically, the time pattern of exports, imports, reserves, GNP, external debt, consumption (or savings) is generated. These are then used to calculate the indicators which serve as explanatory variables in the creditworthiness equations as presented in column (4) of Table 2.

The parameters and initial values are calculated on the basis of data pertaining to a group of oil-importing middle-income LDCs. This preserves some uniformity and also ensures relevance of the analysis since most of the countries in this group had access to commercial credit in recent years and presumably would require continued access to enable the realization of growth objectives.

Since the calculations are based on averages for the group, they do not reflect the situation of any particular country but refer to some hypothetical average. The relative per capita income indicator is by construction constant (the ratio being equal to 1) and has no effect on the simulation (the growth rate of GDP, however, is reflected in the creditworthiness ranking). The two dummy variables (debt-service difficulty, political instability) will be set at zero, as the simple model described in the preceding section cannot simulate these variables. The other values are given in Table 3. Details regarding the calculations are provided in Appendix 2.

For each set of parameter values, a simulation of the growth path over fifteen time periods is generated, with the associated creditworthiness ratings. It is assumed implicitly that any amount of borrowing required to sustain the growth path in the simulation will be available. This is obviously an abstraction designed to avoid the

TABLE 3.
Parameters and Initial Values Used in Simulation Model

Parameters	Values	Comment
α	3.020	fixed
β	1.610	fixed
i	0.062	fixed
i_o	0.034	fixed
g	0.0275	
m_m	0.0962	fixed
m_c	0.1533	fixed
a	0.0975	fixed
Population growth p	0.022	fixed
(B_0/Q_0)	0.3076	fixed
$X_0/Q_0\}$ for trade-gap model	0.230	fixed
C_0/Q_0 } for the savings-gap model	0.83	
c	0.80	
Initial per capita income (U.S. dollars)	1308.96	fixed
Initial (reserves/imports) ratio r	0.250	varies
v	.6644	varies

need of estimating and simulating an endogenous loan-supply equation, which is beyond the scope of this paper.

Given the interest in long-term creditworthiness, we present the rating for the last year of the simulation ($t = 15$) as well as several macroeconomic indicators of interest. Tables 4 and 5 present sets of simulations with several GDP growth rates and various export

TABLE 4.
Creditworthiness Implications of Export and GNP Growth Under Trade-Gap Case

g	ε	Debt-Service Ratio at t = 15 (.2133)[a]	Debt/GDP Ratio at t = 15 (.3076)	Export/GDP Ratio at t = 15 (.2301)	Creditworthiness Ratings t = 0	t = 15
.0275	.045	.4432	.8311	.2991	.3027	.2503
.03	.045	.5324	.9617	.2881	.3079	.2428
.0325	.045	.6241	1.0859	.2775	.3133	.2360
.0275	.05	.3006	.6076	.3224	.3047	.2739
.03	.05	.3834	.7465	.3105	.3101	.2651
.035	.05	.5561	1.0044	.2881	.3208	.2499
.04	.05	.7387	1.2379	.2673	.3317	.2375
.0275	.055	.1711	.3729	.3475	.3069	.2999
.03	.055	.2479	.5204	.3347	.3122	.2898
.04	.055	.5776	1.0433	.2881	.3339	.2575
.0275	.060	.0537	.1262	.3746	.3090	.3287
.0400	.060	.4308	.8388	.3105	.3061	.2796
.0500	.065	.2972	.6238	.3347	.3383	.3039
.0400	.0700	.1758	.3977	.3608	.3405	.3304
.0500	.0700	.4706	.9162	.3105	.3632	.2960
.0500	.0800	.2193	.4961	.3608	.3678	.3451

[a] Figures in parentheses represent initial values ($t = 0$).

TABLE 5.
Creditworthiness Implications of Export and GNP Growth Under Savings-Gap Case

g	ε	Debt-Service Ratio t = 0	t = 15	Debt/GDP Ratio t = 0	t = 15	Export/GDP Ratio t = 0	t = 15	Creditworthin Ratings t = 0	t =
0.0375	0.0401	0.1752	0.2163	0.3076	0.3947	0.2801	0.2911	0.3219	0.31
0.0400	0.0428	0.1800	0.3262	0.3076	0.5810	0.2725	0.2840	0.3285	0.29
0.0425	0.0455	0.1851	0.4377	0.3076	0.7601	0.2650	0.2770	0.3352	0.28
0.0450	0.0482	0.1906	0.5509	0.3076	0.9324	0.2574	0.2699	0.3420	0.27

growth rates. In the trade-gap case, export growth rates are exogenously given. In most cases, the time path of creditworthiness is monotonically decreasing unless a relatively low GDP growth or relatively high export growth rate is assumed.

Some observations can be made on the basis of the results in Tables 4 and 5:

1. A higher rate of GDP growth (holding export growth constant) improves the initial creditworthiness rating, but as it entails heavier borrowings to provide the resources for increased investment, it can reduce creditworthiness in later periods,[9] as demonstrated in Table 5. This result is due to the fact that with the parameter values underlying the present simulations, debt increases faster than GDP in the period under consideration and the negative effect of higher debt/GDP ratio dominates the positive effect of higher GDP growth. An increase in GDP growth of one percentage may reduce creditworthiness at the end of the period by 2.5–4 percentage points.

2. Increases in export growth rate (if sustained over the long run) have a substantial positive effect on creditworthiness within the period considered. An increase of one percentage point in ε will generate a 4.5–5 percentage improvement in creditworthiness at t = 15. This effect is much larger than the static (ceteris paribus) effect of export growth and is due to the fact that an acceleration in export-revenues growth reduces borrowing requirements in every period, thus generating lower debt/GDP ratios—which improve creditworthiness further.

3. The savings-gap model presents better creditworthiness performance compared to the trade-gap model under the same hypothetical GDP growth levels. The inference from these two gap models seems to indicate that the potential for higher GDP growth levels and higher creditworthiness ratings would be

---

[9] Long-run creditworthiness may, however, increase if the capital/output ratio is sufficiently low, since in that case the debt/GNP ratio will eventually decline.

more optimistic for a country in a savings-gap situation than in a trade-gap situation. Being in a trade-gap or a savings-gap situation is not a choice variable for a country. However, recognition of the policy alternatives for the two gap situations would certainly aid in the decision-making process.

We turn now to examine the implications of two other model parameters that can be affected by economic policy. The first is the reserves/imports ratio, which was maintained at the level of .25 in the simulations presented so far. Clearly, an increase in reserves has to be financed by either reducing other claims on foreign exchange (such as imports) or by borrowing more. Simulating a shift to a twice-higher reserves/imports ratio ($r = 0.5$) is associated with an increase in initial indebtedness from debt/GDP ratio of 0.3076 to 0.3852 in both the trade-gap and savings-gap models. The change in initial creditworthiness is quite insignificant, but the end-of-period creditworthiness ranking is lower by about four percentage points (compared to the case of $r = .25$), essentially because the economy has to maintain a permanently higher level of debt/GDP, which dominates the positive effect of higher reserves (see Table 6). These results suggest that maintaining higher reserves for the sole purpose of presenting a more favorable creditworthiness image is not a wise policy. There may be other considerations, however, which can justify high reserves/imports ratios (such as concern regarding increased volatility of foreign-exchange revenues), but these cannot be incorporated in the present model.

The second policy variable with potential for improving creditworthiness is the export-vulnerability index. Unlike the other parameters simulated so far, the *ceteris paribus* effect of changes in the export-vulnerability index would be the same as the dynamic effect. The simulation assumes a reduction of about 33 percent in the share of the three leading export commodities of the economy. This can be accomplished by either promoting the export of commodities that are produced at present mostly for local consumption (e.g., textiles in the early phases of Korea's export diversification) or the development of new lines of export-oriented production (e.g., soybeans in Brazil). As demonstrated in Table 7, there is an improvement of about 3.5 percentage points in creditworthiness due to the simulated reduction in export concentration.

The third policy variable that influences the direction of the creditworthiness ratings is the marginal propensity to consume c. A reduction of five percentage points is assumed in the savings-gap model, yielding a new set of creditworthiness ratings presented in Table 8. Comparing these results with Table 5, the creditworthiness ratings are higher with lower c due to reduction in borrowing and

TABLE 6.
Simulation Results with Reserves/Imports = 0.50

(A) Trade Gap

g	ε	Debt-Service Ratio at t = 15 (0.2670)[a]	Debt/GDP Ratio at t = 15 (0.3852)	Creditworthiness Ratings t = 0	t = 15
0.0275	0.0500	0.3580	0.7236	0.3346	0.2979
0.0300	0.0500	0.4426	0.8618	0.3400	0.2887
0.0325	0.0500	0.5298	0.9935	0.3457	0.2803
0.0350	0.0500	0.6194	1.1188	0.3513	0.2728
0.0375	0.0500	0.7116	1.2381	0.3571	0.2659
0.0400	0.0500	0.8065	1.3516	0.3628	0.2596
0.0275	0.0550	0.2237	0.4875	0.3367	0.3254
0.0300	0.0550	0.3023	0.6344	0.3423	0.3148
0.0325	0.0525	0.4547	0.8853	0.3468	0.2924
0.0400	0.0550	0.6399	1.1559	0.3650	0.2809
0.0400	0.0650	0.3496	0.7338	0.3696	0.3299

(B) Savings Gap

g	ε	Debt-Service Ratio t = 0	t = 15	Debt/GDP Ratio t = 0	t = 15	Creditworthiness Ratings t = 0	t = 15
0.0375	0.0401	0.2193	0.2798	0.3851	0.5106	0.3526	0.3383
0.0400	0.0428	0.2254	0.3908	0.3851	0.6959	0.3594	0.3244
0.0425	0.0455	0.2318	0.5033	0.3851	0.8741	0.3664	0.3117
0.0450	0.0482	0.2386	0.6178	0.3851	1.0457	0.3735	0.2999

[a] Figures in parentheses represent initial values (t = 0).

debt. The policy implication thus calls for curtailing consumption, which could be done through an increase in tax rates or a reduction in government spending in order to free resources for exports. The extent of this policy alternative depends a great deal on the social and economic conditions of the country, taking into consideration the costs and benefits of increasing creditworthiness in the financial markets.

Conclusions

The analysis in this paper covered two very different economic situations: savings gap and trade gap. In savings-gap economies, policies reducing aggregate consumption are effective, but the simulations in the preceding section show that the impact of such policies on creditworthiness is relatively small as compared to the impact of policies affecting exports in trade-gap economies. The simulations for

TABLE 7.
Simulation Results with Changes in Export-Vulnerability Index

(A) Trade Gap					
		Creditworthiness ratings (export vulnerability = 0.6644)		Creditworthiness ratings (export vulnerability = 0.4276)	
g	ε	t = 0	t = 15	t = 0	t = 15
0.0275	0.0550	0.3069	0.2999	0.3456	0.3382
0.0300	0.0550	0.3122	0.2898	0.3512	0.3274
0.0325	0.0550	0.3176	0.2804	0.3569	0.3173
0.0400	0.0550	0.3339	0.2575	0.3741	0.2926
0.0275	0.0500	0.3047	0.2739	0.3436	0.3103
0.0300	0.0500	0.3101	0.2651	0.3490	0.3008
0.0325	0.0500	0.3154	0.2572	0.3546	0.2922
0.0400	0.0500	0.3317	0.2375	0.3604	0.2843
0.0400	0.0650	0.3383	0.3039	0.3788	0.3423
0.0400	0.0700	0.3405	0.3304	0.3811	0.3705
(B) Savings Gap					
g	ε	t = 0	t = 15	t = 0	t = 15
0.0375	.0401	.3219	.3124	.3615	.3515
0.0400	.0428	.3285	.2991	.3685	.3372
0.0425	.0455	.3352	.2867	.3756	.3241
0.0450	.0482	.3420	.2754	.3827	.3119

Note: Average export-vulnerability ratio for the oil-importing LDCs used in the model = .6644. Lowest export-vulnerability ratio for the oil-importing LDCs used in the model = .4276.

trade-gap economies highlight the importance of export promotion and export expansion in preventing a sharp deterioration in the creditworthiness of developing countries. Relatively modest increases in export growth (if sustained over a prolonged period) can bring about a substantial favorable effect in creditworthiness. If reasonable levels of GDP growth are to be maintained, foreign capital will be required over a long period and creditworthiness for commercial finance sources has to be maintained. The acceleration of export growth is, therefore, necessary for sustained GDP growth. Diversification of export industries is helpful but would seem to be of somewhat lesser effectiveness. However, since diversification is often complementary to export expansion, the two policy directions can be viewed as essentially one.

Successful expansion of exports is dependent on both internal policies and external circumstances that are beyond the control of LDC governments. The beneficial effects of what Balassa (1984) de-

TABLE 8.
Simulation Results with Reduction in c Under the Savings-Gap Case

g	ε	Debt-Service Ratio		Debt/GDP		Exports/GDP		Per Capita Income		Credit-worthiness Ratings	
		t = 0	t = 15	t = 0	t = 15	t = 0	t = 15	t = 0	t = 15	t = 0	t = 15
3.75	.0441	.1752	.0992	.3076	.1924	.2801	.3093	1309	1664	.3236	.3364
4.00	.0471	.1800	.1949	.3076	.3705	.2725	.3031	1309	1708	.3304	.3235
4.25	.0501	.1851	.2911	.3076	.5419	.2650	.2970	1309	1754	.3373	.3116
4.50	.0531	.1906	.3878	.3076	.7069	.2574	.2907	1309	1802	.3442	.3006

fines as outward-oriented policies (i.e., policies that do not discriminate against exports) on productivity and growth have been propounded by quite a few studies. These benefits would add to the positive creditworthiness effects of export orientation. But the growth of LDC exports will be limited, in the aggregate, if the economies of industrial nations will not emerge from the period of slow growth and stagnation characterizing recent years.

The interdependence of the industrial and less-developed economies was demonstrated by the recently published *World Development Report* wherein two scenarios of the possible growth for the world economy in 1985–1995 were described. The "low" case illustrates the outcome assuming slow growth in the industrial countries. Under such a scenario problems such as inflation, budgetary deficits, and unemployment in the industrial countries are most likely to trigger increased protectionist sentiment against LDCs' exports. This would pose a serious threat to the capacity of LDCs to accelerate their exports and their ability to maintain or improve their creditworthiness. Lower creditworthiness in turn weakens LDCs' ability to obtain foreign-exchange resources needed to meet their development objectives. Hence, lower GDP growth rates in the developing countries are expected under the "low" case.

The "high" case, on the other hand, demonstrates the results when industrial economies achieve sustained and steady growth. The prospect of LDCs would greatly improve. With higher GDP growth in industrial economies, unemployment and inflation would be under control. As budget deficits will gradually be reduced, interest rates would drop correspondingly and investment would increase. Protectionist measures would subside. LDCs would find it easier to expand their exports and to ease their debt-servicing burden, which would in turn raise their creditworthiness. More capital inflows may be forthcoming, which would facilitate higher growth rates.

The likelihood of either case for the world economy seems to depend to a great extent on the policies adopted by the industrial countries. However, the policy choices of LDCs could also affect the outcome. A variant of the "low" case shows that, given the slow growth in industrial economies, the LDCs could achieve higher growth by adopting policies to raise savings and investment rates and to increase and diversify their exports. As shown in the present paper, such policies affect development prospects also through their impact on creditworthiness and access to capital markets.

The authors are staff members of the World Bank. However, the World Bank does not accept responsibility for the views expressed herein which are those of the authors and should not be attributed to the World Bank or to its affiliated organizations. The findings, interpretations, and conclusions are the results of research supported in part by the Bank; they do not necessarily represent official policy of the Bank. The designations employed and the presentation of material in this document are solely for the convenience of the reader and do not imply the expression of any opinion whatsoever on the part of the World Bank or its affiliates concerning the legal status of any country, territory, area or of its authorities, or concerning the delimitation of its boundaries, or national affiliation.

References

Alter, M. G. (1961) The Servicing of Foreign Capital Inflows by Underdeveloped Countries. In *Economic Development of Latin America* (H. S. Ellis and H. C. Wallich, eds.). New York: St. Martin's Press. Pp. 139–160.

Avramovic, Dragoslav et. al. (1964) *Economic Growth and External Debt.* Baltimore: The Johns Hopkins Press.

Balassa, Bela (1984) The Problem of the Debt in Developing Countries. Paper prepared for the conference on The International Monetary System and Economic Recovery, organized by the Instituto Bancario San Paolo di Torino in Turin, Italy, March 30–31.

Brackenridge, A. B. (1977) Evaluating Country Credits, *Institutional Investor* (June): 13–16.

Chenery, Hollis B. and Strout, A. M. (1966) Foreign Assistance and Economic Development, *American Economic Review* 56: 679–733.

Eaton, Jonathan and Gersovitz, Mark (1981) Debt with Potential Repudiation: Theoretical and Empirical Analysis, *Review of Economic Studies* 48: 289–309.

———— (1980) LDC Participation in International Financial Markets: Debt and Reserves, *Journal of Development Economics* 10: 3–21.

Feder, Gershon (1980) Economic Growth, Foreign Loans and Debt Servicing Capacity of Developing Countries, *Journal of Development Studies* 16: 352–368.

Feder, Gershon and Just, Richard (1977) An Analysis of Credit Terms in the Eurodollar Market, *European Economic Review* 9: 221–243.

———— (1980) A Model for Analyzing Lenders' Perceived Risk, *Applied Economics* 12: 125–144.

Feder, Gershon, Just, Richard and Ross, Knud (1981) Projecting Debt Servicing Capacity of Developing Countries, *Journal of Financial and Quantitative Analysis* 16: 651–669.

Feder, Gershon and Ross, Knud (1982) Risk Assessments and Risk Premiums in the Eurodollar Market, *Journal of Finance* 37: 679–693.

Goodman, Stephen H. (ed.) (1978) *Financing and Risk in Developing Countries.* New York: Praeger.

Kapur, Ishan (1977) An Analysis of the Supply of Eurocurrency Finance to Developing Countries, *Oxford Bulletin of Economics and Statistics* 39: 171–188.

King, Benjamin (1968) Notes on the Mechanics of Growth and Debt. *World Bank Staff Working Paper #6.* Baltimore: The Johns Hopkins Press.

McKinnon, R. (1964) Foreign Exchange Constraints in Economic Development and Efficient Aid Allocation, *Economic Journal* 74: 388–409.

Ohlin, Goren (1966) *Aid and Indebtedness.* Paris: OECD.

Overholt, William H. (1982) *Political Risk.* London: Euromoney Publications.

Sargen, Nicholas (1977) Economic Indicators and Country Risk Appraisal, *Federal Reserve Bank of San Francisco Economic Review* (Fall): 19–35.

World Debt Tables. Washington, D.C.: The World Bank. Various issues.

World Development Report. Washington, D.C.: The World Bank. Various issues.

World Tables. Washington, D.C.: The World Bank. Various issues.

APPENDIX 1
DATA SOURCES FOR REGRESSION ANALYSIS

Most of the data for the indicators included in the regression cover the period from 1978 to 1982 with the exception of export-vulnerability ratio, which uses the latest three years of detailed data on exports that are available. The dependent variable is based on half-yearly data from September 1979 to March 1983. All the independent variables, except for the political dummy variable and the debt-service-difficulty dummy variable, are based on annual data. The oil-dummy variable assumes the same value throughout the period.

The following sources provided input values for the independent variables used in the regression analysis:

1. *World Debt Tables (WDT)*. International Reserves/Imports, Total External Debt/GNP, and Oil-Dummy Variable (where one is given to oil-exporting countries and zero for the rest).
2. *World Development Report (WDR)*. Terms of Trade, Average GDP Growth Rate, Average Exports Growth Rate, GNP per capita/Average GNP per capita for the group, and Debt-Service Difficulty.

3. International Financial Statistics (IFS). Export-Vulnerability Index.
4. Development News–Daily Summary and New York Times index provided input for determining political situations of a country in which a value of zero or one is assigned to the Political Dummy Variable.

APPENDIX 2
DATA SOURCES AND METHOD OF CALCULATION OF THE PARAMETERS FOR THE SIMULATION MODEL

The data for the parameters used in the model are compiled from various IMF and World Bank publications. They pertain to the aggregate statistics of middle-income oil-importing less-developed countries.
The details of the calculations are as follows:

1. α, β

The overall incremental capital output ratio (i.e., $\alpha + \beta$) was obtained first by dividing the average share of investment in the GDP (I/Q) by the average GDP growth rate (g), which yielded a value of 4.63. Both g and I/Q were taken from the World Development Report (WDR), 1983, Tables 2 and 5.

The share of imported capital goods in domestic investment was derived by multiplying the share of capital goods imports in total imports (M_k/M) by imports share in GDP (M/Q), the product to be divided by I/Q. This provides the ratio $\beta/(\alpha + \beta)$.

M_k/M was taken from the World Development Report (WDR), 1983, Table 11. This ratio is equivalent to the machinery and transport equipments percentage share in merchandise imports, which is .28. Total imports (M) and exports (X) were reported in WDR, 1983, Table 9. Given the share of exports of goods and nonfactor services in GDP as reported in WDR, 1983, Table 5, total GDP for middle-income oil-importing LDCs was calculated at 830 billion U.S. dollars. M/Q was calculated as .3103. $\beta/(\alpha + \beta)$ yielded values of .3475. Given the value of ($\alpha + \beta$), the calculation for α and β is thus straightforward.

2. i

The average interest rate on external debt for 1981 was reported in WDR, 1983, Table 17, at 12.2 percent. Adjusting for an average inflation rate of 6 percent for the period, a real rate of .062 was used in the model.

3. i_o

The rate of interest on reserves was assumed to be close to the rate on short-term Treasury bills. The prevailing rate (January 1984) was 9.39 percent. The real rate used in the model is .034.

4. m_m

The parameter for raw-material requirements per unit of GDP was obtained by multiplying the import share of raw materials in total imports (M_m/M) by imports share in GDP (M/Q), which yielded a value of .0962. M_m/M is the sum of the percentage shares of fuel and other primary commodities in merchandise imports as reported in *WDR*, 1983, Table 11.

5. m_c

The parameter for the proportion of imports of consumption goods relative to total consumption was obtained by multiplying the share of consumption goods imports in total imports (M_c/M) by imports share in GDP (M/Q), the product to be divided by the consumption share in GDP (C/Q).

6. a

The average amortization rate was calculated by dividing principal repayments (a) by total external debt (b). Data for (a) and (b) were taken from *World Debt Tables (WDT)*, 1983–1984.

7. ε

The average exports growth rate for the period 1970–1981 was reported in *WDR*, 1983, Table 9. For simulation purposes, different levels of ε were tested in the model.

8. g

The average annual GDP growth rate for the period 1970–1981 was reported in *WDR*, 1983, Table 2. For simulation purposes, different levels of g were tested in the model.

9. c

The marginal propensity to consume was assumed to be approximately .96 of average consumption. The rationale is that the marginal propensity to consume is less than the average propensity to consume—i.e., as income falls relative to recent levels, people will not cut consumption proportionate to the drop in income. This observation has been used to explain the behavior of consumer expenditures in Keynesian macroeconomic theories.

10. r

The initial reserves/imports ratio was set at .25. This follows the suggestion that .25 is the minimal desirable level for LDCs (see Brackenridge, 1977, p. 16; Feder, 1978, p. 29).

11. PCI

The initial per capita income was calculated by dividing the difference of the GDP and interest payments on external debt by the population growth over time (POPGR). POPGR was calculated based on the following equation:

$$POPGR = P_0 \cdot e^{pt}$$

12. P

The average annual growth of population for the period 1970–1981 was reported in *WDR*, 1983, Table 19.

13. C_0/Q_0, X_0/Q_0, B_0/Q_0

These relationships stand, respectively, for initial consumption share in GDP, initial exports share in GDP, and initial external debt share in GDP. The first two were taken from *WDR*, 1983, Table 5. The latter was calculated by dividing total external debt figures reported in *WDT*, 1983–1984.

26

The Employment Effects of Barriers to North–South Trade With and Without Indexed Debt Service Payments

DARRYL L. McLEOD AND DOMINICK SALVATORE

Introduction

Trade barriers between developed and newly industrialized countries have become a particularly sensitive issue. The pressure to keep Northern markets open has intensified in part because a substantial share of many Southern countries' export revenues now goes to meet debt service obligations to OECD financial institutions. At the same time, high unemployment rates in many industrialized economies lead them to view the more advanced semi-industrialized economies as a growing threat to their domestic employment objectives. One widely discussed proposal that explicitly links the debt problem to open international markets is to make debt service payments some fixed percentage of export earnings.[1] One effect of linking loan payments to export revenues would be to alter the gains and losses from protection for both trading partners. Debt service payments become in effect a tax on Southern exports collected by the North.

From Fordham University, New York, New York.

[1] As of December 1985, only two countries, Peru and Nigeria, have officially proposed this type of repayment plan. Bergsten, Cline, and Williamson (1985) argue that "capacity-linked payment" plans that result in forced deferral of interest and principal might cause accounting problems for lenders under current banking regulations. They also point out that this type of arrangement could forestall a country's return to "normal capital market access." However, if the proportion of export revenues set aside for debt service represents the same claim on the country's expected income as the original loan and if credit markets work reasonably well, lenders should in principle find this type of arrangement perfectly acceptable.

551

This chapter explores the consequences of protectionism under alternative debt service arrangements in a general equilibrium model of North–South trade. The North exports capital services and manufactured goods to the South and imports labor intensive manufactures. Because of its prominent role in motivating protectionist policies, special emphasis is placed on the employment consequences of trade barriers. It is shown that the extent of Northern employment gains (losses) from protection depends on the structural characteristics of its Southern trading partner. Protection can lead to reduced Northern employment if demand for its exports falls more rapidly than its imports. One important conclusion of this analysis is that a tariff levied against a traditionally low-wage developing country is likely to reduce employment in the North (mainly because income effects lead to a substantial drop in the South's imports of Northern products). On the other hand, protectionist policies aimed at more advanced "semi-industrialized" countries are more likely to result in short-run employment gains.

Employment in the labor abundant South is always reduced by Northern protection but falls most for the traditional exporter. These asymmetric costs of protection give developing and newly industrialized countries special incentive to discourage protectionist moves by the North.

One might expect that tying Southern debt service payments to export revenues would help discourage Northern protection. However, an analysis of the employment consequences of protection with financial transfers does not entirely confirm this supposition. If debt service payments are fixed in terms of the North's export price, the introduction of debt service payments reduces the North's marginal employment gain from protection and reduces the likelihood that protection will have any positive effect on Northern employment. A somewhat unexpected result is that indexed debt service payments tend to increase marginal Northern employment gains from a tariff or quota. This is because reduction in Southern export revenues caused by the quota also leads to lower real debt service outflows. This means Southern purchases of Northern exports fall less than with fixed debt service payments. In general, indexed financial transfers have a stabilizing effect on demand for the North's exports and on world employment. This is because a fall in the South's terms of trade due to either a quota or a recession leads to smaller reduction in Northern exports and fall in the "world" savings rate.

The North–South trade model utilized here is similar to a number of general equilibrium models recently developed to analyze trade and development issues.[2] These models link specific structural characteristics of each trading partner to different comparative static outcomes. Evidence for the role of structural differences in determining trade policy outcomes is provided by a number of cross-country empirical studies. This research reveals a number of distinct trade and growth dynamics associated with different size, income, and structural characteristics of developing and developed countries. Salvatore (1983), for example, finds that for traditional, small-industry exporters the link between exports and growth is less pronounced than it is for medium-income (an observation not inconsistent with the results obtained here). Similarly heterogeneous outcomes among large and small countries are reported by Chenery and Syrquin (1975) and Chenery and Taylor (1968). Finally, this link between level of development and policy outcomes may provide some justification for the discriminatory most-favored-nation policies already pursued by many OECD countries.

A Model of North–South Trade and Employment

Protectionist trade policies are often motivated by short-run employment and income considerations. The North's concern is with unemployment which it views as a problem of insufficient demand. The South also places high priority on employment and incomes, but perceives its problem as one of insufficient capital with which to effectively employ its large labor force. In fact, the specification of the North is similar to that of Taylor (1981) with a somewhat more elaborate supply side while, following Chichilnisky (1981), the South has both abundant labor and significant disparities in sectoral technologies. The following "stylized" attributes distinguish the two regions:

1. A demand-constrained "Keynesian" North trades with a capital-constrained but labor abundant South.
2. Demand for Southern exports is income inelastic in the North.
3. The South exhibits varying degrees of "technological dualism"

---

[2] Generally, these models have been used to analyze longer term trade and development issues. Chichilnisky (1981) emphasizes the role of "technological dualism" and abundant labor in determining the South's response to changes in its terms of trade. Bruno (1977) and Krugman (1981) focus on the long-run dynamics of technical change, scale economies, and learning by doing: issues that are clearly relevant to the analysis of protection but go beyond the short-run policy horizon adopted here. Taylor (1981) combines a "structuralist" inelastic demand for Southern exports in a Keynesian North with a supply-constrained South. Finally, Findlay (1984) reviews a number of growth with trade models that link a neoclassical or Cambridge-style growth model of the North to a terms-of-trade–constrained South.

in that sectoral capital labor ratios differ substantially, whereas in the North sectoral technologies are more homogeneous.

4. Labor is abundant in the South, in the sense that the labor force is large relative to the available capital stock. Moreover the supply of labor to the formal or urban sector is responsive to changes in the real wage.

THE NORTH

There are two goods: the South's relatively labor intensive exportable, termed "basic goods," and the North's "industrial" export, which is produced using a more capital-intensive technology in both regions. Industrial output is demand determined in the North, reflecting its excess capacity in that sector. Output levels in import-competing Northern basic production, on the other hand, depend on relative prices. Consumer demand is determined in a standard linear expenditure system.

$$PD_B = P\theta_B + \gamma(\Phi - P\theta_B - \theta_I) \tag{1}$$

$$D_I = \theta_I + (1 - \gamma)(\Phi - P\theta_B - \theta_I) \tag{2}$$

where γ is the marginal budget share for basic products, Φ total consumption expenditures, and $P = P_B/P_I$ is the relative prices of basics in terms of industrial goods. Northern basics demand is inelastic, implying a large intercept term θ_B and a small marginal budget share γ.

Total consumer expenditures depend on the uniform savings rate, s, and total national income. To simplify matters, it is assumed that all forms of national income, including capital service payments, are consumed and saved according to the same parameters γ and s, so that,

$$\Phi = (1 - s)(S^I + PS^B + P_I^Z) \tag{3}$$

where S^I and S^B are the output levels of basics and industrial goods, respectively. Capital service payments, Z, are initially fixed in terms of P_I.

The price of industrial goods is determined in the North as a markup over labor costs,

$$P_I = (1 + \tau)(w_n a_2) \tag{4}$$

where a_2 is the labor output ratio for industrial goods.

The rate of profit depends on markup rates τ, labor costs, and output levels S^I and S^B for both goods,

$$r_n = [(P_B - w_n a_2)S^B + (P_I - w_n a_2)S^I]/(P_I K) \qquad (5)$$

Northern investment demand is fixed in real terms, although it could easily be made a function of the profit rate as in Taylor (1984). The world industrial goods market is cleared by quantities as the North's production adjusts to meet exogenous investment demand $\bar{I}$, consumer demand from Eq. (2), and exports to the South, X^I. So that,

$$S^I = \bar{I} + D^I + X^I \qquad (6)$$

The output of the North's basic industries depend on their profitability,

$$S^B = f(P/w_n) = (P/w_n)^\sigma \qquad (7)$$

where σ is the constant supply elasticity.

THE SOUTH

In the South both industrial and basic goods are produced using a constant returns technology.

$$S_B = \min(L_B/a_1, K_B/c_1) \qquad (8)$$

$$S_I = \min(L_I/a_2, K_I/c_2) \qquad (9)$$

where a_1, a_2 and c_1, c_2 are the labor and capital output ratios for basics and industrial goods production, respectively.

Markets are competitive so equilibrium prices yield the dual factor cost relations,

$$P_B = a_1 w + c_1 r \qquad (10)$$

$$P_I = a_2 w + c_2 r \qquad (11)$$

where w is the wage and r the capital rental rate in the South.[3]

Southern capital and labor respond positively to factor prices. Labor abundance implies a relatively flat labor supply curve.[4] The elasticity of labor supply, α, is high and the short-run capital supply elasticity, β, relatively small.

---

[3] Note that the North has a true profit rate, while the South has a capital rental rate.

[4] The abundance of labor itself may prevent any institutional mechanism from effectively raising the Southern wage above its equilibrium level. Short-term changes in the supply of labor can also be interpreted as movements into and out of the formal (urban) labor market.

$$L_S = \bar{L}(w/P_B)^\alpha \tag{12}$$

$$K_S = \bar{K}r^\beta \tag{13}$$

Southern demands are determined in a linear expenditure system identical to that of the North, except that the marginal propensity to spend on basics, γ, is likely to be higher and only profit type income is "saved" (reallocated to I, good demand)

$$PD_B = P\theta_B + \gamma(\Phi - P\theta_B - \theta_I) \tag{14}$$

$$D_I = \theta_I + (1 - \gamma)(\Phi - P\theta_B - \theta_I) + s(rK/P_I - Z) \tag{15}$$

where $\Phi = wL + (1-s)(rK - P_I Z)$.

Solving Eqs. (10) and (11) for the South's factor price relations one obtains,

$$r = (a_1 P_I - a_2 P_B)/D = P_B(a/P - 1)/(ac_2 + c_1) \tag{16}$$

$$w = (c_2 P_I - c_1 P_B)/D = P_I(cP - 1)/(a_1 c + a_2) \tag{17}$$

where, $D = a_1 c_2 - a_2 c_1$, $a = a_1/a_2$, $c = c_2/c_1$ and $P = P_B/P_I$.

In conjunction with the factor supply Eqs. (12) and (13), Eqs. (16) and (17) can be substituted into the factor demand equations to obtain general equilibrium supply functions for both goods,

$$S^B = (c_2 L - a_2 K)/D \tag{18}$$

$$S^I = (a_1 K - c_1 L)/D \tag{19}$$

The magnitude of D provides a measure of the difference between sectoral technologies. "Technological dualism" may reflect differences in capital output coefficients (a large $c = c_2/c_1$), or labor inputs (a high $a = a_1/a_2$). In a traditional developing economy one would expect a high level of dualism in both inputs. In the more advanced "middle income" or semi-industrialized economy these disparities are reduced and D is smaller.

EMPLOYMENT IN THE NORTH

Suppose the North imposes a tariff or quota aimed at increasing domestic employment. Since basics demand is inelastic and the domestic supply curve upward-sloping, protection does tend to increase employment initially. However, this increase must be balanced against a potential reduction in export-related employment. The objective of this section and the next is to determine when the fall in export-related employment is likely to exceed the import-replacing gain and vice versa. Under some circumstances, this change in trade-related employment will dominate the change in total employment. This section elaborates those circumstances and provides a measure of the North's marginal employment gain from protection that turns out to depend primarily on conditions in the South.

Consider the case of a Northern quota on basic imports. The North's marginal employment gain or loss, L_m^n, from a binding quota depends on how output levels change following the reduction in imports

$$L_m^n = dL^n/d\overline{M} = P_m(a_1 S_P^B + a_2 S_P^L) \tag{20}$$

where P is the relative price of basics in the North and P_m is change in P caused by a change in the quota $\overline{M}_B$. Note that because of the tariff or quota P may differ from the South's terms of trade. Since P_m is negative, the sign of Eq. (20) depends on the response of the two output levels to a change in P as indicated by the derivatives S_P^B and S_P^L. An increase in the domestic price of basics affects the North's domestic demand for I goods via the usual income and substitution effects. Setting $Z = 0$, substituting Eq. (2) into (6) and differentiating with respect to P yields

$$S_P^I = \mu\gamma's'[s'S_P^B + (s'S_B - \theta_B)] + \mu p_m X_P^I \tag{21}$$

where $\gamma'=(1-\gamma)$, $s'=(1-s)$, $\mu = 1/(1-s'\gamma')$. Note that μ is the multiplier for a change in the demand for I goods, and p_m is the change in the South's terms of trade induced by the quota. The bracketed term of Eq. (21) includes the income and substitution effects of a change in the domestic relative price P. Since we assume θ_B is large, the negative substitution term tends to offset the positive effect of an increase in S^B. Under these conditions the export demand term $\mu p_m X_P^I$ may dominate S_P^I. The magnitude of X_P^I depends, in turn, on the South's terms of trade, p.

If a higher tariff or lower quota raises the relative price of basics and if demand is inelastic, domestic output will increase by approximately the change in imports.[5] Of course a higher P will tend to reduce the demand for basics, but as $\gamma \to 0$, $D_P^B \to 0$ and

$$S_P^B \to -d\overline{M} \tag{22}$$

Substituting the change in the South's imports of I goods for S_P^I

---

[5] Here we rule out "Metzler's paradox" in which a tariff or quota lowers both the international and the domestic price of the protected good.

and the change in the South's exports for S_P^B, we can write the North's marginal employment gain entirely as a function of the South's terms of trade

$$L_m^n = p_m(a_1 X_p^B - a_2 \mu M_p^I) \tag{23}$$

where p_m is the change in the South's terms of trade induced by the quota. The sign of Eq. (23) indicates the direction of change in Northern trade-related employment. Under the conditions outlined above, L_m^n may also determine the direction and magnitude of the change in total domestic employment following imposition of a quota or tariff.

It will be convenient to rewrite Eq. (23) in terms of the South's cross equilibrium excess supply elasticity ε. Using the balance-of-trade condition with $Z = 0$, the South's import demand M^I can be expressed as a function of ε and p as well so that

$$L_m^n = p_m a_2 (X^B/p)[a_n \varepsilon - \mu p(1 + \varepsilon)] \tag{24}$$

where $a_n = a_1/a_2$ and ε is the elasticity of the South's export supply curve. For the reasons discussed in footnote 8, we only investigate the case in which the South's cross-equilibrium excess supply curve is upward-sloping. This implies that p_m and ε are positive. The first term in brackets, $a_n \varepsilon$, represents the North's employment gain from fall in Southern exports, while the second term measures its employment loss due to lower exports of I goods. Thus the North's marginal employment gain from protection will be negative whenever

$$(\mu/a_n)p > \varepsilon/(1+\varepsilon) \tag{25}$$

If we let $P = \lambda p$ where $\lambda > 1$ is the quota-induced wedge between the relative price of basics in the two regions, the left-hand side of Eq. (25) can be rewritten entirely in Northern parameters. Assuming equal wage rates across sectors the labor-output ratios drop out and Eq. (25) reduces to,[6]

$$(\mu/\lambda)[(1 + \tau_B)/(1 + \tau_I)] > \bar{\varepsilon} \tag{26}$$

where $\varepsilon' = \varepsilon/(1+\varepsilon)$. This version of Eq. (25) is important because it gives us some intuition regarding magnitude of $(\mu/a)p$. Since the right-hand side of Eq. (26) cannot exceed one, if $P_B > P_I$ or $\tau_B > \tau_I$, then it is very likely that protection will reduce trade-related employment in the North. However, Southern competition for Northern

---

[6] Note that τ_B is endogenous and depends on w_n and P, while τ_I is exogenous.

markets makes it possible and even probable that there will be a squeeze on basics sector profit rates implying that τ_B will be less than τ_I and $P_B < P_I$. This means that the North's employment gains from trade may be positive or negative.[7] A very low Southern cross-equilibrium excess supply elasticity makes it more likely that lowering the import quota will reduce Northern employment, if only because the very low P required for the North to gain may imply an implausibly low profit markup in basics production.

In summary, if Northern basic demand is inelastic and its own export supply perfectly elastic, Northern employment changes may be dominated by shifts in the quantity of tradeables, with two offsetting adjustments. The employment-creating effect of a switch to importables is obviously enhanced if basics are relatively labor intensive (i.e., if $a_n > 1$). The multiplier effect of the fall in I sector employment, μ, on the other hand, adds to export-related employment losses. Casual empiricism suggests the multiplier effect would dominate, since Northern industries have relatively similar labor-output ratios. In the sections to follow we make the conservative assumption that these two effects just offset each other, so that $\mu/a_n = 1$.

Given this last simplifying assumption we can restate Eq. (25) solely in terms of the Southern variables p and ε, so that when

$$\varepsilon = p/(1 - p) \tag{27}$$

the North's marginal employment gain from protection is zero. When ε is greater than $p/(1-p)$, the North's marginal employment gain is positive.

The Effect of Northern Protection on the South

How the South responds to a protection-induced reduction in trade depends on how easily it can switch from production of exportables to importables. If factor proportions differ substantially between sectors, changes in the composition of output lead to large changes in factor demands. A shift away from basic exports toward industrial goods, for example, would result in a substantial drop in demand for labor and a large increase in the demand for capital. But since the South's transferable capital stock is limited by assumption, higher demand results in large price changes but little increase in capital services. These income effects may in turn cause a substantial fall in the South's import demand. Under these conditions Northern pro-

---

[7] A higher capital-labor ratio for industrial goods would also lead us to expect $\tau_I > \tau_B$.

tection is likely to reduce its trade-related employment. This section develops several propositions linking technological and factor market conditions to the South's response to terms of trade changes.

Since the South is on its labor supply curve, its employment loss or gain from protection depends entirely on the change in its terms of trade. The Stopler–Samuelson results suggest that a fall in p will reduce the real wage and as long as the supply elasticity α is positive, employment will also decline. This is indeed the case as

$$L_p = \alpha L/Dpw = (\alpha L)[P_B(cp - 1)]^{-1} \qquad (28)$$

where $c = c_2/c_1$ and from Eq. (17) $(cp-1)$ is positive whenever $w > 0$. L_p increases as p or D fall, but it is reduced by a significant disparity in capital-output ratios. Note that sectoral labor-output ratios have no influence on the employment effects of terms of trade changes.

Combining this result with the conditions developed for the North in the previous section, Figure 1 shows the possible protection-induced employment outcomes for both regions when $p < 1$ and $\varepsilon > 0$.[8] The curved boundary labeled $\bar{p}$ follows directly from Eq. (27), where $\bar{p} = p/(1-p)$. Of course, this boundary also depends on the ratio μ/a_n. Assuming $\mu/a_n = 1$, a quota does not change trade-related employment in the North whenever $\varepsilon = \bar{p}$. If $\varepsilon > \bar{p}$, the North's marginal employment gains from protection are positive, while if $\varepsilon < \bar{p}$ employment falls in both regions following imposition of a tariff or quota in the North. If the multiplier effect, μ, outweighs the differences in labor-output ratios, a_n, the $\bar{p}$ curve shifts up to the left. The curve $\bar{p}'$, for example, is the relevant boundary when $\mu/a_n = 1.1$. The range of prices over which Northern marginal employment gains are positive is thus reduced.

Proposition 1 identifies the conditions under which there exists some Southern $p < 1$ for which $\varepsilon = \bar{p}$. The plausibility of these conditions along with the parameters that help determine $\varepsilon(p)$ are explored subsequently.

---

[8] We investigate only the case in which $P < 1$ and $\varepsilon > 0$. As discussed in the preceding section, there are several a priori reasons to expect P_B to be greater than P_I (or for $\tau_B < \tau_I$), not the least of which is import competition leading to low profits and protectionist pressures in Northern basics production. The circumstances leading to $P_B > P_I$ are harder to visualize. Moreover, when ε is negative the employment gains from protection generally do not depend on p. When the South's export supply schedule is downward sloping the North generally gains employment. There are p,ε pairs for which the North loses employment with $p > 1$ and $\varepsilon < 1$, but for this lower segment of the boundary $\bar{p}$ to become relevant, P_B has to be much greater than P_I or ε has to be extraordinarily negative. In general then, Northern employment gains are only open to question when $\varepsilon > 0$ and $p < 1$, and this is the set of p,ε pairs investigated here.

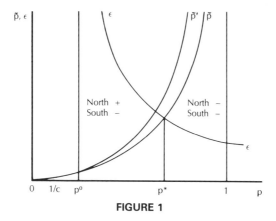

FIGURE 1

PROPOSITION 1: *If when p = 1, there is trade and if c > 1 then there is some* p^*, $0 < p^* < 1$, *such that* $p < p^*$ *implies* $M_p^I < X_p^B$ *and* $p > p^*$ *implies* $M_p^I > X_p^B$ *provided* $X_p^B > 0$ *for all p in the open interval* [1/c,1].

Proof: Suppose $X^B(p) > 0$ when $p = 1$. Since $w/P_B \to 0$ and $L \to 0$ as $p \to 1/c$ and since by assumption $0 < 1/c < 1$ we know that $X^B(p) = 0$ for some p, $1 < p > 1/c$ provided $X_p^B > 0$ for all p in the open interval [1/c,1]. But of course as $X^B \to 0$, $\varepsilon \to \infty$. Let p^0 be the p such that $X^B(p^0) = 0$. Now consider the open interval [$p^{0,1}$]. We know that when $\varepsilon = p/(1-p)$, $M_p^I = X_p^B$. Let $\tilde{p} = p/(1-p)$. Define $f(p) = \varepsilon(p) - p(p)$, a continuous function over the open interval [p^0, 1]. Now as $p \to p^0$ from above, $\varepsilon(p) \to \infty$ while $\tilde{p}$ is positive and finite so $f(p) > 0$. But as $p \to 1$ from below, $\tilde{p} \to \infty$ while $\varepsilon(p)$ is positive and finite so $f(p) < 0$. Therefore, there exists some p^* in the open interval [p^0,1] such that $f(p^*) = 0$ and $\tilde{p}(p^*) = \varepsilon(p^*)$.

Proposition 1 is illustrated in Figure 1. As long as ε is positive when $p = 1$, it will intersect the p curve at some $p > 1/c$, as indicated by the line labeled ε. As ε approaches p^0, $\varepsilon \to \infty$ with $p^0 > 1/c$. At prices above p^* trade-related employment falls following imposition of the quota. If p is less than p^*, Northern employment gains from protection will be positive. Note that prices at either end of this interval are either unlikely to be observed or make the outcome of protection very predictable. A very low p is unlikely because it implies unsustainably low basic sector profit markups. On the other hand, as p approaches 1, implausibly large elasticities are required to create positive Northern employment gains.

Only prices in the middle of this interval, then, create any doubt about the employment outcome of protection. Moreover, this range of feasible prices is ultimately limited by the ratio $c = c_2/c_1$. As technologies become more homogeneous (i.e., as $c \to 1$), the range of feasible prices below one narrows and the ε associated with p^* becomes very large.[9] As capital-output ratios become increasingly disparate or as $c_1 \to 0$ ($c \to \infty$), the South's export demand curve becomes very inelastic.[10] This suggests that only a middle level of capital "dualism" makes Northern gains at all likely. If a reduction in capital dualism is associated with technical progress, this result is mainly relevant to semi-industrialized economies.

Given this middle range of international prices and capital dualism, Proposition 2 explores the conditions that influence the magnitude of trade-flow changes. Specifically, when does a fall in p bring a decline in Southern imports that exceeds the decrease in its exports? Again assuming $\mu/a_n = 1$, this point also determines the North's employment gain (loss).

PROPOSITION 2: *If the South is characterized by a high degree of "dualism" in its sectoral capital-output ratios (i.e., if c is large) and p < 1, then a lower quota for the labor-intensive exports of a low-wage, "traditional" exporter is likely to reduce trade-related employment in the North.*

Proof: Recall that $M_B^n = X_B = B_S - B_D$ and $M_I = M_I^n = I_D - I_S$ (unsuperscripted variables are Southern) so $M_I - X_B = D_I - S_I - S_B + D_B$. Assuming $\mu/a_n = 1$ and referring to Eq. (23) the issue is the sign of

$$M_p^I - X_p^B = (p - 1)p[\gamma' p S_p^B - \gamma S_p^I] + (\gamma'/P_I)S^B$$
$$- (\gamma P_I/P_B^2)(S^B - \theta_I - Z) + s(rK)' - \gamma'/P_I\theta_B \qquad (29)$$

where $(rK)'$ is $d(rK)/dp$. Labor abundance implies that the sign of Eq. (29) is likely to be dominated by the labor component of the first three terms. After a bit of manipulation these labor terms can be grouped as,

$$Lc_1/(DP_B(cp - 1)p) \{\gamma' cp[(p - 1)\alpha + p(cp - 1)]$$
$$+ \gamma[(p - 1)\alpha + (cp - 1)]\} \qquad (30)$$

Note that the sign of Eq. (30) depends entirely on the terms inside the curly brackets. Since $p - 1$ is negative and $(cp - 1)$ always positive, the two α terms tend to make Eq. (30) negative. However if $c = c_2/c_1$ is large, Eq. (30) is likely to be positive, despite a high labor supply elasticity α. Hence a large c makes it more likely that the North's marginal employment gains will be negative. A high c_2/c_1 also tends to raise wages, but a low p and a high a_1/a_2 lower them, so a high c is compatible with a low-wage, labor-abundant South.

Dualistic capital-output ratios, then, tend to mitigate the positive effect of a high labor supply elasticity on ε. Equation (30) indi-

---

[9] As $p \to 1$, $\bar{p} \to \infty$ so for p close to 1, p^* implies implausibly large elasticities. Again for some $p^0 > 1/c$, $X^B(p^0) = 0$. This happens well before the point at which $L(w/P_B) = 0$. But as $c \to 1$, $w/P_B \to (1/p)(a_1 - a_2)$ so that as $c \to 1$, $w/P_B \to 0$. Thus as $c \to 1$ the interval $[p^{0,1}]$ becomes arbitrarily small as $\varepsilon(p^*)$ becomes very large.

[10] To see why this happens, note that as $c_1 \to 0$, $c \to \infty$, $w/P_B \to 1/a_1$ which implies that $L_s \to 0$. When this occurs, the supply response of the South is determined by β, which is assumed to be small.

cates that this effect does not depend crucially on the marginal budget share γ, though certainly a high γ makes it more likely that ε will be low. Protective tariffs levied against a traditional Southern exporter are therefore more likely to reduce trade-related Northern employment. As technologies become more homogeneous and the marginal budget share for industrial goods increases, however, a tariff on the exports of a labor-abundant, "semi-industrialized" South may increase trade-related employment in the North.

Proposition 3 shows how these same characteristics help determine the magnitude of the South's employment loss to protection.

PROPOSITION 3: *The magnitude of the employment loss from a given fall in Southern exports increases with the marginal budget share for basics and with the level of dualism in labor-output ratios, but may decrease as sectoral disparities in capital-output ratios increase.*

Proof: Using the implicit relation between L_s and X_B provided by the South's excess demand for imports we obtain

$$dL/dX_B = L_x = pD/(\gamma'pc_2 + \gamma c_1) = pa_2(ac + 1)/(\gamma'cp + \gamma) \qquad (31)$$

Since from Eq. (17) $cp > 1$ when $w > 0$ and $\gamma' = 1 - \gamma$, it is clear that as γ' increases L_x declines. Similarly, a fall in $a = a_1/a_2$ always reduces L_x. However the cross partial L_{xc} can be of either sign

$$L_{xc} = pa_2(\gamma a - \gamma')/(\gamma'cp + \gamma)^2$$

If $a\gamma < \gamma'$ then L_x increases as the South's sectoral capital-output ratios become more similar.

Since a lower a_1/a_2 and a higher γ' are characteristics one might associate with a semi-industrialized exporter, this possibility cannot be ruled out. For the traditional exporter of consumer goods, however, L_{xc} is likely to be positive. Both a decrease in the marginal budget share for exportables and more homogeneous labor coefficients tend to increase X_p^B, which explains the first two parts of Proposition 3. A smaller change in p is required to bring a given reduction in exports, so incomes and employment fall less. The potentially negative influence of the capital-output ratios is more puzzling, especially in view of Proposition 2 which indicates that as c declines the North is more likely to enjoy positive marginal employment gains.

Taken together, these last two propositions paint a bleak picture for semi-industrialized exporters. More homogeneous sectoral technologies and higher propensities to spend on industrial goods work to increase ε. As a result, a relatively small reduction in p is required to accommodate a protection-induced fall in X^B. Smaller price changes and income effects mean industrial import demand

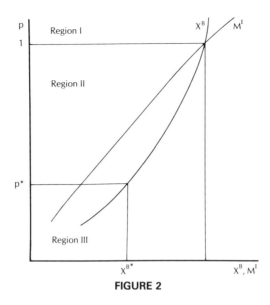

FIGURE 2

may fall less than exports (to the benefit of the North). Yet the fall in
c which contributes to the higher export elasticity also increases the
semi-industrialized countries' employment losses from protection
(Proposition 3).

Figure 2 illustrates Propositions 1 and 2 using the South's cross-
equilibrium excess demand and supply curves. In Region III (with p
> 1), the North's marginal employment gains from trade are always
negative. In Region II, the North continues to suffer employment
losses from protection. At p^* the slope of the X^B curve just equals
that of the import demand curve M^I. If p falls below p^*, the slope of
X^B exceeds that of M^I and the North's marginal employment gains
turn positive. If the X^B curve is less elastic, the North's marginal
employment gains are less likely to be positive, mainly because Region III implies implausibly low price ratios. Figure 2 portrays a
traditional exporter. Labor abundance tends to make the X^B curve
more elastic, but this effect is countered by the capital constraint (a
low β) made binding by technological dualism (a large c). The result
is a low ε. The more elastic excess supply curve of a "semi-industrialized" exporter would expand Region III so that the range of p over
which the North might gain employment would include more plausible terms of trade levels.

Indexed Versus Fixed-Capital-Service Payments

The results of the preceding section suggest that the South may pay a
high price for Northern protection. While a reduction in basics trade

sometimes increases employment in the North, the South always loses. The threat of protection is greatest for the newly industrialized country, not only because its products are generally more competitive but also because its higher export elasticities increase the likelihood that the North will gain from protection, at least in the short run. Tariffs and quotas aimed at traditional exporters, on the other hand, are more likely to reduce employment in both regions, with the South suffering the greater loss. Short of outright retaliation against Northern exports (a course that may be self-defeating if imports are needed for investment), one potential strategy for altering the gains and losses from protection is for Southern nations to tie debt-service payments to export earnings. This sort of arrangement would clearly heighten the already antiprotectionist sentiment of the Northern financial community and would alter the gains and losses from protection in other ways as well.

This section examines the consequences of two different types of financial arrangements on the employment gains from protection: one setup under which transfers are fixed in terms of P_I and another in which payments are determined as a share of export revenues. If the North's price level was dominated by P_I and the South's by P_B and if purchasing-power parity prevailed, the former case would be like fixing debt-service payments in the North's currency.

PROPOSITION 4: *The introduction of financial transfers fixed in terms of* P_I:

    a. *Reduces the range of international prices (export levels) over which the North's marginal employment gain from protection* (L_p^n) *is positive.*

    b. *Increases the North's employment loss to trade when* L_p^n *is negative and reduces the North's gain when it is positive.*

    c. *Increases the South's employment loss to protection.*

Proof: All three parts of Proposition 4 follow directly from the fact that X_p^B falls with the introduction of fixed transfers while M_p^I remains unchanged. With transfers fixed in terms of P_I, the balance-of-trade equation becomes

$$P_B X_B - P_I Z = P_I X_I \qquad (32)$$

where Z is the exogenous transfer. Assuming that capital-service payments reduce Southern savings and consumption in the same pattern as capital income, a positive Z reduces X_p^B. Let $\hat{X}_p^B$ equal X_p^B after the introduction of transfers fixed in terms of P_I. Then

$$\hat{X}_p^B = X_p^B - (\gamma s' P_I Z)/(P_B)^2 \qquad (33)$$

where again X_p^B is dX_B/dp without transfers. Since Z is fixed in terms of P_I, a fall in P_B reduces the purchasing power of the South (i.e., the cost of the transfer in terms of P_B goes up) so that exports fall less quickly as p decreases. Exports are higher at every p, so the elasticity ε falls as Z increases.

Because they are fixed in terms of P_I, transfers to the North have no effect on M_p^I. Recall from Eq. (23) that the North's employment gain from trade depends on the sign of

$$X_p^B - (\mu/a_n)M_p^I \tag{34}$$

Now let $\hat{\varepsilon} = \hat{X}_p^B(p/X^B)$. Again assuming $\mu/a_n = 1$, then Eq. (34) is positive whenever $p > \hat{\varepsilon}/(1 + \hat{\varepsilon})$. Let $\hat{p}^* = \hat{\varepsilon}/(1 + \hat{\varepsilon})$. Since $\hat{p}^* < p^*$ the range $0 < p < \hat{p}^*$ over which $L_p^n > 0$ is smaller, demonstrating part (a). With $\hat{X}_p^B < X_p^B$, the difference in Eq. (34) is always larger, proving (b). Finally, a lower ε implies a given reduction in X^B will lead to a larger fall in p and a larger drop in Southern employment L_s which confirms part (c).

When financial transfers are indexed to export revenues the outcome is quite different. Let δ be the share of Southern exports set aside for debt service, so that the balance-of-payments condition becomes,

$$pX^B - \delta pX^B = X^I \quad \text{or} \quad \delta'P_BX^B = P_IX^I \quad \text{where} \quad \delta' = (1-\delta) \tag{35}$$

PROPOSITION 5: *Starting from an economy in which transfers are zero, the introduction of indexed financial transfers:*

   a) *Increases the range of international prices and export levels over which the North's marginal employment gains from protection are positive.*
   b) *Reduces the North's losses (gains) when L_p^n is negative (positive).*
   c) *Reduces the South's employment loss to any given level of protection.*

Proof: Indexed transfers imply that a fall in pX^B also reduces debt service and therefore consumption in the North. Assuming that the utilization of transfer revenues in the North is identical to that of all other forms of national income and that γ is small, the change in Northern S^I induced by a quota or tariff is increased. Of total transfers to the North, $\delta P_B X^B$, the portion spent on I goods is $s'\gamma'/P_I$. Since $pX^B = X^I/\delta'$, the quota-induced change in Northern trade-related employment becomes

$$L_m^n = P_m \left[a_2\mu[1 + (\delta s'\gamma'/\delta')]\right]X_p^B - a_1M_p^I \tag{36}$$

where s' and γ' are Northern parameters. Note that the term in brackets is smallest when all transfers are saved in the North (i.e., when $s'=0$). Again setting $\mu/a_n = 1$ and writing Eq. (36) in terms of ε, L_m^n is positive whenever

$$[1 - \delta(s_n\gamma' + \gamma)]p > \varepsilon/(1+\varepsilon) \tag{37}$$

Note that ε is not affected by indexed financial transfers. This is because both X^B and X_p^B increase by a factor of $1/(1-\delta\gamma's')$. Since if $s_n > 0$, the bracketed term in Eq. (37) is less than one, part (a) of the proposition has been demonstrated: that is, the North gains from protection whenever $p < \hat{p}^*$ and $\hat{p}^* > p^*$ where $\hat{p}^* = \hat{\varepsilon}[1-\delta(s\gamma'+\gamma)]^{-1}$. Indexed transfers reduce both X^I and X_p^I by a factor of $(1-\delta\gamma s')/\delta'$ (all Southern parameters). Since M_p^I

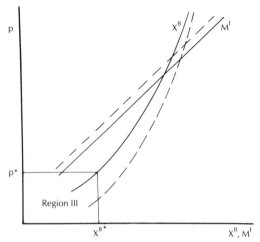

FIGURE 3. Financial transfers fixed in terms of P_I.

decreases and X_p^I increases, L_m^n is always of smaller absolute magnitude with indexed financial transfers, proving (b). Finally since X_p^B increases, a given reduction in M^B will be associated with a smaller fall in p, so that the decline in L_s associated with a reduction in the quota is smaller. This confirms part (c) of the proposition.

Propositions 4 and 5 are illustrated in Figures 3 and 4. Both figures begin with a situation in which financial transfers are zero. Figure 3 shows how the introduction of transfers fixed in real terms

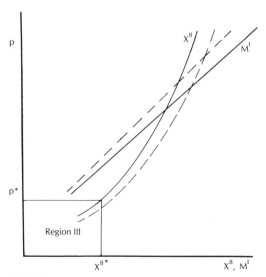

FIGURE 4. Indexed financial transfers.

shifts the South's excess supply curve to the right and makes it steeper. The South's excess demand curve for imports shifts inward but its slope remains unchanged. This has the effect of lowering $p*$ and X^{B^*}, thereby reducing the size of region in which the North gains from protection. Because the X^B curve becomes less elastic, the North's employment loss from a fall in p is always larger after the introduction of the fixed transfer.

The effect of indexed transfers is shown in Figure 4. Again the X^B curve shifts outward, but it also becomes less steep. The M^I curve shifts inward and becomes steeper. The change in the slope of the two curves just compensates for the change in level of trade, so the elasticity of both excess demand and supply curves remains unchanged. This raises $p*$ and X^{B^*}, increasing the region in which the North can potentially obtain employment gains from protection. Viewed in Figure 1, this is equivalent to a shift from $\bar{p}'$ to $\bar{p}$, creating a larger range of terms of trade under which the North may increase its domestic employment. Compared to the no-transfer case, the reduction in trade and employment from a given drop in p is larger. But for a given level of financial transfers, an increase or decrease in p creates a smaller change in the volume of trade with indexed transfers than with fixed transfers. This stabilizing effect of indexed transfers is due to the fact that real transfers from the South decrease with p, dampening the fall in income and employment in that region.

Conclusions and Policy Implications

As the South becomes an increasingly important market for the North's exports of goods and capital services, trade policy must be analyzed in a broader context.[11] The general equilibrium model of North–South trade developed here provides some insights into the economic consequences of alternative methods of managing this interdependence. A reduction in exports from a capital-constrained traditional developing economy requires a relatively large adverse shift in its terms of trade, leading to large income effects and perhaps to a substantial drop in the South's imports of Northern products. Protective policies aimed at this type of economy are unlikely to

---

[11] The dramatic fall in OECD exports to developing countries during the 1982 recession and the associated credit crisis illustrate the increasing level of interdependence between the two regions. A Federal Reserve Bank study estimates that the fall in Latin American imports during the 1982 recession reduced U.S. employment alone by over 250,000 jobs. Branson (1984) also documents the increasing importance of trade between the so-called NICs and the OECD countries. Latin America in particular has become an important market for U.S. capital goods exporters and a source of light manufactured imports, with the U.S. running a significant trade surplus with the region as a whole.

result in any net increase in domestic employment, even under the most favorable conditions for protection in the North. These same income effects increase the employment loss to protection for the traditional exporter.

For the semi-industrialized South, on the other hand, a reduction in exports generally requires a smaller adverse movement in its terms of trade. As a result, the fall in its demand for Northern exports is smaller, and the North is therefore more likely to experience a short-term gain in employment. This is a beggar-thy-neighbor policy in the extreme, however, as the employment decline in the still-labor-abundant South is likely to exceed the North's gain by a large margin.

The imposition of substantial debt-service obligations fixed in terms of Northern export prices makes the semi-industrialized economy behave more like the traditional exporter. The South's export supply schedule becomes more elastic. A fall in the South's terms of trade raises the real cost of the financial transfer, reducing domestic demand and increasing exports at every price level. This income reduction causes a larger drop in Northern exports, making it less likely that a tariff will lead to a net increase in Northern employment.

The switch from fixed-debt-service payments to financial transfers linked to export revenues increases the price responsiveness of the South's exports to pretransfer levels. Since a deterioration in the South's terms of trade no longer leads to an increase in the real cost of financial transfers, the South's export supply schedule becomes more elastic and its import demand schedule less elastic. This leads to generally more favorable outcomes for Northern protection. A disadvantage of indexed transfers for the North is, of course, that real capital inflows fluctuate with the terms of trade. Trade policies which temporarily reduce Southern export revenues automatically "reschedule" that region's financial obligations. A disadvantage of this arrangement for the South is that indexed debt service increases (decreases) the marginal employment gains (losses) to the North from protection.

For the North and for the world as a whole, indexed transfers help stabilize employment. This result follows directly from the fact that only the North saves in the Keynesian sense. During a boom improved terms of trade for the South lead automatically to higher real income transfers to the North where part of the capital inflow is saved. During a recession the South's terms of trade fall and so do real income transfers to the North. A larger share of world income remains in the supply-constrained South, where it is entirely spent. This automatically increases the world savings rate during upturns and reduces it during recessions.

References

Bergsten, C. F., Cline, W. R. and Williamson, J. (1985) *Bank Lending to Developing Countries: The Policy Alternatives,* Policy Analysis in International Economics Number 10, Washington D.C.: Institute for International Economics.

Branson, W. H. (1984) Trade and Structural Interdependence between the U.S. and the NICs. National Bureau of Economic Research Working Paper #1282, Mass.

Bruno, M. (1977) Center-Periphery: Some Aspects of Trade and Development Theory. Harvard Institute of Economic Research Discussion Paper Number 552, Cambridge, Mass.

Chenery, H. and Taylor, L. (1968) Development Patterns: Among Countries and over Time *Review of Economics and Statistics* L (4): 391–416.

Chenery, H. and Syrquin, M. (1975) *Patterns of Development, 1950–1970.* London: Oxford University Press.

Chichilnisky, G. (1981) Terms of Trade and Domestic Distribution: Export-Led Growth with Abundant Labor, *Journal of Development Economics* 8: 163–192.

Federal Reserve Bank of New York (1983) U.S. Trade with Latin America: Consequences of Financing Constraints, *FRBNY Quarterly Review* (Autumn): 14–18.

Findlay, R. (1984) Growth and Development in Trade Models. In R. Jones and P. B. Kenen (eds.), *Handbook of International Economics.* New York: North Holland.

Krugman, P. (1981) Trade, Accumulation and Uneven Development, *Journal of Development Economics* 8: 149–161.

Salvatore, D. (1983) A Simultaneous Equations Model of Trade and Development with Dynamic Policy Simulations, *Kyklos* 1: 66–90.

Taylor, L. (1981) North-South Trade and Southern Growth: Bleak Prospects from a Structuralist Point of View, *Journal of International Economics* 11: 589–602.

——— (1984) *Structuralist Macroeconomics.* New York: Basic Books.

Index of Authors

Subject Index